PRAIRIE FAIRIES

A History of Queer Communities and People in Western Canada, 1930–1985

Prairie Fairies draws upon a wealth of oral, archival, and cultural histories to recover the experiences of queer urban and rural people in the prairies. Focusing on five major urban centres, Winnipeg, Saskatoon, Regina, Edmonton, and Calgary, *Prairie Fairies* explores the regional experiences and activism of queer men and women by looking at the community centres, newsletters, magazines, and organizations that they created from 1930 to 1985.

Challenging the preconceived narratives of queer history, Valerie J. Korinek argues that the LGBTTQ community has a long history in the prairie west, and that this history, previously marginalized or omitted, deserves attention. Korinek pays tribute to the prairie activists and actors who were responsible for creating spaces for socializing, politicizing, and organizing this community, both in cities and rural areas. Far from the stereotype of the isolated, insular Canadian prairies of small towns and farming communities populated by faithful farm families, *Prairie Fairies* historicizes the transformation of prairie cities, and ultimately the region itself, into a predominantly urban and diverse place.

(Studies in Gender and History)

VALERIE J. KORINEK is a professor in the Department of History at the University of Saskatchewan.

STUDIES IN GENDER AND HISTORY

General Editors: Franca Iacovetta and Karen Dubinsky

Prairie Fairies

A History of Queer Communities and People in Western Canada, 1930–1985

VALERIE J. KORINEK

UNIVERSITY OF TORONTO PRESS
Toronto Buffalo London

ISBN 978-0-8020-9777-4 (cloth)
ISBN 978-0-8020-9531-2 (paper)

Library and Archives Canada Cataloguing in Publication

Korinek, Valerie Joyce, 1965–, author
Prairie fairies : a history of queer communities and people in western
Canada, 1930–1985 / Valerie J. Korinek.

(Studies in gender & history)
Includes bibliographical references and index.
ISBN 978-0-8020-9777-4 (hardcover)   ISBN 978-0-8020-9531-2 (softcover)

1. Sexual minorities – Prairie Provinces – History – 20th century.
2. Gays – Prairie Provinces – History – 20th century.   3. Sexual
minorities – Prairie Provinces – Social conditions – 20th century.
4. Gays – Prairie Provinces – Social conditions – 20th century.
5. Sexual minorities – Prairie Provinces – Social life and customs –
20th century.   6. Gays – Prairie Provinces – Social life and customs –
20th century. I. Title. II. Series: Studies in gender and history

HQ73.3.C32P735 2018   306.7609712   C2018-901425-3

This book has been published with the help of a grant from the Federation for the
Humanities and Social Sciences, through the Awards to Scholarly Publications
Program, using funds provided by the Social Sciences and Humanities Research
Council of Canada.

University of Toronto Press acknowledges the financial assistance to its publishing
program of the Canada Council for the Arts and the Ontario Arts Council, an agency
of the Ontario Government.

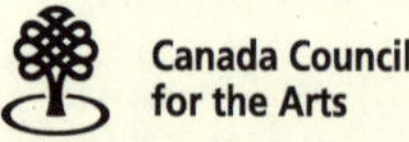

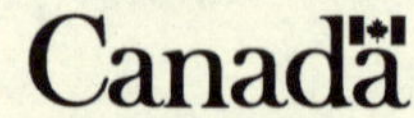

Contents

Contents

Illustrations

Acknowledgments

As I put the final touches on this manuscript it is perhaps fitting that Saskatoon Pride has just wrapped up. The party is over but what remains behind is an enormous rainbow flag still waving atop Saskatoon City Hall. Looking west, across the South Saskatchewan River towards the Bessborough Hotel and the city's downtown, this image dominates the skyline. Such symbols, while significant, do not tell the whole story that brought us to this moment in time when the city, the campus, and the community now flock in record numbers to support sexual and gender diversity in this prairie city. I could not have anticipated these developments when I arrived here twenty years ago from Toronto with little knowledge of the depth of prairie queer histories. It is my hope that this work sheds light on the circuitous path that brought us to this apparent moment of triumph and that it illustrates how hard average prairie women and men fought to make these changes possible – one petition, protest, educational moment, newsletter, and community social at a time. It took generations of queer people, working together and individually, to make that pride flag fly, and while that was not their goal, nor can their battles be reduced to this one symbolic achievement, they would be proud to see what many, in the 1970s, would have thought impossible. Naturally, there are many, many battles still to win, but it is my hope that such symbols embolden people to keep going.

Books and activism have similarities in that you work for years and then finally one day you find yourself with a tangible achievement and the pleasure of writing acknowledgements for a project that seemed never-ending. Writing is so often misconstrued as a lonely, isolated experience, but in reality it takes a community to get authors and their precious manuscripts across the finish line. And I have many debts to people who have toiled in the background: as research assistants, readers of drafts, seminar participants, conference audiences, colleagues, editors, publishers, friends, and family. *Prairie Fairies* has been the beneficiary of so much good will and it is only fitting that I acknowledge people's contributions. Any errors that remain in this book are my own. In the first instance, I want to thank Neil Richards, for donating his wonderfully rich archive of material to the Provincial Archives of Saskatchewan and the University of Saskatchewan Archives and Special Collections that made this work possible. Neil's enthusiasm for this history and his encouragement never waivered, and his tireless suggestions for people to interview, updates about new acquisitions, and positivity were boundless. The staff at both of those archives have been phenomenal, even with the provincial funding challenges, and I want to especially thank Nadine Charabin and Bonnie Dahl at the PAS and Cheryl Avery and Neil Richards at the U of S Archives and Special Collections for meeting every request, including last-minute ones, with grace. My retired colleague, Professor Gary Alan Hanson, who initially gave me a post-it note with Neil's name, phone number, and the cryptic comment "person of interest" deserves credit for starting this whole process! I want to thank all thirty one of my narrators both those who requested anonymity and those who agreed to their names being public: Marion Alexander, Barb Clay, Norman Dahl, Lyle Dick, Bernard Dousse, Bruce Garman, Paul Gessell, Brian Gladwell, Janet Harvey, Gens Hellquist, Elizabeth Massiah, Alan Miller (via email), Margaret Osler, Michael Phair, Peter P. Pratt, Neil Richards, David Rimmer, Mirtha Rivera, Evelyn Rogers, Val Scrivener, Erin Shoemaker, Lilja Stefansson, T, Chris Vogel, and Tom Warner. Everyone took time out from their busy lives to answer questions about their personal lives, activism, and innermost thoughts, and the generosity, helpfulness, and support for this research was much appreciated. Additionally, I want to acknowledge the generosity of Kevin Allen, the research lead and activist behind the Calgary Gay History Project, for his willingness to share materials and his enthusiasm for histories of urban, prairie queer life.

I gratefully acknowledge the support of the Social Sciences and Humanities Research Council whose grant enabled me to travel throughout the country scouring archives, interviewing narrators, and to hire a succession of excellent graduate student research assistants. When SSHRC funds ran out, the University of Saskatchewan provided research funds via their support for department heads, which enabled me to continue the research enterprise while engaged in administration.

I am grateful for the support of the Aid to Scholarly Publishing Program that provided funds for this book to published. At the risk of leaving someone out, I want to thank my research assistants: Noelle Lucas, Erika Dyck, Eric Strikwerda, Jennifer Wilcox, Tonya Lambert, Heather Stanley, Vickie Lamb Drover, Frances Reilly, Erin Millions, and Ryan Eyford for their dedication and hard work.

Earlier drafts of some of this research has been published in scholarly articles and book chapters, and I wish to acknowledge those presses and journals here for permission to reprint those sections. An earlier draft of chapter 1 was originally published as "We're the Girls of the Pansy Parade" published *Histoire Sociale/Social History* in 2012, see: http://hssh.journals.yorku.ca. Excerpts from my article "The Most Openly Gay Person for At Least a Thousand Miles: Doug Wilson and the Politicization of a Province" in the *Canadian Historical Review*, volume 84, no. 4 (December 2003) appear in the chapters on Saskatoon activism, and specifically those dedicated to Doug Wilson's case against the University of Saskatchewan. My thanks to the University of Toronto Press for allowing this material to be reprinted in a revised format here. Finally, I thank the University of Athabasca Press for allowing me to utilize segments of my chapter "A Queer Eye View of the Prairies," which appeared in *The West Beyond the West: New Perspectives on an Imagined Region*, and edited collection from Sarah Carter, Alvin Finkel, and Peter Fornta (Athabasca University Press, 2010).

In addition to the publications above, and the helpful comments from readers and editors I received for those publications, I want to acknowledge the various audiences who have provided enthusiasm and feedback on this research. My work has been workshopped extensively at a series of conferences, most notably the Berkshire Conference on Women's History, innumerable Canadian Historical Association conferences, and at the newly reinvigorated western history conferences. I thank all the faculty and graduate students in attendance for their comments and critique. I am grateful for the opportunities I've had to present my work as a keynote speaker at St John's College, University of Manitoba, and at the University of Alberta, and I thank Adele Perry, Gerry Friesen, and Sarah Carter, for those generous invitations. Presenting this work to keenly interested western Canadian scholars has sharpened my analysis of the contemporary prairies and prairie society immeasurably. My own colleagues at Saskatchewan have been very generous with their time and feedback in faculty seminars. Additionally, I wish to thank Erika Dyck, Simonne Horwitz, Kathryn Labelle, Matthew Neufeld, Lisa

Smith (now at Essex, UK), and Bill Waiser for their generosity in reading earlier drafts of chapters, papers, and in a couple of cases the entire draft manuscript. My department head, Geoff Cunfer, painstakingly created the wonderful maps that appear in this volume. Finally, I would like to thank the McGill Institute for the Study of Canada, and then Director Dr Will Straw, for the invitation to be a Visiting Scholar at MISC for the fall 2016 term. A huge office, the intellectual climate provided at McGill, and the warm welcome extended by colleagues, including by Dr E.A. Heaman, Dr Karen Murray, Dr Nathalie Cooke, Dr Brian Lewis, and Dr Suzanne Morton, were fundamentally important. The charms of Montreal, in particular my Mile End 'hood with its proximity to the Mountain for long dog walks with my golden retriever Scout, and never-ending cafes, restaurants, bakeries, and markets to explore, were vital to recalibrating. One could not ask for a better environment for writing and reflection.

My editors at the University of Toronto Press deserve thanks for their patience, and I am grateful that were always excited by this project from the very beginning. My thanks to then editor Jill McConkey (now at University of Manitoba Press) for championing this book early. Len Husband, who inherited this project, was awesome, always available for a quick email and a timely reminder to keep going. His sage advice on how to stick-handle the system was so helpful. I thank Karen Dubinsky for her encouragement to submit the book, and her firm but kind deadline to "get it done" before she left for Cuba. I made it and Karen read this manuscript in a week, a huge, huge gift to keep the process rolling along as quickly as academic book monographs roll. As series editors, one couldn't ask for better guides and mentors than Karen Dubinsky and Franca Iacovetta, and it is pleasure to have this book appear in the UTP Gender Series. I cannot name all of the individuals at UTP who've touched aspects of this book, including the cover art, its promotion, and the editing process, but it has been a sincere pleasure to work with such a capable team, including my copy editor Dilia Narduzzi, and the always calm, confidence inspiring Frances Mundy.

Finally, of course, no words, however heartfelt, can ever truly thank the families of writers. My sister, Kimberley Korinek, and parents, Shirley and Fred Korinek, have been unfailingly supportive and encouraging of this work, and eagerly read excerpts and chapters. I am grateful to Penny Skilnik for all of her support in the early years of this project, including single-parenting our young sons while I completed the research and oral history trips. Penny's suggestions for people to interview in Saskatoon (from her days running the much beloved queer bookstore cafe Cafe Browse) and her knowledge of prairie life were helpful in the initial mapping of this volume. Thomas and Daniel Korinek grew up with this project as a bit of an unruly step-sibling that was always, at inopportune times, demanding attention. As many feminist writers have observed, having kids and actually writing are often not compatible life pursuits, and yet, in the end, what kids do provide (in fact demand) is that one "balance" work and life. Raising my sportsmen, watching football games in the mind-boggling range of climactic conditions that a prairie "fall" can throw at one, and travelling from one small-town hockey or baseball tournament to another has provided me with a marvelous window into a slice of prairie life and geography that I would otherwise have missed. Season to season, those experiences have proven to be a tonic for the long hours at the computer, and provided us with a tremendous sense of camaraderie, hilarity, and adventure. I would not have missed them for the world. Thus, in their own way, Thomas and Daniel, and our prairie sojourns, have immeasurably enriched this process and the resulting book. Simonne Horwitz came into this project in its final years and she learned more about this prairie world than she might ever have desired. She has been the perfect academic partner: supportive, optimistic, encouraging, and willing to drop her own work to read mine on a moment's notice. She has my thanks for her supreme confidence that this would get done, for her good-natured cheerleading, and for all the laughs we shared as we "made a plan" to deal with the inevitable speed bumps and detours along the way.

Abbreviations

CHR	Council on Homosexuality and Religion (Winnipeg)
CLGRC	Canadian Lesbian and Gay Rights Coalition
EWP	Every Woman's Place (Edmonton)
GARD	Gay Association of Red Deer
GATE	Gay Alliance towards Equality
GCR	Gay Centre of Regina
GFE	Gays for Equality
GIRC	Gay Information and Resources Calgary
GLCR	Gay and Lesbian Community of Regina
LARC	Lesbian Archives of Manitoba and Northwestern Ontario
LASS	Lesbian Association of Southern Saskatchewan
LGBTTQ	Lesbian, Gay, Bisexual, Transgender, Two-Spirited, and Queer
MGC	Manitoba Gay Coalition
NGRC	National Gay Rights Coalition
OWMS	Oscar Wilde Memorial Society
PAS	Provincial Archives of Saskatchewan
PL	Project Lambda
SGA	Saskatoon Gay Action
SGC	Saskatchewan Gay Coalition
SGCC	Saskatoon Gay Community Centre
TBP	*The Body Politic*
U of M	University of Manitoba
U of S	University of Saskatchewan

PRAIRIE FAIRIES

A History of Queer Communities and People in Western Canada, 1930–1985

Introduction

When I was a teenager I used to fantasize about some day discovering a community of other gay people in Saskatoon … After a long evening of walking the streets in the hopes of getting "picked up" I would contemplate the possibility that I was the only gay person in Saskatoon. If I was to find a community of gay people I would have to move to Toronto or Vancouver. It wasn't until I was in my early twenties that I discovered that there indeed was a community of gay people in Saskatoon. At that time it was small, centred around house parties or, in the summer, the park. At last here was a group of people who shared my experiences and could understand what I was feeling. It was an exciting discovery![1]

Gens Hellquist, Saskatoon, 2002

I knew I was gay all my life and I tried to find out about it. In my teens I went to the library and it was under mental illness. I did end up when I was seventeen (1945) in a relationship with a girl a few years older that had been in the army … She wanted me to go to Vancouver with her and at the time I was going with my ex-husband and I didn't know which turn to take, I knew she told me that it was acceptable but society was telling me it was wrong. I became engaged and so she left.[2]

"Dorothy," Saskatoon, 2003

Gay people are everywhere.[3]

Doug Wilson, Saskatchewan Gay Coalition (Saskatoon), 1980

In 1980, Saskatchewan Gay Coalition's Doug Wilson could claim there were "gay people" scattered throughout the province, in small towns, on farms, in the north, and in the big cities. Yet such obvious statements minimized how hard it was for gay people to find others. For Gens Hellquist, his discovery of Saskatoon's queer world, in the late 1960s, was a monumental event and he never looked back. For "Dorothy," finding "gay women" was not difficult. However, despite such knowledge, Dorothy's hesitation about the long-term viability of gay relationships and their diminished status caused her to opt for a conventional heterosexual marriage in 1947. Seventeen years later, she and her husband divorced – "because I was gay." In the 1960s she began a new relationship with a woman and they quietly parented her two teenage children. In 1971, she spotted Hellquist's ad to start a gay organization in Vancouver's *Georgia Straight* and took the plunge undeterred by her girlfriend's reservations. Very quickly, she became the group's "Original Lesbian" and told me that she loved her role in the community. She was subsequently a board member, and eventually vice president of the Gay Community Centre of Saskatoon.[4] This book covers the varied experiences of people like Gens, Dorothy, Doug, and many others through the years of queer subcultural life and later the formation of gay and lesbian communities in the prairies. Searching for queer people then, and historically, was not an easy process, even if we know logically that "queer people are everywhere." *Prairie Fairies* merges those two issues, what British historian Laura Doan calls the "genealogical" work (restoring queer histories and networks) but also the "queer critical history" work that "explain[s] aspects of the sexual past that resist explanation in the context of identity history."[5]

As a work of queer history this book seeks to historicize same-sex desire in the prairies. I use the term same-sex desire advisedly because, as the research will illustrate, not all actors in this world chose to self-identify as gay or lesbian. Prior to the emergence of the political concept of the gay or lesbian individual, many people engaged in same-sex activities but did not define themselves by those activities. "Queer" is a useful umbrella term to capture both those who did self identify as fairies, pansies, men who had sex with men, "married" gay men, lesbians, "gay women," "good friends," or many of the ways that prairie people did or did not reference sexuality, as well as those who were merely sojourners in this world. Similar to Matt Cook and Jennifer Evans, my use of the term queer is also intended to "accommodate individuals who 'disturb' categories" and capture the range of "diverse experiences and identifications" that people held.[6] While I have chosen the word queer to describe these worlds and the actors, when people appear in the text, either my narrators or other protagonists from the archival or oral history collections, if possible I use the words they used to identify themselves. If they did not utilize such terms (particularly if they lived in an era prior to such identification), I have used the word queer for consistency. *Prairie Fairies* is a "queer" history in another sense as it employs a "queer-eye view" of the prairies to purposefully decentre and challenge the heteronormative historiography of the prairie west with its emphasis on Euro-Canadian settlement, agriculture, Indigenous-settler relations, and the economic catastrophe of the Great Depression.[7]

While it has now become commonplace to work from the assumption that queer people were and are "everywhere," one cannot overemphasize how monumental Hellquist's discovery was in the late 1960s. Before anyone with a smartphone and Wi-Fi had access to the world; before the wide-ranging availability of cultural materials, newspapers, magazines, or visual culture; and before widespread sexualities activism, most queer individuals in the Canadian prairies faced the challenge of locating others. Once found, Hellquist and others quickly realized that the people, spaces, and communities they sought were literally right under their noses. And, equally important, that you could choose to stay in Saskatoon, one did not need to move to Vancouver, Toronto, or Montreal, cities that became synonymous with "gay life" (post-1969) and had visible communities and clearly demarcated gay and lesbian spaces. Very quickly, Hellquist discovered that networks of queer men and women had existed within the prairie region for decades, and those individuals had transformed commercial and social places in cities, small towns, and rural areas into queer spaces. But to find queer spaces and people initially took time, persistence, and risk. It meant learning a new language, attention to subtle clues of dress and behaviour, the willingness to be an adventurer who would walk down dark alleys, up rickety staircases, or into the darkened shrubs and trees at the river's edge to find lovers, partners, and friends. The quest to find others is one of the commonalities of the queer experience, and, as this book illustrates, prairie queers were no different than those elsewhere in seeking out their compatriots. But, the terrain, the scale, and some of the challenges were regionally specific. Many literally and metaphorically circled back, waited, and watched from a distance before they worked up the courage to enter these spaces. People like Lilja Stefansson who carried a small classified advertisement in her purse for months before she and her girlfriend, Evelyn Rogers, anxiously phoned the number to ask about the "club" in Regina.

Prairie Fairies historicizes those moments when prairie people, women and men, opened the unmarked door into queer culture and walked through into another world. It wasn't quite Alice's Wonderland, but for men like Bert Sigurdson a successful entry into the world of Winnipeg pansies took him rather far from his working-class Icelandic-Canadian family home on Manitoba Street in Winnipeg. It is in homage to the men like Sigurdson, a Winnipeg "pansy," and his fellow "fairies" and "tutti-fruttis," that the book takes its title. Reclaiming the term "fairies," as they did from a term of diminishment and disrespect to a prideful marker of gendered and sexual difference, is a key focal point of this book. *Prairie Fairies* tells their stories, and in so doing opens a window into a vibrant, larger queer world that has flown under the historical radar for far too long.

The emergence of gay and lesbian organizations, communities, social activity, and activism in the prairies is at the centre of this book. That said, employing the queer framework enables us to move beyond the binaries of gay and straight, "out" and closeted, so as to better capture the daily lived realities of these small and midsized prairie cities.[8] Partly this was necessitated by the fact that *Prairie Fairies* includes the era, prior to 1969 (often referenced as the pre-Stonewall era), when notions of "coming out" and identifying openly as a member of a sexual minority community wasn't a possibility. After 1970, when such open identification as lesbian or gay was well known and increasingly common, there remained sizable numbers of people who did not make this shift. Some older queer women and men continued to practice their well-honed discretionary behaviour, or were not comfortable with the more politicized identity attached to same-sex affection. For others, this discretion was a calculated risk-management strategy for they believed the possibility of revelation might be too high. So they too continued to be "quietly" queer, although in ways that now strike us as hiding in plain view.

This research is part of a transnational historical project to rewrite urban and social histories with queer actors at their core.[9] It has benefited from an extensive historical literature on queer urban histories, staring with the foundational work on New York, Philadelphia, and San Francisco, as well as a theoretical framework that includes historical and cultural geography and queer theory.[10] In American and European LGBTTQ histories (lesbian, gay, bisexual, transgendered, two-spirited, and queer), local studies of queer, lesbian, and gay sexual activity and community formation has dominated the field for the past two decades.[11] British historian Matt

Houlbrook observes that North American and European historians and sociologists have focused so particularly on cities and sexuality that "the city and sexuality appear culturally and conceptually inseparable."[12] In the last decade there has been a growing critique of the urbanities and sexualities scholarship on two fronts. First, in some corners, there is a sense of ennui with these studies. A belief, perhaps, that we've read or heard it all before, and an often unstated but implied question about whether it really matters what the lived experiences of being gay and lesbian were in a succession of cities? Obviously, given the focus of this book, the answer is yes. As Jennifer Pierce argues in *Queer Twin Cities*, positioning the coastal cities like San Francisco as "cities of gay salvation while the Midwest is the place of suicidal despair" ignores a "history of gay radical activism as long and deep as that found in coastal cities" and reifies a problematic dynamic that is both historically inaccurate and dismissive of contemporary queer life in Minneapolis.[13] A similar case will be made for the Canadian prairies.

Queer social histories are not only urban, coastal, and metropolitan but also Midwestern and southern, rural and small town. Another critique of the queer metropolis literature is that it has left the impression that one could only be queer in New York or London, San Francisco or Vancouver, Toronto or Montreal. Those not living the queer urban life were "left behind" in resolutely heterosexual, hostile, or unsophisticated small cities, towns, and rural areas. "Metronormativity," J. Jack Halberstam's shorthand phrase to describe this phenomenon, challenges scholars' tendency to establish a binaristic path from rural, backward "closeted" life to "openly" queer, "liberated" urbanite via the transformative potential of migration. Halberstam challenges this assumption, implied or stated, that positions small town, rural queer people as unsophisticated, apolitical, "closeted" individuals too clueless or fearful to embrace their realities and, in the words of Kath Weston, to "get ye to the big city."[14] More recently, scholars such as Liz Millward, have offered more nuanced analysis of "the rural."[15] This book asserts that prairie people were not "left" behind. Most actively chose to stay, either in prairie cities or in smaller towns and rural areas, creating small pockets of diverse communities and spaces for unconventionality that included sexual minority culture and expression.

Halberstam's intervention accelerated a trend that had, in historical circles, been quietly underway since John Howard's influential *Men Like That* chronicled the lives of queer men in the rural south.[16] Howard's exploration of men who self-identified as gay but also, importantly, "men like that" in Mississippi parlance, those "men who *like* that" – meaning sex with men – was groundbreaking. The latter may frequently have acted upon their queer desires but they did not define themselves by their sexual behaviour.[17] Howard's research made visible those men who had sex with men, their same-sex male peers, and foregrounded the rural and small-town world in which they circulated. A decade later, Colin Johnson's *Just Queer Folks* would take the demand to resexualize rural America even further. Johnson profitably weaves the various strands of medical, agricultural, and popular literature together to remind us that long before the contemporary academic focus on "sex in the city," farms, farmyards, and small towns were awash in discussions of "breeding," both normative and non-normative, of people and animals. Queer people and opportunities for queer lives were part of the fabric of rural American life.[18] Most recently, the encouraging publication of *Queering the Countryside* indicates others have begun to think queerly about the vast tracts of land, communities, small towns, and regional cities where a large number of queer Americans reside.[19]

Canadian contributions to this transnational history of sexualities literature are dynamic, but the Canadian field remains much smaller. Until recently, it has largely been confined to publications focused upon Montreal, Toronto, or Vancouver.[20] Histories of prairie experiences have primarily focused on the early settlement era and, given the use of legal case files, have focused attention primarily on male actors.[21] As those histories, and my own, make clear, "possibilities" for queer companionship and life in frontier, later settlement Saskatchewan's largely male, rural, pioneering world were myriad yet risky. Patrick Gales' 2015 novel, *A Place Called Winter* offers a poignant, fictionalized account of one English man's transformation from married Londoner to queer Saskatchewan homesteader. These publications not withstanding, there is still much research that remains to be done within the Canadian field. In the case of the prairies, the limited literature devoted to sexualities history has largely ignored the contemporary prairie experience. Encouraging signs of change have emerged in the last few years, with the publication of *Making a Scene*, as well as *Overlooking Saskatchewan*, and graduate work on prairie histories of sexuality.[22] In Calgary, an exciting community research project called the Calgary Gay History Project, spearheaded by lead researcher Kevin Allen, is currently underway.[23] Edmonton also has begun a queer community history project.[24] But, as of yet, no other book-length study of urban queer communities exists in Canada. So, responding to the transnational (largely American) question about whether we need more histories of queer urban populations, the answer in the Canadian context is yes.[25]

While *Prairie Fairies* owes a sizable debt to those earlier studies, it takes a purposefully different tack. Unlike single-city studies, this book is unique for offering a multicity, regional study of queer people in five different prairie cities.[26] European and British historians have, recently, begun to explore transnational urban histories and team projects intended to compare queer experiences in a range of national contexts and beyond the well-known queer metropoles.[27] Historicizing four prairie cities – Winnipeg, Saskatoon, Regina, and Edmonton, with partial portraits of Calgary where sources allow (and primarily in relation to Edmonton's history) – provides an assessment of the variety of ways each city created their own civic spaces and institutions as well as their contributions to a regional identity as queer westerners. Offering detailed histories of these four major communities within the prairie region, one can chart the various moments of cross-pollination, migration, and regional networking. "Networks" are not only useful in writing global histories, as Lynn Hunt has argued, but in writing queer histories where migration is such a major facet of the experience.[28] *Prairie Fairies* captures both the movement from small towns and farms into western cities, as well as the movement and interplay between the cities. This regional model has much to offer queer urban histories. Such migrations within the prairies from rural to urban areas, as well as from the north to the more urbanized south, captures a previously hidden world. Occasionally glimpses of the migrations from the region to the gay metropolises (Toronto and Vancouver) are part of this history, but that movement was not my focus. I was primarily interested in those people, like Gens Hellquist and Dorothy, who chose to stay in the prairies. As Dorothy put it, "I travelled a bit and I have never found any place I liked as well as Saskatoon … I'm not a mover."[29]

Prairie Fairies explores what it was like to live as an openly gay or lesbian person. It asks: What queer space existed for prairie women and men? How and when did queer spaces get created? What organizational, cultural, and social spaces, places, and networks were created for gay and lesbian people in 1970s and 1980s? What sorts of gay and lesbian activism emerged from these communities in the 1970s and 1980s? Unlike many works of queer history, largely focused exclusively on male actors, this book is inclusive and historicizes women and men's experiences. This inclusivity, at first, was due to the feminist research design that prioritized lesbian histories and lesbian narrators alongside gay male histories and narrators. But, it also reflects the prairie realities, despite the inevitable gendered and political tensions between and among lesbians and gay men, of the necessity for cooperation. In the prairies settler men and women routinely worked together, coexisted, fought, and were friends. It was also true that in all cities, there were desires for women-only spaces, whether women's dances, lesbian periodicals, or lesbian organizations, and while most of those were not long-lived (Winnipeg's Miss Purdy's Club and Edmonton's Womonspace were exceptions) these were important forums for women. Cooperation has been a defining fact of the Euro-Canadian settler culture on the prairies (among settlers that is) and, not surprisingly, it was transferred to the queer community.

Some will be surprised that this study is set in the prairies, a region popularly identified with religious and political conservatism, with farming and traditional families. That surprise underscores the work that remains to be done in historicizing the post-1945 prairies. The "imagined prairies" are quite different from the realities of these "modern" cities. Small family farms no longer dominate the prairie region even if many people are only one or two generations "off the farm." "The farm" continues to exercise an emotional pull, but the reality is that the majority of prairie people, post-1945, are urban people. Resource development and urban living are the two hallmarks of the contemporary prairie experience. Those urbanites share many characteristics, and have undergone similar changes to those faced by other Canadians. Very quickly, the changes ushered in by cultural and media developments, travel and transportation links, economic development, and trade transformed the west post-1945. The prairies might have had some much needed catching up to do in the 1950s and 1960s, particularly rural Saskatchewan where electrification came late, but even then it only accentuated the exodus to the cities that was underway.[30] By the 1970s, these transformations, as well as the considerable in-migration of thousands of workers to Alberta and the improved circumstances in Manitoba and Saskatchewan where a minor resource boom in potash kick-started a new phase of development, began to transform the region from agricultural breadbasket to resource powerhouse. Events such as the Calgary Stampede may have continued to valorize a mythical "western" region of open ranges, big skies, ranching, farm families, and mountain vistas, but that was more mythmaking and tourism than reality. For queer westerners, as this book will illustrate, these economic, social, and cultural developments have produced greater access to information, brought them more closely into contact with queer political and cultural currents from outside the region, and have in the end made it possible to live queer lives within their home regions.

When one speaks of "the prairies" a number of images arise, including images of grasslands and vast, flat vistas as far as the eye can see. It is a region synonymous with extreme weather ranging from "dry cold" to intense, baking summer heat. Such a harsh climate makes weather a preoccupation and universally unites prairie people in a common cause: survival. Those long patches of winter, where the thermometer fails to nudge above forty below (Celsius or Fahrenheit), have necessitated cooperative strategies and forged a particular pride in toughness and the ability to endure. One of my narrators, Bruce Garman, shared this story from the1950s that encapsulates the role of climate in forging civic-mindedness. In the 1950s, when his "parents first moved to Kindersley [SK] they would be in town on a Saturday. There would be a storm and the men of the town would have to head out linking arms and walk along the roads and find cars because they knew there were farmers who didn't make it home … There is the need to pull together to survive and people were willing to do that."[31]

Weather aside, the Canadian prairies encompass far more geographical diversity than many realize. This area, over 650,000 square miles, includes present-day Alberta, Saskatchewan, and Manitoba. Within this region are a variety of geographical zones, including the southern prairies and grasslands, aspen parkland, portions of the Rocky Mountains in southwestern Alberta, and a large swathe of boreal forest (or Canadian Shield) typography covering the northernmost part of each of the three provinces. There are numerous lakes and rivers, and all major prairie cities, with the exception of Regina, have rivers running through them. Regina has to be content with Wascana Lake, a small man-made lake into which Wascana Creek flows.

Economically, this is a land of tremendous agricultural and mineral wealth. Originally known as the "breadbasket" of the world, in the era when wheat was king grain farming dominated the prairie economy. The classic, iconic, small-town prairie image (repeated in countless Canadian calendars and stock images) was the local grain elevator, taken either at dawn or sunset, so as to capture the building in all its glory. Wheat remains important, but strong export markets for canola and pulse crops, and the desire to move from a monoculture into a more diversified farming strategy, has paid dividends. Not surprisingly, images of place were also deployed by prairie queer activist

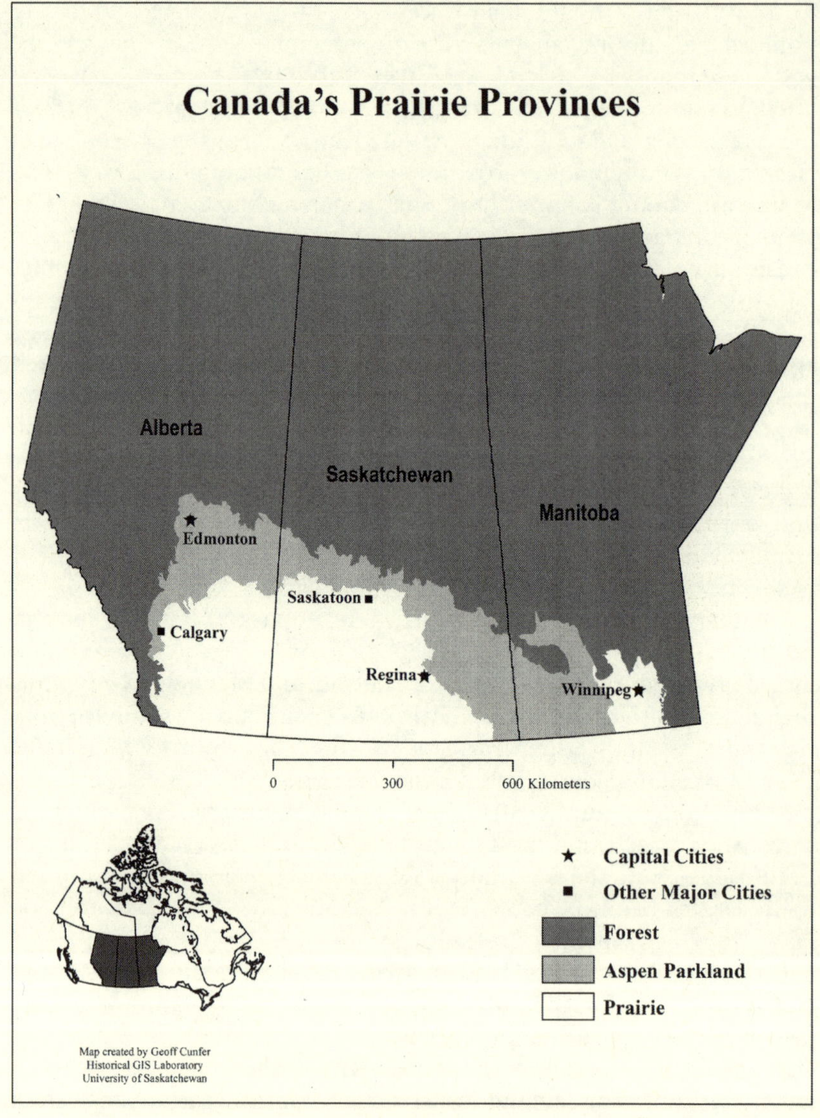

0.1 Copyright Geoff Cunfer, 2017.

organizations, such as Saskatchewan Gay Coalition, whose images of same-sex prairie settlers explicitly challenged the presumed hetero-normativity of the region. Beef production is a key driver in Alberta's economy (Alberta Beef is a provincial trademarked brand). In 1947 the discovery of oil at Leduc, Alberta would usher in an important phase of oil and gas development in Alberta, and later, Saskatchewan. Calgary's wealth is based on the oil industry, and the presence of skyscrapers and office buildings, largely the preserve of international oil conglomerates, dominate the city's evolving skyline. Finally, the northern areas of all three provinces are rich in mineral wealth, and mining is the primary economic activity. Unlike the resource-heavy economies of Alberta and Saskatchewan, Manitoba's economy is more diversified, including a north devoted to mining and minerals. Around Winnipeg and the southern parts of the province are grain and mixed farms. The city of Winnipeg was, initially, a regional financial centre known for its cluster of insurance companies, banks, grain and agricultural futures trading, and manufacturing, but today it is the site of government offices, insur-ance companies, and education.

It is the paucity of contemporary prairie historical scholarship, and the further marginalization of minority sexual histories within prairie histories and studies, that have left the misperception that queer people did not live in the prairies, and that queer communities did not form in prairie cities.[32] Until now, with rare exceptions, they've been largely neglected from regional histories. The reasons for this are twofold. First, many scholars took silences, "discretion," purposefully covert activity, and lack of easily accessible archival documents as "proof" that queer people were not part of the prairie communities. Second, beyond the important early work of Terry Chapman, and later Lyle Dick, few aca-demics thought to look for queer women and men in the prairies.[33] Times change, as do historians and archives. Archival developments and archivists, both institutional and community based, have played a leadership role in collecting materials and, in so doing, made queer historical research feasible.

There are now extensive holdings of queer histories in the prairie region including: the Neil Richards Collection of Sexual and Gender Diversity at the University of Saskatchewan Archives and Special Col-lections, the Neil Richards Collection and the Doug Wilson Collection at the Provincial Archives of Saskatchewan (PAS), and the Manitoba Gay and Lesbian Archives at the University of Manitoba Libraries. The Richards collection at the PAS was one of the first LGBTTQ collections to be "acquired by a Canadian public library" and, at over "17 meters of boxes," it is vast.[34] The Manitoba collection contains the archives from the former Rainbow Resource Centre, including material on Gays for Equality (GFE), Gay Media Collective (GMC), assorted documents from other organizations, as well as the two community-based oral history projects conducted in Winnipeg. Such collections are part of a new wave of archival leadership in queer histories. Adding to these provincial, regional, and university collections are important community history projects in places as diverse as Red Deer, Calgary, Moose Jaw, and Winnipeg. This work could not have been written without all of those foresighted individuals and community iconoclasts who dared to collect queer ephemera and political material in the hopes that "one day" someone would be interested. Where once I feared insufficient primary documents would lead to a partial history, in actuality there is now a huge collection of material for historians to utilize. In fact, there is such a diverse and rich collection of materials that not all of the wealth made it into this volume. Sources for *Prairie Fairies* were drawn from extensive primary archival work in regional, academic, and community archives throughout western Canada, and from oral interviews. There are eighty-two oral interviews in the sample, thirty-one that I conducted in Winnipeg, Saskatoon, Regina, Calgary, Edmonton, Ottawa, and Toronto. The rest originated from three community-based oral history projects in Winnipeg.[35]

Determined to write a feminist, queer history of western women's and men's same-sex, gay, lesbian and queer experiences, the first methodological challenge was to collect sufficient numbers of women to participate in the oral interviews.[36] In the end, I had equal numbers of women and men within my narrator pool, but those simplistic statistics obscure how difficult it was to find women to interview and, conversely, how eager gay men were to share their life histories. A large number of gay men were intrigued by the project and wished to participate. However, while it was difficult to end the interview phase, it became apparent that if I was to finish the research – and given the number of men with similar life histories – I had to set and keep an end date for interviews with gay men. Conversely, I interviewed every lesbian or "gay woman" who agreed to be interviewed. Collecting fifteen usable interviews exhausted all my leads, networks, and narrator referrals. It made me rethink my critique of previous studies where women's voices were absent because it clearly was not entirely a matter of researcher interest or research design.[37]

Not all of my oral histories were with "leaders" or rebels; a few women had more tragic tales of psychiatric institutionalization, of lost children and/or families, or promotions denied. They were cautious about revealing their sexual orientation publicly. Few narrators came from cold calls, advertisements, or media coverage of my work; most were referrals from community leaders or other interviewees. Less frequently, people approached me after public talks to volunteer their stories. Those narrators referred to me by community leaders and activists were referred because of their political involvement or longevity. I only knew two of my narrators before the interviews began. Those introduced by activists often told histories that were disconnected from what their referees thought they might share. In the end, very gratefully, I want to recognize that I was the beneficiary of many very honest, personal stories that affirmed people's decisions to live as lesbians and gays from the 1960s through the 1980s but, at other times, these memories could be heartbreaking.[38] For example, lesbians who never really socialized with other lesbians beyond their partners; lesbians who had been vilified by their communities for being "too activist"; men who identified as gay but had never had sex with other men; men who had never divulged their real name to sexual partners and had never had long-term lovers; men and women who had held leadership positions, professionally or politically, but bitterly spoke to how isolated and lonely those positions had made them. Some leaders of both sexes became so openly identified with gay and lesbian politics that they reported that those who were not shunned them (publicly), fearful that any link with such activists might jeopardize their employment, positions in the community, or family ties. These kinds of memories stung. In the end, taken together, they defy easy categorization or analysis.

Certainly they made any reductive rendering of "communities" highly suspect and erroneous. This book troubles the notion of "community." In actuality prairie queer communities – plural – were stratified by issues of class, gender, race, and educational attainment. This isn't a "community" history, which presumes a united group of actors speaking with one voice. Such a notion is fiction, whether we are historicizing an ethnic, racial, classist, urban, regional, or national community. But a "community" of individuals who were gay and lesbian, participated in community events, had lovers and partners, identified in some fashion as gay or lesbian, includes all sorts and has many stories. I've tried to sample from as many cohorts as possible, because these histories offer a more nuanced, comprehensive record of how people lived as gays and lesbians in the prairies and made it work. Such histories are messy. They include overlapping generations – people who fit best within a homophile generation of activists, and gay people for whom notions of middle-class respectability were paramount, and whose dream was "acceptance" or the space to just be quietly different. Others were part of a liberationist or feminist generation, and they wanted a lot more than merely acceptance, they wanted liberation, the end to second-class treatment, and more equity between men and women. Still others were so discreet and privatized, like the "campus lesbians" in Saskatoon, that they seldom intersected with the community; at least one of my narrators (of a similar vintage) told me that they were not part of the community but they were an interesting type of gay and lesbian experience. One of the strengths of my oral history collection is how candid people were about how they defined communities, and how they understood prairie experiences, and it was not all about celebration. This was very different than the community histories collected in Winnipeg. My life narrators didn't celebrate community or attempt to frame experiences through such notions – although, at times, claims were made for wonderful memories of particular clubs, spaces, eras, and people. Regardless of the tenor of the interviews, a handful of which were persistently downbeat, all of my narrators were revisionists who claimed pride in survival and their choices to forge different paths. These "happy endings" were affixed to many a challenging life history, determined to convince me and perhaps themselves that it was all worth it – after all I was there, in the service of history, recording their stories for posterity.

The collection of community histories gathered in Winnipeg represents a different situation, as male voices predominate and community became an organizing principle starting from their initial proposal for funding support. Winnipeg's oral history project overemphasized activism and self-identification, which meant that they did not capture (or perhaps deem worthy) those more closeted, "respectable" middle-class lesbians who were not "bar people," or who employed discretion as a strategy to enable fulfilling professional and personal lives.[39] Ironically, the low numbers of lesbian narrators in those two collections of interviews inspired Sally Papso, a Winnipeg "lesbian feminist," to aim to locate ten additional women born between 1927 and 1937 to interview.[40] Currently Papso's valuable compilation stands at six archived interviews. She too encountered resistance, and interestingly one of her narratives overlaps with my own collection. After five years only six interviews were completed, while "three others declined to be interviewed as they feared such a public outing." In what amounts to an understatement she noted "lesbians of this age group who are willing to be interviewed are very difficult to find."[41]

While my project wasn't as restrictive about age, accepting narrators who had loved members of their own sex or identified as gay or lesbian from the 1940s to the 1980s, or who had participated in the community events – socials, dances, gay or lesbian political, cultural, or sporting organizations – it still proved difficult to find female narrators. Many women's names were suggested, everyone "knew" of a person who could relate a life history – so I didn't lack for possible interviewees – but those suggestions and my willingness to cast a wide net were not enough. Women were more reticent to put themselves forward. Many simply stated that their own life histories were not noteworthy for an academic project that aimed to "rewrite" the region's history. Interestingly, those who declined all indicated that this was a history they looked forward to reading!

Subsequently, I now realize that one of the first challenges was terminological. I sought gays and lesbians, or queer narrators, but a number of my narrators didn't identify as lesbian. Everyone disliked the term queer intensely, and despite its wide adoption within academic and contemporary LGBTTQ circles there is generational resistance to reclaiming this term. In the interviews I spent much time asking people to define their orientation and how they named their sexual orientation, in addition to asking how important definition was to them (a way to address identity and the centrality of their sexual experiences to their lives). Everyone interviewed indicated that their sexuality was a central facet of their life. Dorothy, and another narrator, originally from Prince Albert, Saskatchewan, indicated they were "gay women."[42] A couple chose dyke with the rest opting for the term lesbian. Many admitted they did not like the word lesbian either, citing its history as a marker of pathology, but nevertheless they identified as lesbians. In addition to disliking the term "queer" they did not warm to my plan to write a "queer" history of the west. As Marion (b. 1934) bluntly informed me: "I hate that word. I am not queer, I am a plain ordinary person."[43] Marion was also an activist; she had worked at the Prince Albert Gay Community Centre in the 1970s. Later, in Saskatoon, she was a stalwart of the city's various gay and lesbian centres, a "grandmother" to many younger dykes who came of age in the 1980s and 1990s. With oral histories, the value is, ultimately, in telling stories that could not be told without them. And it is those who tell their stories who ultimately triumph.

It is their stories you will read, which skews the history towards activists, mavericks, and leaders. Wherever possible, I reference those who tended to avoid interviews (although I have collected three interviews with discrete, compartmentalized individuals who likely would not have responded to calls for interviews had they not been encouraged to speak with me). The stories of those who don't talk deserve to be known, and I have attempted to see that their voices and their experiences are not entirely silenced or marginalized. Sometimes what is offered here are only glimpses, but it was important to include those glimpses so as to most fully capture prairie queer life in all its forms.

Beyond the search for women's stories I was also keen to find Indigenous narrators, and at the very least to critique and complicate the "whiteness" of these queer prairie worlds. As many others have argued, "race mediates how queerness is lived, expressed and indeed remembered," yet unable to locate Indigenous queer participants for the oral interviews, and with very, very limited archival materials upon which to draw, the history that could be told here is largely a settler queer history.[44] In the end, the best I could do was capture those moments where Indigenous actors moved into the mostly white frame – in a handful of the Winnipeg interviews, in interviews with Euro-Canadian narrators (in response to my questions about Indigenous men and women's involvement in settler queer political or social activities), and in a handful of archival documents. This absence is both telling and disheartening. As scholars such as Scott Lauria Morgensen, Andrea Smith, Quo-Li Driskell, Chris Finley, and Brian Joseph Gilley have argued, queer histories and theorists have largely failed to engage with Indigenous people and settler colonialism.[45] And, to be blunt, "queer histories of modern sexualities tend to study non-Natives without examining their formation within settler colonialism." The prairies are the traditional homelands of the First Nations and Metis people, and therefore the glaring absence of Indigenous histories in this work reminds us of the power of the state and the conditions under which Indigenous people lived during this study (initially on reserves, removed from cities and towns). Canada's recently completed Truth and Reconciliation Commission, and its ensuring reports, makes clear that there is much to learn about the oppression and abuse perpetrated on Indigenous families by the residential school system.[46] The enduring, generational legacies of the residential schools, child welfare policies, the failure to respect the treaty negotiations and treaty relationships, and a host of other institutional and state policies that undermined First Nations families, culture and language, health, and economic self-determination were overwhelming. Where the Euro-Canadian narrators I interviewed were fighting for recognition as queer people and perhaps were engaged in gay liberationist activism, First Nations and Metis residents of the prairies were engaged in resistance with provincial and federal governments over these colonial policies.

Having hoped for a more inclusive representation of First Nations queer histories, nevertheless this work does provide glimpses of the formation of some First Nations groups and occasionally actors. For example, the Nichiwakan group, which began in Winnipeg in 1981, was part of a wave of organizations inspired by the Gay American Indians groups in the US.[47] Many of these groups tended to form later, post-1985, and thus the terminal end date of this study has also, unintentionally, affected the ability to include more Indigenous queer histories. Starting in the 1990s, issues of Indigenous sexuality would be framed differently, and that too has had an impact on this history. It was in Winnipeg, in the 1990s, in a meeting of Native activists and scholars that the term "two-spirited" was chosen. This term itself is the subject of much confusion in non-Indigenous communities because it does not merely signify, or name, a minority sexual identity. As Morgensen explains, "Two-Spirited describe(s) an integral location GLBTQ and other Native people might occupy in the shared culture of a Native nation which through kinship, economics, social life or religion linked all Native people in a relationship."[48] As a non-Indigenous scholar, I agree with Morgensen's assertion that we (non-Indigenous queer scholars) need to enter "accountable conversations under … Native leadership" that will ultimately enable a more complex portrait of these parallel worlds to emerge.[49] This study takes the first step, writing a history of settler queer people prior to 1985. Much work needs to be done after my study's terminal date, historicizing the history of two-spirited people and identities in the west, and analysing the impact of HIV/AIDS in the region. What is most likely to yield success is a programme of research specifically focused on two-spirited identities and identified women and men. Greater specificity and a primary focus on two-spirited people will require different strategies and partnerships with two-spirited groups and individuals. I am encouraged that such work has begun, and is being told by Indigenous elders.[50]

My hope is that *Prairie Fairies* enriches prairie history by expanding the frame to include the histories of pride, empowerment, harassment, violence, activism, and homophobia that are part of the modern prairie west. In so doing, though, it asks us to revise what we thought we knew about western Canadian society. Recapturing and analysing the prairie urban queer past complicates and enriches western Canadian history. Queer peoples' struggles to take lovers and carve out lives and social spaces are important because they offer insights into active resistance, accommodations, tolerance, and acceptance in the prairies. The stereotypes of the region as a bleak, persistently homophobic place scarred by violence and police persecutions has some basis in fact but queer women and men were not merely victims of a region noted for valorizing nuclear families, faith, and farming. Larger prairie cities provided refuge. This research reveals many similarities with queer urban practices elsewhere in North America. Yet, the timeline of these developments, the cities' histories, scales, and compositions combined with prairie geographies and cultural sensibilities to produce subtle shadings and differences. What to outsiders may appear to be small western cities with obvious points of comparison with other American cities miss important specifics of the Canadian context. Take the Manitoba capital as an example. Winnipeg exerts a disproportionately strong gravitational pull within the province and western region as the political, financial, cultural, and educational capital of Manitoba. Not surprisingly, it was the queer capital as well. Stereotypes suggest that queer people fled Winnipeg. Rather, it was a destination city for a far-flung queer population of small-town and rural Manitobans, northwestern Ontarians, and, less frequently, former Saskatchewan residents. Equally important, Winnipeggers (similar to many prairie residents) adhered to a set of regional characteristics that could be summarized as comprising a live-and-let-live ethos and resilience. Those who stayed in Winnipeg were a determined bunch, metaphorically and literally, as they had to contend with a harsh social and physical climate. Basic geographical, social, demographic, and organizational practices, which were honed over the course of Euro-Canadian settlement of the prairies, enabled spaces for difference, community building (a prairie necessity), and a pragmatic approach to daily possibilities that were shared with heterosexual prairie residents.

Saskatoon and Regina, the smallest of the four cities, were different. These two cities have, throughout Saskatchewan's history, been locked in a friendly competition to differentiate themselves from each other. Regina, the Queen City, is the provincial capital, and home to the Royal Canadian Mounted Police (RCMP) barracks. The role of government, government offices and services, in addition to the police presence, combined with a smaller, liberal arts university, the University of Regina, skews Regina towards a "government" town mentality vis-à-vis queer communities. Saskatoon is home to the provincial university, the University of Saskatchewan, and is the "hub city" for commerce, education, health, and services for the central and northern areas of the province. A bit edgier, a bit more entrepreneurial and hence a bit wealthier than Regina, there is a more expansive outlook in Saskatoon. It was Saskatoon that developed the better-established lesbian and gay communities, services, activism, and energy. Similar to the other cities, Saskatoon drew queer people from across the province by virtue of these opportunities. It also drew people from elsewhere, such as the expat American activist duo, Walter Davis and Bill Fields, who relocated their queer journal, *After Stonewall*, from Winnipeg to Saskatoon, because of the liberationist politics of Saskatoon. Regina's queer community was more focused on their "club." This club, now called Q Nightclub and Lounge, is owned by the Gay and Lesbian Community of Regina (GLCR). Regina's club is the longest continuously running queer club in western Canada; it was and remains a distinguishing feature of that city and a central hub for various social activities.

Edmonton, the final city in this study, is really the outlier. Ironically, this is where my interest in queer prairie life was initially piqued. In the 1990s, I was fascinated by what seemed like an incongruous story, that of Delwyn Vriend, a lab instructor at King's University College, a Christian college located in Edmonton, Alberta, who was fired in 1991 because it was known that he was publicly gay and involved in gay activism. Those views were incompatible with King's values. Vriend attempted to file a grievance with the Alberta Human Rights Commission and the commission refused to investigate. Because Alberta's human rights code did not name homosexuality as a protected category for employment (unlike gender), the commission informed Vriend that there were no grounds for an investigation into his dismissal. King's was perfectly within their rights to fire him for being gay regardless of the calibre of his work (which both sides agreed was exemplary). Vriend took the Alberta Human Rights Commission to court. And over a series of court cases and appeals, with much regional, and later national press coverage, this case eventually wound its way to the Supreme Court of Canada. In 1998, in a major victory for Alberta's gays and lesbians, the Supreme Court justices declared that sexual orientation must be "read in" to Alberta's human rights code. When that national story broke, and without any context or knowledge of Alberta gay history that preceded it, Vriend's case appeared perplexing. In fact, it appeared audacious to think that in a province with no human rights protection, a gay lab instructor would demand reinstatement at a Christian college. My curiosity was peaked: who and what had inspired Vriend to stand up to this discrimination? From that moment, I became fascinated with knowing more about the queer regional histories in Alberta. Quite quickly, I discovered that stereotypes of Alberta were not entirely accurate. There was a history of queer activism in "Redmonton," as the city is often mockingly or affectionately called.

Edmonton contains a lively mix of government, government agencies, higher education (most notably the University of Alberta), and commerce, namely the West Edmonton Mall (Canada's largest consumer paradise). The city's role as the fly-out city for northern provincial and territorial residents creates a unique vibe. If Winnipeg is one of the more cosmopolitan cities in the prairies, and Saskatoon is a well-equipped small city with culture, education, and resource wealth, Edmonton, for all its infrastructure, wealth, and population, is the toughest city. The gay men's sporting team called themselves "the Roughnecks" advisedly (Calgary used the term "the Apollo Club"). Calgary's wealth, in oil, resources, and finances, skews glitzy (albeit it is a cowboy glamour) with a strong dash of entrepreneurialism. Calgary gets the glory while Edmonton's more blue-collar ethos makes the province work: providing government, bureaucracy, and resource workers. Not surprisingly, queer life in Edmonton was different from Saskatoon and Winnipeg – more furtive, heavily invested in social services, particularly "counselling" and support, and socializing. Pride events in Edmonton began in the 1980s, not the 1970s like Winnipeg and Saskatoon – and there would be no marching until the 1990s. Bath raids that galvanized activism in Montreal in 1977 and Toronto in February 1981 caused much grief in Edmonton in May 1981. In Edmonton, straight residents initiated protests against the police's draconian behaviour, while gays and lesbians watched from the sidelines. For all of that, the notion that Alberta's politics stifles all dissent, or made queer life impossible, was not historically accurate. This research illustrates how the largely middle-class activists and organizers strove to make it safe, physically and mentally, for women and men to be queer in Edmonton. And it makes plain how much further they had to go than their peers in Saskatchewan and Manitoba.

Prairie Fairies is divided into three parts. Part One: Queer Spaces and Opportunities, 1930–1969 historicizes a wide range of queer experiences prior to the formation of explicitly gay, lesbian, or queer spaces. Chapter 1, "The Torch of Golden Boy Burns Bright," focuses on Winnipeg from 1933 to 1969 exploring the diverse queer urban life created in the city. Chapter 2, "A Kiss Is Never Just a Kiss," broadens the lens to explore Saskatchewan queer history prior to 1970, including Regina and Saskatoon, but also small-town and rural experiences. Queer people were inventive, and strategies varied by age, gender, location, and availability of local networks. In Winnipeg many of the spaces of this subaltern queer world encouraged and respected anonymity – the baths, cruising sites, the YMCA, or drag activities – and thus dalliances with heterosexually married men were commonly reported. Even those individuals who subsequently identified as gay recalled that during the 1950s and 1960s they frequently negotiated "double lives" in their attempts to pass as heterosexuals by day while they indulged their queer desires by night.[51] In Saskatchewan lesbian and gay people enacted diverse strategies. The University of Saskatchewan (U of S) campus, in particular, provided spaces for queer activity and later for activism. But it was also true that rural life provided space and pockets of opportunities. It was highly context specific, and using life histories from oral narrators it illustrates how individual determination could make or break these possibilities. You could not pull up to the Tiny Township, Saskatchewan gay and lesbian beer parlour, but you could certainly find lesbian couples quietly living their lives, "bachelor" farmers well ensconced on farms and in their communities, and a variety of queer individuals who fashioned queer lives in places that we might think were anathema to such an existence. Employing a queer perspective, as opposed to writing a gay history, resists affixing historical identity labels and "attempts to understand the conceptual categories and ways of knowing actually used by actors in the past."[52] In so doing, it captures individuals who did not fit into present-day categories of sexual orientation and affords a more nuanced portrait of queer lives in the prairies.

Part Two: Communities, Community Building, and Culture, 1970–1985 explores the creation of explicitly gay and lesbian organizations, spaces, and culture in Winnipeg, Saskatoon, Regina, and Edmonton. Organized into three chapters this section provides an overview of the developments in building queer spaces – institutionally in bricks and mortar clubs, centres, and restaurants, but also the tremendous energy devoted to the creation of cultural materials and programming. These were transformational developments in each city, and illustrate a regional approach to knowledge sharing, networks, and a ready, travelling clientele happy to drive to another city to visit a "club" for a special event. Each city developed a certain expertise: Winnipeg was the cultural powerhouse, heavily invested in education and to that end producing newsletters, radio shows, and later cable television programming, in addition to having clubs, bars, and a restaurant. Winnipeg, and to a lesser degree Edmonton, also had a wide assortment of gay religious groups – those affiliated with the various major Christian churches, support groups for gay Christians (particularly popular with gay and lesbian Mennonites), and branches of the Metropolitan Community Church (the gay Christian church). Regina was known for its club and the ease with which residents of Regina could drive to Winnipeg or Saskatoon for larger queer events. Saskatoon focused on their gay and lesbian centre and activism (primarily covered in part three) but they too produced newsletters, held dances, and created a regional queer cultural event – Metamorphosis – which became incredibly popular. Edmonton had more commercial queer space than the other centres and devoted considerable energy to the establishment of various counselling groups, phone lines, and information sharing. It is suggestive of the challenges of being queer in Edmonton that so much energy and resources went into counselling individuals struggling with their sexual orientation and negotiating the commensurate identities issues. In all cases, these "services" were for city residents, but they were also well used by rural and small-town queer people. One of the old jokes about the prairies is that prairie people measure distance in hours – how many hours it takes to drive from place to place. Car travel mitigated the sense of isolation that had plagued earlier generations of prairie residents. Like their straight counterparts, queer prairie people thought nothing of routinely driving relatively long distances (two–four hours) to attend events in other cities. So, these "visitors" from small towns, farms, and other cities were routinely in attendance in urban clubs, community centres, theatrical performances, and sports events.

Part Three: Activism, Reaction, Visibility, and Violence explores the activism generated with the prairie region. Again, organized by city, the various chapters illustrate the reactions to "rights" cases, American homophobia (Anita Bryant's tour), bath raids (Edmonton), queer-bashing (Saskatoon and Winnipeg), and the creation of pride events. Like elementary science, each moment of activism and greater visibility generated a reaction. Contrary to what one may surmise, not all reactions were negative. Sometimes the reactions were positive and led to moments of alliance between queer and straight residents and neighbours. Other times, visibility provoked anxiety in older members of the queer communities, some of whom did not want to be visible or "political" and resented these newer modes of identity politics supplanting the older forms of discreet subcultural life. For example, groups of middle-class lesbians in Edmonton and Saskatoon continued their practice of discretionary tactics. They never publically acknowledged that they were queer although they lived with same-sex partners and within plain view of their neighbours and colleagues. Sometimes the reactions were violent, from police raids to gay bashings and murder, and those moments were illustrative of the homophobic violence that could easily erupt. These regional similarities and differences are, I believe, part of a significantly "prairie" reaction to universal developments in late twentieth-century queer politics, urban life, and greater social visibility. This section also assesses the surprisingly strong activist impulses and organizations that were created in the prairie west and highlights the fact that in the 1970s, the city of Saskatoon played a leadership role in Canadian lesbian and gay activism. Meanwhile, "five hours down the road" in Edmonton, activism of the sort that propelled Doug Wilson from his graduate degree in education to becoming a well-respected queer activist in 1975, played out rather differently for Delwyn Vriend – who was dismissed from a job in an educational institution because of his "public" gay identity and involvement in gay activism. Vriend's case was launched after a very important development in Canadian legal and human rights law, the creation and implementation of Canada's Charter of Rights and Freedoms. As Miriam Smith has argued, access to this new legal framework (in 1985) would shift approaches to "rights" acquisition in Canada.[53]

Prairie Fairies makes a contribution to a small but important literature analysing the history of gay liberationist activism in Canada and of the ways that Canadian activism was inspired by – and aware of – American developments, while differing from them in important ways.[54] Importantly, in a context where, as Miriam Smith has argued, the "national" movement was never more than a "set of loose networks … rather than a coherent actor," local queer organizations were the source of most activities. The prairies thriving activist scenes, in Winnipeg and Saskatoon in particular, would play an important role in generating local activism and contributing to the "national" liberationist scene. Westerners played a more significant role than earlier pan-national works have acknowledged, including that western activist groups hosted three of the eight national gay and lesbian conferences held between 1973 and 1980.

Gay liberationist strategies and tactics continued to be articulated and used in the west well into the mid-1980s. At a time when many central Canadian organizations would shift to "rights talk" and legal "equality seeking" in the early to mid-1980s, westerners continued with various platforms of the liberationist strategies, including consciousness-raising, education, and human rights matters when they arose. Taking a historical, regional approach to gay and lesbian activism captures continuity and change, offers more perspective into social actors and local organizations, and deepens our knowledge of the breadth of regional queer political work. It was AIDS that changed the focus of western Canadian activist organizations, as well as activist migrations and burnout, not a shift to "rights" talk in the advent of the new Canadian Charter of Rights and Freedoms.

By 1985, AIDS had arrived in all the prairie cities and this plague dramatically transformed the organizational, activist, and queer communities in the various cities, as attention turned from liberationist goals to medical advocacy and support. Hopefully, future historians will research and write that social history. The connections and debates fostered about health, politics, sexuality, and relations between lesbians and gay men post-AIDS offers another vantage point on questions about place, sexuality, and queer politics. AIDS conclusively ended any anachronistic or utopian notion that prairie cities were not home to sizable populations of lesbians and gays, or that LGBTTQ. residents would be content to be second-class citizens with respect to medical care, political representation, or basic human rights protections.[55]

From 1930 to 1985, *Prairie Fairies* demonstrates that queer people created communities; fostered social, educational and social service opportunities; and, indeed, created spaces for prairie residents to be gay or lesbian. People found pockets of urban spaces in which to be queer – this became a precursor to formal politics for some individuals, but also a way to assert a political identity in a place constantly trying to ignore, silence, or eradicate such differences. Putting the queer westerners back into the modern history of prairie cities and prairie societies reclaims important literal and historical space for prairie queer people, and moves them from the margins to the centre of the historical frame. From the 1930s through to the mid-1980s, queer westerners were part of vibrant queer and straight communities, and stories of these "mavericks" ironically fit beautifully within the prairie historiography at the very same time that their existence challenges everything we thought we knew about these provinces.

PART ONE

1930–1969 Queer Spaces
and Opportunities

Chapter One

"The Torch of Golden Boy Burns Bright": Winnipeg 1930–1969

One time these friends of ours, and this other queen, Bobby Turner, well we used to go every week to this place in St. Boniface to play cards – a straight place. We went by streetcar in our drag and we walked in there and they just about fell over. But they enjoyed it. I don't know how wise they were to us, but they thought it was terrific, and many of the men asked me to dance. We did some silly things.[1]

George Smith, Winnipeg, 1990

We used to gather under that [steel canopy at the Alexander Dock] and do our little routine of … chorus girl kicking of We Are the Girls of the Pansy Parade. They still sing that, don't they? At this point Bert sang the interviewer the whole lyric "Our sucking will please, our fucking will tease. We're the Girls of the Pansy Parade!" [interviewer laughs] … I can remember about 25 gays down there on a warm summer night. Just like up at the Legislative Building.[2]

– Bert Sigurdson, Winnipeg, 1990

The geography of queer Winnipeg made possible by Smith's and Sigurdson's oral histories of cruising and drag during the 1930s offer portraits of a vibrant world, largely outside the purview of heterosexual Winnipeggers, where the camaraderie of queer culture and expert knowledge of the city's sexual geographies marked one as a worldly sophisticate in a relatively staid, prairie city.[3] Men discovered this world because they were alert to opportunities and difference – a code word, flamboyant clothes, make-up, or teenagers and young men engaged in "swishy" or "fairy-like" gender transgressive behaviours. Most queer social spaces in Winnipeg were located in the downtown core.[4] Near the train depot, men patronized certain working-class beer parlours (often housed in downtown hotels); Chinese-run cafes; diners and restaurants; the steam baths; the docks; public and commercial toilets (tearooms in gay parlance); the extensive river trails and paths along the Red and Assiniboine Rivers; and, famously, "the hill" behind the legislature. On the hill they were provocatively watched over by Winnipeg's Golden Boy. One of Manitoba's most recognizable symbols, Golden Boy is the focal point of the legislature's domed roof.[5] By day the classically designed statue of a winged male god with his torch held aloft symbolized Western civilization and enterprise. At night, subversively, Golden Boy served as signpost to a nocturnal world of male same-sex experiences.

While Golden Boy and the hill remained a constant from 1930 to 1970, there were other significant changes over this time. First, the subculture became larger and increasingly visible as more men found queer venues and as the lesbian presence became visible in the 1950s. Second, this era would witness a transformation as queer subcultural practices receded into the background and gay and lesbian communities emerged. No longer content to merely participate in a range of queer activities, increasing numbers of Winnipeg residents began to self-identify, to themselves and others, as gay men and lesbians. The adoption and use of those labels, as well as the later establishment of organizations and social venues that were explicitly for gay and lesbian Winnipeggers, politically transformed social and gender relations. Conversely, as the subculture and later the communities became more visible, the dangers posed by the law, the police, and psychiatrists increased as did the risks of alienation from family, friends, and colleagues. To manage those risks men and women used a variety of strategies – evasion, deception, role playing, the compartmentalization of their so-called public and private lives, and sometimes ultrarespectability – to live lives of their own choosing and design. They were also aided by a live-and-let-live ethos shared by the mainstream residents of the city that, provided certain codes were observed, remained willfully naive and ignored "queer" moments occurring at the margins of urban life. For owners of small businesses, such as cafes, bathhouses, or restaurants, this tacit support or tolerance could be financially lucrative.

This gendered and sexual behaviour in Winnipeg shared many commonalities with cities beyond Canadian boarders, yet there were also key differences that made Winnipeg special. First, in the interwar and war years, Winnipeg's relative geographic isolation and the general population's ignorance about queer subculture allowed for tremendous freedoms for those able to locate queer spaces. Bold young queers like Smith and Sigurdson capitalized on this provincialism. Second, in contrast to arguments made about some American cities, the post–Second World War era witnessed an expansion of opportunities for same-sex activity and increasing visibility.[6] Those interviewed whose experiences spanned the interwar and post-war period observed that the 1950s and 1960s brought more openness to Winnipeg's queer subculture as more modern, expanded liquor and commercial entertainment laws increased the possibilities for commercial leisure. At first glance this seems curious because we know that Canada was not immune from Cold War anxieties and purges. However, as the work of Gentile and Kinsman has illustrated, queers were creative about fashioning a wide-ranging variety of public and commercial spaces for socializing and sex despite the risks.[7] Canada was far less affluent than much of the United States in the first half of the twentieth century. After the Second World War there was much "catching up" as average Canadians saw the economy flourish and their incomes rise dramatically. Nowhere was this more evident than in Winnipeg. Winnipeg endured thirty difficult years after the First World War including post-war unrest and class conflict; the searing, long-term effects of the Great Depression; and the psychological blow of having their position as the "gateway," primary western-Canadian city usurped by Vancouver. Such background information provides the vitally important context to understanding the euphoric memories of those queers and lesbians who recounted the late 1940s and 1950s as an era of possibilities, optimism, and exuberance. This tremendous economic rebound and renewed growth in Winnipeg enabled more single, working men and women to afford to rent rooms and apartments. These private spaces alongside the increase in commercial spaces were prerequisites for the expansion of the queer subculture. Greater disposable income also enabled many middle-class men and women to travel to cities with larger gay and lesbian commercial and social spaces. Minneapolis and San Francisco were favourite destinations and further stimulated a sense of queer identity, communities, and, later in the decade, activism.

Third, counter-intuitively, Winnipeg became a destination for queer migrants. As the provincial capital of Manitoba and the largest city within the region, which encompasses Manitoba and northwestern Ontario, queer youth growing up in small towns and rural areas often gravitated to Winnipeg. It was in Winnipeg that one could fashion a queer life. It was possible to meet other women and men, frequenting networks of commercial and public spaces where queer socializing and/or sex might be feasible. Many individuals initially came to the city to study at the University of Manitoba. Others relocated to Winnipeg for work and sometimes, as in the case of dancers with the Royal Winnipeg Ballet, that meant securing employment in a queer-defined workplace. While it was not a "wide-open town," nor internationally recognized for homosexual opportunities or tourism as were San Francisco, New York, or London, provincial and regional knowledge networks marked Winnipeg as a site of possibility.[8] Once individuals found social spaces and a cohort of queer friends, the city took on a different hue. At the same time, they were under no illusions about the limited scope of urban queer activities by comparison with other North American queer tourist destinations. A determined cohort made a decision to stay in Winnipeg. Those who stayed were clear about their attachments to the city and the region: the prairies were home. Their families and jobs were there and Winnipeg struck the right balance – big enough to live as a queer person, but still connected to the places and people that were important. This determination to stay reflects ongoing prairie pride, resilience, and endurance. There are far easier places to live – socially, culturally, or geographically – than the prairies. The bonds occasioned by hardship and the connections established when surmounting those challenges were routinely cited as forging communities and community-mindedness in small towns and prairie cities. This definably prairie attitude, shared by settler queer and heterosexual residents alike, was a recurrent refrain articulated in the Winnipeg oral interviews.

Finally, the politics of gay and lesbian activism in Winnipeg adhered to a slightly different trajectory than in other cities. Although the history of Winnipeg's gay and lesbian activism is addressed later in this book, it deserves to be noted that it was only during the mid- to late 1960s that Winnipeg residents became familiar with gay and lesbian identities and politics as articulated in the United States. News of these developments emboldened a small coterie of university students to import gay and lesbian politics into the city in the early 1970s. Formal gay and lesbian organizing in Winnipeg thus lags behind that of comparable American cities where "some gay men and lesbians were organizing for freedom" decades before the watershed Stonewall Riot of June 1969.[9] Winnipeg was also out of step with Vancouver and Toronto where gay activist groups began to form in the mid-1960s. While this book doesn't posit a simplistic linkage between gay/lesbian identity and activism, recognizing that the majority of gays and lesbians were not seriously involved in activism (as judged by the disparity in numbers between social organizations and activist organizations within the same cities), the introduction of such organizations offer interesting historical opportunities. In particular, Winnipeg's history affords an intriguing perspective on the transition from the earlier predominantly queer subcultural model to the more open, visible gay and lesbian "communities" contemporary model. Thinking critically about this process and why some participants were resistant to such changes (first identity and then, later, activism) offers useful insights into identity formation, social cohesion, and preconditions for gay and lesbian activism.

Methodological Notes and Challenges

As indicated in the introduction, one of the primary reasons queer westerners have not been extensively featured in prairie histories has its roots in methodological challenges and the difficulties of finding sufficient documentation from which to reconstruct such accounts. Recognizing the political value of knowing their histories, in 1990 a small group of concerned individuals initiated the Manitoba Gay and Lesbian Oral History Project. This far-sighted decision has provided an invaluable primary source base without which this book would not be possible. The archive, called Lesbians and Gays in Manitoba: The Development of a Minority, is preserved in the Manitoba Gay and Lesbian Archives at the University of Manitoba (U of M) Library.[10] The value of this archive for sexuality historians cannot be overemphasized. Supplemented and enriched by existing print and cultural documents, including Jerry Walsh's self-published memoir *Backward Glances at a By-Gone Era*, these texts permit the reconstruction of a cultural history of male same-sex desire – in Walsh's words before "homosexuals were called gays."[11] Until now, only a handful of graduate students and scholars have had the privilege of using these documents.[12]

As with all oral histories, these interviews need to be approached with care as they tell us as much about the early same-sex experiences in Winnipeg as they do the era in which they were collected. There are obvious silences, omissions, and absences. Nan Alamilla Boyd recently analysed the ramifications of the field's reliance on oral history sources, questioning their reliability and the precise nature of the "truths" revealed.[13] While the issues of memory, nostalgia, and narrator's propensities to self-edit their lives for the official record are well-known challenges with all oral sources, there is one particular trial unique to historians of queer sexualities: the issue of sexual identity and the political importance placed upon such identities. "Despite the best of intentions and the lightest touch," Boyd observes, "these oral histories are always offered up in relation to the larger gay and lesbian research project" and are "always structured around a certain historical desire for gay and lesbian political visibility."[14] The so-called "coming-out narrative" predominates and those interviewed tend to be individuals who self-identity as gay men or lesbians.

Such was the case in Winnipeg where the 1990 oral histories project was initiated by a handful of local activists intent on creating a gay and lesbian community archive. Their successful application for an oral history grant from Manitoba Culture, Heritage and Citizenship stated that their intention was to "record the experiences of gay men and lesbian women in Manitoba to 1970."[15] The third of thirty-nine questions asked informants to recall "when you realize[d] that you were gay or lesbian?"[16] Not surprisingly, the collective narratives that emerge from the interviews were about self-identification. They chart a progressive chronology from the earlier, informal series of subcultural queer activities and queer spaces, to the contemporary era when a recognizable minority of gays and lesbians emerged in Manitoba. Narrators spoke with evident pride and their personal histories were usually, but not always, affirmative.

Interviewer David Theodore, then a McGill history student, conducted all the tape-recorded interviews in Winnipeg and Selkirk, Manitoba. Telephone interviews proved problematic to record due to their poor sound quality and were quickly abandoned as impractical. Without a travel budget, by default those who were interviewed for this project were city residents. As Winnipeggers they were preoccupied with staking a claim to a differentiated Winnipeg identity and experience. Many informants provided their own individualistic, comparative perspectives about how Winnipeg compared with Toronto, Minneapolis, New York, and London. Some participants were critical of Winnipeg's flaws and limitations for queer people, while others were civic boosters. In addition to their localized, personal recollections, participants were asked questions about major historical events – the Second World War, second-wave feminism – and issues of importance to the queer, gay and lesbian communities such as medical, psychiatric, and social perceptions of homosexuality throughout their lifetimes. It was evident that those who created the interview questions were familiar with American gay and lesbian history and the importance placed on key watershed events such as the Second World War.[17]

Cognizant of the importance of broad representation, the collective carefully noted that "attempts were also made to insure that interviews included individuals from different sub-groups within Manitoba's lesbian and gay community." Initially two hundred people volunteered for interviews and "75 individuals were selected as suitable for actual interviews according to the time frame of their recollections or the singularity of their recollections."[18] Ultimately twenty-two interviews were completed: seventeen men and five women. Ethnically, the vast majority were Euro-Canadians. Only four self-declared First Nations individuals were interviewed.[19] With respect to race and ethnicity, the organizers offered a sample that mirrored (broadly) the contours of Winnipeg's ethnic and racial composition in the post-war era. However, they were keenly aware that the small sample of lesbian interviews would be rightly criticized as unrepresentative. The organizers speculated that women's participation had been limited by the fact that there were "fewer social opportunities … for lesbians prior to 1960" and because "the suicide rate for lesbians was phenomenally high prior to 1970."[20] How they drew these conclusions is unclear.[21] It is overly simplistic to blame the relative absence of women's voices on fewer social opportunities. As Cameron Duder's research illustrates, middle-class lesbians in this era purposefully chose discretion and limited visibility to minimize the economic and social risks of living as a lesbian.[22] Those habits and defences are not easily abandoned. Middle-class lesbian reticence combined with a lack of commitment to locating more women and reassuring them about the value of their recollections are the more likely reasons for the small response rate. Recently, there was an attempt to rectify this imbalance, with the addition of a new oral history collection "Born Between the Wars: Women Who Grew Up Lesbian in Manitoba before and after World War II," which features six lesbian interviews.[23] Lead researcher and interviewer, Sally Papso, also hit a roadblock in her attempt to find lesbian interviewees. She admitted that it was more difficult than she imagined, and that the ingrained patterns of "discretion" and caution about revealing too much of their private lives meant that even a well-connected, long-time Winnipeg lesbian activist faced challenges finding participants. Ultimately, the nature of the original project and the failure to recruit a more representative sampling of narrators shapes the histories that can be produced. My research is sensitive to silences and strives to offer complex analytical assessments of the narrators' histories, but there are hurdles that cannot be cleared. Male voices predominate in Winnipeg's pre-1970s history because of the source limitations not because I intended to exclude women or because lesbians were necessarily rare in Winnipeg.[24]

Setting the Scene: Winnipeg

As Canadian cities go, Winnipeg has received considerable historical attention.[25] Famously located in the "heart" of the country at the confluence of the Red and Assiniboine Rivers, Winnipeg has a lengthy history of settlement, conflict between Indigenous, Metis groups, and settler newcomers, and commerce. Incorporated in 1873, Winnipeg's heyday occurred in the late nineteenth and early twentieth century as railroad construction and then the massive transportation infrastructure within the city laid the groundwork for waves of European and Euro-Canadian settlers and investors. Winnipeg became the primary "gateway city" to the western region.[26] People and goods funneled west into and beyond the city. Winnipeg's growth was meteoric surging from a mere 241 residents in 1871 to 136,035 in 1911.[27] Initially, most of these newcomers were single men and by 1911 the city's sex ratio was still 120 males to 100 females.

Given the rapid growth and the demographic challenges inherent in a city with a disproportionate population of young, single, working men, issues of morality were sources of civic debate prior to the First World War. Winnipeg had two segregated red-light districts. Prostitution was regarded by many, including the city's police force, as a necessary by-product of the large numbers of single male workers and travellers.[28] Winnipeg was "infamous for its saloons and houses of prostitution, which served the tens-of-thousands of single men who passed through the city on their way to work or settle further west. It is doubtless the case, therefore, that same-sex sexual experiences occurred."[29] Civic reformers and first-wave feminist activists opposed this utilitarian view of prostitution and initiated repeated campaigns to eradicate the brothels. Despite such efforts, they remained fixtures in the city until the Second World War. Importantly, then, Winnipeg, like many western North American cities, has a lengthy history of heterosexual licentiousness.[30] Furthermore, this history was often regarded as a colourful remnant of the city's boomtown, western ethos. For our purposes, such histories provide an important context within which to contextualize sexual activities in the city. It was not only queer men who sought sex in particular geographical locations and spaces in Winnipeg. Evidently, there were a plethora of urban opportunities to act upon both heterosexual and queer desires. Prior to sexual activity becoming a marker of identity, men could and did seek opportunities for sex in the city whether it was with female prostitutes or effeminate, young queer men, as the sources below illustrate.

Much of this sexual activity occurred near the railways in the Point Douglas red-light district, or in the railway hotels, cafes, and public spaces near these venues. Railways shaped the spatial and geographical layout of Winnipeg, determining social, commercial, and financial activities within the city. The Canadian Pacific Railway (CPR) yards in Winnipeg were said to be the largest in the British Empire.[31] The CPR lines bisected the city's east and west cutting off the north part of the city from the downtown core. The "north end" was the working-class part of the city and the destination for most of the working-class Eastern European, Jewish, and British immigrants who flooded into Winnipeg prior to the First World War.[32] Not surprisingly, the key commercial, financial, retail, and service industries that supported or depended upon the railways were all clustered in the city's core. Importantly, the city was also rich in cultural and educational facilities. It was home to the University of Manitoba (founded in 1877) and a disproportionately large number of theatres and cultural venues. Such infrastructure meant that Winnipeg was a destination for an international who's who of visiting literati, musicians, and politicians.[33] And it also meant that it drew average people, families, couples, and travellers from the region, including the American Midwest, who were eager to enjoy the range of possibilities it offered.[34]

While the city's geographical location continued to be advantageous well into the twentieth century, it could not retain its title as the pre-eminent western Canadian city. In 1913, Winnipeg was Canada's third-largest city, but by the 1920s it had been eclipsed by Vancouver as eastern manufacturers opted for commercial shipping (via the newly opened Panama Canal) rather than railways.[35] Equally significant, the dislocation after the First World War, the influenza outbreak of 1918, and the Winnipeg General Strike of 1919 were a series of sharp shocks to the city. In 1931 Winnipeg's population was 218,785. The Great Depression walloped the city and further exacerbated its hardships. Twenty years later the population of Winnipeg had increased only marginally to 235,710 residents. The relatively static population figures hide significant demographic changes. In 1931, 56.5 per cent of Winnipeg residents were Canadian-born; by 1971 this had grown to 75 per cent. In 1931, 60 per cent of Winnipeggers chose British as their ethnic identification, while 38 per cent indicated a "European" heritage.[36] While the prairies received a significant stream of immigration from central and Eastern Europe, Winnipeg's ethnic composition differentiated it from the other prairie cities. In particular, the consistently large number of Jewish residents has been a hallmark of Winnipeg's cultural and commercial life (in 1931 17,236 Winnipeggers were Jewish).[37] In the early 1930s Indigenous residents were not yet a presence in the city because the Indian Act regulated them to reserves. In 1971, 42.9 per cent of Winnipeg residents listed British as their ethnicity, while the European ethnic population of Winnipeg had increased. Ukrainians were then the largest ethnic subgroup (64,305 people; 12 per cent of the population) while the Jewish community had grown to 19,380 individuals.[38] Indigenous residents had increased significantly to 4,945 women and men.

The conclusion of Second World War restored prosperity and optimism in Winnipeg as "factories hummed, new industries and head offices located in the city, business was generally good, and housing construction exploded."[39] "Winnipeg also continued to become more cosmopolitan and tolerant in the late 1950s and 1960s."[40] Not surprisingly, queer informants corroborated this in their recollections, observing that the rebounding economy launched more social and commercial venues. Culturally, there were additional important developments. Prior to the war, the Winnipeg Ballet Club, the precursor to the acclaimed Royal Winnipeg Ballet, was formed. The Winnipeg Symphony Orchestra was founded in 1948 and a decade later the Manitoba Theatre Centre was launched under the direction of John Hirsch.[41] Arts and cultural organizations were and remain important to Winnipeg's identity but they were also critical to fostering social and economic spaces for queer women and men. In 1967, the provincial government created a new institute of higher education in the city when the former United College (affiliated with the University of Manitoba) was granted university status and became the University of Winnipeg. By 1971, the population of metropolitan Winnipeg stood at 540,262 people.[42]

Population growth and changing ethnic and racial demographics do not capture the entire story of the post-war changes in the city and province. But immigration is an important part of what defines Winnipeg. As Hans Werner notes, the "presence of large numbers of immigrants intent on becoming part of the community was central to Winnipeg's history" and because it was a "polyglot community for almost as long as it was a city, diversity ... became part of Winnipeg's culture."[43] Another important trend was the desire of Canadians to live in urban areas. By 1951, 57 per cent of Manitoba residents lived in cities or towns.[44] Their city of choice was Winnipeg. Unlike Saskatchewan and Alberta, which each have two major cities, in Manitoba one city predominates. In 1970, 54 per cent of all Manitoba residents lived in metropolitan Winnipeg. Although the city's heyday as a "gateway" city was over, it continued to have a significant position as a major provincial and regional metropolis within Manitoba, northwestern Ontario, and Saskatchewan. While a plurality of Manitobans felt a gravitational pull towards the provincial capital in the post–Second World War era, this was doubly true for Winnipeg's queer migrants.

The Interwar and War Era: Pansies, Fruits, and Dirt

In the late 1930s, according to Bert Sigurdson and others, Winnipeg had a covert circuit of queer spaces in "Chinese cafés on and near Main St, such as the New Moon on Henry Avenue, and a cruising area that stretched along the west bank of the Red River from Union Station north to the Alexander Dock."[45] Bert's experiences (many informants in the oral history collections were referred to only by their first names so this usage is employed for consistency) allow us a glimpse into the lives of Winnipeg homosexuals. Born in 1922, Bert was raised by his Icelandic-Canadian parents in a house on Olivia St in the west end of Winnipeg.[46] The youngest of six children, Bert characterized his household as one where "women had the power," both economically and practically since his mother was the family breadwinner. His father, a former Icelandic newspaper editor, was employed sporadically. Bert attended Principal Sparling elementary school and Daniel McIntyre United College, played sports, and was interested in music and dancing. Bert's first memories of homosexuality and sexual and gender difference dated from 1933 when he met a "precocious homosexual" by the name of Ginger with whom he "experimented" sexually. Ultimately, Ginger decided that he wanted to find "real men" since, as Bert recalled, it was atypical for two "gays" to have sex together, adhering to the then common practice that effeminate queer men had sex with masculine/straight-appearing men. Naturally, we cannot ultimately know how many times this rule was broken by Bert, Ginger, and others! Such structural practices were similar to contemporary homosexual experiences in New York and London, England.[47] This search for real men took Ginger and Bert down to Main St where they met Myrtle, Colin, and Walter at the restaurant of the Brunswick Hotel. Another group of queer men – Percy, Jack, and Mitzi (nicknamed the "society belles") – hung out on Portage Avenue. Employing women's names, or camp names, as they were known, and gender transgressive behaviour, particularly ultrafemininity, were popular practices for younger men. They featured repeatedly in the interviews collected and were well-known queer signs that denoted homosexuality.[48] In fact, in some of the sources the only names utilized were camp names and men's actual names were unknown or forgotten. Because they were pre-teens and teenagers, they were too young to lawfully enter beer parlours. Instead, they hung out in a cluster of Chinese cafes on or near Main St – the Modern Cafe, the New Main Cafe and the Moon Cafe – where as long as they behaved and didn't "camp it up too much" the management tolerated their adolescent behaviour. As he grew older, Bert no longer participated in such gendered transgressive activities, and while the interviews are largely silent about how age differences or life stage affected sexual and gender roles, it seems clear that age, and likely permanent employment, caused some men to alter their behaviour.

Other than Bert Sigurdson's years in the Royal Canadian Air Force (RCAF) during the Second World War, he was a life-long resident of Winnipeg's west end. In the oral interviews, Bert's histories of his queer youth and of his knowledge of queer Winnipeg took centre stage – such was the focus of those interviews. Thanks to his Icelandic surname, it was possible to investigate more of Bert's history and it offers us a more complex overview of his life.[49] In 1942, Bert joined the RCAF and served as a radio operator during the war.[50] Afterwards, he attended the University of Manitoba, graduating with a bachelor's degree in arts in 1949.[51] In the early 1950s, he worked in northern Manitoba with the Canadian National Railway, and later returned to Winnipeg to work as a clerk with the Rock Island Railway. While his widowed mother was alive, she lived with him in a house he owned in the city's west end. In the late 1950s, Bert returned to the U of M to complete a bachelor's of social work, and later a master's of social work degree. He was employed as a social worker at the Society for Manitobans with a Disability for twenty years before he retired in 1983. In retirement he worked as a security guard. Never heterosexually married, his obituary noted that everyone would recall his kindness and that he was a "true gentleman." Guest book entries posted to the funeral home indicated that Bert had been "a

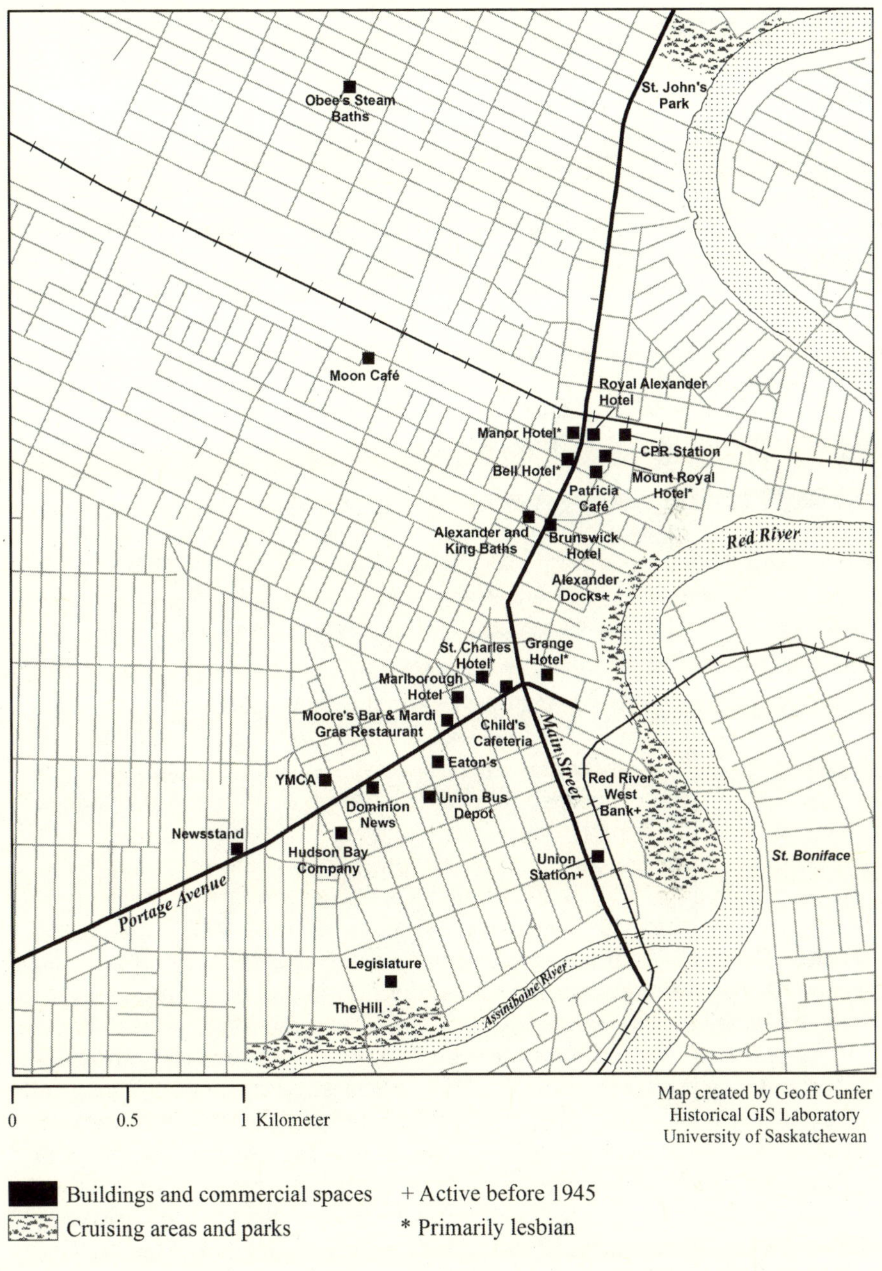

1.1 Winnipeg queer spaces, 1930–1970. Copyright Geoff Cunfer, 2017.

1.2 Bert Sigurdson yearbook photo, University of Manitoba Brown and Gold, 1949. Image reproduced with permission of the University of Manitoba Archives.

beloved friend of my dear uncle J" and another family member noted "we always remembered him at every family get together they had."[52] While his obituary did not mention special friends or partners (perhaps not surprisingly as few people write their own obituaries, and familial and funeral home revisionism has a tendency to soften the edges and obscure differences, in a misguided effort to cast the deceased in the best possible light), it is the guestbook entries that provide glimpses of Bert's adult world. There, two separate entries spoke of his "close friendship" and seamless inclusion at family events with J, indicating that he was well integrated into his friend's extended family. Similar to many of the individual and group histories told in this volume, Bert's obituary and guestbook entries illustrate both middle-class strategies for respectability but also the willingness, on an individual level, for families, friends, and co-workers to accept queer friends and/or lovers within such circles. Ambiguity on both sides enabled queer friends and their families spaces in which to exist, and while we can never know how many recognized people like Bert and J as more than "best friends," some undoubtedly did. At the very least, over time, they become part of familial and friendship networks, quietly demonstrating both the possibilities of queer lives in the prairies, but also of straight prairie and Midwestern families' acceptance of diversity if it was personalized, known, and respectful.[53]

Bert reported that the young men wore a bit of make-up – mascara, and a little Max Factor foundation – but it was really their clothes and their gaits that identified them as homosexuals. Myrtle's mother would create fancy shirts, in eye-catching colour combinations with green fronts and salmon backs. To afford such clothes during the Depression he recalled that they "boosted" (stole) the material from The Bay and Eaton's. While they never wore such attire to school, they routinely sported these outfits on Main St and it often resulted in verbal harassment. Bert recalled that later they cruised an area along the riverbank at the foot of Alexander St and on the docks. Because the practice of cruising can be misunderstood, this book adopts Mark W. Turner's definition of cruising as "a process of walking, gazing, and engaging another (or others), and it is not necessarily about sexual contact."[54]

Not all of Bert's recollections were so rose hued. Verbal and violent assault was not unknown in Depression-era Winnipeg and Bert vividly remembered harassment on the streets. "We used to be so bloody scared of the dirt. And, thinking back, that could be realistic. There were a lot of transients looking for money," Bert recalled.[55] But these attacks were also motivated by gender and sexual differences. "'Dirt' was what we called the gay bashers," he said. "They would be looking out to bash you, trying to take your money. We also called dirt anybody who chased us. When we walked home after our night on the beach … they would call out 'tutti-frutti' and we'd have to take off." Drawing parallels with a later era (by employing the term gay-bashers), Bert is unequivocal that some identifiable queer youth and men drew negative attention on the streets of Winnipeg. Another category of persecution came from those men Bert called "dirt bitches," which he described as other homosexuals, though not "noticeably so," who "would pick on other gays and beat the shit out of them, to prove their masculinity." Those beaten were the more effeminate younger males, like Bert, who were derogatorily classified as "wimps, swishy, fairies."

In addition to these challenges of the street, Bert also spoke forthrightly about commercialized sexual transactions, observing that he was "passive bait for chicken hawks who would pay him for sex."[56] Chicken hawks were older adult men who had a predilection for younger men and newcomers to the queer world. Bert also mentioned the actions of an elementary school teacher whose reputation for assaulting his students in class or in the gym was so widely known that boys who took his gym classes were labelled "Neil's pansies." Over twenty years later, Bert heard that this teacher was formally charged and "jailed in Calgary for having sex with his students" – an outcome Bert applauded.[57] The by then middle-aged teacher, Sidney Neil, was arrested by the Calgary police on charges of indecent assault of a teenage male and contributing to juvenile delinquency. At his trial in May 1956 he was convicted of gross indecency and sentenced as a "criminal sexual psychopath."[58] While detailed analysis of the Neil trial is beyond the scope of this book, it should be noted that he successfully appealed his case to the Supreme Court of Canada in 1957.[59]

Oral historians have written extensively about the challenge and opportunities presented by these sources, and, in particular, about the care with which one needs to address silences, omissions, and people's selective agency in recounting their histories.[60] While I believe it is important to convey the tenor of the recollections provided by Bert and the others, which acknowledges their agency, his recollections are sometimes disturbing and they do raise innumerable, mostly unanswerable questions. Specifically, this interview is largely silent about the ages of the other youth and men with whom he experimented, the power and class relations inherent in those exchanges, and, finally, about the possibilities for exploitation. Bert clearly believed that Neil's classroom conduct was criminal but this contrasts sharply with his more benign and reciprocal view of the streets and his relationships with older males. Without a doubt, those exchanges provided Bert with access to a queer world in which he sought to participate. George Chauncey, Steven Maynard, Jeffrey Weeks, and others have grappled with describing the conflicting "dangers and possibilities" presented by these relationships, concluding that "early twentieth century understandings of sexual relations between boys and men were markedly different than our own."[61] Ultimately, it is seldom possible to know the motivations of the adult actors.

George M. Smith's recollections of the interwar and war years offer a slightly different perspective on those times. George was born in Scotland and his parents immigrated to Winnipeg when he was a young child.[62] In 1933, George quit school after grade eleven to take an accounting programme at Angus Business College. A few years older than Bert, George also reported that he was sexually active in the queer subculture and had two buddies with whom he "hung out." Jack Early (one of the Portage Ave belles mentioned in Bert's interview), Jack Manson, and George frequented a downtown restaurant on Fort St and routinely strolled along in front of Liggett's drugstore across from the post office building. He and his friends used a bit of mascara to "imitate the look of movie stars" but dressed in an ordinary fashion. After dark, they also headed to the Alexander Docks that he remembered as being generally safe from violence. Indeed, the entire "west bank of the Red River from Union Station north to the Alexander Dock" (now Juba Park) was a popular cruising area.[63]

Another interviewee, Gordon C, also noted the popularity of the Alexander Docks area (or the "Hobo Jungle" as it was then colloquially known in a classist, racially-tinged language) and remembered his surprise that there was such a "great mix of people [there] – Natives, Poles, Ukrainians and Hobos."[64] Gordon, who was born in 1926 and raised in the Fort Rouge area of Winnipeg, recalled sexual experimentation from a young age. He reminisced about one friend in particular with whom he engaged in sexual activity from the age of ten through twenty. Asked what terms they used he indicated that "fruit" was commonly employed.

Participant Bruce M's interview effectively bridged the pre-war and war years, and offers a more ambivalent recollection about this world. Born and raised in Winnipeg, he spent a portion of the summer of 1933 at the farm of a family friend. There, at age twelve, he was initiated into having queer sex with an individual he referred to as "Old Uncle John." Nearly sixty years later Bruce recollected that he felt "guilty about the experience" and his friends back in the city ostracized him when he told them what had transpired.[65] Recollections of intergenerational sexual experiences with older family friends, cousins, or siblings were routinely reported in the interviews from this era.[66] However, there were few explicit expressions of anger or victimization in either the transcripts or the recorded interviews. In this case Bruce's guilt and the reported ostracism by his friends are the only clues to indicate these events were not representative of the average experiences of teenage males in Winnipeg.

By coincidence, while swimming near the Norwood Bridge later that summer Bruce met "some gay guys" and then "didn't feel like the only one."[67] He left school and signed up for the Canadian Army but this did not prove to be a positive experience. While stationed in Kingston, Ontario, he was involved in a fight after another soldier called him "queer." After this incident, he was determined to pass as heterosexual and he married a woman while overseas. Despite this attempt at conventionality, the marriage was not enough to provide him with the respectability he sought, and while in the army he was called a "fairy" and a "pansy" despite his capabilities as a soldier. With anger he recalled "he may have been passed over for promotion in the army and later at work because he was 'rumoured' to be queer."[68]

Most of the male informants who were old enough to have served in the Second World War did so. Interestingly, though, their recollection of the war's impact on Winnipeg's queer activity was not a focal point of their interviews. The information they chose to share points to much continuity with queer social and sexual practices of the inter-war period. War meant being shipped out of Winnipeg. Initially they were sent east to central Canada for military training and then usually deployed overseas. Interviewees who shared their memories of those years often identified their experiences in Toronto, Montreal, New York City, and London as highlights of their lives. What transpired in Winnipeg receded into the background until the war's conclusion. For example, the recollections of David B, who was born in 1920 and grew up in the north end of Winnipeg, were typical. David recalled that prior to the war "he learnt about sex from friends [but] had no words to express my feelings" and generally described himself as "naïve."[69] It was in the Canadian Air Force that David discovered how to pick up other men. Acutely attuned to the educational value of queer gossip, David recalled that after he was transferred overseas he "heard another airman make a joke that … Piccadilly Circus was the place for homosexuals."[70] He laughingly reported heading there at his first opportunity. When he returned to Winnipeg after the war, he was a different person, more mature and emboldened about how to locate queer activity. Within short order, he located the city's cruising areas along the Red River, the beer parlour at the Marlborough Hotel, and the local steam baths, which provided him with much needed "private" space since he continued to live with his parents.

By comparison with the bright lights of international queer metropoles, Winnipeg was portrayed as more conservative and furtive. Equally, heterosexual Winnipeggers were depicted as provincial and naive about the homosexual activity that existed within their city. While most of the interviewees focused on international comparisons, many western Canadian service personnel were stationed in southern Ontario and Quebec, which enabled them to offer comparisons between Winnipeg, Toronto, and Montreal. For example, George Smith, who was an entertainer in the Canadian Army's variety show, observed that Toronto during the war years was "the deadest place in the world" compared to Winnipeg. It is worth noting that western Canadian animosity towards Toronto is a beloved facet of prairie culture.[71] In contrast, George "loved New York … we had a ball. We'd go to Harlem and all these places." Still he recalled that though the city was much smaller, "fortunately in those days there was still a lot of fun in Winnipeg. Not like it is now. We had so many places to go then – the beer parlours, etc. It was so fun."[72] Furthermore, he noted, "I could get as much trade [straight presenting / acting men] here as I could in New York, in those days. So it wasn't like coming back to a dead place. I was quite happy to come back."[73] George's recollections offer important perspective on Winnipeg's enduring queer charms.

David S, who turned twenty in 1945, recalled the war as a formative moment for familial reasons. His older brother Bobby returned from his naval service and told his family he was homosexual.[74] The reaction to this shift from covert queer participant to declared homosexual caused shock waves within the family. So did his revelations that he was an active participant in an elite homosexual subculture within the University of Manitoba medical school. Winnipeg's gay and lesbian community archives hold a series of biographical files and records about local people, institutions, and activists. A slim file is devoted to Lennox Gordon "Buzz" Bell (1904–73), the son of a prominent Winnipeg doctor. In 1949 Bell became "the first full-time Dean of the Faculty of Medicine and Physician in Chief at the Winnipeg General Hospital." Remembered as a "gifted teacher, popular with students and colleagues," the information concludes by noting "the medical college gained a national reputation under his guidance."[75] Privately, he was also well known to have discreet affairs with select male students.[76] Bobby S had been one of those students and Dr Bell was frequently invited for dinner in the S household. Dean Bell's circle of students, professionals, and wealthy homosexual men was one of the elite queer subcultures within the city. Bell's discretion and the privileges accorded a prominent professional from a well-established Manitoba family meant that his friendship network largely escaped scrutiny or censure. It helped that the dean was widely respected for his excellent leadership of the college as well as his community service.[77] How much Winnipeggers suspended disbelief about the never-married dean's activities is uncertain, but in this particular case Bobby's family was clearly blindsided by revelations of their son's involvement with Bell.

The final shock came in 1946 when Bobby was charged with gross indecency. Convicted for having sex with two twelve-year-old boys he served six months in Headingley Correctional Institution, a prison just outside of Winnipeg. The family was reportedly in a "state of shock" over the trial, the publicity, and their son's conviction. For David, Bobby's visibility, combined with the stress of the conviction and the negative attention it brought his family, offered a chilling lesson about the limits to Winnipeggers tolerance. After his release from jail, Bobby had his medical licence reinstated and he returned to London, England where he lived in an "openly gay community." By contrast with his older brother, David remembered being very cautious about acting on his homosexual desires, let alone publicizing them. Despite his awareness of the liberating possibilities of moving away from Winnipeg, David purposefully chose to stay there. Other Winnipeg queers actively chose to live there as well, or stay there, despite their knowledge that an openly homosexual existence was possible elsewhere. City residents might travel widely and correspond with friends, family, and former lovers who moved away, but still many remained. Such evidence suggests we need to be cautious about our preconceptions about how individuals make such choices. Sexuality is but one part of a complicated puzzle involving economic and educational opportunities, families and friends, and regional or urban preferences.

David and Bert's interviews were the only ones to mention criminal charges. Criminal court records were not excavated for this book but other historians have profitably used those sources.[78] Scott de Groot's research into Winnipeg's gross indecency charges in the post-war era illustrates a spike in newspaper coverage and convictions.[79] Lyle Dick's case study of the 1942 same-sex trials in Edmonton illustrates the coercive powers of the state to police homosexual or suspected homosexual activities in that city.[80] These two western Canadian case studies support other Canadian research that demonstrates greater media coverage attended the increased gross indecency charges in the 1940s and 1950s. During this time period, Cold War anxieties about social, sexual, and political abnormality, and worries about how best to reconvert from the total war effort to civilian life, preoccupied educators, doctors, governments, and the criminal courts.[81] The relative silence on these topics within the Winnipeg interviews could be due to a number of factors. Informants might not have wanted to dwell on difficult matters or disclose such incriminating evidence about themselves or friends in interviews intended to form the basis for a celebratory community history.

Remembering North Main Street in the Late 1940s and 1950s

After the Second World War, Jerry Walsh settled in Winnipeg. He immersed himself in queer life in the downtown core and, in the excerpt below, recalled those days evocatively:

> Unlike today, back then Main St. was a safe place to cruise day or night. The street's crowning jewel was the Royal Alexander Hotel at the corner of Higgins and Main. It was elegance at its greatest and attracted many queens who hoped that some of its glitter would rub off on them … East of the hotel was the CP Station … It was a bustling place both day and night as train travel was at its peak … Across Higgins was and still is the Mount Royal Hotel, which was where the gay girls hung out, but it also had its share of sleazy drag queens. No other males went there unless in the company of the girls. It was a lively and noisy place with frequent bouts of dikes duking it out … It was the first place that I ever saw two guys dancing together; no one seemed to mind, so next time I brought my patent leather pumps. Between Henry and Higgins on the east side was the Moon Café, a lot of young guys hung out there and were ready to welcome you after the pubs closed. Myrtle an older queen appointed herself den mother and kept all the chicks in check. She demanded respect and if you didn't give it to her, you were told to leave and never come back. It wasn't sex she wanted just control. For a quarter you could get a piece of pie, a coke and a ten-cent package of cigarettes, and spend as much time as it took to make contact. The Chinese owners never bugged you.[82]

Bert Sigurdson also remembered that the Chinese owners were very protective of their cafes. "Chinese fellows were not bad about protecting, they didn't want anything to happen, and they'd shoo everybody out," he said. "You felt more trust with the Chinese fellows that ran the restaurant – they never said anything negative."[83] Whether this was because the owners were averse to trouble, which could have attracted an unwanted police presence, or a calculated business decision to protect their loyal customers is unknown. The preponderance of queer socializing in Chinese-run cafes in Winnipeg demonstrates an important symbiotic relationship that worked for owners and patrons alike.[84]

Peter, who was born in 1935 and raised in the upscale Crescentwood area, remembered "playing around with the other guys" in grade school and "that it was natural … we didn't put any connotation or names to it."[85] As a teenager he discovered the hill behind the legislature and he would ride his bike there in the evenings for sex and then return home. Asked about violence or a police presence during the 1940s, he noted that the "police raids came much later, when they were cracking down." Given the example set by Dr Bell, who Peter remembered as always taking a female escort to public events, he emulated the strategic upper-middle-class public/private duality. "When I was in my twenties," Peter reported, "I remember my lover wanted to go to a movie but I was adamant that we wouldn't be seen together in public going to a movie." Asked if being gay affected his job prospects, he replied "No." Pressed by the interviewer to clarify this statement, Peter shrewdly replied, "well it certainly was possible to work, to become Prime Minister, to do anything you wanted to do you just didn't make your sex life public." Despite the oral history project's goals of chronicling the emergence of a clearly defined gay and lesbian minority, Peter was resistant to this narrative arc. This determination to continue to employ a model of middle-class "discretion" would be paralleled in Saskatchewan interviewees, and while there it was primarily a strategy adopted by lesbians, it is also one that middle-class men used. Peter was critical of "political activists [who] are doing great harm to other homosexuals by publicizing gay activities" because it was his belief that you "can't advance in society if you wear a label."[86] Publicizing the queer world had, in his opinion, brought increased violence to the cruising areas and unwelcome speculation about people's private activities. Corroborating evidence is found in the interview of George Smith, whose youthful memories of drag socializing in St Boniface served as an introductory anecdote. He employed similar strategies to Peter, explaining, "I always had two lives. A private life and a public life." He confided to the interviewer: "I had to keep my hair pinned up at work, we're all scared of somebody."[87]

While there were differences of opinion expressed in the interviews about the degree to which one could be increasingly overt about queer activities as the city shed its economically depressed pre-war malaise, the opportunities for queer socializing increased significantly. Gordon Clark noted that the post-war era Winnipeg bars, such as the Marlborough Hotel, were wide open and on any given night you could find a mixed crowd of "army men and screaming queens." Amendments to the liquor laws, and not the Second World War, were frequently cited as an important lever of change in Winnipeg. 1n 1957, they were revised to include mixed-gender public-drinking establishments, ushering in the era of the cocktail lounge.[88]

Interestingly, all of those interviewed from this post–Second World War cohort reported a loosening up of social mores, which contradicts the dominant characterization of the late 1940s and 1950s in North America as an era of conformity and family values. In part, this was clearly tied to better economic times in Winnipeg generally, resulting in more restaurants, bars, and expanded opportunities for commercial leisure. It also reflected the pre-war teenagers' transition into adulthood, with the commensurate economic and social freedoms. All informants noted that there were increased opportunities for queer male sexual activity and socializing after the war, but stressed that particular codes of behaviour were observed. Newcomers were taught the "rules" by those in the know, including where to sit, what bars to go to, and how to conduct oneself in the baths or on the trails. The paramount rule was to never identify or disclose the men who they had met in queer cruising areas, if they spotted them elsewhere in the city. Unlike their younger selves who challenged gender norms with effeminate and flashy clothes and make-up, in the 1940s and 1950s they largely followed middle-class conventions: they dressed conservatively to go out for the evening in suits, ties, and often hats; they obeyed the drinking rules of the day (patrons had to sit at tables to drink their beer, instead of circulating around the room); and they avoided "camping it up" too much in public establishments. Ironically, the strict nature of the liquor laws encouraged much cruising of the men's tearooms (toilets).

In addition to queer socializing in cafes and hotel beverage rooms, the Grenadiers Club and the YMCA were also popular.[89] The Grenadiers Club, located at the barracks of the Winnipeg Grenadiers, was an unlikely queer haunt but because the steward's son was queer, his friends had access to this space and took full advantage. According to Jerry Walsh, "the Grenadiers was great, plus being a military building the drinks were cheap. Never a night went by that we didn't outnumber the members."[90] By comparison with the 1990s, the cruising spots in the 1940s and 1950s were remembered as being relatively safe. Walsh recalled that the cafes and parks were safe both during the day and the night and bashing was seldom heard of, even on Main St and the hill, two spots that would become increasingly more dangerous in the 1970s. Walsh was particularly proud of the savvy use queer men made of city parks that "weren't as manicured as they are today" and provided ample "underbrush, tall grass and clumps of bush" for trysts. "Banana Park" was the campy, queer nickname for St John's Park. "It was a family park but all the people had to leave by 10pm. The park officers would clear the park and then leave. There were no gates in the fences so at 10:30 the park would start filling up again with those looking for brotherly love."[91] This mixed use of public parks is one example of how multiple communities used the same spaces at varying hours for completely different purposes. Park staff was unwittingly complicit in this queer usage as the park's landscaping and the nightly clearance of people from the grounds enabled queer residents to pursue their activities without harassment or detection.

Similar outcomes but different strategies governed other mixed usage of steam baths in the city. Walsh's testimony offered detailed recollections of the Alexander and King Baths. This bath (the city's oldest) had a primarily queer clientele.[92] Obees, the other bathhouse, was a north end institution. Located at Mountain and McGregor Streets, Obees first opened in 1914 and initially provided access to baths and showers for the local immigrant population. By the early 1940s its mission changed from a purely utilitarian and functional space to a social one. In a recent popular history, writer Russ Gourluck suggests that, "Obees remained a popular destination for men to socialize and play cards, conduct business, perhaps have a few drinks, and enjoy a relaxing steam bath."[93] By contrast, Walsh remembered how this "family" bathhouse attracted a mixed group of older men as well as a newer crowd of queer men who managed to coexist. "The elderly straight men came mainly for the steam, they spent hours steaming and hitting themselves with the oak leaf switches," Walsh wrote. "They also brought food, beer or wine and made a night of it. The gays at first tried to out stay them, but it was a losing battle, so they didn't flaunt it, but went about doing what they had come for. The old timers went about their thing and didn't seem to notice or care what else went on. There were never any problems, mainly because the owner was an ex boxer and no-one wanted to spar with him." In the end, the queer men "took a tip from the straights and brought food" and "for three bucks you could buy a mickey of rye to sip on between sessions."[94] Such descriptions show how the traditions and businesses, originally intended to serve Winnipeg's immigrant populations, were co-opted into homosocial spaces by other men for their own purposes. For the owners of the baths, like the Chinese cafe owners, such queer activity was financially advantageous as it provided an essential new source of revenue. This exemplifies the live-and-let-live ethos in action. It is doubtful that the older immigrant men were unaware of the presence of so many younger, queer men in their midst. But the accommodation between the two groups (one wilfully pretending not to see while the other group did not "flaunt" their business) worked to every-one's advantage. The infusion of new customers allowed the steam bath to stay open, which provided both straight and queer men a private, male-only space away from the prying eyes of wives and families.

Men who first arrived in the city in the mid-1950s, brought with them a fresh perspective on Winnipeg, and in interviews those gay men observed that lesbians were increasingly included in some queer male socializing. Ted Patterson provided one narrative that was particularly detailed about class and gender differences. Raised in Edmonton, Alberta in what he described as a "square, unsophisticated, working-class family," Ted arrived in Winnipeg in 1954 on a scholarship with the Royal Winnipeg Ballet Corps (RWB). Because homosexuality was well known among the members of the RWB dancers and administrators, Ted quickly learned the geography of queer socializing in Winnipeg. He recalled that "gays held court" in the basement beer parlour of the Marlborough Hotel, a primarily working-class venue where discretion prevailed.[95] Ted noted that some Winnipeg bars tried to evict their queer clientele at various junctures in blatant attempts to attract more respectable, and thereby affluent, patrons. These strategies often backfired, such as in the case of the Marlborough Hotel. After queers were barred, they decamped to the St Regis where the staff welcomed them.[96]

Patterson observed that from 1955 to 1970 house parties played a crucial role in middle-class Winnipeg socializing. There were a variety of party circuits, some included the theatre and ballet crowd, others involved more prominent wealthier circles, corroborating earlier comments about the elite queer networks and the class and gender stratifications within the city.[97] Socializing after the theatre, queer patrons tended to head to either Child's restaurant or Moore's bar. Asked to compare Winnipeg's queer offerings to other cities with which he was familiar, Ted honestly observed that "any weekend in Minneapolis seemed like a holiday" and that Winnipeg was provincial by comparison. What kept him in Winnipeg was the RWB because he was able to live in a "gay world" as a dancer with the company. During the 1960s Ted taught dance classes in Brandon, Manitoba, a smaller city he characterized as "a dead end" for gay people.[98] Other interviewees also noted how advantageous the city's strong roster of arts, cultural, and musical venues were to attracting queer migrants and to offering all city resident's economic and social opportunities. Peter explicitly praised the particularities of arts and cultural activities in the city assessing the situation thus: "gays [were] attracted to the arts in Winnipeg" and the "vitality of the arts in Winnipeg [was] due to the work of the Jewish community."[99]

House parties in Winnipeg were popular for a variety of reasons. First, the 10:00 p.m. (later 10:30 p.m.) closing time for licenced drinking establishments meant that people eagerly sought out after-hours social spots. Immediately after the war a housing shortage also meant many young adults were still living at home. In both instances, then, house parties provided much needed spaces for people to congregate. Jerry Walsh recalled eventually being able to afford to rent a bed-sitting room equipped with a kitchen consisting of a coin-fed gas cook stove and an icebox. Though far from opulent, this working-class apartment was the scene of many parties. Initially these parties were basic affairs. The host "would buy the beer and we'd pay a quarter for every bottle we drank."[100] As people began to make more money, living spaces were upgraded to larger self-contained apartments and later houses. More space meant larger parties, now featuring music and dancing. In the late 1960s and early 1970s, Alan Miller observed that house parties were still quite an attractive and enjoyable way for "gay men and lesbians [in Winnipeg] who were in relationships and/or for those who did not visit the bars" to socialize.[101] Ted Patterson noted that he regularly attended lesbian parties and that some of the lesbian couples he met in those years became close friends. He fondly remembered "Pearl and Jean who worked for the Red Cross" because of their great parties in the city and at their summer cottage in Kenora, indicating that both Winnipeg Beach and Grand Beach were also the sites of queer summer parties.[102] Dale Barbour's history of Winnipeg Beach includes gay men's histories of their times at the beach in the 1950s.[103]

For middle-class lesbians in Winnipeg, the house parties were important social venues.[104] One informant, Ruth B. Sells, who was born in 1927 in northwestern Ontario and moved to Winnipeg at age five when her father remarried, remembered a profound sense of isolation during her youth.[105] A tomboy as a child and later a rather solitary teen, she vividly recalled reading Radclyffe Hall's melodramatic lesbian novel *The Well of Loneliness*. Sells worked as a teacher for five years and then subsequently chose to work in a variety of piano and retail music stores in Winnipeg. In those stores she met queer customers and slowly began to build a circle of male friends. In 1950, a male friend who lived in the same rooming house as Sells introduced her to an older lesbian couple. Sells and forty-year-old Joy Boyd clicked instantaneously, resulting in Boyd leaving her girlfriend to move in with Sells. With the exception of one brief hiatus apart, Sells and Boyd were together until Joy's death in 1984 at the age of seventy-four. A frequent traveller to American cities – Minneapolis, San Francisco, and Chicago – Sells remembered that, even though all of them were more vibrant than Winnipeg, Winnipeg was home. They owned a cottage in the Whiteshell area and, looking back on their lives together, Sells reflected that they had been happy to lead quiet, discreet lives.[106] Sells and her partner were the embodiment of respectable middle-class lesbians.[107] Her personal good fortune did not translate into complacency about the challenges of living as a lesbian during this era. She was forthright about the hardships of compartmentalization and living "a lie to survive." This discrimination motivated her participation in the American homophile organizations the Daughters of Bilitis (an American lesbian organization) and the Mattachine Society.[108]

If it was challenging to grow up with lesbian or same-sex inclinations in the city of Winnipeg, it was often more arduous for those raised in rural or small towns. Informants frequently commented upon the impossibility of finding any information about homosexuality, and none mentioned parallel queer spaces in those smaller venues. It was seldom openly discussed and resources were non-existent. Dr A.M. Watts, whose work as a chaplain at the U of M served as a springboard for gay advocacy on campus, remarked that "homosexuality was never seriously discussed" in the 1940s and 1950s, although negative pejoratives like "pervert" could be heard in some circles.[109] Jim H, who grew up in Portage La Prairie, a small bedroom community west of Winnipeg, recollected that he first heard the word "homosexual" in 1959 when he was twenty-three years old. Curious but cautious, he went to great lengths to research this subject. Jim drove all the way to Minneapolis (approximately eight hours by car) to safely investigate the subject in its public library. In Winnipeg he feared the possibility that someone might question his research.[110]

While the 1950s witnessed changes in queer socializing and an increase in venues and opportunities thanks to 1957 legislation that enabled beer parlours to be "mixed" – allowing women to socialize with men – there were also important continuities. Chief among them was cruising the hill and the city's tearooms. Informants provided an extensive list of tearooms that included some of Winnipeg's commercial and public landmarks. Naturally, this use of commercial space was never noted in the commemorative books about Winnipeg. For instance, informants recalled popular tearooms on the third floor of Eaton's, the fifth floor of the Bay, as well as the second floor of the Rialto Theatre, the Hargrave bus depot and the attached Salisbury House restaurant, and the William St library. Such public space was not unique to Winnipeg: "many men, gay identified or not, engaged in public sexual encounters in parks, sauna baths, cheap movie houses, locker rooms, public toilets, highway rest stops and other such places in and around major cities."[111] For some men this activity was merely a sexual outlet, but for others "it could and did lead to self-identification as part of a community bonded by queer male desires."[112] Despite the evident bravado expressed in the interviews about these multiple sites, many men also voiced their apprehensions. Jerry declared that he was always afraid of public ridicule, the risk of losing his job, and fears of police harassment or being arrested, particularly at the hill. Ultimately, he said, "I lived two lives; I did not want my straight friends to spot me with my gay friends at gay spots."[113]

While many gay men indicated that they feared public ridicule and the police, the lesbians interviewed from this time period indicate that what the women feared most were psychiatric interventions. Pat, who was born in 1931 and raised in the north end of Winnipeg, reported that in 1946 she "slept away the summer, afraid that if she told someone she was a homosexual she would be sent to the Mental Hospital in Selkirk."[114] As an adult Pat feared being fired if her work colleagues discovered her lesbianism, so she habitually hid her private life. While Pat's middle-class instincts to remain silent about her lesbianism left her isolated and apprehensive as a teen, as an adult she fared better than working-class or Indigenous lesbians. One Indigenous woman interviewed ("Kate") disclosed that she had spent considerable time in her teens incarcerated in unnamed institutions (one can infer that these were psychiatric institutions or reform schools) where she discovered her lesbianism.[115] She recalled particularly difficult memories of former girlfriends who had committed suicide and her own suicide attempt, which earned her an admission to the psychiatric hospital. In 1965, at the age of eighteen, Kate participated in the Selkirk Mental Hospital aversion therapy programme.[116] Such programmes to "cure" deviant sexual expressions were part of a roster of psychiatric treatments meted out to homosexuals in the era before the American Psychiatric Association removed homosexuality from its list of mental illnesses in 1973.[117] Interviewed in 2006, Jane Smith, a former nurse and volunteer on the Gays for Equality phone line in the 1970s and 1980s, vividly recalled callers who had "horrendous stories of lobotomies, and shock treatment, just because somebody found out they were gay, lesbian."[118] Those experiences, and later working with AIDS patients, were "the driving force" for her committee work and activism.[119]

"The Torch of Golden Boy Burns Bright": The 1960s

By the 1960s, Winnipeg's queer culture had entered a transitional phase. Initially the shifts were subtle, as the post-war expansion of mixed social spaces in cocktail lounges continued to benefit women and men who sought commercial establishments for socialization. By the end of the 1960s, queer and increasingly "gay" culture was no longer invisible to the mainstream of Winnipeg residents. Equally important, numbers of Winnipeggers were now openly referring to themselves as gay or lesbian. The queer subcultural model was beginning to recede into the background (if never entirely disappearing) as an openly gay or lesbian community model began to emerge in the city.

One of those popular cocktail lounges in the 1960s was Moore's Bar on Portage Avenue. This "elegant" lounge was located above a main-floor family-style restaurant and coffee shop. Teenagers and those under the legal drinking age of twenty-one who wanted to cruise the traffic in the lounge sat in the fountain area of the coffee shop where they could observe the stairs.[120] Their queer clientele was so critical to the commercial viability of Moore's that, when the lounge closed, the owners held a party for their gay customers. After the demise of Moore's, the Mardi Gras, which was located next door, began to attract a queer crowd. The Mardi Gras was profiled in journalist Peter Carlyle-Gordge's melodramatic, two-part *Winnipeg World* magazine article entitled "The Hill is Favourite Spot."[121] This voyeuristic article provided a glimpse into Winnipeg's homosexual men and their haunts (the hill, private parties, and the bar). Although Carlyle-Gordge clearly identified himself (then) as heterosexually married, he eschewed the common approach of speaking primarily with psychiatrists and other "experts"; rather, he "decided to talk exclusively with homosexuals themselves and let them explain why they are as they are."[122] Part of his investigation included socializing at "the Madras" (his nickname for the Mardi Gras).

According to Carlyle-Gordge the Madras was the "main centre to meet and socialize," although reportedly "some homosexuals abhor it because such a large proportion of its clientele is made up of exhibitionistic, 'nelly' pretty boy homosexuals."[123] On the night he visited, Carlyle-Gordge found "forty men sitting around the lounge and perhaps four women" in a room that was "brightly painted with dancing scenes."[124] The patrons were "resplendent in silk shirts, sunglasses, bright bell-bottom trousers and whatever else is the latest fashion. Some look like ordinary sober-suited businessmen and probably are. They are the 'respectable' homosexuals, either there with a friend or to eye the younger talent." In his article, Carlyle-Gordge utilizes the terms gay and homosexual interchangeably, evidence of their by now common usage in Winnipeg. "The police know the Madras is gay and make periodic checks, though there is usually no trouble," he wrote.[125] Similar to Moore's, it had a coffee shop at street level, with the lounge upstairs. Young men waited in the coffee shop until the bar closed, when "a drag line form[ed] outside" composed of those from upstairs and downstairs, and "within ten minutes the line ha[d] disappeared, everyone having found a suitable partner. Sometimes a whole group w[ould] troop off to a party if someone suggest[ed] one."[126] The unsuccessful often left for the hill.

The second part of Carlyle-Gordge's series offered a detailed guide to cruising the hill. Beautifully rendered (if dramatic), it is worth excerpting here because it captures the lived reality of this nightly activity and offers a rare observation of how disparate groups of young and old, working-class and elite queers met and negotiated sex and sociability at this famous local cruising spot:

> The Hill is a strange place. Walking there at night – the whole area around the Legislative Buildings in general and in particular that area that slopes down to the river from Assiniboine Avenue – is an odd, unsettling experience. It is even odder if you are a stranger and don't know why the Hill is so famous. Or is it infamous?
>
> The torch of Golden Boy burns brightly in the night, attracting not moths as some lights do, but another kind of night creature, the homosexual. Single men go there. Lonely men. Men looking for other men … They wait patiently and walk endlessly up and down Assiniboine Avenue, through the grounds of the Legislature, down the slope, down to the river, down to the bridge. That's a very favorite spot … On Fridays business on the Hill begins at about 10:30 pm and goes on till 4 am or even later, there being a noticeable increase in business soon after the bars close … A man may go there, walk around for a while ("cruise" is the correct term) and see someone he likes … Two men may pass each other on Assiniboine Ave or in the grounds of the Legislature and be interested in each other. At a reasonable distance, one will turn around and start walking in the other

man's direction, slowly pursuing him at a short distance. After a while, the pursued, if he's interested may walk across to the slope and go down to the riverbank to wait. There the two will meet, talk and arrange whatever they want to arrange …

For every man on foot there are perhaps two or three in cars, cars that cruise round and round, picking up the pedestrians in their headlights. The Hill wouldn't be the Hill without cars … If a headlight blinks and a car slows down to a snail's pace as it passes someone, the driver is very much interested in that someone … This may seem a strange form of "courting," but to hundreds it's quite normal and it goes on every night…

As a rule, those driving cars tend to be older, in their 30's or 40's. Youth almost always walks. Occasionally another kind of car creeps around the grounds by the Hill. It contains not a homosexual in search of a mate, but a policeman or two policemen. The police may scare off a few people, temporarily at least, but they don't interfere too much with the homosexuals, their concern being more with hippies and other "undesirables."[127]

It is intriguing that, in assessing the risks to Winnipeg residents, Carlyle-Gordge observed that the city's police force prioritized hippies and unspecified "undesirables" (we can infer drug users, transients, and/or the indigent, perhaps Indigenous) as posing more of a risk to citizens than homosexuals.[128] The men themselves remained apprehensive of the police and their powers because male same-sex activity was still illegal and "the police could pick you up just for being," Jerry Walsh recalled.[129] After the 1969 Criminal Code amendments, private same-sex acts were no longer criminalized, but "public" sex, whether on the hill or in bathhouses, remained a criminal activity. Murray W, a self-declared working-class male and infrequent hill hustler, reported that "many straight, married men cruised the Hill" in the evenings.[130] For married queer cruisers or those living "double" lives, police harassment or criminal charges of gross indecency had the potential to shatter lives. The increased police presence was also a response to a rash of violence in the 1960s. Gay men who cruised the hill in the late 1960s commented on the risks posed by gay bashers who targeted them for sport, or possibly as compensation for their own conflicted sexuality. Murray W reported that he was "beaten in the washroom of the Mardi Gras" and that "sometimes men would wait outside the MG to beat up patrons." On the hill he was "harassed by the police" while socializing with his group of friends, and later "chased around the city in his car by attackers."

Press coverage of cruising spots and gay practices made them far more visible than previously, and this development brought an attendant increase in anti-gay violence and police surveillance. Queer men recalled that whenever possible they exercised agency in resisting these attacks. Walsh cited the heroic actions of Corina, a man known only by her camp name, who fought back against such attacks: "One night a few of us were at the hill, all of a sudden we heard a great yell, and four guys came a running, being chased by Corina. She chased them all the way across the bridge [Osborne St], then calmly came back and said 'That will teach those bastards they can't fuck around with us.'"[131] In the 1970s and 1980s the anti-gay violence became so widespread that the activist group Gays For Equality created a public education campaign to warn men about the dangers and strongly encouraged them to refrain from cruising on the hill. For the middle-class activists, this was logical and valuable work, much like anti-smoking campaigns appear logical to non-smokers. But reversing decades of queer geographical imprinting that marked the hill as a social and sexual space for a varied group of working and middle-class youth and adults, some of whom identified as gay and others who were there just for the sex, was virtually impossible.

Ironically, one of the safer locations proposed were the baths. The wave of police raids of Canadian bathhouses was yet to come. For many participants these commercial spaces provided the illusion of safety and privacy. Men spoke fondly of the tough owner/operators whose gatekeeper function offered them more protection than in public, outdoor venues. Many frequent bath patrons in Winnipeg continued to be married, middle-class professional males. In his interview Terry observed "the married ones undergo a transformation once they get inside a steam bath; they look ten years younger when they start having 'fun.' It's sad to see them leave because they seem to age as they get dressed. They probably wouldn't speak to you on the street."[132] Perhaps not, but some of them had reportedly worked out flexible accommodations with their wives. Bruce M, the former soldier, told the interviewer that his wife knew that he was "fooling around but considered it a safety valve" to preserve their marriage. Bruce met men through work (at the post office and also while he worked for the railroad) despite keeping his homosexuality "undercover at work."[133] These valuable recollections provide glimpses of men whose participation in the queer subculture remained masked by their public heterosexuality.

The *Winnipeg World* articles, like the oral history collection, provided little commentary about the city's lesbians. Citing space limitations as their rationale, readers were left with only the most fleeting of impressions of lesbian existence. Yet Winnipeg lesbians were staking claims to different social spaces. The Mount Royal remained the venue of choice for working-class lesbians. This Main St bar was derided for both its clientele and its location on Winnipeg's "skid row." Kate, a regular patron of the Mount Royal, recalled that despite its reputation as "grubby and sleazy," there was a sense of protectiveness among gays in the bar.[134] Possibly this was due to the fact that police routinely surveilled and arrested patrons of the Mount Royal. During such raids it was not uncommon for gay people to flee out the back door of the bar, cross the parking lot, and enter the Patricia Cafe, another popular working-class lesbian and gay hangout. Kate recalled that the Mount Royal attracted gay factory workers, hairdressers, cooks, and a number of lesbians, some of whom initially attended the Mount Royal with their husbands. Middle-class lesbians were familiar with the "infamous" Mount Royal, and appear to have attended it infrequently, but reportedly found the hard drinking environment, the mixed clientele, and the routine eruptions of fighting and violence outside their comfort zone. Indigenous lesbians were regarded as "rougher and tougher" according to Kate, and she remembered that they socialized most often at the Patricia, the Bell, and the Manor hotels. According to the abbreviated informal community history, "it was only in the 1960's that lesbians first began to appear at some of the taverns and restaurants that had become popular with gay men. The Grange Hotel and the St Charles Hotel became two of the choicer meeting places at this time. Women also met through less visible friendship networks, softball teams, and acquaintances at work."[135] Perhaps the most successful workplace in which to meet women who were attracted to other women was in the women's service divisions. Interviewees who served in the Air Force (post–Second World War) all indicated that they had relationships with other women there – some managing to fly under the radar though another was dishonourably discharged. Memorable though those experiences were, such relationships did not always correlate with identification as a lesbian. Two lesbian narrators married men, had children, and then only subsequent to their divorces, again began relationships with women.[136]

Kate's interview corroborates the class divide among Winnipeg queers that mirrored the spatial divides in the city between "north-enders" and "downtowners." She reported that the downtown crowd, who patronized Moore's and the Mardi Gras, were more affluent than the Main Street, north-end crowd. Not surprisingly, Main Streeters were often mistrustful of the more affluent lesbians and gays. When community or citywide festivities, balls, or socials occurred, those special events managed to transcend class and geographical boundaries, drawing people from across the city. Race differences were not so easily shed and few oral informants recalled Indigenous people at such events. These histories either confirm the marginalization of Indigenous people within the queer subcultures or indicate Euro-Canadian ethnocentric views that ignored Indigenous participants. These conclusions are very tentative and additional research needs to be done to more fully analyse Indigenous participation in queer, gay, and lesbian activities in Winnipeg. A more inclusive history that included their experiences would better historicize both the queer communities' and the city's demographic changes in the 1970s, when large numbers of Indigenous people moved into the city.[137]

The late 1960s saw the emergence of a new series of drag events, called the Beaux Art Balls, which became popular outlets for Winnipeg's gay and lesbian residents. One such event held in 1969 attracted 250 people for the dinner, dance, and drag fashion show.[138] Paul, a journalist, reminisced, "the queens look forward to this event all year long ... Sometimes the finished product is a riot. Sometimes it's stunning and you would never guess they're really men dressed in women's clothes."[139] It was common to see both men and women cross-dressed at this event intermingling with those who came attired in more cisgendered clothing. In the same era, the first gay boat trips were organized and held on the city's paddle wheel boats. These boats were tremendously popular in the city during the summer. Memorably, drag queens were the featured entertainment that differentiated these cruises from their straight counterparts.

Conclusion

While the history sketched in this chapter may appear linear and progressive given the chronological organization employed, this was not in fact the case. During the interwar and war years, Winnipeg's queer subculture was relatively small and comprised largely of working-class and middle-class men. Those men were the ones who discovered and forged the queer geography of the city's core– the public and commercial cruising sites as well as the cafes, beer parlours, hotels, and transportation infrastructure where men who sought other men congregated. They marvelled at how wonderful it was to see twenty-five men on the docks or on the hill behind the legislature in the evening. Prior to their discovery of these spaces they believed that their experiences were singular. Finding a cohort of other men ended their isolation and was a profound experience. Yet, if their recollections were accurate, the queer subculture was both vibrant and quite small until after the Second World War. Mainstream Winnipeggers were largely oblivious to this secretive world. However, Winnipeg's urban design; the importance of railways; and the constant ebb and flow of settlers, workers, transients, and travellers in and through the city meant that well-known modes of queer sociability were recognizable and available. The absence of lesbians from the extant sources used in this chapter does not, in all likelihood, mean that they were absent from Winnipeg. Winnipeg's pre–Second World War lesbian enclaves, friendships, and social spaces still await their historian.

If the queer sociability of male cruising was an international phenomenon, what was particular and specific to Winnipeg was the city's prominent role in the western region first as the "gateway" city and later as a regional metropolis. The histories of the creation of a queer subculture in Winnipeg deserve to be understood as part and parcel of the Euro-Canadian settling of the west as well as the growth, rapid development, and then stagnation of the city during the first half of the twentieth century. Sexual opportunities abounded in this youthful city, and men took advantage of those opportunities whether under the literal signpost of "Golden Boy" or in the city's red-light district. (See back cover for a contemporary image of Winnipeg's iconic boy.) The queer subcultural world had important parallels with heterosexual men's conceptualization of the city's sexual opportunities. Many of those interviewed had been young, effeminate, gender transgressing "pansies" and "fairies" during the 1930s, but their interviews point to the involvement of "real men" (who presented as conventionally masculine, often known as 'trade'), whose participation in the queer world might have been one of opportunity (an available male sexual partner) but it might also have been one of choice.

During the interwar and war years, and stretching into the post-war era, immigrant small business owners were important in providing spaces for queer socialization in Winnipeg: Chinese-run cafes, European bathhouses, restaurants, and beer parlours. These relationships were mutually advantageous socially and financially. While it would be conjecture to claim that owners recognized and accepted queer diversity, it is not speculation to contend that the region's live-and-let-live ethos (for Euro-Canadian residents) enabled diverse activities and mixed uses of commercial spaces. Queer tables in bars and restaurants, queer areas of bathhouses, and queer uses of public spaces were tolerated as long as "they did not camp it up too much." In the 1950s and 1960s those establishments that attempted to bar queer clients learned harsh economic lessons. Others, like Moore's, recognized their core audience and the importance of such patronage.

After the Second World War, Winnipeg changed, and so did the queer subculture. Winnipeg's economic fortunes finally improved and the city became a major regional metropolis serving northwestern Ontario, Manitoba, and parts of Saskatchewan. As the province's largest city, Winnipeg was an attractive destination for its mix of economic, cultural, educational, and social opportunities. A disproportionately strong arts community differentiated the city from others in the prairies and drew migrants from elsewhere. Queer opportunities expanded in post-war Winnipeg, but, perhaps more significantly, it was in the 1950s and 1960s that Winnipeg became a destination city for queer people. Alongside a demographic shift that saw the city grow to include over half of the province's population, sources indicate that queer, lesbian, and gay men from small towns, rural, and northern areas increasingly chose to migrate to Winnipeg. The reason, quite simply, was because it was possible to be queer and live in Winnipeg. Otherwise, service men returning from the Second World War (with extensive experiences in London, New York, and central Canada) would not have permanently returned to the city. Nor would the next generation of younger men and women, like Ted Patterson, Ruth Sells, or Jim H, have purposefully moved to Winnipeg. These individuals could have chosen other Canadian locations but they did not because ties to the region, community, proximity to family, and employment, combined with their ability to live a queer existence in the city, made Winnipeg a pragmatic choice. The number of commercial spaces, including restaurants, lounges, steam baths, as well as cultural spaces like the ballet and theatre, expanded. Post-war affluence meant that private social spaces in houses and apartments were increasingly available for house parties.

House parties might not seem like a huge innovation, but the creation of a series of house party networks led to the increased visibility of lesbians as they entered mixed private social settings with gay males. Later, women's divergent interests (politically and culturally) would drive a wedge between lesbians and gays in Winnipeg. Continuity with the past was evident in the enduring attraction of public male cruising sites along the rivers and on the hill, but the queer subculture was no longer solely determined by such spaces. People could and did enter it via parties, workplace friends, or while socializing at the theatre or ballet. This indicates that people were not merely discovering same-sex enclaves but beginning to talk more explicitly about previously closely guarded matters. In the 1950s and 1960s, this "subculture" began to be far more visible, making it easier for queer men and lesbians to locate such spaces. They were aided by the city's relatively compact size and the prairie sense of "community" and mutuality that facilitated connections and friendships among Euro-Canadian residents in Winnipeg.

Visibility is not tolerance, though, and one must be appropriately cautious about making overly positive conclusions about how this emerging gay and lesbian minority was viewed by the majority of Winnipeg residents in the late 1960s. Between 1969 and 1970 Carlyle-Gordge reported that there was still "a vast chasm of ignorance, prejudice and irrationality [in Winnipeg] which divides gay society from straight society." Further he believed "that there is a pressing need for more education, research, understanding and tolerance. Until straight society takes a more open-minded attitude to the continuing fact, rather than problem, of homosexuality, a large ... group of the population will remain unhappy, frustrated, third-class citizens, having to hide their true identity and inclinations or, if admitting them, being treated as social pariahs."[140] Both lesbians and gay men in Winnipeg increasingly recognized that the decades of queer subcultural practice combined with the postwar expansion had gradually led to the emergence of "gay and lesbian communities." The language of sexual identities came late to Winnipeg, but by the end of the 1960s people were openly referring to themselves as gays and lesbians. These identities would propel a small minority of often young, university-educated men and women to embrace political activity. Such younger individuals would establish gay and lesbian activist and cultural organizations in the 1970s and 1980s.

For the older cohort involved in this study, those active from the 1930s though to the 1960s, the daily resistance of living openly gay and lesbian lives in a prairie city would be sufficiently political. Their narratives of coming out and staking claims to a sexual and political identity in late adulthood were points of empowerment and obvious pride. Not all embraced this shift from subcultural participant to declared sexual identity. Peter, an elite, upper-middle-class male, was most critical of the dangers involved in this transition, the loss of freedoms associated with openness and visibility, and the potential demotion in status for those now wilfully choosing a minority "label." Men such as Peter (and Dean Bell) were well served by the older model that allowed them to lead double lives of professional success and "private" queer desires, so one could not argue that the new model advantaged all queers. It might have become easier to find others, or to find organizations and spaces for gay and lesbian activities, but such "openness" had its price.

Historicizing Winnipeg's queer subculture from the 1930s to the late 1960s illustrates how western men and women remade commercial and public spaces to suit their needs. Beginning in the 1930s they creatively fashioned a queer circuit within Winnipeg's downtown. These spaces evolved and expanded considerably throughout the twentieth century, although the clearest acceleration was after the Second World War. Western Canadian sensibilities governed how people made sense of such activities. The live-and-let-live ethos that enabled a range of businesses to profit from their queer clients while it provided urban queers and lesbians with much-needed space and services was not unique to Winnipeg, and others have claimed a similar ethos in American western and Midwestern cities. What was unique to mid-twentieth-century Winnipeg were the city's economic and ethnic demographics and the regional characteristics that prioritized resilience, endurance, and community-mindedness at the expense, often, of individual gain or a so-called "softer" life available elsewhere. Not only did people purposefully "choose" to stay in Winnipeg over other more congenial cities, they also migrated there from elsewhere in Manitoba and north-western Ontario so that they could lead queer lives. Contrary to our impressions that queers fled Winnipeg, it was, for many rural, small-town, and northern residents, a regional queer destination city.

Ultimately, the sense of community created within various social networks within the queer subculture during the post-war era led to the emergence of a visible gay and lesbian community by 1970. Not all members of the "pansy parade" joined the gay activist parade four decades later. Geographically, the journey from cruising the hill to lobbying for rights in front of the legislature was a short one. Conceptually, however, to step over that line meant rupturing the tacit tolerance and wilful ignorance of mainstream residents. Politically, conceptually, and practically, the change was profound both within gay and lesbian circles and outside them. While gay politics came to Winnipeg in the 1970s, not everyone embraced them. Some residents would, over time, accept

Carlyle-Gordge's argument that gays and lesbians in the city required acceptance and equitable treatment. Other residents completely disagreed with such notions. The history sketched in this chapter resists closure and, in contrast to the goals of the oral history project, it avoids a linear narrative of emancipation and emergence. Instead, it offers an unique perspective on a "bygone era" when queer social spaces, camaraderie, and expert, insider knowledge of the city provided queer men and lesbians with remarkable latitude in remaking the city's landmarks, commercial, and social spaces to suit their own purposes.

Chapter Two

A Kiss Is Never Just a Kiss: Saskatchewan Queer History

My "coming out" was the most defining event of my life. It changed me permanently. Living as a secret homosexual is like living as a spy in a foreign country. You learn to be fluent in the language, you take on the colouring of that particular culture, you make sure that your mask never slips because your greatest fear is that your true identity will be revealed … For the closeted queer the thought police are everywhere. You can never relax.[1]

Peter Millard, (1932–2001), Or Words to that Effect

Not all of the individuals in this chapter would "come out" as Professor Peter Millard understood that term in the late twentieth century, when he reflected on his life trajectory in his memoirs. In the 1970s, when Millard made this decision, he was in his early forties. Well established in the community as an English professor, art collector, and art dealer, adding "gay activist" to his list of accomplishments was not an obvious development. However, he became a tireless campaigner for gay and lesbian rights, and, in particular, extensions to the provincial human rights code. Despite his choices, and his frustration at times with those who could or would not make similar choices, it was clear that Millard understood the risks and rewards that a shift from private actor to public activist demanded. As was evident in Winnipeg, not all people who participated in queer social and sexual networks – from the 1930s through to the 1970s – would choose to shift from actor to activist, private queer to public gay. This chapter strives to move beyond those limited binaries, representing the range of strategies, positions, and lives that Saskatchewan people adopted throughout the pre-Stonewall era (prior to 1969). Most were not "open" about their private lives, but when we utilize a "queer genealogy" to search for those unconventional people, women and men who left fragmentary evidence of non-heteronormative lives, the fragments – photos, life stories, oral histories, newspaper articles, and some legal cases – add up to a substantive portrait of the ways that women and men in Saskatchewan were "queer" throughout the twentieth century.[2]

Prior to the establishment of explicitly gay and lesbian organizations in Saskatoon and Regina in 1971, finding opportunities for same-sex activities in Saskatchewan was hard work. One had to be alert to opportunities and moments of difference that presented themselves – a random newspaper article about "queer" crimes; sightings of small congregations of men; pairs of "odd" women; a cutting homophobic comment that was double-edged, part warning about transgression, part clue to another, desired world. Unlike Winnipeg, where the gift of interviews with "old-timers" enabled mapping queer activity in the city from the 1930s forward, such a resource does not exist for Saskatoon. Instead, in over twenty-five interviews with current and former Saskatchewan residents, I've collected fragmentary moments of queer lives prior to the 1970s, either individuals' own teen years, or their recollections of "older" members of the community. Many of those fragments overlapped, the same names appearing in multiple oral histories, making it safe to incorporate those histories (not names) in this chapter. Such fragments no doubt represent other elusive histories of the less flamboyant, famous, or charismatic people who remain lost to queer histories of the province. Unlike the previous chapter, where the city of Winnipeg was the focus, this chapter primarily focuses on the province of Saskatchewan, with the city of Saskatoon and to a lesser degree Regina playing secondary roles. It does so for two reasons. First, well into the twentieth century, Saskatchewan was a more rural province than Manitoba. With two major cities, and a handful of secondary, smaller cities, the migratory patterns of Saskatchewan queer women and men encompassed larger swathes of the province as people moved from farm to cities, for business, education, or socializing, before returning "home." Capturing that motion is an important part of the history of being queer in the prairies, and of prairie life. Second, a provincial frame enables historicizing many queer fragments, people, and places, illustrating a tremendous variability of how queer women and men lived. Subsequently, in parts two and three, the focus shifts to Saskatoon and Regina.

Setting the Scene

Histories of Saskatchewan enumerate the province's lengthy history of Indigenous settlement.[3] Subsequently, the Saskatchewan territory was the setting for exchanges between European fur traders and Indigenous, and later Metis, workers and traders. It was, and is, a land with tremendous natural and resource wealth and thus Canada's federal politicians, most notably prime minister, John A. Macdonald, earmarked it as a territory that could enrich the Canadian government.[4] It was not easily secured, and the history of resistance and rebellion; of the creation of the North-West Mounted Police; of the demise of the buffalo; and of the numbered treaties extinguishing Indigenous title to the lands in exchange for reserves, food, and annuities for a decimated Indigenous population are well known.[5] As are the massive waves of settler newcomers, first eastern Canadians and Americans, later Eastern Europeans, who were drawn to the "last best west" by the opportunity of "free" homesteads and their desire to reinvent themselves as prosperous, land-owning farmers. When Saskatchewan and Alberta entered confederation and became provinces in 1905, each province had to designate a capital city. Unlike in Alberta, where Edmonton – the northern, former fur-trade centre – became the provincial capital, in Saskatchewan that honour was bestowed upon Regina, in the province's south-central region. Remarkably ambitious, politicians built a provincial legislature that would serve the millions of provincial residents they anticipated would call Saskatchewan home. Western politicians also anticipated a time when the federal balance of power would tilt westward and Saskatchewan and Alberta would be the power brokers. In addition to being the provincial capital, Regina was, and remains, home to the Royal North-West Mounted Police (later the Royal Canadian Mounted Police), which coalesced two different but important powerful institutions in that city – contributing greatly to the city's character, economy, and demographics.

Unlike the province of Manitoba where Winnipeg consolidated the economic, political, and cultural life of the province, Saskatchewan opted for a more decentralized model. This strategy was intended to stoke economies throughout the province by judicious placement of key governmental institutions. Saskatoon, the former temperance colony on the banks of the South Saskatchewan River, became the home to the University of Saskatchewan.[6] Founded in 1907, the University of Saskatchewan would become the driving force in the city, and this fortuitous decision brought Saskatoon real dividends intellectually, culturally, and socially.[7] In addition to the university, Saskatoon was able to capitalize on its advantageous location in the centre of the province, since, as the "hub city," it was ideally placed to serve the north and central areas. From the city's incorporation in 1906, expansion was rapid and the boom years lasted until the Great Depression. Newcomers surged into the province, and whereas earlier booms had brought Europeans, Canadians, and Americans to small farms dotted across the landscape, this wave of post–First World War immigration was destined for cities – and Regina and Saskatoon were the prime beneficiaries. By 1931, the province's population was close to a million people, making it the third most populous province in Canada after Ontario and Quebec. But, as most know, this boom was not sustainable. Saskatchewan's population peaked in 1936. From that point, it would experience fifteen years of decline and out-migration before the population numbers would once again begin to rise. It would not surpass its depression-era population until 1966. Contrary to the rest of the country, where urban living became the norm in the first half of the twentieth century, it was only in 1971 that the majority of Saskatchewan residents became urban dwellers (52.4 per cent of the provincial population).[8]

Whether through statistics, photographic images of the boomtown, or numbers of students enrolled at the University of Saskatchewan, Saskatoon's growth was spectacular during the 1920s. This boomtown era has captured the attention of academic and public historians, who have found in these heady days of population growth and civic expansion much fascinating social and local history.[9] However, our knowledge of same-sex activities during this era remains fragmentary as sources and, arguably reticence, impedes a fuller portrait of the myriad sexual activities, their private and public spaces of enactment, and the range of opportunities available to residents of such a bustling city. With those caveats noted, the fragments can be stitched into a suggestive history that speaks to the presence of same-sex activities stretching from the settlement years well into the middle of the twentieth century.[10] Terry Chapman's work with criminal court records conclusively demonstrated that western Canadian men were prosecuted for same-sex activity throughout the region (including British Columbia).[11] Proportionately most of the charges were laid in larger urban centres, but smaller communities, such as Humboldt, Saskatchewan (a largely German-Canadian farming community) or Moose Jaw, Saskatchewan, were not immune.[12]

More memorably, Regina, the Queen City, had its very own "Oscar Wilde" scandal at the close of the nineteenth century. Historian Lyle Dick has deftly analysed the intriguing – and rare – example of a prominent Regina merchant, Mr Hoskins, charged with committing "unspeakable" offences with two younger, working-class men in the basement storeroom of his general store.[13] While the force of the law and public and newspaper opinions were opposed to such actions, the men received relatively lenient sentences that consisted of fines and voluntary banishment. Part circumstantial, part the result of class and race-based privileges for the well-connected merchant at the centre of this case, such a decision raises a series of questions about the transition from the early, settlement period to the era of respectable, middle-class urbanity befitting a provincial capital city. Activity that might have been tolerated, if never encouraged or promoted, in a more fluid, largely male population in the western Canadian "frontier" could, at the onset of larger-scale settlement and urbanization, no longer be countenanced.[14]

While the law might have been unequivocal about the illegality of such activity, and could prosecute those caught red-handed, as it were, it is also true that the western region offered significant opportunity for homosocial experiences. As Peter Boag and Adele Perry have documented for the American and Canadian wests, these "frontier" locations, with their predominantly male populations, permitted spaces that could be exploited by the adventurous, curious, or lonely men and women.[15] Sarah Carter's impressive *Imperial Plots* offers a handful of intriguing portraits of single, female settlers, including Isobel "Jack" May, a former nurse, who emigrated to one of the CPR's ready-made farms in Sedgewick, Alberta, in 1911. Known as "Jack," she was a media sensation dubbed the "bachelor girl farmer" who wore men's clothes and did the outside farm work. Meanwhile her friend, Louisa Wittrick, did the inside work and wore conventionally feminine attire. Articles and photographs continued to appear long after May had thrown in the pitchfork, and, a year after arrival, quietly left the Canadian west. This was not uncommon, and many of her neighbours also abandoned their small farms.[16] Certainly her story would fit with many others in this chapter, as it is a "queer" experience that resists easy categorization. Saskatchewan provides compelling evidence of male and female histories of homosocial familiarity, fun, and same-sex activity, which parallel other transnational frontier and western contexts. And it is with one of these suggestive fragments, the dancing Royal North-West Mounted

Police, that this chapter begins our episodic account of queer Saskatchewan histories and people prior to 1969.

The Dancers of Carnduff, Saskatchewan

In 1918, the Royal North-West Mounted Police (RNWMP) launched an investigation into the "inappropriate conduct" of two Mounties stationed in Carnduff, Saskatchewan, a farming community in the province's southeastern corner, close to the Manitoba and American borders. The complainants, the "Dancers of Carnduff" as they signed their letter, alleged that the behaviour of Corporal Bailey and Constable Barker was "insulting to both the Ladies and the Gentlemen" and unbecoming for RNWMP officers.[17] The RNWMP dispatched Inspector Raven, from the Weyburn division, to interview all concerned and report back to the commissioner.

The archival file, complete with transcribed interviews, offers insight into rural Saskatchewan culture. Reportedly, the officers had attended the New Year's Eve and 11 January community dances held at the Odd Fellows Hall in Carnduff. These dances, organized by the young, single men in the district, were open to all men and women. Admission for men was one dollar and women were admitted free. A piano player provided live music and a hot supper was served. This was a dry event but there was a bar in town where men, if they chose, could drink, and some fellows came primed for the evening's entertainment. RNWMP Inspector Raven's work was extensive, as he attempted to interview all sixteen individuals who signed the letter of complaint. In hindsight, it was evident that a handful of men wished the whole event could be forgotten, while others relished the opportunity to enumerate the officers' indiscretions. The prurient reported that Bailey and Barker had been boisterous, perhaps "under the influence of liquor," as they danced with ladies they didn't know well (or to whom they had not been introduced). Equally troubling, they had cursed with ladies present and had accused a pair of local brothers (hereafter known simply as "the brothers" to protect their family identity) of not being sufficiently supportive of Canada's efforts in the First World War. Those accusations escalated and a fist fight was narrowly averted. In the eyes of Carnduff residents, the officers' worst crime had been dancing with each other.[18] The brothers – who instigated the letter – offered the most detailed catalogue of the Mounties missteps and their motivation seems transparent. The officers' had questioned the brothers' masculinity and their patriotism by demanding to know why they had not enlisted. Further shamed by Corporal Bailey's order to Baker not to fight "civilians," the brothers' sole means to restore their honour was with their letter of complaint.

The bulk of Raven's interviews single out issues of intoxication and so-called belligerence, and over half of the reports expressed surprise that the men would dance together in mixed company because, as Dan Lothian reported, "there were nine ladies there that night" and "they were not engaged for all the dances."[19] Dance organizers feared that if the two Mounties continued to attend community dances their behaviour would scare away the respectable, eligible ladies. Stated, rather than implied, were some powerful condemnations of the Mounties transgression of social norms by dancing with each other while ladies languished on the sidelines. What kind of "respectable" men would do that? The only explanation Carnduff residents could formulate was intoxication. And, ironically a by-product of that state, the local women asserted their right to decline the boorish Mounties invitations to dance. The eyewitness reports varied considerably in the finer details of their dancing. One of the brothers fastidiously criticized their dancing technique, noting: "They danced a 'one-step' holding each other around the body. One shouldn't do that. One should place his right arm around the ladies waist and hold her right hand in his left." Farmer Shirley Moore stated that he found it "quite unusual for two men to dance together." Finally, Walter Plews incredulously told Inspector Raven: "I never danced with a man. I think it would be very ungentlemanly thing to dance with a man in a ball room when others were dancing with ladies." The poor Mounties couldn't win. Having imbibed alcohol, been forward with the ladies, and then rebuffed for their advances, their evident enthusiasm at reeling around the dance floor together was the final misstep. Raven's conclusions, perhaps not surprisingly, was focused on RNWMP interests. He closed ranks and aligned himself with the officers and dismissed the complaint of "ungentlemanly conduct" as "frivolous" and the complaint about their intoxication as "not worth serious consideration."[20] He confirmed that the verbal altercation between one brother and Constable Barker occurred but, short of a fight, in his analysis this was best forgotten. Interestingly, this tempest was viewed differently by the assistant commissioner who was not so easily swayed by Raven's tidy dismissal of the fracas, observing that "while there may not be sufficient evidence to warrant a charge of intoxication or disorderly conduct ... their actions were to say the least suspicious." Rather archly he concluded, "there would appear too much familiarity between the H.C.O. and Constable."[21]

Annie Maude "Nan" McKay

While the available sources offer infrequent glimpses of men caught in compromising same-sex activities, whether dancing or having sex, evidence of women's same-sex affection in the same era have proven more elusive. Western Canadian archives, university special collections, and museums contain wonderfully rich collections of women variously classified as pioneers, teachers, homesteaders, journalists, librarians, mountaineers, sporting women, mothers, and wives. With rare exceptions, scholars and students interested in western women's histories confront silences, unspoken assumptions of heteronormativity, or excessive caution about how to interpret "exceptional" western women.[22] Images of these "complex and contradictory characters," sometimes clad entirely in men's attire, such as well-circulated images of agricultural journalist E. Cora Hind whose "uniform" of riding breeches, a Stetson, and militaristic jackets represent, at the very least, opportunities for discussion of gender liberties in the west.[23] Sarah Carter's recent volume *Imperial Plots* makes an excellent step towards initiating those discussions for the settlement era.[24]

Finding evidence of women's same-sex socializing and/or sexuality requires determination and good fortune. And when those glimpses and fragments are found, they require close attention because they raise suggestive questions about queer possibilities. Or, as British historian Laura Doan's work has articulated, these images and moments are "not to provide a usable past but to explain aspects of the sexual past that resist explanation in the context of identity history."[25] The Mounties of Carnduff, Saskatchewan, were not "gay" men in the way we understand that term now, nor was Annie Maud (Nan) McKay a "lesbian," but in both cases their queer presentation, the "facts" of their personal and professional lives, their "single" status, and their actions and activities enable a "queer" critical history. Letters and papers, or occasional publications, require close attention because in many respects they were purposely constructed to foil prying eyes and thwart attention. Sometimes, in serendipitous ways, tantalizing clues remain and then a counternarrative of women's same-sex desires can be made. In the case of McKay, it starts with a University of Saskatchewan alumni project launched to commemorate the institution's first century, an open-minded researcher who allowed for a "nuanced" series of clues to emerge, and, finally, the donation of a cherished university photo album from the 1910s, all of which enabled this queer analysis.[26]

To mark the University of Saskatchewan's centennial in 2007, a series of commemorations were launched. One of the most popular was the "100 Alumni of Influence." This process strove to illustrate the institution's storied past, and, naturally, to position it as a leader – in a way that we understand that term today – so it was clear that one of the goals was "inclusivity," and the search was on for a wide, representative cross-section of accomplished alumni. This undertaking invited contributions from the community and campus, in addition to which a committee of scholars assembled a group of notables. One of the people chosen was McKay. According to the official description, McKay was noteworthy because she was "the first Métis and first Aboriginal woman to graduate from the University of Saskatchewan" in 1915.[27] Interestingly, given the nature of this book, and the methodological debates of making such retrospective historical claims, or claiming queer histories, it is important to note that this was not an identity claimed by McKay in her own published comments or statements.[28] Perhaps it was because everyone knew. Perhaps it was a distancing tactic, as she strove to climb the professional ladder. My point is: she did not claim those identities, and yet they have proudly been claimed for her as a part of an institutional history. In some respects, claiming a queer history for McKay is a similar endeavour, which rests on a slim, but compelling, series of photos. McKay never hid her family background, but her goal of middle-class respectability was dependent on fitting in with the other elites. Overt declarations of Metis heritage would have been rare from middle-class women and men. Having said that, in a small province, where the interconnections between the university, the government, professional society, and professional elites were evident, everyone knew your family, your connections, and your abilities.[29]

Nan McKay was born in 1892 in Fort à la Corne, Northwest Territories, to a prominent English Metis family.[30] Angus McKay, Nan's father, worked for the Hudson's Bay Company at a series of postings in northern Saskatchewan. Initially homeschooled, Nan was eventually enrolled in the prestigious St Alban's Ladies College in Prince Albert, Saskatchewan. Her experiences at this Anglican girl's school were formative, she made a number of close friendships (including with University of Saskatchewan President Walter Murray's daughter Christina), and won an

2.1 Nan McKay, circa 1912–15. Nan McKay Fonds, University of Saskatchewan Archives and Special Collections.

entrance scholarship to the university. She attended the university for three years, graduating in 1915 with a bachelor's in French and English.

By all accounts McKay was a very able accomplished student, and the alumni citation commended her "remarkable commitment to the university both as a student and an alumnus. Active in student life, McKay served on student council, *The Sheaf* editorial board, and played on the University of Saskatchewan women's hockey team. The photo of the women's ice hockey team, with a grinning McKay in the centre (and focal point of at least one of her teammates attention), was clearly a favourite. Other images of the team include two women in the background, skating hand in hand. McKay was also an accomplished artist, painter, and figure skater. McKay served as vice president of Pente Kai Deka, the women's fraternity, as secretary of the campus YWCA, and actively participated in the literary society. Clearly, Nan McKay was a striver. After graduation, she was hired as "an assistant librarian," a position she held for thirty-one years, where she was heralded as the "right-hand man" of a succession of (male) university head librarians.[31] McKay was everywhere on campus – particularly during the First World War when the vast numbers of male recruits marched off campus and to the western front, meaning that those who remained behind did double and triple duty. McKay was one of two alumni co-editors of *The Sheaf* in 1916, and in 1918 she volunteered as a nurse during the flu epidemic. This was in addition to her day job at the library, where she was employed her entire working career, retiring in 1959 after forty-four years of service. Interviewed by the local newspaper when she retired, McKay's reflections about campus were intriguing. "Miss McKay" proudly discussed her participation on the women's ice hockey team, a storied team that competed throughout the west, and asserted that "in those days the young women seemed hardier."[32] An inveterate camper and hiker in her youth (McKay was a member of the alpine club in Banff), her spirit was undiminished. McKay died in 1986, at the age of ninety-three.

If this were all the evidence we had of Nan McKay, then her story would be one of many such suggestive histories of "independent," university-educated women whose personal world of female friends and family – and their passions for sports, camping, mountaineering, and travel – could legitimately open many possibilities about their private lives and inclinations.[33] However, the addition to the McKay fonds of a photo album from McKay's university days provides more conclusive evidence. McKay's album includes photos of parties, theatrical

2.2 Nan McKay and the University of Saskatchewan ladies hockey team, 1915. Nan McKay Fonds, University of Saskatchewan Archives and Special Collections.

performances, camping, travel, and residence life. One-third of the way into the album is a small but significant photo that tilts the balance in favour of claiming Nan and her friends as a lesbian-like cohort.[34] Taken in 1915 outside the university residences, Nan McKay and Hope Weir are pictured locked in an embrace and kiss (see cover photo). It is the only photo of its kind in the album, but this rare image and the series of other images of various social groups indicates that McKay and Weir were a well-accepted part of an established social circle. These photos provide a unique window into campus life. So far, no extant letters between the two have been located and information about Miss Weir's life after graduation is sparse. She moved to Regina and worked at the Regina Normal School as a teacher. It appears she never married. McKay's niece (who donated her aunt's album and other papers) confirmed that McKay never had a boyfriend and, when questioned further by Professor Duff Spafford, she stated that it wasn't uncommon for women of that era not to marry.[35] Technically, this is true – the casualties of war meant that there was a "lost generation" of men, either

2.3 Nan McKay and Hope Weir, approximately 1915. Nan McKay Fonds, University of Saskatchewan Archives and Special Collections.

killed or physically or psychologically maimed by war, which greatly reduced women's marriage prospects. However, a talented, popular woman who had never had a male suitor could, perhaps, have used that respectable cover to avoid divulging other reasons for her decision not to marry.

In a wonderfully engaging essay about McKay's life, former political scientist and lifelong University of Saskatchewan historian Duff Spafford wrote a perceptive short biography of McKay that is notable for the ways that he offers evidence to support a queer reading of McKay's life.[36] He does not make that assertion. But as the expert on her archival papers, and with vast knowledge of the world in which she circulated in Saskatchewan, he provides important signposts for how this daughter of a Hudson's Bay Company trader and English Metis mother, from northern Saskatchewan, with deep connections to the political and academic elite in Prince Albert and later Saskatoon, could navigate a professional life as a single "respectable" woman and still be true to her own unconventionality. His description of a holiday trip that McKay and Christina Henry (later Bateman) took to northern Saskatchewan in 1919, where "both women learned that women wearing trousers, as they did on this journey, were a curiosity to northerners," illustrates his playfulness as a writer but also signals that McKay was unconventional.[37]

Nan McKay would never have self-identified as a lesbian, although that term, and others, did exist.[38] But it is important to remind readers that she never, at least as the written records show, identified herself as Metis or Indigenous either. Eager to become a member of the professional middle class of salaried single faculty and administrators, in an era when Saskatchewan's elite was primarily Anglo-Canadian, it would have been unthinkable to accentuate differences (racial, class, gendered, sexual, or educational). Our "modern" affinity for identity politics was unknown then. So the question remains: was McKay a lesbian? The answer is perhaps, and in that "perhaps" lays important space for queer women's experiences in Saskatchewan. McKay's life was an accomplished one, and she clearly loved the University of Saskatchewan. Her cherished photos from those years were significant enough to be saved, and later donated to the university archives. As this was the only photo album donated, it suggests the importance of those photos with Hope Weir. Discretion prevailed, as it often did when lesbian and queer adults assumed professional responsibilities and put their more adventurous student days behind them. With so few images, letters, or diaries about prairie lesbians prior to the 1950s, the significance of the McKay photo album is amplified. It claims important space for historians to do more than merely suggest that lesbians existed in the prairies prior to the Second World War. And while Nan and her female friends are the focal point of most of her photos, she does have images of co-ed activities, and a couple of male students in their dorm rooms, which are also suggestive – certainly demonstrating that close homosocial bonds were in evidence in the women's and men's residences.

The University of Saskatchewan features prominently in this history of queer activity in Saskatchewan and Saskatoon, because it drew faculty and students from the province and beyond. This infusion of people and ideas brought intellectual, social, and cultural currents to Saskatoon, which might not have otherwise been in circulation. For students, the university's ability to provide space, first for learning, but second for life lessons, as young men and women navigated the transition to adulthood, was critical. For many rural women and men, attendance at the university, whether for regular courses or at a series of extension programmes (e.g., "Farm Week" hosted by the Women's Institute), offered rural Saskatchewan women a taste of the city. Farm Week was a well-known and highly anticipated summer respite for farm wives and mothers, which offered education on nutrition, agriculture, running a prairie farm household, and parenting. It was also an opportunity for socializing and friendship, for much needed downtime away from families, farms, and familial commitments. The full extent of that socializing will likely elude us, but it is not impossible to suggest that the charms of the city were varied.

"Augustus Esch"

As indicated in the introductory chapter, this research illuminates queer experiences in major prairie cities and also rural, small-town, and remote settings. While the material from the cities is more numerous, and has a tendency to give the impression that queer socializing and opportunities were only available in urban spaces – university campuses, beverage rooms, hotels, urban parks, and riverbanks – that was not true. One must be careful to avoid inscribing only cities with the possibility of same-sex activity, spaces, and queer circles. Rural residents found creative ways to organize their lives. Consider the unique narrative provided by "Augustus Esch" about his experiences in Saskatchewan. Unlike McKay (whose photo album enables a queer critical history), in 1978 Augustus Esch (a pseudonym) shared his own history of same-sex love in Saskatchewan.[39]

Born in 1897, and thus eighty-one at the time the article was written, Esch reported that he was born in Belgium, was orphaned as a teenager, and participated as a soldier during the First World War. In 1920, he emigrated to western Canada. Initially destined for his sister's farm in southwestern Saskatchewan, after harvest that year he moved into the city of Winnipeg to find work. In 1921, he headed west again to help bring in the harvest, this time working at a farm north of Saskatoon. In Esch's own words, this was a life altering event: "I stayed with a Frenchman 27 years older than me. I was working for his brother. I had met the man on the boat coming to Canada. He was living alone on a small farm and wanted me to stay with him. He called me his son and I called him my Dad. We loved each other and lived like that for eight years. I got married in 1929. My friend stayed with us; my children called him Grandpa."[40] Widowed in 1943, Esch lost his "Dad" two years later. He concentrated on raising his son and daughter and chose not to remarry. After his children were grown he continued to farm in southwestern Saskatchewan and, "for company," found "elderly lonely men to live" with him. Still spry in the 1970s, he began to place contact ads for older gay men in the *Saskatchewan Gay Coalition Newsletter* that read: "Elderly man in South West Saskatchewan seeks same. He is still in good health, lives alone in a two bedroom house in town and would like the love and companionship of another man."[41]

Esch's original letter, particularly his categorical statement about his views on sexuality – "I believe in love between people of the same or opposite sex (but) not in open demonstrations as shown on T.V." – piqued the curiosity of the newsletter's editor. In 1979, Doug Wilson interviewed Esch as he made his annual bus trek around Saskatchewan, visiting men he had befriended through the years, including a "shop-keeper, a village priest, a grain elevator operator and several farmers." Esch never divulged their names, and, as Wilson astutely noted, "a life of subterfuge had made him wary." He had an uncomplicated view of sexual activity, stating that from a young age he began to "play with men" and found opportunities were plentiful for same-sex activity, as "we [the boys or young men] always slept together," both prior to and during his army service. Attracted to older men, the man he befriended on the boat from Europe "was the major love of his life." Strategically, Esch and his lover were able to exploit their age difference, outwardly constructing the relationship as a familial one – father and son – and hence they avoided detection or censure. Esch claimed that neither his wife nor children ever knew that they were lovers. Claiming that he had a "genuine affection for his wife," her death marked the end of his heterosexual relationships. Leery of being too open about his own sexuality, he was also a dutiful supporter of the Saskatchewan Gay Coalition (SGC) whose goals were to forge links between queer rural and small-town Saskatchewan residents, and, ultimately, to help them "come out" and life fuller lives. On a pensioner's income, he made regular dona-tions of small sums of money to help the SGC defray their costs and wrote frequent letters to encourage the editors in their work.

After his death in 1981, Wilson published an article in *Pink Ink* about Esch's unconventional queer life and loves in rural Saskatchewan. Important for many reasons, including its rarity, histories such as Esch's illustrate how queer activity could be located, framed, and enjoyed in rural communities and small towns. For twenty-four years, he and his "Dad" had managed to carve out a life that enabled them to live and farm together in rural Saskatchewan. We cannot know what the com-munity thought of this arrangement, but he was apparently accepted and well liked in rural small towns. He garnered praise for the care and attention he lavished on lonely, elderly men in the community. Playing a variety of conventional roles – devoted son, a kind-hearted caretaker, or a devoted friend who made annual visits to old acquaintances – Esch managed to coexist in these communities. Indeed, Wilson praised him for providing an inspirational window into a "gay life lived in the very recent pioneer past of Saskatchewan" and for his ability to "thrive undetected in a time and place that would not seem to have been conducive to thriving. The twenty-four year love story with his 'Dad,' the network of loving friends, the elderly men he nurtured indicate the fullness of that life and the many other stories yet untold."[42] Regretfully, Wilson and Esch only met once and therefore any further links to his rural networks did not materialize. Nor did the article jog the memories of readers with similar tales of sexual pioneering on the prairies, particularly of those queer men who chose to stay on farms, or in small towns, rather than strike out for the cities. Given the predominance of agriculture in Saskatchewan, and the fact that majority of provincial residents lived in rural areas until after the Second World War, many, many queer men and lesbians were born and raised in rural communities.

Transgendered Activity and Cross-Dressing Traditions

Transgendered experiences were not a focal point of my research, yet archival work did uncover fragmentary glimpses of transgendered westerners.[43] Those vignettes offer some points of speculation about alternative strategies people might have employed to construct their lives in a fashion that enabled diverse, or more fluid, social and sexual identities. While I do not mean to suggest that transgendered, gender inversion, and "queer" opportunities were one and the same thing – they were not – what I do wish to illustrate by sharing Jean Crandall's story is that gender norms, presentation, and actions were fluid. In settings where most Euro-Canadians were newcomers to the region, removed from biological families, opportunities could be seized for transgendered reinventions as well as "queer" social lives.

In March 1934, Regina's newspaper, the *Leader Post*, published a photograph of Jean (Gene) Crandall under the headline "Scientists are Intrigued." Dressed in conventionally feminine attire, seated at a spinning wheel, Crandall struck a demure feminine pose.[44] Readers learned that Crandall was the heir to a "large fortune" in Elgin County, Ontario. Her attempts to "claim" her inheritance resulted in her brief arrest because her attire and presentation (female) was different from her biological sex (male). The police couldn't charge Crandall with a crime and released her with a "warning to leave Elgin county." As the *Leader Post* reported: "Crandall may be a scientific specimen of rare interest, being apparently a man, but with extreme feminine tendencies. His 'marriage' in Regina (as a woman) still stands on provincial records."[45] Later included in a history excerpt in *Rites* magazine, Crandall claimed that the Regina minister was not fooled by the couple, "The minister heard my deep voice and his only remark was 'you have an awfully bad cold!' We were both very happy. Jim [Crandall's husband] was tickled to death and so was I. When the ring was on my finger Jim grasped me in his arms and kissed me."[46] After their marriage, they moved to British Columbia, living in Pouce Coupe and Cutbank Valley, where Crandall volunteered in the community, taught Sunday school, and sang in church choirs. She was a founding member and first president of the local women's institute. The writers at *Rites* claimed that the western communities were primarily amused by the news of Crandall's arrest and the media publicity.

Crandall's transgendered experience was similar to transgendered westerners discovered by Peter Boag in *Transforming the West*, which reveals the high incidence of transgenderism in the west, the fluidity of social relations, and, perhaps most important, the region's attraction to those iconoclasts keen to "reinvent" themselves.[47] According to Boag, individuals who we would now classify as trans men tended to get more respect, and were treated more favourably, until, often after their deaths, their biological sex was revealed. Individuals who now would use the term trans women often had a harder time claiming a female identity. Those who were most successful were integrated into the community, a factor that had the tendency to mitigate the revelation of their biological sex. Male-to-female transgendered individuals who were more marginalized, lost their partners, or who consistently raised suspicions tended to experience harsher outcomes if and when their biological gender was revealed.

Interviews with Saskatoon residents revealed another long-time transgendered individual, "Bobby," an accountant or clerk who worked in an office in downtown Saskatoon. Dating from the late 1960s, Bobby's story, volunteered by two of my Saskatoon narrators, offers an interesting transgendered experience of gender difference and social inclusion. According to Bruce Garman and T, after his mother's death in the 1960s, Bobby was liberated from worries about embarrassing her and, after work and on weekends, he began to publicly appear as a woman, wearing women's clothes. Garman recalled that when he was dressed in male attire for work he looked uncomfortable and odd, but as a woman he appeared natural and more comfortable. Uncharacteristically, Bobby shopped for women's clothing and shoes in Saskatoon, often using his lunch breaks to pop into his favourite downtown shops. Garman had a friend who worked at Burton's Shoes on Second Avenue. The owner Burt Gladstone's "whole life was selling shoes," and he really cultivated his customers, which included lecturing the staff that when Mr B came into the store he was to be treated with respect. Garman continued, "my friend said that Bobby was in his suit, trying on these high heeled shoes … He would pull up his trouser leg and turn his ankle in the mirror saying 'You know Mr. Gladstone, those pumps I bought last month, I've dyed them several colours, they work with so many outfits and they've given me nothing but comfort.'"[48] This anecdote, Garman admitted, was one he had told many times before and he clearly intended to amuse me with a story of Saskatoon's more innocent days. Yet it can be read on so many levels. It illustrates that acceptance for diversity, and for a range of gendered and sexual presentations/acts/identities could exist – *provided* the right conditions were met. First of all, Bobby was a Saskatonian from a good family, who was a professional, well-established, middle-class client whose patronage was important to Gladstone's business. It doesn't tell us how long it took Bobby to become comfortable purchasing women's clothes and shoes with as much ease and enjoyment that heterosexual women may uncomplicatedly claim. Nor does it tell us anything about the rest of his negotiations outside the store, which cannot all possibly have been this accepting. Still, with those caveats, this vignette of difference does illustrate something suggestive about the city of Saskatoon, and reaffirms the other histories in this chapter. City residents could and did accommodate gendered and sexual differences. Under the right circumstances (in this case a loyal, white middle-class customer), there could be important demonstrations of social inclusion and acceptance. Why that was, in the end, is the more difficult question to answer.

Individuals like Crandall and Bobby were rarities, but western Canadian archives feature plentiful images of cross-dressing. Postcards of men and women cross-dressed in community, school, and university theatricals or for elaborate Halloween parties were common.[49] In an earlier era, the absence of women in pioneering settlements, and all-male environs of mining camps and mounted police barracks, seemingly gave permission for some playfulness at dances, where some of the men appeared in elaborate women's gowns and attire.[50] Throughout this period, and continuing into the contemporary era, community mock weddings were another popular form of gendered, costumed play that proliferate in the Canadian and American Midwest. Folklorist Michael Taft indicates that these events call for further analysis concerning the gendered role playing, social and sexual community norms, and the ways in which these forums provide licence for heterosexual women (conventionally the directors of these plays) to explore the challenges of rural women's work and home roles.[51] One could argue that such weddings also offer opportunities for more critical appraisal of heterosexual sexual and social norms within the region. Parodies of heterosexual marriages, and hard truths about "normalized" gender roles and behaviours, offer important spaces for critique of those norms and, on a more limited scale, an outlet for gendered social and sexual frustrations. If they were launch pads to more sustained queer activities remains a possibility.

The 1940s: Norman Dahl, "Dorothy," Evelyn Rodgers, and Lilja Stefansson

While historians are fond of using major political events as decisive turning points and markers of change, those are never as definitive as our research may appear. Just as the interest and radical potential of cross-dressing continued from the earlier part of the twentieth century well into the post–Second World War era, so did other forms of social and sexual activity. As previously noted, because Saskatchewan remained an overwhelmingly rural province until the post–Second World War era (and hence out of step with the rest of the country, in which the majority of Canadians began to reside in cities beginning in the 1920s), some of the forms of post-war same-sex experiences that Winnipeg underwent in the late 1940s and 1950s (an explosion of same-sex socializing spaces, for example) were not as evident in Saskatchewan until later. Linkages with rural communities, and norms of behaviour from rural areas and small towns, also persisted well into the post-war era.

Norman Dahl was born in 1928 in Birch Hills, Saskatchewan, a farming community in north-central Saskatchewan with a large population of Norwegians. Dahl was raised in a Lutheran household by his Norwegian-Canadian parents. He was the second of three children, and the only son. His father was a prominent member of the community, serving at various times as mayor, as well as a farmer and grain buyer. Dahl's mother worked at home, and in his family education, music, and art were highly valued, thus his parents strongly supported Dahl's aspirations to be a pianist, organist, and singer. According to Dahl, life in Saskatchewan small towns and the countryside in the 1930s and early 1940s was rife with sexual possibilities for boys – from skinny dipping at the local pond, to the fact that time and space permitted much indulgence for boyish curiosity and hijinks. Equally, routine familiarity with the cycle of farmyard life, and animal husbandry, meant a certain basic reproductive knowledge. What was lacking, though, was terminology and descriptors for sexual behaviour. Dahl recalled that the lack of sexual terms and concepts, far from impeding his adolescent sexual activity and experimentations, actually provided him with freedom from fears of censure, since there wasn't any pejorative or medicalized language to describe same-sex acts. It was only once his eldest sister attended the University of Saskatchewan, and brought home stories about a "perverted, homosexual" professor whom he recalled she found "revolting" (all her words), that Dahl remembered hearing those terms for the first time.[52]

Musically talented, Dahl studied piano for years and as a teenager he travelled throughout the province to regional and provincial music festivals and recitals. It was during these travels that he began to notice the other men and teenagers like himself. He attended the University of Saskatchewan for one year in the late 1940s but had to drop out when he was diagnosed with tuberculosis. In the sanatorium he would have his first male love affair – a chaste but intense one – and recalled mourning this man's death for years afterward. After his recovery, he returned to intensive music training and performance with a summer session at the Banff School of Fine Arts. He reminisced that the evening of his final piano recital in Saskatoon in 1949 was very memorable. In the audience that evening was "Brad S," a motorcycle-riding, St Andrews College seminary student.[53] After the recital, Brad and Norman returned to Norman's room at the Senator Hotel, where Norman remembered a night of "wild sex."[54]

Contrary to what some might suspect, neither man agonized over this night, although they did branch off in two very different directions. Afterwards, Brad told Norman that he was "completely heterosexual," and Norman, clearly enjoying relaying this tale, reportedly told Brad that he had "improvised brilliantly." Witty repartee aside, Brad was clear about his intentions, as he chose the conventional path – heterosexual marriage and children. Still, it had an impact, as he continued to have same-sex liaisons on the side. This bisexual dalliance angered Norman, primarily for two reasons. First, he had two sisters and claimed that did not like to see women deceived. Second, because he chose the more difficult road he had little sympathy for those who would not make similar choices. Asked in the interview to recollect his coming out, Norman simply laughed and replied, "I've never been in."[55]

Ultimately, Dahl would leave for studies at the Royal Conservatory of Music in Toronto. On a weekend visit with a conservatory friend to her grandmother's home in Oakville, Ontario, he was introduced to her neighbours, the Wilkes and their son George, who was doing graduate work at University of Toronto after serving with the Royal Canadian Air Force during the Second World War. Smitten, Dahl remembered getting himself invited to Wilkes's Toronto apartment for dinner, and then pursuing Wilkes throughout the following year. After Dahl completed studies at Toronto, Wilkes and Dahl became life partners, splitting their time between Ottawa and their cottage in Gatineau, Quebec (a noted gay Ottawa hideout), that they designed and built themselves. Wilkes was employed by the federal civil service while Dahl worked for a variety of governmental and cultural institutions, including the Canada Council, the Canadian Welfare Council, the National Gallery, and others.[56] Still together when I interviewed them fifty-five years later, they acknowledged the challenges and stresses of living in more homophobic times, and in a city where governmental purges of gays in the civil service were well documented.[57] But they take immense pride in being survivors and their determination to live their lives as they chose. Their life has revolved around work, volunteer activities, social and gay activism, their homes, and travel.

While Norman Dahl's youthful relatively carefree sexual escapades in Saskatchewan seem very daring – and atypical, in that he stressed his family's liberal values and their wholehearted support for his artistic aspirations – his decision to migrate outside the region for advanced education and later employment is a supremely conventional narrative and it is what ultimately enabled his life choices. There would be many others like Norman Dahl, men and women who shrewdly left the prairies in search of better jobs, more cultural opportunities, and, yes, a gayer life. Even the partial list of well-known prairie gay and lesbian émigrés – playwright Brad Fraser; journalist, editor and museum impresario William Thorsell; accountant and activist Tom Warner; musician kd lang; and the late journalist and activist Chris Bearchell – attests to the region's rich heritage of talented expats. According to Chris Vogel, a well-known Winnipeg activist, the large number of former prairie and, in particular, Winnipeg gays now resident in Toronto has immeasurably strengthened and enriched the Toronto queer community while, conversely, weakening Winnipeg's. From the perspective of this work, I did not set out to find and interview expats (that is a different project), but such a study would be a valuable area for future research. For one thing, it may better enable us to differentiate between those individuals who we might label "exceptional" or strongly-identified queers who chafed in these smaller communities (for a host of sexual, occupational, and political reasons), as compared with the relatively "ordinary" people who populate this book, those who happened to be queer, and for whom their sexual identities were not incompatible with their home or chosen region.[58] Intangible differences, and largely unanswerable questions, but in this case Dahl's ambition to excel as a musician propelled him outside the region.

Others were more constrained by conventionality, less driven, and perhaps less inclined to move from their familiar surroundings. Consider the case of "Dorothy" who, born in the same year as Dahl, had an equally precocious sense of her difference from other girls. Such knowledge led down a different path, reminding us of how gender and class differences are major factors in sculpting queer lives and differentiating women's and men's experiences. When she was interviewed, she wryly remarked, "marriage for some of us old timers was the only answer to get away from home. You go into a marriage knowing it probably won't work."[59] And Dorothy was one of the adventurous ones. She identified as a "gay woman" and told me that she knew she was gay her whole life, recalling that as a teenager she had gone to the library and discovered that "it was [listed] under mental illness." More chillingly, during her teenage years, she recalled reading reports in the local paper about a "group of known gays. They were in the drama department." Because "Saskatoon was a very small town at the time," it was reported in the newspaper when their houses were vandalized. "One of them was a female doctor. I remember reading in the paper about their homes being vandalized," an event Dorothy linked with their marginality as openly queer people in a small city.[60] Neither option was attractive – classification as mentally ill or being subjected to random violence and public ridicule. However, when she had the opportunity, in her first job as a seventeen-year-old steno clerk, to have an affair with a slightly older colleague (who had served in the Canadian Army's Women Division), she seized it. During the course of their relationship, they took regular trips to Edmonton on Dorothy's red Harley Davidson motorcycle. When her first lover moved to Vancouver, she found a boyfriend, got married in 1948 at the age of nineteen, and subsequently had two children. Throughout her marriage, she sustained her latent lesbianism by reading lesbian pulp novels that she bought at the drugstore, particularly the work of Ann Bannon. She recalled avidly seeking any information on lesbians and gay people, and eventually she discovered the Daughters of Bilitis, became a member, and was a regular reader of *The Ladder*.[61] Fifteen years later, she divorced, retained custody of her two kids, and remained exclusively lesbian thereafter. Dorothy was very politically active, participating in provincial political campaigns, health care, and social advocacy. In 1970, she answered a contact advertisement in the *Georgia Straight* seeking "gay" people in Saskatoon. She was the only woman who responded, hence her local nickname the "original lesbian." Considerably older than the others in the group, she became a community mother hen and valued counsellor, offering support on gay and lesbian phone-in hotlines and in person, and she participated in human rights campaigns. Despite its constraints for gay people, Dorothy lived in her hometown her whole life, and other than a brief infatuation with moving to New York City, Saskatoon was the only place she wanted to live.

Evelyn Rogers, born in Regina in 1934, also recalled the very limited options for teenage girls and women who were different. In her interview, Rogers vividly recalled that at the age of twelve, she recognized that she was different from the other girls in her classes: "At twelve years old I knew. When all the other girls were looking at the guys I was looking at the girls."[62] Asked how she understood those feelings, she responded, "queer, but I didn't know the word then. Obviously I was the odd girl out." She didn't speak about this sexual discovery until she was an adult, long after she'd taken the expected route and married a male classmate. While born and raised in Regina, Rogers had deep family roots in Rouleau, a farming community a short distance from the city. Her husband was from another prominent Rouleau family, and Evelyn became a farm wife at the age of nineteen. Ruefully, she recalled that "marrying a farmer was a full time job" raising two kids, working on the farm, taking off-farm paid employment, and contributing to the community. In 1975, the "International Year of the Woman," Evelyn's conventional small-town life would be shattered by the revelation of her lesbianism.[63]

Conversely, Evelyn's partner, Lilja Stefansson, the oldest of my narrators, born in 1921, had very different experiences from those of Norman Dahl, Dorothy, and Evelyn. She was born in her parent's bedroom, on the farm in Vestfold, Manitoba. Lilja was the ninth of ten children in a proud Icelandic family. She attended a one-room school until that was forced to close for lack of students, and took her grade eight classes by correspondence. There was no money for her to attend high school and so at thirteen she was primarily responsible for housework. "I never had any teenage years, it was work, work, work."[64] Eventually at seventeen she convinced her parents she should move into Winnipeg for work, and she found a series of jobs as an apprentice to a dressmaker, sewing, and routinely spending time helping an older sister with her family during the sister's pregnancies. She met a man in Winnipeg, and once he enlisted they got married in 1942. They had two kids but her husband was an alcoholic, so she divorced him in 1948. Her sister, then living in Saskatchewan, told her that she could qualify for mothers' allowance as a single mother in Saskatchewan and so Lilja moved there. Disenchanted with how little such assistance paid, Stefansson completed her high school and began working as a teacher's supervisor/ aide. "I worked one year as a teacher supervisor and there was a man parked on my doorstep promising me everything under the sun and I was tired and got married again."[65] Eventually she and her new husband had another child, but "the marriage wasn't going too well" for a host of reasons. Stefansson ruefully told me that she contemplated leaving but "now I have three kids to bring up on my own, that's not fair," and she determined that she "better stick it out and I did for seventeen years. He was a bachelor when I married him, a whole lot older than I am, he stayed a bachelor, he was more concerned about himself and his farm than ever anything for his wife and kids and I think he just wanted a housekeeper."[66] They moved off the farm, into Rouleau, and there, at the United Church as a volunteer secretary, she met Evelyn who was on the church board and also volunteering in a secretarial capacity. They became fast friends, but it would be fifteen years before Evelyn ever felt confident enough to tell Lilja her innermost thoughts.

In our interview, Lilja and Evelyn's fondest discussion was about how they eventually became a couple. Given my previous work on *Chatelaine* magazine, and the periodical's influential feminist material, they were keen to tell me that Evelyn had used *Chatelaine's* article on lesbianism to initiate a discussion about her sexuality and her feelings for Lilja.[67] This was the early 1970s and both women were still married.

Here Lilja describes the experience of hearing about lesbianism for the
first time:

> One day [Evelyn] told me I would hate her if she told me the truth about
> herself. My reply was "Why did you murder someone?" "No," she said,
> "it's worse." I could not think of anything worse and told her so. Finally
> she told me to read an article in the current *Chatelaine*. I went and bought
> it. That was the first time I had seen the word lesbian and had never heard
> of homosexuality. Actually I had to look up the words in the dictionary …
> I held Evelyn in deep regard for many years so eventually that friendship
> developed into an abiding love. Truthfully though if my marriage had
> been a truly loving one I would probably never have realized that it is
> possible to love a woman.[68]

In retirement, Lilja joined a writing group and gave presentations
about being a lesbian, for which she wrote a series of short articles about
her own life history. These are marvellous documents, describing what
it was like to discover lesbianism at age fifty. While they "came out" in
the early 1970s, I have included their story here, because in many ways
it harkens to an earlier model as they were not aware of other groups or
people when they came out as lesbians and became a couple.

It was not easy, initially Lilja was sceptical, and they decided to go
away for a weekend to Williston, North Dakota, to have time to discuss the matter and, Lilja believed, convince Evelyn this was not the
direction they should take. In the end, it was Lilja that discovered that
their "deep friendship of ten years" and Evelyn's love for her was not
an illusion; what's more, she reported that she "found the total fulfill-
ment that had always been missing in my many attempts to have my
needs met by men."[69] This weekend initiated a multi-year affair, and the
women managed to creatively find time for each other, including making "love in a church basement."[70] Their marriages, they assured me,
were irrevocably broken. "Those were exciting but also anxious times.
In all honesty though, our marriages were totally on the rocks before we
got together so we did not break up each other's homes. Rather it gave
us the impetus to break off intolerable relationships."[71] They moved in
together in their small town, which Lilja remembered as a "foolhardy
thing to do," but it did not result in any loss of business for her insurance agency, although the "town gossips had a heyday." The women
went about their business and in 1975 they sold the agency and moved
to Regina so that Evelyn had better employment prospects. Then, they

experienced the full force of small-town condemnation: "The only really noticeable thing was that the community did not throw a farewell function for us, when we moved to Regina. Everyone that left town was usually honoured with a farewell party in the church. Evelyn still feels slighted by that, in spite of always saying she did not want such a function. Truthfully we had both done a great deal of church and community work so in that sense deserved as well as anybody else."[72] This small-minded, small-town rebuke was discussed in our interview, nearly thirty years later, and it was clear that this treatment still rankled. Similar sorts of treatment, largely the silent treatment and shunning, were still being meted out decades later when Erin Shoemaker and Jan Harvey attempted to make a go of rural, United Church of Canada, pastoral charges and found themselves the focal point for many pointed stares and moments of silence. By comparison, for both couples, Regina seemed like a breath of fresh air, a city with spaces for queer life, where there was room for some degree of anonymity and where diversity was better comprehended. Rogers and Stefansson attended Regina's gay club and remembered, initially, loving that space and the joy to be found socializing with other lesbians and gay men. So much so, that when Rogers and Stefansson reflected on their time in Regina, they concluded that it had been largely free of "harassment." Over the years, their families blended, and they pursued varied employment, volunteer, and lesbian experiences. When Lilja died in June 2013, her obituary printed in the *Regina Leader-Post* acknowledged her "partner of 40 years Evelyn Rogers, their children … and grandchildren."[73] (See figure 2.4.)

Lilja Stefansson's experiences were, ironically, perhaps the more conventional of the others portrayed in this chapter. Had my project been to interview older, heterosexual women about their experiences growing up in the prairies, there would have been many stories collected that paralleled Lilja's. Raised on a farm, married young, with little formal education about sexuality, and no family discussions other than of her sister's pregnancies and how that might affect Lilja's life, this was a life of hard work. If my questions about teenage sexual awareness didn't seem absurd to her, it was clear that they did seem self-indulgent. She never had the time to be a teenager, as we understand that term now. Instead she grew up on a family farm, far from "town," and part of hard-working, self-sufficient Icelandic-Canadian family. She was bright and capable, loved school, but if the family couldn't afford to send her brothers to high school, they couldn't afford to send Lilja either. Getting married represented an economic and social strategy, and starting a life

2.4 Evelyn Rogers and Lilja Stefansson, circa 1990s. E. Rogers Fonds, University of Saskatchewan Archives and Special Collections.

of her own meant she wasn't at her family's beck and call. She learned the fate of those who married poorly. The province of Saskatchewan's liberal policy on mothers' allowance enabled her to make a fresh start, and so she moved to southern Saskatchewan. Her second marriage was also far from ideal, but she stayed married for the economic support and, perhaps, some passive assistance in minding the kids. While they were married, she inherited a small sum of money from one of her brothers, and, unwilling to put it into the general revenue of the household, she decided, with her husband's encouragement, to buy a small business, the local Saskatchewan Government Insurance Agency in Rouleau. This decision marked the moment when she would begin to achieve some independence, and it was a critically important step to the next phase – life as a lesbian. Her friendship with Evelyn evolved, and while Evelyn knew she was a lesbian as a teenager, clearly Lilja did not. But, with a little knowledge, she had been "ready for an adventure" and embraced the discovery of what was, by all accounts, a passionate, joyful partnership. This image, taken of the two women the year before Lilja's eightieth birthday, is a marvellous snapshot of a lesbian partnership that was as unlikely as it was enduring.

For other women, migrations feature prominently as they moved from rural areas into the big city to meet lesbians, or to permit their lesbian relationships to flourish.[74] Others moved from outside the prairie region for two primary reasons – employment opportunities or because husbands or partners were transferred. This was particularly true for Alberta, which had a large influx of workers in the 1970s, part of a wave of economic migrants attracted by opportunities in the oil and gas industry. Universities also stimulated western migration, attracting faculty and staff from across North America.[75] In a regional study such as this one, the ability to track individuals throughout multiple locations and cities adds to the research. While I have yet to find evidence that anyone moved to the prairies in the twentieth century *because* of their sexuality, it is also true that moving away from home communities and re-establishing oneself in a new city – and often region of the country – could be daunting but also, potentially, liberating. Ironically, some of my narrators felt free to be themselves in the prairies in a way they had not in their original home towns and cities, and, as part of this shift, felt emboldened to seek out gay and lesbian organizations.

The 1950s

While queer opportunities existed in Saskatoon in the mid-1950s, it would be inaccurate to characterize the city as having an abundance of queer possibilities. Despite an impressive growth rate throughout the 1950s (the city nearly doubled in size between 1951 and 1961), with a population of 95,526 people it was still a smallish city. What outlets adults such as Norman Dahl and Dorothy could locate were not available to those baby boom teenagers coming of age in the city. Gens Hellquist, who was born in 1946, the third of four boys in a devoted baptist family, remembered being very much the outsider during high school. Similar to others I've interviewed, he recalled that the absence of any information about homosexuality sent a "chilling message."[76] He was twelve or thirteen when he first heard the word "homosexuality" and promptly looked it up in the dictionary. Based upon that chance moment, he labelled himself as a homosexual. However, knowing yourself and finding others similar to you are very different matters. Hellquist remembered that no one else in his school, church, or community was prepared to wear the homosexual label publicly, and it took effort to locate others. When asked if he considered moving away from Saskatoon, Hellquist replied: "It is sort of a tradition in this province to grow up here and then move away, but for me I could never decide where I would go ... and, as Joni Mitchell says 'I'm a flatlander, I like to see until tomorrow.'"[77] Mitchell did move away from Saskatoon despite its charms, but Hellquist didn't and in our interview he sketched how he turned awareness about his identity into an ability to locate other queer individuals.

Desire to meet others takes many forms, and similar to other women and men who initially found representations of "queer" characters and personalities in mass media – magazines, tabloids, and pulp fiction with queer content – Hellquist became an avid reader and collector of men's physique magazines. These magazines were nominally identified as "athletic" magazines because many of their models were bodybuilders, weightlifters, swimmers, or gymnasts. In all cases the physique magazines glorified the male body. Physique magazines were readily available on news stands and stores throughout the city because they managed to circumvent censors more concerned about female nudity (most models were either scantily clad, or artfully posed). And, most important, these niche products were commercially successful for news stand vendors. Published under the banner of "athleticism," they supported a general interest in "bodybuilding" among young men. In Canada, the bodybuilding craze was created and popularized by Montreal entrepreneurs Joe and Ben Weider. Weider's memorable ads, which ran in the back pages of comic books, promised teenage males that they could transform themselves from ninety-eight-pound weaklings into real men through the use of weight training and high protein diets. Bodybuilding culture had a variety of heterosexual and queer audiences. Physique magazines (an initial title was published by the Weiders before they turned to more lucrative fitness products and then mainstream fitness magazines) were covertly aimed at an entirely different audience – queer men – and they became a favourite for a generation of queers. Physique magazines flew under the radar of censors who did not concern themselves with this salacious material until the 1960s.[78]

Hellquist began staking out news stands, counting copies of their physique magazines and keeping track of the numbers so as to try to find other purchasers of those periodicals. In 1965, he "met somebody in the Saskatoon News Agency [downtown]" where "they had a full collection of Physique magazines and we sort of perused each other and then followed each other out of the store. I think I asked him 'Where do people meet?' And he told me about the park, so of course I was in the park that evening. And when I ran into him ... I threw about a thousand questions at him."[79] The "park" in question was Kiwanis Park, which runs parallel to the South Saskatchewan River, from the Broadway to University Bridges. Well treed, with an upper level adjacent to the iconic Bessborough Hotel, Kiwanis Park was and remains an attractive location for visitors and residents to picnic, stroll, or lounge. Much like Winnipeg's riverbank and parks, which attracted multiple audiences depending on the time of day, this park was a popular area for socializing. At night-time, the audience shifted to a primarily male one – largely queer – who used it as the city's primary cruising spot. The more private lower level, which was less developed, with considerable natural foliage, bushes, and paths leading to the riverbank, was a key site for queer sociability and sexual activity. In all likelihood, based on the information gathered in Winnipeg, the park had served this purpose for some time, not solely because of its privacy but also because its central location, sandwiched between the Broadway and University Bridges, meant it was within walking distance of campus, the downtown core, and the Broadway and Nutana residential areas. According to Hellquist, by the mid-1960s, the park attracted a wide-ranging group of queer men, including university professors, small business owners, professionals, priests, working-class men, students, and youth. Hellquist remembered that participants ranged from teenagers to adult men, even a few in their seventies, who routinely congregated in the park during the spring and summer months. Although numerically Euro-Canadians comprised the majority of participants, there were Indigenous men in the mix. Finding willing sexual partners was a driving force, but a compelling secondary interest was the desire to connect with other men. In Hellquist's words, this cruising scene was akin to a "community centre" where people met lovers, made friends, and exchanged knowledge. At that time the drinking age in Saskatchewan was twenty-one, so even though Hellquist learned that the Cove, a pub at the King George Hotel, was a queer hang-out, he couldn't legally participate. This challenge faced other teenagers, like David Rimmer, who remembered coffee houses that catered to teenagers and the "4-5 hippies in Saskatoon" and provided alternatives to the indoor and outdoor cruising areas (as in Winnipeg, public washrooms or tearooms were well used in Saskatoon). Rimmer archly noted that he found he did not meet "gentlemen of quality" in those locations.[80]

It was in the park that Hellquist made formative friendships that served as the basis for much queer activism and socializing in the city. One such friend was Dan Nalbach (1935–97), a University of Saskatchewan drama professor.[81] Nalbach was originally from Buffalo, New York, and he brought American styles of queer socializing to the city (including a camp, familial system of social organization called the Stofford family, with himself in the dramatic, central role as Gladys Stofford, the mother of this extended clan of female kin).[82] In print recollections, Hellquist acknowledged the instrumental role that Nalbach had played as "one of the early founders of the Saskatoon organized lesbian and gay community" when he, along with Hellquist, initiated the advertisement in the *Georgia Straight* and rented the post office box for replies in March 1971. Later that summer, Nalbach "hosted a series of parties at his 11th street house where donations were solicited to help raise funds" for the first gay and lesbian group in the city.[83] His obituary in *Perceptions* noted that he could "often be outrageous," but that he was also generous in supporting those gay men who were new to the community. Nalbach served as head of the Drama Department at the U of S in the late 1960s and 1970s, before he left Saskatoon for Montreal, and later New York, where he worked sporadically as an actor. He died in New York City, of an apparent heart attack, in 1997.

Another professor, Don McNamee (1938–94), grew up in rural Saskatchewan, attended public school in Moose Jaw, Saskatchewan, and later received a bachelor of arts degree from the U of S. After completing two master of fine arts degrees from Ohio State University, he returned to the U of S in 1966 and worked in the Art Department.[84] In his obituary in *Perceptions*, Hellquist wrote that McNamee was a "fixture in Saskatoon's gay and lesbian community since the 1960s. Parties at his house in the early 1970s were used to help start the first gay organization in Saskatoon." McNamee left campus in 1985 to start his own architectural design firm.[85] He was a long-time activist, involved with Zodiac Friendship Society, later Gay and Lesbian Community Centre of Saskatoon (GLCCS), and, in the early 1980s, a founding member of the Coalition for Human Equality (CHE). McNamee was also a volunteer at *Perceptions* where, as production coordinator, he designed covers and layouts. "Don will be remembered for much more than his work on lesbian and gay issues," Hellquist wrote. "He was a gracious host and an incredible cook who loved to entertain. For many young lesbians and gay men coming out meant meeting other people at a feast at Don's place."[86]

Both McNamee and Nalbach were a decade older than Hellquist, recalled for their competitive, spectacular parties that drew gay men from across the prairies, and were charismatic raconteurs eager to dish about the city's queer scene and their own exploits. Hellquist, for one, was starved for such personal histories and fondly recollected that both men "mentored this young fag who wanted to know everything about life and about being gay." Nalbach in particular shared much information about the history of queer socializing in North America, and given his travels and connections, routinely brought news, cultural, and activist information to the city. It is difficult now, in the era of ready Internet access to considerable queer and lesbian content – activism, politics, movies, music, and magazines – to remember how literally starved for such representations queer people were in the 1960s.

While this work argues that the University of Saskatchewan was a space where queer students could find others, or for women and men to experiment with same-sex attractions, the situation for faculty members in the 1950s and 1960s was mixed. Nalbach and McNamee had secure employment in "creative" fields where flamboyance would be tolerated if not applauded. Interviewees indicated that neither man was officially "out" on campus, preferring to keep their socializing private, but in a city of this size, and given the infamy of their parties, it was an open secret that both of them were gay. Dan Nalbach and Don McNamee had a competitive relationship, each trying to outdo the other when they hosted parties at their respective homes. These house parties were famous within the queer male community because they featured an eclectic, veritable "who's who" of queer Saskatoon and the prairies. Conversely, Hellquist mentioned that entrée to these exclusive affairs was predicated on keeping in the duo's good books and could, at times, descend into cliques of insiders and outsiders. Bruce Garman recalled Dan's parties attracted "men from Winnipeg, Regina, Calgary and Edmonton. All of the prairie cities, car loads came to these parties."[87] Attending one of these parties in his late teens (around 1970), Garman said the scene at these events were "like some Fellini movie … it was so overwhelming" that he had to leave the house every forty-five minutes to take a break "yet I wanted to be there." A product of the era, these parties were "fuelled by alcohol" and by drugs, which was another part of what drew so many participants to them.[88]

Early 1960s, the Cold War, and the Start of "Liberation"

One of the issues that cannot help but emerge are questions about how this region, and its major urban centres, was different from queer experiences elsewhere. While the study was not designed to be comparative, and it is self-evident that major metropolitan, coastal cities like San Francisco and New York would be different than Canadian prairie centres, there is much fascination about how being queer in the prairies was different from Toronto or Vancouver, and how those who migrated from "outside" the region assessed the possibilities within Winnipeg, Saskatoon, or Regina for a "queer life." One way, as was demonstrated in the Winnipeg chapter, was to compare the recollections of those veterans who had served overseas, or had training in central Canada, with their assessments of Winnipeg's queer subculture. What follows below are the critical observations of outsiders who moved to the prairies for employment opportunities, and who offered interesting insights into the organization of queer life, identities, social inclusion, and community structure as compared with those who had experiences elsewhere. These narratives, although highly personal, naturally, are valuable in terms of trying to understand similarities and differences between prairie queers lives and their peers elsewhere.

Peter Millard first moved to Saskatoon in 1962 after he completed a master of arts degree at McGill University. He took a term position in the English Department at the university. Originally from Wales, Millard (1932–2001) would subsequently complete his doctor of philosophy at Oxford, before returning to a tenure-track position in the English Department. His unpublished memoirs, *Words to that Effect*, offer trenchant observations about Millard's life and experiences in post-war Britain, his academic career, and his impressions of the prairies. This manuscript is historically significant because Millard offers an extended commentary about his "closeted years" and then his decision to identify publicly as a gay man and to participate in gay activism in Saskatoon; he also makes comparisons between life in Saskatoon, Montreal, and the United Kingdom. Valuable for its insights into how he connected with other queer men in Saskatoon, it also serves as a useful corrective to our now oversimplified notion that queer life in larger universities and/or cities – in Millard's case Montreal or Oxford – was significantly more plentiful or more easily located than in Saskatoon. Equally valuable, Millard offers a thoughtful commentary on how those men who came of age in the immediate post-war years negotiated their sexual desires and gradually embraced an identity as openly gay men. Not everyone made that choice, many more remained closeted, socializing privately within their queer friendship networks while outwardly presenting as single men, as did a group of professional Saskatoon women (see below) who also negotiated dual lives throughout the 1960s and 1970s.

While Millard was finalizing his graduate work, he participated in "Saskatoon's pre-revolutionary gay life, in the 1960s, such as it was. There was a particular pub where you could usually find a gay man or two, mingling discretely with the straight clientele."[89] Millard also attended house parties, although curiously not faculty parties, but in his case "the apartment of an older gay man, a pharmacist, who kept a sort of open house for his gay friends, and where newcomers were welcome. His name was B he was kind, genial and was seldom without a glass of rye whiskey in his hand." Similar to the other house parties described above, the adoption of camp names (female) and banter predominated in this world, a charged gendered atmosphere that Millard found challenging: "I still found it difficult to face the fact of my homosexuality, and because I found the atmosphere of the gatherings distasteful. We were very much a subculture, forced into irony and self-mockery, and with our own language. Each man was given a woman's name, and everyone was expected, in the safety of the apartment, to perform in a pantomime of exaggerated femininity." Outside the apartment, the persona adopted was "heterosexual male," which felt equally forced and insincere, and ultimately Millard reflected that this era and this existence was "like a prison." It would take him another decade until he was finally prepared to come out as a gay man and take a political stand, a role that he played both in the community and on campus where, for many years, he was the "token gay" faculty member.

In many oral interviews about this era, queer men recalled the names and importance of a small cohort of university faculty and professionals whose house parties and friendships were a key facet of social life in Saskatoon. While not surprising that a handful of university faculty and staff would participate in the queer cohort within the city, it would be misguided to perceive the university in the 1950s as a "safe" space for queer and lesbian faculty, staff, and students. Much had changed since Nan McKay's time as a university student when such homosocial play could be sufficiently ambiguous or non-threatening to the more naive (or wilfully naive) mainstream majority.

Increasingly conversant with a variety of sexual and social behaviour, and clearly dismissive of those men who were different – enrolled in the "arts" or queer – the University of Saskatchewan campus was coming to terms with the changes of the 1960s. The chill occasioned by the medical, legal, and social pronouncements about this "abnormal," "criminal," and subversive (in Cold War parlance) behaviour meant that many campus queers and lesbians opted for covert activity and official silence. Certainly, McKay herself, as a key member of the administrative team, never flaunted any such differences during the 1950s preferring to live as a respectable, single, wage-earning woman. Others followed her lead, employing this survival strategy and it became a habitual way of life for many professional, middle-class lesbians in Saskatoon.

In the course of finding interview subjects for this book, one group largely eluded me – a group of women that Dorothy called the "on-campus lesbians."[90] According to Dorothy, "everybody in town knows their little secret and yet they don't seem to want to acknowledge that in any way."[91] One interviewee was on the fringes of these groups (of approximately twenty to thirty women in four to six friendship networks). "Selena" (a pseudonym) had been working on campus for over a decade when, finally, one of the "on campus lesbians" invited her to a house party. Her perspective on these middle-class lesbians, largely administrative staff, a few faculty, and other Saskatoon professional women (primarily teachers, nurses, and doctors), has been invaluable.[92] In large part they were born and raised in Saskatchewan, and had met in their teenage years, in a wide range of women's team sports – baseball, softball, curling, hockey, et cetera. Or, they had met on campus, as many of them attended the University of Saskatchewan for their bachelor's degrees and, like most university graduates, made lifelong friendships in the process. As adults, they purchased homes; travelled; and socialized via sports, house parties in Saskatoon, and at cabins at "the lake" in the summer. Their private lives were structured in a series of long-term, seemingly monogamous same-sex relationships. Many people on campus knew that these women lived together, and undoubtedly realized that they were more than roommates or close friends sharing houses to economize. But, as Selena indicated, it was her decision whether or not to tell people she was a lesbian (she did identify as a lesbian) and that any conjecture people made was their issue, not hers.[93] While my other lesbian or gay female informants found Selena's and the other women's positions a frustrating one, it is important to remember that in the era they graduated from university and took their jobs on campus – the late 1950s and early 1960s – queer women and men were vulnerable. There was considerable fear of employment discrimination as the Cold War resulted in purges from the federal civil service. If being considered a political subversive was not sufficient cause for caution, it is worth reminding that being queer was pathologized as a mental illness until 1973, at which time homosexuality was removed from the Diagnostic and Statistical Manual of Mental Disorders (DSM). Women and men were routinely treated by psychiatrists, sometimes undergoing shock therapy or institutionalization, solely because they were lesbians or gay.[94] In such a context, that middle-class lesbians exercised discretion about their private lives to avoid losing their jobs and their families doesn't seem surprising. And once this mode of behaviour was adopted, it was hard to cast aside.

Selena was candid about how she had first-hand knowledge of discrimination and stigmatization in Saskatchewan, observing the mistreatment accorded the disabled, First Nations, and the poor during her own childhood; thus, as an adult, she did everything possible to avoid any "label" that might have impeded her professional and personal goals. As many of the on-campus lesbians were self-made, coming from conventional, working Saskatchewan farm families and small towns, they had little available safety net to catch them should they be targeted due to their sexual differences – hence they kept quiet. Having come of age in an era where discretion prevailed, it was hard to let go of that strategy in middle age, when younger, liberationist colleagues thought this view outmoded, ultraconservative, or, more harshly, politically regressive. And so they remained cautious and private about their personal lives, while making sizable contributions to the campus, the city, and sometimes the province. I hope that one day their histories might be told in a more fulsome fashion, but until the younger, remaining members choose to open up about their lives, I have respected their desire for discretion.[95]

None of my informants specifically referenced a similar group of closeted but well-known queer men. Although, it is important to note that the two faculty members who hosted those fabulously queer parties were not officially out on campus during that era – one would be post-retirement, but not while he was a faculty member. In discussion about men who were a "generation" older than my interviewees, a number remembered people like Bobby, or remembered a very popular priest whose parties at Blackstrap were quieter – but no less fun – affairs.[96]

Another interviewee, T, believed that one of the strategies that protected such "queer" men from criticism, and enabled them spaces in which to be queer in small cities where most people knew one another, was that many straight residents in the community attributed their behaviour "to eccentricity."[97] Colin Johnson makes a very similar point in *Just Queer Folks* about the way that rural communities and small towns can and do harbour eccentricity and, at times, take perverse pride in "their" community's eccentric individuals – this provides some space for queer individuals to indulge in a far broader range of atypical gendered and sexual behaviour.[98]

For all of this, within the city of Saskatoon, what appears to be a bucolic, fairly accepting liberal-minded city, there were episodes of what we might now label homophobic violence, scandal, or crime that chillingly reinforced the reality that queer people had very few legal recourses should they find themselves singled out socially or legally. Contacts and some informants recollected two mid-century scandals: the first was a case of arson at a home owned by two female faculty members, and the raised eyebrows occasioned by the discovery that those women lived together; the second, a story of two male faculty members in the 1950s who had quietly left campus to cover up a queer love triangle involving a student. Searches of the local newspaper and the university archives did not uncover any supporting documents. Neither would people speak "on the record" about whatever back-room deals would have been negotiated to "encourage" faculty members to relocate to another university. Officially, then, there were no corroborating documents, just lingering suspicions and tangible fears of speaking out on the record sixty years later.[99] Which is not to say that such events did not occur. With the federal government pursuing – and purging – queer and lesbian members of the federal civil service during this era, it wouldn't have been unheard of for a prominent provincial institution such as the University of Saskatchewan to quickly act to quell any hints of sexual scandal. In fact, as we shall see in chapter 4, that is exactly how the University of Saskatchewan administration attempted to deal with a controversy involving a gay graduate student in 1974. Initially, the University of Saskatchewan offered Doug Wilson the option to "quietly" withdraw from the university for "publicizing" homosexuality.[100] Wilson refused this gentlemanly offer intended to protect his reputation (to say nothing of the university). Contrarily, Wilson chose to publicize his discriminatory treatment and in the bargain became a gay activist.

In the 1960s, the university was undergoing a transformation on queer matters: some students were openly referencing queer sexuality, closeted queer faculty attended house parties and cruising sites in the city, and many others – old school faculty and administrators – continued to live by the code of silence. While this era of public awakening was slow, it was also bound to be a confusing time with the various mixed messages about what was and wasn't possible, or known, in Saskatoon. For example, the 1964 issue of *The Greystone*, the University of Saskatchewan yearbook, featured the requisite annual retrospective of memorable campus events. One page featured a full page of photos of a College of Engineering event where, in a departure from their traditional rivalry with the "Agros" (agriculture students), the engineers turned their sights on arts students (from the College of Arts and Science). According to the yearbook, "the Engineers managed to get their share of limelight by lynching the 'Arts Fairy.'"[101] Photos of the event depict a pack of engineering students (wearing their collegiate jackets) gazing triumphantly at their work – a three-foot male doll dressed in a letterman's sweater and jeans that they had lynched from a tree in the central campus bowl. This "Arts Fairy" was then "rescued by a daring group in a black Volkswagen," four male arts and science students. The yearbook maintained a tone that suggested that this was just one in a series of campus hijinks that year. How students experienced this event must have been variable, depending on their college, their sexuality, and their maturity level. For engineering students this stunt was intended to offer a moment of group revelry and professional, heterosexual male bonding. For others this was a moment of ridicule and objectification, a blunt reminder that stereotypes abounded about male students enrolled in so-called "arts" programmes. Even in liberating the doll and ending the stunt, the arts and science students were made to look ridiculous, and were ridiculed because their rescue vehicle was a Volkswagen Beetle and not a more macho truck.

Off-campus, the 1960s ushered in an explosion of mass cultural queer and homosexual print materials – pulp novels, physique magazines (mentioned above), and, later, American and Canadian activist newspapers. It was in those cultural materials, which circulated freely throughout North America, including Saskatchewan, that offered the closeted, the questioning, and the openly gay and lesbian residents portraits of queer lives. Future gay activist and historian Tom Warner (b. 1952), who was born and raised in Nipawin, Saskatchewan but grew up in city of Prince Albert, humorously recalled purchasing pulp novels starting from the age of twelve or thirteen, as they were readily available at Frank's Cigar Store on Central Avenue in Prince Albert.[102] Plots varied, and, while heterosexual storylines predominated, many scholars have highlighted the importance of the queer, lesbian and gay plots that, often written by queer or queer-positive authors, spoke to a rapt audience.[103] "One day I ran across a gay pulp novel," Warner recalled. "It was fairly sexually graphic as well, so I bought it." By the time he was near the end of high school he had a "substantial collection of this material, hidden on a shelf in his closet." With no outlet for sexual experimentation in his Prince Albert high school, this pulp fiction offered him both an escape and a glimpse of the world beyond Prince Albert. Many interviewees recalled reading these paperbacks and how they avidly consumed and purchased them, acknowledging the anxiety about having their books discovered by parents or siblings. Warner was eventually busted when his father discovered the materials – although, in a lovely moment of reciprocity, his older brother was also busted for his collection of *Playboy* magazines. Such memories, now framed as humourous stories of youthful exploits, are largely stripped of the shame and power imbalance of that initial moment of parental discovery and chastisement. It also reminds us that both heterosexual and queer teenagers are engaged in these coming-of-age dramas surrounding sexuality – struggling to understand it, experiment with it, and learn about it, in a process too often fraught with embarrassment and fears of parental detection. Queer youth were not the only prairie teens to frequent the cigar-store, pulp-fiction stands seeking diversions and release.

Conclusion

In assessing the queer opportunities in Saskatchewan prior to the 1970 establishment of gay and lesbian activist and social organizations, one is immediately struck by the variety of those experiences. Similar to Winnipeg, women and men actively took their opportunities where they could find them. Records of this time might not be plentiful, and the histories told here are admittedly fragmentary and episodic, but they do illustrate that queer men and lesbians in the Saskatchewan felt able to step outside of the bounds of "normative" behaviour. Youth were freest, indulging in sexual play with friends (largely teenage and pre-teen boys) long before any language denoted such behaviour as inappropriate or "criminal." Later, as university students, the same-sex residences and chaperones' fears of too much heterosexual contact may have unwittingly led to prime opportunities for women and men to act on same-sex desires. Nan McKay and Hope Weir's kiss was not a furtive stolen moment, but a record of a proud and passionate – perhaps brazen – act. And, given the technology of photography from that era, this was no quick "selfie" snapped when people were not around, at least one knowing friend took their photo outside of their university dorm. But, McKay graduated, her friends scattered for jobs, and, once secure in her own professional employment at the university, we know virtually nothing of how she structured her personal life.

McKay's photo album, given the rarity of such early twentieth-century materials, is a marvellously rich document. It corroborates what scholars elsewhere have observed about the homosocial opportunities available in universities. Furthermore, for a smaller coterie of students, such activities led to same-sex activity and friendship networks. Images of the ever-smiling McKay, whether with her hockey teammates, or locked in a kiss with Hope Weir outside her residence, are evidence of her lived realities. The photos don't tell us the whole story, perhaps some classmates avoided them or thought them "queer," but from their *Sheaf* descriptions they both seem to have been popular and well integrated in social and sporting events. So much so that one wonders whether twenty-first-century queer students are as well integrated and accepted? Certainly, officially, there is considerable support for diversity on the University of Saskatchewan campus with our Pride Centre, support for transgender students, and various diversity policies, but in the actual day-to-day lived reality of our undergraduate students the experiences may be much different. Many questions remain, but what is clear is that the photos were taken, saved, and then donated to the university archives. They could have gone "missing" or been destroyed but, thankfully, they were not.[104] Nan McKay embraced her life fully. And her life story deserves to be told in an inclusive fashion even if she lived in an era when such declarations were seldom publicized. Just as the institution has claimed Nan's convocation as a singular achievement for Metis and Indigenous women, we should also highlight her same-sex relationships and sociability with like-minded female friends.

Augustus Esch took an unconventional approach, using a familial cover for his lengthy same-sex relationship with his "Dad." He married a woman, had two kids, and then raised them on his own after both his wife and his partner died. Preferring rural and small-town life, he befriended and bedded men throughout his life. And, seemingly, he flew under the radar as a caring, respectable bachelor. Wilson was impressed with Esch's chutzpah and while Esch clearly regarded organizations like the Saskatchewan Gay Coalition as a positive development, his generation was not one for marching or making public pronouncements about private matters. Norman Dahl's and Dorothy's experiences were dramatically different, even though they were both born in 1936. Dahl never doubted his sexuality nor did he attempt to conform to normative scripts. He also, as an exceptional middle-class male, had complete family support for his musical career, and ultimately it was desire for more education that propelled him from the prairies to Ontario, where he remained the rest of his life. Dorothy also knew she was a lesbian from a young age, but after her first love affair with a woman fizzled, she had few choices as a working-class woman – seek employment or get married. So, she married and had two daughters. She read lesbian pulp fiction, was a member of Daughters of Bilitis, and eventually, postdivorce, found herself involved in a long-term relationship with another woman. Evelyn Rogers followed a similar path to Dorothy – coming out after marriage when she was more securely middle-aged. Lilja Stefansson was the outlier here given her economic and social experiences, but, despite this, she too would navigate a rocky and improbable path, coming out as a lesbian in 1971 at the age of fifty.

Those coming of age in the Cold War, as Hellquist did, had different experiences. On one side there was greater knowledge of gay and lesbian behaviour and increasing access to materials – books, magazines, and geographical sites where queer people congregated (the park, the Cove, and later the Apollo Room at the Ritz Hotel). The flip side was that there was also more persistent negative messaging about this behaviour – whether it was the chill cast by the refusal to even speak of such activity openly or the publicity over local or national scandals involving homosexuality. Campus spaces for queer students changed throughout the twentieth century. Nan McKay was able to exploit a relatively innocent, seemingly open space to socialize in a homosocial world of other middle-class young women. Later episodes like the "Arts Fairy" demonstrated that while greater knowledge of same-sex experiences may have been common, they were not viewed as "neutral." For faculty and administrative staff, job security, propriety, and discretion seemed to be the order of the day. Millard claimed to be the "token" out gay faculty member in the early 1970s. Anecdotal information about campus climate that constrained queer activity, and in which queer faculty may have been quietly invited to leave if they were untenured or in fields that were not as open to diversity (i.e., outside of the arts departments), illustrate a retrenchment from the early 1920s through the mid-century. One might characterize this as a furtive era, where those entering the queer world struggled to find others, and where many insiders were quiet about their sexual proclivities, restricted to house parties and respectable outward performances as single professionals.

PART TWO

1970–1985 Communities, Community Building, and Culture

Chapter Three

Wilde Times: Community and Organizational Development in Winnipeg, 1970–1985

Winnipeg is a city of hard social realities. Gays have to endure the pious venom of the righteous and queer bashing hoodlums. They have to deal with divisiveness among themselves on feminist and racial issues. But beleaguered and isolated as they can seem, in service and love they support a community which provides for those in need, educational programmes, a place to relax or celebrate, a warm welcome for strangers. It is an accomplishment to be envied by larger cities in Canada. I heard it before I went, and I can confirm it now: go to Winnipeg for the people.[1]

Jane Rule, 1984

In 1984, writer Jane Rule was invited to Winnipeg to read and to participate in a writer-in-residence programme at the Winnipeg Women's Building. In an article entitled "Go To Winnipeg for the People," published in the *Body Politic*, she recounted her observations of the city and its gay and lesbian communities. No puff piece, Rule reported Winnipeg's lesbian and gay communities were fractured along gender, class, and racial lines. The Women's Building, "on the brink of closing for lack of funds, was on the north side where many women were frightened to go after dark." By contrast, the Gay Community Centre was in the centre of the city and she found it to be "the most attractive gay centre I've been to. It offers a restaurant where very good dinners are served for less than $6.00, a bar, a small dance floor, a game area with pool table and video games, a meeting room, a library and offices. It is open weekday and Saturday evenings from 5:30 to 1am." While annual dues for the centre were ten dollars, those for Happenings Social Club (Winnipeg's long-time gay and lesbian members club) were fifty dollars, and thus it was clear that Happenings continued to attract a more affluent crowd. Rule observed that more women belonged to Happenings because they deemed it safer and more attractive than unrestricted community space. Much of the annual funding for these organizations came from monthly socials held in places like the Pipe Fitters' Hall, which attracted hundreds of diverse Winnipeg gays – "flamboyant drag queens, men in suits and ties, punks with green and pink hair, the leather crowd, and occasional grandparental types like ourselves." While Rule's appraisal of Winnipeg didn't gloss over the city's challenges nor did it seek to create some fictitiously unified gay and lesbian community, her chief sense of why this "conservative, very churched" city remained livable for those gays and lesbians in its midst had to do with the people: the substantial volunteer commitment to outreach, programming, and genuine caring that she felt differentiated Winnipeg from other gay and lesbian communities. Of course, in this regard, the gay and lesbian people Rule and her partner Helen Sonthoff met over the course of their week in Winnipeg epitomized much of the boosterism that prairie cities, and Euro-Canadian residents of the prairies, routinely highlight as key features of their liveability: volunteerism, community support and pride, and an audacious capacity to dream big dreams regardless of the financial, geographic, or social impediments.

This chapter, the first of two on Winnipeg's queer history from 1970 to 1985, analyses the development of Winnipeg's culture of openly gay and lesbian organizations – the social, activist, and educational groups. In part three, we return to Winnipeg one final time to analyse the key activist accomplishments during those years, mainstream reaction, and moments of resistance. The narrative arc traces the formation of a multitude of groups, cultural products (newsletters, radio, and television programming), religious programming, and support groups and social spaces that, taken at face value, suggests that Winnipeg's explosion of activity represented a great awakening of gay and lesbian residents. Reality is a bit different. This organizational awakening was the product of a small number of extraordinarily energetic and creative individuals. Through most of the period in question, Winnipeg remained ideologically divided between this super cohort of organizers and activists and the majority of city's gay and lesbian residents who eschewed open political support of gay and lesbian initiatives and preferred to remain quiet about their sexual orientation. Organizationally and ideologically, this divide was represented by those women and men who were (primarily) supporters and members of Happenings versus those men, far fewer in number, who were active in Gays for Equality. Politically minded lesbians were rarely found in GFE in any large numbers. Lesbian activists were active in a variety of feminist and lesbian organizations in Winnipeg, including the Winnipeg Lesbian Society, the Woman's Building, Ms Purdy's women's bar, and other more short-lived organizational ventures. There were tensions between lesbian feminists and gay male activists, and sometimes within the women's community between lesbians who were focused on sexuality activism / socializing and those who were more focused on feminist issues. It is only in the late 1970s through to the mid-1980s that one can see these divides being breeched, as an effort was made to foster cooperation with the creation of the Manitoba Gay Coalition (MGC), which then launched Project Lambda (PL), and later the political group "The Lobby," which, in the mid-1980s, organized the final successful campaign to pressure the Manitoba government to add sexual orientation to their provincial human rights code (see chapter 6).

Besides the nature of these tensions in the Winnipeg community, Winnipeg was also distinctive because of the breadth and extent of their educational programming –pamphlets, newsletters, radio, and later television programming – all with an aim to provide constructive information for gay youth and adults. In addition, there were many support and counselling groups launched – starting with the Gays For Equality phone line and later their rap sessions, coffee houses, gay men's discussion groups, lesbian discussion groups, gay father's organizations, et cetera. Another facet of Winnipeg's gay and lesbian community in those years was the significant number of organizations devoted to the intersection of faith and sexual orientation. Those originated because the volunteers staffing the GFE phone lines took many calls from queer Mennonites and Catholics who were grappling with both their sexuality and their faith. The Council on Homosexuality in Religion (CHR), founded in 1976 by Chris Vogel, Richard North, and a former Anglican priest, Reverend Ted Millward, was intended to address the sizable portion of gay and lesbian Manitobans struggling with such issues. CHR would become one of the most well-respected groups in the city.[2] The city was home to a number of religious gay and lesbian groups affiliated with the mainstream religious organizations, including Dignity (Catholic Church) and Affirm (United Church). Demand for gay-positive religious services was so strong that a branch of the Metropolitan Community Church (MCC) was established in Winnipeg in 1983. CHR was also fundamentally important in the cultural life in Winnipeg because it

3.1 Winnipeg Gay Media Collective Staff, February 1981. Left to right:
Sterling Demeshinski, Chris Vogel, Glenn Fewster, unknown & David Granger
University of Manitoba Archives & Special Collections,
Manitoba Gay & Lesbian Archives, PC 292 (A.10–31).

launched a weekly radio program in 1978 called "Gay Christian Forum,"
later rechristened "Gaysweek." "Gaysweek" went off the air in July 1980
when the university radio station CJUM 101 FM stopped broadcasting.
Shortly thereafter, the Gay Media Collective was launched (spearheaded
by Richard North and Chris Vogel) and it created a new, thirty-minute
television program called "Coming Out TV."[3]

Geographically, the city of Winnipeg, as the province's largest urban
centre, continued to pull gays and lesbians into the city from the outly-
ing rural areas and the smaller cities. In particular, the movement of
students into the city to attend the Universities of Manitoba and Winnipeg was a key factor that attracted younger gays and lesbians to the
city. While this chapter focuses upon Winnipeg, it is important to state

the obvious: there were gays and lesbians resident throughout the province. Beyond impressionistic evidence such as letters to magazines or requests for male pen pals from all areas of the province – Brandon, Pine River, Minnedosa, Great Falls and others – more tangibly, formal gay and lesbian groups were established in smaller Manitoba and northwestern Ontario communities.[4] Both Brandon and Thompson established gay groups in 1976. As well, in 1980 a lesbian couple from Winnipeg, Isabel Andrews and Doreen Worden, moved to Rabbit Lake, on the outskirts of Kenora, Ontario, and established the self-published periodical *Voices: A Survival Manual for Wimmin*.[5]

Much has been written about the isolation of the prairies, initially as it pertained to rural women and farm families, and then later to the large distances between cities. This is amplified by the big sky of the southern plains, which even today remains primarily a vista of nearly uninterrupted ranch and farmland, punctuated infrequently with small towns and cities. However, this changed significantly in the post–Second World War era, with the increasing affordability of automobiles and the development of the provincial and national highway system. Car culture transformed the prairies and figuratively shrank the distances. Thus what to other Canadian residents may appear to be long driving distances between cities – eight hours between Saskatoon and Winnipeg, five between Regina and Winnipeg – are routine for prairie residents. Thus, gays and lesbians, like their straight counterparts in the region, were quite adept at making short-haul interregional trips on weekends. Gay residents of Winnipeg frequently travelled to Regina and Saskatoon, while residents of Regina often drove to Winnipeg for special events (for example, the strong women's music scene or the flourishing gay male drag culture).[6]

Those residents of Winnipeg who were looking for an American gay getaway were fortunate that Minneapolis, a five-hour drive away, had a small core of gay commercial spaces.[7] This proximity to an American city with openly gay spaces differentiated Winnipeg from Saskatoon and Edmonton, as cities in North Dakota and Montana were not as queer friendly as Minneapolis / St Paul. When residents in Saskatchewan and Alberta talked about adventures in American cities, they usually flew to well-known American gay destinations (San Francisco or Chicago). This option was also available to Winnipeggers with means or desires, as ads in Winnipeg gay newsletters offered affordable prices for "Super-Spree" weekends in San Francisco that could be purchased for as little as $279. Many lesbians and gay males took advantage of those low charter rates.[8] Such travel provided respite and release – not only sexually, but also culturally and politically. It would result in the importation of a number of American lesbian and gay initiatives that Manitobans sought to duplicate in Winnipeg. It would also, more devastatingly, bring the AIDS virus to Winnipeg.

Locating the Gay and Lesbian World in the 1970s: Continuities and Changes

Gay and lesbian inhabitants of Winnipeg came from a range of backgrounds – from rural and northern small towns in Manitoba and northwestern Ontario, infrequently from other larger Canadian cities, as well as those who had been born and raised in Winnipeg and environs. As in the pre-1970 era, the issue of in-migration and questions of how people located the queer community remained constant. What was new was whether to openly "come out" and identify one's sexuality. The experiences of Dr Dick Smith illuminates the ways in which people continued, even in the early 1970s, to find the community and to make decisions about their degree of political and social involvement.[9]

Smith emigrated from England in 1972, settling in Neepawa, Manitoba, where he was employed as a physician. His first introduction with the Manitoba gay community was the result of a tip from his hairstylist who gave him directions to Obee's Steam Bath in Winnipeg. Though he was only able to drive to Winnipeg every three to four weeks, Smith began to make the trip regularly, and it was through information at the bathhouse that he discovered Happenings socials. He became a founding member of Happenings (chartered in 1973) and he described that organization – and Winnipeg generally – as "very closeted" and "apprehensive about admitting new people."[10] Moving first to Birtle, and then later to Shoal Lake, Manitoba, Smith continued to have rather limited connections with Winnipeg. Within his home communities he found it difficult to find gay people. It was only after he joined a theatrical production in his community that he met another local gay man at a party. While sources such as Smith's are not extensive, presumably other gay men of means also used similar strategies – using time off work to visit "the city" (in this case, Winnipeg) to participate in gay activities. This made life in smaller towns bearable.

In his situation it proved to be insufficient because Smith relocated to Winnipeg in 1976 to do a residency at the Health Sciences Centre and St Boniface Hospital. Once in the city, he noticed ads for GFE coffeehouses on Winnipeg cable television and attended one of them. There he remembered his pleasure "to see gay people talking at a serious level." At the second GFE coffeehouse he attended, he met his partner Doug Arrell. Inspired by the conversations at GFE, he and Arrell discussed starting a gay men's discussion group – and with the encouragement of GFE's Bill Lewis, they began one. Bill Lewis was, then, a microbiology student at the University of Manitoba.[11] Meetings were held at the Idea Centre on Wardlaw Avenue, where another group member, Don Fenwick, described the men who participated as "more intellectual and more politically aware than others."[12] It is this group who would launch the journal *After Stonewall*, with Smith, his partner Arrell, Bill Lewis, Walter Davis, and Bill Fields (the latter two were Americans).

Five years after he arrived in Canada, Smith participated in his first gay demonstration (spring 1977) at the Saskatchewan legislature in Regina, which was attended by gay activists from Saskatoon, Regina, Edmonton, and a small Winnipeg contingent. Smith found the protest energizing, and the post-demo party at the Gay Community Centre in Regina made him realize that Winnipeg should have such an inclusive, congenial space. Regina's centre was open to all and clearly identified as a gay and lesbian space (unlike Happenings, which avoided any signage signalling that it was a gay club). This led to his participation in another venture that emerged from the discussions at the Idea Centre among a group that included Smith, Doug Arrell, Brian Evans, Chris Vogel, Rich North, Larry Laroche, and Don Fenwick – Project Lambda.[13] Brian Evans suggested that Winnipeg should have a gay community centre like one he had visited in England. Don Fenwick suggested the name Project Lambda, and the first committee to establish such a group included Laroche, Fenwick, Smith, and Ted Millward. Smith would become a major funder of Lambda (including the journal *Out and About*), a president of that organization, as well as the founder of the group Manitoba Physicians for Gay Understanding (MPGU), which was based on a similar organization in San Francisco, the Bay Area Physicians for Human Rights. It was there, in meetings, that he first learned about the AIDS virus, and later, when he began to get patients with AIDS, he suggested that Project Lambda should hold workshops about the virus and the impact it could have in Winnipeg. The outbreak of AIDS in the prairies serves as the terminal point for this book, since the surge of AIDS-related organizations changed the organizational and political terrain. Post-AIDS, prairie gay and lesbian life changed dramatically, it became more visible, activism shifted abruptly to dealing with the medical crisis, and these communities, like those elsewhere, entered a far different phase of organizational and activism work. By 1985, there were people living with AIDS in Winnipeg, and Smith was involved with a number of medical initiatives. In 1992, asked to summarize his experiences and reflect on the historical changes in Winnipeg's gay community, Smith offered the important historical overview of an outsider who eventually became a stalwart member of the community. While his interview doesn't gloss over some of the tensions (particularly over the issue of Project Lambda and the Oscar Wilde Memorial Society struggles regarding when to start the centre), in sum he felt that that Winnipeg had made "huge strides." In particular, he cited the passage of the human rights legislation in 1987 as a key achievement.[14]

The Road to Happenings

In the 1970s, the older style of mixed socializing in local bars and beverage rooms would increasingly give way to exclusively gay and lesbian spaces, particularly as visibly gay and lesbian organizing and social institutions finally came to the city of Winnipeg. Ironically, many of the activists and institution builders of the 1970s reminisced about their first forays into Winnipeg homosexual subculture, which all began with a visit to the Mardi Gras. Included in this cohort was Chris Vogel who, in 1972, his first year in Winnipeg, met his long-time partner Rich North the first week he ventured into the Mardi Gras bar downtown. At this time, the St Regis was also popular. When the St Regis closed, people flocked across the street to the Silver Slipper, a more raucous, working-class place that had a crowd that included "queens and natives [sic]," according to Bill S.[15] Yet one still faced the challenge of "finding these spaces" and so, in the early 1970s, small groups of gay men and lesbians embarked on bolder plans to create visibly gay and lesbian social, organizational, and cultural spaces that would fundamentally alter how homosexual Winnipeggers learned about homosexuality, and how they were introduced to the city's scene.

The first such venture, called Club 654 (a cheeky name, which insiders knew meant Club 69), was located in an upstairs location on Erin St in the industrial zone of Winnipeg's west end. According to George Moore, Club 654 was a gay after-hours weekend bar with no liquor licence. Moore recalled that very few women ever attended Club 654, although some informants recall that it was too public – and given this fact, and its isolated location, that may also have affected women's attendance. It was at Club 654 that plans were hatched to start a gay membership club that would have a liquor licence, and would provide dancing, socializing, and drinking space exclusively for queer Winnipeggers.[16] In the late summer of 1971, another group of individuals began to discuss the formation of a different club because there was "a desperate need at that time to have a place all our own. A place and an atmosphere completely gay, where we could dance with our lovers, hold hands with our lovers, communicate with our friends and be ourselves without the hostility we would be sure to get elsewhere."[17] Initially, they met resistance from various members of the gay community itself as they tried to sell tickets for their fundraising socials: "I recall people saying, 'Gay Dance??' 'This is Winnipeg!!' 'Are you out of your mind???'"[18] This core group would later become the founders of Happenings Social Club, which received its charter of incorporation in July 1973 as the Mutual Friendship Society, Inc.

Other attempts to make sure this new club would be successful included outreach in the lesbian community. George Moore went to the Mount Royal Hotel bar, the working-class lesbian hangout, to search for lesbians interested in participating. In a description that sounds a bit as if it were taken from a Hollywood musical, Moore recounted how he approached Kathy, "the leader of the women there." and convinced her to encourage women to support the new club. Furthermore, in the interview he noted that because of the bar's purported toughness, and since he was a middle-class gay male, he was "escorted when he needed to use the washroom."[19] Ted Patterson recalled that people were asked to sign a membership list to start Happenings Social Club and they were informed that the club was "strictly gay for the protection of its members."

To raise funds for their charter, and for rent, the community organized a series of monthly fundraising socials that many women and men remembered with fondness. Pearl Wylie recalled that drag queen shows, as well as dancing and socializing, made these socials "a lot of fun" for the couple of hundred women and men who attended.[20] These events attracted a real cross section of Winnipeg lesbians and gay men, including many "older" women (Wylie herself was then in her early forties) who were eager to participate. Unlike the atmosphere at the Mount Royal, where fights were a regular occurrence, these socials were generally peaceful, although they did have people at the door making sure that only queer people attended. Recalling one humourous incident, Wylie reported: "We'd have two girls at the door, and they would ask, "are you gay?" … this one old girl I know came in and [she] was asked is she gay, and she said 'Well can't ya see, I've got slacks on!'"[21] These socials were held at the Oddfellows Hall, the Steamfitters Union Hall, and other locations. To obtain liquor licence permits they pretended that these were engagement parties. Once the charter was obtained, Happenings dropped the pretence of "engagement, and held regular socials at Immaculate Conception Church Hall."[22] Initially, there were about forty-eight women and men who signed the membership list for Happenings, but a core group of around thirty kept the dream of a dedicated gay club going by attending and organizing the monthly socials until the group was finally able to rent space at 242 Manitoba Avenue. "Happenings membership drew on every circle in town that could be found," and Pat remembered that the first few times she attended Happenings she was "surprised to see so many gay people together at once."[23]

Pat's recollections were echoed by many informants who expressed tremendous pride at the creation of dedicated gay and lesbian space in the city. The ready success of Happenings indicates how starved Winnipeggers were for a dedicated gay and lesbian venue, even if the building was not inviting. Lyle Dick recalled that it was in the city's north end, "the poor part of town," and thus transportation was mandatory. "The building itself had been a synagogue and it was stuccoed over and it was the only game in town. So it was nice to have it for sure. But it was basically a disco bar."[24] Once Happenings secured space on Manitoba Avenue, many gays and lesbians drifted away from the mixed spaces downtown to the new exclusively gay and lesbian club. Happenings Social Club was primarily used as a bar and dance club but it also held other functions, including Sunday brunches and Christmas fundraisers.[25]

Partly as reassurance to those people who were hesitant to openly affiliate themselves with a gay or lesbian club and partly because of the homophobic response to their application for incorporation (discussed in chapter 6), the Happenings board enshrined in their policies two key tenets that would lead to much tension within Winnipeg's extended gay and lesbian community. First, the club had a strict policy "that no straight people are to be admitted to any function of the club, as a guest, or to be accepted as members of the club." Protecting the identity of gay and lesbian patrons was paramount, but this no straights policy was also intended to provide "psychological relief of being free from straight

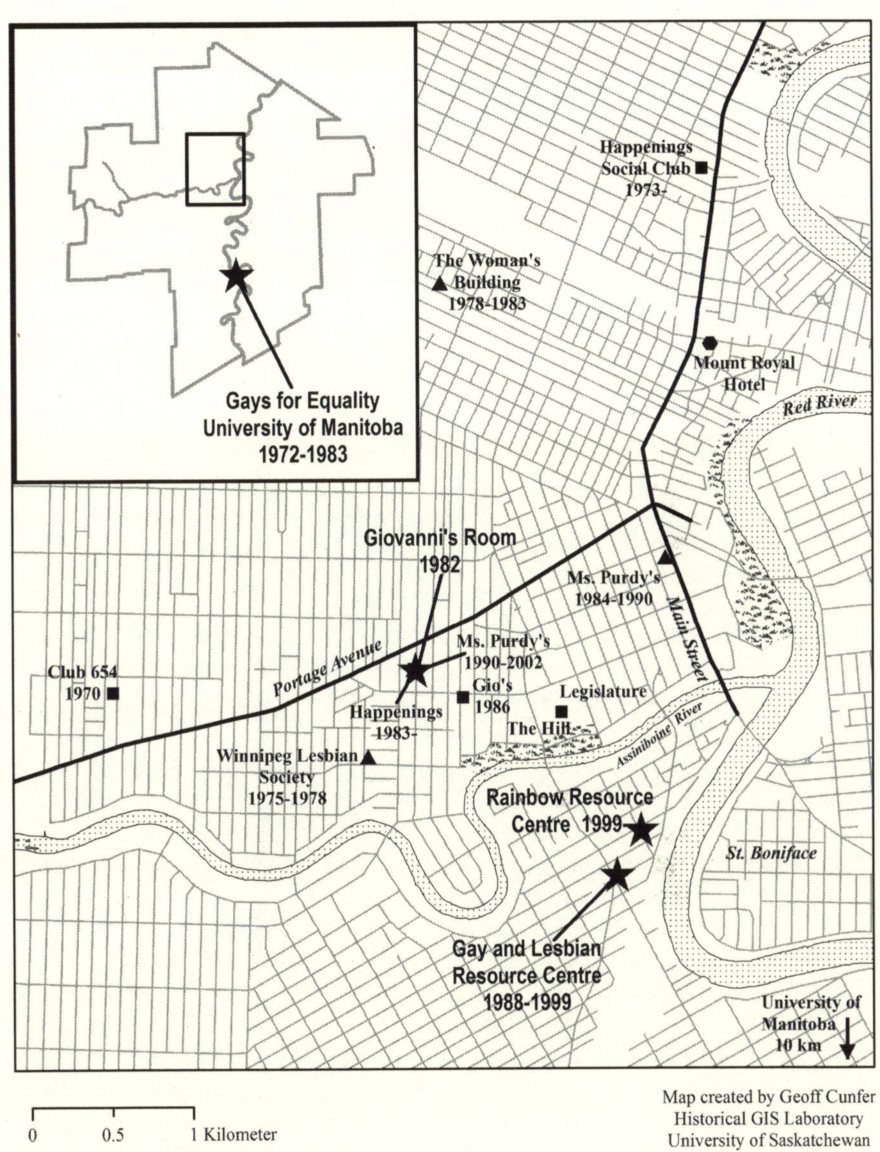

★ **Community centres**

▲ **Lesbian spaces**

⬣ **Mixed spaces**

■ **Commercial clubs**

3.2 Winnipeg queer spaces, 1970–1990, Copyright Geoff Cunfer, 2017.

society's vigilance."[26] The second contentious issue involved gay activism. Because receiving this charter was so contested, and because the provincial Attorney General Al Mackling had publicly denounced their application, stating: "such (gay) groups ought not to be clothed with the same rights and respectability as other groups" as justification for initially declining Happening's charter application, they sought legal advice.[27] This commentary provoked a flurry of radio interviews, talk shows, newspaper reports, and letters to the editors of the local newspapers, all publicity that this group of largely middle-class queer people sought to avoid.[28] Their lawyer, after discussions with the government through back channels, negotiated a compromise solution that would achieve the charter application on the third try. It was agreed that the group would receive their charter in return for three changes to their application: 1) change the name to Mutual Friendship Society, Inc; 2) to explicitly promise to be a non-political, social organization; and 3) to refrain from publicizing when they did receive their charter. Essentially, they were forced into a non-disclosure agreement in return for the charter. These applications took two years to conclude and the bulk of their organizational energies. Surprisingly, only a few people resigned (as gauged from letters in the their newsletter, *What's Happening?*) over anger at how the battle for the charter had been waged (i.e., without public condemnation of the government's discrimination). This approach speaks to issues of class and political appetites. Given the large proportion of Happenings members who were privately, discreetly gay and lesbian, and therefore supremely wary of publicity, particularly adverse publicity, they were willing to agree to these conditions. Hence a negotiated, back-room deal between lawyers suited them fine. They got their club and the conditions were not worrisome to the majority. However, that was not the case for how the other key organization, forming on the University of Manitoba campus, would regard this episode.

Gays for Equality: Winnipeg Liberationist Politics

In February 1972, during the time that Happenings was embroiled in their challenge to receive a provincial charter, another group, the Campus Gay Club, formed on the U of M campus. Phil Graham, then a graduate student at the U of M and one of the early queer political organizers, recalled that he was motivated by his experiences in Minneapolis: "I was involved in the Gay Liberation group at the University

3.3 Phil Graham, founding member of Gays for Equality, August 1980. University of Manitoba Archives & Special Collections, Manitoba Gay & Lesbian Archives, PC 292 (A.08–67).

of Minnesota. That group helped me and many others to come out to accept homosexuality not as a disability or an oddity that has to be constantly hidden from the general public, but as part of their total personality."[29] Graham consulted with counsellor Dr Gordon Tombs and Dr. M. Watts, a campus chaplain, and together the three of them rented a room for the group. Between thirty and seventy people came to the first meeting, which had been advertised in the U of M student newspaper and at Happenings Social Club.[30] Rich North, a Winnipeg resident, and Chris Vogel, raised in Regina and Winnipeg, were also part of this early cohort of Campus Gay Club members. North started in 1973 and Vogel joined because, as he ironically recalled, "I wouldn't have done a damn thing but for him [North], but because I was stuck on him I would have done anything he wanted." And so, very slowly, he started his activist career: "We began by putting up posters downtown that he had made.

3.4 Chris Vogel and Rich North. Gays for Equality promotional images for "Love and Let Love" campaign, 1973. University of Manitoba Archives & Special Collections, Manitoba Gay & Lesbian Archives, PC 292 (A.08–67).

The club changed to Gays for Equality and in 1974 I became the treasurer of that organization through successive changes until last night. Actually, no, in October, when I ceased to be the treasurer for the Rainbow Resource Centre. In 1982 it was the Winnipeg Gay Community Centre, in 1988 or 1989 the Winnipeg Gay and Lesbian Resource Centre, and the Rainbow Resource Centre in 1996/7."[31] Vogel's politicization to gay liberationist politics had occurred in Saskatoon in the fall and winter of 1971–2, at the University of Saskatchewan, where he was enrolled in a postgraduate degree program in soil science. During that year he attended "a meeting of the U of S gay group in December 1971."[32] He had his first, brief, gay relationship in the city and then returned to Winnipeg where he met North.

Initially, Campus Gay Club "got off to a slow start as most people were really uptight and suspicious. Nobody really knew what they wanted or what Gay Liberation was all about. Many, especially those that were already out in the downtown gay scene, were quite negative about the club. They did not want public attention drawn towards homosexuality. They were quite satisfied to remain in the big closet known as the

Winnipeg Gay scene."[33] In the March 1973 issue of *What's Happening?*, GB wrote about his experience with Campus Gay Club reporting that most people in Winnipeg were "misinformed" about what went on there. "The club has changed a great deal from last year. In November it was just about ready to fold so we decided to become a more activist group, to see if we could save it." Equally, he noted that in tandem with their educational and activist agenda, they "also wanted to make the gay scene itself more livable. All I ever hear is what a rotten place Winnipeg is for gays. Some of it we can't change, because the town is too small, but some of it we certainly can change … We are working on a gay cof-feehouse, a dance, and a poster campaign."[34] Their new name, Gays for Equality, reflected their hope that the ideals of gay liberation ideas would circulate throughout campus and the city. GB called on Winnipeggers to evaluate their motivations, writing "some gays say to me, 'I have a good job and a good social life. I do not get hassled, I do not need you because I am already liberated.' If you have to hide from your boss, you family, your friends; if you hate the bar you go to; if you live only for the Hap-penings dances – How liberated are you?"[35] The article concluded with contact names and phone numbers, something not normally included in Happenings's newsletter (which favoured pseudonyms or anonymous editorials), and information about the weekly meetings.

While it might appear odd that Happenings's newsletter included such material about GFE, it was the nature of the community, and the overlapping membership bases, that enabled these acrimonious debates. Bill Lewis, a Happenings and GFE member, openly criticized the city and its gay population since he believed it was impossible to have a sense of pride in being gay "in an atmosphere such as that pro-vided by the MG [Mardi Gras bar]."[36] It would be tempting, and perhaps logical, to view the difference between the composition of the Happen-ings crowd and the Gays for Equality crowd as a generational. And yet, there were always younger gays and lesbians joining both groups, and Happenings was, judging by membership numbers, the far larger orga-nization. The university students, and leaders like Chris Vogel and Rich North who had already completed their university educations, were more likely to be motivated by the student movements, and, according to North, many were involved in leftist politics as well.[37] Those who had founded Happenings, and who had experienced the city's other gay venues (mixed bars with gay clientele), were understandably proud of creating an exclusively gay space. Given the discrimination the club faced in getting their provincial charter, many members needed no further illustration of the hostility of Manitoba residents and politicians towards gays. Such homophobia emboldened and enraged some men and spurred them to activism. But is also evident that such actions also created the opposite reaction in others who, for a host of reasons – employment, family status, the political climate, et cetera – were leery of the costs of further publicity and therefore opted for discretion.[38]

Once established, Gays for Equality became a driving force in Winnipeg's gay and lesbian community because it acted as the incubator for many other gay organizations in Winnipeg. In 1982, Ted Millward published a reflection on GFE's accomplishment in which he cited the importance of student activism and campus involvement in the wider community as the source of GFE's longevity and impact: "It remains the heart and source of almost every local endeavour to improve conditions for homosexual Manitobans. In Winnipeg, as in a large number of North American cities, it was the university which saw the emergence of the first openly homosexual organization, the first one explicitly dedicated to bringing homosexual men and women out of hiding, and to challenging the world myths and slanders."[39] Millward's comments support the analysis advanced in this book about the importance of key regional universities, which offer spaces, organizations, and GLBT political opportunities for their inhabitants, but also play significant roles provincially and regionally. From inception until 1983, Gays for Equality had office space in the University Centre at the University of Manitoba, and although not solely a student organization – in later years it was not run by students – still, it took its campus location seriously, and offered counselling, educational programming, and a variety of resources for students. For Millward, its first priority was "to enable this 'invisible minority' to discover itself, to free its individual members from the feeling that each one is the only one in the world."[40] Life on the University of Manitoba campus (like at the University of Saskatchewan) was not without challenges, yet this was a relatively liberal space in which to be situated, and given that each fall brought new gay or lesbian students to campus, GFE had access to a renewable resource. In 1983, GFE moved downtown to the Winnipeg Gay Community Centre.

Lesbian Organizing in Winnipeg[41]

Although Happenings had, at least in its early years, a nearly equal ratio between lesbian and gay men who purchased memberships, this began to shift during the mid- to late 1970s. As was the case in the other prairie cities, lesbian women's energies tended to be split between their participation in feminist organizations (often their first point of entry into activism) and gay and lesbian organizing. Formal and informal second-wave feminist activity in Winnipeg predated formal gay activism, while "women's liberation" groups originated in 1969. Initially, groups met in people's homes and were focused on political themes and guerilla theatre.[42] While the extant material is much slimmer than those for the gay groups, it is clear that lesbians were often doubly marginalized – first, in the heterosexual-dominated feminist organizations, where they often felt excluded by the heterosexual majority's goals and, second, in the gay organizations where they represented a numerical minority.[43] In both cases, they had to make the case for their concerns – with the feminists they needed to impress upon them the different experiences of lesbian women (particularly with respect to custody issues and sexuality) and how those differences affected their organizational goals. Similarly, with the gay political organizations, lesbians were often at odds with the focus on liberationist policies (e.g., age of consent laws) while they struggled to foreground the importance of child custody issues and the vulnerability of lesbian mothers to state discrimination regarding their "fitness" to parent. Thus, in all three provinces, lesbians attempted to establish political and social organizations that offered them their own spaces. In Winnipeg, lesbian groups were first able to find locations for their organizations within a series of women's civic spaces. In 1972, the first of these to emerge was called A Woman's Place, at 72 Victor Street. This large, rented house accommodated a range of women's feminist, lesbian, and cultural organizations, including the Lesbian Resource Centre, Socialist Women's Collective, Women for Non-Sexist Education, and other groups that used the space for meetings, drop-ins, and as a general focal point for women's activism.[44]

In the autumn of 1975 an alternative organization, called the Winnipeg Lesbian Society, was begun. Starting with a core group of eight women, they sought to make a space that was specifically for women, and that would offer an information line for women who were coming out. In their flyer, they indicated that their numbers had grown to forty women who regularly attended meetings and events, including "all women socials, the formation of an information phone line for women coming out in the community, the formation of a lesbians speakers bureau, the starting of a library of lesbian literature, the picketing of the CBC for discrimination against gay public serve announcements and finally the formation of a support group open to all lesbians."[45] Meetings were held at A Woman's Place, then located at 143 Walnut St, in smaller, more cost-effective quarters. Their goal was an autonomous lesbian organization, and they hoped that lesbians would feel comfortable to attend their Thursday evening meetings and their roster of social events. Addressing some of the tensions in the community, they indicated that they wished to "work harmoniously with other groups in the city and elsewhere," but maintained that there was a need for a social and educational programming for Winnipeg lesbians. Although sources for these organizations are limited, it is clear, from reading through the various extant papers and newsletters from Winnipeg and the prairie region, that one of the primary challenges with these lesbian and feminist organizations were lack of funds. According to the Winnipeg Women's Liberation Newsletter in April 1976, it was hoped that A Woman's Place "could be a centre for organizing women to fight against our oppression, a place of our own where we could be comfortable and open, and grow strong and united. Sometimes it has been that. But not lately."[46] According to the authors, A Woman's Place had not had government funds for two years, and their monthly operating costs imperiled the organization. In December 1976, A Women's Place held an open house, with all of the organizations participating, including the Winnipeg Lesbian Society, Socialist Women's Collective, Consciousness Raising Group, Women's Theatre Group, and others, as a way to stimulate interest and membership in these organizations. Despite their efforts, A Woman's Place was eventually forced to close due to a lack a funding.

Interestingly, a couple of years of fundraising and organizational activity later, a new women's space was able to open its doors to the women of Winnipeg. Located at 730 Alexander Ave, the Women's Building was heralded as the first of its kind in Canada.[47] The Winnipeg Women's Cultural and Education Centre had purchased the three-story brick building from the United Church of Canada in 1978. Renovations were ongoing to outfit the building with office and social spaces, a theatre, coffee house / lounge, and a bookshop. In 1979, a number of women's organizations moved into the building, including Women in Trade, Wages Due Lesbians, Lesbian Phone Lines, and Winnipeg Women's Liberation. According to *Harpies*, a short-lived newsletter produced at the Women's Building, the two lesbian groups in the building had very separate mandates. Lesbian Phone Lines provided counselling for women who were "dealing with the difficulties as well as the good times of coming out."[48] The Wages Due organization was a group of lesbians who sought to politicize the poverty of lesbians and in particular the poor financial circumstances of lesbian mothers. They were in close contact with Lesbian Mother's Defence Fund in Toronto, and were proactively networking to build up legal and social contacts in Winnipeg to assist lesbian mothers with custody cases.[49] Another Winnipeg women's landmark, Ms Purdy's membership club, initially started out in the Women's Building before moving to 266 Main St.[50] Launched in February 1983, Ms Purdy's was a women-only social club that provided spaces for female musicians and artists to perform. By 1984 there were two hundred members of Ms Purdy's, making it a thriving social space for the city's lesbian community. In 1990 Ms Purdy's relocated to 272 Sherbrook Street and was a city fixture until 2002 when it closed. Ms Purdy's twenty-year run made it a very successful queer organization by any standards, but for a lesbian social organization it was unique. Only Edmonton's Womonspace would match this longevity.[51]

Gay Friends of Brandon and Thompson Gay Group

Paralleling the rise of organizational interest and strength within the women's and lesbian communities of Winnipeg, the larger gay community saw a number of new organizations launched between 1975 and 1985. As already noted, in 1976 two gay organizations – Gay Friends of Brandon and Thompson Gay Group – were created. The Brandon group was started by three gay Brandon men who established a phone line that provided information for residents of that city and the southwestern Manitoba region. They were affiliated with GFE in Winnipeg.[52] Gay Friends of Brandon regularly listed their events in Project Lambda's newsletter, *Out and About*, and thus they had the support of the Winnipeg community. For example, a meeting of the Manitoba Gay Coalition was scheduled for 4 February 1978 in Brandon, and thus it gave Winnipeg residents a chance "to drive to our neighbouring city and meet some of our gay neighbours" for a meeting, social, and subsequent tobogganing party in the Brandon Hills.[53] Subsequent issues of *Out and About* indicated that the Brandon group held regular socials, gay and lesbian discussion groups, as well as organized outings to attend some of the cultural and artistic events in the city or at Brandon University – such as film festivals, musical performances, and art exhibits. The group could be contacted at a GFB, Box 492, Brandon

University, or by telephone. Despite their impressive list of activities and contact information, many of the advertised discussion group topics addressed the challenges and struggles gays and lesbians faced in living in a smaller community like Brandon. For instance, on 16 April 1978, the discussion topic was "loneliness and fear."[54] "Edward" who was raised in Brandon, recalled that a "discourse of silence" about homosexuality persisted in that community. Believing that it was impossible to be gay in Brandon, Edward did not come out as gay until he attended the University of Manitoba and went to a Gays for Equality rap group. In our interview, while he stressed that he was proud to be from Manitoba, and proud of his prairie roots, he was also critical of the experience of growing up gay in Brandon, and of the toll it took on those individuals who remained in that community. "I know people were crushed by homophobia. I know I've had friends who couldn't face the stigma of being gay. And who got married to women. I'm sure they were good parents, and to the extent possible were good spouses but to me that is tragic. Because there have been so many lives that have been unfulfilled, or only half-fulfilled because of this overriding stigma."[55] Best-case scenario for small-town gays and lesbians, according to Edward, was to "put on those cha cha heels and cha cha [their] way right out of there." This was his own strategy, moving first to Winnipeg and then further afield after graduation.

In the summer of 1976, a group of gay men in Thompson, Manitoba, a northern mining community, rented a post office box and took out an ad in the local newspaper. Initially, twelve people attended their meetings, but given the hostility in the region, their attendance dropped to five people, including one lesbian participant.[56] Although they changed names a couple of times, from Northern Manitoba Alliance to Gay Friends of Thompson, they had greater longevity than the Brandon group. The participants in Thompson would produce a short, gestetnered newsletter in the late 1970s, which indicated that they had a series of discussions, socials, baseball games, and also often participated in larger regional events (like Metamorphosis in Saskatoon).[57] Membership dues cost six dollars per year in 1978, and with this funding (and regular pledges for other work or activism – for instance, they made a contribution to the John Damien Defence Fund) they paid for advertising in the *Brandon Sun*, in addition to renting a post office box and telephone line. In October 1981 the group was still in existence, as their coordinator was featured on Winnipeg's "Coming Out" TV in an episode entitled "Great Northern Gays."[58]

Organizational Explosion, 1977–80

In the late 1970s, there was a flurry of organizational activity in Winnipeg. So much so that a one-day conference was held in May 1977 at the University of Winnipeg to bring all the groups together. Invited to attend were the religious organizations: Council on Homosexuality and Religion & Dignity; the activist groups: Gays for Equality and Winnipeg Lesbian Society; the gay and lesbian political journal: *After Stonewall*; the discussion and counselling groups: Gay Men's Discussion Groups and GFE Counselling Unit; and the various community-based and social groups: Gay Friends of Brandon, Thompson Gay Group, Winnipeg Gay Youth, and the Mutual Friendship Society. Organizer Bill Lewis (affiliated with GFE and *After Stonewall*) invited all gay groups to participate and share their histories and organizational goals; what's more, he wanted to see if there was any interest in ongoing communications and affiliations.[59] The end result of this meeting was a published directory that contained short institutional histories of the establishment of those organizations now within the umbrella of the Manitoba Gay Coalition. While MGC was never as vibrant as Saskatchewan Gay Coalition, it did lead to some discussions and networking. As noted above, CHR indicated that they continued to offer assistance to those whose "acceptance of their homosexuality was obstructed by religious sanctions," and thus the CHR provided individual counselling along with information to churches and other agencies that might enable them to more effectively counsel gay and lesbian individuals.[60] Composed of clergy and lay people from a variety of religious backgrounds, CHR also offered religious services on the second Sunday of every month. Unlike CHR, which was ecumenical, Dignity was an international Catholic organization, founded in 1970 in San Diego, California. The Winnipeg chapter, launched in 1976, offered gay Catholics services, study, and fellowship, all with the ultimate goal of providing information on "the way in which Catholicism and homosexuality can be reconciled."[61]

Taking a different approach was the gay liberationist journal *After Stonewall*. *After Stonewall* indicated that their goal was to capture the essence of the "prairie provinces … particular outlook on gay liberation which we believe to be just as valuable and just as much a part of gay life as is that of Toronto, Montreal, New York or San Francisco."[62] Some members of *After Stonewall* were also part of the Gay Men's Discussion Group. Gay Men's Discussion Group (launched in January 1977) offered Winnipeggers the chance to meet and discuss a range of social and political issues, including: "gay oppression, self oppression, men's liberation and sex roles, gay relationships and youth sexuality," among others. Limited to a dozen participants, and meeting in individuals' homes, the group proved popular and by spring of that year two other men's discussion groups were established.[63] Another forum for conversation and counselling was the Gays for Equality Counselling Unit, which had ten non-professional peer counsellors available to handle a variety of counselling and information services, as well as hosting monthly coffee houses / rap sessions, a referral service, and a recorded message line. Many oral interviews with Winnipeg residents indicated that it was with GFE that they met their first gay people, and, through phone counselling and rap sessions, become comfortable with their sexual orientation and began to meet other gays and lesbians in Winnipeg.[64] Winnipeg Gay Youth also had space in the University of Manitoba Student Union. While recognized by many as a necessary area for gay programming and counselling, then, as now, the politics of socializing and interacting with gay youth, particularly those who were under legal drinking age of eighteen, was difficult. The synopsis that this organization provided indicated that finding space for their meetings was difficult, and that their brochures and pamphlets directed at high-school students met with a mixed reaction.

One of the major moments of the day-long event was the interaction between Gays for Equality and Happenings (Mutual Friendship Society) representatives. For the first time since their early years, the 1977 meeting offered something of a rapprochement between the Mutual Friendship Society and GFE. MFS stressed their social goals and indicated that they were willing to work with other organizations in the city to better the lives of all gays and lesbians in Winnipeg. Beyond the chance to clear the air, to strategize and share organizational information, the tangible outcome of this conference was the creation of the Manitoba Gay Coalition (MGC). MGC also hoped to be a force for political action, sponsoring a candidate's debate in the 1978 provincial election, and polling provincial candidates about their stand on gay human rights. MGC later created PL in August 1977. PL's sole mandate was to fundraise for and purchase space to create a gay and lesbian community centre in the city, since the constant movement from temporary locations, and concerns for their collection (library and archival materials from early Winnipeg organizations), made the notion of a permanent space very attractive.

By 1978, organizational growth in Winnipeg lessened, as most of these newly created groups strove to keep their fundraising and finances solvent. Many initiated their own in-house newsletters. There were also concerted efforts towards community building, educational and cultural programming, and civil rights. Not until 1982, when Giovanni's Room, the name of the Gay Community Centre of Winnipeg, opened at 275 Sherbrooke St, would Winnipeg witness more organizational development. A year later, the Mutual Friendship Society moved across the street, when they purchased 272 Sherbrooke St. This accomplishment was lauded by all organizations in the city because, after many years of work, gays and lesbians finally owned their own public space and were no longer at the whim of landlords. 1983 also saw some negative developments in Winnipeg, as it was the year that the Women's Building closed due to lack of funds. More ominously, it was also the year in which the first AIDs awareness session was held at MFS, after the news broke in the October 1982 issue of *Out and About* regarding a disease referred to as "immune collapse," which was rapidly affecting gay men in New York, Los Angeles, and Toronto. Despite the belief that Winnipeggers would be safely removed from such disease, gay medical professionals realized that it was only a matter of time before it came to the city. In April 1984, Winnipeg had their first support group for persons with AIDs and Winnipeg's first AIDs diagnosis came in 1985.

Educational, Social and Cultural Developments: Happenings

"You will never know" … of how it used to be many years ago. How a few of us used to meet at our apartments or homes to sense the feeling of belonging and to enjoy our lives together. How terribly secretive things were. It was a very hidden society, plagued with a sense of public ridicule and harassed by the police. Now … when I attend one of our socials, so open and completely free I feel a deep immeasurable pride in our gay and lesbian community and how it has come out, into the sunshine and clean air, no longer furtive, no longer hidden, no longer fearful. *Wilde* Times Editorial, 1982.[65]

Once Happenings got their charter, they began to use the funds they had raised from their socials (held in a series of rented halls) as cash for rental accommodations while saving for a permanent location. In addition to socials (usually held monthly), Happenings featured a series of special parties (Halloween and New Year's were the most popular), drag shows, and, in October 1973, a Beer and Borscht night that, as part of the city's Folklorama, featured "hosts attired in authentic Slavic dancing girl costumes passing out treats to one and all."[66] They organized a bowling league called the Tuberose 5 Pin Mixed Bowling League, and added some outdoor recreational pursuits – field days and picnics.[67] Turnout for these events varied, but for a key annual event such as the Halloween dance – when 365 people showed up – the hall was overcapacity.[68] They also provided VD clinics, particularly after they received word from Edmonton's Club 70 that there was a outbreak of syphilis in the city. Although it is difficult to get a clear idea of numbers, because no membership lists of Happenings members were archived, from their printed commentary it would appear that, in the early years, women and men joined this club in roughly equal numbers. This ratio would change once women's only clubs started in Winnipeg. Gays for Equality was always overwhelmingly male in focus, in large part because the more political women were in feminist and lesbian organizing. In interviews Chris Vogel noted that their best fundraising socials attracted many women, and that they were always advised not to hold any socials that conflicted with softball tournaments because lesbian attendance was critical to success.[69]

House Parties and the Hill

While these exclusively gay events did draw lesbians and gays away from the mixed bars, they did not completely change other patterns of queer life in Winnipeg. House parties continued in their popularity, as did cruising the hill. Hilary Osborne-Hill, the Happenings social commentator, wryly questioned the natural challenges that Winnipeg gay males had to overcome when cruising on prairie summer nights: "do Arpege and OFF! really do something for each other???" Such campy statements about the popularity of nighttime cruising at the hill minimized the risks that gay men took in cruising this Winnipeg landmark – as it grew increasingly risky.[70] In the 1970s there were a series of gay bashings on the hill, something that GFE tried to publicize so as to alert men to these dangers. GFE urged men to avoid the hill but this proved difficult for a host of reasons, starting with the long history of this queer cruising site. Another major challenge was the diverse range of men who congregated at the hill. In addition to openly "gay" men who had alternative venues, there were also men who "had sex with men" (men who were married, not openly gay, or unwilling to label themselves). Men who had sex with men could not or would not "risk" attending gay-identified spaces and so had to take the "risks" posed by the hill. A larger issue was that it was anathema to liberationist queers to curtail sexual activity, or "privatize it," because of civic concerns about violence – far better the police actually curtailed gay bashing and prosecuted bashers.

Queer organizations expended much effort on encouraging people to pick up their cultural materials, attend sessions, socialize, but awareness that such groups existed was only part of the equation. It fell to individual lesbians and gay men to actually choose to participate. Even those individuals who later were active in queer politics expressed initial reservations about joining gay groups or being "seen" reading gay materials. For example, Don Fenwick, who would become an involved community member and Project Lambda organizer, avoided the GFE booth and information during his undergraduate days at the University of Manitoba in the early 1970s. Originally from Flin Flon, Manitoba, Fenwick indicated that he spent his university days partying largely due to his discomfort with his homosexuality and his nervousness about participating in GFE events. Fenwick's recollections serve as an important reminder that despite the gains in access, programming, and availability of information, it does not necessarily follow that all gays or lesbians can or will participate. Fenwick remembered seeing GFE booths at university-wide events like Festival of Life and Learning, but he believed that there was much hostility on campus. However, four years later, "on the first sun tanning day of the season, he was walking and stopped by 'The Hill.'" He took off his shirt and shoes and sat. It didn't take long for him to be noticed. A man introduced himself and Fenwick and the individual ended up having sex. After that experience, he reported many visits to the hill. As he met more gay men, he learned about other places gay men frequented – such as the St Regis Hotel, Silver Slipper Lounge, and Detour. He heard about the "Club" on Manitoba at this time, but during his interview noted that he found Happenings "closeted, paranoid, racist and bigoted."[71] Fenwick would become a participant in more "left-wing" organizations, like the Idea Centre discussions and, subsequently, Project Lambda.

Gays for Equality

In contrast to the social activities at Happenings, or the informal cruising at the hill or along Winnipeg's riverfront paths, the cultural and educational activities at GFE were primarily educational and political in focus. First, the wide-range of programming, groups, and sessions that GFE ran – both on campus, and later from their downtown loca-tion – offered members of the gay and lesbian community a place where gay and lesbian history, culture, and community were fostered. Largely working to counteract the silence and negativity about gay life, GFE strove to positively portray coming out and to assist gay and lesbian Winnipeggers to "come out," which they hoped would, ideally, lead to activism. For example, in their annual report for 1973–4, GFE indicated that they had been involved in counselling work, via their recorded message machine. The three-minute message, which was changed fre-quently, offered an anonymous way for Winnipeg residents to learn about gay activities in the city. According to GFE records, which were routinely kept for both the recorded line and the telephone counselling service, there was an average of five seconds between calls to their mes-sage line, which attests to the popularity of the phone line.[72]

GFE faced a number of obstacles to setting up the phone line, and these obstacles make clear the ways in which various governmental, media, and commercial organizations engaged in a clear form of obstruction-ism to "protect" citizens from hearing or reading about homosexual-ity. Such official homophobic pronouncements, whether from crown corporations, government offices, or mainstream media, made life very difficult for gay and lesbian groups, and illustrates how "openness" and visibility could cut both ways – allowing queer people to find gay and lesbian organizations, but conversely, they paid a price, in lawsuits to achieve basic services, harassment, and media battles, which caused some men and women to question whether this truly was "progress" from the older, more covert days. In interviews and published reminis-cences, many activists recalled that local papers at first refused to print ads for GFE because they feared offending readers. Similarly, Manitoba Telecom Services initially refused to print the GFE phone number in the phone directory. After negotiations and legal assistance, this decision was overturned. Attempts to put up posters about GFE services in the city were met by a City of Winnipeg by-law against postering. Obvi-ously, this was not a coordinated harassment campaign – the players and the goals were too diverse. But the energy gay organizations had to expend to enable themselves to have the basic requirements other organizations and groups took for granted – a phone number and tele-phone directory listing, event publicity, posters, media exposure, and the ability to incorporate and host social events – illustrate the pow-erful, systemic homophobia at play. Various individuals, government organizations, and crown corporations found GFE's existence threatening to the status quo and strove to kneecap them at every turn. GFE always prevailed, but such battles made gay activists of this generation critical of government motivations and of the presumed homophobic reactions that lay at the core of these denials of service.

Once some of these hurdles were cleared, members of GFE were able to actually concentrate on their programming! One of their early – and quite successful ventures – was the free Friday coffee houses. They also hosted eight socials throughout the year. Subsequently, GFE held "rap sessions" on the first Friday of the month. These sessions offered participants a structured discussion, involving an experienced group leader, and then a mix of experienced attendees and newcomers. Held in neutral settings, usually on campus, the purpose of the rap sessions were "to help newcomers not only talk with someone about being homosexual, but to become comfortable in a gay setting, to begin the process of making gay friends."[73] GFE indicated that they "continuously distributed" information, including their own pamphlet *Love and Let Love*; Toronto's *The Body Politic*; the Canadian Gay Liberation Movement's *Operation Socrates Handbook* (published at the University of Waterloo), and the *American Library Association Bibliography*, et cetera. As a campus organization, GFE was given space at the University of Manitoba's Festival of Life and Learning, and, through these outreach methods, GFE was able to get their materials out to people in a fairly accessible fashion.

For many Winnipeg people, GFE was their first point of contact in the gay community. This was true for Ted Millward, a trained Anglican priest, teacher, and librarian, who recalled that his first contact with the Winnipeg gay community was on Christmas Eve 1975 when he phoned the GFE phone line and learned of their coming-out rap sessions.[74] Although it was not common for middle-aged men to decide to come out of the closet, friend Chris Vogel recalled that Millward felt that the times had changed significantly and he had to acknowledge his true self. Such acknowledgment came at a high price, as he resigned his priesthood and position as school chaplain, although he maintained his position as the head librarian at St John's College, University of Manitoba.[75] He attended the rap session early in 1976 and began to make some friends in the gay community, and subsequently attended a fundraising dinner for the John Damien Defence Fund. There, Millward met Rich North and Chris Vogel, and eventually Vogel asked Millward to participate in the launch of the couple's new venture – the Council on Homosexuality and Religion (CHR).

Besides serving as the intake organization for lesbians and gay men searching for like-minded friends, GFE was an important participant in a range of campus events, like frosh week and educational activities. GFE organized the first gay pride week events in Winnipeg starting in 1973, which included Winnipeg's first gay parade (see figure 6.1). Held in October, the organization and programming for the week was largely organized by Rich North. Pride activities included screening the film "Sunday, Bloody Sunday," as well as informational lectures, a dance, coffee houses, and a special invited guest speaker, Barbara Love, an American lesbian author who promoted her popular book entitled *Sappho Was a Right-On Woman*. Finally, they held a well-attended symposium on gay rights and experiences, which included representatives from the Manitoba Department of Education, Manitoba Human Rights Commission, GFE, Vancouver GATE, the Unitarian Church, and the University of Manitoba Student Counselling Services.[76] Similar to Saskatoon, after a promising early start with gay pride activities, they would not be held in Winnipeg again until the 1980s. GFE's final activity for the year was the drafting of a brief for the Manitoba Human Rights Commission, which encouraged the attorney general to include sexual orientation in the province's human rights code. "Manitoba Homosexuals: A Minority Without Rights" offered evidence of the discrimination gays and lesbians experienced in Winnipeg – specifically with respect to housing, employment, violence, and exclusion. While obviously educational, such documents were also part of GFE's second major organizational goal – educating the broader populace to the gay minority, and, in so doing, actively demanding that politicians and the public respect the rights of this minority group.[77]

The Council on Homosexuality and Religion (CHR)

The first, and perhaps most important "spin-off" from GFE was the Council on Homosexuality in Religion.[78] Starting in November 1976, CHR meetings were held in Vogel and North's house. CHR was a non-denominational group whose main goals were to serve as a "counselling, information and resource centre on questions of homosexuality especially in a religious context."[79] Eventually the CHR moved to space on the University of Winnipeg campus, and, although they had a broad-ranging mandate, they tended to stick to producing and disseminating literature about homosexuality and religion. In addition, they held monthly, ecumenical worship services. Given his educational background, Millward was a driving force in this organization – writing popular booklets such as "What the Bible Says to Homosexuals." "What the Bible Says," which was reprinted multiple times, offered readers an analysis of "biblical passages which are chiefly used to maintain the traditional condemnation of homosexuality," and offered alternative interpretations and contextual information for those oft-lauded biblical "truths." CHR also produced an "occasional publication" called *Gay Christian Witness*, which provided news of its work, and offered reviews of books, articles about the challenges gay religious adherents faced in their churches, and similar information.

In June 1982, *Gay Christian Witness* published an article by Harry Wiebe entitled "Gay Mennonites: A Look at a Few of our Experiences," which summarized research Wiebe completed for a Mennonite Studies class at the University of Winnipeg.[80] Based on his interviews with several gay Mennonite men, Wiebe analysed their common experiences. In all but one case, the men's families continued to support them, but their faith communities did not accept their homosexuality. Mennonite churches were not prepared to accept "out" homosexuals in the congregations. Similar to the position taken by the Catholic Church, the Mennonite churches advocated celibacy for gay and lesbian members. Interestingly, Wiebe reported that the Brethren/Mennonite Council for Gay Concerns (BMC) had been founded in the US in 1976 to assist homosexuals, their families, and their communities through the dissemination of educational materials and information.

The men profiled in Wiebe's article had all moved into the city from rural areas and small towns. In Winnipeg, most of the men reported that they were no longer religiously affiliated with the Mennonite faith, preferring to think of themselves as ethnoculturally Mennonite. For instance, "Gerhard," a twenty-four-year-old Winnipeg resident who had devoted much energy to trying to educate his urban church about homosexuality, ruefully discovered the inherent conservatism of that congregation.[81] "Being a Christian is important to me, but being a Mennonite is not really that important. I was a member of a Mennonite church but with my 'coming out' came also pressure to be celibate and to ignore my homosexual tendencies. If I refused to conform, my membership would have been challenged. To avoid embarrassment to my family and friends, I quietly resigned my membership with no reason given. The pastors, however, knew the reasons. From my church, I do not know of any other gay Mennonites, and from what I've heard, I'm the only one to 'come out' in our community."[82] Other men were not as open about their orientation, worried about the reactions of family, friends, and faith. The article did not minimize these men's struggles with the Mennonite faith, nor the challenge that lay ahead to convince the conservative religious group to change its religious and social pronouncements about homosexuality. Yet it was not an entirely depressing article, as it provided a window into gay men's resilience and determination not to retreat to the closet. These difficult decisions – whether to be openly gay or to maintain their ties with the Mennonite faith – had strengthened them. A significant number had proudly accepted their sexual orientation and they were moving forward with their new lives. The tone of this article is not surprising, as one of the key roles of CHR was to offer religious gays and lesbians "hope" for the future. While they left the Mennonite faith, the men interviewed by Wiebe did not sever their ties with organized religion. The connections between queer sexuality and religion is an important, if often underexplored, issue within queer histories, where religion is primarily viewed as antagonistic to queer people. Little work investigates how those who wish to stay within faith communities, or keep religious practices, reconcile their sexuality and religiosity. For Winnipeggers, many of whom had strong faith backgrounds, religion was a key issue for those grappling with diverse sexual identities/practices. For men like Gerhard, one of the options was moving into other more accepting Christian congregations. Gerhard joined the Anglican congregation, where he felt more accepted, and his story (and countless others that were printed in various publications) offered readers inspirational personalized narratives from which they could learn and, potentially, assist in their own transformative moves.

Religiosity was an issue for urban and rural queer people, but it was also true that those residents of southern Manitoba, particularly around Steinbach, had particular challenges given the close connections between families, faith communities, and employment/occupation. Queer farmers, for example, working on family farms, had great difficulty "separating" their private and public lives, or in making the step towards queer identification without risking their livelihood. One of my Winnipeg narrators, Frances Williamson, who participated in staffing the GFE phone line, recalled that "a lot of people I worked with on the line came from Mennonite groups from the predominantly Mennonite areas like Steinbach, Winkler, Morden and they were just absolutely terrified that something would get out into the community … It was always difficult to guide them in any direction because it was brick wall no matter where you went."[83] Her recollections echoed those of Doug Nicholson, another phone line counsellor, who remembered that "religious conflict was a frequent concern among callers."[84] For those callers, there was no easy solution for their questions and concerns about how to live gay lives – given the conservative social and religious climate, as well as the economic realities in which commercial, educational, and agricultural employers and employees were often bound by kinship ties and faith. "Coming out" in those settings was simply not feasible as it put individuals at risk for losing their families, their friends, their communities, their livelihoods, and being ousted from their churches. Many queer people from those communities lead the "double lives" model from an earlier era, or, conversely, they made the move into the city (as Gerhard had) and transformed themselves into urbanites.

While the work of CHR was largely educational, formed to respond to the callers to the GFE phone line who had questions requiring religious counselling, there were other reasons for such an organization. In the 1980s, all the mainstream churches in Canada were engaged in debates, studies, and administrative and religious questions about how to address demands for greater inclusiveness for gay and lesbian members, and, potentially, gay and lesbian ordinands. The importance of religiosity in the prairies, where churches and religiosity infused daily discussions and politics, practically necessitated an organization that could counteract the tremendous power of the churches to pronounce on appropriate social, sexual, and spiritual behaviour. One of the beloved tactics of conservative religious organizations, particularly those based upon a literal interpretation of biblical teachings, was (and remains) the power to utilize biblical quotes as "evidence" of the sinfulness of homosexuality. CHR's most popular publication offered historically specific explanations and context for those passages. It also offered examples of how to rebut such simplistic homophobic statements that had a tendency to be produced as "commonsensical." In so doing, like many organizations, it was both educational and political.

CHR participated in the demonstrations against Anita Bryant's tour; it held forums with Winnipeg churches discussing the issue of Christianity and homosexuality; and, as well, the group – often in the person of Ted Millward – wrote many letters to the editors of the Winnipeg newspapers, offering clarification and critique of government statements about homosexuality.[85] Millward capitalized on his expertise and his well-respected position at the University of Manitoba to propose continuing education classes about the history of homosexuality.

In 1979 he offered a continuing education course called "Homosexuality in History and in Contemporary Society," which was markedly different from the other offerings in French, Spanish, German, and Chinese language instruction, or more popularly oriented classes such as "Mushroom Identification," "Antiques for the Amateur," or "Law for the Layman."[86] Millward's course offered interested students a sweeping survey of the history of homosexuality from ancient times to the present, artistic and cultural commentary, and information about the current legal situation of gays and lesbians in Canada, and in Manitoba specifically. Interestingly, CHR was the first Winnipeg gay and lesbian organization to obtain a charitable status, and thus it served as a popular organization for those gays and lesbians who wished to make financial donations.

Out and About in Winnipeg

In 1977, the short-lived Manitoba Gay Coalition launched Project Lambda. Project Lambda was a non-political group whose primary goal was the establishment of a gay community centre in Winnipeg to which all gays and lesbians, including youth, would be welcome.[87] PL followed the well-established practice of holding monthly socials as fundraisers, as well as collecting an annual membership fee. Shortly after inception, PL launched *Out and About*, their monthly bulletin, billed as a "light reference guide" to the city's attractions and events. Rather naively, the organization believed that *Out and About* would become a moneymaker for the organization, but such small periodicals never broke even, let alone turned a profit.

Reading through issues of *Out and About*, one is immediately struck by the diversity of events held in Winnipeg – fundraising socials, river cruises, women's-only events, educational and cultural programming on the two university campuses, political activity, cultural events (theatre, ballet, the symphony, a range of live music from jazz to folk to rock, and visual arts), sports, and more homespun, informal events – potluck suppers, coffee houses, cards and game nights, picnics, tobogganing, et cetera. While editors and readers of *Out and About* often complained about the lack of venues and activities, for those prepared to brave the interminable winters and get out there, considerable programming was available. Though it is impossible to mention all the various groups that existed, they ran the gamut from self-help groups (Lesbian Alcoholic Group, Families of Gays) to political activities like Wages Due

Lesbians or groups for middle-aged gay men such as the Forty–Sixty Club.[88] Despite some of the vitriol that raged between the small group of liberationists in Winnipeg and those who preferred gay socializing to politics, it was evident that many queer Winnipeggers were extremely cautious about revealing their sexuality "publicly." For example, the editors of *Out and About* stressed that readers must not make presumptions about the sexual orientation of people whose names appeared in the little journal. They were also sympathetic, and cautious, in their profiles of groups like Forty–Sixty. For instance, the editor's politically correct description of a typical evening for the Forty–Sixty Club speaks volumes about the city's political and social climate: "At a typical meeting, the members gather in a quiet, home-like atmosphere to chat about mutual interests, discuss current affairs and spend a quiet evening of social exchange. The members come from all walks of life and met freely on common ground. There is no pressure to divulge your name or occupation, *so none feel threatened – a common feeling among older, established gays*" (emphasis mine).[89] *Out and About* also made considerable effort to advertise events in other prairie cities, in particular noting the gay and lesbian bars and their addresses and the formation of gay political and social groups. The bulletin's scope extended beyond the Winnipeg city limits, events and organizations in Brandon and Thompson, Manitoba, received coverage, as did similar organizations in Grand Forks and Fargo, North Dakota. It was not uncommon to have announcements printed for special American activities; for instance, in September 1980 a weekend workshop was held in Fargo/Moorhead, North Dakota, sponsored by the Fargo/Moorhead Lesbians and Gays to highlight the work of the American organization the National Gay Task Force.[90]

Another strength of *Out and About* was its coverage of women's events. This was one of the ways in which it differentiated itself from *What's Happening?*, particularly in its later phase, where the editor mused openly that he routinely heard complaints from the "girls" about the lack of women's content. Having a female editor of *Out and About* was one key factor (although the revolving door on the volunteer editor's office door meant little consistency at the bulletin). It may have reflected women's greater participation in PL or, additionally, the way in which *Out and About* tried to offer something different from the two other newsletters that jockeyed for Winnipeg gay and lesbian reader's attentions in the late 1970s to the early 1980s – *What's Happening?* and *Wilde Times*, the quirky entry from the Oscar Wilde Memorial Society.

Lesbian and/or Feminist Organizational and Cultural Events

Winnipeg women's/lesbian cultural, political, and educational programming was quite separate from the gay male events. It was only in community socials, and later at demonstrations, that both sides of the community came together. Chris Vogel recalled:

> at first, most lesbians who were out in Winnipeg did not want to participate in gay liberationist activities because they feared or were suspicious of the men, but equally, because they believed their true calling, their best efforts, were devoted to feminism. And they formed lesbian organizations and groups, but on the other hand when we had demonstrations they were much more successful in recruiting each other to participate in the demos. So while the organizations were almost entirely, but not solely, conducted by men. In some ways women exceeded the male participation.[91]

Beyond their political work with feminist and lesbian organizations, social events for lesbians tended to consist of drop-ins, coffee houses, potlucks, dances, and women's music concerts. This activity was strengthened in 1979 with the launch of the Women's Building and the renovated basement space that served as the first home of Ms Purdy's Social Club, which was a women's lounge. Initially located in the basement of the Women's Building, Ms Purdy's moved to Main St a couple of years later, becoming one of the longest running lesbian social spaces in the city.[92] Entertainment at Ms Purdy's was eclectic, as the organizers provided Friday and Saturday night canteens where women could participate in bingo, films, concerts, drop-ins, and potlucks with subsequent music and dancing. For those more interested in pub activities, pool and ping-pong tables were available, as were darts, chess, checkers, and cards.

Other programming in the Women's Building consisted of organizational meetings for the variety of resident groups, including: The Winnipeg Women's Cultural and Educational Centre; Women in Trades Association; Painted Ladies Theatre Company; Native Women's Advocacy Group; Media, Arts, Graphics and Ideas Company; Winnipeg Committee Against Violence towards Women; Artemis Reproductions and Brigit's Books. Games nights were held every Sunday, and women were encouraged to drop in for an informal evening of socializing and games. Programming on Thursday's consisted of Wen-Do courses, a form of women's self-defence, and the rest of the week was rounded out with organizational meetings.[93]

One part of the larger urban cultural scene that intersected with Winnipeg's queer communities, particularly the lesbian communities, was Winnipeg's rich musical scene. In 1974, the first Winnipeg Folk Music festival was held in Bird's Hill Park, and it quickly became a popular annual event. Perhaps because of the city's famously bad weather, a disproportionate number of accomplished rock and folk musicians and bands hail from Winnipeg. The folk and women's musical scene, while not as commercially popular, was also strong in the city, and includes such luminaries as Heather Bishop (originally from Regina), whose self-distributed children's and women's music made her a draw on the women's and folk music circuits. This deep pool of musical talent in the city led to the creation of a series of Canadian women's musical festivals in Winnipeg in the 1980s. These summer festivals, often coinciding with summer solstice, offered local lesbians and feminists important cultural and political events to attend. Performers came from across the country, including well-known musicians and singers such as Rita McNeil, Lorraine Segato, Lillian Allen, Connie Kaldor, and a host of lesser-known performers, including a cappella groups, Inuit throat singers, and musical/dramatic performances. Accompanying the music, and an equally important part of the event, were workshops, craft and artistic wares for sale, and the opportunity for women to socialize in like-minded company.[94]

"Coming Out TV"

Another important cultural vehicle for the gay and lesbian community was radio and television programming. As already noted, the gay radio program ran for two years, from 1978 to 1980. When it ended in the summer of 1980, plans were launched to take advantage of the CRTC regulations that required cable providers to provide local programming, via a local television station, in their markets. These laws, known colloquially as "Can Con" regulations, proved to be serendipitous for Winnipeg's gays and lesbians. They could offer local programing and the station was receptive to airing the programme. Beginning in September 1980, "Coming Out TV" aired on Winnipeg channel Thirteen for thirty minutes a week. "Coming Out TV" aired from 1980 to 1994 and was unique to Winnipeg. This was years before gays and lesbians in other Canadian cities would have access to such programming, and well before cable television providers offered gay-and-lesbian-themed packages for subscribers. In short, Coming Out TV was a Winnipeg landmark. Over the years, all possible angles on gay and lesbian life were highlighted – whether political, cultural, religious, social, or medical. Programming consisted of interviews, news, music, local announcements, and features. Although the local community was their primary source of talent, the Gay Media Collective were able to capitalize on gay and lesbian visitors to the city, and, given their engagement with developments in national, regional, and international activism (gleaned by reading *The Advocate*, *The Body Politic*, and assorted other print materials), they were able to provide an eclectic mix of programming which highlighted cultural, religious, political, medical, and academic issues. A veritable who's who of Canadian and American performers, politicians, historians, and medical professionals appeared on the show, including: George Hislop, Robin Tyler, Jonathon Katz, Ian Young, Heather Bishop, Nicole Brossard, Suniti Namjoshi, Meg Christian, Ed Jackson, Betsy Warland, Ted Millward, Chris Vogel, Dr Dick Smith, Jane Rule, and Holly Near.[95] In contrast to the way in which gay and lesbian organizational activity was often quite distinct, the lesbian programming on Coming Out TV was strong. Programs featuring lesbian celebrities, or those devoted to discussing lesbian parenting, lesbian socializing, activism, medical and health issues, and legal concerns, were routinely highlighted.

In additions to these special guests, the program featured a wide-ranging line-up of rebroadcasts of documentaries and short films. For instance, the first episode rebroadcast the documentary film "Truxx," which explored the Montreal police raids on that city's bathhouses and the political outcome of those actions. Along with such programming, "Coming Out TV" also routinely featured leaders in the city's gay and lesbian community, profiled community organizations, featured discussions of local and national news, and announced community events.[96]

Given the nature of this community-based programming, it is doubtful that ratings were ever compiled for the show. But, one can gauge its importance in a couple of key ways. First, the length of time the show was broadcast (over seven hundred shows were produced) suggests that there was demand for this programming. Second, Collective participants recalled that people in the community spoke about the show and promoted it. Third, the members of the Collective applied to be included in a new CBC series called Take Thirty Access Series. This initiative provided successful community groups with the opportunity to broadcast in Take Thirty's timeslot. Likely an attempt by the CBC to increase regional programming (probably cost effectively), the Gay

Media Collective's application was successful. After two months spent writing, taping, and editing their feature, the show aired on 11 March 1983. In letters, Robert Dame, a member of the Collective, noted, "we believe (as does the CBC) that we have produced a good program. Its various segments link into the same meaning: we are people too; we do not fit any stereotype. We hope you will agree that this program is not only worth viewing for itself, but also that it is one step further in assuring the recognition of our legal rights."[97] The Collective kept the letters that CBC received after the program, ten of which were favourable and seven of which were negative. They also received letters from various gay organizations, including Gays of Ottawa who wrote to congratulate them on their achievement. "We saw the program and thought it was excellent," wrote John Duggan for Gays Ottawa. "This project is extremely valuable in supporting gay people across the country who would have seen it, and in changing negative attitudes of some heterosexuals."[98]

The program featured interviews with members of the Collective (all men) in which they discussed their relationships, homophobia, coming out, and lives as gay men in Winnipeg, Manitoba. Reading through the letters, one is immediately struck by the way in which the positive and negative responses may be classified. Those positive letters were primarily from other gay men or those with knowledge of the gay community, while the negative mail came from people who sought to position themselves as "normal" (their words), heterosexually married, religiously observant Canadians. Obviously, given the size of the Take Thirty audience, the receipt of seventeen letters is hardly representative, but it does provide one means by which to assess people's reactions to the program. Those who wrote affirmative, appreciative letters were not only from larger cities in southern Ontario and Quebec, but also small towns in New Brunswick, Manitoba, Saskatchewan, and British Columbia. Most people openly identified their orientation – and the bulk of the positive letters were written by gay men or, in one case, the mother of a gay son. One heterosexual woman wrote that the program changed her impressions of gay people, and challenged her presumption that she was a liberal thinker. Gay male letter writers claimed the program was representative of their experiences and applauded the portraits of "average gay men." For instance, a woman from Lynn Lake, Manitoba, wrote: "as a mother of a recently come out homosexual young man I wish to express my appreciation for your recent documentary on this subject. My son could fit in the group of men you showed …

and I appreciate that you did not choose the *extreme types* with whom we usually associate homosexuality" (emphasis mine).[99] The language used in the letter is important because, as with many such positive testimonials, it praises as much as it critiques, privileging the more conventional, middle-class gay men viewed in the programme and not the "extreme" types (not defined) that the mother, and viewer, felt might distort or damage people's views of gay men. More poignantly, from Vernon, British Columbia, this writer offered the CBC his thanks for a "straight forward [programme with] no put-on or cover ups. I truly enjoyed, appreciated [it] and raised my opinion of the CBC a hundred fold." Continuing, he offered this biographical information to contextualize his comments, "I am 55, a grandfather of two and father of two. I was married for 20 years and came out 5 years ago, after working for 30 years, I am now retired."[100] Similarly, another gay man, resident in London, Ontario, thanked the CBC for depicting "a bunch of responsible, level-headed adults in a relaxed and open atmosphere, and I thank you for that. We are not all hairdressers, clothes horses or all-around wimps and people have to realize that. We are everywhere. We are fathers, doctors, politicians, your friend your neighbour." Moving beyond the statements regarding affirmative images, and non-stereotypical role models, Mr S., another viewer, also addressed the issue of displays of affection, which distressed or shocked some viewers. "God knows you've rubbed some fur the wrong way showing men embracing and (horrors) kissing … it was one of the most beautiful things I've ever seen on television. Thank you CBC."[101] In our contemporary era, where our multiplicities of television channels, networks, and specialty programming regularly offer viewers gay, lesbian, and transgender characters (however problematic or stereotypical some of those portraits are), it is worth recalling that then it was incredibly rare to see positive images of gay and lesbian people, or displays of affection between same-sex actors, depicted on network television. Those fleeting moments were incredibly powerful, both for queer people who vividly recalled such programs but also for those who reported being "assaulted" by viewing such "displays."

The negative letters were extreme, filled with biblical imagery and teachings about Sodom and Gomorrah, archly notifying the CBC that "God's wrath" would befall the "immoral beings" from Winnipeg.[102] Most found the scene of the men kissing "blasphemous, evil smut" that was best kept from impressionable viewers. Negative letters laced with Christian imagery and teaching came from viewers in Ontario and

Nova Scotia. The negative responses from the prairies struck a slightly different tone. From Garrick, Saskatchewan, a reader wrote: "I really think they need medical help ... they all looked so pale and sickly. You'd think they would realize that they're not normal."[103] From Winnipeg, one married woman wrote to protest the use of public money to air such programming, and then offered her enlightened view of homosexuals: "If a number of people feel that *that* lifestyle suits them and they do not interfere with children, I do not think they should be persecuted or discriminated against, but they should, in all decency live quietly and discretely and not flaunt it" (emphasis in original).[104] "Flaunting it" was often the criticism when gays and lesbians poked through the omnipresent heterosexual mainstream culture. That gay male Winnipeggers dared to visibly depict their lives or to claim explicitly gay spaces in a city that was both multicultural and racially diverse, yet also hard-working, conservative, and often cautious about change, would continue to shock some viewers and residents throughout the period of this study.

Giovanni's Room

One of the hallmarks of the post-1970s era was the goal of diversifying gay and lesbian socializing away from its traditional venues – bars in particular – into more inclusive space that might enable a wider range of community members to participate. This was a particular goal for lesbian activists and community builders.[105] That was one of the driving forces behind the creation of PL in 1977. Despite their best efforts, three years later their goal of a community centre remained unrealized. In August 1980, Richard North submitted his proposal to PL for "Giovanni's Room."[106] North had been one of the key ideas men behind many of the innovative initiatives that emerged from GFE, and, in this regard, the proposal for Giovanni's Room was something markedly different from other ventures in the city, and indeed the country. Drawing his inspiration from James Baldwin's novel, in which Giovanni's Room "becomes a symbol of the struggle to make a place for homosexuality in the hostile heterosexual culture," North wrote that now, in a more congenial time, "that space exists, and it is simply up to gay people to occupy that space. There is room for Giovanni's Room now, and it is up to us to realize that possibility."[107] North sketched plans for a simple cafe that would have a menu of sandwiches, coffee, light supper, and would also be eligible for a liquor permit to serve beer and

3.5 Giovanni's Room, 1983, University of Manitoba Archives & Special
Collections, Manitoba Gay & Lesbian Archives, PC 292 (A.08–67).

wine. Located in an upstairs location, specifically chosen so that patrons
would relax knowing that they were not visible from the street, this
cafe could serve as social space in which people could meet, congregate, hear live music, read, et cetera. As a socialist, North indicated that
he was not interested in a commercial venture; rather, he hoped that
the revenue from Giovanni's Room might subsidize office and meeting
spaces for PL. Embedded within the document was North's rationale
for why Winnipeg should have such a space and his reflection offers a
valuable analysis of the city's gay community. Borrowing from feminist
writer Virginia Woolf, in a section subtitled "A Room of One's Own,"
North lamented the situation in Winnipeg.

> The failure of an adequate gay scene to develop in Winnipeg has severely
> limited the development of a gay identity and a sense of community. What
> happens is this. After people have come out in this city and have devel-
> oped a sense of their identity as gay people, they want to live gay lives.
> They quickly realize that Winnipeg has very little to offer the gay person
> who is Out and About. Consequently, they leave Winnipeg for Toronto,
> Vancouver, Montreal or even Saskatoon – places where a more developed
> gay scene exists. One needs only to think of those who have been active
> in the gay movement in Winnipeg to confirm the validity of that analysis:

many of those who were involved in Happenings during the early years have left the city … Many of those who become involved in gay liberation through GFE have left … And the organizers of the *After Stonewall* collective have moved to Saskatoon … Until there are actual places where gay people can meet and socialize, the broader process of liberation and social changed will be truncated. Winnipeg needs a gay scene if a strong identity and community are to flourish in this city.[108]

After commentary about various downtown locations that he was already scouting for a suitable location, North indicated to the PL board that he was offering them this proposition, and he agreed to run the venture. If they were uninterested he would go elsewhere. While the news of the proposal, and of the mailed ballot that all members of PL were to receive in the mail was presented enthusiastically in *Out and About*, the result was that Giovanni's Room did not get approved to proceed.

Published commentary in *Out and About*, prior to and after the Giovanni's Room proposal, indicated frustration with PL's inability to bring the centre to fruition. PL's ongoing financial conservatism (originally they wished to wait until they could purchase a building rather than spending money on rental space) and their lack of volunteers stymied the project. It was a long-term fact in Winnipeg that attendance for social events, socials, balls, and other events could be quite significant (well into the four hundred to five hundred participant range), but getting people to volunteer to host and run such events was another matter. This was a challenge in the other cities as well – people loved to dance but few lived to serve, clean up, or organize.

Into this stalemate, came a new organization, campily called the Oscar Wilde Memorial Society (OWMS), whose goals were twofold: to get a gay community centre running and to offer Winnipeggers more cultural, athletic, and social venues for gay people. The brainchild of Richard North, North brought his concept of Giovanni's Room with him. From the launch of *Wilde Times*, OWMS's newsletter, it was clear that some version of a cafe was in their future. Plans for a gay bookshop were included with the cafe concept. The editor of *Wilde Times* indicated how difficult it was for gays to find cultural materials in the city: "Having just moved to this city … I find it shamefully apparent that there is no satisfactory source of gay literature to be found in this city. I've gone through the usual nerve-racking experience of buying a copy of *Blueboy*, *Mandate* and the lesser stars at public newsstands, but somehow that doesn't seem to be enough. Sooner or later even beefcake can get boring. Coming out in this city you need all the support you can get. It would be nice to see that there was more to gay literature than that found on the backshelves of Dominion News."[109] While it was apparent that OWMS was in some regard a competitor with PL, very quickly the two organizations joined forces and advertised each other's social events in the other's newsletter. *Out and About* retained the flavour of a television-listing guide at times (with the exception of the regular Lambda update), providing monthly news and events. *Wilde Times* was more focused on a broader range of cultural programming in the city – theatre, ballet, new movies, the symphony, et cetera, and usually offered readers an article about gay culture or history. In part this made astute publishing sense, given that the city had, at times, three monthly newsletters serving gay and lesbian members in Winnipeg – *What's Happening*, *Out and About*, and *Wilde Times*. Where once tensions within the organizations had been quite strong, particularly between Happenings and any organization deemed to be "political," financially, this was no longer tenable. At various times, the groups were partnering and sending out joint newsletters to their members.

Another way that increasing interaction was evident was that with three organizations holding fundraising community socials, the community reached the saturation point. In November 1981 the first joint social held to benefit Happenings, OWMS, and PL was held and over six hundred people attended.[110] Because records were kept of attendance, published reports indicated that 13 per cent of those in attendance were from outside the province, people from Saskatchewan, North and South Dakota, Minnesota, Alberta, British Columbia, and northwestern Ontario and, high praise, "one flew in from Toronto the same evening when he found out about the social."[111] At its height, Doug Nicholson, a founding member of OWMS, remembered that the organization had over six hundred members.[112]

Another way to gauge success, and a really important one given the fissures within Winnipeg's community, was that the board of Happenings committed itself to working with PL and OWMS to make a gay community centre a reality. According to Happenings directors, "the co-operation between the Winnipeg Gay Organizations which began to be channelled formally last fall into the Manitoba Coalition of Gay Organizations, is beginning to result in projects of real value to our community."[113] In that same issue, members were informed that rental space on Sherbrooke St was being considered for leasing for the Giovanni's Room, The Winnipeg Gay Community Centre. The PL board and OWMS decided to go ahead, PL committing $10,000 of their reserve fund and OWMS $4,000 to renovations, most of it done with volunteer labour and energies. By March 1982, they took possession of what would become Giovanni's Room, The Winnipeg Gay Community Centre, on Sherbrooke St. Opened later that spring, the centre was a source of pride for those who had the dream through the 1970s (and earlier) of such a place where people could proudly assert their identity. In "Lambda Update," the author commented upon the accomplishment the centre represented in terms of determination and cooperation within the community. Equally, he noted:

> I sat with an older friend the other night at the Centre who told me he thought he would never see the day this would happen ... He was so wrought up their were genuine tears in his eyes and he only wished some of his friends, now departed, were here to see it.[114]

Not everyone felt pride when they looked at that sign. First, it clearly did not opt for the conventional yoking of "gay and lesbian" but was clearly a "gay" centre. In subsequent published comments many well-intentioned organizers behind the centre bemoaned the lack of women's participation. While those were genuine concerns, it seems curious that they did not realize that inclusive signage (which is now common) might be partly responsible. For others, any overt indicator of sexuality created a backlash. By coincidence, Gio's (as it would later be called) was located across the street from Happenings Social Club, an organization that continued its practice of eschewing any visible public signage. While its board might have supported the gay centre venture, some members did not because they remained closeted and fearful of both violent reprisals from straight harassers and of revealing their sexuality. Such individuals would not enter spaces marked "gay." Furthermore, some were enraged that such signs existed, for example:

> I stood in line one Friday night at the Club (Happenings) waiting to get in and heard some goon talk. It alarmed me and my friends ... These are some of OUR PEOPLE talking about going outside, finding some rocks and smashing the neon sign at the Centre! ... Great this is just what the straights want. Lets murder ourselves! Remember, it's our dollars that are going into the Centre. Lets ALL have the sense to understand times have

indeed changed. We do not all necessarily changed with them. Its personal freedom of choice … but do respect your gay brothers and sisters that have and are changing! [115]

More positively, in May 1983 the Mutual Friendship Society approved a grant of two hundred dollars per month to the Winnipeg Gay Community Centre to "pay the rent on one of the suite annex that will be used to house counselling, clinical and meeting purposes for gays and lesbians."[116] Perhaps even more momentous than this entente between Happenings, OWMS (managers of the centre), and PL was the news that Happenings had purchased their building at 272 Sherbrooke St. Property ownership had been part of Happenings goals from the beginning, hence their determination to get incorporated and raise funds. With considerable pride they announced this accomplishment on their twelfth anniversary.

On Saturday at four pm the plaque, placed on the north wall of the building was unveiled amidst great fan-fare and celebration. It as a proud, nostalgic event … Many officials of our organizations were present including Lyle Dick, Chairman, Project Lambda … Chris Vogel of Gays for Equality and Ted Millward of the Council for Homosexuality and Religion who read a most commendable letter from the Council congratulating the Club as being the pioneer leader of our gay/lesbian history. Benny B. (a Charter member of Happenings) cut the ribbon. The Club was decorated with huge white banners proclaiming in brilliant letters… It's ours … we OWN the building.[117]

Later that evening, at an anniversary social on Higgins Avenue, Paul S. "put on a 21 minute nostalgic review of music from Manitoba Avenue and there were indeed misty eyes on the dance floor."[118]

Conclusion

Community building in Winnipeg took many forms in the years 1970–85. In contrast to the previous era, where gays and lesbians met in mixed commercial spaces, socialized at home in house parties, or cruised well-known landmarks such as the hill, 1970–85 witnessed the growth of gay-owned and -operated spaces. Prime among them was Happenings Social Club, which operated from 1970 to 2009, making it one of the longest-running gay and lesbian social spaces in Canada.[119] Many cities had such spaces and thus this was not unique in terms of queer socializing, nor was it as activist and visible as it could be, avoiding the use of the terms gay or lesbian on the doors until the late twentieth century – long after clubs in cities such as Regina, Saskatoon, and Edmonton had pushed through that barrier. And well after other shorter-lived ventures in Winnipeg had explicitly claimed gay and/or lesbian spaces. "Big closet" to some detractors, "safe space" to others, Happenings was a place where many Winnipeg gays and lesbians went to socialize – even, sometimes, the activists who were so critical of what they perceived as a failure of confidence.

Happenings's chief foil during this era of significant community and organizational building was Gays for Equality. GFE, originally created on the University of Manitoba campus, and based upon an earlier, American model at the University of Minnesota–Minneapolis, was the driving force for education, counselling, culture, and liberationist politics in the city. Drawing upon a small nucleus of gay male activists, notably the duo of Richard North and Chris Vogel, GFE offered wide-ranging services – indeed it approximated a gay social services organization, with its information and counselling hotline; various support and information groups; coffee houses; library; and at various times, newsletters and cultural materials. GFE was the incubator for many other separate organizations – most notably the Council on Homosexuality and Religion – but also Project Lambda, the Oscar Wilde Society, the Ideas Factory, and more. Some shared personnel with GFE, others sprang from GFE initiatives, or with modest funding from GFE, such as the gay radio programming and later "Coming Out Television." Only the short-lived *After Stonewall* Collective was entirely independent of GFE personnel, thanks to the originating collective, but also their more leftist political perspective. GFE was not terribly lesbian friendly, although a handful of women did participate on the phone line and in various activist ventures with gay male activists. GFE was often at odds with the conservatives who dominated the membership at Happenings, and by turns, GFE was either polarizing or persuasive. Winnipeg lesbians were active in a series of their own social, community, and activist spaces, at times organized in the Women's Building, at other times in a series of venues and locations in the north end or downtown. The women's groups came and went more quickly, largely due to the fact that they were financially more tenuous than GFE's male activists (many of whom were employed by government, government agencies, or in various university positions) or than the mixed audience of wealthier members at Happenings. Part of a broader framework of feminist and women's cultural activities, these lesbian organizations were in the anomalous situation of both having greater support upon which to draw (particularly for spaces, et cetera), and yet were more hampered by political debates within the feminist groups and their organizations over how openly they wished to be identified with lesbian politics and to support lesbian issues.

From 1970 to 1985, Winnipeg residents had opportunities to engage with a variety of gay and lesbian organizations, media, cultural products, and a range of spaces in which to discuss, debate, dance, and socialize. It was a far cry from the "old days" when house parties of ten to fifteen people had seemed exhilarating. It brought Winnipeg into line with developments in other major North American cities, and made the lesbian and gay community visible in a way that it had not been before. Support for newcomers to the city, for those individuals coming out as lesbian or gay, as well as many cultural and educational materials about gay and lesbian history, literature, music, et cetera, were all readily available in Winnipeg. Despite North's description above of Winnipeg's conservatism and provincialism, the fact that a program such as "Coming Out TV" was scheduled in the prime evening hours, on a local cable television station, and that it continued for seven hundred shows, featuring a range of politicians, cultural producers, academics, local activists, and queer performers was astonishing. Many years later, the creators of Pride TV would face an uphill battle against the discriminatory tactics of Shaw Cable whose decision to keep it listed as a separate, "adult" channel (which cost subscribers a premium) disastrously affected their audience share. Pride TV was really aimed at the urban, metronormative gay viewer; it was not, as packaged or characterized by Shaw Cable, an adult channel (meaning porn) that should command a premium subscription and marginal categorization to the "adult channel" periphery. Winnipeg's savvy crew of dedicated activists and cultural producers exploited a cablevision loophole (local programming), and, in so doing, beamed "queerness" into every Winnipeg household on Saturday evenings. Apologies to Stompin' Tom Connors, but this was not your typical "Winnipeg Saturday night."[120] Such visibility, as we shall see in the final chapter about Winnipeg activism, could elicit support and certainly made it easier to be gay and lesbian in the city, but it could also induce reprisals. There was violence in the city, gay bashings were not uncommon, but beyond such physical violence, there were also reprisals from government, media, and big business, who feared the increasing openness of the lesbian and gay population. The visibility stimulated by GFE programming, politics, and community building also sparked internal tensions between those women and men who were content to socialize at Happenings (and "live their lives") and those liberationist activists who dreamed a bigger dream of a more inclusive Winnipeg.

Chapter Four

Grassroots: Organizational and Social Opportunities in Saskatoon and Regina, 1971–1985

I got involved in everything, the dances, the phone line, God I can't forget Metamorphosis, one of the highlights of my life. Every year at Thanksgiving we had a three day event, people from all the over the country used to come, Winnipeg, Regina, Calgary, Vancouver, Toronto … Metamorphosis gave me that outlet (to volunteer), gave me that connection with the rest of the world and the rest of the prairie provinces, gave me a feeling of belonging.[1]

Marion Alexander, Saskatoon, 2002

In 1969, *Maclean's* profiled the city of Saskatoon and proclaimed it a place where you could "live the good life."[2] Writer Jeannine Locke's story started with some compelling "facts" to prove her point. She enumerated Saskatoon's history of economic challenges (the lingering effects of the Depression), the pros and cons of geographic isolation, and it's recent transformation as the "potash capital of the world." However, the city's 130,000 residents were fortunate to have two other longstanding advantages: first, its central location, the "hub city" for various agricultural and transportation networks, and, second, the provincial university, the University of Saskatchewan (U of S). U of S was a large enterprise, complete with medical, veterinary, and other professional colleges, which gave Saskatoon a key advantage – economically, culturally, and socially. Long before Richard Florida's notion of the "creative classes" emerged as a trendy way to categorize energized, livable cities, Locke's description of Saskatchewan fit that bill.[3] Government workers, RCMP recruits, politicians, and the province's key bureaucrats called Regina home while Saskatoon took the cultural and economic laurels. In this "civilized city," people "enjoyed amenities that in other cities are reserved for the rich" such as art galleries, symphonies, and theatre.[4] Urban historian Alan Artibise, characterized Saskatoon as "one of the more dynamic prairie cities" in the post–Second World War era.[5] One of the major drivers of these changes in the 1970s was a resource boom, "based on minerals rather than wheat," and Saskatoon faced "problems of rapid growth first experienced in the boom era of the 1900–1913."[6] Wealth and amenities certainly were central, but Saskatoon's livability was also attributed to the ethos of Saskatoon residents. "Passivity" according to Locke, "is not socially acceptable in Saskatoon. Its people have always been remarkably ambitious, not only for themselves and their children, but also for their society. Prosperity has not withered either their pioneer spirit or western chip on their shoulder ... the fact that easterners and even their coastal neighbours to the west have long regarded them as prairie rednecks has something to do with the eagerness of Saskatonians to find their own solutions to their problems and prove that they belong in the national big league."[7] After all, in their desire to win the bid for the 1971 Canada Winter Games, this was the city that promised to "build" a mountain for the ski events!

Maclean's 1969 snapshot of Saskatoon offers a timely introduction to this chapter, as the growth of the queer, and later gay and lesbian communities, also began to accelerate in the late 1960s through the early 1970s. Based upon oral and archival materials, this chapter summarizes the important lesbian and gay social, cultural, and organizational developments in Saskatoon and Regina from 1970 through to 1985. This exploration of "queer" life and networks in those cities includes an analysis of the integration between lesbians and gay men and of the mainstream population's reaction to the queer minorities in their midst. While the smallest cities in this study, evidence illustrates that Saskatoon was punching above its weight. Regina, always in Saskatoon's shadow when it came to queer organizations, nevertheless had a well-established gay and lesbian club and episodic moments of political activity worth highlighting.

Saskatoon's Good Life: Gay and Lesbian Style

While Jeannine Locke did not feature any gays or lesbians who were living the "good life" in Saskatoon, in 1969 some clearly were. Unlike Winnipeg, which had a very strong folk music scene, or the attractions of Vancouver's climate and vibe that drew hippies, iconoclasts, and queers to the west coast city, Saskatoon's good life and charms were more circumscribed. Initially, other than the park and a series of popular cruising sites in tea rooms (public toilets) in the downtown core, or the beer parlours in downtown hotels, the selection of "queer" spots in Saskatoon was limited. Indeed, for those intent on moving beyond the search for same-sex male partners to an engagement with building self-identified gay and lesbian spaces, it became evident that organizational development was a requirement. Younger gays and lesbians, largely but not all baby boomers, wanted more than just cruising spots and watering holes. As David Rimmer so eloquently noted "there was no place to go, no organized groups or anything of that nature which meant just basically the toilet culture which I didn't find particularly appealing."[8]

As in Winnipeg, Saskatoon residents carved out pockets of "queer spaces" where gays and some lesbians could congregate. In the late 1960s and early 1970s the Cove at the King George Hotel was the place to be seen, while others frequented the Carousal Room (a beverage room) at the Bessborough Hotel, Saskatoon's landmark "railway" hotel on the city's riverbank. While it was true that select bars had functioned in this way previously, Bruce Garman and Gens Hellquist actively recalled trying to establish one key downtown bar, so that gay men (in particular) but also a few lesbians had access to commercial social spaces.[9] In a city flush with cash, and short on amenities to handle the pent-up demand, even bar space was at a premium, and gay drinkers soon found themselves pushed out of both of those prime, downtown locations. In 1971, the Apollo Room at the Ritz Hotel, at 118 21st E, became their new local. Decorated with murals of the lunar landing on the walls, the Apollo was variously recalled as seedy or romanticized as a "hippie" hangout. Fans of the Apollo were legion, noting that upwards of fifty gay people could be found there many evenings, socializing and drinking, and that its relaxed ambience and reputation for attracting an alternative mixture of downtown working-class residents and workers, university students, and queer people made it an easy place to congregate. Apollo staff was aware of their diverse clientele, protective and particularly keen to avoid police harassment, and this bar became a fixture in the downtown core until its closure in 1985.

Various house party circuits were also operational. Lesbians had, potentially, opportunities to meet other lesbians via team sports. Women's baseball and softball leagues were popular while in the winter attention shifted to curling. But, and this is often forgotten when historians reflexively enumerate the importance of the house parties, you had to be invited. Waiting and hoping for an invitation could, in some cases, take years to materialize. Selena described the process as "having to be in a situation where it evolves, this particular person [teammate] might invite you to something at their place." It would be a casual invitation to a party, and when you arrived it might be a conventional party, with straight couples, or it might be a party where "the first thing you realize is they are all women."[10] This could take years to play out. And once it did, the onus was on the neophyte. Could she fit in? Could she learn this largely middle-class lesbian code of conduct (discretion, privacy, respectability)? Asked to comment on the nature of these parties, Selena reported that these lesbian sporting circles were not rowdy affairs. Groups of women, largely couples, enjoyed food, some drinks, conversation, and music. All appreciated the rare ability to let down their hair within an all-female social circle. Selena remembered little, if any, physical affection on display, no dancing, just an evening of socializing.

While the "rules" at those house parties were specific to the middle-class women who hosted and attended them, the desire to secure an invitation to exclusive house parties was also recollected by many male narrators. The A-list gay male parties, hosted by the faculty bon vivants, Dan Nalbach and Don McNamee, were highly coveted.[11] The male parties were more ribald affairs. And, in retrospect, interviewees' recollections of them were more mixed. Some narrators enjoyed these parties for their bacchanalian adventures, wild clothes, camp bitchiness, and the way that Nalbach and McNamee held court. Some men were buttoned up and nervous, and those individuals preferred to come early and leave quickly. Some others famously arrived in drag. Trendsetters arrived wearing "mustard bell bottom trousers" prepared to fully embrace the evening's liberatory possibilities.[12] Nalbach's networks were extensive; narrators remembered he had recipe cardholders filled with contact names in Saskatoon as well as within the region. When he hosted parties he made sure that word reached gay male residents in Regina, Winnipeg, Edmonton, and beyond. Years later, Tom Warner, writing for *The Body Politic*, described these parties as "sordid and sad."[13] One issue concerned the "rules" for these parties – some were uncomfortable with the rules that Nalbach set. According to Gens Hellquist, challenge arose over the matriarchal "family" system, in which men were given women's camp names (by their hosts) and linked in elaborate "families" with mothers, aunts, and sisters.[14] Nalbach "was known as Gladys Stofford, the matriarch of the Stofford family."[15] When he died, in 1997, his *Perceptions* obituary indicated he was "survived by his three Stofford daughters in Saskatoon, and blood family in Buffalo, New York." Some enjoyed this style of gay male camp culture and others loathed it.[16] And, for younger gay men, many of whom were interested in gay politics, this older preliberationist socializing was at odds with their views of gender and sexuality.[17] Those who made their views strongly heard were excommunicated. Such shunning was not subtle, and it proved painful in a small city like Saskatoon with limited alternatives. Dedicated spaces, which could be open to all gay and lesbians regardless of their age, political views, identities, or social capital, became an increasingly attractive option.

Regina: In Search of a Few Good Men

In 2003, I interviewed Leonard Lawrence* (b. 1943), a retired SaskTel employee, a founding member of the Gay Community of Regina, and former Happenings (Winnipeg) member. He generously provided me with a candid, often poignant, life history of his experiences from a rather idyllic youth in a small southwestern Saskatchewan town, through his career in banking and crown corporations, and his experiences as a gay man in Regina.[18] Here, he tells of the process by which he finally located queer space in Regina, in 1968, at the age of 25:

> LL: I got in touch with one of the people who [I] used to fool around with as a kid who moved to Regina. He didn't live there anymore but I was desperate to find people and he gave me a name of someone to call. He wasn't all that helpful, all he wanted to do was have sex. He told me about a place where they busted people, which they did, but I never had the guts enough to go in there. So I used to sit outside, and I noticed this one guy went in and out about five or six times and I followed him. He's dead now, E. And we talked … He asked me if I was looking to fool around with another guy? … I said I wasn't really looking to fool around, but I wanted to know where the other men were. And he said, "oh, they all go to the Hotel Saskatchewan basement to drink." Then I was too chicken to go so he took me, it was 1968, I believe …
>
> VJK: What was it like to go to the Hotel Saskatchewan for the first time with a gay man?
>
> LL: Scary … They called it the Coachman … the north end of the bar was just about all gay, the south end was straight and they never really intermingled.

VJK: Did the south end know about the north end?

LL: A lot of them didn't ... And yet there would be forty people sitting there at a time.

VJK: Primarily men, some women, or all men?

LL: Primarily men and the big deal then was everyone was going drinking on a Friday or Saturday night hoping that somebody would have a house party ... At the first house party I went to ... I saw two men dancing together and I thought it was disgusting and I left, but I went back – ha ha ha – the next time there was a party! E clued me in, that men didn't just have sex together they did other things.

Similar to many other prairie cities, queer space in the railway hotel beverage rooms, usually located in the basement of these buildings (not the more upscale lounges, which still remain to this day), was well known to those insiders and travellers. But, as LL's history reminds us, this was a rather indistinguishable crowd who were purposely trying to blend into the space, and so everyone had a story to tell of their initiation into this world. Venues changed over time, as Regina entered the era of clearly defined gay and lesbian spaces, most notably with their beloved, long-standing Gay Community of Regina club, but the emphasis in Regina was primarily on creating social spaces.[19]

Saskatchewan's capital city was, in many respects, an entirely different sort of "queer" town than its northern neighbour. It was more furtive, it tended to lag slightly behind Saskatoon in the creation of explicitly gay and lesbian community spaces, and politically it was far less inclined towards overt gay and lesbian activism. Archival information, corroborated by my narrators, provides evidence that Saskatoon was a more queer politicized city and, conversely, that Regina residents were more interested in socializing at their club, which now holds the title as the longest running queer club in the prairies.[20] Participants attributed Regina's difference to three factors. First, this conservatism, which many called "paranoia," was attributed to being the provincial capital city. Those interested in working for government, whether in the provincial civil service or the various crown corporations (SaskTel, SaskEnergy, Saskatchewan Government Insurance, et cetera), were cautious about jeopardizing their careers. Unlike Winnipeg and Edmonton, also provincial capital cities, Regina's smaller size meant that it retained a more "small-town" mentality with respect to matters of surveillance and lack of privacy.

Lesbian narrator Debbie Simmons (b. 1955) recalled: "It [the University of Saskatchewan] is certainly part of a more liberal attitude of the people who live here [Saskatoon]. I always make a real stark comparison to having grown up in Regina. Regina is a government and RCMP town and when you move from that to Saskatoon, which is a university town, the differences are … night and day."[21] Pushed to elaborate further, particularly about the RCMP presence in Regina and how that affected her recollection of her teenage years in Regina, Simmons said: "You only have to be young in that city, with F Barracks full of cadets to recognize how the cities are different. It's like living in a military town. It changes the flavour of the community."[22]

Curiously, while Saskatoon had the stronger gay and lesbian political movement, producing gay and lesbian political leaders whose creation of various organizations, political events, cultural initiatives, and political lobbying/protest organizations were legion (see chapter 7 for more details), it would be mischaracterization to leave the impression that residents of Regina were uniformly "less political." Narrators recalled strong leftist organizations in Regina; for example, Jan Harvey (b. 1953) said: "Regina was a very politically active place on the left. There was a lot happening, the U of R was more political than the U of S," but "Saskatoon also had an active women's movement and active gay movement."[23] The University of Regina was originally established as Regina College, a liberal arts college affiliated with the provincial university in Saskatoon. It received its charter as a separate university in 1974. And yet, when Jan Harvey "came out [in 1979] if you wanted to be active as a gay person in Saskatchewan you moved to Saskatoon. Because that seemed to be where most of the activity was."[24] Aware that this was a "gross generalization," Debbie Simmons reported that the "visible gay community in Regina was all about socializing. The gay community in Saskatoon was about organizing. That's what made it different." Neither city was immune from violence, and in interviews lesbian narrators matter-of-factly spoke about homophobic violence as well as fights among lesbians at dances and how this necessitated extra security. In Simmons's recollections, Regina was a tougher crowd, even in the 1980s. She reported, "the women used to come to the bar with knives in their boots. [I]t was [like] the fifties."[25]

While residents of the two larger cities did drive back and forth for events, Regina drew participants from the southern areas of the province, and evidence suggests that it was also a draw for Americans living in North Dakota.[26] Regina was the largest major centre in the region and so it appears to have been a destination for rural and small-town North Dakota residents. In the 1980s, there were attempts to engage in regular outreach with residents of Estevan, Saskatchewan, and points south. By car, both Calgary and Winnipeg were within an easy day's drive, and so residents of Regina routinely travelled to Winnipeg for gay and lesbian events, including socializing at Happenings, drag shows and celebrations, and for the lesbian, folk music scene in Winnipeg.

As Leonard Lawrence's history at the outset of this section enumerated, informal socializing in Regina had followed established patterns similar to elsewhere with the mixed use of railway hotel bars. The Hotel Saskatchewan's Coachman bar, on Victoria Ave in Regina, was a key destination. In the 1960s and early 1970s, the north end of the Coachman bar was home to a group of gay male patrons, ranging in ages from twenty-one to seventy. The south end was largely straight, and popular with university students from the University of Regina.[27] One of those students, Brian Gladwell, wryly noted in his interview that he had been one of the student activists from the University of Regina drinking in the south end of the bar: "For years, I had not a clue that the people I was most desperate to meet were in the same bar as me."[28]

Opposite the Hotel Saskatchewan was Victoria Park, a small, urban park that was popular for cruising given its proximity to the hotel, but also for its relative safety. Leonard Lawrence recalled "pickups" being made in Victoria Park. While most interviewees recalled learning about cruising venues from other men, or by happenstance, as they were strolling, driving, or bicycling around the city streets, one recalled being warned about such places by his parents. Paul Gessell who grew up in Moose Jaw, Saskatchewan, recalled staying with his family at the Hotel Saskatchewan. Gessell's mother "warned him about the park" and the men who congregated there in the evenings. As a child he remembered being mystified by what she meant, but sensed not to ask for more details. Later, as an adult, he was shocked when it dawned on him that "you are that person," the "deviant" who his mother had warned him about.[29] Working-class and poor inner-city residents eventually displaced Victoria Park's gay male population. Then, gay male cruising activities in the downtown core took place on city streets, particularly the 2,000 and 2,100 blocks of Scarth Street.[30] Another major green space in the city, Wascana Park, a treed area of the city near the provincial legislature, was another cruising site (particularly the College Avenue section). Wascana Park was recalled as more dangerous because it was more isolated and had little evening foot traffic. Regina's downtown shopping mall, the Cornwall Centre, also featured gay male contact and cruising areas, primarily tea rooms. The Copper Kettle, a popular Regina institution, was a convenient spot for lunch, or postwork drinks.[31] Its proximity to Victoria Park, which it faces, made it a "nice spot" for a meal and conversation, according to Lawrence.

Saskatoon's Age of Aquarius

While interviewees laughingly estimated that there were only a handful of hippies in the 1960s, the value of an ever-changing population of students and faculty at the University of Saskatchewan meant that cultural trends and currents eventually reached the city.[32] David Rimmer recalled that when he was in his final year of high school, in 1969, he spent time hanging out at a downtown coffee house, the Shad Rack. Part of its charm was its illicitness, as it was spot for trendsetters thrilled to enter via a back alley "front door," smoke cigarettes, drink coffee, and indulge in the occasional joint. Rimmer wasn't certain he had enough street cred for this place, but he persevered and eventually met another young man, a recent transfer from Vancouver who revealed that he was "bisexual," and they initiated an affair.

The optimism sparked by Saskatoon's economic and cultural expansion in the 1960s was shared by a handful of queer people. Saskatonians could read Vancouver's alternative newspaper the *Georgia Straight*, which providing tantalizing glimpses of a "gay world" that existed beyond the parks, bars, and tea rooms. The *Georgia Straight* brought news of gay-owned and -operated spaces, and of the stirrings of political arguments in favour of legal recognition for gay people. For example, Canada's first gay political organization, the Association for Social Knowledge (ASK), was launched in Vancouver in 1965. Encouraged by news of the establishment of gay social clubs in Calgary and Edmonton, Gens Hellquist and Dan Nalbach took the pivotal first step for Saskatoon, when they placed a simple one line ad in the March 1971 issue of the *Georgia Straight*'s alternative listings section of the paper: "Saskatoon Gay Liberation, Box 3043, Saskatoon, SK."[33] Hellquist shared that he had never relinquished that post office box number (over thirty years later) because of its significance to his work and life in Saskatoon. As mentioned previously, it is important to highlight that Nalbach, and a handful of other early activists, were Americans or had studied in the US (McNamee). This meant that they drew upon transnational queer networks – social, political, and cultural – and thus enriched the queer culture and politics emerging in Saskatoon. Nalbach left in the mid-1970s and so his local contributions appeared to cease at that time, but he was remembered for an influential role as an "early founder."[34] A few men and one woman, Dorothy, "the original lesbian," responded to the *Georgia Straight* ad.[35] That original trio decided, after conversations, to send letters to the other people they knew who were gay – all twelve of them!

That fall, Hellquist, Nalbach, Bruce Garman, and Tom Warner launched two campus gay organizations, The Gay Students Alliance at the University of Saskatchewan and Saskatoon Gay Action (see below).[36] At the same time, respondents to the *Georgia Straight* ad met to discuss the creation of dedicated gay social spaces. Fundraisers were held, often in McNamee's home, to help kick-start these efforts. Progress was swift, and initially Hellquist recalled "in many ways things have been too damn easy for us." Zodiac Friendship Society received its provincial charter in March 1972.[37] Similar to other prairie cities, they purposefully chose a slightly playful, coded name that would not trigger concerns or cause cautious members to avoid the group for fear of exposure. According to their newsletter, the name Gemini was chosen because, as the astrological sign of "twin warriors," Hellquist wrote, "many of us feel like warriors at times fighting to hold our heads up in this bigoted society. Hopefully Gemini Club will be a place where all gay people can hold their head up and be proud to be gay."[38] Within this organizational umbrella were two primary wings: the social wing, the Gemini Club, which was tasked with organizing dances and other social events, and the political wing, Saskatoon Gay Action, which was dedicated to activism. Saskatoon Gay Action used the funds raised by the dances and community fundraisers to provide funds for government lobbying and activism. This organizational structure was modelled after the members-only clubs established in Edmonton (Club 70), Calgary (Club Carousel), and Winnipeg (Happenings).

Notably, Zodiac Fellowship Society did not face the hurdles that the Winnipeg groups faced – either in chartering their non-profit organization or in advertising themselves in the city's local newspaper, *The Star Phoenix* (SP). The SP willingly ran their small classified ads. Dorothy remembered some readers were confused by the ad: "Our first ad in *The Star Phoenix* asked interested gays to phone or write. We quickly learned that the word 'gay' seemed to mean 'merry band' or 'swinging singles' to many people so we coerced the *Star* into taking an ad wherein we called ourselves 'homosexuals' – a major effort. Anyway,

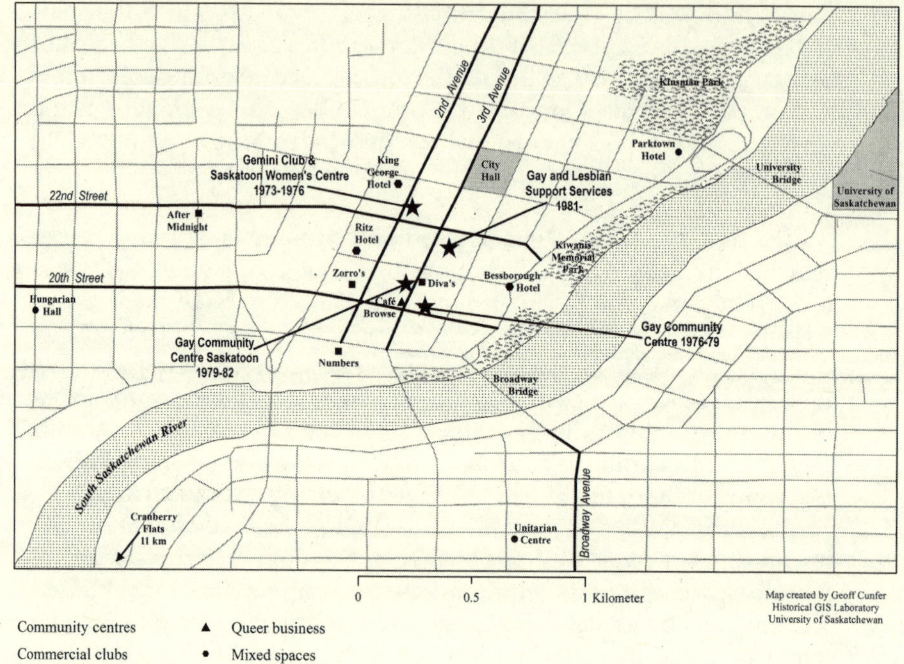

4.1 Downtown Saskatoon queer spaces, 1960–2000. Copyright Geoff Cunfer, 2017.

we've come a long way since then when ten was considered a crowd."[39] As I've indicated elsewhere, terminological issues are of prime importance to historians of sexuality. The fact that some residents of Saskatoon still did not know what "gay" meant in the early 1970s, and that to clarify their advertisements Zodiac Fellowship Society used the term "homosexual," illustrates a gap between insiders and outsiders. Dorothy's comments also clearly explain that using the term homosexual – a word many queer people considered pejorative – was not the group's first choice, but local confusion necessitated it.

As news spread about the organization, they began planning for the first Gemini Club dance, held on 11 February 1972 at the Unitarian Centre, 502 Main St E, a couple of blocks off Broadway on the city's east side. Paul Gessell was one of those earlier responders to the advertisement and he attended that first dance. Attendance at dances was very strong in contrast to political action groups. Gessell remembered a varied group of people from Saskatoon, but also people from other cities including Prince Albert, North Battleford, and rural areas, including a farmer from Davidson, Saskatchewan.[40] A journalist, Gessell's observations were particularly useful as he remembered the crowd as an all-white group in which university students predominated, but that also included professors, students, farmers, more "conservative" types, and married people. In the early 1970s, he remembered that people were more sympathetic to the presence of heterosexually married men, viewing the gay and lesbian "community" as a diverse one, in which, he wryly recalled, they were "all in it together."[41]

These dances were incredibly popular and they raised funds (in addition to those from the earlier house parties), which allowed the Gemini Club to begin renting space in March 1973. Located at 124A 2nd Avenue N, the main downtown commercial artery, this upstairs location gave Saskatoon the distinction of having the first gay centre in the prairies, and only the second centre in the country (Toronto had the first). The Gemini Club was across the hall from the Saskatoon Women's Centre.[42] This proximity was an educational opportunity for both groups. My narrators recalled that a small core of feminist lesbians began to participate in local gay activism, changing the groups' focus and analysis. The Gemini Club housed a small library of fiction and non-fiction books and provided a space for gay and lesbian drop-ins (Friday night was the lesbian drop-in night). As it evolved, it would include a telephone information and helpline; coffee houses; spaces for political meetings; and either a location for, or organizing committee space for, community dances.

Gay and lesbian socializing at community dances was a formative development in the early 1970s. People routinely flocked from surrounding cities, smaller towns, and rural areas to attend. These dances also enabled a growing public awareness of gay and lesbian residents. The vast majority of gay and lesbian participants were primarily focused on the dances and pleasure derived from mingling with other gays and lesbians. However, it would be misguided to view those moments as "merely" social or to discount the value of such socializing. Gessell recalled, "it was like being a Communist in the McCarthy era … sitting in a room with other gay people was a very political act" because "family, church, and school said it was wrong."[43] In addition to the value of being surrounded by other queer people, dances and social events served to draw individuals into gay and lesbian organizations, familiarizing them with individuals outside their own, smaller circles, and gradually participants were exposed to varying views about "gay liberation" politics – in discussions, via support for activist causes or legal cases, and by virtue of the access these events provided to newsletters, literature and, in particular, gay and lesbian publications. The "national" gay and lesbian newspaper, *The Body Politic* (produced in Toronto), was sold at dances. *The Body Politic* wrote a series of articles about Saskatoon's community and its accomplishments in 1977, and ranked them as the "best" gay and lesbian community centre in the country.[44] One could not dispute, that in resolutely heterosexual western Canada, there were substantial liberatory possibilities inherent in same-sex couples dancing together to a mix of popular and country music. Fundraising dances, as opposed to the regular Gemini Club membership nights, also offered the possibility of outreach to the straight community, and it was not uncommon for straight allies – friends, colleagues, neighbours – to attend these dances. Some "straights" were motivated to support the cause because of their friendships with gay and lesbian colleagues and students, but also because it marked them as liberals. Gay and lesbian participants were divided about this support. The more conservative were worried and fearful that "straight voyeurs" (their words) might spot them at these events and out them. This was a legitimate concern given the city's size and given the risks discreet queers faced when they ventured out for an evening of socializing. Those who practiced "discretion" (their words) about their sexuality resented the fact that with all the bars and clubs to choose from, straights opted for the only space that was available to queer people. Those people who were comfortably out and open about their sexuality, or more political about sexual identity, "were anxious to make the dances as open as possible; what we were fighting for, after all, was nothing less than complete integration into society."[45]

Peter Millard, a professor of English at the University of Saskatchewan, wrote an article about one such night, an honest rendering of the alliances and tensions found on the dance floor: "When I arrived at the little hall, it was packed. It was a fancy-dress affair and people had entered into the spirit. Men with a body that could get away with it were stripped to the waist, lesbians seemed to favour black tie, and there was colour and excitement everywhere. Straight and gay people danced with each other, straight couples and gay couples mingled, all without any sense of unnaturalness." Reflecting on this scene, Millard poignantly wondered, "Why on earth it could not always be like this?" Marvellously, one of those straight participants published his views about what it was like to participate in a gay and lesbian community dance. William Slights, a colleague of Millard's, reported that he didn't hesitate to buy tickets to a benefit dance for a lesbian mother at risk of losing her child but he worried, "what if some gay woman made sexual advances to my wife when I left her alone? And if she liked it, where would that leave me?"[46] Where indeed? Historians of sexuality have tended to frame such alliances and inclusivity as signposts of political engagement, yet Slights's anxieties remind us that human motivations and experiences are seldom so one-dimensional. We need to be alert to the tangled webs of motivations, feelings, anxieties, and fears that underlay both straight and queer participation in such evenings. They were far from uncomplicated affairs, and in their rareness were memorable for a host of reasons, even if the prevailing narrative is to read them as moments of respite and release in a sea of heterosexual dominance.

If the mere act of socializing could be construed as fraught with tensions, anxieties, and fears of disclosures, then the corollary step of engagement in explicitly gay and lesbian politics was an even larger bridge to cross. And, not one the majority of Saskatonians were comfortable making. Millard's insights into why this was are helpful reminders of the tensions, class, and educational privileges potentially forfeited, and the very real fears of violent retributions: "Like so many older, closeted gays, I was made uneasy by the actions of gay liberationists. The fear was twofold: first, that their actions would make the public more aware of homosexuality thus increasing the danger of being exposed, second, that they would prompt an unleashing of heterosexual hatred against us."[47] Similar to the fears expressed in Winnipeg over the overt actions of Gays for Equality, Millard observed that despite increasing "tolerance" of gay activity "homosexuals like me still depended on invisibility and people's ignorance; this Gay Liberation rocking of the boat was alarming." It is important to note that in Millard's reflections, his language choices were deliberate – those closeted types were "homosexuals," whereas the out activists were "gay." Despite his concerns, Millard crossed the Rubicon in dramatic fashion, coming out publicly during a boisterous University of Saskatchewan Student Union (USSU) debate in 1974 (see below), and henceforward he was fearless in his defence of gay faculty members and students, taking pride in his status as the token gay faculty member.[48]

"Pride" in the Prairies

Another landmark achievement in 1973 was the city's first pride celebration, held on Labour Day weekend. The Gemini Club organized a picnic and social events at Cranberry Flats. Cranberry Flats is a well-known recreational area (nicknamed "bare-ass beach" for its popularity as a nude sunbathing spot) on the bank of the South Saskatchewan River at the city's edge. This daylong event was not without controversy (see chapter 7 for details of the city's refusal to designate this weekend as an official civic event). However, it demonstrated that the activists in Saskatoon Gay Action were eager to develop events that merged social, political, and community outreach goals (to attract larger numbers of lesbian and gay people to the centre's activities). A month later, Winnipeg hosted their pride week events. The vast majority of contemporary pride events tend to commemorate a key American moment in GLBT activism, the Stonewall Riots in New York City, which occurred in June 1969. However, in the early 1970s, a number of pride events and initiatives emerged across North American cities. Some, like those in New York City, referenced the Stonewall Riot dates and were held in June. Others were held throughout the summer and fall – commemorating a variety of dates or selected in conjunction with particular campus, urban, or activist dates/events.

Within the Canadian context, the hosting of two pride events in 1973, in Saskatoon and Winnipeg, was significant. Vancouver, Montreal, and Toronto would all inaugurate their pride traditions later, in 1978, 1979, and 1981 respectively, although there is evidence to suggest that early pride-like events were held in Vancouver in the early 1970s. Sexualities histories resist progressive narratives. These early pride events were not sustained, and due to a variety of circumstances, particularly the demands on volunteer organizers, provincial and urban politics, and the onset of the AIDS epidemic, many cities had long fallow periods before pride events were resurrected. For example, pride events were not held in Saskatoon for a decade, between 1980–90. Calgary and Edmonton would not introduce pride events until the 1980s, and then it took a few years before organizers felt confident to launch pride parades (now considered a central focal point of pride celebrations). Regina hosted their first pride events, including a parade, in 1990. Jean Hillabold recalled that the pride committee organized a mask-making party before the parade, so that people could make masks and hence feel more comfortable to participate. Hillabold recalled that many

Regina gays and lesbians felt that they might risk their employment, or perhaps be attacked, if they marched in a gay pride parade.[49] The later start date of the Alberta pride celebrations, and such experiences as those described in Regina, led to the impression that all prairie cities lagged in celebrating pride – but that was not the case.

Regina's Odyssey 1972–1977

Official gay organization came to Regina in winter 1972. Don Murdoch and a small group of gay men and lesbians visited Saskatoon to inquire about the Zodiac Friendship structure and organization. In February 1972, at a party at Murdoch's house, the Atropos Friendship Society was adopted as the name of Regina's gay and lesbian group.[50] In 1994, David Darrel Hockley produced an unpublished history of Regina's gay community called "A History of the Gay Community of Regina," and it is a treasure trove of information about queer Regina. Based on interviews with old-timers and Hockley's own memories of community events (starting from the 1980s), it offers a window into the city's queer life. However, there are some limitations to his history. Hockley's desire to protect the privacy of those involved in the history of Regina's queer community has resulted in a document that is strong on institutional facts and completely silent about who participated in this world. People are referred to by their institutional titles (directors, presidents, treasurers, for example); otherwise we get no glimpse of the individuals involved. This document reinforces the dramatically different culture that existed in Regina, where secrecy and conservatism seems to have been a long-standing community priority. In the preface, he notes "writing a history on a group of people can be quite difficult, especially if it is a minority like gays and lesbians who due to the environment around them, tend to be secretive and very sensitive to heterosexuals knowing anything about them. For that reason, I have written this history without mentioning the names of those persons involved in the events stated."[51] My interviews in Regina, along with documents from Odyssey newsletters and other publications, have permitted a more inclusive history of the city's queer activities.

Initially Regina's club was called the Odyssey Club, and it was located at 2242 Smith Street, in the downtown core.[52] This three-story house was rather ramshackle, but in interviews it was nostalgically recalled by all participants, once they managed to find it.[53] Long-time member, Brian Gladwell, whose activity with the club dated to 1974 when he started driving from Fort Qu'Appelle, Saskatchewan, recalled finding the group and the vetting process for admission. He got a contact number from a "crisis line," and when he dialed he was invited to a member's house to see if he was "legit" before he was escorted to the club's next open night. This level of surveillance – having a member vouch for your "identity" – was also routine practice at Winnipeg's Happenings in the early years. None of my Saskatoon narrators reported this phenomenon.

Gladwell remembered the house on Smith St well, "the place would be packed, there was dancing and a fireplace with a couch in front of the fireplace ... people would be milling around in the dining room, and a DJ and dancing on the other side of the couch." As it was unlicenced, individuals brought their own bottles and handed them over to a bartender in receipt for tickets for the course of the evening. At the start, dances were held Saturday night, and they were really popular with forty to fifty people in attendance. The installation of a "complete music system" was an important moment for the club, according to Hockley. Members enjoyed a mix of "popular disco, rock and roll, and country and western music," which, sometimes, when the "beat was strong," encouraged everyone in the club to join in a "snake dance," parading up and down the staircases and into and out of each room.[54] Eventually the club started opening on other nights of the week due to demand. Even though he recalled feeling like "an outsider" at the club, Gladwell eventually moved to Regina so he could be closer to the club.[55]

Others located this queer space by spotting the tiny classified ads placed in the local newspaper. Evelyn Rogers cut one such advert out of the *Regina Leader Post* and told me that her partner Lilja Stefansson carried that phone number around in her purse "forever and ever" before they worked up the courage to call it. When they did finally make that telephone call, the woman they spoke to, Heather Bishop, invited them to her house in Regina, and over the course of their first conversation she volunteered to take them to the club whenever they wanted to go.[56] Bishop was in the early days of her recording and performing career then, but subsequently became a celebrated Canadian folk musician, children's performer, and activist. Over thirty years later, Rogers's recollection of that first time they ventured to the Smith St house, was memorable: "It was scary at first, you had to go around a dark, dark place and up rickety stairs and into the back room." Jean Hillabold, another member who participated in the Smith St location, remembered that the windows were boarded up so people could not look inside.[57]

Heather signed Rogers and Stefansson in, which was standard protocol for newcomers. "The guys were in the dining room and the women were in the living room, gathered around the fireplace and that was our space," Rogers remembered. She recalled the dancing being located in another space, further away from the "women's space" in front of the fireplace. Rapidly the place went from foreign territory to a place Rogers described as "like home, a good place to be and be who you wanted to be."[58] Initially, a woman resided in the house, enabling the organization to claim it was a private house with private parties – so people could bring their own alcohol without necessitating a liquor licence.

While primarily remembered as a site for socializing, regular dance nights, and the annual special events such as New Year's and Halloween, the Odyssey Club did try a variety of ventures to foster a lesbian and gay community in Regina. They produced a newsletter that highlighted their activities and informed people about club initiatives and rules. After the investment in the music system, the next priority was the purchase of a "Gestetner 145" duplicating machine for "$463.50," because it meant the club could independently, in-house, produce their own newsletters.[59] In 1977, assessing their first five years, the president wrote, "a sense of community is no longer quite as spontaneous and needs more conscious development and support … An 'old gold' atmosphere once a week is not what I believe we're after, nor is it an atmosphere of underground subculture with no visions of daylight and leaving ourselves inaccessible for the general community."[60] One initiative they inaugurated was a phone line to provide information about upcoming events and also counselling and support for newcomers to the lesbian and gay community. They organized a public relations committee to "create awareness of issues involving homosexuality," "to educate the public," and to "develop better communication between 'the gay world' and 'the straight world.'"[61] Not surprising, given the name of the committee, and its parting words of advice – "let's make a good impression" – the truncated goals here were about acceptance, and education, not liberationist activism.

Hockley notes that 1977 was a "turning point" in Regina because that year "younger" members of the community wanted the club's name to acknowledge that it was a gay organization: "They pointed to the fact that Regina was a member of the Prairie Gay Coalition that also consisted of the gay communities of Saskatoon, Calgary, Edmonton, Winnipeg and Thunder Bay."[62] Perhaps more important, the fact that Saskatoon had changed their organization's name in 1974 was a strong motivator, "since Saskatoon could be open about what kind of club it was, why not Regina?" There were financial difficulties, due to decreasing memberships, and this younger cohort believed that more transparency would encourage more memberships. Some members of the board, "were generally of a more conservative nature and were not prepared to go along with the proposed changes," while others indicated they were "tired of being in office and wanted to retire," so the result was that the entire board resigned to "allow the membership to elect a new board of directors."[63] On 14 August 1977, at a special membership meeting, the name was changed to The Gay Community of Regina (GCR), and a new board was elected.[64] This non-profit organization has operated continuously since 1972, and primarily hosts the community's club that has moved to a number of different locations, from Smith Street, to 2069 Broad Street, to 1422 Scarth Street (where they owned the building), and now their current location on Broad Street. This venerable institution was the focus of Glen Wood's 1999 documentary *Community Building*.[65]

University of Saskatchewan

The University of Saskatchewan remained a key site for gay and lesbian community and organizational building. This should not be construed as some simplistic equation that university faculty and students were uncritically "liberal." As the examples of campus chill during the 1950s and the Doug Wilson case (1975–6, see chapter 7) illustrate, it was not easy to be openly identified as gay or lesbian on campus.[66] It was achieved incrementally, one faculty, one class, and one student at a time. Queer people fought for recognition and made savvy use of the resources campus provided – libraries, meeting space, the student newspaper, and an era of questioning authority – to create changes. My narrators spoke with pride of those accomplishments of forging gay and lesbian spaces on campus – but they were a small minority of people who attended or worked on campus in those years. Neil Richards, who worked in the university library, recalled that there was other gay and lesbian staff and that the campus library was a supportive workplace.[67] One of the important ways that universities served to stimulate queer spaces and activism was by virtue of the fact that they attract faculty, students, and, less frequently, staff from all over, not just the urban communities in which they are based. According to Richards, the large numbers of early Saskatoon leaders who were from elsewhere was a key facet of Saskatoon's gay and lesbian leadership. With the exceptions of Gens Hellquist, Bruce Garman, and Doug Wilson, most of the more openly gay and lesbian activists and organizers in Saskatoon either had family far away or were estranged from their families. "Lots of us" (Richards was from Ontario originally) including "Peter (Millard), Kay Bierweiler, Roger Carriere, Dan Nalbach, Val Scrivener had this particular freedom" to appear at protests, write letters to the newspapers, and be "openly gay" in ways that those who lived in the same city in which they grew up were often constrained.[68] Other, older, quietly queer women and men watched from the sidelines, uncertain about whether to embrace this shift towards openness or to continue their practice of discretionary behaviour.

Concrete evidence of "gay" students and politics was introduced to the University of Saskatchewan in fall 1971 when two organizations were established – Gay Students Alliance (SGA) and Saskatoon Gay Action (SGA). The organizers, Gens Hellquist, Bruce Garman, Dan Nalbach, and Erv Warner were a small collection of staff (Hellquist), students (Garman and Warner), and faculty (Nalbach).[69] This presence was an important shift in campus culture, because, as a student group, they were provided with space at welcome week activities and other small resources that enabled them to fund guest speakers and events similar to Gays for Equality in Winnipeg. SGA members appeared on local radio programs and discussed anti-gay discrimination with the Saskatchewan Association on Human Rights. They sponsored various speakers to campus, including a 1973 visit by Del Martin and Phyllis Lyon, the founders of Daughters of Bilitis and authors of *Lesbian/ Woman*.

Perhaps one of the more dramatic initiatives, and certainly a well-attended one, was the January 1974 campus debate sponsored by SGA and the University of Saskatchewan Debating Society, in which Peter Millard and Beth Foster squared off against Rev Michael Horban and Hetty Clewes on the topic "Gay is Good for God and Man."[70] Millard was involved with the University of Saskatchewan debating club, and each year the group hosted an exhibition match intended to draw attention to "debating." In 1974, homosexuality was, according to Millard, "one of the hottest topics around the city." His memoirs devote much attention to this event, not surprisingly both a memorable one for campus, and a significant turning point in Millard's life. As he explained, "I began one sentence casually with the words "as a homosexual myself." There was an almost audible gasp from the audience, and I noticed the students from my freshman class look at each other in surprise."[71] Two hundred and fifty students, faculty, and staff attended this debate. *The Sheaf*, the student newspaper, also reported there were audible "gasps" at Millard's announcement.[72] Looking back, Millard remembered the moment and its aftermath: "it was an extraordinary feeling. I had broken cover, and was standing in the brightly lit open. There was fear, but it was overwhelmed by a surge of euphoria. No more hiding, no more lies, no more deception; there was no going back now."[73] From that point on, he became the "token homosexual" faculty member and while he acknowledged that there were "snide remarks, the occasional joke, and some more serious opposition … by far the more common reaction, however, was either support or more often, indifference."[74] There were other queer faculty on campus at the time, but only Millard chose to be more open about his sexuality and to become a gay activist. In his memoirs he recalled that another colleague spoke to him afterwards and asked, "Why did you do that? You friends won't be able to talk to you, now." Millard's response was not noted, but in his memoirs he wrote: "It was sad to see what fear could do to this man who in all his relationships was more than ordinarily generous and loyal." It was, he thought, "an example of how blind many gay people are about themselves. No-one who had anything to do with this man was under any illusion about his sexuality … yet it was so unthinkable to him that anyone should know about his homosexuality that he went about convinced that his secret was safe."[75] Millard's observations about his colleague's impression of his sexuality were identical to those expressed by Selena, who told me that unless she explicitly told you she was lesbian you could not "presume" to know.[76] It speaks to widespread anxieties about "openness" but also individual desire to control the message. I have not referred to these individuals as "closeted" in this book because that was not entirely the case and the term doesn't fit. Most were out to groups of friends, perhaps family, but in the workplace they were discreet about their sexuality, meaning they did not talk about it. While they did not talk about it, they also did not hide that they lived with same-sex "friends" and they attended events like this debate, which could, in the eyes of other work colleagues, clearly position them as queer even if they did not say they were gay or lesbian.

Whereas most faculty and staff had vested interests in discretionary practices, students continued to find university a liberating experience. Many of my narrators spoke of the opportunities campus life provided. For example, Debbie Simmons knew she was "different" as a teenager

4.2 Peter Millard. Fifth National Gay Conference, Saskatoon,
29 June–3 July 1977. Image courtesy of Charles Dobie.

but couldn't really articulate what that meant. Here she describes the importance of attending university, and the campus environment:

> DS: Most of my high school years were spent avoiding the issue, and it wasn't really until I moved to Saskatoon [1975] and started University, that I started trying to find out more information. I would sneak off to the library, and find every copy I could of local, not local, but Canadian newspapers like … *The Body Politic* …
>
> VJK: You found that here in our U of S Library?
>
> DS: Yes, that's right … It was all about being at University. I took some sociology classes in my undergrad program and one of the profs brought in speakers from the local gay community, unfortunately they were in classes like deviance, but he also brought them in in a class about family, and I think, honestly that was the most important thing that happened to me. Because for once I had a face to identify and people who had positive things to say.
>
> VJK: So despite the fact that they were coming in under the guise of deviance they [the speakers] spun it very positively?
>
> DS: Absolutely. They were there to promote all the positive things about being part of the gay community and it was the first time that I had been introduced, even in a group setting, to someone who identified themselves as a lesbian.

Many of my narrators in Winnipeg, Saskatoon, and Edmonton later participated in such educational sessions, and spoke of those events as game-changers for gay and lesbian students. These moments of opportunity and revelation were counterbalanced by the majority views that circulated on campus. The University of Saskatchewan in the mid-1970s was not an inclusive space where diversity was uniformly recognized and supported. Later in the interview, when I asked Simmons to frame her experience within the larger campus culture, and notions of the "majority" views (admittedly a problematic term), she responded:

> DS: I certainly never heard any positive comments. [I]t was quite common for the University men to call each other faggot in a derogatory way, you didn't hear a lot of slang words about women unless of course you were out with students where everyone was drunk and some woman wasn't appreciative of advances, they got derogative comments. Generally you didn't hear anything about lesbians, and what you heard about gay men

was negative. This environment was quite different though, because the University was still reeling from the Doug Wilson incident, so it was a little more sensitive about these issues.[77]

One wonders what it would have looked like if it had not been "reeling" and "sensitized" to gay issues and politics via the Wilson case. Such memories, and others, remind us of the bravery required to identify as different from the heterosexual majority. "We were queer and we were dykes," Simmons proudly stated.

Most universities towns, particularly smaller cities and communities, have town/gown divides and Saskatoon was no different. Many of the lesbian narrators noted divides between middle-class "campus lesbians" and working-class queer women. Off-campus the lesbian "community" was not an uncritically affirmative space in the city. Class, racial, occupational, generational, and political differences bifurcated it. Simmons was involved in various reproductive lesbian feminist issues (lesbian parenting, custody issues), yet she candidly admitted that there was often a gulf between her and others: "I was an anomaly. I was in university, in a professional program and most of the people I met that were my age group were women who were trying to find an alternative way through life, largely through trades. And so, if you didn't wear the plaid shirt and the steel-toed boots you weren't part of the group ... I used to get called capitalist all the time."[78] Happy to don the "look" of flannel shirt and jeans for weekend socializing, on Monday morning Simmons was back on campus in her professional program.

Saskatoon Organizational Development and Evolution, 1975–1984

Originally created by gay men, SGA was supportive of including lesbian perspectives. In May 1974, SGA organized the first Prairie Gay Rights Conference of gay activists. Delegates from Winnipeg, Edmonton, and Saskatoon focused on two key issues: an exchange of political strategies and the "role of lesbians and community cooperation."[79] In January 1975, ZFS and SGA officially merged to become the Gay Community Centre of Saskatoon. University of Saskatchewan students continued to be involved in this organization, continuing the links with campus while, at the same time, opening membership to the city's queer residents. That summer, the GCCS got a federal government youth grant to create educational materials about sexual diversity. It employed four

FEATURES

Saskatoon

**It has one of the biggest gay centres in the country.
A report on the people who make it work.**

by Tom Warner

It's not as I remember it. I recognize only a few of the faces in the crowd, faces that are familiar and comforting. The other hundred or so people jammed into this room are strangers. It's an odd feeling. I used to know *all* of the faces. On the crowded dance floor bodies bob and bump to the sounds of disco music; on the periphery intimate groups of men and women are clustered around a dozen tables... a lot of laughter, more than a little gossip. Another group winds its was carefully between the tables, delicately manoeuvring their trays out of harms way. In an adjoining room, two women are playing pool. In a closed office, away from the noise, a woman offers some gentle advice to a very nervous young man.

It's not as I remember. And everywhere there is a feeling of warmth and hospitality.

I have come home, after five years, to Saskatoon. A lot has changed. For gay people, it represents a kind of transformation of this city of 140,000 people, plopped incongruously down beside the South Saskatchewan River.

For one thing, it is no longer quite the bastion of heterosexuality it once was — where being openly gay often meant moving to a larger city. Not so long ago a gay man or woman could spend years looking for a gay community only to discover a lifestyle revolving around the park, public washrooms, a couple of 'mixed' bars and a few indescribably tacky parties.

Today, Saskatoon is a city with a visible and growing gay community which operates a full-time community centre on a busy downtown street. Where I am, dancing, this particular Christmas vacation.

Fall, 1971. I stumbled upon a copy of the *Georgia Straight* and found an ad which read simply, "Saskatoon Gay Liberation, Box 3043, Saskatoon." It seemed unbelievable. I answered the ad, worried about who might receive the letter. A few days later Doug Hellquist phoned. He had placed the ad because he wanted to form a gay organization in Saskatoon.

Right: Doug Hellquist, 30, Executive Director of the Centre. "Doug has a woman's soul - he *feels* and deals with his feelings. He's a benevolent leader and a true supporter of women's issues - not in a partonizing way like so many other men." I'm listening to a lesbian member of the centre. Doug attracts support like that - he *is* a warm and generous personality and many, many of us owe our coming-out as gay people to him.

He says "I believe the biggest contribution the Centre has made to Saskatoon is the development and growth of a supportive gay community." Participation in the Centre has grown from 30 or 40 five years ago to somewhere between 800 and 1000 today.

Incredibly, over the next few months a small group of people discovered the same astonishing little classified, answered it, and formed the nucleus of the future organization. For nearly two years we functioned precariously out of a post office box and the nearest available living roon.

By January of 1972 the group had a Board of Directors and was calling itself the Zodiac Friendship Society. Admittedly closety, but the political arm of the ZFS was a little more upfront — Saskatoon Gay Action.

The first priority was to provide a social milieu which would permit the gay community to grow and prosper. Without this, political action would hat not have been possible.

February 11, 1972. Saskatoon had its first gay dance. We were exhilarated and inspired by the turn-out. Over fifty men and women attended that night, and the future looked entirely rosy. Buoyed by the success of this first dance, ZFS decided to hold them on a weekly basis at the Unitarian Centre. But nothing ever quite lived up to the promise of that first dance. On a good night we might get forty people. I remember one disastrous evening when there were only five — someone had held a party and everyone was there...

Nonetheless, just one year later, ZFS took a calculated gamble. It opened its own community centre in downtown Saskatoon, smack in the middle of everything else legitimate, and offered counselling, phone-lines, drop-ins, dances and political action meetings. It has never looked back.

Successes. The group has had its share: hosting the first prairie regional conference of gay activist groups in 1973, obtaining a pro-gay statement from the Saskatchewan Human Rights Commission (setting a precedent for the movement in Canada). It pressured prairie newspapers to carry gay advertisements; helped a lesbian mother to fight for custody of her children; intervened in two federal and one provincial elections... and finally launched the famous case around Doug Wilson, the gay educator discriminated against by the University of Saskatchewan.

There was some opposition to the organization in the old days. "Saskatchewan is too small, too conservative" they said. Not any more. The group is attracting the old, the young, men, women — a good cross section of the city's gay population. And they're committed — to being out, and making the centre work.

It's not called the Zodiac Friendship Society anymore. It's been the Saskatoon Gay Community Centre since 1975 — a new upfront name symbolizing a new, upfront gay community.

People make it work. Hard working, determined people like those shown on this page — Mavis and Elizabeth, Neil and the two Dougs.

The fifth anniversary of the Saskatoon Gay Community Centre is an important milestone in the history of the gay movement in Canada. The success of this small band of gay activists in this prairie city has shown that gay liberation is not just a phenomenon seen in large urban centres. But most important, the people at SGCC have shown that with a little bit of effort, you *can* build something out of nothing. And it took only five years. □

Above: Doug Wilson, 26, President of Saskatoon Gay Community Centre. "My firing and what happened as a result? I feel very positive... very happy about everything that happened. It has been the catalyst for a multitude of positive things... support for and awareness of gay rights."

Not shown: Mavis Carleton, 48, founding member of SGCC, member of Board of Directors. "I feel as though I have found my home and my family at the centre. I was very apprehensive when I answered that ad five years ago...there seemed to be so few female homosexuals in those days." Mavis was the first lesbian that many of us had ever met. Now she's only one of many women actively involved in the running of the Centre - she pointed out that 4 of the 9 board members are women.

Neil Richards, 26, SGCC member. "The University of Saskatchewan library's gay collection is twice the size of the University of Toronto's." Neil is a librarian who spends a lot of time organizing the Centre's library and placing gay books in local libraries. The Centre now stocks 337 titles, available to anyone who wants them.

Above: Elizabeth Noton, 22, formerly co-director of the University of Saskatchewan's Campus Women's Centre; currently a member of the SGCC Board of Directors. "There are times when it's important for me to relate exclusively to women around concerns that we have in common, and bring the energy of the experience back to the mixed group in the gay movement." Saskatoon's gay community is not divided along sexual lines. Lesbians in this city are not separatists - but they're not just token women either. "When I need support... it usually doesn't matter what the sex of the person is," notes Elizabeth

4.3 "Saskatoon: It has one of the biggest gay centres in the country," *The Body Politic*, 1977. Images provided courtesy of DailyXtra.com

people, Gens Hellquist, Anne Lawrence, Elizabeth (Lesley) Noton, and Doug Wilson, two of whom would play central leadership roles in the community.[80]

Throughout the mid- to late 1970s, campus and city activity continued, spurred in the first instance by the Wilson case, which resulted in campus debates, special features in the *Sheaf*, and much political work (see chapter 7). Peter Millard re-established the Gay Academic Union on campus, which ran until 1982 when it was replaced by Gays and Lesbians at the University of Saskatchewan. One of its initiatives was an annual gay film series at Place Riel Theatre on campus. In March 1976, the Gay Community Centre opened a new club at 310 20th St. A month earlier, they had been profiled in Toronto's *The Body Politic* with a glowing review that ranked them as the best community gay and lesbian organization in the country. But changes were on the horizon and that proved to be the high watermark. In 1977, committees were struck to explore the organizational structure of the GCCS. Archival documents and interviews illustrate that there were interpersonal tensions within the organization.[81] In our lengthy, and candid interview, Gens Hellquist recalled the terrific labour that fell to volunteers, and admitted that he and Wilson disagreed about how to move forward: "In 76–7 it centred on Doug Wilson and myself. Doug and I didn't see eye to eye on a lot of things ... We had different philosophies. I realized at that time that if we were going to grow and become successful we needed to start hiring people to do tasks. You can only burn out so many volunteers before things crash and burn. Doug didn't agree on that. He wanted to continue to run everything on volunteers."[82] As becomes evident in chapter 7, there were more philosophical differences than merely this issue of hiring more staff (Hellquist was paid staff at that point), but, impressively, he also admitted that a large part of this situation was stoked by the interpersonal dynamics between himself and Wilson. In what was a powerful moment of the interview, Hellquist said, "I also think there was ego stuff involved. Doug didn't come out until later in the 70s. And by that time I was already heavily involved and I think that Doug decided the he should be the premier star in the community and I was young and stupid. So there was quite a split at this time."[83] Despite this, they pulled off a highly successful national conference for gay political and community groups. But change was imminent. Hellquist resigned from the centre and starting working with the Community Resource Centre where he eventually became the executive director;

it would be a couple of years before he returned to volunteering in the community.

In 1978, a new organization, Saskatchewan Gay Coalition, was created, which was intended to be provincial in scope and to include, as a founding principle, equal participation of women and men. In reality, this group was largely directed by members of Saskatoon's community, notably Doug Wilson and Kay Bierweiler, who made presentations throughout the province; created *Grassroots*, the newsletter of SGC (see below); and performed considerable outreach work to encourage urban, small-town, and rural gays and lesbians to realize that "gay people are everywhere."[84] Wilson was critical of urban queer activists, who might acknowledge small-town and rural lesbians and gay men, nevertheless still believed that "everyone with the where-with-all to do so will leave Sioux Lookout, Moose Jaw, and Medicine Hat for the 'bright lights' and 'safety' of a larger place." According to Wilson, such migrations to urban areas, and the concentration of gay activism there, had led to a "top-down" movement focused on urban issues, which SGC wished to work against. Their journal started modestly with only thirty-seven subscribers, but by "August 1979 we had established over 1400 contacts in at least 127 Saskatchewan communities, as well as in every other province, the Yukon and more than twenty states in the U.S." Once a sufficient mass of people were involved in various Saskatchewan communities, the SGC travelled to those communities to initiate meetings, and, by the late-1970s, SGC had organized social groups in "Moose Jaw, Prince Albert, Meadow Lake (Wilson's hometown), the Melfort-Tisdale area, and the Kindersley-Eston-Rosetown areas," with a community centre established in Prince Albert in 1978.[85] The Prince Albert Centre materialized quickly, going from an organizational meeting in April 1978 with two local gays and lesbians, to its opening less than two years later. Tangible gains, though, were not primarily in more centres or spaces, but rather in groups, awareness, and networks. For example, "gay Native people and gay education workers" had begun to talk about organizational options as part of this grass-roots networking style. For Wilson, the key political achievement was "the long term prospect of gay people living and working positively and openly not only in Saskatoon and Regina (not to mention Toronto, Montreal and Vancouver) but also in Mortlach, Loon Lake, Swift Current and Langenberg, indeed on the farms and in the small towns of every province."[86] He conceded that this would take a "long time" but they were invested for the long term. Regretfully, Wilson, who died from complications from AIDS in 1994, was not around to see such moments materialize. Many decades later, and in a different political climate, the city of Humboldt, Saskatchewan, (5,678 people in 2011) hosted a gay pride parade in 2016.[87]

In January 1979, GCCS was on the move again, into a new location at 245 3rd Avenue South. George Taylor, alderman for the city of Saskatoon, attended their grand opening, widely viewed as an important acknowledgment of the centre's visibility in the city. The national gay and lesbian movement also took notice of Saskatoon's accomplishments. According to *After Stonewall*, Saskatoon was then "the only city in Canada with a gay community centre. It is self supporting, raising money by holding weekend dances and through membership fees. It provides telephone and personal counselling services, has library facilities available to the general public, and houses political action meetings."[88] Other cities had taken note of this achievement, and in June 1979 members of the Vancouver gay and lesbian community sought to establish a gay centre in their city. A follow-up conference, planned for September, indicated that the "Vancouver gay centre wishes to model itself after Saskatoon's centre, which along with Saskatchewan Gay Coalition, has the 50% lesbian control written into it's constitution."[89]

Taylor's participation signals greater public recognition, but this important symbolic gesture masks as much as it reveals because not everyone in the city was comfortable with the growing presence of gay and lesbian residents. Within the year an arsonist would set fire to GCCS. Thankfully no one was injured but the property damage was in excess of $10,000. The centre reopened two weeks after the arsonist attack, but this homophobic violence, combined with the opening of Saskatoon's first commercial gay club, After Midnight, at 102 Avenue B South, created severe financial difficulties. It was during this time, that Hellquist re-engaged, concerned that the centre was "pretty much strictly a social club. And there were some of us who were concerned about the phone lines, people coming out, the support stuff, and the education stuff. So we started another group called Gay and Lesbian Support Services."[90] Gay and Lesbian Support Services (GLSS) opened at 217 - 116 3rd Avenue South and the Gay Community Centre closed in March 1982. Their library was transferred to the GLSS. Where they differed was in political ideology. GCCS had been liberationist, keen to advance a political agenda for lesbians and gay men, whereas GLSS had a broader mandate with social services in the forefront and politics receding a bit into the background. Still, there were many people who viewed the providing of social services for lesbian and gay Saskatoon residents as highly political. Community building, however, remained a priority in Saskatoon. Various social and cultural vehicles were created to nurture gay and lesbian identities; in particular, the Metamorphosis cultural festival in 1979 and a succession of gay and lesbian periodicals (see below).

If we could characterize the 1970s as a decade of optimism and expansion of gay and lesbian organizations and initiatives, this all began to change in the 1980s due to a dramatically different political and medical climate. In April 1982, the Saskatchewan Progressive Conservative Party, under leader Grant Devine, won a landslide victory. Support for the PCs was largely but not entirely rural, and they had a strong core of fundamentalist Christian supporters who believed that the heterosexual family and traditional gendered roles of breadwinning husbands and homemaking wives and mothers were the foundation of Saskatchewan life. Similar to other right-wing governments, they favoured smaller government, and in particular less support for social services. PC voters and many politicians were openly hostile to gay, lesbian, and feminist activism.[91] Homophobic newspaper headlines became shockingly commonplace. That these views were held and publicly expressed by senior cabinet ministers – and Premier Devine himself – made the situation critical. Social Services Minister Grant Schmidt is best remembered for his 1988 statement that homosexual practices were "not normal, not moral," and similar to "drunkards, slanderers and swindlers, they [homosexuals, like Svend Robinson whose "coming out" as a gay politician elicited these comments] should not be exposed to children for fear of setting a bad example."[92] In addition to these routine homophobic pronouncements there was a dramatic contraction in provincial funding.[93] As Hellquist recalled, the 1980s were a dark decade for provincial government funding, and a sharp reversal of the more supportive, sometimes expansive climate of the 1970s in which gay and lesbian residents felt that Allen Blakeney's NDP government was amenable to discussion, if not action. In addition to the province's PC majority landslide, the gay community began to battle the AIDS virus. In 1983, Saskatchewan had its first confirmed AIDS case. Two years later, AIDS activism, support, and education transformed gay and lesbian activism and community organizations in Saskatoon much as it did elsewhere in the prairie region. Then, a terminal diagnosis, the severity of the AIDS epidemic, and the need for community led education (as right-wing governments failed to act, either to fund necessary research or initially to make safer sex information available), as well as social supports for people living with AIDS, brought lesbians and gay men together in a variety of activist and volunteer organizations. But it also took a toll on Saskatoon. Longtime Diva's club manager, Kelly Faber, indicated that she stopped counting how many friends and members had died from AIDS once she realized she had lost over one hundred people.[94]

All of these factors (arson, political regime change, and the AIDS epidemic) coalesced to change Saskatoon's gay and lesbian community organizations. In addition, after over a decade of really innovative activism and organizational building, the handful of key Saskatoon women and men who were the masterminds behind all of these activities were exhibiting signs of burnout. In 1982, the commercial club, After Midnight, was renamed Numbers. In June 1983, it met the same fate as GCCS, when an arsonist attempted to set its front and back doors alight. Everyone evacuated safely, but it was a reminder that homophobia couldn't be ignored. Numbers moved to 493A 2nd Avenue North and reopened on 2 September 1983. In November 1984, Zorro's, a private gay members club, opened at 249A 2nd Avenue South. It operated only Friday and Saturday nights, which drained customers from Numbers and proved to be a shaky business proposition – it closed in early 1985. Numbers however, would prove to be a community stalwart. Eventually renamed Diva's, they've had a successful tenure in the city, and currently are located at 220 3rd Ave South. One final, decisive moment that marked the end of an era was the closure, in 1985, of the Ritz Hotel. The new owners, the Royal Bank of Canada (RBC), had the building demolished to make way for a new RBC building and shops. The loss of the Apollo Room was mourned as yet another sign that the 1980s were, for Saskatoon gays and lesbians, the end of an era.

Regina Organizational and Social Developments, 1973–1985

Although Regina lagged Saskatoon in developing a full roster of social and cultural events given the paramount focus on "the club," there were a few other organizations in the city. In January 1973, students at the Regina campus of the University of Saskatchewan created the University of Saskatchewan Homophile Association.[95] Bev Stiller, who would become the first female president of the Atropos Society in 1975, and Gary McDonald launched this group.[96] A year later it was renamed the University of Regina Homophile Association when the University of Regina received its independence from the University of Saskatchewan.

That November, Del Martin and Phyllis Lyon, the founding couple behind the American lesbian organization Daughters of Bilitis (and authors of the book *Lesbian/Woman*), were sponsored to speak at both the U of R and the U of S.

No information existed to explain why Saskatoon chose Saskatoon Gay Action and Regina chose Homophile Association. While there had been a history of such groups in Canada, including the inaugural group, the University of Toronto Homophile Organization (1969–73), homophile was still an old-fashioned term to choose in 1973. Regardless, the University of Regina Homophile Association counselled gay and lesbian students and participated in educational sessions in various university classes. In 1980, the organization ceased operations because they reportedly could not "recruit new members."[97]

Since approximately 1975, the Gay Community of Regina (GCR) had a "Gay Information and Support Service Line," which provided callers with information about gay and lesbian activities in the city. According to Hockley, in November 1978, a group of lesbians and gay men formed "Gay Regina" whose purpose was "educational and political, especially in promoting legislative (both Dominion and Provincial) human rights for gay people.[98] GCR was short-lived, disbanding in 1980 after they hosted a successful gay rights conference.

Like Winnipeg, GCR had a series of gay and lesbian religious groups. Starting in the "late 1970s–1983" there was a support group called "One Loaf" that was held at St John's United Church, on 4th Avenue and McTavish Street.[99] A chapter of Dignity, the Catholic gay and lesbian support group, was launched in 1984. Like the United Church of Canada (UCC) group, it hosted socials, potluck dinners, and support group discussions. Two lesbian associations, Lesbian Association of Southern Saskatchewan (LASS, founded in February 1982) and the Lavender Social Club (founded in August 1984) were also started. Both groups held social events, LASS published their newsletter *Second Wave*, and they hosted potluck dinners. The Lavender Social Club hosted women's dances in various locations throughout the city of Regina. Those dances were, Hockley recalls, very popular, particularly as the warehouse district location of the GCR in the mid-1980s drew smaller numbers of lesbians due to its isolated location.

It was not uncommon for Regina residents to participate in rallies or protests (often organized by Saskatchewan Gay Coalition) at the provincial legislature in the late 1970s and early 1980s. Saskatchewan Gay Coalition attempted to partner with Regina groups and individuals, but it proved difficult to keep sustained Regina participation going within the group during the late 1970s through the early 1980s. An expansion of gay and lesbian organizations did not occur in Regina until the late 1980s and early 1990s, propelled in part by the AIDS crisis and generational changes in those openly involved in the community. For example, as previously mentioned, Regina first hosted gay pride events in 1990.[100]

While women did participate in the club, and were prominent in membership lists, volunteer positions, and on the roster of the newsletter, the evening dances and socializing were predominately male (approximately 60 per cent). Female interviewees often commented that they found the music choices, the male predominance, the alcohol consumption, and some of the challenges of a club venue less desirable. In the late 1970s, a series of lesbian organizations began to form in Regina. Similar to Saskatoon, feminist organizations had existed in the city during the late 1960s through the 1970s, but there were tensions over lesbian participation and lesbian goals. One of the founders, Jan Harvey, remembered that feminism and lesbianism was the primary focal point of LASS, which despite its name, was primarily composed of women from Regina.[101] In a nod to be inclusive to a few members who attended from Moose Jaw, they chose a more inclusive name, but it was primarily a Regina organization.

A 1983 *Briarpatch* profile of LASS provided a rationale for the group's existence, a demographic breakdown of membership, and an analysis of the politics of women's and gay groups in Regina. Occupationally, LASS members came from a variety of backgrounds, including: "tradeswomen, students, health care workers, public servants, educators, lawyers, musicians, and business owners."[102] The women ranged in age from mid-twenties to their forties. While they were out to their immediate families, none of them admitted that they could be "totally open" about their lesbianism for fears of how it might affect their employment, housing, children, or community standing. While the article was judiciously written, to explain to the uninitiated why LASS existed, it offers insight into Regina's activist circles. Women's organizations in the city were (similar to situations elsewhere in the prairies) not completely welcoming to lesbians. And, some LASS members weren't comfortable working in predominantly gay male organizations either because they were irritated that their issues and goals were often of secondary concern. So, LASS was intended to "create alternative space for lesbians to build our own community."[103] Politics were interwoven in this goal of community building, as LASS aimed to "support lesbians who find themselves losing their children in custody battles solely on the grounds of their sexual orientation, to women who are trying to 'come out,'" as well as those women who were "facing the hostility of our society because they are already 'out.'"[104] The group was active from the late 1970s until the mid-1980s. A combination of burnout for the original group of fifteen women combined with the rightward turn in Saskatchewan politics really curtailed much activist work. In its later years, LASS served a primarily social function, hosting monthly potluck dinners. In the mid-1980s, a *Lesbian Newsletter* was produced in Regina, at a subscription cost of ten dollars per year (one dollar an issue). It was, like LASS, a means to break isolation; the newsletter primarily offered information about activities and events of interest to the city's lesbians, such as a notice for a "Woman's Dance" to be held at the Schnitzel Haus, on Hamilton Street in Regina in February 1984.[105]

Asked, retrospectively, to comment on issues of homophobia in Regina, and how that has changed over time, lesbian Jan Harvey offered this perceptive comment about the commitment required to live openly as a lesbian in Regina: "I feel fairly comfortable because I dare to be. Because I feel I have the right to be so I just do things like [hold hands] going down the street ... I don't have any male friends who would do that, but it is different for men."[106] There were no illusions that Regina offered some queer paradise for lesbian and gay men. What Harvey articulated explicitly, more explicitly than many interviewees, were her choices about where to live and her sexual identity, and the small moments of daily activism she felt necessary to square these two apparently reconcilable notions. She had not been "stuck" in Regina. She chose the prairies, and the midsized city of Regina in particular, in which to live. Yet, she also wanted the opportunities available elsewhere and so she felt compelled to push for recognition. Pragmatically, she came to realize that two middle-class, middle-aged women walking together doesn't spark an incendiary reaction in residential areas of the city. However, she and her partner Erin Shoemaker, an ordained minister, had experience with small towns while Shoemaker was posted to a rural Saskatchewan, United Church of Canada ministerial position. They were often ostracized and subject to the silent treatment when they entered stores, and she believed that it was "still very isolating to be a lesbian in rural Saskatchewan." As a former Winnipegger and urbanite, Harvey said, "I don't have Saskatchewan rural roots ... so I don't romanticize rural life. If you are not from there it doesn't matter how long you live there … you are still outsiders … I find a place the size of Regina or Saskatoon is nice."[107] Like Rogers and Stefansson's experience leaving Rouleau, when the town refused to host a farewell event, such experiences of rural and small-town intolerance are illustrative of the quiet yet effective way that such messages can be sent.

For all the talk, from residents of Regina, about Saskatoon being the more "political" city, and of their envy of the vibrancy and possibilities of life in Saskatoon, they were also contented to live in Regina. The club – for all of the personal challenges, years of tenuous financial circumstances, and politics – had survived, and, in the end, it was Regina that maintained their member-owned and -operated club far longer than Saskatoon and even Winnipeg. Forging community takes many forms, and while some will lament Regina's focus on "merely" social space, having the tenacity to keep that space afloat, to find creative ways to use the funds from the club to support other ventures – if only sporadically – has paid some dividends in continuity and visibility in the city of Regina. As Brian Gladwell observed, "when we moved to 2070 Broad St., and put the rainbow flag on the front of the building, that was a significant statement."[108]

In August 1980, the Scarth Street location was sold and the GCR moved into rental space at 2069 Broad Street.[109] *Gay Saskatchewan* provided this admiring description of the new space: "The Regina gay community's new Centre is one of the largest in Canada. A beautiful dance room, lounge and pool table, areas for talking … as well as a large kitchen and bar facility make this an exceptional gathering place for lesbians and gay men … To reach the Centre, go to 2069 Broad Street, walk around to the back lane behind the country music bar (straight). Centre door is marked 'The Rear Entrance.'"[110] Then listed under "Gay Regina" in the phone book, it is notable that the entrance was still in the back alley and, while the doorway sign was intended to be a cheeky fun name for those people who knew what kind of a bar it was, one cannot help but wonder how much confusion might have occurred given the proximity of the straight western bar and these instructions. Alley entrances remained common for both Saskatoon and Regina. Since then it has had a few name changes, but is currently called Q Nightclub and Lounge. With its prominent rainbow flag sign, Q is a Regina institution (it is now located at 2070 Broad St). All of my Regina narrators attended "the club" at various junctures in their lives; served on the board of directors; and had a variety of views about the institution's longevity, the rationale for why the club occupied the primary attention of Regina residents, and, naturally, the politics and personalities involved in running this vital but financially precarious venture. This rich oral history awaits a community historian to unpack all the twists and turns.[111]

Key Cultural and Educational Developments

One of the more remarkable and admired cultural gay and lesbian festivals in Saskatchewan was Metamorphosis. This "prairie celebration of lesbians and gay men" took place in Saskatoon from the 1978 until 1989.[112] Initially sponsored by Saskatchewan Gay Coalition, Metamorphosis was all about transformation and celebration. Using the image of the butterfly (now more recognizable as an image for trans people), the organizers intended the event to celebrate diversity within the lesbian and gay community, and of its "continued growth."[113] Held over the Canadian Thanksgiving weekend this three-day festival promised "laughter, loving, dancing, singing, art, crafts, photography, music, theatre, books, film, poetry, good food, good company, good times, women loving women, men loving men, sharing, building, growing, flaunting it and more, much more."[114] Organizers viewed this as a unique opportunity not only for the queer community but for the straight community as well: "It will be a unique opportunity to present ourselves to the straight world in a very positive, highly visible way. But more important, it will bring us closer together and will allow us an opportunity to be together and celebrate ourselves and our lifestyles. Culture is an important part of our lives and opportunity to experience gay culture on such a large scale is rare indeed, especially on the Prairies."[115] An ambitious line-up of performers, including Blackberri from San Francisco and Ferron from Vancouver, along with prairie singers and comics, provided entertainment.[116] According to reports in *The Body Politic*, over two hundred people attended this event, with seventy-five at the Thanksgiving Monday feast. Torontonians in attendance told *TBP* that it was a "total high energy weekend, stronger than Toronto's August Gaydays celebration." Another was impressed by the "cohesiveness" of Saskatoon's gay community. As another Toronto woman reported, "Metamorphosis was a good name for it. There was a tremendous strengthening of people, culture and community over the weekend. We changed, metamorphosed, gained a lot of strength from each other, and we were able to bring this back to our own cities."[117] Participants like Marion Alexander, whose recollections are the epigram at the outset of this chapter, recalled Metamorphosis as a highlight of her life.

4.4 Metamorphosis poster, 7–9 October 1978, Saskatoon Gay Coalition.
Artist: Mark Erikson. Neil Richards Collection, Provincial Archives
of Saskatchewan A821 VII.14b. Image courtesy of Neil Richards.

One of the hallmarks of the weekend was a savvy combination of co-ed events for gay men and lesbians, and then men's and women's coffee houses and lesbian-only events. For example, in 1979 there was a women's-only dinner and dance and a fundraiser for Meg Christian, a feminist singer and songwriter.[118] Eventually, Metamorphosis became more and more focused on lesbian events and was increasingly organized by women. In 1980, the Gay Community Centre could no longer provide funding for the event given their financial challenges. Organizers submitted a grant to the Saskatchewan government's Cultural Activities Program. The initiative was sponsored by the Saskatchewan Gay Coalition, whose member groups – "Prince Albert Gay Community; Carrot River Gays; Regina Gay Community; Moose Jaw, North Battleford and Fort Qu'Appelle" – were listed as supporters. The ten-member volunteer organizing team hoped that the event would "provide a positive cultural environment for gay people and all people to express the richness of gay contributions to the prairie environment."[119]

No word on the fate of this grant, but Metamorphosis did happen in 1980 and it was a resounding success, attracting three hundred gay men and lesbians. Writers for *TBP*, in an article titled "Prairie Festival Blooms," offered an outsider's view of the long weekend which, while generally positive, seemed a bit taken aback by the Saskatoon scene: "It was unstructured and yet organized; in the middle of a workshop on the nuclear industry someone got up and sang a song about seagulls ... The Saskatoon community has always been characterized by an intense emotionality. Visitors are frequently surprised by the kissing and embracing that accompany meeting and parting here."[120] Not all visitors liked this, as one critic reported, "It's like a goddamn evangelical movement." Concluding by claiming Saskatchewan as the "conscience of Canada," the *TBP* author observed that there were "extraordinary warm relations between the men and women; unusually high number of children around; dismal technical quality of the arts and crafts; startlingly positive coverage by the local radio stations; and the unstated conviction that grassroots organizing with occasional boosters like Metamorphosis is the only way for the national gay movement to go."[121] Subsequent years were equally successful at attracting large numbers of attendees, and, in 1982, Walter Davis reported that Metamorphosis had made a profit. This accomplishment spoke to the dedicated volunteers who organized this event, and of support from the community, particularly in the wake of the challenges posed by the Gay

Community of Saskatoon Centre's closure in 1982. Davis's letter was bittersweet because, at the same committee meeting that next year's Metamorphosis organizers were named, the SGC dissolved itself for lack of interest and attendance at its annual general meeting. Clearly, cultural, social, and artistic events were huge draws for queer prairie residents and visitors; gay and lesbian politics and "provincial cooperation, outreach, and education," however, were no longer as interesting priorities.[122]

Many of my Saskatoon narrators recalled Metamorphosis with pride, and were nostalgic about the good times and the community engagement. Lesbians like Marion Alexander recalled it as "one of the highlights of my life" in our interview. Women spoke of the importance of positive spaces provided for gay and lesbian people who were estranged from their families of origin during this holiday weekend, and how grateful attendees were for the community festival and Thanksgiving feast.[123] Bucking the trends elsewhere in the community, Metamorphosis remained a highly anticipated annual event until 1989. In fact, it was so beloved that it was revived for another shorter run in 2001–2.[124] However, given the fact that it used incredible amounts of volunteer labour to organize, it was no longer sustainable. Over the years, it changed from an event that included equal male and female organizers with many events for gay men, to an event largely organized by and for lesbians.[125] Whether this feminization of the event contributed to its eventual demise is difficult to assess. However, the reality was that the volunteer-run committee tasked with providing entertainment, social, cultural, and political activities for upwards of three hundred attendees could not sustain the energy and effort necessary to host.

Sperm "Running Back to Saskatoon"

One of the significant components of the Metamorphosis weekends, particularly given the leadership role lesbians played in organizing these events, was education about sexuality (lesbian and gay), health, reproductive rights, and custody laws. By all accounts, both from my narrators and from the published reports in queer periodicals and newsletters about the conference, these sessions were the best attended of all the workshops and panel discussions. Only the dances and social events attracted more participants. Debbie Simmons, a member of the community centre, was involved in organizing these events with other lesbian feminists. She recalled that the idea that lesbians would have children using donated sperm was one that led to tense exchanges between lesbians and gay men, and between lesbian feminists and straight feminists in Saskatoon. As she recalled, "women were starting to realize that being a lesbian didn't mean you couldn't have children, and so there was all kinds of discussions about those 'hot topics': adoptive rights, reproductive rights, and legal rights of couples."[126] Straight feminists who might claim lesbian friends, or activist colleagues, regarded them very differently "when they started thinking about these gay women having children and raising children without men in their lives … it was a very hard concept to get people to look at without being emotional about their prejudices at that time." And, shockingly, gay men were not as supportive as Simmons had hoped. Rather sarcastically, she reported that gay men in Saskatoon "weren't at all" interested in reproductive rights for lesbians. "Gay men who prior to this time had never given two thoughts [about] their sperm all of a sudden had ownership issues over it. It was very bizarre. And for the most part they continued to act that way."[127] Eventually, she and her partner found a gay male couple who consented to be donors for them.

Once they were successfully pregnant, given that Saskatoon was a small town and most everyone in the queer community knew each other, the news spread: "There was more shock and concern then there was support. But there were some women in the community who also wanted to have babies. So informally, some of that information was shared … at one of those Metamorphosis weekends … we even put on a workshop literally about how do you get pregnant and how do you do your own inseminations." Long before the Canadian government and Health Canada would introduce legislation about sperm and egg donors, this enterprising group of Saskatoon lesbians set up an informal network of donors. Simmons proudly, and rather hilariously, reported that "as a result of that experience we ended up being involved in sort of an underground sperm operation and so people had lined up sympathetic men in the community, in the straight community, who would agree to be sperm donors but didn't want to know anything else about it … We had a couple of women who were trying to get pregnant. I'd get a phone call at 9 o'clock at night, 'okay now,' and I'd run across town and pick up the sperm and then deliver the sperm." According to Simmons, these men were feminists, whose female partners were feminists, and they saw themselves as "enlightened" enough to assist in this venture.

In the interview I asked about what this "sperm-running ring" indicated about Saskatoon, and whether Simmons felt this version of "community politics/engagement" characterized Saskatoon's atypically left-of-centre ethos. "At the time, I didn't think about it. To be honest I didn't think about some of this stuff for years until I knew I was coming for this interview ... it didn't seem odd until I started to reflect about it. And then I thought, well you know, I guess there weren't too many women driving around the city with a condom under their arm trying to keep sperm warm," she replied.[128] Pointedly asked about the broader significance of these events and the political implications, Simmons reminded me that the personal was political: "We wanted children. In some cases all it takes is that recognition that it is possible."[129]

"Are Straight Folks Normal?"
The Quinlan Sisters, 1981–1984

Peter McGehee (1955–91), Doug Wilson's lover, was a talented musician, artist, and singer. Originally from Pine Bluff, Arkansas, but raised in Little Rock, he had lived in a number of major American cities before meeting Wilson at gay pride events in San Francisco in 1979. He moved to Saskatoon to join Wilson, and there his creative energies led to a series of memorable musical performances and novels. Thinly veiled autobiography, McGehee's archly comic novels were about men like him, small-town, southern queer men whose eccentric families of origin clashed dramatically with their gay adult children.[130] While fiction, *Boys like Us, Sweetheart,* and *Labour of Love* were comedic, bittersweet novels about living and loving in the age of AIDs, and a window into his life with Doug Wilson. The final book, aptly named *Labour of Love,* was published posthumously, a true labour of love by Wilson himself, who died of AIDs two weeks after he finished writing and preparing McGehee's manuscript for publication.

In addition to his novels, McGehee was also well known for his songwriting, musical, and theatrical performances as part of the musical cabaret act *The Quinlan Sisters,* which he originally created in San Francisco and later brought to Saskatoon, where he wrote new songs. Performing with Fiji Robinson and Wendy Coad, McGehee's satirical, political commentary about the gender wars, sexuality, and "normalcy" won over audiences with edgy, hysterically funny lyrics packaged in dynamic sets of a cappella harmonies.[131] *The Quinlan Sisters* became a cult fixture in Saskatoon, performing at the Broadway Theatre, and then later touring and performing in western Canada, Toronto, and San Francisco. They had a brief sojourn as artists-in-residence in Kingston, Ontario.

Perhaps their most famous song, "Are Straight Folks Normal," nicely probes the question of who and what gets to define "normal." This song mocks the notion of "normalcy," turning the tables on "straight folks" in its attempt to make the political point about the absurdity of life, relationship categories, and strict definitions of appropriate behaviour.[132] Later, with Robinson, as part of a performing duo called *The Fabulous Sirs*, McGehee toured nationally and recorded their performance at the 1987 Edmonton Fringe Festival.[133] The *Fabulous Sirs* also performed in New York and San Francisco. While McGehee's time in Saskatoon was short, only a few years, his energy, creativity, and performances were memorable – another outlet for queer people and their allies to enjoy, and an important interlude of queer cultural critique within the city.

Queer Periodicals

One of the key means of community building that all Saskatchewan gay and lesbian organizations used was the newsletter or, later, in a more polished format, the small magazine. In the Internet age, print media – magazines and newspapers – are imperiled, but before 24/7 newsfeeds on social media, access to "news" magazines, newsletters, and newspapers were key cultural and political documents for the queer community. Post-Internet, it is important to remind readers of how essential those early newsletters were for providing basic directories and information about prairie clubs. All narrators whose experience with the gay and lesbian worlds predated the establishment of queer organizations spoke poignantly about how difficult it was to locate other queer women and men. Newsletters overcame these challenges and transformed access to queer spaces. No more endless searching, subscribers could have this information conveniently mailed to their home in a discreet envelope. Today, these slim, photocopied newsletters look rudimentary and basic, but then their creation was eagerly anticipated and emancipatory. In all cases, newsletters were the top priority for prairie queer clubs after their formation – they served as a means to send out information, keep people updated on news and politics, and were a recruitment opportunity.[134]

A large number of narrators, most notably Gens Hellquist, Tom Warner, Dorothy, Debbie Simmons, and Neil Richards, spoke to the strategic importance of these cultural products. A large part of Hellquist's education came via the *Georgia Straight*, the alternative newspaper produced in Vancouver. "We were able to get magazines like *The Georgia Straight* in Saskatoon ... it was very counter-cultural ... In the late

1960s and early 1970s we heard about Stonewall through the *Georgia Straight*, I would hear about a new club opening in Calgary or Edmonton"; he started to wonder, "why don't we do something like that in Saskatoon?"[135] Undergrads in the early 1970s could read Toronto's *The Body Politic* in the University of Saskatchewan library. There were also American queer newsletters or papers, pulp novels, physique magazines, and fiction that opened up both cultural worlds of differences and social experiences.

In addition, Hellquist began his search for queer people at the Saskatoon News store in the city's downtown, where the teenager routinely staked out the store trying to catch a glimpse of men reading or buying physique magazines. Tom Warner had his stash of pulp novels that, ruefully, his father found and confiscated.[136] Dorothy subscribed to the Daughters of Bilitis newsletter, *The Ladder*. DOB was an American lesbian organization whose influential newsletter served as an important cultural text for American lesbians in the 1960s and 1970s.[137] Delivered to her home address, she assured me that since she was a housewife she was home to collect the mail, so her husband never had any idea she received these lesbian magazines.[138] In the early 1970s, Neil Richards was an avid reader of Toronto's *The Body Politic* at the University of Saskatchewan library, where he worked. By whatever means, these cultural products were important because they were the entry point to gay and lesbian representations and, ultimately, social and political participation. Similar to Winnipeg and Edmonton, Saskatoon, Regina, and even the much smaller centres such as Prince Albert, Saskatchewan (where a gay centre was established in 1978), placed importance on establishing lending libraries of queer cultural materials. This trend of creating libraries, making community histories, and archiving were widespread in liberationist circles throughout North America, partially due to the fact that a number of gay activists were either academics or, like Richards, library staff.[139] A number of catalogues and presentations were given to highlight gay and lesbian holdings in the university and public libraries. For example, in May 1983, Frances Rooney gave presentations at the Saskatoon and Regina public libraries about "Finding Lesbian History."[140]

When Saskatoon and Regina residents created their own gay and lesbian organizations intended to provide social and political spaces, one of their first decisions was to create newsletters. *Zodiac Friendship Society Newsletter* (Saskatoon) and *Odyssey News* (Regina) were the earliest iterations, respectively created in 1972 and 1973. By the mid-1970s, there would be more specialized publications, which provided information for lesbians and gay men that was explicitly political. One notable was the special "Gay Liberation Supplement" that appeared in the 7 October 1975 issue of the University of Saskatchewan student newspaper, *The Sheaf*. This issue, available free to all members of the University of Saskatchewan community, provided widespread publicity for political and social developments in the community.

In the late-1970s, two important publications appeared in Saskatoon – *Gay Saskatchewan* (1977), the newsletter of the Saskatchewan Gay Coalition, and *After Stonewall* (1979) – that deserve dedicated attention. These periodicals attempted to be the prairie equivalent to *TBP*, seeking to politicize provincial and urban residents to gay and lesbian politics. Unlike *TBP*, they were primarily regionally focused, and both publications made it a cornerstone of their mandates to be inclusive. The goal was to have equal participation and representation of lesbian issues. This goal was not achieved, but it continued to be an ideal that both publications pursued.

Gay Saskatchewan explicitly made it a part of their mission to engage in provincial, and to some extent regional, outreach within the province. Doug Wilson, one of the key editors and activists in this group, spent time encouraging the formation of local gay and lesbian groups in Carrot River, North Battleford, Prince Albert, and Moose Jaw. In between visits, film screenings, and small socials held at community bars and hotels (where attendance seldom reached double digits), the newsletter provided political news, offered a reader's forum where lesbians and gay men described their lives in small-town and rural locations, and encouraged readers to be proud. Because Wilson had great familiarity with small-town Saskatchewan, he did not preach "being out" as it was conventionally understood (self-declaring to family, friends, and colleagues), but rather that small town gays and lesbians take pride in themselves, and begin to find others, and allies, within their communities. Acknowledging the different strategies necessary for life in small-town and rural western Canadian places was a key part of Wilson's place-based queer politics. He did not diminish people's experiences, or presume that they hadn't yet worked up the courage or initiative to migrate to a larger centre. Instead he strongly believed that gay and lesbian Saskatchewan residents had the right to acceptance and self-determination anywhere. If they could make the next step to active political work, even better, but that was not a necessity. This perspective made SGC's message of support for small-town queers of all ages grappling with the realities of being queer in very different, potentially

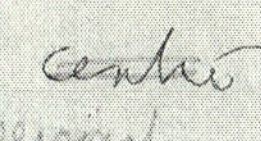

4.5 *Grassroots/Gay Saskatchewan*. Newsletter of the Saskatchewan Gay Coalition, vol. 1, no. 5 (June 1978). Neil Richards Collection, Provincial Archives of Saskatchewan A821 VI.4. Image courtesy of Neil Richards.

difficult, situations than their city brethren. It was also both a recognition of the realities of prairie life, but, in terms of queer politics, ahead of its time as many urban queer activists continued to hold out the promise of the urban, queer metropolis as the solution to small-town, rural life. Wilson himself inspired many people, such as Val Scrivener who remembered, "I was never that political until I met Doug Wilson and just watching him the way he stood up for things that he believed in … he could get people on his side."[141] Scrivener offered much reflection on how Wilson's personality and charisma affected people in the city, but ultimately it was personal: "He made you feel that way too. I was proud to be gay with Doug."

Considerable energy went into the newsletter, much of which Wilson wrote himself. Originally *Gay Saskatchewan* consisted of four pages of mimeographed paper stapled together, but it eventually grew to twelve pages. Started in February 1978 from a small list of thirty contacts throughout the province, the editorial committee encouraged readers to pass along the names of friends and acquaintances they thought would enjoy the discreetly wrapped periodical. Advertisements were also placed in other gay papers and journals, as well as in the classified section of many community newspapers, to alert gay men and lesbians to the newsletter. Archived letters indicate that the vast majority of people who received *Gay Saskatchewan* were pleased, although many expressed initial surprise at their inclusion on the list – evidently others knew their secret! Of course, some people asked to be removed from the mailing list. Considering the snowballing method of contacts and subscription that *Gay Saskatchewan* employed, there were surprisingly few letters of complaints about the content. More notable were the few requests from women who asked that their husbands be removed from the mailing list.

Each issue offered readers news about gay political and current events in the province, a calendar of gay attractions and organizations – primarily in Saskatoon, Regina, and Prince Albert – in addition to classified ads and readers' letters. Unlike the personals sections of urban gay newspapers and periodicals, with their specificities and arcane jargon, these ads were characterized by their yearning for any gay friends in the area. Ads such as this one were common: "Are there any males 15–35 that would like to share a career in farming with a kind, sincere gay farmer, non-drinker, non-smoker? I need a helper, good buddy, and we both need the companionship, love and respect of another person."[142] Ads placed by women were less prevalent, although they were more likely to come from small towns. One ad read: "Quiet, lonely

Medicine Hat gal wishes to meet or correspond with other women; only sincere persons need reply."[143] Less common, but nevertheless routinely published, were ads from married men who wished to balance their "stable" family lives with gay male liaisons on the side: "Professional, middle-aged family man in Regina who wishes to honour his family commitments, desires the companionship of other males, younger or older, possibly in similar situation. Those replying can be assured they will be treated with discretion and respect."[144] At its peak, 2,100 readers scattered throughout western Canada and the northern plains states subscribed to this periodical. Another way to gauge success was through financial or in-kind support. Members of SGC supported *Gay Saskatchewan* with financial donations, some of which came from "including regular monthly donations from several old age pension cheques," and in-kind donations (stamps, stationary, volunteer labour).[145] A large reason for this support and success was due to its unique audience:

> The people being reached are a different breed from those found in small activist circles and the largely ghettoized urban gay population for whom the urban, middle-class white male perspective of the *The Body Politic* ... has to this point been the major articulation. That articulation too often speaks neither for, nor to, the middle-aged farmer from all over the province [or] the dyke couples operating small businesses, throughout the province; the newly politicized eighty year old gay man in the South West of the province; the native lesbian in La Ronge. This is a different, and a broader constituency ... The sense of emerging community is tangible."[146]

Saskatchewan Gay Coalition was not the first provincial coalition (Ontario and Manitoba created coalitions first), but it was in Saskatchewan that such an emphasis on rural, northern, and small-town community building occurred. Endeavouring to meet "individuals in their own communities, provides an end to isolation" and support. And, ultimately, this "support engenders collective and individual strength and awareness and from that in the long term comes more openness. This coupled with exposure to positive articulation of gay liberation gives confidence and further movement toward the crafting of a larger, positive and open provincial gay community."[147] The success of this periodical speaks volumes about how receptive people were for these messages, and for the no-pressure encouragement to be themselves.

A publication that was influenced by SGC, and had, for a short period, overlapping editorial personnel (Wilson), was the periodical

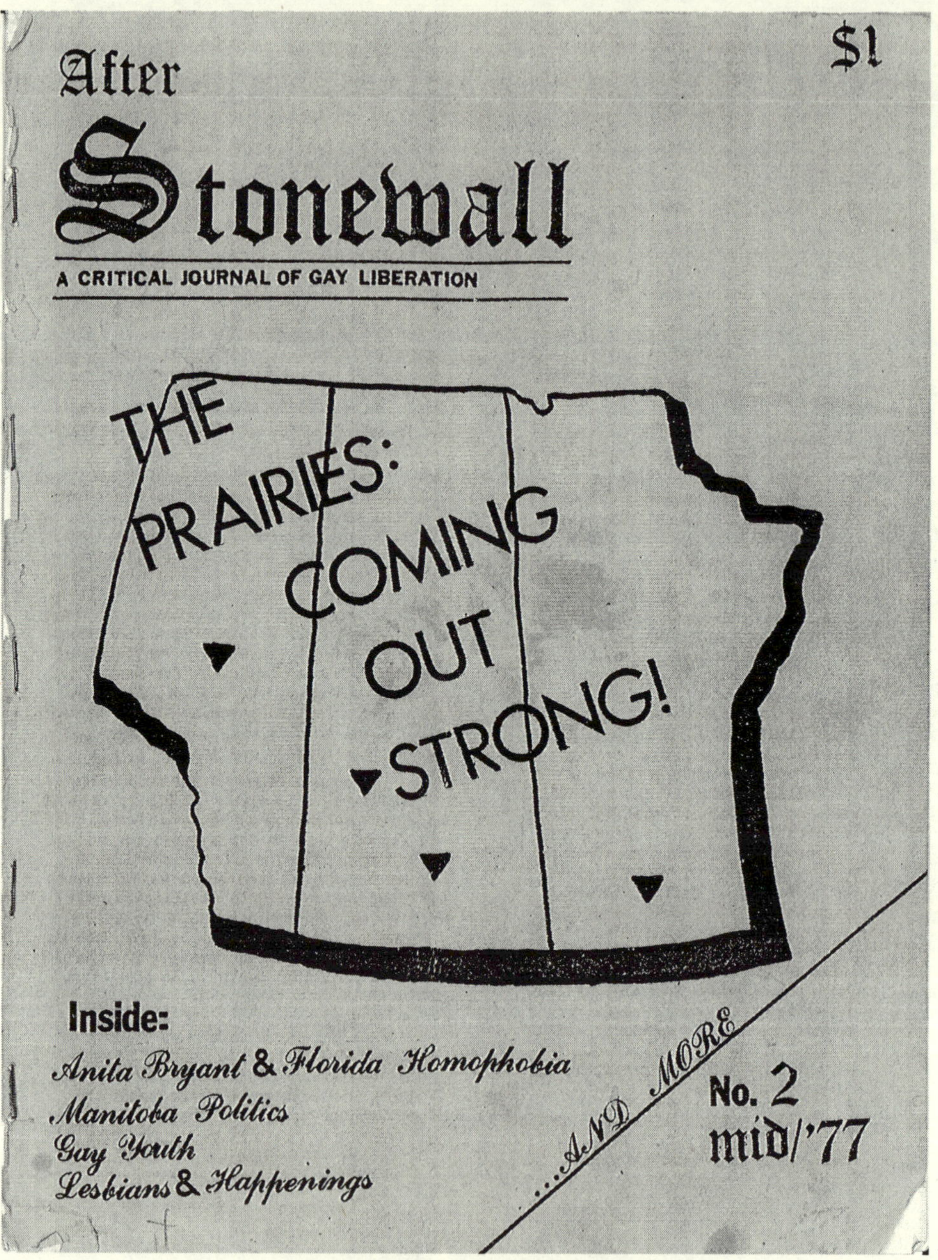

4.6 *After Stonewall*, 1977. Neil Richards Collection, Provincial Archives of Saskatchewan A 595 II.2. Image courtesy of Neil Richards, Creators: Walter Davis and Bill Fields.

After Stonewall: Critical Journal of Lesbian and Gay Liberation in Prairie Canada. Originally launched in Winnipeg in 1976, this collectively produced journal moved to Saskatoon in 1979: "Walter and Bill came from Winnipeg ... Wiesia and Amy came down the road from Toronto. Wiesia returning to her prairie roots. 50% lesbian control is now a real policy of this journal."[148] The fall 1979 issue also included work from Doug Wilson and Mark Erickson. This newly organized collective continued to be liberationist, viewing "orientation towards civil rights as a strategy as fundamentally wrong"; instead, they believed in "no compromise."[149] They wrote evocatively about how Saskatoon was more in alignment with their liberationist politics than Winnipeg, and of how Saskatoon's leadership role attracted Davis and Fields to the city.

Similar to *Grassroots*, *After Stonewall* had a primarily western Canadian audience, although they tended to attract more urban readers with pockets of "readership in rural Manitoba and western Ontario." Again, the goal was outreach as editors indicated they hoped "to break down some of their isolation through these pages."[150] In this way, like *Gay Saskatchewan*, they were on a mission to spread gay liberationist politics and to encourage gays and lesbians throughout the prairies to become aware of political issues; to participate in political events in addition to social events; and to craft a specifically western Canadian version of queer politics that was more cooperative, grassroots, and gender inclusive. "The east" – which practically meant Ottawa (national gay organizational offices) and Toronto (home to *The Body Politic*) – was deemed out of touch with how regional queers experienced gay and lesbian lives and politics. This was a persistent frustration voiced in many of the periodicals. In reality much leadership actually seems to have come from the west, and, at many times, it is noteworthy how, despite the sense that they were ignored, forgotten, or trailing behind, various initiatives – gay history classes, community centres, or periodicals – were, if not appearing "first" in the west, appearing very shortly after their central Canadian counterparts. One reason for this was because of the ways that gay and lesbian periodicals were shared and exchanged between groups. Thus western or eastern groups could readily replicate initiatives from other areas of the country. No periodical was better at reporting on political, cultural, and social events happening elsewhere than *Perceptions*.

4.7 *Perceptions*, 11 July 1990. *Perceptions* was edited by a collective of members, Gens Hellquist was the editor. Neil Richards Collection of Sexual Diversity in the University of Saskatchewan Archives and Special Collections Image courtesy of Neil Richards.

Perceptions was the most successful, longest-lasting prairie queer periodical (1983–2013). As I indicated, many organizations had their own newsletters and in 1983 *Gay Times,* the newsletter of the Gay and Lesbian Support Services (Saskatoon), merged with *GAZE,* the newsletter of the Gay and Lesbian Community Centre, to create *Perceptions.* Launched in Saskatoon, this production was the brainchild of Gens Hellquist, and it was his vision and energy that enabled it to continue for thirty years. The first issue of *Perceptions* appeared in March 1983. It was small, only three sheets of paper folded and stapled; yet its mission was large – forging community. When they marked their fifth anniversary (the fortieth issue), the collective took a moment to proudly reflect on their accomplishments:

> We knew that we wanted a publication that would present gay lives through the eyes of gay men and lesbians in the prairies. We also knew that a healthy gay and lesbian community needs a means to communicate and exchange information, that we can't relay on the non-gay media who often treat us with disdain when they aren't treating us to silence … Many of our readers in rural areas of the province have informed us that PERCEPTIONS is an important part of helping them feel connected to the larger gay and lesbian community.[151]

One of the interesting aspects of *Perceptions* was how frequently it used "western" or rural motifs, often black-and-white line drawings; while simple, these images attempted to visually demonstrate the rural, western reality of some of their readers and, similar to *Grassroots,* this differentiated the publication from comparable queer periodicals in which images of urban queer life predominated.

Initially produced by a collective of twelve volunteers, eight men and one woman, at their one-hundredth issue, only two of the original twelve were still involved, and eight of those people had moved away from Saskatoon.[152] In 1989, *Perceptions* became larger, issues routinely topped nearly forty pages and it was now a prairie-wide magazine. According to Hellquist, in the late 1980s there were "no other gay and lesbian publications in the prairies and out here in the hinterland we have always felt that our community encompassed more than our own cities and towns. When we don't hesitate to hop in our vehicles and drive the three to seven hours it takes to get to another large city's lesbian and gay community for the weekend, it makes sense that we keep in touch with what is happening in those communities."[153] This regional coverage of queer activities and politics no doubt accounted for some of their subscriber success. Other queer magazines came and went during the 1990s, but *Perceptions* endured until 2013 when Hellquist, its founder, patron, and long-time volunteer editor, died. Only two final issues have appeared since his death, so it appears that this periodical has run its course.

Perceptions offered political and cultural materials; listings of queer social, political, and community spaces; and advertisements for various gay- and lesbian-owned enterprises (bars, guest ranches, bookshops, et cetera). It also republished much news from North American queer periodicals. It was a treasure trove of information about social, medical, cultural, and political developments. While it really took their mandate to keep their readers abreast of queer current events seriously, their coverage of AIDS and health-related issues became a distinguishing feature of the periodical. Towards the end of their impressive run, lesbian readers routinely complained that there was very little content for them – and they were right. For his part, Hellquist always countered that the editors had little success attracting lesbians to write regular columns or to join the editorial collective. *Perceptions* had a wide subscriber base throughout the prairies, particularly thanks to the extensive listings, index, and contact information provided in each issue for various groups, clubs, and cultural events in BC, Alberta, Saskatchewan, and Regina, and while much "coverage" of queer activities has moved to digital formats, this periodical played an important role in keeping queer political news and discussion alive during its run.

Conclusion

Saskatchewan, the "flyover province" in twenty-first-century slang, a foreign world to all but those who live here, was a very different place for queer residents in the 1970s and early 1980s. As this chapter makes clear, there was a significant amount of community, cultural, and social spaces developed in those foundational fifteen years. It built upon the longer history of covert sexual and same-sex friendships, cruising spots, and bars, and was stimulated by the great changes taking place elsewhere in North America. For Saskatoon, the impact of scholars and students, with their ideas, experiences, and drive for change, was a key propellant. But that "expert" import shouldn't be overdrawn; it was also a product of a long-standing Saskatchewan immigrant ethos of "improvement" and ambition for the city. Saskatchewan born and/or raised activists, such as Hellquist, Garman, Dorothy, and later Doug Wilson and others, were engaged in these North American currents and developments: reading periodicals and novels, subscribing to organizations if they could, and aggressively seeking out any glimpse of sexual difference or opportunity that resonated with their sense of themselves as gay or "queer."

Much of this queer community development radiated outwards from Saskatoon, where early leaders like Gens Hellquist and Dan Nalbach initiated gay organizations by placing their small classified ad in Vancouver's *Georgia Straight* newspaper. Events began to snowball, and soon both Saskatoon and Regina had gay community organizations, social clubs, and modest newsletters. The 1970s were heady days, full of expansion of services and groups, and year after year there was more activity and greater openness in the city. Conversely, the 1980s were a decade of contraction and retrenchment, and, by 1985, one could see tangible signs that it was the end of an era. The Ritz Hotel and the Apollo Room were demolished in 1985.[154] The election of Grant Devine's Progressive Conservatives had, from 1980 onwards, put a chokehold on financing for community organizations, particularly those that advanced feminist or "radical" ideas at odds with the right-wing, conservative government keen to defend "traditional families" against so called "special-interest" groups. Shortly thereafter, the AIDS crisis arrived in the prairies. This epidemic exacted another toll, personally and politically. Saskatchewan's first AIDs death occurred in 1984. This medical crisis created a rapid reorganization of gay and lesbian activism, and voluntary organizations focused on acute needs: assisting people living with AIDS; lobbying for medical resources and research; intensified lobbying for human rights legislation; and community-based safe-sex educational campaigns. Those initiatives, with AIDS as the driving force, took the vast majority of community resources.[155]

From 1970 to 1985, changes in community organizational development and awareness of gays and lesbians in Saskatoon and Regina were not linear. For every bit of "progress" with the creation of new organizations or periodicals – film festivals, clubs, dances, political organizations, or newsletters – there could be reprisals. In chapter 7, on Saskatchewan activism and resistance, the key moments of reaction and reprisal will be analysed. Some of them were harsh reminders that "difference" wasn't always appreciated or accepted – Wilson's case at the University of Saskatchewan in 1975, Anita Bryant's Christian revival meeting in Moose Jaw in 1978, a handful of attempts to torch the city's gay social spaces, and a murder in 1985 offered harsh reminders that not everyone applauded the changes to "livable," liberal Saskatoon.

Regina residents, in their own words and in the words of their northern rival, were often more pragmatic; disinclined to make too much of a political fuss; more cautious; and perhaps constrained by the city's confluence of politics, bureaucracy, crown corporations, and the RCMP presence. Given the imbalance between the activity in Saskatoon and Regina, they appear to have been given short shrift here. That wasn't the intention but it does illustrate two key points. First, that Saskatoon really did have a unique concentration of activists who stimulated organizational activity in the city. No simplistic analysis of Saskatchewan as the birthplace of Medicare or as the first province led by a NDP government explains Saskatoon's gay political ascendancy and Regina's caution. But, it is also important, that what Regina did accomplish, to sustain and nurture their "club" from the early 1970s to the present day, represents much volunteer cooperation and work. That rainbow flag sign on Broad Street was an important moment and it remains significant, particularly since it is a major downtown artery with a large volume of car traffic. It is visible and it was and continues to be noticed. Gay and lesbian space, and community and organizational formation take many forms, and in Regina it focused on their club – and that endures. In 2016, Saskatchewan now has a pride network (funded in part by Saskatchewan Community Initiatives Fund), which supports "community development, inclusion, leadership and vitality."[156] This year, Moose Jaw, Saskatchewan, held a pride parade; Humboldt, Saskatchewan, had pride events, and a number of other smaller towns, including Yorkton, Melville, Weyburn, and Estevan, had various events – flag raisings, queer-identified groups, or events within other special civic celebrations that provided visible participation and evidence of the queer people living in those regions. In the final chapter, in section three, we shall see how the community organizations and community building stimulated activism and responded to resistance.

Chapter Five

"Outlaws": Organizational and Social Activities in Edmonton and Calgary, 1969–1985

I felt when I arrived in Edmonton [in 1980] that I was in Toronto in 1965 ... Here it was terribly hidden. There are two discos and a bar and GATE. And that's that. Now we have a lot more. We have MCC and Dignity and ALGRA, which is a provincial gay rights organization ... we have privacy defence committee, a gay father's group, a gay youth group, a choral group called the Vocal Minority, a gay study group, a drag group (the Imperial Court of the Wild Rose) and a women's group.[1]

> Walter Cavalieri, July 1983

Edmonton was such a paradise compared to Moose Jaw.[2]

> Paul Gessell, August 2006

Perception of the queer "scene" within the prairie region was highly individualistic and relative. Small-town residents', like Paul Gessell, impressions of "the big city" often tended to marvel at the opportunities for queer socializing. Those individuals who had a wider point of comparison for queer social spaces or came from outside the prairie region, like Walter Cavalieri, could have exactly the opposite impression. Each one is true, to a point, but in this chapter we move beyond the first impressions, and those of the newcomers to the city, to detail how queer residents of Edmonton and Calgary experienced queer social space, organizational formation, and cultural production.

Collecting information about rural experiences proved even more difficult to capture. Oral histories offered one such route, although they were far from perfect. In my interview with historian of science, Professor Margaret Osler, a New York–raised academic who took a position in Calgary's History Department in 1975, Osler offered a fascinating perspective on outsiders, writing history, and Calgary's gay and lesbian politics. Her recollection of accompanying her colleague, Dr Elaine Leslau Silverman, on one of her 1976 oral history trips to collect Alberta women's experiences is illuminating:

> Do you know the book that Ellie Silverman did on the *Last Best West* ... she went up to Northern Alberta to do those interviews and I went with her on that trip and we encountered a couple ... somewhere outside of Boyle Alberta ... in the middle of this parkland is this lovely old farmhouse and a pond with baby ducks and a woman who must have been 70. She seemed old at the time, great big woman, she was right out of some stereotype and another woman who was more normal looking who lived with her and they lived together in this house for hundreds [of] years and I forgotten what they did. This was a married couple, now I don't think I was there for the interview and I'm sure that Ellie didn't ask the direct question ... But I have no idea what that would be like and how the community would treat them?[3]

The Last Best West was a "collective autobiography about migration and adaptation" in Alberta from 1880 to 1930 and, while nuanced, there were precious few single women or women who lived without men. Only one photograph, of a female couple labelled "Homesteading Women, Square Deal, c. 1912," offers a glimpse of non-heterosexual women's experiences.[4] I am not surprised that in 1976, no "direct question" was asked of the female couple in Boyle, Alberta, but it is yet another moment of how researcher discretion, or reticence, creates gaps and silences. Years later, it is difficult to write such histories without materials. It is not, as many suspect, that queer people did not reside in the prairies, it is that sources for them, and moments such as the one described above, have tended to only partially capture their histories, if they are captured at all.

Osler's interview was remarkable for her own candour. Well aware of queer culture and activism in North America, and in Calgary, in her own life she adhered to that compartmentalized model adopted by Saskatoon lesbian administrators and academics. She seldom intersected with any community or queer activist work in Calgary. The reasons were multiple. As an academic she felt she was an outsider to this world. She admitted that she was fearful of the militance of activists, telling me "gay activists certainly seem fearless in a certain way ... they're much more aggressive or militant about whom they are." She was further constrained by her partner, a prominent Calgary professional woman who expected complete discretion about their relationship. That put Osler in a difficult situation. And yet she identified as gay, telling me "I call myself gay and am burdened to use the name lesbian, but I don't like it." Asked to clarify what she meant she told me that she found lesbian to be "clinical" term.[5] She was also a feminist, and was shocked by the conservative politics of Calgary. Asked about living in the west, she laughingly told me that she was as far east as she felt she could live, because she loved the Pacific northwest and the hiking and recreational opportunities there. When her partner died in 2003, there was much debate among a close circle of her and her partner's friends, but ultimately it had been her closeted partner's wish that Osler be officially recognized as her "companion" in the newspaper obituary. During her illness, her partner's views on revealing her sexual orientation relaxed. Her history department colleagues reaction was a surprise: "When [partner] died and this notice went around, and this is a pretty conservative department … and for years I was almost the only woman there. The people I was most concerned about were sending me cards, said something nice to me in the hall. I think there were only two people who didn't say anything to me … but I was amazed and for the first time I felt I really live here, it was okay"[6]

Reflecting on this interview many years later, and the layers of information that Professor Osler shared with me, clearly processing her own life decisions as we spoke, it was very evident that she would never have consented to our interview had she not been encouraged by colleagues, and willing to assist a younger scholar. She was forthcoming but uncomfortable, thus one of those rare interviews that historians of sexuality seldom capture. During our interview she was generous with her stories of growing up in New York as a "red diaper baby," her perceptions of Calgary when she arrived in 1975, and was not in any way oppositional as a narrator, or classically "conservative," but she had been cautious. She had purposefully chosen to be an outsider to this world for a variety of reasons she felt were defensible (class, career, nationality, partner's preferences, and the University of Calgary's culture). Her colleagues reaction to the obituary had caused a bit of a reappraisal of her decision to compartmentalize, but after nearly thirty years, she wasn't going to change her well-established practices. My decision to reveal her life choices and history is not to critique her motives. It is to amplify the challenges posed by oral histories, both with those we do interview, and of the many, many other women and men who never consent to an interview. That self-censorship, added to researcher biases or reticence, has resulted in our limited sources, at times, from which to write these histories. This partly explains why there is very little material in this volume about "early Edmonton," unlike early Winnipeg and Saskatchewan.

In this chapter Edmonton receives the lion's share of the attention for the simple reason that fewer narrators were located in Calgary, and fewer archival holdings for Calgary's queer history were located. Thus, in this volume, Calgary is cast in a supporting role. However with their community history well underway, under the direction of lead researcher Kevin Allen, I am confident that a more fulsome history of Calgary's queer history will soon appear.[7] Calgary appears here, then, primarily in relation to Edmonton, as residents of Edmonton and Calgary were often travelling back and forth between the cities, sampling cultural and social events, sometimes active in activism, and this participation and interconnection reflect on both of their cities unique experiences. In that spirit, let's start with reflections (circa 1985) about the early days of Calgary's queer socializing.

"The first public function in Calgary was Halloween 1968, at the Highland Golf and Country Club. About 100 nervous gays showed dressed to the nine's. This led to the formation of the 620, located at the Odeon Theatre at 620 8th Ave."[8] In 1974, the president of Club Carousel wrote about early Calgary and its evolution into a city with one of the earliest membership clubs in the prairies. She observed that about 150 members had initially joined the private business venture, the 620 Club. But, that was only the tip of the iceberg of Calgary's gay population because police harassment made many leery of attending: "It was a nice little club for the braver of the gays to go too. The place was frequently visited by police and cars parked in the vicinity of the club were often towed away or the license numbers were taken down and list was made of those who attended. Consequently many of the older professional people of our groups were afraid to go."[9] When Club Carousel began in 1969 it had over 600 members, making it "the largest private gay club in Canada."[10] An early membership card, with a stylized carousel horse, was the ticket to Calgary's gay and lesbian community as well as reciprocal entry into the other gay and lesbian clubs in the prairies. By the mid-1970s the novelty of this club and space was on the wane. The president was optimistic that they would turn their fate around, praising the "totally mixed club with 75 female and 275 male members" in

5.1 Club Carousel membership card, 1975. Neil Richards Collection, Provincial Archives of Saskatchewan A 1067.145. Image courtesy of Neil Richards.

1975.[11] One persistent issue in Calgary was the police, and eventually the community would create a liaison committee with the police.

Police harassment was also common in Edmonton. "Cal," interviewed by Maureen Irwin for her "Partial Chronology of Edmonton Lesbian and Gay History" in the mid-1990s, remembered that prior to the establishment of queer clubs, private, mixed parties in houses were characterized by "special relationships and valuable friendships" between gay men and lesbians in Edmonton "like you don't see anymore."[12] However, house parties had "lots of drinking" and invariably the "police showed up" on noise complaints. Cal remembered that the police were "not violent with anyone but it was harassment, they took your ID and always broke up the party." To surmount these challenges, mixed parties were held outside the city, sometimes on an acreage, while another group went to "Mann Lake fishing."[13] The experiences in Calgary and Edmonton were different from Winnipeg, Saskatoon, and Regina where police harassment was not mentioned nearly as frequently as Calgary and Edmonton.

Queer people did live in Alberta and, as the two chapters devoted to Edmonton illustrate, they were able to carve out pockets of queer culture, commercial spaces, and sometimes activism. But being queer in Alberta, historically and contemporarily, was never easy.[14] The recent federal government decision (2016) to posthumously pardon Everett Klippert, the Calgary man who was, in 1965, "the only person to be labelled a dangerous sexual offender simply for being gay," underscores the dangers of living in a "bad town" in a "bad time to be gay," as *Globe and Mail* journalist John Ibbitson has characterized Klippert's misfortune.[15] Klippert's 1960 trial and incarceration, on eighteen counts of gross indecency for consensual sex with other men, resulted in a four-year prison sentence. Upon release Klippert moved to the Northwest Territories but his criminal record followed him. He was questioned in 1965 for another unrelated crime, (which he did not commit), and again admitted to police that he had consensual sex with four other men. Incarcerated again, this time the courts applied for a dangerous offender status for Klippert. They were successful in that application because he was a repeat offender who, logically, they believed would reoffend if given the opportunity. Klippert's family challenged this designation and his case eventually went to Canada's Supreme Court. The Supreme Court's 3–2 decision to keep Klippert incarcerated indefinitely received widespread media criticism, even in Calgary, where the *Calgary Albertan* wrote, "the spectre of a life sentence seems to us a little severe." Ultimately, Klippert's case served as one of the rallying points for the 1969 decriminalization of consensual, private same-sex sex between adults. Inexplicably, for three years Klippert languished in jail until his July 1971 release when he resettled in Edmonton. According to family members, lawyers, and friends interviewed by Ibbitson and Kevin Allen, the working-class man was not keen to be a hero or to be cast as a gay rights pioneer.[16] He merely got on with his life, choosing to be quietly gay, involved with his family, friends, and later his wife. Klippert died in Edmonton in 1996.

Restoring individuals like Klippert back into the histories of Alberta disrupts the dominant historical narratives that largely excluded queer people from provincial history.[17] This work challenges, and revises, our notions of Alberta that continue to focus upon social and fiscal conservatism; natural resources, agriculture and ranching; faithfulness and small-town values as the defining facets of Alberta. Alberta was also, in the post–Second World War era, an increasingly urban place and in those two large cities, Edmonton and Calgary, and smaller cities, such as Medicine Hat and Lethbridge, queer people were beginning to become more visible parts of the urban fabric. Bereft of contemporary histories of urban Alberta, in particular the histories of Calgary's rise as a resource and financial centre; or of the massive post–Second World War migration and immigration waves that transformed Alberta; or a historical assessment of the various social, political, and cultural currents in the province – the stereotypes of an old, reactionary, largely rural Alberta continue to hold sway.[18]

Queer histories have been marginalized within western Canadian and prairie history for another key reason, and that is due to the limited sources from which to reconstruct and write them. All of these organizations generated materials – newsletters, posters, minutes of meetings, for example – but the emphasis on privacy has, ironically, the effect of further erasing queer histories. For example, in 1973, Calgary's *Carousel Capers* included this warning in the pages of the newsletter: "this is a private newsletter, published by a private club and the contents are confidential ... Names of members appear in the newsletter and these individuals do not wish publicity."[19] Furthermore, they warned careless readers that if they revealed people's names the newsletter might have to close. They were aware of politics elsewhere in North America, but Calgary was different: "Out of the closets and into the streets is a great battle cry for gays who don't have too much to lose but then there are the rest of us."[20] Until such newsletters and documents started appearing in civic, provincial, and university archives, as donations from former gay and lesbian activists and/or members, histories such as this one were nearly impossible to write. This work owes a supreme debt to GATE, the gay and lesbian activist organizations in Edmonton, Gay and Lesbian Community Centre of Edmonton (GLCEE), and GALA (Gay and Lesbian Awareness), as well as long-time activist Maureen Irwin's community history of Edmonton, and Calgary activist Doug Young, whose recognition of the importance of gay and lesbian history encouraged them to preserve their documents and, in so doing, the all too fragmentary links with the queer past.[21] These papers, housed at the City of Edmonton Archives and Glenbow Archives, and the work of John Cooper, who provided contextual information in his own family fonds at the Glenbow, alongside author interviews collected in Edmonton made the following chapters possible. Still, as noted above, there are significant gaps, and perhaps more than most works of history, this one resists closure. Calgary and Edmonton were challenging cities in which to live. They were not even able to muster the "scene" available in Saskatoon, in terms of possibilities for living a queer life, but they did have queer spaces, gay and lesbian clubs, cultural products, small groups of political activists, and, as destination cities for queers from many smaller towns and rural areas, they have a queer history worth writing.

Setting the Stage

Edmonton, Alberta, is a city of contrasts. Formally incorporated as a settler city in November 1904, with a population of 8,350 people, the city has experienced sustained growth throughout the twentieth century.[22] Provincial capital of the most conservative, resource-rich, Canadian prairie province, its nickname "Redmonton" indicates that internally it is regarded as a more politically liberal city than Calgary, its southern competitor and the hub for the southern ranching communities and small towns. Part of that difference is economic. Edmonton is not as wealthy a city as Calgary. It has a large proportion of working-class Albertans (some unionized, some not) and civil servants, which imparts a distinctive flavour to the city – modest, hard-working, and in some ways grittier. For example, in the 1980s, when both Calgary and Edmonton had competitive gay male sports clubs, gay men in both cities chose appropriately campy, cheeky names – Calgarians styled themselves as "Club Apollo," whereas Edmontonians chose "The Roughnecks." As the histories of gay organizational and social development in this chapter illustrates, Calgary lagged behind Edmonton in developing organizational infrastructure and they trailed the rest of the western provinces in their abilities to host protest marches or "gay pride" parades. What's more, with the exception of Gay Information and Resources Calgary (GIRC), they tended to be far more focused on gay religious, social, and commercial spaces rather than political activism.

Edmonton is home to the largest university in the province, the University of Alberta, and, as the provincial capital, there are a disproportionate number of government workers, university employees, students, medical professionals, and researchers attached to the teaching hospitals. The North Saskatchewan River bisects the city, creating a lush parkland with a series of parks, running trails, and an attractive valley setting for many of its historic government, educational, commercial, and recreational institutions. It is located in the central part of the province, on the Yellowhead Highway, the northern major highway route that links Winnipeg with Edmonton (via Saskatoon). Edmonton serves as the gateway to the northern parts of the province, and is thus a hub for resource workers and companies. For many northern resource communities and, indeed, residents in the Northwest Territories and parts of Saskatchewan, Edmonton is their closest and most popular destination for work furloughs and those seeking urban attractions – dining, music, professional sports, shopping, and social and sexual opportunities. A river also runs through Calgary. The famed Bow River, and this valley, alongside the foothills and grasslands adjacent to the city, with the Rockies a short drive outside the city limits, provide Calgary with considerable geographical advantage. This fortunate location, a magnet for sports and recreational opportunities in Banff, Lake Louise, and beyond, has brought Calgary the Olympics in 1988 and much international tourism. Calgary is also famously known for its Stampede and annual two-week cowboy celebration, which is inaugurated by the famous Stampede parade. This "Wild West" culture is fictional, a construct by savvy settlers who saw commercial and tourist opportunities in creating this western rodeo event. Much has been written about the Stampede, but for our purposes what matters is that Calgarians have had no difficulty "parading" as cowboys and cowgirls. So when conservative elements in the gay and lesbian communities claimed that "parading" and "flaunting" difference is not a Calgary trait, it was disingenuous. Flaunting western heterosexuality was perfectly acceptable in the city yet flaunting queer sexuality was an entirely different matter.

The discovery of oil at Leduc, Alberta, in 1947 (just south of Edmonton) sparked the Alberta oil industry and transformed the province into a magnet for international investment, workers, and new residents. This transformation of the provincial economy really accentuated the Albertan difference, particularly from its twin province Saskatchewan.[23] Unlike Winnipeg, Saskatoon, or Regina, both Edmonton and Calgary would experience exponential growth in the post-war years, as in-migration from other parts of Canada, and also the United States, caused a population explosion. While Calgary is synonymous with oil company headquarters and activity, Edmonton's population growth has also been impressive. In 1945, 111,745 people resided in Edmonton, by 2000 over half a million others had moved to Edmonton and the city's population topped 614,665 people.[24] In 1971, according to Statistics Canada figures, Edmonton had a population of 436,264 people and Calgary slightly less at 403,319. Obviously, this influx of people had a tremendous social, cultural, and economic impact on the province. For our purposes, it is important to note that such migration brought many "outsider" concepts of gay and lesbian organizations, politics, and community building to Alberta. Indeed, in sharp contrast to Winnipeg and Saskatoon, civil servants, academics, and students who were newcomers to the city and the province dominated gay and lesbian organizational activity in Edmonton. Thus, they were able to replicate activities and organizations from elsewhere (Vancouver or San Francisco). Equally, if not more significant, since these newcomers left family and friends when they moved west they were free to reinvent themselves as queer, away from the watchful gaze of family and childhood friends.

Edmonton Queer Spaces Prior to 1969

While there are no oral history collections, as there are in Winnipeg, to permit the rich personal insights into the pre-organizational world in Edmonton, fragments of pre-activist and associational life did emerge from interviews and recollections with "old-timers." These recollections are partial, but nevertheless they enable a valuable window into Edmonton's queer scene prior to the emergence of gay and lesbian social and organizational groups in the 1970s.

In 1979, the Alberta Lesbian and Gay Rights Association newsletter *Gay Horizons* extended birthday greetings to eighty-year-old Swen Sandberg – "probably the oldest gay activist in Canada," who had lived in the Edmonton area since 1926.[25] Subsequent issues of *Gay Horizons* noted that Sandberg had donated the organization's gestetner machine, a vital contribution that allowed them to print their newsletters in house. Dorothy, one of my Saskatoon narrators, recalled Edmonton fondly, remembering her weekend trips with her first lover, by motorcycle, from Saskatoon. Later she returned to Edmonton with her lesbian partner because they enjoyed socializing as part of a group of forty to fifty lesbians, many of them former Canadian service personnel, who congregated for camping weekends at an acreage outside the city.[26] Or like Paul Gessell, who routinely made the trip from Moose Jaw, Saskatchewan, to Edmonton for gay clubs and socializing. A "mere" four-hour drive from Saskatoon, Edmonton's size, more liberal alcohol and tax policies, and far greater retail opportunities made it a favourite destination city for straight and queer Saskatchewan weekend trips. Edmonton activist Maureen Irwin's "A Partial Chronology of the Edmonton Lesbian and Gay History" reported a similar subcultural world as those that existed in Winnipeg and Saskatoon.[27] According to Irwin's research, "long before there were clubs [dedicated gay spaces] there were drinking places, the queens frequented bars in the Mayfair Hotel, the gay and lesbian university crowd went to the Corona." Meanwhile the "King Edward Hotel and Royal George Hotel were patronized by gay men and lesbians."[28]

Irwin was a transplant to Edmonton, and in her own autobiographical materials recollected some of the challenges lesbians faced in the 1950s. Originally from Windsor, Ontario, Irwin was in the Canadian Air Force, stationed near Montreal, and she recalled that lesbian life in the early 1950s was a "secretive, rough life in late night gay bars. Most women wore campy leather or distinct mannish outfits. Often there was violence." But, Irwin noted "the only place you could be yourself was in the gay bars for men, which wasn't for me" because "there was a lot of heavy drinking and a lot of women were into the heavy butch image."[29] Instead, Irwin unwittingly found other lesbians through sports: "They didn't call us lesbians in those days. They called us baseball players. Sports was [sic] one of the ways that women of this self-identity could come together." On the first women's baseball team that she joined, there were only two straight women. After the game, "the team would go to a straight bar and just 'laugh and joke and sometimes touch,'" and thus it "just started to become obvious to me."[30] Well aware that such behaviour was taboo and could result in her expulsion from the Forces, Irwin noted that they never talked about these feelings or named them. Other women had similar experiences, both in the services and also on baseball, softball, and curling teams.[31] Despite a brief affair with a fellow servicewoman, Irwin eventually met and married a "nice man" in 1955 because a lesbian existence was "against everything that was going on in society." Married for twenty-three years and the mother of four children, she and her husband separated in 1978, and, three years later, Irwin officially came out as a lesbian. The numbers of women – and men – who made similar decisions are lost to us now, but this issue was often broached in interviews with many of my openly gay and lesbian narrators, and nearly all cited friends, family, and acquaintances from their formative years, who, though probably queer, took the more conventional path. Some, as Irwin did, eventually left their marriages while others were not as bold. Irwin and her husband moved to Cold Lake, Alberta, in 1965, and then again to Edmonton in 1974, where Irwin found employment as a librarian at the *Edmonton Journal.* Although not part of the community until the early 1980s, in her chronology, she noted that similar to Montreal there were all women basketball and baseball teams that played in organized civic leagues. JD, one of the women cited in Irwin's chronology, recalled that "there were many dykes on those teams, women ages from 20 years to 45 years, and most socializing was in women's homes" after games.[32]

In 1972, a sensationalistic exposé of gay and lesbian life in Canada entitled *A Not So Gay World* implied that life outside of the three major cities (Montreal, Toronto, and Vancouver) was dire for Canadian gays and lesbians. In the appendix, though, were resources for many major Canadian cities, including Edmonton. Edmonton's listings included the gay activist group GATE and the authors had contacted GATE for some information about the city. According to a "well dressed older man we spoke to … You can figure on ten thousand homosexuals in each city (Edmonton and Calgary). Seven thousand men. Add another three thousand women. The thing is, it doesn't really show. For one thing, here in the Midwest we haven't got bars that are exclusively gay. So there's no one place you can point a finger at and say 'Look at all the queers'"[33] Still, improvements were happening as the Alberta individuals contacted noted that "the Scarth Street Society, with about 750 members meeting at centres in Calgary and Edmonton" had just been created. "The Society, as it is known to members, is the only club of its kind in Canada that has a charter from the Federal Government."[34] It was in Alberta – with its unique prairie social structure – that the gay membership clubs were first created. Interestingly, Calgary and Edmonton's groups had started out similarly and then diverged, as Calgary remained a primarily social centre and Edmonton would become far more diverse in its gay and lesbian community, eventually supporting sports, artistic, political, social, commercial, and social service groups.[35]

GATE routinely received requests for information about Edmonton's gay "scene" and subculture from other organizations (and they reciprocated with newsletter exchanges, and sometimes waived membership fees for guests from out of town). The valuable concise descriptions written for outsiders offer some preliminary perspective on the city in the early 1970s. For example, in 1972, a communiqué arrived from the managing editor of Sydney, Australia's *Butch Magazine* asking GATE Edmonton to supply them with "urgent information on local scenes and places" for their December issue.[36] The reply, dated November 1972, offers a wonderfully detailed overview of Edmonton's gay male social, cultural, and activist milieu in the early 1970s: "The gay scene in Edmonton is very quiet, in the sense that it is hidden. There is a great deal of paranoia in this city, caused in part by the basic conservative nature of the province and general fears. Therefore a majority of the 'scene' would involve groups of people who interact on a personal level in small numbers." However, the response from GATE's secretary noted that changes were underway, thanks to the "young gays who seem to be unwilling to remain in their closets – they rightly believe that it is not necessary to hide homosexuality from society or themselves."[37] According to this letter "the social scene consists of a couple of bars frequented by gays and a gay club."[38] Because there were no exclusively gay clubs, a handful of straight bars were frequented, and in 1972 the most popular were "the Grand, the Ambassador, and the Mayfair," although it was noted that the "the Ambassador has begun refusing service to gays." The Ambassador's decision meant the Grand became the most popular mixed queer socializing spot. By 1972 there was also a dedicated gay and lesbian space, a social club called Club 70 (see below), which reportedly had 350 members: "It is open on Wednesday, Friday and Saturday evenings. Liquor is available on Saturdays only with dancing to records on all three nights." In addition to the club, another organization, Workshop 70, "has just been organized" to work in the field of entertainment "putting on plays, musical reviews, film series, etc." Finally, of course, there was GATE.

Gay Alliance towards Equality (GATE)

In sharp contrast to the numbers involved in Club 70 (approximately 350), GATE's secretary noted that the Gay Alliance towards Equality had "approximately 15 voting members" and several others who attend meetings. "GATE holds business meetings every Thursday evening and a social drop-in once a week, generally on Saturday evening at 7:30pm."[39] It was founded by "radical left wing students from the university" and was located near the University of Alberta campus in a rented house. Early organizers were Michael Roberts, Bob Emery, Bill Booth, Tom Hutchinson, and M.A. Mumert."[40] GATE was devoted to gay activist concerns, primarily lobbying work to change discriminatory laws, including the Alberta provincial human rights code called the Alberta Individual Rights Protection Act. It was hard to be an activist in Edmonton; Irwin's history notes such moments as a planned 1972 demonstration (concerning self-determination for Vietnam) only attracted two individuals and was cancelled.[41] GATE provided "drop-ins," where newcomers to the gay and lesbian world had the opportunity to meet others and to "talk and listen to music. We attempt to keep the atmosphere as relaxed and informal as possible. After the drop-in many of the people present go down to Club 70."[42] There was an internal tension in GATE between those most interested in activist work, who would form a regional affiliate of Canadian Lesbian and

Gay Rights Association in 1975, and those who wanted GATE to be focused on social services to the community. As Irwin's interviews revealed, the majority felt that GATE should be focused on "education and social services, coffee houses, camping events, picnics, and other social events."[43]

A similar description was offered in 1974 when Saskatoon hosted the first Prairie Regional Gay Liberation Conference. The conference attracted some twenty-two representatives from Alberta, Saskatchewan, and Manitoba. Organizers in Winnipeg and Saskatoon were favourably impressed by GATE's entry in the annual Klondike Days festivities in Edmonton in 1973, and thus it occurred to them that regional networking and information sharing would be beneficial.[44] As this was the first time the groups had attempted such an event, much time was spent cooperatively sharing histories, organizational goals, and activist strategies. Edmonton had the most diverse representations, as they sent delegates from three organizations. Calgary did not send any representatives (nor did Regina). Club 70 indicated it was the city's oldest group, having been formally chartered in 1969. With a membership hovering between three hundred and four hundred people (and an equal number of non-members who participated), they were the largest gay and lesbian social group in Edmonton. Rather critically, they noted "there was little desire to get out of their 'giant' closet as there they were protected from the police, the public and perhaps even themselves" by their membership-only policies.[45] As a way of moving forward, they hoped to provide more support to GATE's activities in the future. GATE indicated that they existed since 1970, but had been known as GATE for only the past year and a half. At that time, they offered male and female telephone counsellors, referrals, drop-ins, and were the point group for Edmonton gay activism. Finally, the third Edmonton delegates were lesbian-feminists. This group indicated that they emerged out of the women's movement activism of the late 1960s, and had little contact with gay male organizations or gay men during their formal period of organizational activity, from 1971 to 1973. Some of the women were participants in Cybelline House, "a lesbian coop house in Garneau where men weren't even admitted to read the electric meter."[46] Although participants indicated that they had disbanded in 1973, at the time of the conference efforts were being made to re-establish the group. In 1974, a handful of these women were active as GATE telephone counsellors, and believed that such work would lead to a "growing involvement with the gay community."[47]

Club 70 (1969–1978)

Club 70, Edmonton's members-only gay and lesbian social club, was the city's oldest institutional gay group.[48] Narrator Paul Gessell recalled attending opening night at Club 70, an environment he found relaxed and inviting.[49] In addition to this exclusively gay and lesbian space, there had also been cruising sites in the city and mixed use bars that catered to a gay clientele. Gessell recalled that the back five tables at the Mayfair Hotel were known as gay – even the doorman was aware that this was gay space. Interviewee Michael Phair noted that, historically, Edmonton's riverbanks had offered opportunities for gay male companionship: specifically the hill by the *Edmonton Journal* offices and the current Crowne Plaza Hotel, the riverbanks by the Royal Glenora Club, and the city's bus station washrooms.[50] In this regard, Edmonton featured similar outdoor and commercial cruising spaces as Winnipeg and Saskatoon. Men accustomed to cruising practices in their home communities could readily locate them in Edmonton.

In its early years, Club 70 had to overcome a series of bureaucratic obstacles and commonplace homophobic challenges (similar to Winnipeg) to establish gay and lesbian social spaces within the city. Club 70's first location, on the southeast corner of 101 St and 106 Ave, in a basement location under a Greek restaurant, only lasted a month before the restaurant owner discovered the nature of the "club" who had rented his space. Patrons arrived one night to find the door nailed shut. The club took the owners to court, and he was ordered to pay their relocation costs to 10242 106 St.[51] Given the liquor laws, they could not obtain a permanent liquor licence and hence each month they applied for one licenced evening per month. They were hassled by both the liquor board and the police to make sure they conformed to the liquor regulations. Patrons recalled that the police routinely checked that there were no bottles of liquor on the premises on the dry nights. Despite the rules, and frequent police presence, there was nostalgia for the "wonderful friendly atmosphere" available to both men and women. Gessell corroborated this view, when he told me that it was heaven to be in a gay space, listening and dancing to music with other gay men and women. He remembered that Anne Murray's 1970 hit song "Snowbird" was an anthem for city lesbians, and whenever it was played it caused lesbians to flock onto the dance floor. This memory provides evidence that significant numbers of women attended these dances.[52] In this, as in the comments below from William Thorsell, the issue of nostalgia for the old times – and of the ways that adversity forged identities and communities – was a routine recollection in oral and print interviews. Beyond dancing, Club events included socializing and drag shows. The drag organization, The Court of the Wild Rose, was established in Edmonton in the 1970s and proved popular.

As part of a membership drive, and to facilitate knowledge of their events, Club 70 started a simple newsletter in September 1970 called "Club 70 News."[53] At only a few text-heavy pages, this newsletter provided a basic summary of club news, special social events, club rules, and, less frequently, local issues or political activity. Physically located in Edmonton's industrial zone, in a converted garage, this rather modest club became a mecca for those queer people who desired exclusively queer space. In April 1972, membership stood at 260 members, and the club offered reciprocal guest member privileges with two other western clubs – Club Carousel in Calgary and the Gemini Club in Saskatoon.[54] Guests ranged from 50 to 100 people on any weekend night, and they had to be signed in with a paid member. Members were required to show their cards at the door, be of legal drinking age, and were prohibited from using drugs on the premises. Originally, they only had a liquor licence for a few nights per month: Saturdays were traditionally the evenings when beer and liquor were sold, Fridays were restricted to beer and soft drinks, and Wednesdays were normally dry. In subsequent years, those were renamed "coffee house" nights to put a more hip spin on this teetotal legislative restriction. Aside from drinking, the other burning issue for members was that straight guests were prohibited from attending the club. Those who brought straight guests into the Club were subject to a thirty-day suspension.[55]

Interviewees recalled that both women and men were members in the club, and that a small number of First Nations men attended.[56] Lists of board members confirm women's participation but – at least at the board level – men vastly outnumbered women. As with other such members-only social venues, Club 70 ran on volunteer labour. In the newsletter the president welcomed new members, informing them that "you've become a member of a pretty progressive club with a friendly and intimate atmosphere. It's acquiring tasteful decorations and the operation is apparently running smooth … We come from different and varied backgrounds, with almost every profession and trade in our membership. So let yourself be known … It's up to you – we need your help to make Club 70 the best club in <u>North America</u> – or the world for that matter."[57] Western boosterism was as prevalent in gay

5.2 *Club 70 News*, vol. 4, no. 10 (October 1974). Neil Richards Collection, Provincial Archives of Saskatchewan A 595 II.33. Image courtesy of Neil Richards.

organizations as it was in straight organizations in the prairies. Part exaggeration, part competition with Calgary's Club Carousel, nevertheless such hyperbole underscores the evident pride in the club's creation. At the time of writing, the club was only open three nights a week: Wednesday night from 8:00 p.m. until midnight, Friday and Saturday nights from 9:30p.m. until 3:00 a.m. Dancing and socializing continued to be key activities, but theatrical and special events were also held in the club during holidays and civic celebrations (such as Edmonton's summer festival Klondike Days). Ethnic-oriented theme nights were also popular, the club frequently staged events such as Bavarian night (free beer), Hawaiian night, and St Patrick's Day festivities. Live bands appeared monthly. Another all male gay space, the Gymini Health and Sauna, located in the basement at 10166 100 St, opened for business in the fall of 1972 and advertised in the club's newsletter.

By all accounts, the club was a success as memberships expanded considerably each month. Equally impressive, the club's guestbook indicated that many gays and lesbians from within the prairie region routinely attended the club. Occasionally, they attracted international visitors. In June 1972, a visitor from Berlin, Germany, attended Club 70 and indicated that the club was listed in the Berlin gay "who's who" guide. Ironically he had to tell "an Edmontonian that there was such a club here."[58] Affluent members were avid travellers, and the newsletter frequently promoted ski trips to Banff (skiing optional!), Calgary, Vancouver, Toronto, as well as San Francisco and New York. Closer to home, places like Spokane, Washington, promoted their two gay clubs as welcoming destinations for Edmontonians.

As the years went on the newsletter and the group grew more established. By 1974 membership cost $15.00 for the year, and member's rate for Friday and Saturday admissions ranged from $1.00–$2.50, depending on the type of event. In the mid-1970s, the club was located at 10242 105 St. By then they had branched out into more diverse social events, hosting a series of distinct events including musical plays. Their production of Hello Dolly was promoted heavily across the various regional gay newsletters and periodicals, and ticket holders came from Calgary, Saskatoon, Regina, and Winnipeg to attend the sold-out musical theatre performance.[59]

While the club remained "officially" apolitical, it did offer GATE much-needed space to sell gay and lesbian periodicals, primarily *The Body Politic*, to raise funds. They promoted GATE events on a noticeboard dedicated for their use and within the newsletter. One political view that both the club and GATE shared was the importance of gay men and lesbians to work cooperatively. This policy of inclusivity could, at times, be problematic and largely theoretical, but both organizations viewed it as an important goal to attract more lesbian participation. The example that follows, though, is indicative of how these well-intentioned notions were often compromised by their assumptions and stereotypes about lesbians.

Edmonton Lesbians

In January 1974, Club 70's "Roving Reporter" offered this observation about lesbian difference: "We came across a household of Lesbian Feminists and had a brief but thoroughly enjoyable visit. We learned that the term 'girls' is not an endearing one, but 'women' is. Like that men? The women are seriously contemplating a Lesbian-Feminist magazine. I won't elaborate as they are going to tell us more."[60] They discovered that a perennial problem in Edmonton was that lesbians found it difficult to find others: "The women present told us that lesbians tend to be more closeted than the men (generally speaking) and have a more difficult time in finding out where things are happening." The lesbians interviewed were positive about the "24 hour telephone service. Many women have called looking for information on the women's scene."[61] Commensurately, a "number of women were showing up" for GATE drop-ins, which the organization "found encouraging."[62] To facilitate more discussion about the unique situation lesbians faced, GATE organized a successful lesbian drop-in in February 1974.

A month later, one outcome from that drop-in was the publication of a personal essay by an Edmonton lesbian. The writer spoke about her own fears and isolation, and those larger issues which plagued the city's middle-class lesbians. "BT" wrote "though I lived with another lesbian, we were very careful to appear as roommates in public; we dared NOT use endearing words, touch each other, sit in any but a lady-like fashion … wear slacks or associate publicly with other known lesbians."[63] Though this relationship was undated in the essay, it was likely from the late 1960s or early 1970s, thus providing a window into what was a very limited existence for "respectable," middle-class, closeted lesbians, including that wearing slacks might trigger derogatory comments from Edmontonians. "In desperate fear we lived in a twilight world of our own making somewhere between the dull heterosexual way of life and the gayer style of other lesbians who were proud to be just that. Yet, we longed to meet other gays and to socialize with our own people hidden somewhere in our city," BT wrote. Those familiar with lesbian and gay pulp fiction of the 1950s and 1960s will note the use of the phrase "twilight world" – a pulp fiction favourite. By contrast with men's experiences of seeking out same-sex connections through well-known urban cruising grounds, the recollections of BT speak to different challenges lesbians faced. Self-knowledge and awareness was insufficient; even those women in relationships struggled to locate other lesbian friends with whom to socialize: "Where to safely meet other gays? How to approach them? Ah! That was the puzzler … We drifted apart, my friend and I and, whereas she is still hiding from her own shadow, I luckily met 'Mary-Lou' who pulled, prodded, pushed and argued until I dared to venture into the sunlight … now I am a member of Club 70 and love it there for I can mingle freely with my own people and I can truly be myself."[64] BT's recollections are worth highlighting here because they speak to concepts of identity formation. It reminds again about being careful to avoid an implicit critique that such spaces were "merely" social clubs. Club 70 may not have explicitly engaged in activist activities, nor did they use clear language to identify the club as a gay and lesbian space, but such organizations did encourage women and men like BT to come out into this world. They were a launch pad for identity.

Empowered with a born-again convert's zeal, BT's essay concludes with an encouragement to her fellow sisters to "come out amongst our own." Helpfully she clarified what this meant, in practice, in Edmonton. "I don't mean the hauling out of banners proclaiming our lesbianism, nor shouting of our pride in what we are, for all the world to hear – no, not that, but simply the abandonment of our self-imposed isolation and fears in order to mingle with other lesbians." For middle-class lesbians this was pride, Edmonton style. In future issues, BT wrote updates on the lesbian world for readers of Club 70's newsletter. Those reports indicated that BT found her newly liberated status invigorating, but not all the local women she spoke too were convinced by this message, many remained fearful of being more open. These fears were unspecified, but, naturally, we can surmise that they involve fears of job loss, fears of rejection by family, friends, and neighbours. The issue of queer politicization and identity – whether feminist, lesbian, or gay activist – has parallels in all the cities, where women and men struggled to define whether they would be political, and if they could, where to direct their energies.

Womonspace, a lesbian organization founded in the early 1980s (see details below) offered another perspective on openness, identity, and politics. From the fragmentary evidence that exists, it appears that some Edmonton women were interested in working with gay men on practical matters (e.g. staffing the volunteer phone lines at GATE), while others in the universities may have been focused explicitly on feminist issues. Extant evidence suggests that the depth of commitment to lesbian feminism and overt gay activism among Edmonton women was limited in the early 1970s.[65]

The End of "the Club"

After a successful eight-year run, Club 70 began to find that financial problems and competition from other commercial spaces were insurmountable and therefore they closed their doors.[66] The building was sold and the new owners opened another gay and lesbian bar in the fall of 1978 called the Cha Cha Palace. This venture proved problematic with management issues and reported fights among the lesbian patrons and it closed soon after opening. In 1979, the space reopened as Boots, a men's-only private gay club where women were "allowed only by the invitation of a member."[67] During this period, other commercial clubs catering to the gay and lesbian crowd had begun to open. The first was Flashback, originally located on 11639 Jasper Ave, which opened in 1976. In 1977, the Roost, a private men's club opened at 10345 104 St. The Roost's owner had originally been the manager at Club 70 yet, despite the fact that Club 70 was mixed space, the Roost also initially barred lesbians. Whatever the physical, ideological, or financial motivations for creating these male-only spaces, this proved financially unviable, and, in 1978, the Roost partially rescinded the rule and allowed women to attend the club on Friday evenings. Edmonton gay bars' decisions to prohibit lesbians (either completely or partially) were not replicated in Winnipeg, Saskatoon, or Regina. However "women's dances" were popular in all of the cities for a host of reasons, including the music played, the "vibe," the ability to carve out lesbian-only spaces, and, in some cases, the opportunity to hold dances in more central or "safer" areas of the city that were more accessible to women reliant on public transportation. Saskatchewan narrators also recalled fights among lesbians at some of the dances.[68] Narrators spoke about the periodic outbreaks of violence among women, which they attributed to heavy drinking and the butch-femme roles that were "very much part of the scene."[69] When Womonspace dances started in Edmonton in the 1980s, they had strict rules about fighting and hired security to maintain order.[70]

Similarly structured to Winnipeg and Saskatoon, Edmonton's succession of social clubs and venues emerged in the same time frame as their prairie peers, although there tended to be more social spaces in Edmonton. Edmonton gays and lesbians were well read and well travelled, they knew of activist causes throughout the region, the country, and internationally, but, similar to many of the members of Happenings Social Club in Winnipeg, there was apparently little desire on the part of the majority for political work. In a revealing interview with *FAB* magazine, William Thorsell, the former editor of the *Globe and Mail*, recalled his formative years in Edmonton. Thorsell provided a brief biographical snapshot, including that he was a top graduate from city high schools, and the University of Alberta (Bachelor of Arts in 1966, Master of Arts in 1970). After a second master's degree at Princeton University, he took a position at the *Edmonton Journal* as a writer and was later promoted to associate editor.[71] Thorsell remembered that at that time his "personal" life and his public life seldom merged. Joking that back then the trendy look consisted of white T-shirts, Levi's 501s, and a moustache, he remembered that "people used to say I looked like an RCMP officer in those days." There wasn't much of a gay neighbourhood, but Thorsell recalled feeling an adrenaline rush when he hit the club. According to Thorsell, "you'd drive out in 20 below at night, where there's no cars anywhere in sight, and suddenly you'd see this clench of cars in an abandoned area of town around a one storey cinder-block building with a little light over the door, and that's the gay club and it's suddenly quite thrilling. It was as close as you got to being an outlaw. I'm glad in a way that it doesn't happen [that way] much anymore. But it did create a sense of community."[72] Many individuals offered similar reflections – that adversity created community, particularly in the prairies where isolation and climactic hardship were and still are routinely cited as conditions for forging strong community bonds. Such recollections speak to nostalgia for one's youthful "old days." Edmonton gay outlaws were, according to Thorsell, satisfied with the thrill of sexual nonconformity, disco music, and a warehouse space for their club: "It wasn't a politically active community. It was just 'Let's go dancing,' and we didn't cause ripples otherwise. You'd get *The Body Politic* and it was another world, a politically charged world that just did not happen in Edmonton."[73] It bears highlighting that Edmontonians were well aware of events elsewhere and interested in reading gay political news, so it is not, as some might surmise, that life in the provinces meant lack of awareness of gay and lesbian politics – that was not the case. But knowledge is not action, and applying those insights and activist models into the local scene was not always the logical next step. When it was, not everyone embraced this shift – as the creation of GATE (Edmonton) well illustrates.

GATE (Edmonton)

Vancouver's Gay Alliance towards Equality (GATE) was formed in May 1971, and according to Donald W. McLeod's chronology was one of the first "Canadian groups to plan civil rights strategies ... and became known for its no compromise positions" in opposition to police liaisons, age of consent laws, and Quebec self determination.[74] GATE (Vancouver) came to prominence on 28 August 1971 when they held a demonstration of twenty gays and lesbians outside the Vancouver courthouse at the same time that "the first large scale gay demonstration in Canada" was held on Parliament Hill in Ottawa.[75] In the brief released to the press, entitled "We Demand," members of Toronto Gay Action highlighted the discrimination that gays continued to face in housing and employment as well as their ongoing hassles with the legal system – despite the so-called "de-criminalization" of homosexuality in the 1969 Omnibus bill. GATE Vancouver's Chairwoman Marion Cantie stressed, "gays cannot expect equality to fall from the Heavens, and we can't go on living in a Fool's Paradise, accommodating ourselves to being oppressed, living in what we call 'the closet' ... Our rally is aimed at more than police authorities, landlords, the government and employers; we want to talk to the ordinary people of Vancouver and to begin to educate people about who we are, and why our demands are just demands." The GATE spokespersons concluded by urging all persons and groups who supported gay liberation and civil rights to attend the rally. Cantie added, "After 2,000 years of persecution, what are we waiting for?"[76] As part three illustrates, these were heady days for Canadian gay liberation and civil rights groups. The first gay liberation group in Canada, University of Toronto's Homophile Association, was organized in October 1969. A year later, Vancouver Gay Liberation Front was created, followed six months later, in June 1971, by Vancouver Gay Alliance towards Equality.[77] In the fall of 1971, Saskatoon Gay Student Alliance formed, making it the first prairie liberationist group. Edmonton would follow the next year, when Michael Roberts, a member of GATE Vancouver, enrolled at the University of Alberta and brought formal gay activism to Edmonton.[78]

The charismatic and determined Roberts was initially a one-man band of activist activity, hinted at in his November 1972 press release where he stated that he had been "crusading for equal rights for homosexuals throughout Western Canada for the last two years."[79] Chapter 8 provides the analysis and overview of GATE activism in the early 1970s as the group lobbied the provincial government about the provincial human rights legislation. Extant minutes from GATE indicate that it was a very small organization. The membership listed a mere ten names – only one of whom was female. All members resided in Edmonton. Primarily, they were an organization geared to university students and faculty. Their classified advertisement in the University of Alberta student paper, *The Gateway* read: "Gay Alliance for Equality (GATE), Edmonton, holds regular meetings and a social drop-in every week. All gays welcome. For further information call GATE at 424-2011 or write to us at Box 1852 Edmonton."[80] Roberts had paid for the post office box, and the phone number listed was his private home phone. GATE was located in Robert's house, close to the University of Alberta campus. Meeting minutes indicate that there were tensions within the organization and as well as some "ill-feelings" between Roberts and members of Club 70. Hence it took time for the much larger social club to come around to supporting the activist group. At the first Western Clubs conference held in Saskatoon in 1972, GATE Edmonton and Roberts were excluded, while Club 70 organizers attended.[81]

Beyond outreach in the city, Roberts also corresponded with other gay and lesbian organizations in the west. An exchange of letters with Gays for Equality in Winnipeg, in 1973, offers interesting behind-the-scenes information about the role that Edmonton played in offering guidance to Gays for Equality as they became firmly established as an activist organization. Roberts sent them a copy of GATE's constitution and other promotional material. Asked about some of the challenges Roberts's faced, he replied: "You ask what some of our problems are; I could go on for pages and pages but will stick to some of the most important items. First, regarding money. We have a $12 per year adult membership fee and $6 for students." Additional money was raised by selling issues of *The Body Politic* at local dances and in the club, and asking for donations, but this left them with a fairly meagre amount of funds. The second major problem was their small membership: "Although we 'bring out' an average of five people per month, only a few of them become members of GATE. We have tried to rectify this by making the organization more appealing to people less militant by holding more social activities. There is a small core of militant people who do most of the letter writing, picketing and leafleting but the greatest number can't because of their job situations or other reasons." Regarding the city's political climate, he wrote, "paranoia is a major problem here in Edmonton … we have a hard time persuading people that the telephone line is not bugged, the apartment is not watched, and that it is legal for gays to meet without fears of recrimination."[82] Obviously, the Cold-War climate that other historians have addressed with respect to gay purges in the civil service (notably in Ottawa), and the surveillance of student and activist groups, cast a chill over Edmonton, and they were cautious about surveillance and the possibility of recrimination or criminal charges.[83] The Moose Jaw Rally to Answer Anita Bryant (see chapter 7) was surveilled by the RCMP, so queer women and men were correct in their assumptions that they were being watched – what wasn't known, naturally, was what, if anything, might be done with the information.[84]

Roberts's letter notes that Edmonton's bar, like Winnipeg's, had a thriving membership and perhaps this was working against the growth of more explicitly activist groups: "The Club is great for socializing, dancing and drinking, but many gays feel that this is all they need. It is difficult to show them that they *need* liberation as well as liquor. They end up voluntarily confining themselves to a ghetto of their own making."[85] Unlike Winnipeg, where frictions between the social club and the activist club were more overt and acrimonious, Edmonton's situation seems less polarized. Indeed, the social club did allow space for GATE to sell periodicals, and to post messages on their bulletin boards and later in the newsletter – so they were not anathema to working with the activists. Roberts closed with encouraging GFE in Winnipeg to call themselves GATE: "this would not mean that you would have to be connected with us in any way other than information exchange as each GATE group is autonomous." However, in terms of perception, Roberts saw clear advantages: "using this name would show straights that gays are united and are organizing on a national scale. There are GATE groups in Victoria, Vancouver, Edmonton, Regina and there is one being organized in Calgary, and GATE is the political arm of Saskatoon Gay Action."[86]

My research on Saskatoon and Regina indicates this was both promotional overstatement (Regina) and overreach (Saskatoon). Regina campus had informal discussions of queer politics, Saskatoon was far more politically advanced than Edmonton, and their connections with Vancouver were direct, that is, not mediated via Edmonton. Regardless, the use of the term GATE in Saskatoon was abandoned quickly, and links with Vancouver (if they persisted) were more informal ones between queer political leaders and workers, not formally institutional. While the current literature on gay and lesbian organizations and activism in Canada focuses upon Ontario, and in particular Toronto and Ottawa where there were sustained attempts to create "national" gay political organizations and to call themselves "national" in stature, many of the western activists and western organizations had a healthy dose of scepticism about how central Canadian organizations could claim to know their particular interests and needs, let alone claim to represent them.[87] As with many such notions of "national" political or media coverage that originate from central Canada, what is lost in the "logic" of these statements was that these were not one-way migrations, nor the only activist conversations. As this research indicates, a number of prominent activists who worked in central Canada moved there from western Canada (a partial list would include Tom Warner, Doug Wilson, Bill Lewis, Gary McDonald, and Chris Bearchell). At the same time, many activists in the western region were mobilizing regionally, hosting prairie gay and lesbian conferences for their social organizations and, later, activist organizations. Those individuals were influential participants in national discussions and demonstrations, including: Gens Hellquist in Saskatoon, Doug Young in Calgary, Michael Phair in Edmonton, and Chris Vogel and Rich North from Winnipeg. Conferences, workshops, and demonstrations all drew gay and lesbian activists, artists, and scholars together. A number of influential "national conferences" were held in the prairies, which meant they were also accessible for those prairie members who were interested and yet could not afford to travel to activist conferences in Ottawa. Scholar Gary Kinsman described these annual conferences as an important "cross country political forum for people to come together every year."[88] Prairie and western Canadian lesbian and gay activists deserve their due when we speak about "national" Canadian lesbian and gay activism. Given that the cohort involved in gay and lesbian activist tended, at least in the 1970s, to be quite small and disproportionately weighted to university undergraduates, it was even more likely that migrations to and from universities in other areas of the country would create much interregional migration.

In November, citing his decision to move to attend university in Toronto, Roberts resigned from GATE Edmonton. In September 1973, his lawyer negotiated the transfer of the telephone number to the remaining core of Edmonton members.[89] While this was often the fate of organizations dependent upon university students, it also seems likely to have been a case of burnout and discouragement over the glacial pace of changes. In November 1974, when the next Western Clubs conference was held in Saskatoon, Bob Radke, another University of Alberta graduate student, was listed at GATE's president. The services they offered were the increasingly standard gay centre complement: telephone information line, ideally staffed by male and female counsellors; consciousness-raising groups; and plans for a library of gay and lesbian materials.

Histories of GATE, written in its formative years by insiders, give much credit to Bob Radke for returning GATE to solid ground. People recalled that had it not been "for his dedication and foresight ... there would probably not be GATE today. And, he too carried an enormous load, as he sold *Body Politic* at all functions and at Club 70 to pay the organization's bills. He operated GATE out of his residence for a long time. Finally, in late 1974 the organization was solvent enough that they were able to rent premises on 109 Street, just north of Whyte Avenue (between 82nd and 83rd Ave above Bruno's Restaurant)."[90] As was common for such gay or lesbian offices, they were located upstairs, hence giving members and participants some degree of anonymity from passers-by on the street. While the key goal of GATE was raising awareness about gay and lesbian political issues, they could not implement those goals if people were struggling with their own identities and acceptance. Thus, GATE placed a very strong emphasis on counselling. In particular, they began to benefit by having volunteers with strong backgrounds in educational psychology or social work, and thus they placed significant emphasis on a professional, rigourous training program for their counsellors. According to organizer's recollections, over one hundred people participated in those mid-1970s training sessions. A persistent issue was gender imbalance as GATE was a primarily male organization. Though they received periodic requests for female counsellors and phone-line staff, Edmonton lesbians preferred to work with lesbian organizations. GATE kept scrupulous telephone logs, recording the names of people who phoned the organization and the telephone numbers of callers, which were classified in three categories: "serious, tourist information & nuisance."[91] During a four-year period, from 1975 to 1979, GATE volunteers took 15,998 calls. Of that total, "56.7% were nuisance calls, and the volunteers concluded that because of the volume, and the constancy of those calls "public attitude toward homosexuality has not changed much. Despite an increase of 'liberal tolerance' we are still surrounded by vicious homophobics."[92] Serious calls were for information, referrals, medical advice, or were from individuals seeking assistance during the coming out process, a category that represented 4,148 (26 per cent). The remainder of the calls sought the location of bars, clubs, baths, and cruising areas in the city, from city residents as well as travellers.

In 1974, GATE organized a day-long discussion with local lesbians to see what dialogue and political/community solidarity was possible. As reported in the *Club '70 News* it was evident that the situations faced by Edmonton gays and lesbians were similar to those faced elsewhere – "age of consent issue, experiences of discrimination (such as in employment and immigration), how people new to the gay scene can meet other gays, political activity, and the general social atmosphere in Edmonton."[93] Still, the similarities and differences logically led to questions about how the two groups could work together. One important note is the use of the phrase "gay women." This phrase, one that emerged in interviews in Saskatoon, was obviously also used in Edmonton and may suggest (as it did in Saskatoon) women who tended to work with gay men, in "gay" organizations, as opposed to those interested in lesbian or feminist organizations. "Can and should Edmonton's gay women be assimilated into GATE's organizational framework, traditionally male, and still maintain some degree of autonomy or identity? Should the lesbians form a group of their own and then work with GATE as needs arise?" At the end of the day, participants recognized that while integration could be beneficial, and sexism alone was not regarded as a valid reason for not working together, lesbian participants had a range of opinions on working with GATE. Some of the women did not want to "commit to political activism," but others thought they would like to participate in the hotline. Ultimately, decisions were left with the women to decide what role they wished to play in GATE."[94] One indicator of the lesbian political terrain in the city came from Edmonton expat Chris Bearchell, who moved to Toronto to work with *The Body Politic* collective. In an article in a local paper, she was interviewed about her career, and indicated that after being an activist at Jasper Place Composite High School, and as a member of the student movement at the University of Alberta, she found it impossible to find a forum for activism after graduation, and hence in 1973 she moved to Toronto.[95]

In January 1974, GATE established a lending library. The catalogue of ten available books is evidence of the organization's financial situation as well as the dearth of gay and lesbian novels and non-fiction works. The fiction-dominated list included such canonical books as *City and the Pillar* by Gore Vidal, *City of Nights* by John Rechy, *Giovanni's Room* by James Baldwin, *Maurice* by E.M. Forster, and *Boys in the Band* by Mark Crowley. Interestingly, *The Lord Is My Sheppard and Knows I'm Gay* by Pastor Troy Perry, founder of the Metropolitan Community Church in the United States, was the sole non-fiction offering. By summer, the list had expanded to thirty-nine titles, and material on gay activism and lesbianism were now offered, including: *Homosexual Liberation*; *Cases and Materials on Civil Liberties*; *The Gay Militants*; and *Lesbian Women*, by Del Martin and Phyllis Lyon.[96]

In May 1975, the *Edmonton Journal*, which previously had been hostile to GATE (refusing, for instance, to accept their ads for civil rights work, and later for advertising that copies of the *Body Politic* could be purchased at GATE offices), published an exposé of homosexual life in Edmonton. Given the dramatic title, "Gays Quit the Shadows, Seek Place in the Sun," and accompanying silhouette of two men holding hands, it was a voyeuristic portrait of what it was like to be a gay Edmontonian. Nevertheless, it provided much free publicity for GATE as members of the organization were interviewed for the article. Don, a member of GATE, indicated that he was angry "because very few people are willing to listen," including politicians, who largely ignored GATE's questionnaire in the last provincial election in March 1975. Furthermore, he indicated that the local media were not interested in publicizing GATE's issues, and the school system did not want homosexuality discussed in sex-ed classes.[97] In another article, entitled "Get It Straight; We Don't Want to Change" *Edmonton Journal* feature writer Jim Benthein began with the requisite statement about his heterosexuality and feelings by stating, "I am in a room full of homosexuals and lesbians and I'm frankly, uptight." Quoting a variety of GATE members, including women, the article enumerated various forms of discrimination they had faced and the difficulties of their life in Edmonton. Jean, a lesbian in her late twenties, reported that "isolation is the big problem for gays in Edmonton. You can come down here and meet other gay people but association with the outside community is limited. You can't be a part of any social functions in the straight world." Those men and women interviewed spoke of employment discrimination, difficulties in obtaining housing, and, for the two younger males interviewed, the trials of coming out to families. "'The hardest thing to cope with is your family,' says Doug, a recent high school graduate … It was important for me to tell my folks, because they were important to me. At first their reaction was 'goodbye.' Then they apologized and moved to the point of tolerating me. I'm hopeful of acceptance in the future.'" "Chuck, a grade 12 high school student … says he is being 'strangled' by school life. It's so oppressive there. Everything is so blatantly heterosexual and hostile. It's all 'You homo this and you homo that.'"[98] Some of these forms of discrimination would be reiterated when GATE made presentations to the Alberta Human Rights Commission (see chapter 8 for analysis of their political work).[99]

In the mid-1970s, GATE was very activist. As well, a few lesbians began to volunteer and their analysis proved valuable: "The women brought a lot to the organization – very involved, very articulate and committed."[100] Presentations were given in the city and beyond in the smaller communities, including places such as Grande Prairie, Alberta. They began to sponsor dances at the Little Flower School and subsequently at the South Side Orange Hall. In 1976, the offices moved to an upstairs location at 10144 101 St, north of Jasper Ave. Their new location – downtown – offered better access to their services. Counselling and social events – dances, coffee houses, camping, sports, and picnics became the key GATE pursuits. In this time period, Anita Bryant came through Edmonton on her Western Canadian tour, and GATE and others organized a march to protest her evangelical concert. Such openly political work had, according to some recollections from more closeted members, an impact on membership as "the high level of visibility of these activities caused a lot of people to leave or not to join GATE in the first place." Those who were strongly activist banded together to form ALGRA, the Alberta Lesbian and Gay Rights Association.

In 1978, the majority of GATE members voted in favour "of refraining from a direct or indirect political affiliation … this marked a new maturity and a new direction for GATE's affairs, and from that point on … GATE placed its emphasis on social service to the gay community of Edmonton."[101] This shift towards less political "work" at GATE towards a fully social service model was described by one member as representing a "new maturity." While I argue that continuing to advocate for and assist lesbians and gays in Edmonton to embrace their sexuality, and to participate in community organizations, falls within a broader definition of "political," which includes claiming spaces in prairie cities that were identifiably gay, it was clear that overt politicizing – marches, demands for governmental action on the human rights file, and speaking out about homophobia in the press were viewed as risky, and not something the majority of Edmonton gays or lesbians might choose. Student activists might indulge in such risky activities but "mature' members realized that service was more essential. Womonspace would have their own struggles over politics, and ultimately eschew politics in favour of providing "space" to be lesbian. Tempting as it might be to set up a contrast between conservatism and retrenchment in Edmonton, versus Saskatoon's liberationist and later liberal activism, that would be an oversimplification. In the mid-1970s and throughout the 1980s, there was a conservative backlash, partly political, partly the rise of evangelical Christianity, that while most pronounced in the United States, as Marc Stein has argued, created ripple effects in Canada.[102] In Alberta, a province governed by Peter Lougheed's Progressive Conservatives from 1971 to 1985, was in some ways bucking those trends. Lougheed's PCs represented a departure from the previous government of Premier Ernest Manning and his Social Credit Party, which held explicit fundamentalist Christian views. In 2012, when Lougheed died, "Mr Alberta" was extensively praised and eulogized as a "red tory."[103] Lougheed was commended for his excellent leadership on resource issues, intergovernmental trade and constitutional talks, intelligence and political skills, and for modernizing Alberta into a more outward-looking, business-friendly, less agrarian province. At the same time, social issues such as "gay rights" did not, it is fair to say, achieve much traction within the provincial legislature. In 1977, GATE's incorporation documents claimed "to improve the quality of life for lesbians and gays in Edmonton" as their primary objective.[104]

In the late 1970s, GATE moved to a series of successively smaller, more cost-effective locations within Edmonton's downtown core. While GATE's role as the central organization for Edmonton's gay community seemed to be diminishing, judged by their continual need to relocate to smaller, more affordable office spaces, the transfer of activist work to ALGRA and the growth in various niche groups in the late 1970s also drained some momentum and energy away from GATE. Regardless, GATE continued to provide some financial support and it became the central organization, and often the point of contact (like Gays for Equality in Winnipeg) for community activity. GATE assisted people in establishing groups and organizations, things that ultimately undercut

GATE's financial viability. Similar to Winnipeg, religious groups were popular. The group Edmonton Gay Christians was launched in 1976. In February 1978, a branch of the Metropolitan Community Church (MCC) was established in Edmonton with the Reverend D.A. Gunton as the pastor. MCC received a sponsorship from GATE that provided them with the funds to cover their telephone costs in that year. Two months later, Dignity Edmonton, the Catholic gay organization, was launched. Many of these groups had Calgary counterparts, and it was not uncommon for them to hold joint meetings. For example, Dignity Calgary and Dignity Edmonton met in Red Deer for a "mass and picnic" in September 1978, and at that time proposed that they "amalgamate their newsletters," ultimately publishing under the title *Dignity Alberta*.[105]

Also in this time frame, the Gay Fathers group was launched, as were two new activist groups: the Edmonton Lesbian and Gay Organization (ELGO) and the Gay Association of Red Deer (GARD, see below). Finally, ELGRO, the Edmonton Lesbian and Gay Rights Organization, a student organization at the University of Alberta, formed in July 1978. In the late 1970s, GATE also produced a newsletter called *Communigay*, which appeared bimonthly and was mailed free to those members of the gay and lesbian community in the city, and throughout the province, interested in learning about their activities.[106]

By the 1980s, GATE prioritized their social service work. In this regard, they were different from organizations like GFE in Winnipeg, which had a more educational, social, and media focus. Indeed, when one of the key people who had been involved with GATE moved to Winnipeg for graduate school, he wrote a lengthy letter describing the differences between the two gay communities, and in particular the differences between GFE and GATE. "Winnipeg's arrangement is different than ours," he wrote. "The Gays for Equality group has a community centre with an entertainment facility (bar, dancing, games room) which pays for the whole operation (including library, clinic). Their peer counselling service is quite underdeveloped – much like GATE's ten years ago. They weren't keen on my offer to change that."[107] Importantly, he noted his own observations about the differences between the two cities and about his greater involvement in Winnipeg: "so far I've been on the GFE cable TV program 'Coming Out' talking about peer counselling and the Edmonton scene. I'm much more out here (Winnipeg). One of my profs commented to me today about the TV program – no apparent concern."[108] It wasn't entirely, as one might initially presume, that Winnipeg was a more open place (remember many Winnipeg residents feared being too open). Instead, this man, originally from Grande Prairie, Alberta, and later a university student in Edmonton, was further away from his family and friends. Politically, though, Manitoba's NDP governments were more progressive than the pro-business PC Party of Alberta, which did have an impact on social and political organizing.

In 1983, GATE was in difficulty: "For a year now, GATE has been trying to guarantee its continuance through fundraising and dances but neither has produced the revenue needed to support its 104th Street Centre." With rent and utilities costing over a thousand dollars per month, and no government grants, it was on the verge of collapse – moving to a part-time information line. Their social services director was angered that the organization was not receiving support, as "the drop-in centre and the library have been and should continue to be essential elements in the coming-out experiences of very many gay men and women, offering something no club or disco can offer." Well informed about services elsewhere, he continued: "I have had a chance to talk with people who run gay community services in Los Angeles, Phoenix, Baton Rouge, St. Louis and Saskatoon, and to compare the services offered by their centres and those offered by GATE. Not one of them offered a program equal to GATE's in continuity, comprehensiveness or quality."[109]

That same year Walter Cavalieri taped an interview with activists in Saskatoon and Winnipeg in July, in which he reflected on his time in Edmonton, the changes he had witnessed, and the differences among gay and lesbian communities in the American and Canadian cities in which he had resided. The former New Yorker had been living in Edmonton since 1980. Asked how he found things in Alberta, he replied:

Bible belt. Terrifyingly so at times. It's a very closeted place. Probably the most closeted place I've lived. There are probably 50,000 gays here, if you go by the Kinsey estimate, which seems to be fairly standard, and yet I don't think that you see more than a hundred turn up ... Two years ago when we had our "bath raids" here, the straights staged the political rally outside of City Hall ... I find the community as a whole homophobic. I was working at the Citadel Theatre for two years and I had to be in hiding ... Since I moved my job into the social services, its different ... they knew I was gay and active in the gay community when I went to it – all I have to do is do a good job and they're happy.[110]

Although more optimistic about Edmonton's surging number of gay and lesbian groups in the mid-1980s, Cavalieri indicated that "I don't like Edmonton per se it's a city without history ... I also find that for a frontier city, it lacks daring ... but what this city has given me is the opportunity to work. To work in areas that are to me special, and personally very meaningful." Being able to work as the social services director of GATE and to direct the counselling program was very important. Cavalieri's comments about what Edmonton gave him are important to underscore. Gays and lesbians, like their straight counterparts, live in various cities, small towns, and rural areas for a host of reasons, but employment and educational opportunities are two of the prime ones. While many scholars have discussed migratory patterns pertaining primarily to issues of sexual identity and the "search" for communities, such a focus on sexual identities obscures the other reasons for mobility and residency. Alberta cities were, in the postwar period, in a period of rapid expansion due to the economic booms that required both resource workers and then a whole compliment of service, governmental, commercial, and social service infrastructure to support the resource sector. People might not have "dreamed" of moving to Edmonton, but they did eagerly seek the employment opportunities it offered, and, once there, some of these migrants contributed significantly to the small gay and lesbian communities and organizations that they joined or founded.

GATE's history has an interesting twist at the end, as a series of issues reached a crescendo in 1987 when the board had to inform members that due to the inability to produce audited financial statements from 1980 to 1985 they had lost their society status. Unable to utilize the name GATE, they brought forward a motion to create a new organization that would assume GATE's role and operate with a constitution that was only slightly modified. This new organization recognized the need to refer to both gay men and lesbians, and also sought to achieve one of GATE's long held goals – to establish a community centre. The new name reflected both of those changes, and in 1987 the Gay and Lesbian Community Centre of Edmonton (GLCCE) was created.

Womonspace

During the decade in which GATE attempted to solidify its position as the key organization serving all of Edmonton's gay and lesbian residents, one of its ongoing challenges was gendered. Specifically, women in Edmonton sought their own space and opportunities for socialization. To that end, Womonspace was created as a non-profit social and recreational organization for gay women (their terminology).[111] Although a number of groups for Edmonton gays had formed in the late 1970s, there was a distinct lack of women's programming. Ironically, one of the reasons cited for this was GATE's policy to be a "mixed" organization – and thus all social, educational, and activist initiatives they organized were to be for both women and men. The few women who volunteered at GATE, "as trained peer counsellors," reported that what they "heard over the phone, in the office, and almost everywhere else was 'How come there is nothing happening for women in this city?'"[112] There was a demand, then, for women's-only spaces, and, in particular, a strong demand for women's dances. The first initiative was to approach GATE to establish a women's dance. Though GATE indicated that they could not explicitly support such a venture given their policy of trying to forge alliances between gay men and lesbians, they would, unofficially, underwrite such an initiative. Thus, with GATE's financial stake and their expertise on how to organize a dance – permit application, security, drinks, et cetera – a group of eight women decided to organize a women's dance in Edmonton in September 1981. This initiative was a great success. From there, they grew more confident at organizing dances and eventually decided to form their own group. Initially Womonspace meetings were held at Every Woman's Place (EWP) located at 9926 112 St on the second Tuesday of every month.

EWP was an interesting concept in its own right. Located downtown, in the community of Oliver, this six-room, non-profit centre served women's "social, cultural, educational, physical and metaphysical" needs.[113] Established in June 1981, this self-financing group had attracted 125 members in their first six months. They were not explicitly lesbian, nor were they radical feminists, stating, "radical feminism is not a priority of EWP but it lends it support to groups and individuals fighting violence against women, sexual discrimination, nuclear weaponry, boredom and similar concerns." Beyond providing space for causes and consciousness-raising, they offered the usual gamut of social activities and educational activities – a library, lectures and workshops, pub nights, coffee nights, films, and games. While they were inclusive about providing space for all women (and children), men were prohibited from the place because, quite simply, they believed that there were plenty of spaces for men in male-dominated organizations. Sources on this group are limited, but, from their own published information, it appears that they attracted a diverse group of women from teenagers to those in their sixties, from a "gamut of different lifestyles." This was the first time since 1975 that Edmonton had a women's centre. Annual membership fees were based on sliding scale, depending upon income, and ranged from five dollars to twenty-five dollars per year.

Beyond the Womonspace dances, the group also worked with other women's or lesbian groups on special initiatives; for instance, in July 1982 the Edmonton Lesbian Collective and Womonspace screened the American film "Word is Out." Women interviewed by graduate student Noelle Lucas for her master of arts thesis on Womonspace indicated that the group's members were divided over overt political activism and, indeed, overt identification as a lesbian organization remained a contentious issue for the group.[114] Hence, while they were identified in gay and lesbian newsletters as a lesbian social and recreational organization, they were seldom so identified in more mainstream publications. In their own newsletter, first published in 1982, Womonspace defined themselves as a "social, recreational and educational resource group" for women.[115] Similarly, to protect the needs of women who were still discreet about their sexuality (because they feared the loss of their employment, children, or family members should their lesbianism be divulged), they eschewed political involvement. This choice was not without controversy, as more political lesbians (including those affiliated with the University of Alberta) disparaged Womonspace's members.[116] Similar to the experiences of membership disparities between gay activist groups and gay social groups (whether in Winnipeg, Saskatoon, or Edmonton), Womonspace's emphasis on creating a community, through their dances and later their very well-produced newsletter, *Womonspace News*, attracted a far larger membership. One member, Maureen Irwin, who was active in a host of social, organizational, and activist groups, recalled that while some people dismissed Womonspace for its emphasis on socializing, the number of women who came out into the community through the Womonspace organization and went on to participate in other ventures was impressive. According to Irwin:

> The legislation in Canada did not change because Womonspace had their dances, [Womonspace] provides a place for people to come out and provides community supports. It's a place to meet with others and meet new

partners. It provides the needed social support for many. [Members] tend to downplay that part of it. I think we have to recognize that those people who were marching for change stood shoulder to shoulder. Most of them were lesbians which included GALA (Gay and Lesbian Awareness) people and people associated with Womonspace. We changed in 20 years in ways I could never have dreamed possible. If everyone had just joined Womonspace to have fun, the world wouldn't have changed. I think the biggest thing anyone has ever done is coming out and leading our own lives. This is how we change things – by being out. That means being out in the banks, the grocery stores and in the public as much as possible. That is where the activism really takes place.[117]

Individual activist recollections of Womonspace varied dramatically. Elizabeth (Liz) Massiah who had moved from Waterloo, Ontario, to Edmonton in 1983 remembered that when she arrived "there wasn't very much" in Edmonton's lesbian and gay social calendar. It "was Womonspace and Womonspace has done a wonderful job of creating a social community for lesbians. They had mostly dances and potlucks ... You could go to two or three bars and the men would go too. It wasn't very integrated at all. Dignity was very active and that was mostly Catholic men."[118] However, because Massiah refused to be "discreet" about her lesbianism and was very focused on activism, particularly working on successive campaigns to achieve legislative changes in Alberta, she clashed with Womonspace's decision to be officially non-political and to forgo explicitly mentioning their lesbianism in the media. Massiah was expelled from Womonspace for her openness, and, in our interview, naturally, she still reflected bitterly on that difficult time, "it cost me a lot over the years, I have suffered more for it [being out] within the women's community."[119] Such a perspective also cost Womonspace, as they had to cover a significant financial shortfall after a board member embezzled funds, and the organization refused to go to the police because they didn't wish to divulge the nature of the organization publicly, nor did they want to receive any negative publicity.[120] Naturally, such refusal to seek any form of redress for this white-collar crime speaks to two key issues: internalized oppression and worries about revealing the members' sexual identities in the first instance. But, second, it reflects the local climate; undoubtedly Womonspace's board had cause to worry about how the police, courts, and the media might treat allegations of criminal activity in a lesbian social organization.

Gay Association of Red Deer (GARD)

While the bulk of attention in this chapter focuses on the city of Edmonton, as in Manitoba and Saskatchewan, work was also underway in smaller cities to establish queer organizations. In 1978, "Bruce" recalled that Gay Information and Resource Centre (Calgary) and other organizations had been influential in encouraging him to create an organization in Red Deer, Alberta. Here, he offers his own perspective on why he felt the Gay Association of Red Deer (GARD) was important and the challenges involved in establishing a gay organization in a small, central Alberta town: "Having lived in Red Deer for many years, and having a reasonable knowledge of the City and Central Alberta, I knew the time had come to unite gay people throughout the region."[121] "It was a long slow process," and one that Bruce noted involved "placing ads in the personal column of the *Ad-Visor* community newspaper, and being refused advertising privileges at the *Red Deer Advocate*. But eventually the letters began to flow in, originally to the *Ad-Visor*, and subsequently to the Association's own Box 356."[122] The advertisement, much like the one Doug Wilson placed a few years earlier in the University of Saskatchewan's *Sheaf*, seems relatively benign now: "Gay Association of Red Deer. For details and information write Box A.D. Advisor. Strictly Confidential."[123] People wrote from a variety of cities, small towns, rural, and recreational communities in Alberta including Red Deer, Alix, Calgary, Camrose, Caroline, Edmonton, Hughendon, Lacombe, Olds, Rimbey, Rockey Mountain House, Sylvan Lake, and Tees, as well as Prince Albert, Saskatchewan, to express interest. Emboldened, a date was set for their first meeting, 24 February 1979 at the G.H. Dawe Community Centre, and fourteen people arrived to discuss planning an organization, watch a screening of the National Film Board's "New Romance," and socialize. Neither GIRC nor Gay Saskatchewan, both of which promised to send representatives, was able to attend.

In subsequent newsletters, Bruce described the organization's meetings, their goals, and some of the challenges they faced. It is instructive to note his reflections about the first meeting: "Attending one's first meeting can be a rather frightening experience for some gay people in the process of 'coming out.' Almost everyone was very apprehensive at first but it was found to be a very worthwhile and rewarding experience for all."[124] Bruce recalled he was "completely inexperienced and incapable of running a meeting," but he found his footing and the group discussed a range of issues, including their goals to meet regularly and plan some social events, to not become a "tricking agency" or "dating service," and to investigate getting a "a place of their own." With five dollars in their bank account, such dreams were not going to be realized. Bruce encouraged people to subscribe to the free papers produced by Saskatchewan Gay Coalition (*Grassroots)* and GIRC. When the meeting adjourned everyone headed to Choppy's Disco in the Capri Centre for drinks and socializing.

In early April, members of GIRC were on hand, hoping to encourage GARD to formalize their organization and establish some goals, such as a telephone line and the creation of "gay space." The GIRC representative, unnamed, said that it would be "interesting to have Gay people frequent a certain centrally located tavern (or corner within a tavern) so that this area would acquire a Gay reputation and serve as an informal place for Gays to meet. Any ideas?"[125] In June, it was announced that the Valencia Lounge of the Granada Inn was "quickly acquiring the reputation as a Gay Bar" and, with an excellent "cruising area," it was chosen as their informal location.[126]

April 1979 was a busy month in Red Deer as five members of GATE (Edmonton) spoke at Red Deer College. Later that month, Doug Wilson of SGC was in Red Deer, discussing gay organizations and goals and screening the film *Word Is Out*. Support from the larger urban and provincial groups helped to bolster Red Deer's small community as part of their own goals of coalition building. This support was critically important, and while it is presumptuous to claim that such smaller centres would not have managed to organize their own groups, two of the more successful small cities to organize gay groups / gay centres – Red Deer, Alberta, and Prince Albert, Saskatchewan – were certainly beneficiaries of support from SGC and GIRC. That said the goals of urban activists were often different from those residents of these smaller cities and farming areas. The recurrent requests from the local attendees at GARD were for social events, often at members' homes or at community locations. Activists tried to encourage them to create organizational spaces and activities, such as telephone information lines, libraries, and discussion groups. Activist mentors hoped that such developments would foster more awareness and pride. Doug Young (Calgary GIRC) and Doug Wilson (Saskatchewan Gay Coalition) were both originally from small towns (Medicine Hat, Alberta, and Meadow Lake, Saskatchewan, respectively), and so they were familiar with these men's situation. However they were also proud, tough gay activists who were defiantly "out" to everyone who knew them. Having long since moved to larger cities and gained reputations as regional gay activists, their advice and suggestions were beyond those of the neophyte organizers at GARD who initially struggled to chair meetings.

Ultimately, GARD established three goals for itself: "To get lesbians and gay men together in an association for self betterment and to provide social activities"; to "represent Lesbians and Gay men in Central Alberta"; and to "promote self awareness and to provide a counselling service in the future."[127] Twelve people voted on these motions, eleven in favour and one undecided. They elected four officers, all men, to run the organization. While lesbians were welcomed, clearly this was a primarily male group. Those members of GARD prepared to discuss policies, institutional goals, and perhaps politics were a small fraction of the lesbian and gay population of central Alberta. Adopting appropriately cautious goals, they hoped to foster more interest in GARD and increase their membership base. However, within a few years, the enthusiasm for this organization had waned, the newsletter ceased, and "gay life" in Red Deer returned to normal. Doug Young, one of the Calgary organizers who had encouraged this initiative, reported that GARD was a victim of its own success: "all the people who did come out and get involved ended up moving to Calgary! Which isn't really the idea."[128]

These glimpses from GARD newsletters might be have been all we knew about Red Deer gay and lesbian life if not for a fortuitous decision, on the part of the Red Deer and District Museum, to initiate a cultural history of lesbian and gay life in Alberta in the late 1990s.[129] This project was funded by the Alberta Museums Association Research Communities Grant programme and resulted in nineteen interviews with lesbians and gay men. Part of a larger project to collect the social histories of central Albertans, this project with lesbians and gays resulted in sixteen usable interviews (equal numbers of women and men participated) and the collection of a few boxes of gay ephemera. Those interviewed came from "a variety of backgrounds, including highly trained professionals, writers, hospitality industry workers, artists, teachers, health care workers, and skilled small business owners."[130] Over half of them were self-employed so, in many respects, their sexual orientation was not a liability to employment. However, because of "the volatile environment" of central Alberta, which was recognized as a "growth area for religious groups ... belonging to the Christian Right and to white supremacy groups," the research director wrote that it was "critical to ensure that the identities of individuals participating in this study be protected."[131] Red Deer Museum provided me with access to these interview transcripts, the letters of support and protest that were received when the provincial grant was made public, and the cultural materials collected. Yet, "anonymity, confidentiality and a low profile became guiding principles for the study," and so while I was provided access to these documents I was prevented from making reference to any material from the transcripts.[132] Most of the interviewees expressed the need to be constantly vigilant, and fears about their physical safety and economic livelihoods abounded, as this example illustrates: "God, you (interviewer) hold all of our futures in your hand, cause you could really [unstated] – but you know that. I can't afford to go out and have my face in the newspaper, so the people that have nothing to lose are the ones that are visible to the community."[133]

Visibility and openness were calibrated in degrees. According to the researcher, with "few exceptions" the narrators were out to their "families of origin and, after some struggle, had been accepted."[134] One of the key challenges, naturally, was finding other queer people: "Study participants often reported meeting their partners in larger centres like Calgary and Edmonton and some either carried on commuter relationships or their partners moved from large cities to be with them." Others reported "creative solutions" that included community centre dances (which would have been those organized by GARD) and later the use of a local bar called The Other Place (TOPS).[135] No information was provided in the report summary about the reaction to having lesbian or gay partners move into Red Deer to live with narrators, which, given the reality that everyone's business was known in smaller communities, seems an odd issue not to pursue. Descriptions of the bar are illustrative of the ways that even in a small city like Red Deer, making queer spaces was possible:

(TOPS) is the only place in town where someone can come in and be who they want to be. It doesn't matter whether they are gay, straight, bisexual, transgendered. We have transgendered people who have been in here. We have guys who are straight but like dressing up in women's clothes, and they want to go out in public. Well, they're accepted here but they're not accepted any other place in town. They feel comfortable here and they can come here and be who they want to be. The minute they walk through the door, they have to put on their other role. They have to go into the pretend mode again. This is not a pick up place really. Here, it's more a sit and visit – oh, you're new, introduce yourself, sit, play pool. Like last night there weren't many people here, maybe 7 of us, but we had a lot of fun because we were having pool tournaments, just having a good time. And nobody got drunk, we sat and visited a lot.[136]

While the description of the bar scene at TOPS was a contemporary rather than historical one, I've reproduced the quote in full because it challenges some of the testimony about "vigilance" and suggests ways that spaces were not impossible to find, showing how word of mouth would build about this pub's clientele. And, it points again to the importance of social spaces for identity formation and community building. In the interviews, perhaps not surprisingly, one hears echoes of the GARD members goals for gay and lesbian life in Red Deer, with narrators expressing less interest in "organizational and advocacy groups than to those with purely social intent."[137] Thirty years later, a wide range of queer people living and loving in Red Deer still expressed little enthusiasm for "politics" or creating organizations; instead, they were most interested in "social" opportunities and spoke with praise about the enlarged social spaces in Calgary and Edmonton, and of the ongoing challenges of living in a small, central Albertan city. The museum's leadership in proposing this gay and lesbian oral history project was admirable, particularly in the face of the firestorm of controversy that hit them when their grant was announced in the press. They were, as museum professionals, first following up earlier oral history project leads that had uncovered a handful of gay and lesbian residents, from which the museum was able to build a network of queer narrators to interview. Second, this group was of sufficient size that they felt it was important, from a social history perspective, to collect their histories and cultural documents. Third, even in places as religious and apparently right wing as central Alberta, spaces could be found, queer lives could be created, and aware and accepting straight allies could see their queer neighbours for what they were: part of the community of Red Deer.

From a Vocal Minority to the END
(Edmontonians Networking Discretely):

By the mid-1980s, a number of new organizations had sprung up in Edmonton, including a middle-class professional social group, called the END Club, which stood for Edmontonians Networking Discretely. These mixers were held after work, providing middle-class gay and lesbians with alternatives to post-work drinks with their work colleagues.

Later, when the group was better established, they held a series of Sunday morning brunches and special events, including Christmas and New Year's events. Membership lists indicate that both women and men participated in this group during their three-year existence.

Specific social and cultural groups, sports groups, and parenting groups accelerated in the mid-1980s as the older one-size-fits-all "clubs" or groups (such as GATE) withered away. Partly this shift should be seen as an interest in niche events, but it was also true that this was a move away from political organization and social service work that fostered "coming out." These groups did not require volunteer staff or office spaces. They did still require coordinators and organizers, but that was less onerous than finding funding, space, and volunteers to keep enterprises like GATE viable. Perhaps the most successful of these ventures was the choir: The Vocal Minority, which participated in a series of public concerts, pride day events, and travelled through western Canada to participate in choral events. GALA (Gay and Lesbian Awareness) was formed in 1984 with members from all the key institutions in Edmonton. Originally given the task of organizing the pride week events, it eventually had a hybrid purpose as it had a pride committee and an activist committee. Edmontonians celebrated pride activities starting in 1981, however official recognition from the city of Edmonton would not occur until the mid-1990s (under Mayor Jan Reimer). The activist wing of the committee was devoted to lobbying the government for increased rights for homosexual Albertans (in particular the inclusion of sexual orientation into the provincial code).

Conclusion

This history of Edmonton gay and lesbian organizational and social growth through the 1970s and 1980s (alongside extant glimpses of life in Calgary and Red Deer) illustrates similarities and differences with the other cities in this study. It is possible to chart a progressive growth in Edmonton from small groups with a handful of members to a roster of gay and lesbian groups organized around social, sports, cultural, and political interests. Such an analysis needs to be resisted, as it masks much change over time. GATE was a constant throughout the era, although it really struggled throughout the late 1970s and particularly in the 1980s to maintain a toehold and role within the community. In moving from a political organization to an explicitly social services organization, they hoped to continue to be relevant to the largest number of Edmonton

gays and lesbians. Womonspace, a lesbian social group, was more successful at carving out spaces for themselves during this time period, but
again, they explicitly eschewed politics within their organization. Many
members of Womonspace were active in other gay and lesbian political
groups, and thus political discussions were stimulated by Womonspace –
or kick-started by debates there – but operationalized elsewhere. A
demographic breakdown of membership in various political, social,
and cultural groups would reveal tremendous overlap, as members
of GATE were also members of other organizations and Womonspace
members who were interested in politics were members of ALGRA or
other subsequent political groups.

What Edmontonians did accomplish, sometimes in coalitions with
activists from Calgary (more details follow in chapter 8) and within their
own city, was that they claimed spaces to be gay and lesbian. Edmontonians were more conservative than the other cities in this regional
study. As Cavalieri's comments suggest, there was a "delay" in comparison with initiatives and degrees of openness elsewhere. He was closeted at the Citadel Theatre, whereas men in Winnipeg spoke of the city's
arts institutions as welcoming spaces for queer employees. Having said
that, Cavalieri was able to be out in his social service work in ways that
was not possible for Doug Young in Calgary. Equally important, gay
and lesbian organizations in Edmonton were more likely to be led by
individuals who had migrated to Edmonton as adults, for work, not
those who were born and raised in the province. That is an important
distinction. Gay and lesbian organizations tended to draw leaders from
outside of Alberta to the provincial capital. But, those organizations did
attract Edmontonians, both those who liked to dance (the majority) but
also those smaller numbers of women and men who felt compelled to
work towards more political goals. Those gay and lesbian spaces were
few, and they were not well known, but they did exist. People attended,
they picked up periodicals, danced, socialized, networked "discreetly,"
and managed to keep organizations moving forward. When the toll of
work proved too much for the too few volunteers it was a recurrent
pattern that organizations might lie fallow for a year or two, only to
re-emerge a couple of years later in a slightly different form. All of the
alphabet soup of Edmonton gay and lesbian organizations speak to this
determination to keep going, recalibrate, and move on.

The focus on social services, which was the primary focus of GATE
for so many years, speaks to real needs within Edmonton to provide
those gays and lesbians who were struggling with coming out, and in

particular with handling their families, or their faith groups, or with worries about how this might affect their employment, with some tangible information and assistance. It fit the needs in that city. Community building was a tenuous juggling act in Edmonton, and, in chapter 8, with the focus on activism, reaction, and homophobic backlash, the challenges of being visibly gay or lesbian in Edmonton will become even more clear. In so doing, it reiterates an important argument of this book, that "community building" and "socializing" should not be mistakenly declared non-political. It was not apolitical to attend events advertised as gay or lesbian, to dance in isolated warehouse settings, or to be a sexual "outlaw" in Edmonton because so much of the rhetoric of the place, anachronistically, continued to valorize heteronormative Albertan small-town, rural, and heterosexual family values.

The research collected here suggests that it was harder to be gay and lesbian in Edmonton than elsewhere in the prairies. Such resilience deserves recognition for the fortitude it required to endure, and in various small pockets, to thrive. At the same time, a very small crew of activists attempted to push back against a provincial majority hopeful to ignore or will away the queer residents in their mix. And there was tangible pride expressed at how their contributions had improved lives for Edmonton gays and lesbians. For example, in 1983, Cavalieri, GATE's social service director, wrote to an organizer at Vancouver's GAYFEST to protest their dismissive comments about Edmonton. Cavalieri starting by reminding him that "I'm not an Edmonton chauvinist. How could I be? I grew to maturity in New York City." Yet, he felt compelled to stand up for his adopted city, writing,

> however, Edmonton has changed a great deal since you were a youth ... and it continues to change. What people go through here is, for the most part, not much different from what they go through in other cities, even in Vancouver ... Growing up – and self acceptance for a gay man and woman – is an individual process, and I would guess that about the same percentage make it here as in your (admittedly much more beautiful) adopted city. So, let's not be TOO smug! Many of us find true freedom only when we manage to escape from our home towns – regardless of how exemplary those home towns may seem to others, and how dismal to us.[138]

Comments similar to Cavalieri's were repeatedly expressed throughout this volume, important reminders that cities like Edmonton can and do offer liberation for a variety of queer people. Some, such as the transplanted Edmontonian living in Vancouver, could think of nothing worse, clearly, than being stuck in Alberta, and while such views are often repeated, in their oversimplifications they miss how people chose Edmonton, carved out lives, and make the places accessible for those who wished to live there. And they could be very successful, as the trajectory of Michael Phair illustrates.

Today, early gay activists, such as Michael Phair (HIV Edmonton, Edmonton city councillor 1992–2007), are embraced and lauded for their volunteer and professional work. Recently appointed chair of the University of Alberta's board of governors, Phair's accomplishments and his gay activism are evidence of tremendous changes in Edmonton from the period described here. Winnipeg also achieved impressive firsts when Glen Murray was elected as the first openly gay mayor of a major North American city in 1998. By comparison, Saskatoon has lagged such developments, illustrative of the circularity of "progress" and of the ways that such histories, however carefully calibrated, resist closure. Michael Phair holds a series of awards for service, and has a public school in Edmonton named in his honour. It was a long road to get to the point where a prominent gay activist can be publicly celebrated and acknowledged for his extensive contributions to the city and the province. And part of that was the continual, Sisyphean battle throughout the 1970s and 1980s of organizational birth, death, and reincarnation, which in some form or other played an important role in keeping political discussions alive and finding spaces for lesbian and gay men to be queer.[139] Such work did not directly lead to the different circumstances today – one cannot simplistically connect the dots – but it did forge identity and create space. It offered possibilities and opportunities that, with an advantageous Supreme Court decision in 1998, could finally turn the page for Edmonton, and Alberta, queers.

PART THREE

1970–1985 Activism, Reaction, Visibility, and Violence

"Love and Let Love": Activism, Reaction, Visibility, and Violence in Winnipeg, 1970–1985

Gay liberation is alive in western Canada. Every day we hear new reports in media of this or that event which reaffirms that gay people will not accept their lot in silence. Whether it is lobbying for a resolution on human rights at the Manitoba NDP Convention or protesting the anti-gay practices of the Canadian Broadcasting Corporation, we are organizing and active.[1]

After Stonewall Collective, Spring 1977

In the early years the nature and level of activity [gay activism] was as high in Saskatoon and Winnipeg, I don't know about Alberta, as it was in Toronto and Montreal. In some cases higher. That is we had phone lines, and offices and lending libraries, that have continued in existence more durably than elsewhere. Than any of these places. We held demonstrations, we engaged in publication and broadcasting, at a level not evident there ... The things that were remarkable in Toronto and Montreal were the very large demonstrations they had on certain occasions, steam bath raids, Truxx, and we could [not] have demonstrations of that size but we did not bad with the Anita Bryant demonstration.[2]

Chris Vogel, 2002

In 1977, in *After Stonewall*'s inaugural issue, their editorial entitled "So Much to Do" enumerated the various goals for the movement and their estimation that gay liberation was in good shape, as it was proceeding on a number of fronts including human rights legislation, challenges to anti-gay media practices, and general homophobia and violence. Retrospectively, Chris Vogel, a long-time Winnipeg activist with GFE, recalled the strength of Winnipeg and Saskatoon's activism, which made for a unique situation within the prairies. This chapter and the succeeding one on Saskatoon provide an analysis of those activist initiatives. One marvels at the level of energy and dedication expended to create change, but changes took a long time to materialize and not everyone could maintain their motivation. Six years later, in 1984, Darryl Kippen published an article entitled "After Stonewall" in Winnipeg's *Out and About* newsletter. Using the then prevailing notion that the Stonewall Riots in New York City had launched the lesbian and gay liberation movement, Kippen rhetorically asked what Winnipeg gays and lesbians had learned during those fifteen years? "We in Winnipeg are a small community, not very politically aware or active. We will begin to change things only when we begin to realize we are an oppressed minority. We still await human rights laws to protect us, 15 years after Stonewall … Lesbians and gay men must consciously work together to end discrimination and oppression."[3] Written in response to Manitoba attorney general Roland Penner's press statement that a revision to the province's human rights code was not a governmental priority, Kippen's article burned with indignation. Tired of the governmental promises that never materialized, Kippen ended his call to arms by bluntly calling on Winnipeggers to stand up for their rights: "The community must react swiftly against acts of discrimination and accept nothing less than equal treatment. We must take pride in ourselves, in our diversity, and never forget the lesson the Stonewall riots taught us."[4]

These three observations illustrate the challenges, and in particular the cyclical nature of activism, moments where activists felt they were poised for gains alternating with moments where they felt far less optimistic, perhaps resigned, about the glacial pace of change. And so, while it might seem, from the proceeding chapters, that the experiences of Winnipeg's gay and lesbian communities went from strength to strength, with an expansion of explicitly gay and lesbian organizations building on the foundations of the pre-1970s queer subcultural activities, organizational building and activist strength should not be conflated. Gay activists could point to some tangible accomplishments between 1970 and 1985, including that Manitoba became the first prairie province to add sexual orientation to their provincial human rights code in 1987. But they also faced sizable challenges including opposition from the provincial and municipal governments as well as from fellow citizens. Gains were always counterbalanced by retrenchment and reprisals. Such realities mitigate any analysis that it became "easier" to be openly gay or lesbian in Winnipeg, despite the plethora of groups, events, and newsletters. While Winnipeg became an increasingly multicultural city, a city with tremendous educational, cultural, and economic opportunities, it was and remains true that Manitoba's capital was also a dangerous city.

Homophobic violence was a disturbing, if routine, part of queer life in the 1970s and 1980s. Gay bashings were routine, but the violence escalated in the late 1970s. Sadly in a couple of cases these beatings proved fatal. In September 1978, Peter Petkaw "was found unconscious on the bank of the Assiniboine River with a broken skull, leg and six fractured ribs."[5] Two weeks later the thirty-one-year-old gay man was dead. Protests and a trial ensued. In February 1979, an eighteen-year-old Winnipeg man received a life sentence for Petkaw's murder. Six years later, another sensationalistic murder, of Desmond Smith, received significant media coverage and left many outraged. Smith's death shocked the city because he was a prominent local accountant, pillar of the Anglican Church, and vice president of the board of the Winnipeg Art Gallery. Unbeknownst to many he was also gay. According to news reports, he was routinely in the habit of picking up homeless or working-class young gay men, and one evening he misjudged – and the trick murdered him "in self-defence." Voyeuristic newspaper coverage of the Smith murder accentuated his double-life, his homosexual "lifestyle," and his questionable practice of "helping" out young gay men, many of whom made their living hustling on Winnipeg's streets. This murder had some eerie parallels with Marvin Klepsch's in Saskatoon, another middle-class professional male whose "lifestyle" (the RCMP investigators' terminology) had led to his unfortunate demise in a field north of the city. People's reactions were split – some believe Smith's murder represented the reality of homophobia within Winnipeg society, and they bemoaned the tragic loss. Other residents were not moved by such liberal-hearted perspectives, instead adhering to old-school, biblical truisms such as "as you sow, so you reap," which cast Smith as the architect of his own demise. Victims of sexual assault and violence are often victimized after the fact by questions about their character, behaviours, mode of dress, and presence in "dangerous" areas of the city. Smith's case caused tensions in Winnipeg because it was uncommon for middle-class Euro-Canadian men to be the victims of such crimes. In the end, though, the conventional narratives critiqued Smith for his sexual choices and amplified Christian views that were sharply critical whenever gay and lesbian activists dared to "flaunt" their sexuality. Flaunting included a wide range of behaviour, from public displays of affection to demands for legal rights and appropriate medical care, safeguards that other Manitobans took for granted, as well as health education about the AIDS virus.

Looking back, activist Chris Vogel recalled that the fundamental work of activism in Winnipeg was "to show that gays and lesbians were not monsters, were not different from heterosexuals ... At first we were left with very little. Occasional brief to some form of government body. But essentially holding gay events to keep the organization alive, support gay and lesbian people in coming out, and services, public education – pamphlets, broadcasting, speakers, demonstrations."[6] Much of the work of organizations like GFE focused on two issues – education of the queer and straight communities about the realities of gay and lesbian life and liberationist activist work to change the laws in Manitoba, to make discrimination against homosexuals illegal. One of their earliest brochures, "Love and Let Love," featured images of lesbian and gay couples (see figure 3.4, page 126) and an explanation that though such sentiments "may seem simple enough" for "those persons who wish to relate emotionally and physically to another of the same sex, this statement assumes enormous significance."[7] Intended to provide a summary of GFE's civil rights, public education, and counselling work, the back of the brochure offered a concise statement about gay love and liberation. Particularly important was the itemized list of gay liberationist goals that GFE held alongside the "twenty-five other gay organizations from Victoria to St John's" that were part of the National Gay Rights Coalition.[8] Enumerating goals and pressing for changes took sustained efforts and was far from simple. Conservative religious views were deeply entrenched in Manitoba, backlash and oppression were commonplace, and large numbers of the queer community feared the repercussions of being too open about their sexuality. For instance, in 1973, GFE was awarded a federal government Opportunities for Youth Grant to compile material for an educational booklet entitled *Understanding Homosexuality*, only to find, ironically, that they could not get their original publisher to publish the volume. GFE versus Derksen Printers (detailed below) illustrates how contested publicizing sexual difference could be, and vividly reminds us of the hatred, censorship, and hostility that were easily stirred up by basic, educational materials.[9] Thus, in this final chapter on Winnipeg, focused on activism and resistance, it is apparent how much hard work went into demanding change, being visible, and claiming spaces within urban and provincial society. And, in Winnipeg, one of the hardest and longest-running battles was an internal one, between the members of Gays for Equality (GFE) and Happenings over whether one should be an openly, activist gay person or rather adhere to the older model of quiet discretion, happy to socialize in queer spaces and "live their lives."

GFE versus Happenings

These two Winnipeg institutions, Happenings, with its large membership, drawing upon many social circles in town, and GFE, a small, group of more radical gay liberationist men, were often at loggerheads in the 1970s and 1980s. Tensions came to a boiling point in February 1974 when the University of Manitoba student newspaper published an article entitled "Struggling On: Winnipeg's Gay Liberation Movement 2 Years after."[10] The article was sharply critical of the members of Happenings for their conservatism; at issue in particular was their refusal to publicly criticize Attorney General Al Mackling's statement that "such [gay] groups ought not to be clothed with the same rights and respectability as other groups." Mackling initially justified declining Happenings's application for a provincial charter solely on the grounds that they were a gay organization. *The Manitoban* article criticized Happenings decision to remain silent as well as their decision to "disassociate themselves entirely from GFE's political activities" to achieve the goal of a chartered club. Three applications were necessary for Happenings to secure their charter, and they were only successful after back channel negotiations between their lawyer and the government. When GFE publicized this government mistreatment, imperilling the negotiated settlement, tensions flared. According to the article, Happenings retaliated and attempted to get GFE's U of M funding revoked by raising questions about whether they were actually a student organization. Furthermore, Happenings claimed that "GFE had no support within the community" and hence did not require continued funding.[11] "Struggling On" drew an analogy between what was then called "black liberation" of African Americans and gay liberation, illustrating how frightening and self-defeating it would be if African Americans opposed their own liberation, in the way that conservative, middle-class gays in Winnipeg seemingly opposed gay liberation.

This article generated much discussion in the community and received further international attention when it was republished in the American queer newsmagazine *The Advocate*.[12] In response, Happenings clarified that their charter was achieved through legal channels. Their response, entitled "Am I an Uncle Tom?," refuted the claims of GFE.[13] Beginning by noting that the author of "Struggling On" was a former editor of *What's Happening*, the author indicated that the article had generated much anger and frustration. Happenings "didn't wish any publicity" and therefore didn't want GFE publicizing their organization. While many members of Happenings, as gays and lesbians, supported the general goals of GFE they disliked the tactics: "rather than march with placards and make speeches I choose to pay my rent and feed and clothe my body. I suppose I should feel guilty, but I don't because to me it's a simple matter of being realistic rather than idealistic ... I fail to see what good is accomplished by groups of Gays marching down the streets of North America. In fact, I am embarrassed by them".[14] Elsewhere in the same issue, Happenings's gossip columnist Hillary Osborne-Hill (a camp pseudonym) remarked: "loved the rotten things that GFE said about Happenings in *The Manitoban* – Proves we are a success! When people are jealous they just can't be kind." Furthermore, she urged people to join the social fun that occurred at Happenings's events, "we don't carry flags, wave banners or man the barricades, but we have a good time."[15]

Happenings was, in terms of members and participation, the far larger organization. And even with the controversies between liberationist ideology and the so-called "realistic" discretionary policies, according to Vogel, "everyone went [to Happenings] because there was no where else to go." Unlike the social clubs in Saskatoon and Edmonton that offered spaces for activist materials (periodicals, a message board), Happenings "wouldn't promote the activities of the liberationist groups, in the early years they even refused to put up posters on the premises," Vogel recalled. When pressed about the demographics of those who were most invested in privacy, Vogel said, "the manager recalled that some of the most hostile to liberationists were women."[16] Both groups were open to lesbians and gay men, but various sources indicate that they were predominately male. By the early 1980s, this view softened a bit and Happenings was tentatively beginning to work cooperatively with the other groups (see below). The influx of newcomers to the community allowed for generational changes. Happenings endurance also made it a Winnipeg queer tradition. Happenings is one of many groups that merits its own history for its influential, at times controversial, role in Winnipeg's queer community. During its thirty-plus years of operation, it changed dramatically from the closed "members-only" place to the more visible, open queer space in its final years. To claim it was "merely social" does it a disservice, as it was the first place that many Winnipeggers, from the 1970s–2002, experienced gay and lesbian space. It would be rare to find a queer person in Winnipeg who wasn't familiar with Happenings. At this community bar, queer men and women realized that they were part of a larger, collective group of fellow gays and lesbians. Some patrons would be politicized by those discoveries, using Happenings as a fun place to dance and drink, but also finding their way into a host of other activist, medical, political, and cultural queer groups. GFE was always far smaller, largely a handful of key players led by Rich North and Chris Vogel, whose energy and work stimulated so many organizational developments in this chapter, including their decision to wed in 1974.

Going to the Unitarian Chapel: Getting Married in Winnipeg

Many Canadians would date the first gay marriage to early twenty-first century after changes to the provincial and federal laws made it possible for same-sex couples to legally marry.[17] Throughout this roiling debate, and despite much active commentary in the newspapers, on television, and on talk radio programs about the historic nature of this shift in Canadian social policy, one aspect of this story has not received much coverage: the February 1974 "marriage" of two Winnipeg men.[18] Chris Vogel, twenty-two, and Richard North, twenty-six, held their same-sex marriage ceremony in Winnipeg, a few days before Valentine's Day in February 1974. Their service, held in the Unitarian Church, was officiated by Rev Norman Naylor. In interviews North was quoted as saying "our commitment to each other is fundamental in our lives ... and in our society, formal recognition of such a fact is accomplished through the custom of marriage. The fact that homosexuals are not permitted legally to marry is an attempt by society and by government to reject the validity of a homosexual relationship."[19] North and Vogel's decision thrust themselves, and Winnipeg, into the media spotlight, including a feature interview with Barbara Frum on the CBC radio program *As It Happens*.[20] Clearly bemused, and a bit bewildered, Frum asked the couple "what on earth is marriage for" if they were not planning to have children, be monogamous, make a lifetime commitment or even wear wedding rings?[21] Patiently, Vogel and North explained that they did not believe in "ownership" nor did they believe there was a connection between "a loving relationship and sexual exclusivity." Simply put, they stated that, "homosexuals should be able to do everything heterosexuals can do," and, most important, because "marriage has status and homosexual relationships should have the same status." Frum wished them good luck and as a parting shot quipped, "I hope you stay out of the divorce statistics."

Years later, they stated that their reasoning had been multiple – to publicize discrimination gay men faced, to offer a positive image of queer couples which contrasted with the more common demonizations of homosexuality, and additionally to push the Manitoba government to realize the inequity of their laws. Their principle objectives achieved, Vogel and North met some opposition from their "politically correct friends" who were upset at the notion that they would wed. Vogel's mother, who worried about them wearing wedding rings, was also critical. In that respect, Vogel recalled that people worried erroneously, because "in a sense we were feminists who didn't do things like that." Interestingly, in the Winnipeg interviews conducted in 1992, many of the gay male activists vividly remembered this historic moment and stated that the widespread media coverage of the Vogel and North marriage gave them a favourable impression of Winnipeg. For instance, John Robertson, who lived in Calgary and worked at the *Calgary Herald*, believed that this was an indicator of Winnipeg's acceptance of the gay community. Donn Yuen felt that the marriage distinguished Winnipeg. Finally, Ken Steffenson remembered reading positive news reports in the *Regina Leader Post*, and thus believed that Winnipeg was a good city in which to live as an openly gay male.[22]

Over thirty years later, Vogel recalled that they tried to do everything by the book, including going for the then mandatory syphilis tests. He recalled:

> we were trying to do everything legally, we were unsuccessful but we tried, and we went to get them. I was explaining to my secretary that I was getting this paperwork to the typing pool, get it signed, and then take it back to the doctor. And one of the older women on staff had a hawk's eye or an eagle's ear for this sort of thing and she came charging down the aisleway saying "you're getting married." And I said yes, but I'm getting married to another man. Well my secretary who I'd given rides to work, asked if it was Rich. The older woman just stood there with her mouth open. But they got together and bought a pair of silver goblets which the director gathered everyone together to present to me and wish us well. I never had problems with her ever after.[23]

Naturally, their decision to wed was about more than acknowledging their relationship, it was a brilliant piece of activist theatre geared to publicize discrimination and create dialogue. And one that Midwesterners seemed determined to make. In 1970, air force veteran and lawyer Jack Baker, and Mike McConnell, a librarian, applied for a marriage licence in Minneapolis, Minnesota. They were turned down, and their case went to the US Supreme Court, which denied same-sex couples the right to marry.[24] In 1971, they used gender-neutral names (Baker legally changed his to Pat Lyn McConnell) and were able to get a legal marriage licence and married wearing "white bell bottom pantsuits and macramé headbands."[25] News of the Baker and McConnell marriage was widely covered in straight and gay media. Given the proximity between Winnipeg and Minneapolis, personal connections between gay activists in those cities, and the fact that liberationist politics did not respect national borders, the American same-sex marriage proved influential. Because Vogel and North anticipated that they were not going to be approved for a civil marriage licence, they followed the religious practice of having the banns read in the Unitarian Church. This religious practice was perfectly legal for heterosexual couples who, after three readings, would be able to legally register their union after the church ceremony. In this case, ten months after the ceremony, the attorney general declined their application, clearly indicating that this practice was not open to same-sex couples and that same-sex couples could not wed.

In retrospect, of course, it was not surprising that North and Vogel's quest was not successful. What did work brilliantly was the publicity it shed on same-sex relationships, marriage laws, and politics. Given the rift between the activists at GFE and Happenings, it was inevitable that some pronouncement would be forthcoming about the Vogel and North nuptials. Gossip columnist Hilary Osborne-Hill archly wrote, "weddings, weddings, weddings – I don't like cheap sensationalism with the recent gay wedding at the Unitarian Church, the GFE must really be digging deep. Since when do two gay people need a straight minister to tell them they love each other? Rumour has it that the marriage ... is rather shaky – Will the divorce get as much publicity?[26] Confounding their skeptics, a decade later, they held a benefit dinner to mark their tenth anniversary. The twenty thousand dollars raised went to support a new activist resource for lesbians and gays, called the Manitoba Gay Legal Defense Fund. The fund was sponsored by GFE, CHR, and the OWMS. Coverage in *The Body Politic* quoted Vogel as saying, "these cases are too important for an individual's financial status to determine whether or not they will receive a full hearing."[27] The priority areas for which they would fund legal costs were: child custody, criminal charges, recognition of same-sex unions, and Charter challenges. In 2014, Vogel and North were once again the focus of CBC attention, this time in a glowing interview with CBC Winnipeg where they reminisced about their forty-year marriage and the continuities and changes in queer activism.[28] Forty years later, one fact remained consistent – Manitoba continued to refuse to recognize their 1974 marriage!

GFE versus Derksen Printers

As mentioned above, in the summer of 1973, GFE had been awarded a $5,000 federal grant through the Opportunities for Youth Program to research and produce a booklet entitled *Understanding Homosexuality*. Aimed at an audience of younger gays and lesbians, particularly those struggling with coming out of the closet to family and close friends, the booklet offered what was intended to be reassuring viewpoints of scientists and clergymen about homosexuals and homosexuality. Once completed, the manuscript was sent to Derksen Printers, in Steinbach, Manitoba, for printing. The owner, Eugene Derksen, refused to honour the contract and was eloquently quoted in the *Winnipeg Free Press* stating, "I don't have to dig in the garbage to make a buck. Why should I have to work for a bunch of bastards like that?"[29]

Steinbach (and the surrounding farming areas in southeastern Manitoba) was, and remains, a German Mennonite community. Economically prosperous, this small city and its surrounding area is a region where religiosity, ethnicity, and culture have forged a tight-knit community and family, church, business, and farming are strongly interconnected. Thus, unlike Winnipeg, there was a strong bias towards a conservative, religious view predicated on Mennonite religious teachings in many facets of life. For example, Steinbach was a dry town, and successfully fought against liquor sales in restaurants or stores until its first liquor store opened in 2008. In 2016, Steinbach made the national news because for the first time ever they hosted a gay pride parade.[30] Participation exceeded expectation, and many people came from as far away as Winnipeg to support Steinbach queers and their allies in their historical moment. However, it was also not without controversy, as Ted Falk, the federal Conservative member of Parliament, issued a press release to explain his planned absence. "I've been clear on this issue many times" Falk said, "and have made my position public on my values of faith, family and community." Furthermore he reiterated that even without a scheduling conflict (a beloved tactic employed by other politicians who have ducked out of pride day events), he would not attend the community's parade.[31] Derksen Printers had a history of censorship. Previously they refused to print movie advertisements in the local newspaper, and thus their refusal to print gay literature was part of a larger worldview that regarded many aspects of contemporary North American culture as immoral. In reaction, GFE lodged a human rights complaint. They were summarily informed that since the provincial code did not offer any protection for discrimination stemming from issues of sexual orientation (unlike sex, religion, race, ethnic background, or political viewpoints, which were protected), Derksen's refusal was both legal and there were no avenues for formal complaint or recourse.

With their options limited, GFE staged a picket of the printing plant – mustering eleven marchers (eight of whom were lesbians) onto the sidewalks. The description printed in the American gay newsmagazine, *The Advocate*, vividly captured the mood of the demonstration and the counterdemonstration. For those familiar with novelist Miriam Toews work (who was born and raised in Steinbach), the scene described in *The Advocate* could have been lifted from one of her novels.[32]

> A dozen Mennonite ministers … appeared, several towing children. Carrying their own placards, the clergymen from the ultra conservative, frontier sect paired off one-on-one with the gay pickets, and preached the evils of homosexuality to them individually. Gays responded by setting up a chant of Gay is good, and the ministers increased the fervour of their preaching. The cacophony finally brought the RCMP, who convinced all present to break off the demonstration or face arrest under the village's public disturbance law.[33]

Besides the publicity and the opportunity to demonstrate against religious homophobia, the only tangible outcome of the Derksen Printer's picket and protest had been to offer the group a very clear case in which the province's human rights legislation was found wanting. According to Vogel, after the experience with Derksen's, local activists realized that a central focus of their work had to be civil rights. In particular, an amendment to the provincial human rights code was necessary so that such blatantly discriminatory practices could be challenged. GFE

was emboldened to set up a meeting with Attorney General Howard
Pawley to discuss the anti-gay bias prevalent in Manitoba on 26 September 1974.[34]

GFE Conferences, Pride, and Politics

In the overview of the more significant moments in gay and lesbian
activism that follows, GFE's leadership is unmistakable. According to
Ted Millward, this was due in large part to its origins as a university,
student protest organization:

> Gays for Equality was formed during the period of student political activ-
> ism, and it has continued to be uniquely the political voice of the Manitoba
> gay community. It has instigated and sponsored all of the public dem-
> onstrations drawing attention to the unwarranted discrimination against
> homosexual persons. It has supported and taken part in public protests on
> other social issues. Through briefs, presentations, public discussions and
> workshops, it has maintained pressure upon political parties and upon
> all levels of government to correct the variety of legal injustices to which
> homosexual persons are subject.[35]

Oral and archival information indicates that such activism did not
always work in their favour, and, in fact, could alternatively make them
a lightening rod for critique. Their membership numbers were always
far fewer than social or community organizations. Millward corroborated this, writing, "this, consequently, has been the area which has
brought the most criticism upon Gays for Equality, not only from outsiders who resent any mitigation of social disapproval of homosexuality, but also from that segment of the homosexual population which
fears any attention focused upon it."[36]

Similar to Saskatoon, Winnipeg and GFE initially played a leadership role in the Canadian lesbian and gay rights activism. Miriam
Smith's work cautions against any presumption of a "united and
coherent movement" for lesbian and gay activism in Canada.[37] Yet
her focus on developments in Ontario and British Columbia, and with
organizations devoted to the acquisition of federal rights, namely the
National Gay Rights Coalition, and later EGALE (formed 1986), flat-
tens regional differences and minimizes the prairie contributions.
The National Gay Rights Coalition, which existed from 1975 to 1980
(with a name change in 1978 to the Canadian Lesbian and Gay Rights

6.1 1974 National Conference Parade, Winnipeg, 31 August 1974.
University of Manitoba Archives and Special Collections, Manitoba Gay &
Lesbian Archives, PC 292 (A08–67).

Coalition), had very limited funds, a handful of affiliated activist organizations scattered across the country, and little organizational apparatus or personnel from which to generate a program of activism. During its years in existence, one of the primary focal points was the annual conference, which was held in various major Canadian cities so as to provide access to a wide range of participants. Prairie cities hosted the conference three times: Winnipeg in 1974,[38] Saskatoon in 1977, and Calgary in 1980. It is significant that Winnipeg's GFE were the second hosts chosen for these foundational national events. A year after GFE's first week-long gay pride festivities, the organization felt confident enough to host the national conference on the Labour Day Weekend. On the opening day of the conference, delegates marched through the city's downtown core. Such an activity

6.2 Winnipeg contingent and others at the National Gay Rights Coalition Conference Parade, Ottawa, 1975. University of Manitoba Archives and Special Collections, Manitoba Gay & Lesbian Archives, PC 292 (A.00–67).

proved an impossibility in Calgary six years later, a rather sharp contrast between different activist and urban cultures. A year later, in 1975, the Manitoba contingent would be featured prominently in photos of the Ontario parade in Ottawa.

The University of Manitoba Archives and Special Collections has a wonderful collection of archival photographs, in all their 1970s splendour, that depict pantsuit-clad gay male liberationists "flaunting" their sexuality and their pride.[39] Such events and images do underscore the activism – and the activists – that emerged from the prairies. Some, like Bill Lewis, would move to Toronto; others, like Rich North and Chris Vogel, remained in Winnipeg. In either scenarios, Winnipeggers were making contributions in a time where liberationist activists were small in number. Later, after NGRC had folded, local activism was of primary importance to advancing issues of gay and lesbian identity, consciousness-raising, and politics within Canada.

The Women's Building and Lesbian Activism

Importantly, while gays and lesbians engaged in separate activist agendas, it was often in public demonstrations that they came together and there the women often had a much more significant presence then the men. One person who vividly recalled the various types of lesbian activist work underway in Winnipeg was folk singer Heather Bishop, who moved from Regina to Winnipeg in 1975. Having cut her teeth on activism in the Queen City, where she remembered doing many "speaking engagements on homosexuality," she first got to know Winnipeg through regular visits and then attendance at Happenings.[40] After relocating, Bishop was active with the Winnipeg Lesbian Society. In 1980, six members of the WLS wrote a history of their organization for *After Stonewall* and carefully explained their desire for autonomy, not separation from gay male politics: "We have to get together on our own. Lesbian women are very close to the bottom of the power structure. Access to power comes through organizing autonomously ... We seek power over our own lives, not separatism."[41] The WLS collective eventually folded because of conflict between members over "consensus" versus "democratic" decision-making. At that point, Bishop's touring schedule picked up and she was often on the road, hence unable to participate directly in Winnipeg's community, although she did play at numerous local benefit concerts. According to her, Winnipeg's "women's community is wonderful" because it is "close-knit with a small town feeling." Asked to contrast the gay male activists from the lesbian activists, Bishop noted that the "local lesbian community has always been more politically active than the gay men's community. Even on the issue of AIDs ... women and lesbians were in the forefront – doing the political fighting." Without naming names, Bishop noted, "a few gay men are heavily involved and they receive little credit from their own community."[42]

She most certainly meant Vogel and North (as well as Dr Dick Smith). Vogel and North noted in their various interviews the way in which they became "notorious" for their political work and the price they paid for these political views. One narrator candidly recalled, "[I] wasn't interested in political work ... [I] leave that to people like Chris Vogel"; although this individual did add that he valued "Chris' contribution to the gay community."[43] In the second series of oral interviews conducted in Winnipeg in 1992, this tension between "activists" and "average" gay men doesn't come through as clearly as it might because the focal point of that interview project was activists and community builders. In my interviews, in emails with former activists, and in archival documents of interviews with those individuals (like Doug Wilson and Doug Young, who I did not have the opportunity to interview), such sentiments were widely expressed. In every city there was a divide, and often lingering bitterness on the part of those activists, often a small handful of men and women who were willing to be openly identified as activists, and the much, much larger group of individuals who were cautious about "politics." A major focal point of the activist work in the prairies was focused on consciousness-raising and encouraging people to identify as gay and lesbians – very basic gay liberationist strategies. And there was engagement with this process. Starting with a series of concentric circles, women and men who socialized in the clubs, or joined organizations or sports teams, managed to tell their family and close friends, sometimes close work colleagues, but then many stalled, unable or unwilling to be more "public" or more "political." This challenge was evident in every city, and certainly in the smaller towns and communities. While more people seemed comfortable to be "political" in Saskatoon or Winnipeg, it was equally true that this was not the case for the majority of queer residents even in those cities, let alone the more cautious situations in Edmonton, Calgary, and Regina. Given the small numbers of gay men involved, burnout was a persistent issue that caused activists to leave the fold.[44]

Women were involved in a variety of initiatives, like Take Back the Night marches, lesbian conferences, women's cultural events, Ms Purdy's women's social club (1984–2002), and the religious organizations.[45] D. Wood, who moved to Winnipeg from Toronto to be with her partner, indicated in her oral interviews that she found the women's energy at the Women's Building, 730 Alexander Avenue, was very impressive. Although it was officially called the Women's Building, it was "primarily lesbian" according to the oral interviews. The building's mandate was to provide space for a variety of women's groups and initiatives and it was largely funded out of the pockets of members. In the final years, it was reaching more straight women and this, in part, led to its demise. Wood claimed that the feminist emphasis shifted to more liberal feminist goals, at which point lesbian politics were being co-opted. Add burnout and financial stresses to the dissension, and the demise was inevitable. Wood bemoaned the fact that the Women's Building closed in 1983 due to lack of funds, while Ms Purdy's, the social club, was still vital and popular.[46] Not all lesbians believed that social space, with a heavy emphasis on bars, drinking, and dancing, were sufficient or healthy for queer people. Woods organized a group called Making Our Own Way, which held coffee houses for a couple of years. Another outlet for lesbians in Winnipeg was the Women's Resource Centre at the University of Winnipeg, which, in the late 1980s, had a membership that was entirely lesbian.[47]

At the University of Manitoba, Professor K. Louise Fulton's prominent position as the Margaret Laurence Chair in Women's Studies allowed her to sponsor some feminist and lesbian work in the university and community. This included the highly successful Lesbian Issues Conference in 1986, which a number of women cited as highly productive for initiating discussions around a host of lesbian issues – sexuality, addictions, violence, and politics.[48] This institutional support, similar to that given to GFE in the 1970s by the U of M Student Union, greatly assisted the causes of lesbian activism and women's and feminist organizations, since it provided campus space, recognition, and stimulus for dialogue. If the gay male community was often split over issues of "publicity" and being "openly gay," the lesbian and feminist communities were often fractured over different political goals. In particular, there were tensions in Winnipeg, and elsewhere, concerning the way that the mainstream feminist movement often did not allow spaces for lesbian issues and initiatives to be discussed, nor were they comfortable acknowledging all of the lesbian feminists in their organizations. Despite the comments of many of the Winnipeg women interviewed who nostalgically recalled the city's "close-knit" lesbian and feminist communities, other archival evidence suggests a competing version of events. Despite the terrific value of the community oral histories, there were shortcomings. And one of the key issues was about the very question of creating a "community" historical legacy project. Those interviewed were keenly aware that this community resource would be viewed as celebratory as well as official. Most narrators were keen to stress the positives, and the accomplishments, rather than dwell on difficulties. What difficulties they did mention tended to be oppression from outside the queer community – not tensions and debates within it. Archival evidence suggests a competing version of events for the lesbian communities in Winnipeg, in which radical lesbian women who felt marginalized – whether in leftist organizations, feminist groups, or the gay and lesbian community – spoke out about these challenges. Yvette Parr provided the most succinct summary. She wrote:

> lesbians are constantly being silenced, censured and generally put down.
> No struggle has come easy for us. It has always been considered a lesser
> lifestyle in which the social pressures keep us quiet. Blatantly or subtly the
> pressures are always there ... Wimmin who identify emotionally, mentally
> and physically with other wimmin are in for a rocky road but in joining
> hands we find the strength to survive ... Many times over the years splits
> have occurred in feminist endeavours. Often it's the lavender menace syn-
> drome. Why cannot all wimmin learn from herstory? All hetero wimmin
> should listen to Meg Christian's song "Leaping Lesbians."[49]

Parr's anger references American political and cultural references, further evidence of how aware many Winnipeg and prairie activists were
of political activity elsewhere, and of how tapped in they were to lesbian and queer cultures. Such national and international knowledge
did not always mitigate the local circumstances and the tensions she
and her colleagues Isabel Andrews and Doreen Worden would express
about Winnipeg's feminist and left political scene. Stratification of the
community on class, gendered, racialized, and political levels was very
real. Such tensions are not surprising for volunteer-driven organizations with limited funds and with political positions that contrasted
sharply with heteronormative values of middle-class Winnipegger's
gender, sexual, and social relations.

Dissenting Lesbian *Voices*

This perspective on the Winnipeg lesbian activist scene was really
best epitomized by the breakaway cell of lesbian feminists – Doreen
Worden, Yvette Parr, and Isabel Andrews – the creators behind the
periodical *Voices*. Self-produced and funded, and "published" on a
gestetner machine in Kenora, Ontario, *Voices* was a persistently dissenting voice. In 1982, they described their ventures as a "publication [that] exists because of the stubbornness of a couple of dotty
old dykes who, 3 and 2/3rds years ago, decided to get an early start
on their second childhood in the bush country of Ontario. *Voices* is,
without question the first and only and last lesbian publication that
will ever come out of what has been called the Alabama of Canada."[50]
In a response that Worden and Andrews wrote to the Combahee
River Collective Statement on Lesbian Separatism, they provided
more details about their political views and life histories: "We are
lesbian lovers and companions who define ourselves politically as

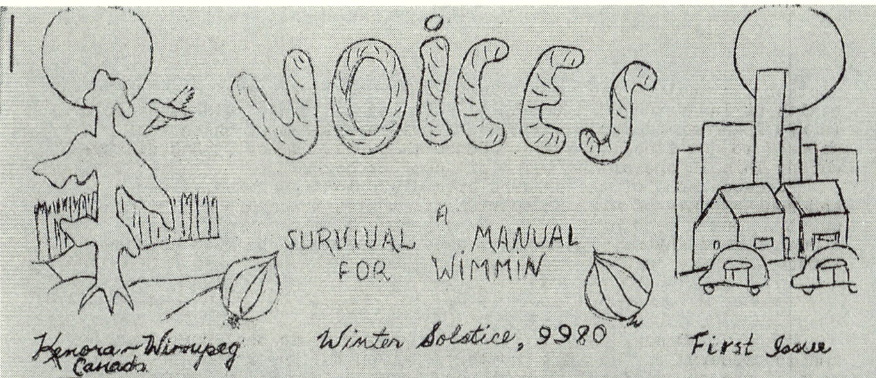

* __Winter Solstice__ occurs in our hemisphere this year on December 21. This is when the days start to lengthen again. Matriarchal cultures celebrated this day as the first in a New Year and rejoiced at the rebirth of the sun -- the return of more sunshine. So do we. * * * We use the year 9980 to remind ourselves that many many centuries of herstory occurred before the origin of the christian calendar.

So begins Voices, "a survival manual for wimmin," in its first issue. Voices, c/o I. Andrews. RR #2, Kenora, Ontario P9N 3W8

THIS SURVIVAL MANUAL FOCUSES, ON WIMMIN'S HEALTH, OF BODY MIND AND SPIRIT. OUR PURPOSE IS TO PROVIDE A FORUM FOR SHARING INFORMATION, IDEAS, EXPERIENCES, SKILLS AND DREAMS.

On this continent we face a human-created environment which is increasingly hostile to health and peace of mind. We believe there are resources available to help us cope (e.g. from the traditions of natural medicine) but they are seldom reported on in the daily press, TV, radio or in popular magazines. It is mainly the alternate press (e.g. Wimmin's publications, Rodale Press, etc.) who are popularizing them. So we have decided to join this small but growing stream of information-sharing.

Some of us remember pre-medicare days when we could not afford to scoff at "Old Wives' Tales". As services under medicare are now being eroded, the time is again coming when, as individuals, families and groups we will rely on such knowledge. Probably we will be better off for it. Who knows some of us may even see the day when methods of healing called unorthodox or quackery today will be honored as they deserve.

This survival manual is all about "Old and Young Wimmin's Tales" of one kind or another. It is intended for personal support, to strengthe wimmin, rather than for any short-term 'political' purposes. We welcome discussion and debate. Please send us your ideas, experiences, information, etc.

Some of the topics we plan to focus on in future issues are:

6.3 *Voices*, Winter Solstice, 9980, first issue (1980), Kenora-Winnipeg, Canada. Creators: I. Andrews and D. Worden. Neil Richards Collection, Provincial Archives of Saskatchewan A 595 II:207. Image courtesy of Neil Richards.

lesbian separatist sympathizers. We are white, ages 47 and 50, and 'came out' at the ages of 41 and 45. We have chosen to live in semi-retreat, devoting our energies to economic necessities, clearing out our heads, enjoying and strengthening those areas of our communities which are supportive to women, especially to lesbians and other poor women ... We are poor and always will be."[51] Women like Worden and Andrews seldom leave behind such rich documents. While they were clearly a unique offshoot of the Winnipeg lesbian community, in other respects, their experiences were expressed by other lesbian narrators (both those interviewed by myself and in community oral history collections) who came out later in life and faced health and financial pressures that underscored their double oppression (as women and lesbians). Their ability to articulate their positions, to create a newsletter for other wimmin like them, and their radical solution to their experiences of oppression – lesbian healing retreats – were not popular in Canada, although some lesbians in the United States did create "women's land" rural farms, retreats, and communities that bore similarities to Worden and Andrew's retreat.

A 1981 article provided three critiques of International Women's Day (IWD) events in Winnipeg. Worden's article "Nobody Cheered for Me" captured the scene "at a celebration party at the Grant Motor Inn in Winnipeg ... I waited until the end but nobody cheered for me and my oppressed group, lesbians ... Fifty percent of the women in that room were part of a group no one seems to want to cheer – even when the party is to celebrate *women*."[52] Yvette Parr, in her article "The Closet's Getting Stuffy," analysed the reaction to a display of lesbian literature at the IWD events, and of the silencing lesbians faced. Writing from personal experience, Parr wrote:

> I feel that we're just tolerated on I.W.D. Many of us are active politically on many diverse issues such as daycare, abortion, welfare rights, etc. We concern ourselves with all wimmin's needs, but for some the price is too high so they drop out to give energy to their own lives and the lives of their lesbian sisters. They have to, their sanity is at stake. A display of lesbian literature was held in Winnipeg as part of a cross section of Winnipeg wimmin's groups. This did not just 'happen.' It took a lot of energy and persistence on the part of the three lesbian wimmin who took the initiative. One womin [sic] passer-by literally dragged her children away so they would not be exposed to those "atrocities"; another's comment was "we live in a sick society!"[53]

Regardless of these homophobic responses, Parr viewed the literature table as an important accomplishment: "The lesbian display was able to pass on info to the lesbians who saw us, of the activities and outlets for lesbians in Winnipeg. This is reason enough to become more visible."[54] In activist circles one takes debate and dissention for granted: the hours are long, rewards few, and goals seem impossible to achieve. Still, such seemingly impossible initiatives like creating a self-funded lesbian newsletter in the remote Canadian shield country of northwestern Ontario demonstrates a level of commitment to concrete action against insurmountable odds.

Voices: A Survival Manual for Wimmin (1978–84) focused on "wimmin's health, of body, mind and spirit," and their purpose was to "provide a forum for sharing information, ideas, experiences, skills and dreams."[55] The collective that produced the magazine was coordinator Isabel Andrews, her partner Doreen Worden, and, for the first few issues, Yvette Parr. Lee Laning, an American lesbian journalist, described a visit to Kenora to meet Worden and Andrews: "In September we visited Isabel and Doreen … they are the wimmin who put out *Voices*, and who house the Lesbian Archives of Manitoba and NW Ontario (LARC). They live outside of Kenora in a lakeside cabin perched on solid bedrock." Clearly, they were into sustainable agriculture before it was a trendy, urban pastime: "In addition to the usual potatoes, tomatoes and squash, Isabel nurtures a growing number of herb[s] which she sells from their little store next to their home. From this store Doreen also sells Watkins products, eggs from her leghorn chickens, and sundry other useful goods."[56] Worden and Andrews had met in Winnipeg in 1975, when the forty-one-year-old Worden came out as a lesbian. In the city they had been heavily involved in feminist groups, lesbian feminism, and labour activism, particularly at Winnipeg's Women's Place. But, in 1978, burnt out and frustrated, they set out on a "healing journey … Moving out of the city, fighting addictions, learning about herbs and reflexology, healing rituals and" becoming more politicized.[57] In LARC's press release they indicated that "for too long cities have absorbed most of our lesbian energy, but in some parts of this continent the trend is now beginning to reverse."[58] The move was also an attempt to live more authentically women-focused lives. There, on their own land, they hoped to restore their health, cultivate their lesbian feminist ideals, and politicize the issue of rural lesbians.

LARC was intended to preserve the histories of rural and western experiences with a particular emphasis on Winnipeg organizations and women's healing.[59] In 1985, in a letter of introduction to the Women's Movement Archives in Toronto, Andrews announced the new venture's ambitious goals while she admitted, in a classically self-deprecating manner, that their self-funded, owner-operator approach to archiving was perilous: "The lesbian archives has had an inauspicious beginning, opening in September 84 and closing temporarily in December because of low energy and not enough money to heat the building through the winter."[60] Going forward, they planned for LARC to be open between summer solstice and fall equinox.

Neither their newsletter nor their archives endured beyond the mid-1980s due to financial challenges (they, like many radical liberationist groups, were opposed to government funding and wished to be independent from the state). In spring 1983, they wrote to various newsletters and organizations, asking for support for *Voices* in the form of additional subscriptions or donations. As they explained to readers of *Thunder Gay,* the newsletter produced by Gays of Thunder Bay, Ontario, "we are the only lesbian publication between BC and Toronto, the only rural lesbian publication in Canada and one of the very few on the continent regularly featuring natural healing from our perspective. We are no longer able to help finance *Voices* from our own funds."[61] This letter marks the end of the archival trail for *Voices,* although not the work of Worden and Andrews. Worden remained active in various lesbian and women's activism, including the establishment of the Kenora Lesbian Phone Line in 1989.[62] She was also active in feminist organizing against violence, volunteering at the Kenora Sexual Assault Centre and participating in the annual Take Back the Night Marches.[63] There were many other short-lived lesbian and/or feminist periodicals in the prairies including: *Labyrs News* (Saskatoon); *Saskatoon Women's Liberation Newsletter;* *Prairie Woman;* the *Lesbian Newsletter* produced by the Lesbian Association of Southern Saskatchewan, and, later, the *Sensible Shoes News,* a lesbian newsletter from Regina. *Sensible Shoes News* offered a similarly eclectic mix of cultural materials, politics, and community outreach.[64] Such periodicals kept lesbian activism alive in the prairies, although none were as original and iconoclastic as *Voices.*[65]

CBC and Human Rights Activism

In 1977, GFE was active in a national protest against the CBC's anti-gay policies. In Winnipeg, the CBC was the only radio/television station that refused to air public service announcements by GFE. The picket held outside CBC headquarters on Portage Avenue was a combined venture between GFE, the Winnipeg Lesbian Society, and some CBC Winnipeg staffers. As well, their continuing campaign for Manitoba to revise the provincial human rights code to include homosexuality intensified in 1977 when Quebec became the first province to include sexual orientation as a defined category in their provincial human rights code. Manitoba's would not pass until 1986, the third Canadian province to include protection for gays and lesbians in their human rights code (Ontario was second). It took repeated efforts for Manitoba's gay and lesbian activists to achieve this goal. As detailed below, this lobbying campaign, similar to Saskatchewan's, experienced delay and setbacks when the governing NDP party proved averse to making the changes. They stalled on revising the legislation even after this item was approved by the NDP convention as part of their legislative goals. As in Saskatchewan, this defied past practice, as policy items approved at convention were supposed to be introduced in the legislature when the NDP next formed government. So, on one hand, it was evidence of support in theory, but activists were tired of lip service and "signs" of support and wanted action. Politics, as that oft-repeated truism captures well, is the art of the possible. And thus while members of the NDP, ideologically, appeared to be in favour of human rights extensions for gay and lesbian Manitobans, it was not until the 1980s that such a legislative change finally seemed possible – after successive rounds of activism.

"Answering Anita Bryant" Winnipeg Style

In the late 1970s, one of the important stimuli to North American gay and lesbian activism was provoked by Anita Bryant's campaign, in Dade County, Florida, to repeal a 1977 ordinance that protected gays and lesbians from discrimination.[66] Sexual orientation had been protected in Dade County and, as part of a group called "Save our Children," Bryant worked to rollback this achievement and have the ordinance overturned. Bryant, a former beauty queen, was a popular American Christian singer and spokesperson for Florida orange juice. She was sufficiently well known and mainstream that she had a platform to promulgate her evangelical Christian views. In 1978, Bryant and her entourage toured large and small Canadian cities, starting in Toronto in January, Edmonton and Winnipeg in April, before arriving in Moose Jaw, Saskatchewan on 1 July to spread the gospel

of evangelical Christianity, the joy of heterosexual marriage and traditional families, couched in an explicitly anti-homosexual message.[67]
Renaissance International, a Canadian evangelical organization led by
Ken Campbell (a former United Church of Canada minister), sponsored Bryant's tour of Canadian cities. In Toronto, the gay and lesbian
community attempted to silence the "Christian Liberation Crusade,"
and urged the city to prohibit her performance. Western cities took
an alternative approach, attempting to "answer" her assertions about
the sinfulness of homosexuality by picketing her concerts and critiquing her homophobic message. Regardless of whether western gay and
lesbian activists saw this as an opportunity or resigned themselves to
the futility of demanding an evangelical event be cancelled in the heart
of the Canadian Bible Belt, the Bryant tour stimulated cross-regional
activism and strategizing. It also sparked gay and lesbian residents'
realization that quiet forbearance was not an entirely useful strategy.
These "coalitions to answer Anita Bryant" staged demonstrations,
gave press conferences, and engaged in dialogues about religion,
homosexuality, and region.

When local gay activists realized that Bryant would bring her message and her music to the Winnipeg Convention Centre on 30 April, a
committee of local activists – both lesbians and gay men – was formed
to counteract her concert. The groups in Winnipeg, Saskatoon, Edmonton, and Calgary were all in close contact with each other – sharing tips
on what had worked vis-à-vis the events, and lending support to each
other as the date of Bryant's visit approached. Thus, in some respects
Bryant's "love the sinner, hate the sin" message served as the means to
foster interregional cooperation. In *After Stonewall*, activist Walter Davis
described this as a "spirit of unity." In a dissection of her tour, Davis
wrote:

> The west has handled Anita Bryant. Both Edmonton and Winnipeg saw
> attempts at broad coalitions of both gays and straights with significant
> supports from women's organizations. While Edmonton's gay commu-
> nity was divided on the type of actions held and while the traditional gay
> organizations in Winnipeg played little role in organizing the protests, it
> was generally agreed that the success of the actions were proof of the need
> for high visibility in response to Bryant. The Winnipeg delegates urged
> that the focus of the answer to Anita Bryant not be on religion and that the
> presence of lesbian issues and lesbians be assured in order to build real
> unity in action.[68]

It is noteworthy that many of the collected interviews with activists indicate that people recall the Bryant tour vividly and that participation in the demonstration was formative. Glenn Fewster recalled that opposition to Bryant helped "solidify the gay community."[69]

Winnipeg Lesbian Society was part of this protest against Bryant, involving some 350 marchers, which organizers believed set a Winnipeg record.[70] Another group, Lesbian Mothers, scheduled a musical festival to coincide with Bryant's performance, and this too proved a very popular form of cultural protest.[71] While in hindsight the demonstration could be cited as a proud moment for gay and lesbian activism, one protest participant, Lyle Dick, recollected the imbalance between those who attended Bryant's performance and those who protested differently: "I remember going to a demonstration against Anita Bryant in 1978 … [she] was addressing a huge crowd in the Convention Centre in Winnipeg … And there was this tiny little demo … And I remember thinking to myself is this a good idea or not? It sends out the message that we're really marginal … It was important to have done it, but at the time I wasn't so sure."[72]

The previous Bryant demonstration in Edmonton was a similar size. There, activists of gay and women's rights staged an anti-Bryant rally. According to press reports, "more than 300 people, including at least 40 Calgarians demonstrated opposition to Bryant's appearance" at Edmonton Coliseum on April 29, 1978."[73] A wide-ranging alliance of support included "church groups, labour unions, a staff member of the Alberta Human Rights Commission," and gay activists. According to the Calgary gay paper, "media coverage of event was mostly positive and often supportive with some of the best editorial comment on gay rights in the history of Alberta."[74] Later that summer, the demonstration in Moose Jaw, Saskatchewan, was larger than the Winnipeg one, and featured alliances of churches, labour, academics, feminists, and gay and lesbian rights activists. Saskatchewan Gay Coalition bussed in protesters from Saskatoon and Regina, alongside those from Moose Jaw itself, which produced an impressive protest march and rally (see chapter 7).

No doubt one of the reasons Western groups were keen to provide a critique, and answer Bryant's claims that homosexuals lived perverted, sinful, sick lives, was of the ways in which her form of fundamentalist Christian "beliefs" were widely embraced in the region. Thus, while Toronto residents could legitimately demand to "Stop Anita" and what they regarded as her anachronistic messages from receiving publicity, that approach would not find favour in the west. Interestingly, the prominence of lesbian women during the Bryant visit – both within the committee and in protest marches outside the Convention Centre – demonstrated the ways in which Anita's message was particularly galvanizing for lesbians, feminists, and members of women's organizations, not just gay male activists. Isobel Andrews, then living in Winnipeg, wrote to *After Stonewall* to critique some of the "leftist male mistakes" and to note that in response to Bryant's visit to Winnipeg, she, as a member of Wages Due Lesbians, had "participated in the Committee to Answer Anita Bryant, and in the Lesbian Benefit concert that answered Anita by establishing a lesbian mother's defense fund."[75]

Press coverage of the event concentrated on the gay protestors outside the Convention Centre. In response, there were many critical letters to the editor published in the *Winnipeg Free Press* from citizens critical of gay disruption and the gay "lifestyle." The critics laced their letters with biblical passages to support their views. Astutely, Ken DeLisle, the founder of Dignity Winnipeg (the Catholic gay organization), offered this well-considered response:

> Due to many recent letters printed in the *Free Press* against the homosexual community for their actions protesting Miss Anita Bryant's recent visit to the city, I feel I must speak up against the myths they continue to spread. The first myth … is the suggestion that the homosexuals not only want do deny Mrs. Green her freedom of speech, but that we wanted her physically silenced by taking her life. Mrs. Green does have a right to speak, but we also have a right to speak – to argue with her statements and explain our views … We do not want special rights. Just the right to stop living a lie. Those of us who are homosexual by nature want to live honestly and contribute to our society, country and world. To do so we need help to protect our rights, to break the chains that keep us in our closets – our prisons.[76]

Evaluating the reactions to events like the Anita Bryant concert resist simplistic analysis. By virtue of the letters in the local papers, it was evident that there were Winnipeg residents in agreement with Bryant's anti-homosexual, pro-Christian family message. Whether sanctimonious, self-righteous, or just smug in their conventionality and so-called "majority views," it does not automatically follow that they represent the majority of Winnipeg residents. Far fewer letters were published condemning Bryant or supporting the gay activists. And one might easily conjecture the way in which the stirring up of homophobic commentary prior to and after the event was a trial to the gay and lesbian community, particularly those grappling with their orientation, or those for whom these hateful messages propelled them deeper into their closet.

However, in giving activists a focal point for action, events like Bryant's tour also, paradoxically, strengthened the communities. Certainly, it offered an opportunity for the women and men to unite against homophobic hatred and it offered a teachable moment about ongoing oppression. Bryant's views demonstrated the ways in which homophobia was still a scourge – one that could more easily be defeated with some basic human rights tools in the arsenal. Thus, it reinforced the drive for political changes. Finally, Bryant's sanctimonious message was off-putting to many people, religious and otherwise, including those who were not members of evangelical churches. Within a few short years, the tide would turn, and it would be Bryant herself experiencing a reversal of fortune – first divorce proceedings, then later losing her lucrative sponsorship contract before recanting her anti-homosexual beliefs. For lesbian and gay activists who organized to "Answer Anita," it was a moment of Schadenfreude.

"Queer Bashing in Winnipeg: Survivors Talk"

In the fall 1978 issue of *After Stonewall*, Bill Fields wrote, "today, here in Winnipeg" a "man dies from a beating he took on the legislative grounds. Nice well trained men out queer bashing. Queer-bashing. Teaching faggots a lesson."[77] This sombre news of Peter Petkaw's death, and the ongoing reality of violence on the hill, provided the topic for a special exposé entitled: "Queer Bashing in Winnipeg."[78] Field's article is difficult to read, but provides important evidence about the vitriolic nature of homophobic violence in the city so I've included excerpts of Bill Dwyer's first-hand account of his gay-bashing. Dwyer was introduced to readers as a forty-year-old man from Detroit, Michigan. A craftsman, member of a men's consciousness-raising group, and practicing Quaker, Dwyer had only lived in Winnipeg for a year at the time of the attack. Dwyer described sitting on the steps of the legislature with a friend, watching the sky and chatting after an evening meeting and dinner. His friend left, he lingered for another smoke, and then a truck and car pulled up, full of young guys, and the ringleader demanded a blow job. Dwyer refused, at which point "he answered by jumping out of the truck and hitting me, knocking me off my feet. Then others, there had been three in the truck, four or five in the car, joined him in kicking me again and again." They asked if he was "queer" and he didn't respond; the kicking continued, two men urinated on him, still the kicking continued, until "finally, some of them said, 'he's had enough. Leave him there crying, like a queer.'"[79] After they left, he got to his feet, another car pulled up and a gay male told him to get in. At home he surveyed the damage: "two black eyes, a bad bruise on my head, a couple of cracked ribs. My face was covered with blood and I had smaller bruises all over." He did not report the attack to the police nor did he seek medical care, preferring to patch himself up. Given the late model of the truck, the assailants clothing, and their ages (late teens to early twenties), Dwyer told Fields that he believed they were "all from middle-class white families."[80] Similarly, Petkaw's attacker was only eighteen at the time of his conviction in 1978.[81] As this attack had not been provoked, Fields asked him to speculate on why he was targeted. Dwyer said, "homophobia takes a lot of forms. The leader of the group that night was trying to prove his manhood." More generally, Fields and Dwyer spoke about the upsurge in violence on the hill and attributed it to a host of factors, one of which was visibility.

> The media gave attention to the Hill as a place where gays hang out. The number of incidents does seem to have increased about the same time as the [security] gates and the news coverage. Since my beating, I have heard of at least six others. A fifteen year old riding a bicycle on the Osborne Bridge was hospitalized. I read of another man who was beaten with a chain on Assiniboine and then there was the man who died. A friend of mine who wouldn't tell me how he got his eyes blacked told a mutual friend it happened there. And those are only the ones I have heard about.[82]

Little wonder that GFE had attempted to publicize the danger of continuing to use the hill as a cruising ground, a practice, as previous chapters illustrated, that had a long history in Winnipeg. Asked to explain what, beyond hate, might motivate such actions in the city, Dwyer, who had lived as openly gay in Toronto and Detroit said, "it is a real Winnipeg scene for cars and trucks of kids to ride through town yelling 'fag' at people walking. They're all around 18 and 19. At the top of their lungs they scream, 'Fucking queer, I'm going to kill you' while shaking their fists."[83] Dwyer speculated that part of the increase in such homophobic violence, and also homophobic graffiti in the downtown core, might be due to "Anita Bryant and her kind. There has always been some uptightness among young men about homosexuality, but Anita Bryant's 'cause' and the controversy created by some fundamentalists inflames the climate, and lends social approval to hostility." Dwyer was not anti-religious, in fact, as a Quaker, he believed that education, not retributive action or imprisonment, was the solution to this outpouring of violence and hate. He encouraged more emphasis on male discussion groups, and a wider range of male role models provided for boys and young men, which might counteract the overwhelming messages men received about being macho and tough. Such education might help to defuse such situations before they ended in violence.

Activism sparked, in all prairie cities, a number of reactions, and one of them was violence. It is also likely, though, that activism encouraged people to speak out and potentially report crimes, if not with police, then at least with gay and lesbian organizations. Few were as immediate as this one, where debates about the role of homosexuality created by Anita Bryant's visit to the city may have sparked a wave of anti-gay reprisals. But, it was true that however much liberationists urged openness, urged people to stand up and be counted, part of that process of greater visibility was, in the minds of some prairie residents, clearly incendiary. There is no other rational explanation for the wave of bashings (Winnipeg), club violence and club arson (Saskatoon), bath raids (Edmonton), or murders (all cities) in which gay men, less frequently lesbians, found themselves assaulted, arrested, their property and clubs damaged, or, in the most extreme cases, murdered. If the intention of these waves of violence was to turn back the clock to a bygone era of quiet discretion, limiting public visibility of gay men and lesbians, or "to teach" gay men a lesson, they were not successful. Strong political voices in all cities continue to demand that such violence be met with resistance. Queer activists urged people to be savvy, use various strategies to stay safe (including moving around in groups later in the evenings), but they did not countenance backing down. That said, many more conservative members of these communities no doubt decoded these messages differently, and, in chapter 8, and in the discussion of whether to hold a march in Calgary, one of the key points raised by those who opposed the march was the fear that marching might trigger violent reprisals from "Christians" or "cowboys." The anti-gay "groups" were not organized as a movement to push back against queer visibility and claims to urban spaces. But anti-gay and lesbian opposition was part of the fabric of prairie life. Throughout the 1970s and 1980s, a series of events reminded gay and lesbian people of how tenuous and vulnerable their position could be in these cities.

"Unbecoming Behaviour": Homophobia in the Workplace

One of the prevalent themes in my oral interviews and in the oral histories collected in Winnipeg was the issue of workplace homophobia and discrimination. People had stories to tell of being passed over for jobs, having been marginalized because their sexual identities were known, or, conversely, of having been underemployed because their volunteer work as queer activists was too widely known to make them "employable" in certain forms of work – most notably teaching, but also in social services or government employment. Other than education, this phenomenon was not universal, and each circumstance was highly unique. One interesting case that merits sustained analysis was that of Frances Williamson in Winnipeg. Williamson was trained as a nurse and very well regarded professionally. She had been married for twenty-seven years (1945–72), and, after the dissolution of her marriage, she entered a lesbian relationship. In our interview, she admitted that, "I knew as soon as I got married that I'd made a big mistake. But because we both came from good Christian homes we tried to make it work out. We had lots of good times but it didn't work. He knew there were problems."[84] While working in public health, she had encountered materials, nonfiction and fiction, about homosexuality – lesbianism specifically – that provided her with a window into same-sex activities. Such information led her to realize that her high school crushes were more than a phase and she acknowledged she was a lesbian. She volunteered at the GFE phone lines, worked the door at dances, or tended bar (she joked that as a non-drinker she was not a risk to sample the booze or to have difficulties handling the cash), and so was well integrated into Winnipeg's queer community. Williamson had a six-year long lesbian relationship with another nurse. That relationship ended when her partner's family intervened. The loss of this relationship, and her old-fashioned views on partnerships (she told me that had her partner died, she would not have remarried), meant that she did not seek another relationship.

All of which is to say that Williamson's knowledge of queer Winnipeg, and her political engagement, was extensive – she read *The Body Politic* and authors like Jane Rule (in fact she actively corresponded with Rule, and eventually became friends of her and her partner, Helen Sonthoff, which included annual visits to their home on Galliano Island,

British Columbia).[85] She was a participant in Winnipeg's community, attended dances at Ms Purdy's, answered the hotline, and knew Chris Vogel and other male activists well. She was also active in her church and worked towards fostering a more inclusive climate for queer congregants. So, when I posed the question about homophobia, and in particular, about costs in the workplace, Williamson told me, "I was never able to prove it but I was blacklisted" by the Manitoba Association of Registered Nurses (MARN). Here Williamson tells her story:

> I had been accepted for a very good job in B.C. ... at the end of the interview, when I had been accepted, the interviewer asked me do you know so and so at the MARN offices and I said yes, I did. And she asked me if I minded if they called for a reference. I had nothing to hide. Three days later I got a call saying they had decided not to accept me. This [the person they asked to speak too] was one of the women who was terribly homophobic in the nursing group. That was in 1980. I had just finished my Master's. Well I tried to find out and hit a brick wall everywhere I went. I didn't come right out and ask, but when I had been President of the Manitoba Association of Registered Nurses I was the one that had to take the registration away from somebody that was in a lesbian relationship. It was passed by the Board and I had to do it ... I did not stand up and say you're talking about me too. Which in hindsight I should have done.[86]

At this point in the interview, I asked if standing up for that other nurse, approximately four years earlier, would have made a difference. "No," Williamson replied, "I would have been booted out too." According to Williamson, the nursing act gave three reasons for revoking a nursing licence: "drug addict, poor standard or care [work] and unbecoming behaviour." When she was president, she asked the board chair to clarify what was meant by "unbecoming behaviour," and learned that this was the code word for lesbianism within the nursing profession. Frances Williamson retired in 1985, and when we spoke, in 2002, these moments of workplace and professional homophobia were, as she put it, "still all pretty fresh."[87]

Understandably, this was a challenging moment in the interview, and like many of my narrators, I was impressed at Williamson's candour and bravery. She readily admitted to having been placed in the no-win situation of being obliged to strip another lesbian of her licence when she was the president of MARN. She also candidly spoke of her own challenges with homophobia within her family of origin, her profession, and within her church. This white, middle-class professional woman's experience serves as the cautionary frame of reference for assessing the strategies employed by the "campus lesbians" in Saskatoon. Well credentialed and well thought of professionally, such workplace discrimination against gays and lesbians now strikes us as patently unfair. But these were routine occurrences and there were just enough of them to sow fears in the minds of middle-class professionals. Those individuals who circumvented such events, particularly very prominent ones, had some extra clout or protection. I asked Williamson about Dr Bell, gauging that her time as a nurse and his as dean of the Faculty of Medicine at the University of Manitoba must have overlapped. Yes, she responded, she did know Dr Bell, and then she added that while rumours always circulated about Bell he was "always very good to all the staff, he was one of the better people. Very sensitive. Very kind." She had clear admiration and respect for Bell. How had Dr Bell managed to have such a prominent career, I asked, in spite of the reality that he was, for the time, as "openly" queer as a middle-class professional doctor could be? She said she did not believe this was a double standard for men, or for doctors, but that the key to Bell's ability to navigate the system was that he was from a well-respected, well-connected Winnipeg family. Had he not been, his ability to keep his position might also have been jeopardized. One of the strategies that enabled queer people to lead successful lives in the prairie region was this issue of being "one of our own," a phrase that earmarked those who lived and later worked in their hometowns, whether rural areas or big cities. Not everyone was accepted – class, race, and community engagement were important factors in whose orientation might be accepted, or at least ignored, versus those whose difference marked them for difficulties.[88]

Censorship: *The Joy of Gay Sex* in Winnipeg

In 1980, after a complaint from a Winnipeg woman who claimed that while looking for the *Joy of Cooking* she had instead found the *Joy of Gay Sex* and the *Joy of Lesbian Sex* at a Classic Books store in the city, city police were called. The bookshop chain was warned about selling these books. Subsequently, Coles bookshop in Winnipeg was also warned about selling this material.[89] Attorney General Gerry Mercier's press conference indicated that such "obscene" literature had no place being offered for sale in Winnipeg, and the province was going to move to ban the sale of such materials. In response to these actions, in November

1980, one hundred members of the gay and lesbian community, along with supporters, marched outside the legislature to condemn these actions. Photographs taken of the Stop Police Book Banning Censorship Demonstration, organized by lesbian activists and Liberation Books, held on 1 November 1980, show people bundled up against the cold, carrying placards protesting police censorship and interference. The photos formed some of the visual images for a "Coming Out Television" program on censorship.

Issues of censorship would continue to feature prominently in Winnipeg. In 1983, a Winnipeg-area school principal made headlines for complaining that a collection of books from the Canada Council had included a book promoting homosexuality. The book in question – *Flaunting It!* – was a collection of reprinted essays from *The Body Politic*.[90] Press reports claimed that he intended to return the book to the council and "explain his view on the subject." In the same article, another principal in Amaranth, Manitoba, claimed that he "threw the book in the garbage."[91] In April 1985, school trustees in Winnipeg voted to have the women's magazine *HERizon* removed from their school library, because it was "anti-male and promotes lesbianism."[92] Winnipeg was not the only city in Canada that was riding a wave of book-banning hysteria, fearful of literature's impact on impressionable minds, notably teenagers. Peterborough, Ontario, had famously banned the works of Canadian literary icon and resident Margaret Laurence. In the 1980s, gay and lesbian bookshops in Toronto and Vancouver found themselves under siege from Canada Customs.[93] Equally important, within feminist and activist circles, an acrimonious debate about pornography divided activists over issues of women's oppression and sexual violence versus those who argued that state censorship was a dangerous – and blunt – means to address those concerns.[94]

Human Rights Activism, 1982–1987

In the fall of 1982, GFE and Chris Vogel filed complaints with the Manitoba Human Rights Commission, charging that the Manitoba government, a union, and an insurance firm discriminated against Vogel with respect to benefits for his long-time partner and "spouse," Richard North. In the claim, GFE said that the issue was denial of benefits in the employee health and pension plan. In March 1985, one of the more dramatic efforts to publicize gay discrimination and to urge the government to include sexual orientation into the human rights code was

Richard North's hunger strike. North's hunger strike lasted fifty-nine days. During that time he demanded that Attorney General Roland Penner amend the code. Neither Penner nor the NDP government of Premier Howard Pawley was swayed by these radical tactics.[95]

All of this occurred despite the fact that the Manitoba NDP was on record as stating that they were in favour of amending the human rights code in the province to include sexual orientation. The government's failure of will frustrated gay and lesbian activists as they lost faith in the government's reassurances that they would eventually, in due course, modify the code. In large part, this dickering on the attorney general's part was what precipitated Richard North's fifty-nine day hunger strike, starting on 8 March 1985.[96] In February 1986, a group of activist lesbians and gay men in Winnipeg formed a group called the Sexual Orientation Lobby, to "persuade politicians to entrench their rights."[97] Nicknamed "the Lobby" this group met with all the provincial MLAs, and asked organizations like the Manitoba Federation of Labour and the United Church of Canada to endorse their cause. According to Daryl Kippen, the UCC turned out to be a "valuable supporter and presented a brief at the hearings," while "the Anglican church only provided a letter of support."[98]

The public hearings were held in July 1987. The Lobby's motto, "the sun shines on all of us," represented the fifth or sixth attempt by the gay and lesbian community to achieve modifications to the human rights code – an initiative that Vogel and North had initially demanded and lobbied for in the mid-1970s. Some of the key organizers were Margie Cogill, Joan Miller, Deb Dunstan, Joyce Rankin, Darryl Kippen, and Glen Murray (future mayor of Winnipeg and Canada's first openly gay mayor).[99] Rankin recalled that Vogel and North lobbied on their own behalf for the modifications, and many other interviews noted that a variety of other Winnipeg lesbians and gays offered briefs on behalf of feminist or gay organizations. For instance, K. Louise Fulton helped with the brief presented by the Manitoba Action Committee on the Status of Women while Lyle Dick presented a brief on behalf of Project Lambda. Fulton recalled that her experience with the public hearings convinced her of the importance of bridging the feminist and lesbian communities and of making lesbian advocacy a priority.

Over the course of approximately four days of hearings, in rooms packed with participants and the press, Cogill and other Lobby organizers worked well into the night, scrambling to find speakers to support their cause because they had not "anticipated the number of people who came to speak in opposition to the legislation."[100] Recalling the scene, participant Sally Papso remembered that the hearing room had been divided into two parts: "Gays and lesbians were on one side and the Fundamentalists and Homo-Haters were on the other side." After listening to many fundamentalists speak, especially ones talking about child sexual abuse, [Papso] decided a rebuttal was necessary. Having extensive experience in counselling these children and their abusers, she couldn't "tolerate the lies and hatred being spread by these people."[101] The United Church was the only religious body to voice its support of the legislation. Ken DeLisle noted that there were important links between feminist and gay and lesbian activists within the United Church. Space doesn't permit coverage of the importance attached to the United Church of Canada's decisions, at Victoria General Council in 1986, to begin studying homosexuality and its implications for ministry and membership in the church body. In Winnipeg, there was some convergence between these religious events (activists and supporters, like Frances Williamson, Dr A.M. Watts, and others, who were involved in both the Manitoba Conference and the national conference discussions) and the course of secular gay and lesbian activism.[102] Ken DeLisle cited the UCC's feminist awareness as a beneficial factor when the church began to grapple with homosexuality.[103] An Affirm United group (gay and lesbians within the UCC) was created in Winnipeg in the mid-1980s. In addition to the fundamentalist adherents who spoke against the legislation, the Catholic Church was openly opposed to the amendment. Articles and letters in the *Winnipeg Free Press*, quoting Bishop Exner, entreated the politicians not to amend the legislation. This contrasts sharply with Saskatchewan where, in 1996, the bishop from Saskatoon diocese wrote an open letter to all Catholics in the province supporting human rights extensions for gay and lesbian people.[104]

Margie Cogill recollected that the process the government initiated (meetings and presentations to the government) allowed for representatives in the community to get their message across. Lyle Dick reflected that it had been so effective, in part, because lesbians took the leadership role, and that the community offered a unified response to the commissioners.[105] Joyce Rankin concurred, stating that because women were in the leadership position, it made it more palatable for the homophobic MLAs to deal with women and not gay men. In terms of the lesbian and gay community, 1985 marked a turning point with the election of a woman, Belle Sherlock, to the presidency of Project Lambda for the first time. Donn Yuen, Lambda's treasurer from 1979 until 1992, recollected that under Sherlock's leadership membership of PL soared to an all-time high (over two hundred people) because she encouraged lesbians to join.[106] Rankin also recalled that lesbians and women in the local community and NDP party were urged to pressure their NDP MLAs for support. With the Lobby providing educational information for Roland Penner, and because of the NDP's approved support for the human rights revisions, the party finally amended the legislation. While the Conservative Party was vehemently opposed to the legislation, the support of Liberal Leader Sharon Carstairs was another important factor in the passage of the legislation.

In July 1987, Howard Pawley's NDP government passed Bill 47 by a narrow vote of twenty-nine to twenty-five and only after a last moment amendment to the bill inserted language stating that the government was not condoning or condemning any lifestyle.[107] Manitoba's provincial human rights code now included sexual orientation as a prohibited category for discrimination – the goal was finally achieved. Given Pawley's narrow majority, and the strongly held Christian views expressed by members of the Opposition, as well as a few members of the governing NDP, it was evident that this legislation would attract much debate. Many of the politicians who spoke in the legislature indicated that this was a very contentious issue for Manitobans. In their speeches, speakers who opposed the bill quoted biblical texts and interpretations; utilized farming and agricultural metaphors about animal husbandry and sexual "normality"; and also offered blatantly discriminatory and scarifying images of how these "special rights" for homosexuals would negatively affect the educational system, jeopardize the province's youth, and sanctify perversion. One particularly prominent opponent, former NDP Premier of Manitoba and former Governor General Ed Schreyer, was quoted in press reports as classifying homosexuality as an "affliction" that would "grant special status to gays and lesbians."[108] Those who were in favour of the legislation repeatedly discussed matters of equity and spoke to the issues of discrimination in employment, access to services, housing, and the like that would be rectified by the passage of such legislation. Never did they discuss the six years that they had supported the notion of amending the human rights code to include sexual orientation, nor of the way in which their neighbouring province Ontario's decision to amend their code in December 1986 had, in some ways, finally encouraged Manitoba's NDP government to pass the legislation. Kippen recalled that at the annual Christmas open house at Government House activists provided "small cards to everyone present saying 'We support the inclusion of sexual orientation in the Human Rights Code.'"[109]

In the aftermath of the vote, there continued to be articles devoted to criticisms of the government's action. One critique, from Native leaders, indicated that they believed that their provincial representative, Elijah Harper, had failed to convey the Indigenous viewpoint on homosexuality. Chief Guy Wood stated that homosexuality was contrary to "Indian values," and was "against their traditional teachings" and "could undermine the family." For his part, Harper did not comment on why he had chosen not speak out on the issue.[110]

Conclusion

One feature of the 1992 interviews with Winnipeg gay and lesbian activist leaders was a culminating assessment of the community's accomplishments and, additionally, questions about how Winnipeg's situation compared with other prairie cities. Few people had experiences elsewhere. But for those that did a few salient points were repeated. First, many noted that in comparison with other centres Winnipeg gays and lesbians were quite concerned to maintain their privacy, and hence were preoccupied with issues of public disclosure of their sexual orientation. According to Bev Baptiste, a MCC minister who moved from Calgary to Winnipeg: "In Winnipeg the gay community is more closeted because most members were born here and fear family and friends living here will reject them if they learn about a person's homosexuality."[111] Of the leading activists, most had moved to Winnipeg for work or educational opportunities and hence did not have to carry that burden. Only Rich North, whose family was from Winnipeg, was the exception to that rule. Others, of course, had migrated from within the province, and given Winnipeg's predominance (and that the city's papers were taken throughout the province), news of what happened in the capital reached the small towns and rural areas very quickly. For instance, Lyle Dick's family was quick to comment on his publicized views in the *Winnipeg Free Press*, and he knew, before he allowed his letters to be published, that such statements amounted to a public assertion of his homosexuality. Still, by comparison with life in Brandon, Neepawa, or Thompson, being gay in Winnipeg, the province's largest and capital city, home to two universities, a plethora of cultural activities (ballet, symphony, theatre) and with varied queer spaces, enabled political and social activity that was impossible elsewhere in Manitoba.

The support of the universities – in terms of personnel, funding, and physical space – was incalculably important. This characteristic would be repeated in all of the prairie cities, and where the universities were best established; with strong roots in the community, one often found gay activism and organizational support. This, more than urban size or whether the city in question was a political capital, seems to define the gay and lesbian prairie experience. Thus future chapters will detail how the success of gay organizations and communities in Saskatoon and Edmonton – and their links with the provincial universities – was a key support for activism, particularly in the foundational years when gay groups were small and funds were limited. The small amounts of funds, office space, and access to small student service/club funding envelopes were tremendously important.

For all the battles, within and with the media, against queer bashing, and within professional and religious organizations, it would be in Manitoba, in 1987, that gay and lesbians on the prairies had their first success with revisions to a provincial human rights code. Saskatchewan took until 1993 and Alberta until 1998. It marked years of work by Gays for Equality, and later ad hoc groups, like Project Lambda and The Lobby, to achieve this milestone. The crew of activists in Winnipeg was never large, but they were determined and, as the histories and archival evidence illustrate, that determination eventually proved successful. This achievement needs to be evaluated against the other reactions within the city and the region. Not everyone supported gay and lesbian rights by a long shot. Winnipeg had a couple of hundred activists rallying outside the auditorium when Anita Bryant rolled through on her Christian revival tour, while inside thousands of attendees heard Bryant's message. Winnipeg had more challenges getting their club charter, in advertising themselves, even in selling books about gay and lesbian sex than the other cities did – including Calgary. It is a wonder, in some respects, that they accomplished the human rights legislative revisions when they did. It appears to be the result of organization, compelling statements, hard work, and serendipity. Manitoba wanted to be seen to be a leader in extending these rights after Quebec and Ontario had done so in 1977 and 1985 respectively – never underestimate the power of interprovincial rivalries to the "get 'er done culture" of western Canada. Manitoba, like Saskatchewan, had NDP governments in power at the time of these legislative victories, but both NDP parties had resisted for years, long after these matters had been approved by their annual conventions, so it is important not to simplistically regard the NDP government as uniformly more progressive on social issues. It is clear that each city, province, and to an extent their rural hinterlands were unique in how they created moments of gay and lesbian activism, responded to discrimination and homophobia, and resisted calls that they "quietly" return to a less political, less visible presence in these cities. In Winnipeg, the organizational drive has been particularly strong and enduring, and one can point to the continued presence of a gay community organization from the early 1970s to the present day. Campus Gay Club started in 1972, and later quickly became the Gays for Equality organization. In the late 1970s, Project Lambda and the Oscar Wilde Memorial Society started fundraising drives to purchase their own spaces, a quest that was finally realized in 1982. That year, Giovanni's Room opened at 275 Sherbrooke St and Happenings Social Club purchased their building across the street, at 272 Sherbrooke St. Gays for Equality moved out of their space at the University of Manitoba campus in 1983 and into the community centre space.[112] Ted Millward, from the Council on Homosexuality and Religion, donated his organization's library to the centre, offering patrons a lending library of queer materials.[113] In 1988, this centre was renamed the Winnipeg Gay and Lesbian Resource Centre, and it relocated to 222 Osborne St. Over a decade later, that organization would rebrand itself as the Rainbow Resource Centre (and it moved to 170 Scott St), where it remains to this day, "serving Manitoba's Gay, Lesbian, Bisexual, Transgender and Two Spirit Communities."[114] Although their name changed and they moved from campus to the community, arguably the core work of what was Campus Gay Club, later Gays for Equality, and now the Rainbow Resource Centre, has continued from the early 1970s until the present day. That is a record few cities can match. Equally important, and clearly linked to the organizational continuity, is the fact that a handful of key activists remained involved, including Chris Vogel and Rich North. In 2018, Vogel and North were still together and still fighting for recognition, which is emblematic of the ways that such activists continued to live their activism and to stand up to the authorities – governmental, social, or urban – that challenged their ability to live their lives.

Chapter Seven

"Towards a Gay Community":
Activism, Reaction, Visibility,
and Violence in Saskatoon, 1970–1985[1]

I have come home after five years to Saskatoon. A lot has changed. For gay people, it represents a kind of transformation of this city of 140,000 … It is the people that make it work. Hard working people, determined people, like those shown on this page – Mavis and Elizabeth, Neil (Richards) and the two Dougs (Hellquist and Wilson) … The success of this small band of gay activists in this prairie city has shown that gay liberation is not just a phenomenon seen in large urban centres. But most important, the people at SGCC (Saskatoon Gay Community Centre) have shown that with a little bit of effort, you *can* build something out of nothing (italics in original).[2]

Tom Warner, The Body Politic, 1977

I think there were a lot of people who had unhappy lives and that has been a sin. Life is much better now, with more opportunities. History has to show that there was a great deal of repression, double lives or no lives.[3]

Paul Gessell, Ottawa (formerly Moose Jaw), 2006

"Well [being a lesbian] it's been a freeing of the soul. You know being the one who didn't know anything about it [lesbianism] it has broadened my outlook on life and awareness and it's been a very positive thing for me to be out … We've had all kinds of things thrown at us at various times and we're still weathering the storm.[4]

Lilja Stefansson, Regina, 2003

Evidence from interviews and archival documents illustrate that Saskatoon had a unique history of gay and lesbian activism and tremendous organizational continuity and growth throughout the 1970s and 1980s.

7.1 Towards a Gay Community button, Fifth National Gay Conference, 29 June – 3 July 1977. Creator: Saskatoon Gay Community Centre. Neil Richards Collection of Sexual Diversity in the University of Saskatchewan Archives and Special Collections. Image courtesy of Neil Richards.

But people's experiences varied immensely. Not everyone was as brave as fifty-four-year-old Lilja Stefansson who left a difficult marriage, and officially came out as a lesbian, in small-town Saskatchewan in 1975. Paul Gessell's observation, and his decision to speak for many that would never have spoken with me, cautions about framing this history in too positivistic terms and of the submerged iceberg so seldom visible in histories based on oral histories, of those queer people who couldn't make the leap from no lives, or double lives, to open acceptance. Previously, I've written at length about the campaigns for human rights protection (1993) and the Doug Wilson case (1975).[5] The successful conclusion to these battles for human rights coverage in Saskatchewan occurred in 1998 and hence is well outside the scope of this volume, which concludes in 1985. Two decades of activism were required before the Saskatchewan government legislated the changes to the province's human rights codes. Saskatchewan was the seventh Canadian province to recognize sexual minority rights, and on the face of this legislative landmark it would hardly seem fitting to argue for the province as a "beacon" of gay and lesbian activism. However, in the space available here, concentrating on the years from 1970 to 1985, I do want to make that claim, because in taking the long view of these various, disparate moments of activism, the ongoing educational campaigns, and the publicity of queer politics and issues, a strong case could be made for Saskatoon's leadership role in Canadian gay and lesbian activism.

SGA Activism and Opposition 1971–1975

Just to recap, gay and lesbian activism formally arrived in the city in spring 1971 when Gens Hellquist proposed the creation of Saskatoon Gay Liberation. Later that fall, two gay organizations were formally created: Gay Students Alliance at the University of Saskatchewan and Saskatoon Gay Action. Reflecting on the accomplishments of their first year, Hellquist wrote, "We've made great strides in Saskatoon last year. Three different groups (including Gemini Club) have been established to work for the gay community in Saskatoon." However, what would be a constant irritant – too few activists and organizers and far more free riders – was also evident: "Without the support of all the gay people in Saskatoon, these groups will fold so let us hear from you. Let us know that you are alive and that you give a *damn what happens* … let's all get together and make Gemini Club the best club in Canada" (emphasis mine).[6] Hellquist's roles and institutional affiliations would change over time; he was sometimes in an official leadership role, at other times it was unofficial, but he was always the conscience of the community, and right up until his death in 2013 he continued to issue such edicts, trying to rally the closeted and complacent to get out and participate.

In 1972, Hellquist was the president of SGA and he, along with Bruce Garman, Tim LeMay, Peter Millard, and others were pragmatic about their chances for change. According to Hellquist, the "SGA had no clear political philosophy because it must rely on a relatively small membership, whose attitudes cover a wide spectrum, few of them radical."[7] Members ranged from sixteen to seventy-one years of age and, although the Saturday evening dances were the most popular activity, there were clear political goals. Saskatoon took a lead role within the province and region, hosting delegates from Regina who were keen to replicate this structure in their city. In November 1972, they hosted forty delegates from all five prairie membership clubs at the First Western Canadian Gay Clubs Conference.[8] In May 1974, Saskatoon Gay Action hosted the first conference of prairie gay activists. Approximately twenty delegates came from Winnipeg, Edmonton, and Saskatoon.[9] Even at that early

7.2 Gens Hellquist, February 1977. Images provided courtesy of DailyXtra.com

juncture, topics of discussion were national activism, community relations, lesbian and gay cooperation, fundraising, and counselling. And, most important, unlike the other four cities, where the social membership clubs were formed first and activist groups, if they formed at all, came second, in Saskatoon the activist group was formed first, making it the community leader, and, in many ways, the activists used the social club fundraisers to help support their work.

In their first few years of operation, Saskatoon Gay Action was busy on a number of activist fronts, requesting changes to the provincial human rights code, changes to the immigration laws, and working to promote awareness of gays and lesbians in Saskatoon. Initially, this often consisted of being alert to opportunities, particularly on campus, to question visiting speakers or politicians about gay and lesbian issues, which garnered publicity and built awareness. For example, in October 1972, during a Liberal campaign rally at the University of Saskatchewan (in advance of the federal election later that month), Bruce Garman asked Prime Minister Pierre Trudeau "his position on the place of homosexuals in the Bill of Rights and on restrictions against homosexuals in the Immigration Act."[10] Trudeau shrugged it off and was reportedly "non committal," but Justice Minister Otto Lang subsequently replied, "the majority of Canadians felt there were already enough homosexuals, drug addicts and prostitutes in the country."[11] There was a recurrent tendency by politicians, police, and, sometimes, civic leaders to group homosexuals with drug addicts and prostitutes, trigger words intended to signify criminality and marginality. Clearly, those in power weren't expecting the margins to speak up and demand their rights.

In addition to these moments of politics and publicity, SGA's work towards human rights extensions began in earnest in winter 1973, when Garman and Hellquist were encouraged by the Saskatchewan Association of Human Rights to prepare a brief on anti-gay discrimination for the government.[12] That August, SGA presented the document, which requested that the Allen Blakeney NDP government amend the human rights code to include protections for Saskatchewan's gay and lesbian citizens. A positive reaction to this meeting, with Attorney General Roy Romanow's assistant, and the positive comments later attributed to Romanow, inspired hope.[13] Further encouragement arrived on 25 August, when the Saskatchewan Human Rights Commission (SHRC) officially recommended that the code be expanded to include sexual orientation. This decision by the SHRC made it the first human rights commission in Canada to make that recommendation.[14]

At the same time as SGA was working on human rights activism, they initiated a series of other points of publicity/activism intended to forge awareness and foster change. For example, Bruce Garman, on behalf of SGA, approached Saskatoon City Council to request that they proclaim the week of 19–26 August 1973 gay pride week.[15] Garman informed councillors that this week commemorated the anniversary of the Canadian federal government's legislation to decriminalize homosexuality between consenting adults.[16] Furthermore, SGA hoped that in designating this week gay citizens could "demonstrate their pride in their sexuality and their desire to be allowed to live their lives without the fear of discrimination and oppression."[17] The city disagreed. Alderman Penner dismissively replied: "I think there are certain matters that are subject to privacy of the individual, that don't need any proclamation or public statement made about them."[18] Gay pride events went ahead without the proclamation. Pride events in the prairies offer moments of revelation, both historically and within contemporary prairie cities. In 2017, the city of Saskatoon was proudly flying the pride flag, and the city's mayor, Charlie Clark, and city councillors were happy to support the flag raising and attend the parade. The city's previous mayor, Don Atchison, never had space in his calendar to attend pride events – over his five terms in office.[19]

Saskatoon City Council was not the only organization that dampened the spirits of SGA and their various early 1970s requests for legal and social changes. Local and gay community newspapers and newsletters routinely reported on various forms of homophobic opposition or repression: court cases, particularly surrounding child custody; refusals to print advertisements or publicity information; refusals to rent spaces for community dances; and, occasionally, episodes of homophobic violence. In August 1974 the provincial farm newspaper, *The Western Producer*, refused to publish this small classified advertisement: "Zodiac Friendship Society, an organization for homosexual men and women, for information phone." The identical ad had run without controversy in the *Star Phoenix* for two years. *The Western Producer*'s business manager explained their rationale: "this is a family paper, we do not want to upset any readers, our main concern is to make a buck."[20] Zodiac filed a complaint with the provincial Human Rights Commission. An investigation was conducted, but, without a category in the human rights code protecting sexual orientation (like gender) from discrimination, there were no legal grounds from which to challenge the *Western Producer*'s decision.

The Advocate, the American gay and lesbian newsmagazine, published a short article in their 11 September 1974 issue about a lesbian custody case in Saskatoon. In May 1974, Darlene Case's ex-husband illegally took their nine-year-old daughter into custody claiming that Case's sexual orientation made her an unfit mother for their two children. *The Advocate* reported that this was the first case in which a lesbian mother had fought back, declaring that her sexual orientation was insufficient grounds from which to "establish her unfitness for parental custody."[21] SGA was rallying for her cause, supporting her, and soliciting funds to help her pay her legal fees.

Not all aspects of gay and lesbian life in Saskatoon made it into the press and so it is difficult to assess how much day-to-day "opposition" there was to signs of lesbian and gay emergence. What this sampling suggests is that early support for gay and lesbian organizations could be accommodated. And perhaps, under some circumstances, queer people could be tolerated in particular environments, but fundamental changes to the status quo – demanding human rights, lesbian parenting, publicizing gay and lesbian organizations in rural and farm communities – were forms of lesbian and gay self-determination or "activism" (opponents would use the term "special rights" or "flaunting") that were strongly opposed.

In winter and spring 1975, SGA began more actively lobbying the NDP government for human rights protection. In February, every MLA was sent a short brief entitled "A Minority without Rights" (originally prepared for the Saskatchewan Human Rights Commission) and a questionnaire to elicit their views on this request for human rights coverage. Only twelve of the sixty MLAs responded. Only three responses were positive. It was an election year and while SGA wanted to make gay and lesbian human rights an election issue, the politicians, recognizing a wedge issue, were leery to touch it for fear of alienating voters. Some chose silence, others chose to pass the buck. The premier stated, "that the matter fell under the jurisdiction of the Attorney General Roy Romanow." For his part, Romanow "declined to comment on the grounds that he [was] a Minister of the Crown."[22] Undeterred, SGA decided to publish the results of this questionnaire in the newspaper, timing the ad to appear right before the election. The *Saskatoon Star Phoenix* refused to publish the ad.

The newspaper's decision was curious. They had routinely published classified ads for SGA. When management attempted to justify their decision, it merely inflamed matters and sparked Saskatoon's first

7.3 *Star Phoenix* Protest March with Neil Richards in front, 10 June 1975.
Image courtesy of Neil Richards PAS S-B 13421.

gay protest. Fifteen members of Saskatoon Gay Action picketed outside the *Star Phoenix* building.[23] Interpreting such moments, and many
others that followed in Saskatoon, are challenging. At the time, the
gay and lesbian community, through their spokesperson Richard Nordahl (a faculty member at the university), decried the paper's actions
as obstructionist behaviour. The *SP*'s counterclaim was that without
the candidates' consent they could not run the ad. Jim Struthers, the
paper's executive vice president, indicated that he wanted to ensure
that "all candidates have a chance to reply before the ad was carried."[24]
By then, naturally, the election was over.

Queer protestors were outraged at the paper's complicity with the
politicians' attempt to silence discussion of sexual politics/rights during an election campaign. On the picket lines, activists handed out pamphlets enumerating media silencing of gay issues, stating "the refusal

to run the ad is just one more instance in which the press discriminates against gay people and refused to allow free access to the press which is a right that is supposed to be guaranteed in this country." They highlighted the hypocritical situation where the paper proclaimed to champion both democracy and free speech but caved when they feared angering politicians. Their masthead quote, from Canada's Supreme Court – "Democracy cannot be maintained without its foundation; free public opinion and free discussion throughout the nation of all matters affecting the state within the limits set by the criminal code and the common law" – appeared on the editorial page in each issue of the newspaper.[25] The community newspaper *The Saskatonian* lambasted their decision and their politics: "The *SP* has never pretended to be unbiased. But events this week have shown that this talk of free public opinion and free discussion is only that."[26]

Ironically, while the paper wouldn't print SGA's election advertisement, they saw no inconsistency in publishing a photograph of the protestors on the newspaper's front page. Such actions effectively outed those photographed, in Saskatoon and beyond, as many small-town and rural families had subscriptions to one of the two major urban dailies, the *Regina Leader Post* or its sister publication the *SP*. In fact, this protest made a big splash as it was covered in all the regional papers, including the *Calgary Herald*, the *Prince Albert Daily Herald*, the *Edmonton Journal*, the *Vancouver Sun*, and the *Moose Jaw Times Herald*.[27] Some, like Nordahl, a Princeton University graduate and scholar, who came to Saskatoon in 1969 for a tenure-track appointment at the University of Saskatchewan, were many miles away from family and had job security.[28] Others, like Hellquist and Garman, had been out to their families for years. At least one protestor, Doug Wilson, quickly informed his family about his participation in this gay rights protest before the newspaper arrived at his family's farm. Wilson recalled that this protest marked his entry into formal gay and lesbian politics and that the news ricocheted around Meadow Lake, Saskatchewan.

In the end, the *Saskatoon Star Phoenix* was a conservative, pro-business paper, keen to boost the city's fortunes. It was not inclined to question the status quo politically, and so it was cautious about creating a controversy during a provincial election campaign. Gay and lesbian protesters were not treated with the same level of deference. The paper knew that photos and a story about a gay protest in Saskatoon would sell papers. And the goal of the protestors was media coverage and the opportunity to highlight discriminatory treatment. When it served the *SP* (financially), they were prepared to publish a photograph of gay activists that sold newspapers or, conversely, classified advertisements advertising a gay and lesbian organization. Contextually, the *SP* actually published quite a bit of gay and lesbian material. These articles, painstakingly cut and archived by Neil Richards, are now part of a massive Saskatchewan Archives Board collection. They illustrate that the *Star Phoenix* printed thousands of materials about lesbian, gay, and queer people from 1970 to 2000. Yet the "majority of the clippings do not deal with local stories but were picked up by Saskatchewan editors from wire services – i.e. international and national stories, entertainment reviews and personal advice columns."[29] Such material was usually filler in the inner pages of the paper, but it provided an important context for the material about Saskatoon gays and lesbians and provides a sense of the paper's editorial policies. Given the frequency of these wire service articles, they must have attracted readers and sold copy.

From Zodiac to Gay Community Centre of Saskatoon

Much attention is paid in histories of sexualities to terms and taxonomies – what people call themselves and why – because terminology is an important facet of changing views about same-sex practice. It also denotes a change in concepts of identity formation. While same-sex sexual activity has existed for a long time, what these acts are called and how individuals themselves understand this sexual activity has changed dramatically. Very briefly, throughout the twentieth century, the shift from terms such as homosexuality to "gay" – one imposed by medical experts, the other chosen by gay people themselves – recognized a shift from pathology to self-identification and pride. Such changes in terminology mark important political developments, and historians of sexuality utilize these shifts as watershed moments in queer history. Organizational names trod a similar path. In the 1950s and 1960s in the United States, queer organizations tended to chose organizational names that only insiders understood. This was a logical practice in a time of tremendous oppression. When Canadian gay organizations began, in Vancouver in the mid-1960s, they tended to follow that pattern. In the 1970s, post-Stonewall, and in the era of gay liberationist politics with slogans such as "gay is good" and "out and proud," organizational names were explicitly identifiable as gay. This was a political decision to be public and to demand to have spaces and organizations for gay and lesbian people.

The situation in the prairies was a bit different, as their first organizations in all cities were not explicitly gay, even though they were formed in the 1970s. There were many debates about names of queer organizations – from members, government regulators, and participants. Each city was unique in their history of chartering gay and lesbian spaces, but none of the five prairie social clubs initially chose names that were explicitly identifiable as gay or lesbian. Although it is important to note that while the official names might have obscured the group's purpose, in Saskatoon the original ad placed by Gens Hellquist and Dan Nalbach did ask for those interested in forming a "gay group" to contact their post office box address. Then they pragmatically chose a campy, insider name so as to allow those who were less confident or open about their sexuality to participate. In our interview, Neil Richards recalled that in Saskatoon the Gay Centre came first and elsewhere in the prairies the social clubs came first, which in his analysis, meant that activists were controlled by the clubs.[30] In 1975, Saskatoon reached an important milestone when it became the first of the cities to abandon their original coy name, the Zodiac Friendship Society, for a readily identifiable name: the Gay Community Centre of Saskatoon. Peter Millard, president of GCCS President, explains the rationale:

> We are now the GCCS. This change of name, which has been approved by the Registrar of Societies in Regina is symbolic of our progress towards a goal ... to provide a fully supportive environment for gay people, in which we can discuss matters of mutual interest with each other, get help with problems, try to enlighten the community about the nature of gayness and to press for political and social change ... We have managed to avoid the divisions between the social clubs and activists that trouble other centres, and both Edmonton and Winnipeg have begun to take notice.[31]

While members applauded this new name, it is important to point out that in labelling themselves the *gay* community centre, it also marked the organization (intentionally or not) as male focused and less inclusive. Had they chosen the term Gay and Lesbian Community Centre, which would have formally recognized the lesbian community activists and members, an important nod would have been made to equity.

Doug Wilson's Case

In 1975, Saskatoon and the U of S campus received national attention when graduate student Doug Wilson's experiences in the College of Education become headline news.[32] Wilson was born and raised on a farm in Meadow Lake, Saskatchewan, about 250 kilometres northwest of Saskatoon. After high school he attended the University of Saskatchewan in the early 1970s, successfully completing his Bachelor of Arts and Bachelor of Education and, after teaching for two years, returned to campus for a master's degree.[33] In the fall of 1975, Wilson and a group of students placed an advertisement in the University of Saskatchewan newspaper *The Sheaf*: "Anyone interested in participating in a campus gay organization. Contact Doug Wilson, Box 203, College of Education."[34] Again, a modest advertisement sparked the crisis – demonstrating the ways that "publicizing" gay organizations (and the implications of those actions: greater openness, political demands, and the end of furtiveness) – upset norms of prairie society, and in this case, the U of S campus. Furore ensued, because Wilson had misjudged a number of factors. First, he dared to be both publicly gay and to link a gay organization with the College of Education. Asked to explain himself to the dean of Education, and subsequently the university president, Wilson was given the option to quietly resign from the College. This "old-school" approach was evidently one that university administrators thought was fair and they expected Wilson to gratefully accept their offer. Here he made a second, calculated decision that broke with past practice: he declined and went public with his situation.[35]

Photogenic, with long blond hair and blue eyes, charismatic, and determined, Wilson made a compelling spokesperson for gays and lesbians, vividly demonstrating the discrimination they could face if they were "out" about their orientation. A group of straight and gay colleagues, activists, and campus staff (including Wilson's office mate Skip Kutz, as well as Pat Atkinson, Gens Hellquist, Peter Millard, Neil Richards, and many others) created the Committee to Defend Doug Wilson. This organization was modelled on the Committee to Defend John Damien, a group created in Toronto earlier that year to support Damien's wrongful dismissal case. This is further proof of how connected Saskatoon activists were to gay activism elsewhere. The Wilson committee kept the focus on Wilson's excellent academic record, his skills as a teacher and supervisor of student teachers, and the discrimination that seemed out of step with the times. They also, as my narrator

7.4 Doug Wilson. Image courtesy of *The Sheaf* vol 66, no. 23, (3 October 1975).

Neil Richards recalled humorously, encouraged Wilson to do media while they plotted strategy.[36] Given Wilson's eloquence and charm, he excelled at media interviews, and he gave a series of important national CBC radio interviews with luminaries including with journalist Barbara Frum, as well as *Maclean's* magazine, and *The Body Politic*. He was also interviewed favourably by regional television and press, including all Saskatoon television stations, CBC Saskatoon, commercial and campus radio stations, the *Star Phoenix*, and *The Sheaf*. In interviews, Wilson stressed his desire to live "honestly" and "openly."

Campus was galvanized by this debate, and it politicized many "liberal-minded" people to the challenges gay and lesbians faced on campus and in the community. It also marked a sea change in mentalities, from the "old school" ways of privacy to the new reality that gay people did not want backroom justice; instead, they wanted equality and transparency. In 1993, on his retirement from the U of S, the University of Saskatchewan Faculty Association newsletter, *The Vox*, interviewed Peter Millard about his years on campus, his perspectives on faculty unions, collective bargaining, and his observations about how campus life had changed during his career. One issue Millard highlighted was gay activism. Millard noted "we've made a vast amount of progress" since his arrival when "homosexuality wasn't mentioned." For example, he recalled: "In the English department ... years ago somebody went to the Head and said somebody was a homosexual, and that person simply 'resigned,' and the department head considered himself a very civil person for having allowed the man to go off and do the 'right thing.' It was a subject that wasn't brought out into the open, which is a filthy state of affairs."[37]

Then the Wilson situation hit campus, and Millard recalled his contributions with pride. He characterized the case as one that moved the whole campus from an era of darkness, privacy, and special back-room dealings, to a more transparent, even equitable one where such actions could no longer be condoned. Millard remembered that people simply "did not want to know about it [homosexuality]." And that went for the liberal-minded as well as the conservative parts of campus. "People, even liberal people, would come and say: 'Why are you bringing this out in the open? I'm tolerant. If somebody's causing problems well I can have a cup of coffee and explain things to this person.'" Millard's line, his vintage liberationist political stance, was that such tolerance was no longer enough: "We said 'Thank you very much, those days are over. It's my battle and I'm going to fight it, and what's more, I don't trust you to do it over a cup of coffee."[38]

Beside this sea change in values and openness, there would eventually be a human rights lawsuit filed, claiming gender discrimination, which the university's lawyers successfully fought (arguing that Wilson was not discriminated against because he was a man but because he was gay – an area not covered in human rights legislation). Wilson's teaching career was effectively over. He rightly assessed that no school boards in Saskatchewan would hire an openly gay teacher, however well qualified and talented. But, more significantly, the public attention of his case did have some very positive outcomes. First, it provided Saskatchewan residents with concrete evidence that gay and lesbians were provincial residents and not just residents of distant places with explicitly gay communities. Second, learning about Wilson's situation graphically illustrated the experiences lesbians and gays could face in the school system, higher education, and in the workforce. Those with conservative religious views tended to believe Wilson precipitated his own fall. Others who were more amenable to learning about difference, and for whom Wilson's articulate, wholesome Saskatchewan story resonated, tended to see his treatment as unjust. In this way, while the battle might have been lost (the human rights case against the university), a major moral victory had been achieved. And, later, various collective agreements on campus – and in the province – moved to include anti-discrimination statements for homosexuals; therefore, belatedly, subsequent graduate students, staff, and faculty would not face the same fate. In March 1995, the University of Saskatchewan Gay and Lesbian Students created the Doug Wilson Award to recognized LGBTTQ leadership on campus. Peter Millard was the first recipient of this award.[39]

Saskatoon Gay Community Centre in Action, 1975–1977

In February 1977, *The Body Politic* applauded the energy and accomplishments of the fifth anniversary of the Saskatoon Gay Community Centre, which was "one of the biggest in the country."[40] The centre had moved to larger accommodations at 310 20th St to handle its buoyant mix of programs and events. In the laudatory article, Tom Warner wrote that Saskatoon "is no longer the bastion of heterosexuality it once was – where being openly gay often meant moving to a larger city. Not so long ago a gay man or woman could spend years looking for a gay community only to discover a lifestyle revolving around the park, public washrooms, a couple of 'mixed' bars and a few indescribably tacky parties."[41] Warner offered short profiles of key women and men, an assessment of their accomplishments and key issues, and quotes from community leaders. In the end, Warner concluded that it is "people that make it work," a point that has much historical and contemporary currency in the prairies. Warner recognized this fifth anniversary as an important milestone for the organization but also for gay activism in Canada: "The success of this small band of gay activists in this prairie city has shown that gay liberation is not just a phenomenon seen in large urban centres. But most important, the people at SGCC have shown that with a little bit of effort, you *can* build something out of nothing" (italics in original).[42] Reports in 1976 indicated that in the first five years of the centre's existence, the number of people who used services (including attending dances) had grown from a handful of individuals to nearly a thousand people per year.[43] Later that same year, Saskatoon hosted the National Gay Conference from 29 June–3 July 1977. This was the fifth conference for Canadian gay and lesbian activists, and a mark of distinction for Saskatoon's community organizers that they were able to host such a successful meeting for the country's activists (see below).

During the years when Doug Wilson was president, his annual report indicates that there were tensions in the community over relations with the police. As well, they were struggling to keep their full-time staff person (director Gens Hellquist). Organizationally, they had become "paralyzed by personality conflicts" and divergent views about the Centre's mandate(s).[44] Tom Warner provided some invaluable information when he shared that there was a growing political gap between those who believed in a more militant form of political work and those who felt that political issues needed to be balanced with continuing to provide the social experiences and services necessary to the larger majority of the city's queer residents. The vast majority of whom would never become liberationist activists. Carefully framing his comments to make clear to acknowledge that he had not lived in Saskatoon during this era, he had merely visited and kept up with local friends, Warner said: "I think he [Wilson] was one of the polarizers … he was not an outsider but he was well connected with activists in other places and on the left, the NDP … and I have a feeling that he and a host of other people tried a little too hard to bring what they genuinely believe was a more progressive and militant politics into an environment in which it wasn't going to work. I don't think you could take the tactics that they would use in downtown Toronto or Vancouver and apply them to Saskatoon."[45] Others have commented on the ways that Wilson was profeminist, and, as the challenges with the National Coalition and the larger numbers of women involved in Saskatchewan Gay Coalition would indicate, this too was a possible cause for the tensions. In my Saskatoon interviews, I asked everyone about Wilson and received (as expected) a variety of opinions. Most said he was charismatic, Neil Richards recalled that he was "bright and warm" and that he had "a talent for friendship" but could also be "very determined."[46] Val Scrivener, who volunteered at the Gay Community Centre "a couple of times a week," found it a beehive of activity and, given that it was a small core of volunteers, she found it a bit like a family. She recalled that either "Doug Wilson or Gens Hellquist would be there ... they were very political and they were always getting some letters prepared or getting some demonstration organized and you just went up there and whatever had to be done was done."[47] Originally from the United Kingdom, Scrivener had come out as a lesbian in Australia, and then followed a girlfriend to Saskatoon. She remembered that Hellquist and Wilson "didn't get along very well," which she attributed to their different politics, but for her Wilson's positive energy and his friendship was key: "I think what made me love Doug [Wilson] so much was just his total acceptance of himself and he made you feel that way too. I was proud to be gay with Doug."[48] Scrivener was also involved in Metamorphosis organizing, and her then partner was a vice president of the Gay Community Centre for a year, so she had a very good opportunity to comment on the day-to-day interactions.

Divisions over feminism, political goals, and approaches were not uncommon within liberationist politics in Canada or elsewhere. As I argue throughout this volume, prairie activists were well aware of the political events, organizations, and strategies elsewhere. Wilson, and a couple of the female activists later involved with Saskatchewan Gay Coalition, including Kay Bierweiler, had spent considerable time in San Francisco. Tom Warner, Neil Richards, and other Saskatchewan interviewees cited outsider strategies for some of the differing perspectives held by Wilson and Hellquist. It was also personal, as Hellquist himself acknowledged. Warner's book *Never Going Back* covers these debates across the country, but in our interview he was able to elaborate on the local, Saskatoon situation.[49] He had strong praise for Hellquist's ability to know what political strategies would work best in Saskatoon: "I think that Gens and other people in the community also would have said you can't overlook the social side. You still need your phone line and your counselling and your dances and that sort of thing. You need the political, and Gens has always been a political activist who has always been visible. But he is always at the same time saying people have to live in the city, they have to be able to come out, they have to have a space, and make contact, so you need phone lines, and dances and that sort of thing."[50] These debates were also the product of volunteer activist organizations, as too much work, too few people, and the requisite burnout that ensues created many organizational ebbs and flows throughout time. Prairie organizations were similar to those elsewhere in experiencing such growing pains, and they frequently had to contend with the migration of activists to larger centres, notably Toronto. Those major issues, combined with more minor but perhaps more controversial personality rifts between members of the community, were also grist for the mill. Those challenges aside, the centre still had momentum and was trying to realize some of their long-held goals. They were participants in the "largest gay rights demonstration" in the prairies, held outside the Saskatchewan legislature in Regina in March 1977, where a coalition of groups organized by the Saskatchewan Association of Human Rights protested the provincial government's intransigence.[51]

National versus Regional Activism: National Gay Coalition, Saskatoon 1977, and the Aftermath

Saskatoon hosted the National Gay Rights Coalition conference from 29 June–3 July 1977. The conference theme "Towards a Gay Community" summarized the belief in the power of grass-roots community involvement, an expansion beyond the select group of activists (particularly those from central Canada) who felt that they spoke for the diverse collection of lesbians and gay men in Canada. Over the course of five days there were conference presentations, coffee houses, socials, dances, a march, and workshops on lesbian and gay politics. A coalition of Saskatoon groups organized this event, including the Saskatoon Women's Liberation group, which sent a lesbian caucus to the conference. Many political issues were addressed, including ongoing support for John Damien, support for lesbian mothers dealing with custody issues, issues of lesbian autonomy (which resulted in a statement recognizing that parity between lesbian and gay male activists would be an operating principle of NGRC going forward), and general support for human rights protections. While the outcome appeared positive, the plenary sessions were characterized as "raucous and bitter" debates about issues of lesbian participation within the movement, particularly issues of parity, and tensions around regional and "national" views on lesbian and gay politics.[52] Nominally successful, the concluding march managed to salvage the desire for unity and for foregrounding lesbian's experiences. The image chosen for this conference – the patchwork quilt of prairie farms – is distinctive for a gay liberationist conference (see figure 7.1, page 301). The image is a very familiar one in the west, but, in using this rural image, the conference organizers purposefully strove to accentuate their difference from larger, queer organizations with their resoundingly urban focus. This, and the Saskatchewan Gay Coalition emblem, two same-sex farmers with a field of wheat behind them, offers an image that is both regional and divergent from other images used by gay liberationists in Canada and elsewhere. Years before academics would begin to argue against the overwhelming bias towards "metronormativity" in the queer urban histories, these Saskatchewan activists were critiquing the movement for its failure to include rural queers and rural perspectives.

In the synopsis provided in Saskatoon Women's Liberation newsletter, author Pat M. wrote: "the spiritual high of the conference was the gay rights march through the streets of Saskatoon on July 1, which ironically also happened to be Canada Day. A contingent of about 80 lesbians led the total parade of 300 gays and supporters, as we chanted our demands."[53] The route for the march, for which the GCCS had a parade permit issued by the City of Saskatoon police, took them through the core of the city's downtown. Marchers assembled at the foot of 20th St, near the Kiwanis Memorial Park, and walked west along 20th until they reached 2nd Ave, the city's main downtown street, they then turned and walked towards 23rd St where the parade ended at Saskatoon City Hall.[54] Her numbers were slightly higher than those provided in *The Body Politic*, which claimed 75 lesbians and 250 delegates in total who attended the conference. Michael Lynch, an activist and academic from Toronto, lauded the organizing committee's hard work and praised the local organizers Neil Richards and Roger Carriere (Regina).[55] The heady feelings created by the Canada Day march and the reactions of straight people to gays dancing alongside them were fond memories of many of my narrators, including Neil Richards. This moment, reported in the queer and straight presses, all highlighted the joy to be found in this intersection of gay pride, holiday festivities, and a receptive if perhaps stunned city: "By the end of the afternoon, gays were dancing makeshift polkas in the streets as well, to the bemusement of the Saskatoon onlookers who had gathered for the Liberal Party's Canada Day celebrations."[56] Bill Fields, from *After Stonewall*, also depicted that golden moment as a highlight: "We danced in the sunshine, free and naturally to a Canada Day Band. Hets [sic] stood back and watched while men danced with men, women danced with women … we moved our bodies to music on roped off streets while signs proclaimed, 'Canada, I want to hold your hand.'"[57] But it was not all fun in the sun. In retrospective interviews decades later, academic and activist Gary Kinsman indicated that "the most significant developments in cross-country organizing occurred at the Saskatoon conference in 1977, where there

7.5 National March, Fifth National Gay Conference, Saskatoon,
29 June–3 July 1977. Image courtesy of Charles Dobie.

were a series of workshops on organizing in unions and other topics, and a group of lesbian feminists managed to pass a motion entitling lesbians to 50% control of voting decisions."[58] Followed, in his estimation, by the "most devastating conference" in Halifax.[59]

A year later, in Halifax, those resolutions were reversed and the prairie regional reps who strongly supported lesbian parity were outmanoeuvred, resulting in a walk out of the conference and a split in Saskatoon over how further to respond to these actions. Weisa Kolansinka, a Saskatoon lesbian feminist and participant in the conference wrote, "many prairie gay and lesbian delegates came away from the conference saddened, frustrated and angry."[60] The Prairie Gay Conference held in Saskatoon in May 1978, with sixty delegates in attendance, by contrast had set the stage for these challenges. In Saskatoon, delegates had overwhelmingly voted for lesbians to have parity with gay male activists in decision-making. They had also overwhelmingly supported reorganizing the national coalition to make it more responsive and reflective of regional groups. Saskatoon had been a driving force for those changes, with the city's representatives highlighting that the "Gay Community Centre of Saskatoon and the Saskatchewan Gay Coalition operate and function on the principle of lesbian parity – and both have been successful in building a sense of community and solidarity amongst the women and men."[61] Representatives in Halifax wanted none of this. Kolansinka characterized the opposition as "eastern chauvinism" by "the male-dominated central Canadian organization" that made it clear that the lesbians welcome to participate were those who "buy the conservative, bureaucratic, civil rights package, and not lesbians who want to talk about lesbian needs, concerns and ideas." In her opinion, the direction taken by the newly renamed Canadian Lesbian and Gay Rights Coalition (CLGRC) showed a lack of interest in the realities facing lesbians, rural queers, and youth. Those activists who supported this perspective, including Doug Wilson, SGC, *After Stonewall*, and others, walked out of the plenary sessions in Halifax. In a letter to *The Body Politic*, Doug Wilson wrote, "from our perspective here in Saskatoon, we have a very clear understanding of the nature of CLGRC: the point is we find the nature of CLGRC (narrowly civil libertarian, Central Canadian dominated, and lacking any real commitment to lesbian and women) to be unacceptable."[62] When they returned to Saskatoon, they debated the outcome in the GCCS and, in the end, a majority opted to formally cut ties with CLGRC. As sections below will indicate, these decisions, while democratically achieved, were challenged locally. It would become a point of bitter contention that this decision was made on behalf of the entire GCCS – which had long-standing ties with central Canadian organizations and activists.

Saskatchewan Gay Coalition

In December 1977, while working at the Saskatoon Gay Community Centre, a desire to create a provincial voice for gay activism led Wilson, Kay Bierweiler, Wiesia Kolansinka, Susan Langer, Terry Nelson, and Marg Taylor into discussions with gays and lesbians in Regina.[63] The individuals represented a range of groups, including: the Gay Community Centre of Saskatoon, the Regina Gay Community Centre, the Gay Academic Union at the U of S, and the Lesbian

Caucus of the Saskatoon Women's Liberation group.[64] This meeting led to the formation of the Saskatchewan Gay Coalition (SGC).[65] A critical part of the mandate of the SGC was to foster and encourage other gay groups throughout the province, including Regina, where they felt activism needed support. Apropos of the debate with the national organization, SGC was a feminist organization, determined to give women an equal share in decision-making and was supportive of feminist concerns. SGC initiated outreach with rural gays and lesbians through a volunteer-produced monthly newsletter initially called *Gay Saskatchewan* and later renamed *Grassroots: The Voice of Gay Saskatchewan*.

While Wilson's work with the Gay Community Centre was important, his unique attempts at grass-roots organizing throughout the province permit observations about some of the differences in the prairie gay experience. The concept of a provincial coalition was not original to the Gay Community Centre of Saskatoon since coalitions already existed in three other provinces: Manitoba, Ontario, and Quebec. But the SGC was an important organization for the large numbers of Saskatchewan residents living in rural areas and small towns. In their statement of purpose, the SGC vowed "as lesbians and gay men we believe that we must work for liberation as a means for change in our own lives and in the communities in which we find ourselves. We choose to do this collectively, as a coalition, for we know that no single gay community can achieve liberation in isolation while others remain oppressed."[66] In 1977, members of the centre, along with activists from Regina, participated in a demonstration outside the legislature to lobby for human rights protection for homosexuals.

That "march" was billed as the "largest in the prairies" by organizers. Those who attended it marvelled at the display of strength and of unity, as it attracted "gays from across the prairie provinces." Winnipeg's Dick Smith, a member of *After Stonewall*, wrote an article about his "first" gay march. His trenchant observations capture the mood, but also the characteristic differences that set Saskatchewan apart:

Gays from across the Prairie provinces gathered at the bandstand in the dale. 85 of us in all; a poor representation for Canada's two million gays – but the ranks were swelled by children brought by their lesbian mothers, and a few dogs barking enthusiastically! A colourful friendly crowd all in high spirits gaily greeting friends from Edmonton or Saskatoon ... the

forum for discussion was excellent and thoughtful. We were brought up
to date on developments across Canada; heard that this was the largest
gay march on the prairies; discussed the important issue of lesbian autonomy, mused over how gays could be so respected in one city (notably
Saskatoon) and so disorganized and split in squabbling factions in other
places.[67]

The march was held in Regina for a couple of reasons. First, as the provincial capital, mobilizing in front of the legislature was symbolically
important. It was also a central location that could (and obviously did)
draw activists from Saskatoon, Winnipeg, and Edmonton. Regina's gay
activists were, Smith admitted, "few in number but they have a great
clubhouse. Open fireplace, fine wooden dance floor, comfortable chairs
and a great taste in music."[68]

In addition to organizing provincial moments of activism and the
newsletter, members of Saskatchewan Gay Coalition travelled throughout the province to foster gay support groups in rural areas. All those on
the contact lists for a particular region would receive a mimeographed
note from Wilson, inviting them to a meeting at a discreet location. "I
will be in Yorkton, May 29–30, so I'm taking the opportunity to call
a meeting of Gay Saskatchewan contacts in the area," Wilson wrote.
"The gathering will be at 8pm … at the Corona Hotel. The room is
registered in my name so just phone ahead or ask at the desk … We
hope by bringing people together we can begin to lay the foundation
for some sort of local support system for sisters and brothers in your
area … Only Gay SK contacts in East Central area of the province have
been informed about this meeting so, as much as possible, discretion
is assured."[69] Meetings such as this were held throughout the province
from 1979 through 1982. Though urban areas of the province could offer
residents and visitors gay nightclubs and social events, Wilson's decision to become something of a gay circuit rider, holding meetings in
small-town hotels, was a bold gesture. No word on what hotel regu-
lars thought of the lonely, nervous men who inquired after Doug Wilson's room number, but one can imagine that these meetings did not go
unnoticed. Small-town hotels generally contained the local bar, which
did double duty as informal community centres in the evenings. While
Wilson was comfortably out, most of these men no doubt took calculated risks when they decided to accept Wilson's invitation. Reading
through the correspondence, one observes a very clear pattern emerge
as contacts in each area wrote or phoned Wilson to indicate, belatedly,

that they were unable to attend, but they requested that he send them detailed letters of what transpired and, most important, who attended.

Wilson's published articles about these meetings were inspirational reading, although he acknowledged that attendance was small. For example, in one report of a meeting, Wilson wrote:

> The hotel room in the remote northeastern Saskatchewan town was so tiny that the projector had to be set up and run from the bathroom. There, as part of an outreach programme, members of Saskatchewan's Gay Coalition were showing the film "Word Is Out" to four gay men from the area: two teachers, a reporter and a priest. None of these local people had ever been to a gay meeting. They had never met each other, or any other gay people in the area. Tense and nervous at first, they began by discussing the film, then talked about their own experiences, laughed, visibly relaxed. The process had begun.[70]

Wilson's official reason for the coalition building was based on a genuine concern to help rural gay people access support and social networks, from which, he believed, political action would follow: "Maybe someday they will join us when we rally at the legislature. In the meantime, each individual reality is altered. The building has begun."[71] Unofficially, of course, had it not been for Wilson's decision to return to the university for graduate work, after he completed two years of high school teaching in Makwa, Saskatchewan, a small town in northwestern Saskatchewan, he too might have continued to live an isolated existence as a closeted gay male. Wilson's personal experiences of the reality of small-town life likely made him empathetic to these men's existence.

Few letters exist from people who attended one of Wilson's small-town gay outreach socials, but a letter from a male reporter in "northeastern Saskatchewan" matches the time frame and general description of the event above. In contrast to the inspirational message of *The Body Politic* article, this man's version of events spoke to the more pressing realities of small-town life – fears of exposure and secrecy, as well as the reticence of small-town folks: "Maybe I'm expecting too much but the four people who came (including myself) said little and I opened up a bit but not very much ... I could lose my job if it became known I was gay ... but I'm willing to take chances ... I was rather disappointed and just got further depressed by the whole thing and furthered my resolve to go somewhere else than 'le petite' Tisdale."[72]

In 1979, in a lengthy essay in *After Stonewall*'s first issue published from Saskatoon, Wilson reflected on the outreach program's goals and accomplishments. He noted the widely held liberationist view that "gay people are everywhere," yet "the assumption seems always to have been, that although we are everywhere, that everyone with the where-with-all to do so will leave Sioux Lookout, Moose Jaw and Medicine Hat for the 'bright lights' and 'safety' of a larger place."[73] He spoke of SGC's goals to lessen isolation, to meet gay and lesbian rural and small-town residents on their own terms, and that such initiatives "immeasurably strengthens and heartens those of us who for years have lived in fear and isolation." Beyond attendance and newsletter circulation statistics, SGC was beginning to see some progress. To cite one issue, "gay native people and gay education workers have moved closer to some real organization as part of the grassroots organizing effort."[74] Saskatchewan Gay Coalition was, along with *After Stonewall* and *Voices*, one of the few organizations then working to encourage the formation of queer Indigenous groups. Ultimately, "the long term prospect of gay people living and working positively and openly in Saskatoon and Regina (not to mention Toronto, Montreal and Vancouver) but also in Mortlach, Loon Lake, Swift Current and Langenburg, indeed on the farms and in the small towns of every province is exciting." He acknowledged it would take a long time for that vision to materialize, but the organization was focused on the long term.

SGC also organized the Prairie Gay Conference of May 1978. Held in Saskatoon, this event drew over one hundred registrants from across the region who participated in workshops and discussions about gay activism, regional collaboration, and their relationship to the Canadian Lesbian and Gay Rights Coalition (formerly the National Gay Rights Coalition). Unlike the national conference in 1977, this regional conference illustrated some of the fault lines between regional and "national" gay and lesbian activism. Mirroring contemporary Canadian federal politics, many members of the SGC were suspicious of central Canadian gay activist's goals and tactics as well as resentful of their continuing claims to speak for and represent all Canadian gays and lesbians. Not all members of Saskatoon's gay activist community were in agreement with that decision, and it was one of the major fault lines that developed between the SGC and GCCS. Importantly, some of the original founding members of what would become the GCCS (Hellquist, Garman, and others) were not in agreement with this move because they were well connected with many of the leaders in Toronto (e.g., Tom Warner, who had moved to Toronto and was working with CLGRO), and thus they were less inclined to view "Easterners" critically.[75] Hellquist also had a long history of participating in national activism. In 1997, he reflected on attending his first gay demonstration on Parliament Hill in 1973 when the crowd was merely "a few dozen," but "we were an earnest group intent on changing society to allow us to attain full expression of our humanity."[76] It bears reminding that those activists who "stayed" in the prairie region – Hellquist in Saskatoon, Vogel and North in Winnipeg, Young in Calgary – were active participants in national queer activism via their attendance at these conferences. Hellquist and Richards also noted, in their interviews, their links with gay activists in Toronto. Richards, originally from Peterborough, Ontario, spent time in Toronto annually, and, while there, he volunteered at the Lesbian and Gay Archives, went to Glad Day Books, and became friends with Ken Popert, Ed Jackson, and Gerald Hannon, key members of *The Body Politic* collective.[77] Such mobility, now taken for granted but often overlooked in historicizing the lives of queer activists outside the queer metropoles, was important on a number of fronts, not the least of which was in demonstrating that there were important connections and contributions made by westerners to these national activist groups, and that such messages and political insights were brought home, debated, and discussed in regional centres. Less frequently, but also important, was travel and participation in American queer culture and activism. And finally, as a university town, queer activism in Saskatoon was further stimulated by those newcomers to the city – faculty, students, and staff – who contributed to the energy within the local activist organizations.

The large number of activists within Saskatoon who were newcomers from the United Kingdom, the United States, and other parts of Canada were important, as was the international outlook embraced by their born-in-Saskatchewan peers. For example, David Rimmer regarded Wilson as a "cultural innovator" whose more radical vision was "extremely important" for Saskatoon.[78] In part, this was due to Wilson's American connections – he repeatedly travelled to San Francisco, and lived there for awhile; his lover, writer and performer Peter McGehee, was originally from Arkansas; and among Wilson's coterie of close female friends, both lesbians and straight women, were a number of Americans including Kay Bierweiler, his co-organizer at SGC. Nevertheless, there is no disputing

that Wilson's style was a hybridized one that drew upon Saskatchewan's cooperative ethos but also found inspiration in American
gay cultural developments. Two of the influential *After Stonewall*
members (who also were, for a time, involved in SGC) were Americans (Walter Davis and Bill Fields). I don't mean to suggest a simplistic analysis about American-style gay and lesbian organizing
and its influence on Saskatoon. In those years flights to San Francisco from Saskatoon were affordable and easily accessible. Hence
many Saskatoon gays and lesbians who could afford to travel to
San Francisco and other American cities did. Instead, such evidence
underscores the important fact that the prairie queer communities
may have been geographically isolated from major queer centres,
but they were still connected to American and Canadian activist
developments. Given the evidence of considerable travel, American
periodical subscriptions, American émigrés in local activism, plus
the strong emphasis on shared cultural materials (among Canadian
and American organizations), they were well aware of North American activist currents. By contrast, the larger cities in Canada and in
the United States were often not terribly well versed in the realities
of local organizing, unless it was in the form of sporadic coverage of
regional highlights in the queer press. This one-sided relationship –
where the "regions" avidly follow queer metropolitan trends, report
on them in local, regional queer periodicals but the larger centres are
largely unaware of these prairie activities – has been duplicated in
our queer histories. The result leaves the impression that not much
happened in western Canada, which is inaccurate. People, information, and politics travelled easily up and down, integrating the prairies into a network of queer activism. Community members in some
cities, like Calgary, said such outsider activist strategies would not
work there, but other cities, like Saskatoon and Winnipeg, embraced
some of these tactics and politics. Lynn Hunt has encouraged historians to focus on "networks" as ways to better explain globalization
and global history, an important point for those writing histories of
sexuality as well – queer activists and queer people were/are often
in motion, moving for work, lovers, conferences, activism, and so
forth. And, in these migrations and "networks," important linkages
were made between cities, political organizations, and people.[79] Less
frequently, but in one important departure, the American Christian
right inserted itself directly into the prairies via Anita Bryant's 1978
fundamentalist tour.

Anita Bryant in Moose Jaw

The Saskatchewan leg of Bryant's tour visited the small city of Moose Jaw, located forty-five minutes outside of Regina and approximately two hours southwest of Saskatoon. Bryant's visit was a hundredth birthday present to the city from the Moose Jaw Fellowship for Evangelicalism.[80] Gay and lesbian activists in Saskatoon organized an opposing event, lead by Reverend Colin Clay (a queer ally and University of Saskatchewan Chaplin): "At noon on July 1 several hundred gay men and lesbians, concerned church people, union members and other supporters marched from Moose Jaw's CP Rail Station, up Main Street to Athabasca Street" ultimately ending in the band shell in Crescent Park.[81] According to participants, this event was multi-denominational and featured singing, messages of support from a variety of organizations, and was an alliance of gay and lesbians and their heterosexual supporters. This differentiated it from Winnipeg's protest picket, in place outside the auditorium where Bryant performed, which consisted primarily of gay and lesbian activists.[82] Now we would characterize the Saskatchewan reaction as a gay-straight alliance, and while that terminology was not employed then, it was a strategy that Saskatchewan activists utilized time and again, taking advantage of supportive allies and the province's record of such alliances between labour unions, political parties (particularly the NDP), and activists to achieve societal changes. The busload of Saskatoon protestors, added to the local protestors, marched down Moose Jaw's Main Street chanting, "Women, workers, gays unite – same struggle, same fight. Gay rights now!"[83] Clay's ex-wife, Barb Clay, who also participated in this rally, remembered it as a pivotal personal moment. In our interview, Barb Clay explained, "we took a busload of people down from Saskatoon to have a counter protest and that was an 'aha moment.' That's when I threw my wedding ring over the fence in Moose Jaw. I just took it off!"[84] Then forty-five, Clay told me she had lesbian tendencies from her teenage years; she and her ex-husband discussed how they would go forward. In 1980, on the eve of their twenty-fifth wedding anniversary, they separated for good, and within a few months she met her partner Lynn. This reaction to Bryant's tour is exceptional, but beyond being a good story, it illustrates how such events – a revivalist, anti-queer rally – can and did produce radically divergent results. For every Calgarian who worried that a gay protest march might end in homophobic violence, there were other people who would be liberated. Although few would have such a dramatic reaction as Barb Clay, her recollections remind us of the complexity of people's lives and motivations.

After the rally, the majority of Saskatoon activists returned to the city on their chartered bus. A few gay and lesbian protestors stayed behind to watch the spectacle unfold. Peter Millard was part of that small group of curious observers and he wrote an evocative analysis of how the "good" folks of Saskatchewan could (in the name of religion and with classic Canadian politeness) be encouraged to take part in an explicitly anti-gay and lesbian event. The power of a particular "mean spirited theocracy where values of small business private enterprise were evident"; "women were denied dignity and independence"; and, above all, "where homosexuals receive short shrift."[85] In the final, penultimate moments of the rally, Ken Campbell asked the crowd to stand and recommit themselves to the Christian religious and social values endorsed at the evening's gathering. Peter Millard's description of this "frightening moment" reminds us of the views that openly circulated in the province: "stuck in our seats, a tiny group of gay people and friends, we found ourselves surrounded by 1,000 ordinary, decent Saskatchewan people dedicating themselves to work for a society in which we might as well not exist."[86]

Reaction to this rally came from all corners. The RCMP sent undercover surveillance operators to observe the rally. In heavily redacted documents of the security services D ops marked SECRET, RCMP special operatives described the participating groups in this protest: Saskatoon Human Rights, Regina Gay Community Center, Regina Community Women's Center, Saskatoon Students Union, University of Regina Student's Union, Women's Action Collective on Health, Saskatchewan Gay Coalition, and Saskatoon Women's Liberation.[87] The Mounties were ostensibly there to monitor members of the Revolutionary Workers League who were also in attendance at the rally. Violence was not anticipated, and the RCMP knew that the goal of these protests was media coverage. However, given notification by Moose Jaw's deputy police chief, the RCMP report indicated that they "would have coverage at the rally and this office will likewise be present and a concluding report can be expected."[88]

After Stonewall and *Gay Saskatchewan* both proclaimed the event a success (judged by numbers and coverage), and praised the coalition efforts to bridge provincial and regional activism alongside local activism in Moose Jaw. Truth be told, Anita Bryant's crusade was already running out of steam as she began her Canadian tour. During the Moose Jaw rally, Reverend Ken Campbell had asked the crowd to make donations to Bryant's Christian Liberation Rally, and as part of the pitch mentioned that Bryant's income had declined by $100,000 last year as a result of her "brave stand against homosexuality."[89] A year later, she announced that she was divorcing her husband, resigning from the Anita Bryant ministries, and prepared to "live and let live." She claimed that she wanted to move on from those whose "personal vendettas about gays" had turned her off fundamentalist Christians.[90]

Making sense of the Moose Jaw rally between those who supported Anita Bryant's Christian version of the "right life" and those who were opposed encapsulates the key tensions at the heart of this study. How can we fully understand the various layers of gay and lesbian community, activism, resistance, and accommodation within the prairies? It's complicated, while a glib answer, is actually the most accurate. The Moose Jaw rally has captured the attention of activists, writers, journalists, popular historians, and academics because of the unique setting and confluence of issues: gay activism in an improbable place, the dream showdown between evangelical Christians and their critics (believers and non-believers), and the gender politics of "traditional femininity" versus radicalized "feminists." Much has been read into this rally, or projected onto participants, and much work remains to be done at teasing out the nuances of what actually happened.[91] Joseph Wickenhauser has provided a fascinating comparison of the insider-outsider dynamics of the rally comparing articles in the local newspaper, the *Moose Jaw Times Herald (MJTH)*, against the activist materials published in a variety of queer magazines and newsletters. Articles in the *MJTH* tended to portray those opposed to Bryant's visit as outsiders or gay militants bent on disrupting a Christian service. Yet, not all Moose Javians supported Bryant's visit to the city. It was equally true, though, that those Moose Jaw residents opposed to her visit were also suspicious of the outside activists who descended on their city. Those imported activists, largely from Saskatoon, who presumed to encourage and assist "locals" to protest and be visible were not sympathetic to the issues on the ground in Moose Jaw or the accommodations gay and lesbian people living there took to make their lives possible.[92] It was this issue of "visibility" upon which the gay and lesbian residents of smaller cities often diverged from their big-city peers. What was possible in Saskatoon wasn't possible or even necessarily desirable in Moose Jaw. Wickenhauser's assertion that more conservative strategies befitting smaller centres should not be incorrectly labelled as non-political is apt.

In much the same way that Saskatoon could not be Toronto – with its plethora of activist groups and cultural and commercial spaces – so too Moose Jaw couldn't be Saskatoon.

After Stonewall Politicizing

In fall 1979, *After Stonewall* welcomed readers from their new location in Saskatoon: "We found new homes. We unpacked our suitcases and crates. We had arrived in Saskatoon and a new *After Stonewall* collective was about to be born." Walter and Bill moved from Winnipeg, and Wiesia and Amy came "down the road from Toronto," which meant 50 per cent lesbian control of the journal.[93] Walter and Bill had been attracted to Saskatoon's activism, and with their other Winnipeg cohorts moving to Calgary (for employment), they sought out Saskatoon to set up shop. Doug Wilson and Mark Erickson joined them on the first issue of the journal. Unlike other Saskatoon gay periodicals (in particular *Perceptions* 1985–2014), which had long print runs, *After Stonewall* disbanded in 1980. Their duration in Saskatoon was not a long one, but it merits attention here for a few reasons. First, for choosing to move to the seat of prairie gay activism – Saskatoon – Davis and Fields' decision demonstrates that the city was known for activism, and, in particular, a kind of activism that was politically sophisticated, well entrenched, and strong. Numbers of those attending board meetings for the Saskatoon Gay Community Centre might only number between twenty and thirty people, but the volunteers' energy, determination to be self-supporting, and leadership was well known – whether as a model for Vancouver to follow, or as a beacon for the American expat activists.[94] The December 1979 issue of *After Stonewall* announced that a delegation from Vancouver had visited Saskatoon, and was prepared to follow Saskatoon's lead in establishing a dedicated, self-funded gay centre in their city.[95]

Second, *After Stonewall* published photos, essays, book reviews, and editorials that demonstrated the varieties of queer work underway – cultural, political, social service and counselling, and rural outreach (it included much attention to Saskatchewan Gay Coalition's outreach activities) – and provided a glimpse into the interests of the community and some of its leaders. Visually, none of these early newsletters and small periodicals had much sustained artwork, but they did capture politically evocative moments worthy of note. Cover art images depicted "The Prairies Coming Out Strong" (figure 4.6, page 206) or, later, a photo taken of two gay men embraced in a kiss on the steps of the University of Saskatchewan administration building. The sign they held, "it takes a fairy to make something beautiful," spoke loudly of the politics and possibilities on offer in Saskatoon. It offered profiles about people like Don Jones, the teacher from Smeaton, Saskatchewan, whose lawsuit against the school board for wrongful dismissal was championed by SGC and written about in *After Stonewall*. Jones's victory was regarded as a textbook case for coalition building within the province. There were articles about gay bashing in Winnipeg. There were liberationist articles about women's rights, lesbian autonomy, and gay politics and space. Third, *After Stonewall*'s members, particularly Walter Davis and Wiesia Kolansinka, threw themselves into activism in Saskatoon. *After Stonewall*'s collective impact on Saskatoon's activism is debatable. On one hand, they brought terrific energy and ideas to the city; their liberationist message, feminist engagement, and "no compromise" views encouraged debate about activist goals. On the other hand, their time in Saskatoon coincides with the Gay Community Centre's financial difficulties and personnel challenges. The role that various people in the collective played in the centre's insolvency, the role of the new commercial clubs, and activist burnout can never completely be unpacked from archival documents.

Smeaton, Saskatchewan: An Unlikely Gay Victory

In March 1979, Don Jones, a high school teacher with ten years experience, was pressured to resign from his teaching position in Smeaton (near Nipawin) in north-central Saskatchewan for allegations that he was gay. In May, Jones contacted the Saskatchewan Gay Coalition looking for help because the school board, his principal, and the Saskatchewan Teacher's Federation had all urged him to resign. Jones resisted and on 15 May 1979 he was fired. In his letter of dismissal from the school board, Jones was accused of "immoral behavior," "unprofessional conduct," "neglect of his duties," and was characterized as suffering from "mental instability."[96] Jones denied those charges. During the two days of hearings, in August 1979, Jones admitted that he was gay but denied the "vicious, false innuendo concerning my alleged sexual activity and mental abilities." Jones admitted to having had consensual sex with adult men in the community. In fact, it was the accusations of two local, married men, who claimed that Jones had assaulted them, that launched the complaint. Jones claimed that he had sex with one of the men and kissed the other, and claimed that both of them were willing partners.[97] The appeals board agreed that Jones reputation as an effective educator was not in question but they noted that going forward his "effectiveness as a teacher would be severely limited to the point of possibly causing impairment to his pupils' progress."[98] While Jones did not agree with this assessment, he did resign his position stating the "board members, my principal, and the director of education acted in an entirely unethical and dishonest manner throughout the affair, I just couldn't continue to work with them after the way they'd treated me."[99]

Like the Wilson case years earlier, the issue wasn't about any criminality because Jones also had a clean employment record and was held in high regard by his colleagues, students, and members of the community. It was, quite simply a case of homophobia involving a teacher whose sexual orientation was, critics claimed, sufficient reason to remove him from the classroom. Like Wilson, Jones initially refused to quietly resign. According to a representative from the SGC, he also refused the suggestion of the Saskatchewan Teacher's Federation to move to another division.[100] That the Federation, Jones's union, recommended moving school divisions illustrates the minimal support he received for his case. When the appeals board agreed that he should be reinstated and the dismissal was overturned, true to his word, Jones officially resigned. What to make of this moot victory? In interviews about the case, Doug Wilson pointed to Jones's victory as evidence of changing times in the province, one that he felt spoke to the work of SGC in supporting various small-town, rural and remote gays and lesbians via the SGC outreach programs. Along with moral support, the SGC raised funds to cover his $7,000 in legal costs. In the Spring 1981 issue of *Grassroots*, the Saskatchewan Gay Coalition congratulated Jones who had obtained a new teaching job in central British Columbia. The editors reminded readers that Jones still had large legal bills to pay, and that donations to the organization in his name would help to lessen his burdens.[101]

Lesbian Activism

Between 1970 and 1984, Saskatoon had a succession of lesbian activist groups. Though short-lived, they demonstrate that lesbians in the city were involved in feminist, gay liberation, and lesbian activism throughout this time period, and often women were involved in multiple groups at the same time. In December 1972, an "independent gay women's group" was founded in Saskatoon to provide lesbians with a group focused on their interests.[102] Announced in the *Gemini Club Newsletter*, this group only lasted a few months, the last record of its meetings were in February 1973. That fall, Erin Shoemaker was listed as the organizer for a lesbian feminist group in the city. Shoemaker, like a number of lesbians I interviewed for this project, came out as a lesbian after her marriage ended. Born in Neepawa, Manitoba, in 1943, she married in 1960 at the age of seventeen, had three children, and in 1971 she and her husband divorced. A friend in Saskatoon suggested she move there, and she did, relocating to a communal house within walking distance of campus. She enrolled in university classes and it was in a U of S sociology class she met her first gay male – Bruce Garman – a guest speaker from Saskatoon Gay Action.[103] She invited him to her house for tea, they chatted about the Zodiac Friendship Society and mutual interests, and eventually she recollected he invited her to a attend one of Zodiac's community dances.

Shoemaker's own recollections of this process, and the fluidity of moving from feminism, women's issues, and community involvement to lesbian feminism, provides an interesting observation about the era, and about her life in Saskatoon in the early 1970s:

> When I came out I was in Sociology, I was a feminist and I was politically active and when I came out my friends used to say, you know I just burst out of the closet and the door slammed shut and I didn't realize what I had done. I had left my kids with my ex-husband because I didn't see myself having marketable skills to support them … I regretted that decision since, but that's the decision I made at the time. So they weren't living with me, they were with me for part of that first summer on holiday and then they moved to Finland [with their father] … I expected people to be excited and I think that was one of my big shocks cause when I went back to my feminist group and I said I'm involved with a woman they were shocked and I thought what?! … People had been talking about how they thought this was a good idea [lesbianism], all this academic debate about lesbians but [the reality was] it was threatening.[104]

She and her then partner, Beth Foster, were active in lesbian feminist and gay and lesbian activism in the city. Foster served as the third president, and first lesbian president, of the Gay Community Centre of Saskatoon.[105] Shoemaker remembered that they walked around the U of S campus holding hands and while they got "a few stares, we didn't get a lot of overt harassment."[106] Prior to coming out she was involved in activism around access to abortion, take back the night marches, and the women's centre (Saskatoon), but once she came out, "I got more involved in gay and lesbian stuff ... early marches, demonstrations in the 70s, Metamorphosis was really a highlight." Much of the Metamorphosis organizing was done by lesbians, and as the years went on programming tilted in favour of lesbian attendees.

In the mid-1970s, the *Saskatoon Women's Liberation Newsletter* published a series of articles describing their goals, activities, and varied memberships. They had a lesbian caucus and for many it was clear that just talking about their sexuality and meeting other lesbians was considered key activist work. One member who attended the Montreal lesbian conference in January 1974 wrote "between 150–200 lesbians were present ... One of the most exciting aspects of the conference was meeting women who had never been to a conference of any kind before and who had never talked to other lesbians about being lesbian."[107] That February the Saskatoon Women's Centre had their grand opening, and the newsletter proudly reflected on their struggles to keep a centre afloat: "The Women's Centre is our proudest accomplishment after years of existing in holes-in the wall. We counted our locations since 1969 recently we are now in our sixth!" In their location in the Ross office building they were unable to afford electricity "and had to hold meetings at night by candlelight." This current location, the third on 2nd Avenue, was "the best and most comfortable of all!"[108]

My lesbian narrators were all involved, at one time or another, in gay and lesbian activism and in particular in the GCCS. As indicated previously, a number of them struggled with the term lesbian, preferring gay women, and others wanted to just be ordinary people and resisted labels. However, as the 1970s progressed, it became evident that the absence of formal recognition of lesbians rankled. Whether the battles at the national level, or the policy changes of SGC, or *After Stonewall*, it was increasingly evident that lesbians required formal recognition. In 1981, the newsletter of the GCCS contained a proposal, from Diane, that the name be officially changed to "Gay and Lesbian Community Centre of Saskatoon." She acknowledged that, "Saskatoon has long been known, across Canada, as a city where lesbians and gay men work together and actually like each other. The GCCS has a policy of equal power sharing between lesbians and gay men."[109] So, now, she believed the time had come for a more inclusive name. "As lesbians, we need an identity, we need to be recognized as women, lesbians by the media ... The more the courts hear of us, they will realize that there are women loving women and that they will not get away with taking our children, harassing us and restricting our loving."[110] When the new organization, Gay and Lesbian Health Services, was founded in 1982, lesbian was in the organizational title.

While it is evident that many women worked within co-ed activist groups in Saskatoon, another cultural venture exclusively for lesbians was launched in Regina in the 1982 when a trio of Regina lesbians created *Lesbian Information Note*. A year later it was renamed the *Lesbian Newsletter*. *The Lesbian Newsletter* ran from 1983 to 1985. In 1985, the *Labyrs News*, under the editorial direction of Jean Hillabold, was created. Jan Harvey, one of the creators of the Lesbian Association of Southern Saskatchewan (LASS, started in 1983), remembered that the group's goals were both political and social, but, over time, and with a diverse collection of participants, the group eventually became primarily social in their focus, hosting monthly potluck dinners and occasionally dances.

Not surprisingly, given the range of political ideologies evident within the gay community and among gay male activists, there were also tensions among Saskatoon lesbians about politics. Some easily and readily called themselves feminists. They had been part of feminist organizations, feminist activism, or had taken women's studies or sociology classes where they were introduced to such issues (and many openly declared feminists tended to be university educated). In one interview, Erin Shoemaker most clearly delineated the differences between herself as a "feminist lesbian" versus the "real lesbians":

> Donna* [a pseudonym] was a very outgoing attractive friendly, very butchy kind of woman ... They came over [to the house] and it was kind of like a face off between the feminist lesbians and the real lesbians and I mean I was just an arrogant academic I think at that point. I thought I knew it all, and ... Donna was simply lesbian who had always been a lesbian in the womb I'm sure, even though she has been married and had a couple of kids and I think in truth we were probably threatened by each other, although you'd never know it from Donna cause she was just really in your face kind of person ... we became friends further down the line and have remained friends actually ... I just have a tremendous amount of respect for those lesbians. I know I didn't then.[111]

At the time of this interview Donna and her partner were living in Niagara Falls, Ontario.

I had a similar exchange with Marion Alexander from the opposite perspective, and it provides nuance on this issue of identifying as a "feminist." Alexander said "I am a feminist," but she had challenges with the group she called the "bra burners" – the university feminists she felt were more radical in their lesbian feminism and who, often, did not stay in Saskatoon (perhaps she was thinking of the women involved in SGC who ultimately gravitated to larger centres, including Toronto, after their prairie sojourn). Alexander had not been privileged enough to attend university, and so she had an immersion course in lesbianism and feminism when she entered the Saskatoon community. She recalled, "when I first came out, I'm an ordinary person, if I thought a lady was foxy, I said foxy. I was not saying that woman was an animal. Boy they pounced on me like I was shit you know!? ... I tell you I had a real education after I came out."[112] Asked about these tensions within the lesbian community, she said "it always seemed to work itself out," and Shoemaker's narrative corroborates a similar sentiment. Given the class and educational differences between these women, it isn't surprising that initially it was difficult finding common ground. How it got worked out, for those who stayed in the community, was that in the trenches of volunteering – for Metamorphosis, for GCCS, for AIDs Saskatoon – volunteer organizers and activists worked together, shared stories, and broke down these barriers created by class differences. This was not an easy process and clearly both sides had anxieties about it, but it did help that many organizers recognized the importance of education and discussion; of providing lesbian and gay novels and non-fiction at the centre; of starting discussion groups, rap groups, and consciousness-raising groups as such groups were variously called; and, above all, of providing resources and materials that fostered knowledge of sexual identities, and recognized the knowledge of disparate life experiences and different viewpoints. All prairie activists, in various cities, spoke of the ways that such groups had to be big tents, welcoming people with different backgrounds and politics because of the realities of scale and of the cities. Separationist, hard-line views, which occasionally did occur, challenged the realities of life in these cities where volunteer community builders, leaders, and activists were a small cohort and they had to find ways to work together, or they would surely fail together.

This section on lesbian-focused activism is small because it was primarily the case that Saskatoon lesbians worked with their gay male counterparts in larger, co-ed ventures. They might not have been recognized in the titles of those organizations, but membership lists, directories of board memberships, photographs, and recollections of my narrators indicates that lesbian volunteers, activists, and organizers were essential to these organizations' operations, as Val Scrivener's earlier recollections attest. Barb Clay recalled that 80 per cent of the workers organizing Metamorphosis were women, and that "everybody said good old Saskatoon can pull this off, Calgary can't, Edmonton can't, Winnipeg can't, and there was a real sense of community in Saskatoon."[113] Clay worked with Hellquist and Erin Shoemaker as one of the organizing committees for gay and lesbian support services – she "volunteered and did counselling" – and when it became Gay and Lesbian Health Services she continued her work.[114] In the mid-1980s, when AIDS came to the prairies, it would be teams of lesbians and gay men, particularly in Saskatoon and Regina, who pulled together to lead those volunteer organizations. Clay was training as a social worker and spent time working in San Francisco, and later brought some of her knowledge and training with AIDS patients back to Saskatoon. Lesbian narrators remembered women taking a leadership role as volunteers and less frequently paid employees. Erin Shoemaker was the first executive director of AIDS Saskatoon. Ultimately, Clay observed that this ethos of volunteer support was not just within the lesbian and gay communities, but broadly based within the community: "[G]enerally the prairies are strong in volunteerism….We just all pitch in if you want something done and there aren't many dollars behind it well it gets done by volunteers and that has certainly worked very well for us. Unfortunately it tends to be the same volunteers."[115]

Violence

While Saskatoon had a liberal ethos, and many of my interview participants looked back on the early years of gay community organizing and activism fondly, there were many episodes of violence directed against gay and lesbian club patrons. For example, at Zodiac's first location they faced harassment from local high school students. Asked to elaborate on what that meant, T recalled they threw "beer bottles, causing general disturbance outside the club, hooting and hollering from across the street or in cars. Or harassing people coming out the door at night when the club closed."[116] To avert these challenges, club goers chose to enter or leave in pairs: "we always left with people. Or met somebody at a bar and then went over. The odd time you went to the club solo, you made sure that you were close enough to the door to make a good exit or entrance."[117] The Saskatoon police force was called, on occasion, and according to my narrator, "we brought the police in, but the police at that time were just as bigoted … the police had quite a dim view at the time," and so they were less than helpful to curtailing this activity.[118]

As chapter 4 indicated, numerous times arsonists attempted to set the various gay and lesbian clubs on fire and it was miraculous that no one was injured. Patrons also were vulnerable to muggings as they came and went from the centre. For example, in April 1976, the *SP* reported that members of the Gay Community Centre had appeared in front of city council requesting extra police protection: "In a letter to council, Doug Wilson, the centre director, said several persons leaving the centre March 28 were attacked by a group of youths. The attack left several persons injured and led to hospital treatment for two others."[119] Furthermore, Wilson indicated that lesbian and gay patrons were routinely subject to verbal and physical assaults outside the centre at 310 20th St E. This Riversdale location was the site of much homophobic violence. Currently Riversdale is the new "hip" area of Saskatoon, the site of ongoing gentrification, with many coffee bars, art galleries, and restaurants. Then this core neighbourhood was a largely poor, working-class area of Saskatoon. This violence was unacceptable, perhaps shocking to white, middle-class gay and lesbian club goers, but was regrettably routine for the many Indigenous and Metis residents, along with new Canadians, who lived in Riversdale. Additional tensions arose because the centre was upstairs from the Indian and Metis Friendship Centre (see below), and this fact seems to have lead to episodes of homophobic violence.

In September 1979, arson was suspected in a blaze at the Saskatoon Gay Community Centre that caused $10,000 in damages. According to press reports, the fire was set in the sound booth and destroyed the club's sound system and entire library (which was used as the fuel for the fire). The damage was covered by insurance, but it was volunteer labour and incredibly long hours that got the centre up and running again in two weeks time.[120]

No narrators mentioned being personally targeted by the police, but in March 1980 a *The Body Politic* report indicated that Gens Hellquist had his home raided by the RCMP as part of a porn raid / censorship sweep.[121] The Mounties told Hellquist that his name was on the mailing list of a gay male porn producer in San Francisco. The RCMP seized a small number of films and magazines, material, according to Hellquist, that anyone could order from a mail order distributor, and gave Hellquist a Canada Customs receipt for his seized films. Interestingly, it was Hellquist's impression that the RCMP lost interest in their raid – and in him – when he indicated that his employers' were aware he was gay and there were no possibilities for entrapment or leverage to get him to reveal names and addresses of closeted gay men in the city.[122]

Gay Indigenous Groups and Activities

One of the limitations of the archival holdings, and my oral history sample for Saskatoon and Regina, was that information about gay and lesbian Indigenous people was severely limited. It was a standard interview question to ask about Indigenous women and men's participation, and most of my Saskatchewan interviewees recalled a number of Indigenous men at gay and lesbian dances during the 1970s. One such exchange between my narrator T (b. 1953) and I was fairly commonplace:

> VJK: Any Aboriginal members of the gay and lesbian organization?
>
> T: Oh very much so, very much so.
>
> VJK: Women and men?
>
> T: Women and men, yes. And a lot of very good people, because they themselves [are] considered a minority … and then on top of it having to be gay or lesbian, then to deal with both.
>
> VJK: was a lot
>
> T: was a lot exactly. The prejudices were just astronomical.
>
> VJK: How well were they accepted in the gay and lesbian community?
>
> T: Very well and still are.[123]

Beyond those broad strokes though, my primarily Euro-Canadian informants could not usually recall names of Indigenous acquaintances they socialized with, nor did any report a lover, partner, or friend who was Indigenous. There were clear limits to the inclusiveness of the Saskatoon community and to the likely small cohort of Indigenous women and men who attended queer events.

David Rimmer (b. 1951) was one of the only interviewees to recall any Indigenous men by name and to indicate that this group had been sizable. It was "primarily men if not exclusively … probably eight to ten and they identified as gay."[124] He recalled the most active years for these groups was while the GCCS was above the Indian and Metis Friendship Centre, in this case offering opportunities for the groups to interact. This group put on a "traditional feast for the rest of us one night … it wasn't something that lasted for years … but it left an impression with me. I think it's important because it is Saskatoon." Rimmer believed the Indigenous men were Cree; one of the men was from Duck Lake, another from the Piapot Reserve. Asked what became of this group, Rimmer (who at the time of our interview, lived in Ottawa) wasn't entirely sure. Some, he had heard, had passed away from AIDS. It bears reminding that the prairies were not immune to this scourge, and so interviews with gay men are rife with references to this missing cohort of friends, activists, and lovers. Other archival documents suggest that for some Metis and Indigenous gay men, GCCS's move away from this location provided the opportunity for more groups to organize, as it provided them with a bit more distance and anonymity to attend Indigenous discussion and social groups. Starting in the December 1978 issue of *Gay Saskatchewan*, brief announcements calling for the creation of a "Native Gay Group" were published. "The Coalition has been approached by Native people regarding problems encountered by Native gays and we will give every assistance possible" to organization of such a group.[125] The following year it was described as a "priority" for the organization. In November 1979, a small group of "Native" lesbians and gay men met at the Gay Community Centre, and their main concern was to get the word out to other Indigenous gays of their existence. The last mention of them in the Saskatchewan Gay Coalition newsletter came in March 1980, with this report of an "authentic Native dinner" held on 26 January. It is little wonder David Rimmer recalled it so many years later, as the newsletter's editor described the event in detail: "We had food like moose, duck soup, fish, corn, bannock and blueberries. The turnout for the dinner was great with friends from Prince Albert, Regina and Fort Qu'Appelle. The guests expressed their thanks and praised the food very much. After the dinner, the audience was given a demonstration and a history of traditional Indian dancing and music and then were asked to participate in some of the dances. A good time was had by all. The proceeds of the dinner will go to future events of the Native Gay Group.[126] The level of detail provided speaks to the novelty of this event, but then information about this group ceases to be published. Other groups would emerge in the mid-1980s, but with little archival trail to follow other than these glimpses in the newsletter, finding more information proved impossible.[127]

Of all the fragments of histories woven together in this book, the absence of Indigenous gays and lesbians haunts me most. I know they were there, interviewees remembered men and less frequently women, but for a host of reasons, with the passage of time, these names and faces were forgotten. This is an avenue for much further historical investigation, and I hope queer researchers or allies from within Indigenous and Metis communities will restore these two-spirited histories to the history of queer people on the prairies. Or, potentially, for other Indigenous elders to come forward, as Ma-Nee Chacaby has recently done in her moving book *A Two-Spirit Journey: The Autobiography of a Lesbian Ojibwa Cree Elder*.[128]

Homophobia / The Costs of "Discretion"

Homophobic violence was rarely reported in Saskatchewan, largely because those who suffered were not certain their claims or experiences could be remedied by reporting them. The few cases here are, as in the other chapters, suggestive of what could occur in the prairies, not an exhaustive enumeration of what did. However, "homophobia" is broader than physical violence, and here, in the experiences related by one of my gay male narrators from Regina, was another perspective on the costs of living a queer life in Saskatchewan.

After a decade working for one of Canada's major banks, Leonard Lawrence quit and took employment with SaskTel in Regina, where he moved in the early 1970s.[129] Shortly thereafter his father died, and since he was the only unmarried son he moved his widowed mother to his home – an arrangement that lasted for over twenty-five years. He recalled that this suited him because she was independent and "bought the groceries and paid the utilities," so he was free to do what he wanted. However, at various junctures in the interview Lawrence indicated how constant vigilance "compartmentalizing" his life had been draining. Other than a close gay friend from his banking days, who also lived with his widowed mother, he never had gay male friends to his home, never officially disclosed his sexuality to his family operating on the "don't ask, don't tell" ethos, never gave out his home telephone number, nor, finally, did he ever divulge his real name to gay men he met. He had, he noted, "spent a fortune on hotels," and with his friend Joe (a pseudonym) had travelled the world, to Europe, Thailand, and Mexico, where they had toured historic and cultural sites by day and explored gay nightclubs in the evenings. For all this covertness, it is important to indicate that he had been one of the founding members of Happenings Social Club in Winnipeg, supported drag activities in Winnipeg and Regina, and was a key player in Regina's gay- and lesbian-owned club. Lawrence's interview was fascinating for a variety of reasons, not the least of which was his long, institutional memory of the clubs in Winnipeg and Regina, and the difference between the bigger, more cosmopolitan Winnipeg scene where doctors, drug salesmen, and "businessmen" might mingle at pretheatre drinks, take in a theatrical performance as a group, and then head off for dinner and a night of dancing. Regina's world was far less expansive, a factor both of less cultural and social opportunities, but also its size, demographic factors, and the paranoia that characterized individuals like Lawrence himself. Lawrence firmly believed that the risk of public display, or even all-male socializing, let alone explicit gay identification, would jeopardize his employment and social standing. Some readers will attribute this to age or "generational" differences, but that isn't sufficient explanation. Lawrence knew some of the activists from Saskatoon, – some were older (such as Dorothy), others slightly younger (Hellquist) – and while he admired their ideas he felt that they "didn't care" about employment or personal risks. Similar to Selena, this middle-class, privately gay male felt that his hold on middle-class respectability – employment, home ownership, standing within his large, extended family – was too tenuous to risk by being open about his sexual orientation. Or, in his case, to drop his strategy of a double, compartmentalized life. Asked to assess how important his sexuality was to his identity, he replied, "a lot of my life is structured around that, and keeping a secret."

Homophobia in Saskatchewan was very real. In 1975 Neil Richards, on behalf of the Gay Community Centre of Saskatoon, wrote to Huntley Schaller, director of the Saskatchewan Association of Human Rights, describing the various impacts that accrued to those who were openly gay or lesbian:

> the homosexual resident of Saskatchewan, male or female, who chooses to live with a degree of honesty and integrity can expect to encounter a great deal of overt and pervasive discrimination. We know of many individuals who have been refused employment, accommodation, commercial services and educational opportunities on the grounds of their sexual orientation ... fear of discrimination by employers, landlords and teachers is one of the main reasons why the great majority of homosexual men and women seek to hide their sexual identity.[130]

Furthermore, he added, such discretionary tactics were not without their own, albeit different, toll, "It is the belief of this organization – supported by psychiatric research – that secrecy of this type is fundamentally unhealthy and can contribute in some individuals to serious emotional problems."[131]

In a number of interviews with narrators, women and men, the matter of counselling, mental health issues, and, in a smaller number of interviews, institutionalization arose. While we know that mental health issues are prevalent, if often unacknowledged, within Canadian society, there is a long history of pathologization of queer people by the medical profession. From early twentieth-century sexologists through to contemporary psychiatrists, lesbians and gays have been subjected to pathologization. They have also been the recipients of a range of treatments, including shock treatments, surgery, pharmaceuticals, and talk therapy all intended to "cure" them. In extreme cases, lesbians and gays were institutionalized for their sexual activities, choices, and, later, identities. A cohort of lesbian narrators in the interviews for this project, both my own and those collected in Winnipeg, spoke directly about experiences in the psychiatric ward, a fate that (if the interviews are anything to go by) tended to affect working-class, high school educated and/or Indigenous women in larger numbers than their middle-class, university-educated, Euro-Canadian sisters.

One of my best interviews was with Marion Alexander, a woman who many in Saskatoon's community considered a beloved lesbian "grandmother," friend, volunteer, and activist.[132] Alexander was a community stalwart and it isn't going too far to say that in many senses she was adored for her energy, her work, and her sheer determination to make a difference. But her road to beloved lesbian elder had been a challenging one. Born in 1934, she grew up in a "lower class" family of seven kids in Swift Current, Saskatchewan. Alexander had been labelled the "bad girl" (her words) and she spent a year and a half in a home for "wayward girls" in Regina. When she emerged from that institutional experience (aged fifteen approximately), she lived briefly with a foster family before rejoining her biological family in a small town near Prince Albert. There, as a teenager, she met her future husband, who worked for the grain elevator company, and got married at age seventeen. They had seven kids together, and she worked part-time at the regional hospital in Prince Albert. Asked to describe how she came to identify as a lesbian, she indicated, "I was different right from the beginning," but, because she had found no books or resources to help her, even with crushes on women as a teenager, she proceeded with a conventional life, getting married and having children. She came out in 1979 into the Prince Albert community before moving to Saskatoon in the 1980s. Initially, in the interview, she glossed over this, and indeed the whole experience in Regina as a teenage girl, but when it became clear that there was a real gap in her story between marriage, kids, and coming out in 1979, she circled back and shared this narrative:

> Maybe I should go back a bit here, I had a nervous breakdown in 1974 and I was sick for the next five years in and out of the psych centre. It was just too much for me, I had too much to handle and that was my way out. Some people go to alcohol, some go to drugs and I decided to have a nervous breakdown and then in 1979 our house burned down and I lost my twin grandsons … it was after we built our new place, after the fire, I sat down and started reading the paper [*Prince Albert Herald*] and the personals were there, there was a little ad Support for Gays and Lesbians, call this number in PA …
>
> I thought, what am I sitting here for you know? It was just like a light bulb went on in my head. What am I sitting her for and I got up, this was November, the first part of November, and I said I have to go to the corner for cigarettes so I jumped in the car and drove to the corner and used the pay phone there and phoned and a fellow by the name of Mother, we always called him Mother, answered. He said there were no women there right now but when one came in he'd have her call me. I said careful because I'm on a party line, so I went home and sat with my elbow on the phone and when it rang the first thing Jan said "you called the Gay and Lesbian Community Centre." I said "we're on a party line." Then it just seemed like I was home you know, the weight of the world went off my shoulders.[133]

Despite her anxiety about being on a party line, and the realization that her "secret" was out, it was really instructive that in this memory she also expressed relief and joy at, as she put it, "being home." Very shortly afterwards she moved out, got an apartment in Prince Albert, ironically in the same building where the community centre rented space, and a year later she moved to Saskatoon. Marion's interview was a rich one, and she was proud of her life, kids, grandkids, coming out, role in the community, and the long-term friendships, support, and love she had experienced at the GCCS and its successor organizations in Saskatoon.

Mental health issues / histories were not a focal point of my oral history questions, and when people disclosed them or other health issues (and with older narrators, it was common to hear about health issues), I listened respectfully but did not ask follow-up questions because I was acutely mindful of privacy issues, worried that in the rapport developed in the interviews people might reveal more than they wished to see in print, and mental health wasn't my academic focal point. But, stories of institutionalization, mental health issues, counselling, and therapy emerged repeatedly in many interviews – indicators of the both the system's treatment of lesbians and gays but also clear evidence of the impact of being "different" and in many cases closeted for a portion of their lives. It was also evident that this burden was disproportionately felt by my working-class narrators, or those raised in working-class households. In those families, often with large numbers of kids and fewer resources, the "state" (schools, health care institutions, social workers) was quick to label them – in this case as a "bad girl." And such labelling, or any deviating from the middle-class script, could result in involuntary incarceration, treatment, or apprehension by social services. Later in the interview, in answer to a question about the importance she placed on being a lesbian, Marion told me that it was fundamentally important, otherwise, "I wouldn't be me … I would probably still be that woman that was going in and out of the psych centre." Since coming out, she reported that she had never been hospitalized for mental health issues.[134]

Given the necessity of archival and oral sources from which to write history, it is important to underscore the obvious, that without sources we can only go so far in interpreting silences, omissions, and gaps. Lawrence's and Selena's interviews were important, in the first instance, for their own histories that they shared, but when one realizes that these were two of the silent, more closeted, gay and lesbian people living, working, and loving in Saskatchewan, the importance of their histories were magnified. Alexander's interview provides the counterpoint, the person who leapt out of the closet, societal perceptions be damned, and left behind the revolving door on the mental health care system. The toll exacted by silence, vigilance, self-monitoring, and discretionary behaviour was played out throughout Regina, Saskatoon, and across the region.

As mentioned previously, violence was not unheard of in Saskatoon. Beatings at club closing, arson attacks, and fears of violence in cruising grounds were all registered in the city. Narrators did not dwell on those episodes in their recollections, but they did occur. Both Saskatoon and Winnipeg recorded murders during the time frame of this study that were clearly motivated by homophobia. In August 1985, Marvin Klepsch, a forty-four-year-old Saskatoon child psychologist, was found dead in a "farmer's field north of Sutherland" a suburb of Saskatoon.[135] Members of the queer community were outraged that the RCMP, who were investigating the murder, appeared more interested in interviewing Klepsch's friends and colleagues about his "lifestyle" than in finding the murderer.

While one could cite many instances of homophobia, and a range of criminal, medical, and social experiences to exemplify experiences with homophobia in the prairies, an important one concerns families of origin. Throughout the oral interviews, narrators commented on their degree of openness with their families of origin. Some, like Lawrence, were not open about their sexuality. Others were, and were able to report they had varying levels of acceptance; still others were merely tolerated (or their partners were tolerated) at family functions. Few told of being purposefully excluded from those families, although it was clear that these most personal of memories were emotionally difficult for my narrators, and not an area in which it seemed ethical to push for more details. A few broke down in tears relating their experiences of coming out to parents or siblings, or having breakthroughs in later years as Canadian society became more accepting of queer people, and as laws about human rights, or in fact gay marriage, become more prevalent.

In the July 1994 issue of *Perceptions*, Gens Hellquist wrote an editorial about family homophobia, and since it pertains to one of the early queer community stalwarts, it is worthy of inclusion here. Hellquist wrote:

> It's amazing how so many aspects of life in our homophobic society work at making our lives invisible. A couple of weeks ago I attended the funeral of someone I've known for over 25 years. This individual had been part of Saskatoon's gay and lesbian community for all those years. He had been involved in numerous lesbian and gay organizations and during the last decade was one of the key people in the fight for human rights protection. You would never know that if you attended his funeral … No mention was made of his life after the time he finished his school. The funeral was for someone who was not known to me or anyone else at the funeral. The funeral was arranged by his mother who apparently never did accept the reality that her son was gay … The part of his life between university graduation and death was obliterated. His life and work were

made invisible in an attempt to deny who he was. I find it rather sad and ironic that after 25 years of struggling for liberation our lives can so easily be erased and attempts made to eradicate who we are. While we made enormous gains in 25 years we can still be shoved back in the closet at any time.[136]

Hellquist attributed the mother's reaction to "fear" and the desirability of erasing the existence of queer lives. While the family remained unnamed in the editorial, given that the issue was dedicated to the memory of Don McNamee, and an obituary, likely written by Hellquist, appeared in that same issue of *Perceptions*, it seems safe to conclude that it was McNamee's family to whom Hellquist's rage was directed. Such treatment underscores how, academically and socially, it would be misguided to simplistically reference "progress" with respect to queer peoples' experiences in the prairies. This vignette illustrates that "gains" are not forever, and can, without warning or vigilance, be easily erased. McNamee's treatment also offers a window into the ways that such "visibility" often triggered episodic homophobia. Hellquist emphasized that point in the editorial's concluding paragraphs: "There are certainly other forces active in our communities who want to deny our existence and deny the diversity of our community." He encouraged *Perceptions*'s readers to "remain vigilant to make sure they are not successful. As we make inroads in the campaign for total equality there are those who will fight harder to try and prevent those gains." Standing up to them, being prepared to "confront them and their lies," was, in his opinion, the only way forward.[137]

Not Just a Building ... The Closure of GCCS

In 1982, *The Body Politic* reported on the closure of Saskatoon's gay community centre. The same place that had received such fanfare five years earlier was now, as of March 1982, officially gone. Their building at 245 3rd Ave in Saskatoon was padlocked by the landlord for failure to pay the rent. In part, the centre was the victim of a series of events, including downtown renewal in Saskatoon, which saw the demolition of many older buildings for newer facilities. In that transformation, many low-income tenants were displaced. According to Bill Kobewka: "gone are those incredibly concentrated years following the 1977 National Conference when anything seemed possible and was. From Sunday community dinners, to the cable television committee, the centre cultivated a host of ideas. Cohesiveness helped get things done." In addition, the urban transformations in Saskatoon brought more money, population, and gay people to the city: "This new group is more conservative and complacent than those who had the fundamentalist spirit of the earlier years. Life is comfortable. They haven't been threatened by anything as catastrophic as a bath raid, police brutality, or the invasion of private residences."[138] An ever-widening rift between the social and political crowd further accelerated in these years. The financial impacts of fire, flood, problematic relationships with landlords, and the opening of a commercial gay disco in town all played a role, as did leadership transitions.[139]

The writing had been on the wall in 1981, when outgoing president Walter Davis offered an emotional report at the GCCS annual general meeting. He opened by setting the context of what had been achieved in ten years of hard work, reminding those present that Saskatoon had a proud history of gay and lesbian activism and achievement: "The gay community centre is a precious acquisition. Few cities in North America have a member-run democratic centre of our sort." He praised the foresight of early leaders who were "bold enough to take those first steps a decade ago," "dared to host a national conference, to launch Metamorphosis, to give lead to building a provincial coalition, to give aid and assistance to our own people here in Saskatoon and miles beyond."[140] Davis was one of those outsiders attracted to Saskatoon specifically because of the dynamism and political work of the GCCS, and the "central commitment to a multi-faceted community of social, educational, political, and counseling" work for "as many possible lesbians and gay men as could be served." And yet, as the audience knew, Davis would have to address the dramatic reversal of fortune. From revenues of $60,000 in 1979 to near insolvency in 1980 was, he indicated, a product of their own success: "Our focus on disco music both led to spectacular increase in attendance *and* created a potential market, a moveable audience. We welcome people here who only come here for the music *but* with no other relationship with the centre, it was inevitable that they would be drawn to a commercial club that, after all, can provide a disco-only function better than we can." The launch of After Midnight meant the end of capacity crowds. Because the GCCS did not attempt to compete with them, revenues declined dramatically. Reading between the lines of the report, After Midnight wasn't keen on cooperation with the GCCS, which further affected revenues. Davis stressed that individuals were not at fault, but this financial shortfall and rising rent costs exacerbated interpersonal issues, so people turned "inward" and "rumours" flew about how and what would happen.

Despite "suffering a lot at the cash box," Davis summarized the year's other tangible accomplishments: sexuality debates opened in the United Church of Canada, "labour, Native, Women's and other organizations join[ed] us in demanding human rights for lesbians and gay men. We saw Anita Bryant say 'live and let live!' We enjoyed some *favourable* press coverage in this city ... we saw major and minor union contracts protect lesbians and gay men. We saw Don Jones, with virtually no support, win a very important moral victory." Reaching the crescendo of his report, Davis ended on this social gospeller note: "if that is a climate of defeat indicating a time to throw in the towel, what would be a hopeful time? We, all of us, made it possible. We, all of us, will make it better."[141] Other decisions, not indicated in the annual report, were also at play. There were tensions about the decision of GCCS and SGC to leave the CLGRC. Internal letters, alongside those published in *The Body Politic*, indicate that there was not agreement about this decision. There were even debates about whether Saskatchewan Gay Coalition was an autonomous organization, or whether it was a subsidiary of GCCS, and hence acrimonious questions about who had the authority to make such decisions arose. Given the dedication and energy invested in the centre and in SGC, it was perhaps inevitable that at a time of a major economic crisis, long-simmering political debates would boil over.

In March 1982, Brenda Vallelee and Doug Wilson, representatives of the board of directors for the Gay/Lesbian Centre of Saskatoon, made a final plea for funds: "The Gay/Lesbian Centre of Saskatoon is in dire need of financial assistance. A series of misfortunes have forced us to close ... and have left us with overwhelming debts."[142] They attributed the crisis to a break in, in which their amplifier was stolen and vandals damaged the centre. Subsequently a flood caused $3,000 worth of further damages to the newly renovated space – space largely restored with volunteer labour, further overburdened the small core of volunteers. The decline in attendance combined with a rent increase proved to be fatal. The board of directors sought donations and also advertised mixed fundraising dances to be held at the Hungarian Hall, 323 Ave F S, where they hoped to raise monies to help pay off the accumulated debt. They also pledged that "a great deal of time w[ould] be devoted to reaching out and mending some of the rifts."[143] It wasn't to be. The emergence of another agency, Gay and Lesbian Support Services, meant that the Gay Community Centre's goals of a phoenix-like rise were clipped.

Gay and Lesbian Support Services (GLSS)

This crisis created by the loss of the Gay Community Centre served a catalytic effect on "old community stalwarts," which led to the creation of Gay and Lesbian Support Services. The new organization took over the library, started peer-counselling sessions, a telephone message system (GAYLINE), and supported the creation of a host of social, sports, and self-help groups. GLSS was the brainchild of Gens Hellquist and had this mandate: "GLSS is a group of concerned lesbians and gay men who have joined together to offer much needed services for the Gay community in Saskatoon. The goal is to create a healthier, happier and more supportive gay community … Support groups include gays with dependencies (alcohol or drugs) a men's discussion group, parents of gays, older gays, gay teens."[144]

Under Hellquist's astute leadership, GLSS became the driving force within Saskatoon. Its primary focus was on serving the communities' needs, but that should not be construed as a code word for apolitical. The politics of daily life, for Saskatoon gays and lesbians in the 1980s, meant that they were battling the provincial government and their homophobic agenda for access to health care; access to the far less robust pools of government funding that existed for community organizations; and for the right to continue to work for educational, counselling, employment, and legal rights of the gay and lesbian community. Notably, it should be pointed out that GLSS was the first group to actually acknowledge lesbian members in their title – Gay and Lesbian Support Services. Their offices were located downtown at 116 3rd Ave S, in the Ross Building. GLSS continued until 1987, which was an accomplishment given the dearth of funding for all social agencies during the Devine years, let alone one devoted to gay and lesbian issues.[145]

Conclusions

During the 1970s, within the prairies and indeed wider afield (Toronto and Vancouver in particular), the success of Saskatoon's gay community centre and of Saskatoon's leadership role provincially, regionally, and nationally were well known. Their activism was broad-ranging, including employment discrimination cases; rural and small-town outreach; political demonstrations for human rights extensions; multiple turns hosting regional and national gay and lesbian conferences; agent provocateur, at times, within the "national movement"; and, throughout most of this time, Saskatoon made a concerted effort to sustain a local community centre that funded activism one dance, social, and membership fee at a time. By the mid-1980s, though, fire, flood, AIDS, volunteer burnout, and political machinations, as well as the political chill and funding scarcity of the Devine years, ushered in leaner times. There would also be fissures and debates internally, less often between lesbians and gay men in Saskatoon than elsewhere on the prairies, but between insiders and outsiders, between those invested in a "no compromise" position, as the editorial collective at *After Stonewall* put it, and those who were pragmatic about politics in the prairies. The no compromisers tended to leave. The pragmatic liberationists stayed, kept talking, kept working, and sometimes recognized the value of compromise. Sometimes they knew that when one organization folded, another one would materialize, in a slightly different form and with a slightly different mandate, but often with a similar crew of paid and unpaid activist volunteers, and with goals of some sort of "community" centre – whether organized around politics, community, or health. There was continuity there – groups, telephone lines, libraries, and, above all, political work.

But Saskatoon, for all of its leadership and strength, was not immune to cross currents of homophobia – from families, employers, the media, fellow citizens, and in the 1980s and early 1990s, the provincial government. Newspapers were visibly threatened by small classified ads for the formation of gay organizations, not only in small towns, but also in Saskatoon and on campus. Violence was a part of those years, and clearly a form of resistance – perhaps "payback" for visibility. The fate of Martin Klepsch (while thankfully not commonplace) was attributed to his "lifestyle," by which the RCMP meant being a gay man who had sex with men and socialized in gay clubs. Trauma from such violence, bashings, the multiple club arsons, and the seeming police indifference (at times) imposed another chill on the community. Medical forms of pathologization as "bad girls," treatment for a range of mental health issues, and, in extreme cases, institutionalization also created their share of trauma for those lesbians and gay men attempting to forge different paths through heteronormative Saskatchewan society.

Saskatoon's history of activism and reaction, resistance and violence, is one that has been forgotten. This was a city that received significant national coverage in the pages of Canada's national gay newsmagazine *The Body Politic*. *TBP* might have, initially, profiled Saskatoon because there were multiple personal connections among its crew of activists, journalists, and prairie expats living in Toronto. But that is only a partial explanation. Equally, if not more important, was that Saskatoon did, for a city of its size, have an incredibly active and dedicated gay and lesbian community. A handful of volunteers, including many long-term Saskatoon residents – Gens Hellquist, Bruce Garman, Neil Richards, Peter Millard, Dorothy, Doug Wilson, Richard Nordahl, Val Scrivener, Marion Alexander, Erin Shoemaker, Barb Clay, and others – kept activism and cultural activities alive in this city. Where many cities, such as Winnipeg and Edmonton, lost critical masses of gay and lesbians to larger centres, Saskatoon managed to hang on to a core group of people who kept a sense of continuity going. Some activists, such as Davis and Fields, Kolansinka and Bierweiler, and others, shone brightly for a few years and then moved on, partly for work opportunities, partly for larger gay and lesbian centres. AIDS took a toll on Saskatoon and Regina, and thus there is a missing generation of men – like Doug Wilson, or Dr Gary MacDonald (Regina) – whose potential contributions remain unrealized.

It would be inaccurate and simplistic to leave the impression that this was some sort of gay and lesbian "Brigadoon" on the banks of the South Saskatchewan River.[146] It was not. Homophobic violence, institutionalization, lost children, lost jobs, and social and economic marginalization were real facets of life during this time. Archival and oral history sources all recalled such episodes, the fear they created, and the reactions these events set in motion. Some narrators and gay and lesbians fought back, were defiant, refused to slink away quietly – Doug Wilson and Don Jones are perfect examples. Others were defiantly activist and open; they talked about discrimination, called politicians, neighbours, colleagues, and residents on their behaviour in public lectures, in the pages of *Perceptions*, on the op-ed pages of the local newspaper, and at rallies. They demanded equality, and spoke truth to the fact that Saskatchewan's often vaunted sense of itself as a province of social justice support and radical history could be remarkably blinkered at times, and often blind to issues of sexual orientation, homophobia, and sexism. A smaller cohort of women and men took an older approach. They strategically chose to be quietly gay or lesbian, to live double or compartmentalized lives, and to socialize very minimally within the larger community of gay and lesbian peoples. As many informants reiterated, they were not part of the "community" but they were an "interesting part of gay life." This isn't a "community" history, which presumes a united group of actors speaking with one voice. Such a notion is fiction, whether we are historicizing an ethnic, racial, classist, urban, regional, or national community. But a "community" of individuals who were gay and lesbian, participated in community events, had lovers and partners, identified in some fashion as gay or lesbian includes all sorts and has many stories. I've tried to sample from as many cohorts as possible because these histories offer a more nuanced, comprehensive history of how people lived as gays and lesbians in Saskatoon and made it work. Such histories are messy. They include overlapping generations, people who fit best within a homophile generation of activists, and gay people for whom notions of middle-class respectability were paramount, and whose dream was "acceptance" or the space to just be quietly different. Others were part of a liberationist or feminist generation, and they wanted a lot more than merely acceptance. They wanted explicit recognition: they wanted to claim their space in the city, to sing about loving other women, or to dance with their male lovers on a beautiful Canada Day afternoon at a party beside the city's Bessborough Hotel. This smaller group made great strides for the whole through their activism, their defiance, and their sheer determination to keep on going. In the mid-1980s, when this history ends, they were at a low ebb, demoralized by an overtly homophobic and hostile provincial government, waking up to the harsh reality of AIDS, and beginning to regroup to fight that medical onslaught. That would be an interregnum, and they would re-emerge – smaller, more focused, but vitally engaged in taking queer activities in Saskatoon into the twenty-first century.

Saskatchewan has a history of being "next year country," a phrase originally invoked during the Depression as farmers reassured themselves that with hard work and perseverance, plus some help from the climate gods, their fortunes would improve. So too this phrase describes the queer community, it would continue to push forward with, among other achievements, the launch of AIDS Saskatoon; Gay and Lesbian Health Services; later the Avenue Community Centre; Diva's, a longstanding commercial club; and, for a wonderfully brief interregnum, Cafe Browse, a lesbian-owned and -operated bookshop cafe. The history from 1984 to the present offers many vitally important stories awaiting a historian. Politically, sexual orientation would finally be included in the provincial human rights code in 1993. Pride events would be relaunched and a pride flag would fly above city hall, dominating the downtown skyline. Few in the early 1970s could anticipate how their work, and the small ad placed in the *Georgia Straight*, would turn out. But, as the recollections of my narrators and the archival materials make abundantly clear, change isn't linear. Writing a history of prairie queer communities is the historical equivalent of describing a two-step of advancement and retrenchment, victories and defeats, increasing numbers of openly proud and visible queer people and small, but persistent, pockets of quiet, discreet, closeted individuals.

Chapter Eight

Found-Ins at the Pisces Spa: Moments of Activism, Repression, and Public Education in Edmonton, 1970–1985

Out of the closets and into the streets is a great battle cry for gays who don't have too much to lose but then there are the rest of us.[1]

Editor, *Carousel Capers*, Calgary, 1973

The first time I said to a good friend that I am a lesbian … she said … be careful, people will think you are a pervert. I was very astonished and indignant … I was so stunned that I didn't have the legal rights when I came out and then when I just instantly moved into this weird category where I was in danger. I gave up all of my privileges I was just astonished and said "why the hell didn't somebody tell me that?" It's like I never really knew until my friends said you could lose your job because of it and I thought what the hell has that got to do with anything?! I was just stunned and very indignant and naive, I thought well we'll just go get this changed.[2]

Liz Massiah, September 2003, Edmonton

The sentiments of two middle-class lesbians, one writing anonymously in Calgary's gay organizational newsletter in the early 1970s, the other reflecting on her experience coming out in the 1970s and 1980s, offer two different perspectives on "politics." As this volume has argued, socializing as a queer person in the prairies was political, insomuch as it involved identifying as lesbian or gay, the conscious choice to socialize with others who identified as queer, and staking a claim to spaces within the heterosexual majority. But in this chapter, devoted to snapshots of activism in Edmonton and Calgary and moments of reprisal, repression, and resistance, the frame shifts to political lobbying, education, and campaigns to articulate queer political issues within Alberta.

One of the more dramatic changes, in visibility and organizational development, occurred in Edmonton as the previous chapter illuminated. But not everyone could embrace activism. The lesbian editor at *Carousel Capers* obviously believed that activism was for those gays who didn't care and by implication not those resident in Calgary. Liz Massiah held a very different perspective, and her indignation and anger about her second-class status (from married, heterosexual Euro-Canadian woman to lesbian) spurred her to a decidedly different conclusion. Individuals like Massiah were very much in the minority in Edmonton, and while demonstrable changes in visibility and access to organizational, social, commercial, and political opportunities were evident, not all embraced them. It was not an easy trajectory from consciousness-raising and organizational development to activism in Alberta. Of all the provinces and cities profiled in this book, it was Alberta where, fittingly, the chinook of intolerance could blow in at any moment. This chapter charts how moments of visibility, activism, and significant accomplishments, for example, the election in 1992 of Edmonton's first openly gay city councillor, Michael Phair, must be balanced against the moments of violence, homophobia, and retrenchment. Perhaps no one knew how quickly the political winds could change than Delwyn Vriend, whose case thrust himself, Edmonton, and Alberta into the media glare.

Oral interviews with Edmonton activists and archival records clearly indicate that Vriend's case, which initially broke in 1991, was an absolutely pivotal moment. With the exception of the Pisces Spa raid (May 1981), Edmonton queers never made much of splash on the national gay and lesbian consciousness until Vriend, a twenty-five-year-old lab instructor, was fired from his job at King's University College in Edmonton. The president of the private Christian university offered Vriend the option to quietly resign (which parallels Doug Wilson's case at the University of Saskatchewan, fifteen years earlier). Vriend refused. Like Wilson he resisted resigning when his only "crime" had been being openly gay. After his dismissal, he went to the Alberta Human Rights office to launch an investigation. They refused to take his case because Alberta's Individual Rights Protection Act did not include protection for sexual orientation. In an interview Vriend recalled how it felt "to walk out of the Human Rights office and realize they couldn't do anything. That was a shock." [3]

Canadians living outside of Alberta were not so shocked because Vriend's treatment confirmed stereotypes of the province – as a religiously conservative place where gay people were unwelcome, often persecuted, and thus deeply closeted and fearful. Many people no doubt wondered why Vriend, an openly gay male who was active in Edmonton gay organizations, was so naive (perhaps misguided) to work at a private, Christian institution such as King's. Looking back on the episode and the ensuing legal challenge, Vriend credited the experience with making him confront the contradictions between his church's teachings (he was a member of the Dutch Reform congregation) and his identity as a gay man. He became a poster boy for gay and lesbian rights in Alberta, and, unlike many children from fundamentalist Christian families, was supported by his parents. In 1998, the Supreme Court of Canada rendered a historic decision to have sexual orientation read into the Alberta provincial human rights code. Premier Ralph Klein fumed and initially claimed he would invoke the notwithstanding clause, but very shortly it became apparent that such a move would not be a winning one, even in Alberta. Much had changed since Everett Klippert's case went to the Supreme Court in 1965. In particular, the Canadian Charter of Rights and Freedoms had been created, which gave gay activists more legal tools with which to pursue redress. Equally important, Vriend's case was strengthened by the precedents established by the inclusion, in all other Canadian provinces except Alberta, of sexual orientation to provincial human rights legislation. Subsequent media reports praised Vriend's decision to fight, and he credited his family's support, and in particular his parents' experiences as organic farmers and vegans, for instilling in him the importance of standing up to discrimination. In Alberta, where cattle ranching and the beef industry are major economic drivers, identifying as a vegetarian or vegan can be challenging.[4] In fact, vegetarianism and animal rights politics (which, admittedly, are not always linked) were polarizing issues. One could claim, as I have elsewhere, that "vegetarian" was as contested an identity in Alberta as being queer.[5]

While Vriend's situation and his determination to proceed with his legal case all the way to the Supreme Court of Canada are well covered elsewhere, few have addressed the backstory.[6] Given the absence of work about queer Albertans, the critical information necessary to understand how Vriend could have thought, rather audaciously, that being a queer instructor was a possibility at a private Christian school is missing. Hopefully, this chapter provides evidence of some moments of queer resistance, political awareness, and community building that began much earlier, in the 1970s, when organized gay and lesbian clubs began to form in Edmonton. Unlike the Winnipeg and Saskatoon chapters, this chapter is organized around "snapshots" of activism and activists and is less comprehensive. This is purposeful for two simple reasons. First, despite rapid strides in historicizing the queer experiences in Calgary and Edmonton, particularly their community history projects, the source base for these two cities was not as plentiful. Yet it was important to keep Alberta's cities and regions in this book because, rightly or wrongly, that province so often "represents" the west in the Canadian national imagination. Prairie residents are well aware of Alberta's unique histories, immigration streams, and economic base, but for those outside this region, who may erroneously regard Alberta as representative, or the most fascinating of the western provinces, the contrasts between Alberta, Saskatchewan, and Manitoba offers important context to regional variations and similarities. The perspective on how queer life in Alberta was and was not similar to other prairie cities engages with important historical and contemporary attempts to understand Albertan exceptionalism. Vriend's case did not appear in a vacuum, and, regardless of his and his supporters tremendous resilience and strength, his case drew upon a couple decades of political work in the city from a small community of politicized gays and lesbians, and straight allies, who had managed to carve out moments for politicizing and educating the province about sexual diversity. Those successes may have emboldened him – and others – to perceive that Alberta was now ripe for more concrete changes in acceptance of sexual minority communities, colleagues, and citizens.

Lobbying for Human Rights: GATE and the IRPA

As chapter 5 indicated, GATE arrived in Edmonton in November 1970. It was transplanted from Vancouver to Edmonton by activist and university student Michael Roberts. One significant accomplishment during Roberts's tenure was a brief that he presented to the Alberta legislature in 1972 requesting that the new legislation, the Individual Rights Protection Act (IRPA), include sexual orientation as a protected category.[7] The IRPA, introduced by the Conservative government of Peter Lougheed, was intended to protect the rights of Albertans in matters of employment and housing. Interestingly, the legislation didn't employ the usual human rights terminology, but, in nomenclature more acceptable to the government's entrepreneurial ethos, it protected people's "individual rights," particularly in the area of employment, so that all Albertans could share in the provincial prosperity.[8] Alberta came late to such legislation as it was only introduced in 1972. By comparison, Saskatchewan's CCF government, under Premier T.C. Douglas, introduced the Saskatchewan Bill of Rights in 1947.[9] Thus, this was the only province where gay activists were able, prior to the bill's passage, to lobby for sexual orientation to be included. Robert's press release concluded with this optimistic assessment of the meeting: "Mr Roberts has received assurances from many of the members of Alberta legislature, including the Premier (Lougheed) that his submission will receive their fullest consideration when they again debate Bill 2. However, he failed to convince them and when the IRPA was originally passed it did not include reference to protection for sexual orientation. These rights were finally secured through the culmination of an on-again off-again, twenty-six-year battle waged by various gay and lesbian organizations.[10] The lateness of this achievement (human rights protection) is but one marker of how the gay and lesbian minority were regarded provincially. An important piece of the struggle involved which provincial parties held power. NDP parties were far more likely, eventually, to revise human rights codes to include coverage for sexual orientation. This was the case in Manitoba in 1987 and Saskatchewan in 1994. Conservative provincial governments, such as Alberta's Conservatives or British Columbia's Social Credit party, were ideologically opposed to these changes. In 1992, BC's NDP swept into office and they made revising the provincial codes to include sexual orientation one of their early legislative priorities.[11]

Alberta Gays and Lesbian Version of *A Minority without Rights*

In 1976, a succession of organizations lobbied the provincial government and the Alberta Human Rights Commission to consider revising the IRPA to include sexual orientation. All of the major western cities used the same format and title, "A Minority Without Rights," but they used evidence of discrimination culled from their unique provincial and urban situations. So, Gays for Equality (Winnipeg), Saskatoon Gay Action, Edmonton's GATE, and Calgary's GIRC (Gay Information and Resources Calgary) all shared the same title and, in successive iterations of this document, were able to provide more detailed lists of individuals who had faced discrimination in housing and employment, faced custody battles because of their orientation, or had been physically assaulted because of their sexuality.

In 1976 when GATE drafted the brief, their purpose was "to supply background information about the homosexual minority in Alberta"; "human rights and civil liberties"; and "public education" to eradicate "prejudice against homosexual people."[12] GATE claimed to speak "for the needs of all the homosexual and bisexual people of Alberta."[13] These documents are fascinating, not only for the information they provide about homophobia and political activism but also as cultural documents in their own right. They conventionally began with projections of the number of homosexuals in the province (using Kinsey's numbers and Statistics Canada population statistics) to illustrate that this advocacy was intended to help a sizable number of Albertans affected by prejudicial treatment. Addressed to rights commissions and sitting members of provincial legislatures, the documents were aimed at a broad cross section of individuals. Some readers, it was anticipated, had virtually no knowledge of gay and lesbian people. Others whose primary knowledge might derive from religious teachings, conversely, were presumed to require re-education and information that framed "homosexuals" as responsible citizens whose orientation (not sexual behaviour) caused them to experience inequitable and unfair discrimination in daily life. Christian anti-gay views were prevalent and demonstrated in a variety of forms in Alberta, including letters to the editors of local newspapers, attendance at Anita Bryant's Christian revival, or, more unconventionally, a break-in at GATE which, the perpetrator claimed, was religiously inspired. In spring of 1975, GATE Edmonton was broken into "by a man who informed police that he was "working on behalf of Moses." He destroyed several hundred dollars worth of furniture and caused substantial structural damage to the building."[14] According to activists, the way to correct this homophobic treatment was to amend the Individual Rights Protection Act to include sexual orientation and amend the Alberta Bill of Rights to include the term "sexual orientation. Doing so would "ensure that homosexual people in Alberta would have the same rights as other citizens."[15] Framing such concepts as matters of "equity" was very important because opponents frequently referred to such human rights protections as "special rights," implying that such coverage for gays and lesbians would diminish the rights of the majority.

Activists were not optimistic that this would be an easy process. And so, they endeavoured to present a range of cases to illustrate the discrimination gays and lesbians in Alberta faced. Furthermore, they cautioned that many cases were never reported because with few options for redress unless crimes were committed there was little point to further subject oneself to adverse publicity. They could marshal reams of evidence of discriminatory treatment, including censorship, lost housing, employment terminations, and violence. Censorship battles were waged across Canada, some at the federal level (with Canada Customs seizures of books and periodicals destined for gay and lesbian bookshops in Vancouver and Toronto), others, as has been addressed before, involved publishers, bookshops, and newspapers.[16] In Alberta, an advertisement for GATE promoting sales of *The Body Politic* – "Canada's leading gay liberation newspaper" – was declined by "*The Edmonton Journal*, the *Calgary Herald*, the *Grande Prairie Daily Herald-Tribune*, and the *Red Deer Advocate*. The *Grande-Prairie Daily Herald-Tribune* failed to publish the advertisement but kept the money order."[17] Refusal of service in bars and restaurants provided another large category of discriminatory treatment. For example, an Edmonton tavern "with a large, though not exclusively, homosexual clientele" began carding long-time gay patrons and arbitrarily refused to serve them if their identification was "unacceptable." A managerial change created this new policy. Housing discrimination was also a persistent issue. Two gay Calgary men were denied an available, vacant apartment. When they asked why, they were told, "we don't rent to single men, especially your kind."[18] Most significant of all was employment discrimination. Evidence provided listed teachers whose contracts were not renewed in southern Alberta and in the Stettler School Board. Elsewhere a daycare worker with twenty years experience was asked to resign and told "you already know what your problem is."[19] Moving from the list of discriminations to the more positive request goals for further public education, the brief requested that changes be implemented to the province's high school curriculum. GATE asserted that education about homosexuality would dispel myths promulgated by bigotry or allowed to run unchecked due to ignorance. Evidence in support of their requests were slim, but they included a January 1976 letter from Carole Fogel, director of the Saskatchewan Human Rights Commission, to GATE's R.E. Radke confirming that "the Saskatchewan Human Rights Commission has recommended the addition of 'sexual orientation'" to Saskatchewan legislation.[20] Given that these reports were shared among gay and lesbian organizations, and each city or region modified their own document, it is not surprising to see material from other cities and provinces. While the Saskatchewan Human Rights Commission was widely applauded for their recommendation that the province's human rights code be revised to include sexual orientation (in response to Wilson's case), it was still a recommendation at that point, not policy.

In August 1979, the Alberta Lesbian and Gay Rights Association took up the cause, making a presentation to the Alberta Human Rights Commission. They explained that unlike previous briefs prepared by groups based in Edmonton and Calgary, "ALGRA includes a substantial rural membership. In addition, urban local organizations are affiliates."[21] Politically astute and striving to demonstrate a broader based coalition of gays and lesbians throughout the province, this document indicated substantive progress in finding allies since the last submission from GATE. Namely, they cited the Alberta Federation of Labour's support for revision to include sexual orientation in the labour code. Alberta Conference of the United Church of Canada also supported code revisions, as did the Alberta NDP. Quebec's passage of human rights extensions to lesbians and gay men was highlighted. Further evidence of societal change was provided, including a recent Gallop poll that claimed that "52% of Canadians were in favour" of such extensions and, finally, that the Alberta Human Rights Commission requested the IRPA be amended.[22] This iteration's catalogue of discrimination included a wider variety of experiences and, for the first time, named individuals. For example, it was reported that "in 1977, Russ Pritchard, then president of Gay Information and Resources of Calgary was interviewed by the *Calgary Herald* for an article on the Calgary gay community. Several days after the article appeared he was fired. Following an informal investigation by the Human Rights Commission he was rehired."[23] Refusal of service in bars and restaurants continued to be reported. In Calgary, it was alleged that the Kings Arms tavern in the Palliser Hotel refused service to "gay patrons," which was the "culmination of a series of arbitrary acts by a new manager."[24] Many of the cases were repeated from the original document, and a section on the precarious situation of teachers received more sustained analysis and condemnation.

One issue that received brief attention in these documents, but more extensive coverage in the *Gay Calgary* newsletter, was the discrimination that GARD faced in Red Deer. A November 1979 article reported that the local Red Deer paper, *The Advisor*, had "refused to continue to allow the Gay Association of Red Deer the use of its mail forwarding facilities." When GARD called and asked for an explanation they were informed that ads for GARD had elicited "a number of negative phone calls and letters." When GARD representatives collected their mail at *The Advisor* offices, they were dismayed to find that the envelopes had been opened and then taped shut. So much for confidentiality. GARD demanded an explanation and the paper unconvincingly replied that, "the letters had been included in the regular business mail and opened accidentally."[25] These sorts of chilling events underscore precisely why many rural and small-town queers remained cautious about greater visibility. Their fears were real. Various organizations attempted to police gay and lesbian activity, and closely followed who attended queer events or was interested in queer materials. Alberta newspapers were often oppositional, if not always actively surveilling, gay and lesbian residents. Another Red Deer paper, *The Advocate*, "refused outright to print an advertisement giving the name and address of GARD." An employee of the *Advocate* is said to have stated, "It's bad enough having gays around. Why do you have to advertise it? We don't advertise we're not gay."[26] Such deceptively simplistic questions about "advertising queerness" ignored the realities of the "advertisements" of heterosexuality, which abounded throughout the prairie west in the form of announcements and published photos for engagements, weddings, milestone anniversaries, "stag and doe" parties, and myriad other, less showy, moments of heterosexual pageantry. In a culture where people married young, often right after high school, and could, if they stuck it out, celebrate fifty, sixty, and sometimes seventy years of wedded bliss (all milestones proudly announced in community newspapers), partnering up was a prairie passion. Claiming that heterosexuality was not "advertised" was incorrect, it was routinely advertised and celebrated in prairie newspapers.

In 1980, Gay Information and Resources Calgary (GIRC) revised the brief again and made an appeal to the minister of labour, Lester Young. GIRC identified itself as "an organization working in the areas of education, counselling, community development, and civil liberties for homosexual men and women in southern Alberta." GIRC was an affiliate of Alberta Lesbian and Gay Rights Association (ALGRA) and a member of the Canadian Lesbian and Gay Rights Coalition (CLGRA). Their goal, as in previous documents, was to "draw attention to the large numbers of homosexual men and women in Alberta who remain legally defenseless to combat bigotry and prejudice in such important areas as employment, housing and accommodation."[27] The document and letter, spearheaded by Doug Young, again urged the minister to have sexual orientation included in the provincial human rights code. And, most important, Young stressed that "in our opinion no exceptions be made in the areas of sexual orientation or physical disability as the Alberta School Trustees Association has suggested. We feel it is unnecessary for school boards to retain special powers to interfere in the private lives of students or staff."[28] In addition to cataloguing some of the previous issues of discrimination from earlier versions, they offered a handful of new cases. Including one in which the GIRC was refused a booking at the Victoria Community Hall earlier that year during the controversy over the national gay and lesbian conference in Calgary (see below). Media reports indicated that the community association explained their decision (which reversed past practice) as a precaution due to "children being present in the neighbourhood."[29] Events at the Palliser Hotel in Calgary had now escalated to the point that "an entire section of customers, approximately forty people, were denied services and required to leave the King's Arms Tavern" in November 1978 after several "gay patrons objected to being called derogatory names ... by the manager of the tavern. The Kings Arms is well known as a gay-frequented beverage room and most of the patrons asked to leave were publicly known to be gay."[30]

There is a dreary repetitiveness to these documents. The cases cited were, as readers were often reminded, the mere "tip" of the iceberg, as few individuals reported routine discrimination because they feared further hostility. Beyond governmental intransigence, the successive issues of *A Minority without Rights* provide a counterbalance to the expansion of social, activist, cultural, and commercial spaces for gays and lesbians in Edmonton and Calgary in the 1970s (see chapter 5). More organizational space cannot simplistically be interpreted as "progress" and acceptance within Alberta. The ability to be broadsided by homophobic bar managers, employers, landlords, or media, and sometimes from more conservative factions within the gay and lesbian community itself, happened with sufficient frequency to undercut complacency about "gains." And, no matter how persuasive, no matter how much evidence was amassed demonstrating discrimination, or how eloquent the gay and lesbian activists were, Alberta's government proved resistant to change. Whether the premier was Peter Lougheed or Ralph Klein, the results were the same – no action. Until, finally, the Supreme Court acted. In part, this may have been the Klein government's goal so that they did not alienate their rural, religious base. Klein, while mayor of Calgary, denounced the police's heavy-handed tactics with parade permits for the gay pride march, which, while not supportive of gay politics, was an acknowledgment of democratic rights to assemble. Such dramas, and the recitation of such discriminatory episodes, demonstrate the ongoing challenges of being openly queer in the province. Those events also amplified impressions, beyond the province's borders, that Alberta was a more virulently homophobic province. This second point, virtually a truism, is debatable. Until we have more histories and comparisons of gay and lesbian experiences throughout the country, this generalization may not be entirely accurate. Rural areas and small towns, in the interior of British Columbia, Ontario, or Nova Scotia, where sizable numbers of religious, evangelical Christians lived, could also be intolerant. The point is not to absolve Alberta or to dismiss the legitimate criticisms of homophobic discrimination in the province; rather, it is to nuance this history. This comparative, provincial, and regional analysis illustrates that multiple notions of inclusiveness and exclusion, tolerance and homophobia, could coexist and circulate within the province and its two major cities. But such was also the case in Manitoba and Saskatchewan where discrimination, violence, repression, and hostility were not unknown.

Anita Bryant in Edmonton, 1978

Similar to the other prairie cities, Ms Bryant arrived in Edmonton in April 1978 to share the same Christian revivalist message that was, as covered earlier, pro-heterosexual family, traditional gender roles for women and men, and anti-gay and anti-feminist. The experience in Edmonton was little different than Winnipeg or Moose Jaw, and so it doesn't merit additional coverage of the city's experience – except with one notable exception. In Edmonton, the daily newspaper, *The Edmonton Journal*, had a lengthy editorial essay, written by William Thorsell, which called out Bryant's dangerous, intolerant message. Entitled the "Anita Syndrome," Thorsell struck hard at the key issue: "How far can people legitimately go in advocating the unequal treatment of others on religious grounds? Do we accept the denigration of a minority because the intolerant majority says it is following orders? Historically, we have never accepted that excuse."[31] Thorsell shared some of Bryant's comments from an interview she gave with *Playboy* magazine where she explained that she didn't hate gays, or Jews (another of her targets), but because of her interpretation of the Bible all non-believers were "doomed." This disingenuousness extended to women as well, as Bryant was quick to note that she realized it was "God's will" that women submit to men "because God says women are the weaker vessels ... That's biblical."[32] While she freely espoused these views, she also claimed that she wasn't personally responsible because she was merely repeated Biblical truths. That, for Thorsell, was the key – Bryant's lack of responsibility for her position as an "honest" broker of Christian belief.

Thorsell wrote that a "coalition of groups is demonstrating against Anita Bryant's Edmonton visit this weekend, in large part because of her aggressive attitudes towards them in particular, but also because of the dangerous process on which her political action is based: faith rather than thought."[33] Labelling her discourse a "profound issue," one intended to "deprive whole classes of people of their normal rights in Canada," he cautioned against complacency. In his concluding statement, he strongly denounced her visit, her views, and encouraged readers to be vigilant about what was at stake: "There are some who say Anita Bryant should be ignored, that she isn't significant. But this is a powerful woman leading a political fight for unequal treatment of millions of people. Democrats in a free society will ignore this phenomenon only at their peril."[34]

The significance of the *Edmonton Journal* publishing this anti-Bryant editorial was important. It was widely cited throughout the queer press, and reprinted in the *Saskatchewan Gay Coalition Newsletter* – a sign of respect for this rare 1970s mainstream press article in support of gay and lesbian human rights and anti-discrimination. At the time, Thorsell's rationale wasn't entirely clear; now, naturally, it was evidence of a rare moment when he felt compelled to break through his own silence about such matters, and neutrally champion gay rights against the views of the Christian right.

"Coming Out in the Hat": Politicizing
Medicine Hat and Other Small Alberta Towns

Gay Calgary, in their October 1979 issue, provided a "heartening" front-page story about plans to start a gay group in Medicine Hat, Alberta.[35] Two members of GIRC, working in tandem with their partners in ALGRA, spent two days in the southeastern Alberta city encouraging lesbians and gay men to form a local group. Ads placed in the *Medicine Hat News* yielded a few responses and the group planned to go back in October for a follow-up meeting. This process was similar to an earlier effort in Red Deer (see chapter 5), which led to the creation of GARD. While small-town participants were eager to meet others in their community, and, in the case of Red Deer, most desirous for socializing opportunities, the author of this news item spoke to the politics behind these initiatives: "The purpose of rural outreach is to bring together gay people who live in areas where no gay group exists. GIRC has been active in Medicine Hat and Lethbridge, as well as in Red Deer ... Plans have also been made to contact gays living in Banff area."[36] They acknowledged that this work was similar to the outreach program launched by the Saskatchewan Gay Coalition (upon which ALGRA was based), where "in less than two years the coalition has been contacted by over 1200 lesbians and gay men living on farms and in more than 100 communities."[37]

In December 1979, *Gay Horizons* published another article on efforts to meet and encourage gays and lesbians in Medicine Hat. The author, a resident of Calgary wrote: "It isn't easy being gay in Medicine Hat, but it's by no means impossible. The gay underground though difficult to locate, exists there."[38] A trio of gay and lesbian activists from Calgary set out to explore Medicine Hat and reported on their challenging day, as they sought to find spaces where gay people hung out, to find bookshops and venues to leave copies of *Gay Horizons* newspaper (ALGRA's newspaper), and to talk with local gays and lesbians about their experiences. One newsstand that carried the American gay periodical, *The Advocate*, refused to accept copies of *Gay Horizon*, dismissively calling the paper "that shit." Other venues in the city were also a bust, odd since a newsstand in Brooks, Alberta, was prepared to take the newspaper. They reported on their dinner with two gay contacts that emerged from the newspaper ads, and learned from those discussions that gays and lesbians "have a group that meets regularly in one Medicine Hat bar that does not intimidate them." After dinner, the group went to a "classically straight small city disco" where the three Calgarians had the "unnerving experience" of "having to sit through an evening of drink and dance playing 'straight' which they did for the "sake of local gays who were with us."[39] Their conclusion was "the closet is despicable." There is a tendency in the articles to discuss "creating spaces" in small towns and rural areas and to gloss the challenges, striving to positivistically report on every meeting and coffee as a step on the path to greater visibility – if not explicit activism. Clearly, Medicine Hat had a long way to go, and even by Calgary standards of openness (which, as we shall see below, was limited) they were still in the "underground era."

Six months later, *Gay Horizons* published another article about small-town Alberta activities, this time in Lethbridge. Entitled simply

"Lethbridge Dance," *Gay Horizons* reporters described an event at the city's Hungarian Hall attended by sixty people.[40] This community dance was sponsored by Gay Alliance of Lethbridge Alberta (GALA). The second gay dance in the city attracted people from "Lethbridge and surrounding area (about half the guests), Medicine Hat and Bozeman, Montana. Nearly 20 Calgarians journeyed to Lethbridge for the dance."[41] Still, organizers were not pleased with the turnout as a number of other Lethbridge gays and lesbians did not attend because they were "afraid to show up." Another dance was planned for the fall, supplementing a roster of social activities that including house parties, camping, and barbecues.

Adjacent to this article was a different report from Lethbridge, which highlights some of the routine hassles and homophobia of life there. In February, a GALA meeting, held in a Lethbridge apartment, was interrupted by "unruly neighbours."[42] According to the article, K.J.K. of Lethbridge crashed the meeting to tell the gay male GALA crew to keep the noise down. Discovering that it was a meeting and not a party, as he originally believed, "K accused the people in the room of being faggots. He returned a few minutes later with 3 or 4 of his friends and allegedly struck" GALA's secretary.[43] Apparently there had been previous episodes of "general harassment" of two GALA members who, by virtue of sharing the apartment together, were "suspected of being gay." Lethbridge City Police were called and K.J.K. would be charged with assault once he was located by the police. Interestingly, neither the police nor the landlord involved in this situation were informed of the nature of the meeting (although in the gay press article it was fully described), which illustrates the "vigilance" that Red Deer narrators reported was necessary to successfully live as gay or lesbian in small Albertan cities.

Doug Young (1950–1994)

I did not have the opportunity to interview Doug Young, the mastermind and driving force behind many GIRC initiatives, because he died from AIDS in 1994 in Calgary. His close friend, John Cooper, who oversaw the donation of Young's papers to the Glenbow Archives (a significant collection, particularly given that the GIRC institutional files were destroyed), indicates that the interviews that he and Young hoped would transpire did not due to the rapid progression of Young's disease.[44] Instead, we have Young's papers and notebooks; press coverage from the *Calgary Herald* and *The Body Politic*; Cooper's notes of their conversations; Cooper's reflections about the challenges of attempting to distil the life of a "gay warrior" and "Calgary pioneer" into mere words, namely his published obituary; and the contextual information provided in the Cooper fonds at the Glenbow.

According to Cooper, Young was "one of the progressive members of the gay rights movement and worked in harmony with other progressive leaders such as Doug Wilson of Saskatoon and the Body Politic Collective." The list of his accomplishments was astonishing: member of GIRC, 1976–81, president of GIRC (1977–9), member of the Right to Privacy Committee responding to the bath raids in Toronto and Edmonton, member of the Gay Political Action Group (post-GIRC). Young also served as southern Alberta's representative in ALGRA and had served nationally as Calgary's delegate to the Canadian Lesbian and Gay Rights Coalition and National Gay Rights Coalition, its predecessor. Young had attended those national gay rights conferences held in Saskatoon, Halifax, Ottawa, and Calgary (1977–80), which permitted much cross-regional and national discussions, and were remembered as "significant in defining the modern gay rights movement."[45] Although he was instrumental in lobbying for human rights inclusion in Alberta, Cooper was adamant that Young was not a narrow "rights" activist.

In 1980, *The Body Politic* profiled Young, Richard Kinsman, and Henry Berg, the three primary GIRC activists. Photographed sitting outside the old YMCA building where GIRC was based, Young provided a fantastic interview contrasting his experiences in Ottawa with those in Calgary, his perspective as a former small-town Albertan, and his thoughts on the movement's future. Born in Taber, Alberta, and raised there and in Medicine Hat, Young attended Medicine Hat College, and later the University of Calgary, before striking out to see more "liberal parts of the world – Montreal, Ottawa, and Toronto." After his stint in central Canada, he returned and settled in Calgary.[46] Reportedly, Young had not experienced homophobic discrimination or harassment in the west because he "didn't fit the stereotype" ("queens" and "fairies" were those routinely harassed during Young's youth). However, he did have a taste of discrimination in Ottawa. One evening, prior to attending a Gays of Ottawa dance, he and his friend were on the receiving end of homophobic harassment:

20 kids started harassing us. I tried to talk to them, but they were only interested in hassling. These kids lived in my neighbourhood, and after

that I was constantly harassed by them. I couldn't go in or out of my house without being called names, and they always followed me around – always a large group of them. I'd tell them that I knew who they were, knew their licence numbers of their bikes – that they couldn't intimidate me. But they did. Up to that point, I'd never felt any real overt oppression. I never thought I'd get into a situation where I would. But for three months that I continued to live there, it was like a living hell … I came back to Calgary in '74, and the city suddenly seemed very liberal.[47]

However horrible it was for Young, one doesn't want to overanalyse this one recollection in order to demonize Ottawa and applaud Calgary liberalism. Such assessments of oppression and liberal tolerance are far more complicated, and often highly individualistic. No doubt Young was trying to surprise or unsettle readers of *The Body Politic* by claiming Calgary as a "liberal" city. Yet it is also true, as revealed in work of Kinsman and Gentile, that Ottawa was repressive for gays and lesbians.[48] Conversely, prairie cities did, counterintuitively, offer pockets of liberal-minded tolerance where people were content not to look too hard, or ask too many questions, which, as I argue, enabled queer lives. This-live-and-let-live ethos is an important framework in which these city's cultures need to be understood as it created much space for unconventional people, queers among them, to exist. Equally, though it was not my intention in this book to make it nationally comparative, such moments arise and they offer important contextual information about other cities in Canada. Ultimately, such recollections ask us to revise our historical stereotypes about queer possibilities and spaces throughout Canada, not only "the west."

Upon his return to Calgary, and with a background in social agencies and mental health work, Young reported that he felt compelled to start some organizations for Calgary queer people, and in particular, that there should be an "information line" and counselling "support services." He started talking with a few people he thought might be involved. The early radical organizers of GIRC – Myra Lipton and Windi Earthworm – "had come out of the old People's Liberation Front," and Young recalled them as fantastic people, although far more radical than most of the others. Their radicalism resulted in Lipton and Earthworm being squeezed out very shortly after GIRC was created. Into this vacuum came Young, whose involvement began in 1976. He fell into activism, and candidly admitted, "Up to that time, I'd always thought of myself as a closet case. I didn't see myself as having any

particular familiarity with gay organizing, or with the issues involved."
But, over time, he and others around him evolved, developed an analysis, and willingly embraced activism.

Young was wide-ranging in his gay politics. He was interested in
lobbying the Alberta and Canadian Human Rights Commissions while
also a critic of activist focus on the urban queer experience. As he said,
"I'd like to see our rural outreach working a lot better, too. Bob Harris
and I are both from Medicine Hat. We sit down and talk about it sometimes, and I remember how much I hated the place and realize that there
must be thousands of people there and in other places who feel trapped
there."[49] He found that there were people in Medicine Hat and Lethbridge eager to get involved – eager to do something – but that support
was key. Young also reflected on the controversy over the gay march
and of the divisions within the gay community in Calgary over the pros
and cons of marching. He disagreed with the conservative gay perspectives, particularly those individuals affiliated with MCC Calgary, but,
publicly at least, valued those "opinions being represented. Eventually, it's going to be a good thing. We're going to grow."[50] And they
did, launching the Gay Political Action Group (after GIRC imploded),
Gay Youth Group, Gay Fathers, Gay Academic Union, the Lesbian and
Gay Community Police Liason, Gallac, Apollo, *New Horizons*, and other
groups, all of which Young helped to encourage.[51]

Almost fifteen years later, after more conservative elements seized
control of GIRC and the organization's demise, Young gave his final
interview. Notes of Young's last interview with Cooper about his activism, his organizational work, and his legacy were less optimistic, more
resigned about the significant challenges and differences between
progressive, liberationist activists and their more middle-class, conservative cohorts. With an AIDS diagnosis, and having witnessed the
discriminatory treatment of AIDS patients, Young spoke bluntly and
honestly about his life's work. For a start, Young had paid a financial
price for his activism in lost jobs (activist notoriety and steady employment were not compatible), and this partially accounts for his anger
with what he called "the middle class sheep" within the community.
Periodically, in Calgary (see opening comments from Club Carousel)
as elsewhere in the prairies (Saskatoon, Regina, and Winnipeg interviews and print materials), more conservative gays or lesbians made
critical, simplistic statements about "those with nothing to lose" such as
Young, who they imagined as being cavalier about employment, willing to commit fully to activism. For activists like Young those words

stung. He had lost, and yet still kept on fighting and advocating for gay people regardless of the toll it exacted from him financially and emotionally. When he first became publicly identified as a gay activist he was working at Canada Customs, but very shortly afterwards he found himself out of work and "took to driving a cab. He also worked as manager at Jay's Relaxation Centre, a gay bathhouse."[52] Labelled a courageous "gay warrior" in a posthumous tribute essay published in the *Calgary Herald* (the irony of which would have amused Young and his friends, who knew of his battles with the *Herald* over their refusal to print classified ads for GIRC), writer Brian Brennan summarized the costs of such a role:

> Sometimes his was a lonely road to hoe. Within the gay community, there were conflicting interests at work. Doug often found himself on the opposite side of the fence to those who wanted to create a kind of hermetically sealed hothouse community for gays within the larger mainstream society. Young wanted gays to have a strong voice in the mainstream chorus of the cities. As a small-town Albertan, he also wanted gays to have some visibility and comfort in the rural areas, where they often felt trapped and vulnerable. "You might call him, in jest, one of the agrarians of the gay rights leadership" says a friend.[53]

According to Cooper, Doug Young and Doug Wilson were "uncompromising men." And in 1995, in handwritten notes that are included in the papers donated to the Glenbow, Cooper wrote "to see [Young's activism] in terms of 'social justice' and liberal radicalism as most who come here will be determined to do, is highly mistaken … The movement, at least as Doug conceived it began with a negative concept of freedom, as freedom to be left alone." Paramount in his conceptions of western gay activism was "pride and desire for autonomy" with a "local society with its own literature, and institutions." Young felt very strongly that gay rights groups should not accept government money because it compromised their autonomy, nor should western Canadian groups take direction from the central, national gay political movement that might not represent their issues. He was proud that during his time at GIRC they were entirely self-funded from dances and donations. Finally, Cooper explicitly noted that he disliked middle-class, urban paternalism, "Young had not despaired of rural society, or of small city and small town society. This differentiates [Wilson and Young] from the comfortable middle class ghetto gays … It is disrespectful to rural people to believe they are innately less tolerant or able to understand."[54] Young, Wilson, and others were ahead of their time with their political arguments for and support of rural and small-town queers, and particularly their beliefs that it should be possible to be gay or lesbian in farming communities and small towns, not just in larger, urban centres..[55] Their contributions to the prairie gay and lesbian movement offered a distinctive variant of gay activist thought and an explicit rebuke to outsiders' dismissive notions of rural and small-town prairie people.

(Not) "Everyone Loves a Parade": Calgary 1980

In May 1980, the secretary for GATE Edmonton sent a strongly worded letter to GIRC Calgary advising them of a motion the Edmonton group approved at their recent meeting: "Although we at GATE recognize that GIRC and other gay groups in Calgary are in the best position to decide what activities are acceptable in their own city; Nonetheless GATE regrets the decision to not hold a public march during the forthcoming CLGRC conference and urges GIRC and the Calgary gay community to reconsider; Further GATE especially regrets that groups which have chosen not to belong to CLGRC are attempting to influence legitimate CLGRC activities."[56] Awarded the opportunity to host the national gay and lesbians rights conference, Calgary's GIRC found themselves in a challenging situation with other Calgary organizations and businesses, notably the owners of the gay social clubs, Metropolitan Community Church and the drag organization (the Imperial Court of the Chinook Arch), all of which initially urged caution and ultimately demanded that plans for a parade be shelved.[57] These conservative groups (in interviews the Imperial Court of the Chinook Arch likened themselves to Rotary in drag) felt that such a march, a routine feature of Canadian national gay and lesbian conferences, would draw "unfavourable" attention to gays and lesbians. This was an odd position. Saskatoon's 1977 march had been a conference and city highlight. Winnipeg's 1974 march, while small, was also a success. GIRC went back and forth on the issue before they formally requested a parade permit. At which point, Brian Sawyer, Calgary's chief of police, denied the application. This also contrasts sharply with Saskatoon and Winnipeg where parade permits were readily obtained from the city police forces. The reaction to this chain of events, as it played out in the local paper and in the pages of *The Body Politic*, offered interesting insights into the local, provincial, and national fault lines. It also made bedfellows of interesting factions and individuals. For example, Calgary's mayor (and future Alberta premier) Ralph Klein was part of the minority group of city councillors who argued that "the discretionary powers of the police are too wide," and he and other councillors were concerned that Calgarians right to free assembly was compromised by the police decision to ban the parade.[58] As mayor, Klein had a history of contentious relations with the gay and lesbian community of Calgary. At times spontaneously supportive, he could also backpedal quickly when his read of the political tea leaves indicated he had overstepped and misjudged Calgarians appetite for diversity.[59] *Gay Horizons* reported that: "widespread media coverage was received for the Eighth National Conference of Lesbians and Gay Men when the *Calgary Albertan* the city's morning daily ran a front page story on March 2. The story unleashed a torrent of coverage in the print and electronic media that was greater than any single gay event ever received in the city." What had caused most of the interest was the "fact that the conference will include a gay parade through downtown Calgary. Parades or protest marches are virtually unknown in this city of over half a million people."[60] Yet, of course, this was not entirely true as Calgary was internationally renowned for their annual Stampede Parade with its pageantry of cowboy and western themes. In response, Robert Harris of GIRC wrote, "religious fundamentalists crashed from their closets calling for public morality and decency." But it wasn't just fundamentalists, gay organizations were also vehemently opposed. In April, GIRC had to change its plans "after considerable opposition was voiced at a meeting of the gay community." In particular, GIRC's information services director claimed "he was pressured by Brian Sargeant, past President of the Imperial Court of the Chinook Arch" and presented with a financial ultimatum: "Brian Sargeant told me that if GIRC didn't cancel the parade, the Court would withhold the money it had set aside to give to GIRC for the conference. He also said they (the Court) would keep the money we gave them for the benefit the Court is putting on for us."[61] Given assurances that GIRC would acquiesce to their request, the "petition started by unidentified members of the gay community opposing the march was destroyed after the march was cancelled."

A wide range of letters were printed over the parade controversy from within the city and from outside. Not all can be analysed here, but this episode offers insights into queer activities in Calgary and within Alberta. David Garmaise, with the Coordinating Office of the Canadian Lesbian and Gay Rights Coalition, the national group working with

Calgary to host the conference, sent a letter to clarify the process in Ottawa the previous year that, while no doubt intended to be helpful and to share strategies, starkly accentuated the differences: "At Celebration 79 in Ottawa we applied to our regional government for a permit to hold a demonstration and we included in our application an outline of the route of the demonstration. As a matter of course, the Ottawa Police were informed and it was they who escorted the demonstration through the streets of the Ottawa." Furthermore, Garmaise indicated that there was "no increase in violence against gays after the demonstration."[62] Comments such as these were regarded as tone-deaf to the local, Alberta situation, and were invariably cited when western activists critiqued the "national" activists for their recommendations. Patronizing, unaware of Calgary specificities, and seemingly unwilling to acknowledge that one-size-fits-all conference activism did not fit each local organizing situation, it merely fanned the flames of discontent. And queer Calgarians, no matter their politics, did not like to be upstaged by Ottawa. Another black mark against the Calgary conference was that the city's mayor refused to open the conference as Ottawa's Mayor Marion Dewar had the year before.[63] Adding insult to injury, the Victoria Park Community Association refused to rent its hall to Gay Information and Resources Calgary for the dance, on 28 June, to be held during Celebration 80. Victoria Park President Rick Penlington said, "his association does not rent to motorcycle gangs, or stag parties either, claiming the association did not want riots in the community. He made reference to the presence of children living in the Victoria Park neighbourhood." The dance was relocated to MacEwan Hall, University of Calgary campus.[64]

George Edin, a former editorial board member of Winnipeg's *After Stonewall* collective, then living in Calgary, wrote to *Gay Horizons* expressing his outrage over these debates and the fissures within the gay community: "As plans for a national gay conference have been unveiled, the bigots and Bible Thumpers have come out of the woodwork. That was to be expected. But what has prompted me to write this letter, is the totally unexpected attack on G.I.R.C. by other gays: Lloyd Greenway, pastor of M.C.C., Vance Campbell, owner of Myrts and the Parkside [bathhouse and social clubs]; and an unnamed representative of the Imperial Court of the Chinook Arch." After pointing out their business interests, and deriding the drag court for having the temerity to remind people not to "flaunt" their sexuality, Edin wrote, "Gay men and lesbians will only get their equality and freedom by being proud and strongly protesting the existing injustices."[65] From the opposite perspective, Calgarian Bill Holmes a Court wrote:

> Why should we antagonize the whole community of Calgary? They know we exist and have been more than happy to let us exist in the Community without much undue harassment ... I feel that if there is a march in Calgary, the slogan, "Kill a Fag for Christ" could well become a reality. We must remember that we do happen to live in what is commonly referred to as the Bible Belt of Canada. How many innocent Gays in Calgary want to become a martyr for the Gay Rights Movement in Canada???[66]

Holmes a Court's critique, while politically divergent from western queer progressives/liberationists, makes a similar, important point concerning *regional* challenges to *national* strategies – westerners of all political and non-political stripes were at odds with national views and disinclined to take direction. CLGRC disbanded in 1980 so Calgary's conference marked the end of national conferences. It reflected the reality that Canadian gay and lesbian activism was strongest locally and regionally. The precarious finances of local and "national" activist groups was also a factor since there were few government funds available (many groups would have refused such funding had it existed), and hence they were sustained by fundraisers, memberships, and donations.

In the end, no march was held. Approximately forty activists held a silent picket outside of Calgary's City hall on 28 June, and at the conclusion of their thirty-minute picket they sang O Canada before heading over to St Patrick's Island for their rally.[67] The debate over this issue and the cleavages it revealed between gay business interests, "discrete gays and lesbians," gay and lesbian activists, and straight and queer media illustrated many of the challenges and contradictions in the city. It was possible to be quietly gay in Calgary. In Holmes a Court's words, the city was "happy to let them exist" and many were grateful for this tolerance. Clearly they did not think anything more was possible. Others were not so comfortable taking the status quo for granted, given that it wasn't based on similar rights to privacy, assembly, or employment safeguards, things that their heterosexual colleagues, neighbours, and friends took for granted. Much hand-wringing went on about "marching" and "flaunting." Warnings about violence were intended to cast a shadow over the activist organizers goals for a "celebration" and for their desire to mark Calgary's emergence as a worthy centre of gay and lesbian activism. As the events that transpired in Edmonton in 1981 would remind people, rights are better than tolerance.

Pisces Bath Raid (1981)

Similar to the raid on Montreal's bathhouse in 1977 and Toronto's in February of 1981, the raid on Edmonton's gay bathhouse – the Pisces Spa – on 30 May 1981 became a major politicizing moment in the city. Newspaper accounts and oral histories all agree that this was an important watershed moment. My Edmonton narrators, both women and men, regarded this as a formative juncture. Interviewed about his experiences in Edmonton, Peter Pratt told me that if he were writing a "history of gayness in Edmonton" volume one would conclude with Pisces Spa raid. The Pisces "was radiant" and "the bath house raid would be the end of volume I because that was a major damper on what was then a growing community."[68] Another narrator, Michael Phair, dated his engagement with gay activism to the raid.[69] Edmonton's reaction (gay and straight) provides another vantage point on activism and resistance within Alberta.

Pisces Spa, a gay bathhouse, had operated in Edmonton for a couple of years without any overt hassles from the police or the city. In fact, as Phair recalled, gay men were under the impression that the Pisces, which was "considered the highest quality bathhouse in western Canada in terms of its standards" and located in a modern purpose building, was a safe space. Word on the street was that if one kept quiet, went to the baths and "stayed out of the way the police would not bother you."[70] According to the *Edmonton Journal*, "John," a member of Pisces Spa, called in a tip to the police because he was "disgusted" by the sexual activities there. Quoted in the paper, the unimaginatively named "John" said "being gay is obviously a difficult lifestyle. There are a lot of people who think we're sick or mental cases and places like the spa make it seem so."[71] Phair claimed that despite what the police said in press interviews about an anonymous tip, it was unclear who instigated this raid. At the time of our interview, Phair was then an elected city councillor in Edmonton, the first openly gay local politician in the city, so he was well placed to comment on these matters. Phair claimed it was still a mystery to him whether it was politically motivated within Edmonton City Hall or was inspired by the raids in Montreal and Toronto, and hence part of a wave of political repression.[72]

What was known was that starting in January 1981, the Edmonton police began staking out the Pisces Spa. Undercover police officers were sent into the premises, other officers taped men entering and leaving the building for five months before the raid was launched.[73] At two o'clock in the morning on Saturday 30 May, fifty-seven Edmonton policemen and RCMP police officers burst through the spa doors and rounded up sixty men found on the premises. Writing for *The Body Politic* Chris Bearchell wrote, "the cops played dirty, using video cameras, and middle-of-the-night trials. The mainstream press was suitably dismayed. Supportive straights staged a demonstration."[74] These men, who would later be charged as "found-ins" under the bawdy house laws in Canada's criminal code, were arraigned in a special five o'clock in the morning court hearing. The owners of the spa were charged with keeping a common bawdy house. A year earlier, newspaper reports of frequent gay bashings of hustlers on Edmonton's gay male stroll, on McDonald Dr between 100th and 101 St, criticized the police for their ineffectual presence. Warning of a "bloodbath," the article reported that "groups of ten men armed with knives and baseball bats have attacked hustlers working the strip," with several male prostitutes reporting that they "rarely see police patrolling the strip."[75] The president of the Edmonton gay club Boots n' Saddle told the *Journal* that he had "pieced together about four dozen assaults in the last five months, ranging from scare tactics to terrorizing gays in their own homes."[76] The police spokesman maintained that they were patrolling that area of downtown as frequently as the other areas.

Michael Phair was one of the found-ins and wrote articles about his experience in *Fine Print* the local gay newspaper. In our interview, he was also generous with his reflections about this galvanizing event: "I was really annoyed with myself with not knowing enough about what was going on … I remember distinctly … how mad I was and how ignorant I was about what was happening with the police and the judge that was there at that time… and what rights I did or didn't have."[77] He became one of the men willing to serve as a spokesperson, which, given his employment in the Department of Education, was a brave move. Others would be scared back into the proverbial closet by these events, but Phair and others recognized that "you couldn't just be quiet and gay and everything would be okay" – it was political and he realized he had to be politically involved.[78]

The day after the raid, GATE issued a "Gay Alert" claiming that this was the "first offensive by Edmonton police against gay people in this city."[79] GATE, Dignity (the gay Catholic organization), and MCC (Metropolitan Community Church) mobilized to help people, in particular those charged, to deal with the aftershocks from the media publicity. Counselling and support were available, and they contacted a lawyer to provide the men with information about their charges and the process. An evening meeting was scheduled for 3 June at Flashbacks Bar. GATE urged people to call the chief of police and the mayor "to make sure the responsible authorities are informed at our outrage at this violation of our private lives." Gay activists had long asserted, and various raids on bathhouses made clear, that while patrons believed such spaces were private (and they were intended as private commercial sexual sites), in the eyes of the police and the law these businesses were "public" spaces. Furthermore, those present asked the key question that many in the community and supporters outside were asking: "How so many officers could be mobilized for this raid concerning activities which have no victims when the police department's response time to trouble calls is so dismal?"[80]

Following precedents established in Montreal and Toronto where similar police raids had galvanized and politicized the gay communities on 1 June, the Privacy Defence Committee of Edmonton was created to "give support and protection to those arrested at the Pisces raid by raising funds to help defray their legal expenses; to offer assistance to others who may find themselves in similar circumstances; and to advocate for changes in the privacy provisions of the Criminal Code."[81] The committee had already raised $3,000 towards legal fees, and the Privacy Defence Committee included people from gay political, religious, and social agencies, with Doug Whitfield, from GATE and ALGRA, chosen as their spokesperson. Their release indicated that monies had also been received from Toronto. A rally, organized by a heterosexual Edmonton couple, Ken Bolton and Kathy Rankin, was held outside of City Hall to support those arrested and to protest the police raid. "The issue isn't homosexuality and it isn't prostitution," Bolton reported to the *Edmonton Journal*, "it's what we see as a misuse of the law to legislate private morality."[82] The Pisces raid was widely covered in local queer periodicals, such as *Grassroots* and *The Body Politic*. "Attack on Edmonton Gays" indicated that "gays and defenders of civil rights fought back" in their 3 June rally with a "crowd of 150" hearing statements of support for gay rights to sexual expression from women's, civil rights, and labour groups."[83] Support was not forthcoming from the management and owners of the Pisces Spa, which provoked a sense of betrayal in the gay community in both Edmonton and Toronto.

Within the city, this raid stirred up considerable media interest. It was breaking news, reported on the front pages of newspapers and on the nightly radio and television newscasts. The 2 June edition of the *Edmonton* Journal editorial warned "Chief Robert Lunney should remind his officers that they are servants to the law; they are not the law itself."[84] Phair recalled that the media were more negative about the raids than some might have anticipated, and he believed this "surprised the police" who had not anticipated criticism for their actions. Phair remembered various media raising questions about police resources, about whether they didn't have anything better to do, particularly since no drugs or alcohol charges were laid, no underage participants were found, and given that everyone there was a consenting adult.[85] Support came from many corners, although sensationalism and titillation were part of the attraction as residents speculated openly about who was charged and the "sort" of men who engaged in such activities. The newspapers did not publish a list of the found-ins names, but CFRN TV published the list of names for "5–6 seconds," which was, for one of the men charged, "long enough for people I work with to see it plus others and ask us."[86] Beyond those arrested in the raid, news reports that the club's two-thousand-person membership list had been seized by police created another set of worries and further fanned media interest. Talk radio host Eddie Keen, from CHED 630 AM, aired a short commentary on 8 June about the raid and the firestorm of debate it ignited. His commentary, a transcript of which was included with the Privacy Defence papers, offers some insight into the reaction of straight Edmontonians, both the homophobic and the supportive. Keen wrote: "there's been a lot of snickering and whispering and wondering since that raid on a gay club last week ... everywhere I go people are calling me over and asking ... have you seen the list ... any big names on it?"[87] Keen admitted he had no knowledge of the people on the list. He said media and observers were split into two camps: "one says reveal the names of all of those found in there ... punish them, ridicule them ... the other point of view is that what grown men do behind the walls of a private club is their business." Continuing, Keen explained that the club's owners were making $24,000 a month off this venture, and hence in his books it wasn't "private" but rather a sexual establishment catering to gays – and in this regard little different from a brothel. Interestingly, the most prominent Edmonton resident involved was not a found-in but one of the owners, Dr Henry Toupin, "the city's foremost neurologist." Toupin and his two business partners appeared in court for an unscheduled, late-afternoon appearance where they quickly plead guilty, and Toupin was fined $10,000. The Defence Committee was shocked (perhaps naively) that while they counselled the found-ins to plead not guilty and to challenge the laws, management's primary objective had been to minimize bad press, publicity, and to cut their losses. GATE strongly condemned their actions. In a press release, they stated: "GATE feels that the owners of Pisces acted irresponsibly; for several years they made money on Edmonton gays, and then, when those gays were under attack, the owners betrayed them."[88] Furthermore, the owners of the Pisces pled guilty and refused to offer any help whatsoever to the Privacy Defence Committee, which was set up to assist the found-ins and to contribute to their costs. In retaliation, GATE indicated that henceforth it would not provide referrals to the "new bath" in the city unless the owners of The Courtyard Club would confirm that they would cooperate and financially assist patrons should a similar event occur.[89]

Keen was critical of the special treatment Toupin received, and he stressed to listeners that though the situation seemed novel because it involved same-sex sexual activity this was little different from much illicit heterosexual sexual activity that routinely took place in Edmonton. In his concluding statement, Keen admonished listeners about the inherent dangers of calling for queer men's names to be released and harsher penalties: "Be careful about being hypocritical ... if we are going to expose customers in a gay club, then we had better start identifying johns picked up with prostitutes ... can you imagine the howling if that happened? ... I can tell you that some days that list would read like a who's who of big business, big politics, corrupt religion and pillars of the community."[90] Keen was not a "liberal," nor was his news talk program routinely progressive in the views expressed. What is interesting here is how he succinctly reminded Edmonton listeners that illicit sexuality was prevalent. He made explicit the similarities around illicit sexual acts and behaviours, gay and straight, encouraging male listeners to be aware that the exposure of one group's sexual adventures could have repercussions on another – far larger – group's adventures. Many prominent "pillars of the community" might not like to find themselves in a similar spotlight. Men should, Keen believed, stick together.

Beyond the salacious details, what appeared to perplex some Edmontonians was the question: just what sort of men would use such facilities? Newspaper stories indicated that the men ranged in age and background and that not all were Edmonton residents, some were from small towns or rural areas. Demographically, there were single and married men, new immigrants, and Euro-Canadians. Some articles tried to explain (ostensibly to the naive, but there was a prurient interest expressed as well) what motivated men to participate in activities at the Pisces Club. For example, an *Edmonton Journal* article told the story of a "closet gay," a "27 year old Athabasca farmboy," who reportedly told the court that the Pisces Spa was "'like a refuge.'"[91] Shrewdly ascribing him as a wholesome, ordinary Albertan with the use of the term "farmboy," his lawyers led him through a narrative that stressed why such facilities were necessary. Farmboy told the court that twice monthly he left his small town and came to Edmonton, "where he could drop the 'dual personality' he adopted in his early twenties, when he recognized his homosexuality and began hiding it." At the Pisces he "could meet his friends and relax and socialize in an atmosphere he couldn't find in his home community." Interestingly, he told the court about half of his visits involved meeting the same person. Such commentary speaks to the coping strategies of some small-town gays, whose livelihood (farming) seemed incompatible with an explicitly gay life. Hence, he made routine sojourns into the city for companionship and sex, before returning to the farm. A number of the other found-ins were northern resource workers on furlough. They too had a long tradition of using their furloughs to head into cities in search of urban pleasures and recreation: food, drink, sex, socializing, and shopping. What might have been viewed as "blowing off steam" if oil rig workers were found with female prostitutes or in a brothel was depicted very differently when it involved same-sex activities. Though the police sought to reassure citizens that they were not harassing gays – nor were the raids the beginning of a gay purge in Edmonton – Staff Sergeant John Torgenson, the head of the morality squad, nevertheless told the papers that the Edmonton City Police "take a very hard line here in morality, the integrity of the police department is at stake." Furthermore, he sought to reassure people, "I want people to know that if they deal with us they're dealing with a scrupulously honest bunch."[92]

Few of the people rounded up in the raid willingly went public with their stories. One who did was Michael Phair. For Phair, the raid proved a defining moment. Phair offered very effective public and print recollections of the experience – and the terror, shame, fear, and outrage he felt about being subjected to such homophobic treatment by the police, the courts, and the media. In a series of essays in *Fine Print* he wrote, "as justice unfolded Alberta style I was appalled at the dark underside of bias and injustice that I witnessed in the courts." For instance, "the owners of Pisces were fined over $45,000 more than ten times the amount of any previous bawdy house case."[93] Similarly, "in the vast majority of similar cases in Alberta, charges against the found-ins have either been dropped or discharged, especially when the owners plead guilty." Lawyers Sheila Greckol and Barrie Chivers, who represented one of the Pisces found-ins, concurred with Phair, noting in media interviews that "the raid was conducted in an offensive manner ... reminiscent of more authoritarian times."[94] Chris Bearchell remembered that Edmonton gays "were desperate and felt trapped ... The gay organization in Edmonton has a long, continuous history. But like a lot of smaller communities they had limited resources." Importantly, though, "the raid was a test by fire. Edmonton's gays went through it and came out stronger."[95] For the sake of comparison, in Toronto, the February 1981 bath raids led to massive street protests and rallies on Yonge Street, and in front of 52 Division. Thousands of queers chanting "no more shit" challenged the police – but also the city at large – about harassment and homophobia. Edmonton's protest rally was considerably smaller. The "Straights against Discrimination Rally" on 3 June outside Edmonton City Hall "to which an estimated 100 people turned out."[96] Gerald Hannon, from *The Body Politic*, arrived in town to cover the events and brought support from Toronto. He discovered that after the shock of the raids, and the ensuing exposure, Edmonton gays and lesbians were less inclined to angrily take to the streets and garner more notoriety.

Many wondered what purpose the raid served. Indeed, much talk focused on the ways that the police and courts system set out to vilify the men arrested and the community at large, with their heavy-handed tactics and overtly homophobic statements. To cite just one example, in his concluding statements in the first Pisces found-in trial, Crown Prosecutor Morrey Ferries told the court that the spa was a place for "depraved" and "pathetic individuals." While he adhered to the standards of the law, which meant stressing that "homosexuality is not an offense" Ferries explained what was offensive about the activities in the Pisces Spa, was that, in his opinion, "it is an offence for people to rut like animals in place specifically designed for that purpose."[97] Concluding one of the trials, Provincial Court Judge R.E. Hyde took the opportunity to admonish the members of the audience from the Privacy Defence Committee and a few found-ins, stating "you're criminals, all of you, criminals."[98] For his own part, Phair's journey through the system was harrowing and depressing, having plead not guilty, on the advice of the Privacy Defence Committee lawyer, he represented himself and was ultimately found guilty and fined $250. He appealed to a higher court and was eventually exonerated after nearly two years of fighting. In Phair's estimation, the raid "rattled our complacency just enough to ensure that it will never happen again." Few took the route Phair did, as most men plead guilty to get the court exposure over with quickly and with a minimal amount of attention. The spokesperson for the Privacy Defence Committee, Phil Knight, was critical of the costs to the community and the province: "The raid clogged up the courts for months, cost a lot of money, and for what? ... It wrecked some people's lives, some had to come out to wives and families, and others had to leave town." Not surprisingly, some men were driven back into the closet, others suffered from "alcohol-related problems," and one individual "was almost suicidal, and had to be watched over day and night during the trials ... he was from a smaller community and was afraid of his home town finding out about his involvement in the raid."[99]

In interviews and retrospectives, many people who were active in gay and lesbian activism in Edmonton noted the importance of the Pisces Spa raid for the way in which it spurred the community into action. It pointedly illustrated how the absence of sexual orientation in the provincial human rights code was a severe liability, as well it illustrated that people were not "safe" in their chosen clubs, bars, and organizations. It also pointed to the wide discretion in interpretation of the bawdy-house legislation:

> At stake is the right of gay people to engage in sexual activity in a place that is in fact private. Because of the wording of the law, a private home or any other place can be interpreted as being a common bawdy house. Any place to which one or more people visit to engage in "indecent acts," whether prostitution is involved or not, is a bawdy house ... The police in Toronto have already charged 2 people for being keepers of common bawdy houses in respect to their own private homes ... The law effectively denies the right to privacy, and this aspect of the law has already been applied in a very discriminating way against gay people.[100]

Equally, it made some members of Edmonton's community far more visible to the public at large. In that July's Klondike Days celebrations, the Privacy Defence Committee entered a bathtub in the bathtub races, entitled the S.S. Pisces II. These "six intrepid and foolhardy soldiers sailed the notorious pink triangle down the North Saskatchewan River" on board their "Gay Nineties Bathhouse."[101] This defiant entry openly tweaked the media and assembled observers, particularly when the participant's sang their revised version of the Sesame Street song "Rubber Ducky You're the One" for the judges. They didn't win the race, but this gay political theatre was a considerable success in terms of visibility – both that day and in press coverage, as their photo was featured on the front page of the *Edmonton Sun*. The individual losses for the found-ins were substantial but this episode gave the community some resolve to fight back and to begin a more concerted effort towards politicization. Some took this as a cue to be more open and activist so that liberal-minded Edmontonians (who were starting to be supportive) had alternative, positive representations of gay and lesbian lives, not just the stories related by courts, police, and the media of the "depraved" and "pathetic" individuals rounded up in the darkness of an early morning raid.

One of the ways in which it is clear that the raid did turn the tide in Edmonton can be seen by the increasing growth of gay and lesbian organizations and of civic visibility within a few years after the raid. For instance, for the first time ever the city's lesbians and gays celebrated gay pride festivities in 1982 with the theme "pride through unity." The gay pride committee was composed of people from a variety of groups – including GATE, Dignity/Edmonton, Gay Fathers, the Imperial Court of the Wild Rose, the Privacy Defence Committee, and Womonspace.[102] The newsletter *The Gay Gleaner* pegged attendance at this first pride week at 450 to 500 people. While the newsletter was quick to note that "there were no marches or demonstrations," those who attended the city's pride events had a wide range of activities from which to choose, including an open house at GATE, dinner and show organized by the Imperial Court of the Wild Rose at Flashback's, a baseball tournament organized by the Roughnecks (a gay men's sports club), a pride dance, and then, the final activity, a barbecue held on the outskirts of Edmonton, at Camp Harris, where Dignity sponsored its fourth annual picnic. In analysing the success of this venture, the *Gleaner* reported, "in the past gay groups in Edmonton have functioned more or less independently, although GATE has occasionally co-sponsored dances with other organizations. For the first time Edmonton's gay community really was a *community* in the full sense of the word; a group of people sharing, co-operating, supporting. As a result new friendships have been formed, understanding between the city's various groups has improved, and

Edmonton gays have a greater feeling of pride" (emphasis in original).[103] Phair remembered that after the raids, "there was a huge growth of new organizations, gay and lesbian organizations and groups and activities that sprang up … That really came out of that sense that we've got to do more. We wanted to do more. Some of them were just sports groups and were not politically aimed," but he sensed that all felt compelled that it was "time to get moving here a bit."[104] Pratt echoed that view, stating that the next phase of Edmonton's history – that is, post raid – was one he would characterize as "the agency phase." The most important agency to emerge would be founded around Michael Phair's kitchen table – AIDS Network of Edmonton – in the mid-1980s.[105]

Documenting Edmonton Queer Life:
"The Gay Straight Jacket," 1981

Momentum and interest in Edmonton's gays and lesbians continued to build after the bath raids. In November 1981, CBC Edmonton aired a twenty-minute documentary entitled "The Gay Straight Jacket," which was intended to explore a broader spectrum of gay and lesbian life than what was portrayed in news reports of the bath raids and ensuing court coverage.[106] The gay community newsletter, *The Gay Gleaner*, carried significant coverage of what was described as "one of the most important television events of the past few months."[107] Aired in prime time, this short documentary provided a "tour of the clubs, a visit to the hill and into peoples' homes. We met bar owners and patrons, a hustler, two gay couples, a transvestite, university professors, G.A.T.E. peer counsellors and clergy. With the exception of the hustler and one clergyman, all were gay."[108] According to the gay journalists, the majority of phone calls about the program were positive, which was mirrored by the views of the gay journalists/activists who wrote short reviews of the programme for the community newsletter. Gay and lesbian viewers expected a "patronizing, distorted heterosexual view," and thus, while "flawed," it was, with a couple of important exceptions, deemed "non-judgmental."

Viewers criticized the time devoted to interviews and images from the hill and voyeuristic comments about sex. Most criticism was reserved for the interview with "Marcel" (all names were aliases) where the bar patron was pointedly asked if his parents knew he was gay. Marcel indicated they did not know, and then the interviewer blasted the young man, telling him: "If they don't accept you, it'll kill you,

you know that!"[109] Given the use of aliases, and with a camera technique that alternated between shooting people from behind or obscuring their faces, it further led to the impression that gays in Edmonton had to lead covert lives. Walter's analysis of the program highlighted those concerns: "Until we can freely show our faces on television, and reveal our identity, we reinforce the public's image of us as people who hide because we are *ashamed*," he wrote (emphasis in original). "The rear view interviews distressed me. They were a sad reminder of the oppression which we are often, alas, forced by circumstance to accept and endure in order merely to survive."[110]

In the following issue of the *Gleaner*, Lena, one of a lesbian couple interviewed in the program, voiced her upset over the criticism of anonymity in the program. Lena wrote "both Lynn and I are (or were) out at work, to our friends, and to our families, and so we were not concerned about these people. But we were concerned about redneck straight men who might want to 'straighten us out,'" and neither one of them was willing to risk an assault or rape for the sake of the documentary.[111] Having recently lost her job, she also did not wish to risk a job search by openly identifying as a lesbian on local television. Lena's wrath was reserved for the imbalanced coverage allotted to gay men and lesbians. She was resentful at the time she provided to the "obnoxious male chauvinist interviewer only to see it cut out. Not one word was mentioned about lesbian lifestyles, the particular problems of lesbians, or feminist issues. I am really angry about our five-second token appearance when so much time was devoted to male hustlers: there are more of us than of them!" As with so many other media portraits, unless lesbians were the sole focus of the programme or article, they tended to get ignored or marginalized in articles about the "gay world." In her analysis, "women making it on their own was probably too threatening for most Edmontonians to handle."

GATE Revisited: Being "Passively Political" in Edmonton 1982

In 1982, Edmonton's *Gay Gleaner* printed an editorial debating the issue of how or whether the city's long-standing organization Gay Alliance towards Equality was or was not political. While its name suggested as much, the confusion had been sowed by the organization itself, which accentuated their so-called "non-political" contributions: "educational, supportive, social" in a fundraising brochure produced in late 1981.[112] The rationale for this positioning was due, the writers' claimed, to a widely held view in the city that GATE was too political for most tastes. The recurrent refrain, similar to that expressed in Thorsell's recollections (see chapter 5), was "I don't go there it is too political."[113]

The writers believed this was a mistake and a mischaracterization of an organization that might not be "militant" but that deserved commendation for their support in the city. Instead of militancy, they characterized GATE as a "passively political" organization as necessitated by the current needs of its membership. In particular, they highlighted GATE's social and political work, providing an important frame for readers to think critically about the politics of everyday socializing, consciousness-raising, and education: "Establishing and maintaining a freely available drop in centre, a setting in which our alienation, for a moment, ceases to exist and in which the open flow of thought and feeling, unfettered by fear of exposure to hostility, away from the censoriousness of society, can take place – that is political."

Counselling work, sometimes derided as social service work, was also applauded for its political value: "To counsel gay men and women to appreciate not just their equality … but their self worth – that is political." Sending speakers to schools, creating libraries "to educate … that is really political. For education is the most fundamental, the most radical thing a political organization can do." They applauded the growth of discos, bars, spas, and sports teams, but claimed that such spaces were not as keenly invested in change. Instead, it was the "quiet political work of organizations like GATE, like the perpetual drops of water falling from the roof of an underground cavern, can and do shape things, albeit slowly and quietly."[114] Clearly, they thought GATE was underselling itself or attempting to downplay its "political" work in an effort to launch a successful fundraising campaign, but the newspaper's view that quiet, less flashy politics should still be viewed as politics is an important one.

Mid-1980s Gay and Lesbian Activism

Elizabeth Massiah arrived in Edmonton in 1983 (having come out as a lesbian in 1981), and remembered her shock and anger at her diminished status in society from married, heterosexual woman to lesbian: "I was so stunned that I didn't have legal rights when I came out and then when I just instantly moved into this weird category where I was in danger … I gave up all of my privileges I was just astonished and I said why the hell didn't somebody tell me that!? … I was just stunned and very indignant and naïve, I thought well we'll just go get this changed."[115] Such personal discoveries fuelled many of the Edmonton gay activists, a small core of a dozen or so activists in the mid-1980s and early 1990s. Massiah's experiences were, like many activists', highly personal and individual (with respect to her own trajectory of identification as a lesbian and embrace of identity politics) and spoke to a particular sense of middle-class professional overconfidence that, having articulated the "problem," solutions could be easily found. It was not, as she and others discovered, merely about naming the problem, solutions involved sea changes in political views about queer people and that required much public education and lobbying.

Interviewees who were knowledgable about Edmonton's gay and lesbian activism credit three major galvanizing events/issues for stimulating gay and lesbian activism. The first, the Pisces Spa Raid (above) made it abundantly clear that it was not sufficient to be "quietly" gay in Edmonton. Risks posed by inadequate laws and the lack of human rights legislation could have perilous consequences. One could be charged with a crime for participating in consensual sex in a private commercial space and subsequently risk one's employment, family, and friendship networks. That moment, and many smaller personal moments of discovery of second-class status, fuelled successive waves of activism within Edmonton. Activism in Edmonton was, like elsewhere, two pronged – lobbying the government for legislated human rights protection and striving to educate the populace about gays and lesbians. The second major game changer was AIDS and activism surrounding people living with HIV. In the mid-1980s, when AIDS came to Edmonton, there was an explosion of organizational development, activism, and attention paid to gay men (in particular), which stimulated health activism. Third, as already noted, was the Vriend case in the early 1990s – which sparked an activist trend.

Because AIDS and Vriend happened outside the parameters of this study, the activism in Edmonton seems more truncated than in Winnipeg or Saskatoon. Partly this is about resources and sources, which were not as plentiful for Edmonton, nor were lesbian and gay narrators as willing to do interviews. Some activists, like Maureen Irwin, were already deceased, others had moved away, but others were frankly burnt out and not keen to talk.[116] However, it was also because activism was a smaller force in Edmonton and personalized within a small coterie of individuals – whether in the 1970s with GATE, GIRC in Calgary, and the formation of ALGRA. In 1979, Bob Harris wrote "the gay movement in Alberta took a major step toward cooperation and increased inter-group activity at the Alberta Gay Conference in Edmonton, April 21, 1979 by creating Alberta Lesbian and Gay Rights Association (ALGRA). This was the first Alberta conference ever, and the event attracted over 20 delegates from Calgary, Edmonton and Red Deer."[117] Groups attending were Edmonton Lesbian and Gay Rights Association (ELGRO), Gay Alliance towards Equality (GATE), Dignity Edmonton, Metropolitan Community Church Edmonton, and the Edmonton Women's Coalition. The Gay Association of Red Deer attended with one Calgary group in attendance, Gay Information and Resources Calgary. They agreed to be part of the national organization, CLGRC, and elected two reps to serve on that body – Clare McDuff-Oliver from Edmonton and Doug Young of Calgary.

Institutionally, much change occurred in the 1980s, which meant that it was a transition period for queer activism and issues. In the 1980s there was GALA and later GLCCE. Liz Massiah in her interview credited a few key players – Phair, Irwin, Barry Gross, Katharine – with keeping much of Edmonton's organizational core going. In Calgary, Doug Young, Bob Harris, and Henry Berg were equally hard-working. Massiah recalled, "we had the Tories convinced that we were this huge group … they thought there was thousands of us in GALA and we had all this money. We never told them any different."[118] In reality they were about ten people, and, as she recalled, "a lot of politicians weren't very smart," we sent "three versions of the letter and put it on four different colours of paper, it's a hell of a long letter and it comes to your office all signed by the same ten people. And these 'stupid Tories' would say 'God you guys, how do you do it? We just smiled.'" One of the driving forces was Maureen Irwin who Massiah described as "everybody's great grandmother. She was just powerful because she was this strong, feminine out lesbian, had more grandkids that she could shake a stick at … She had the trust of the United Church … everyone loved her and she didn't put up with crap from anybody." When Irwin died Massiah recalled that they flew the provincial flag "at half mast."

Maureen Irwin

Irwin came to lesbian activism late, after a heterosexual marriage and raising four kids. Employed as a librarian at the *Edmonton Journal* newspaper, and through her friendships with some of the feminist journalists at the paper, she discovered the local independent bookshop Common Woman Books. It was there she first discovered positive books about lesbianism and in volunteering at the store she met a larger circle of feminist friends. In 1978, her husband asked for a separation and subsequently a divorce. After discussions with a counsellor, she was determined to kick-start her life again and in 1981 she came out as lesbian. Immediately, Irwin began to get involved with a host of activist activities in Edmonton – she was one of the founders of Womonspace, which provided an alternative space for lesbian women to socialize (outside of the bars), worked the phone lines at GATE (later GALA), and eventually got involved with the drive for gay and lesbian rights. The recipient of a number of civic, gay, and national honours for her extensive volunteer work, in 1993 the Pride Committee of Edmonton created the Maureen Irwin Award for Committee Service. When Irwin died in 2002, she was treated to a glowing Life and Times feature in the *Edmonton Journal* that eulogized her as one of "Edmonton's leading lesbian activists."[119]

One of Irwin's finest moments came in 1990, at a Edmonton conference entitled "Flaunting It!," which brought activists, lawyers, and prairie and federal human rights commissioners together for two days of discussion and debate about how to successfully advance the agenda for gay and lesbian rights in Alberta. Irwin was one of the co-organizers in her capacity as a spokesperson for GALA. In a poignant and very effective speech, she reflected on her life, stating:

> During the 23 years I was married I had all the rights of a Canadian citizen. But since my separation and divorce I have lived for the last 13 years as a lesbian in Alberta without most of the rights that were afforded to me before. Am I any less a person now than I was when I had a Mrs. in front of my name? Of course not, but let me tell you how the laws of Alberta have treated me and you may understand why I feel the need to work to change them. It is not just so my children and my grandchildren can live in a better, fairer, province but because I am a person and it is the right thing to do. We should not have to pay our dues to get admitted to the Club of Equal Rights.[120]

Irwin went on to describe how her lesbian status resulted in her inability to get a mortgage or insurance with her same-sex partner; her failure to receive medical and dental coverage; her challenges negotiating the hospital system, where she had to constantly explain her situation so as to be with her hospitalized partner and was barred from acting as next of kin when it came to treatment decisions; and the final indignity was that she was told that her will could be contested by her children. The speech was a powerful one, and at the conclusion the audience erupted in applause. The following day, the *Edmonton Journal* carried a quote from Irwin, criticizing Fil Fraser, then Alberta's chief human rights commissioner, for his admonition to gays and lesbians to "try and show people that you're okay" in a non-confrontational way. To try to emphasize his point, and to make his message more palatable, Fraser revealed that he too understood the challenges of being a minority, sharing his autobiographical experiences as a black, Protestant, middle-class man raised in a working-class, Catholic area of Montreal. Visibly angered by this patronizing advice, Irwin told reporters, "I need these rights now ... not in ten years or when Mr. Fraser thinks I've earned it!"[121]

In 1993, Irwin and her partner, Sheryl McInnes, flew to Ottawa so that Irwin could receive the Canada Volunteer Award Medal and Certificate of Honour. She was the first "openly lesbian activist" to receive this award.[122] The award recognized her over thirty-year history of volunteering with a wide range of organizations, including the United Church of Canada, the Girl Guides of Canada, Urban Manor (Edmonton homeless organization), Multiple Sclerosis Edmonton, Diabetes Canada, Take Back the Night Marches, the National Action Committee on the Status of Women, and International Women's Day to cherry pick from an extensive list of board memberships, leadership positions, and volunteer activity. It was her work in Edmonton's gay and lesbian community – recognized with an award from GALA – that meant the most to her. Irwin was a "member, board member and founder of four major gay and lesbian organizations in Edmonton: the Gay and Lesbian Community Centre, Womonspace, Parents and Friends of Lesbians and Gays, and Gay and Lesbian Awareness Society (GALA)."[123] She won the GALA "Woman of the Year Award" (which was later named for Irwin), showing just how foundational a figure she was within the city.

Such simple but effective calls for equity were made by other prairie gay activists, including Winnipeg's Chris Vogel and Richard North, Saskatoon's Gens Hellquist, Peter Millard and Doug Wilson, Calgary's Doug Young and Stephen Locke, and Edmonton's Liz Massiah, Michael Phair, and Delwyn Vriend – to name just a few prominent advocates for gay and lesbian rights. What impresses with all these and other unnamed activists, in work that spanned from the late 1960s through to the present, was their bravery in stepping into the harsh media spotlight. Every call for gay and lesbian rights triggered an onslaught of homophobic, often religiously inspired, critique. While this has lessened over the course of time, it remains a defining fact of life in the prairies. Similarly, it would have been far easier to take their activism to

8.1 Maureen Irwin, *Perceptions*, 28 July 1993. Neil Richards Collection of
Sexual Diversity in the University of Saskatchewan Archives
and Special Collections. Image courtesy of Neil Richards.

other, more congenial cities, but these people's determination to work
to create changes for gays and lesbians in the prairies demonstrates
their commitment to making the prairie west a more equitable and livable place for all queer westerners.

Conclusion: Out of Adversity, Pride

The impetus for the first gay pride celebration in Edmonton emerged
from the anger and chaos occasioned by the raid on the Pisces Spa. The
fight against another more potent foe – AIDS – would prove a sober rallying cry for renewed activism and visibility in Edmonton. Edmonton's
first confirmed case of AIDS occurred in 1984 and the community's first
death, of an Edmonton expat then living in Toronto, followed the next
year. Michael Phair, along with others, would work to found the AIDS
Network of Edmonton in 1986. Initially, the network operated out of

Phair's home, and was an all-consuming voluntary effort. In recognition of Phair's tireless work, the *Edmonton Journal* named Phair Edmonton's Citizen of the Year in 1987 – the first time this award recognized gay activism/volunteerism and was awarded to an openly gay activist.[124] He went on to run successfully for Edmonton's city council, where he became the first openly gay elected official in Edmonton when he was elected in 1992.[125] He served on council for fifteen years, representing the downtown and south side, and helped to launch a wide range of programs for children, the arts, queer people, and the city's disadvantaged.

The history of overt gay and lesbian activism in Edmonton began in the 1970s, starting slowly and cautiously with attempts to lobby the provincial government for amendments to the proposed IRPA. While it was clear that social activities, whether the membership-only Club 70 or later the commercial gay bars, were far more popular than activism, it would be simplistic to view these two types of gay and lesbian spaces and organizations as parallel or competing ventures. They were clearly connected. People bought *The Body Politic* at Club 70, they had occasion to read about political developments in the club newsletter, and were provided with information about how to get involved in activism. As Womonspace founder Maureen Irwin acknowledged, through social activities, friendships, partnerships, and a renewed sense of identity and pride, women and men, came to a variety of political conclusions. A determined handful openly embraced politics and activism. Others, like the Pisces found-ins, had it thrust upon them. Not all, naturally, became energized to the degree that Phair and Irwin did in their respective battles for justice.

It is evident that Edmonton was a cautious place, and gay men and lesbians were not as keen on "publicity" as they would be in other cities, namely Toronto, Vancouver, or even Saskatoon, where gay politics managed to merge more successfully with the province's leftist tilt and offered gay and straight activist alliances tremendous scope for change. But, by comparison with Calgary, Edmonton could and did often seem remarkably liberal. In this they drew upon Edmonton's lengthy tradition (by Alberta standards) of political activism; they drew upon the students and sometimes faculty of the University of Alberta; and they were enriched by the coterie of gay professionals who came to Alberta for employment – Roberts, Irwin, Phair, Massiah and others – who then found themselves contributing not only their professional skills but their gay and lesbian activist perspectives. Unlike Saskatoon, which sought to be explicitly political, Edmonton was political when provoked. But, when they were provoked, whether in Pisces or via the scourge of AIDS, they created a host of organizations to meet those challenges.

Beyond the top tier of gay and lesbian professionals and leaders who migrated to Edmonton and served as important organizational leaders, the city attracted many more queer migrants from the region and beyond. Some were infrequent sojourners and visitors – gay farmers who came into the city to meet queer friends at the baths before heading back to the farm and their "conventional" lives. Others moved into Edmonton to take part in the larger opportunities available there. Where they differ from Saskatoon and Winnipeg, naturally, was in the scale of the boom and the particularities of the resource and governmental surge of employment. Given their proximity to BC and the ease of travel, Edmontonians were also adept at travelling to Vancouver, as well as to American cities; because of this, they imported various American and Canadian gay organizations to the city – Metropolitan Community Church (originally from California); Dignity (American Catholic organization); pride festivities; Privacy Defence Committee (Toronto); and the list goes on. Some might argue that such imports lessen the distinctiveness of Edmonton, making it a branch plant town for queer activities and organizations. Those who would make these arguments probably have not lived in Alberta where, faced with the onslaught of right wing, often "Christian"-infused media (including the provocative "newsmagazine" *Alberta Report*, 1973–2003), gays and lesbians faced battles over their ability to determine their own lives. Of the cities in this study, Edmonton was perhaps the most challenging in which to be queer.[126] And, most important, Alberta was the very last province in the country to recognize gay and lesbian human rights to employment and housing.

This chapter illustrates the history upon which the Vriend case drew, the organizations and activists who were working towards the achievement of the human rights extensions beginning in the early 1970s, and the growing demands for justice and visibility. It also illustrates the level of general homophobia both within the straight community but also through the fissures with the queer communities in Edmonton and Calgary. The Pisces raid was a dramatic reminder of police oppression. But the depressing list of discrimination enumerated in "A Minority without Rights" – lost jobs, careers, apartments, violence, and refusals to be served in bars *with reputations as queer spaces* – illuminates the challenges of Alberta. The quotes at the outset of the chapter speak also to the Edmonton paradox – a more enlightened city in a province not noted for such accommodation and tolerance. As well, similar to the other two cities, Edmonton was a place where, despite its challenges, queer people could find friends, partners, clubs, and groups – they could be gay or lesbian in a way that small towns (like Moose Jaw) and rural communities couldn't possibly accommodate. Assessment of Edmonton's livability is all relative. These cities should not just be judged as wanting by outsiders and expats. They were destinations for small-town queers who believed that Edmonton and Calgary represented significant improvement on smaller towns and rural areas. Doug Young's experiences in Medicine Hat and Ottawa were both hellish by comparison with Calgary. Similarly, the early group of men who created GARD all subsequently moved to Calgary for greater gay opportunities. Few experienced the highs and lows more than Michael Phair, and his experiences – of oppression and opportunity – perhaps best explain the inexplicable. Queer life was not merely possible in Edmonton, Alberta one could thrive there but you had to be tough. And additionally, it helped to be determined, creative, and energetic – those with fewer resources tended not to fair as well. Recently installed as the chair of the University of Alberta's board of governors, Phair's talents are widely respected by a government that he once strenuously lobbied against. Few would have thought his trajectory possible in the early 1980s, but his example, and Maureen Irwin's many years before, illustrate the cyclical, non-linear nature of changes in matters of social justice, equity, and activism. None of this is predictable, retrenchment and new forms of repression/conservatism await queer activists and people. Histories of movements and queer players have a tendency to pick some snapshots of triumph, but it is hoped that balancing triumph with repression and retrenchment provides a more nuanced window into how gay men and lesbians navigated politics in Edmonton. Taking a broad view of "politics," and analysing Edmonton and Calgary within their provincial and regional context, offers a means by which to better understand these queer histories. Furthermore it challenges outdated perceptions of a unified, reactionary "Alberta" because it was possible to be queer there, but it took a handful of activists with bundles of energy to push and prod the larger queer population to think critically about being satisfied with tolerance and to work towards a more public acceptance of diversity.

Conclusion

The prairie provinces of Canada may not have big city gay communities but we do have a particular outlook on gay liberation which we believe to be just as valuable and just as much a part of gay life as is that of Toronto, Montreal, New York or San Francisco. We have come together at a particularly exciting time here in western Canada but it is also a time of gathering clouds. We believe that it is more than ever a time for gay self esteem to be shown and for the walls of alienation to be challenged and breached.[1]

After Stonewall, 1977

I think it's part of that prairie mentality where out here it can be pretty brutal and we gotta stick together … I have had lots of people who I've known who have gone to Vancouver and said the community is not nearly as welcoming … They come back here and like our community better. I know we have seen tremendous change … Being an activist I have learned the importance of politics, like it or not it makes a difference.[2]

Liz Massiah, Edmonton, September 2003

People in places like Edmonton, Calgary, Winnipeg and Regina, et cetera, have *had* to build stronger communities outside of ghettos. I think there is a greater sense of inclusion within smaller gay communities because we cannot segregate ourselves, we have to be strong in a fragmented way. And I also think that there is a great sense of humanity about people on the prairies – we have had to work together in isolation from larger centers.[3]

Glenn Murray, Winnipeg, 1999

This regional history of queer people living and loving in the prairie provinces from the 1930s through the mid-1980s offers a number of important contributions to histories of sexuality, gender, and, more specifically, western Canada. In the first instance, it conclusively demonstrates that queer people carved out spaces for socializing, community building, and activism within the prairies. *Prairie Fairies* contributes to a well-developed field of transnational urban histories of queer people and communities. Most urban histories of sexual community formation, activism, or identity focus solely on one city so this multicity, regional analysis of queer life in the Canadian prairie cities and the rural areas surrounding them is unique. Within the field of Canadian prairie history, this work challenges the overwhelmingly heteronormative focus, shifting the gaze from the majority to the margins. A regional approach better captures migrations within the region, as women and men moved from farms, small towns, and smaller cities into the larger cities as they sought out educational opportunities, employment, and sexual opportunities. It has conclusively disproved the impression, largely one of conjecture and stereotype, that all queer people, particularly those with initiative and drive, moved away from the prairies, while those who stayed were "closeted" or "left behind." People chose to move, regionally or outside the region, but they often chose to stay. This third path – moving within the region, to a larger city with queer resources, people, and activities – allowed people to fashion queer lives. In Winnipeg, Saskatoon, Edmonton, Calgary, and Regina, varied spaces – mixed use bars, cruising areas, membership clubs, community centres, cultural and sporting groups, religious groups, and activism – proved highly attractive. Affordable car travel, a culture of "road trips," and a sense of regional interconnections fostered by gay and lesbian periodicals, newsletters, and conferences further stimulated this network of regional queer possibility.

Yet, it is clear from newsletters, conferences, and organizational minutes that not only were prairie people networking and moving within the region, they were also contributing to national gay activism and organizational discussions. And those residents of large Canadian queer communities were familiar with their western peers. Activists from Ontario and British Columbia wrote about them in *The Body Politic*, attended Metamorphosis and other regional and Canadian national gay and lesbian activist conferences held annually from 1973–80. What has been lost in the decades since the national conferences ended, and with large gaps in our histories of contemporary queer politics, is how interconnected the "national" scene was with the west. There were tensions, to be sure, in political approaches to gender inclusivity and above all about who was able to define the strategies and speak as the "national" queer political voice. Western voices were strong, and some articulated a different vision for activism, whether the "no compromise" *After Stonewall* crew, or the more moderate but nonetheless proud grass-roots, regional perspective offered by Saskatchewan Gay Coalition. Other queer activists had worked extensively with their Ontario counterparts – at the Lesbian and Gay Archives, *The Body Politic*, or various political groups based in Toronto and Ottawa, because they often travelled to Toronto and because some of those individuals were transplanted western Canadians. It is important in the Canadian context to pay attention to regional contributions and voices within the "national" gay movement because the Canadian movement was never as large or as organized as the American national lesbian and gay activist movement (or as well funded).

The absence of much sustained historical attention to gay activism and gay sexuality in Canadian history has contributed to the amnesia about prairie queer life, activism, and organizational development. As I argued in the introduction, little attention has been paid to queer histories, people, or communities. With the passage of time and the passing of activists, community organizations, newsletters, and magazines, this vibrant history was in danger of disappearing. Thankfully, the dedication to archive building and oral history projects meant that key individuals and communities were intent on saving their histories and providing resources from which they could be written. Studies such as this also make an important contribution to western Canadian histories, as they revise contemporary histories to demonstrate that queer women and men were part of prairie cities and communities. Going forward, I hope that contemporary histories of the west will be more inclusive of sexual minority communities and contributors.

Turning now to the key questions: What was it like to be gay, lesbian, or queer in the prairies? How did people organize their lives? How did they create organizations, social spaces, and activism? Was it more difficult, or dangerous, to be queer in Alberta? How did lesbians and gay men interact? *Prairie Fairies* illustrates that the context, individual initiative, and city/regional setting affected being queer in the prairies quite dramatically. There were two distinct eras, one pre-1970 (part one) in which queer activity was largely subcultural, queer people making spaces where they could, converting tables, corners of bars, men's washrooms, parks, and house parties into queer space. Post-1970, with the creation of explicitly gay and lesbian membership clubs and then gay and lesbian organizational and activist groups, gay and lesbian networks became more public. As part two illustrates, from 1970 to 1985 there was a dramatic expansion of spaces in which to be gay and lesbian in the prairies. People responded enthusiastically to these new members-only clubs, and dancing, socializing, and opportunities for friendship were recalled as formative experiences. Many similarities were evident across the region, as the clubs shared tactics, encouraged visitors with reciprocal membership cards, exchanged newsletters, and as staff and organizers attended annual meetings to further refine the network. All strove to start libraries, to provide telephone information lines, perhaps later a counselling service, each had a newsletter, and all strove to make their club "the best" part of a regional rivalry among prairie cities. These social spaces were, as many narrators made clear, political insomuch as they required people to self-identify and to take some level of risk to inquire about, enter, or join such groups. Once navigated, those evenings of socializing, solidarity, and sex were, as some recalled it, nothing short of "revolutionary." Taking those steps, however strong the incentive, could still be a challenge, as the quest for "identity" as a member of sexual minority communities did not come easily. It was not without backlash, violence, and repression, but as part 3 illustrates, in all cities and provinces, smaller groups of activists were not prepared to be threatened back into older days marked by discretion and subterranean life. Activists also shared tactics, most notably the quest for human rights legislation, but they also fought specific battles that exemplify how the cities could be so disparate in their queer organizing and opportunities. Saskatoon was the most political, Winnipeg the most invested in education, religion, and media work, and Edmonton the place where counselling programs predominated alongside a plethora of commercial bar spaces. Calgary was the most cautious of the cities, a city where even the club newsletter, mailed only to club members, came with a privacy warning. Regina residents were not far behind in their concern for privacy. In Regina, their club took the lion's share of their community energies and, notably, it alone survives of all the membership clubs.

The first section offers a window both into Winnipeg's preorganizational life from the 1930s–1970 and the episodes of queer visibility in the province of Saskatchewan prior to 1970. These are remarkably varied and, at times, vibrant worlds. But one must be careful to remember that these histories are based on a source – oral interviews – that have specific challenges and biases, however liberating in their potential. The oral histories only enable writing histories about those individuals who consented to give interviews. This seems self-evident, but what that means is that a number of groups are marginalized or missing entirely. In the Winnipeg chapter there are very few lesbian voices, which was not because lesbians did not live in Winnipeg but because they did not volunteer to provide oral histories as readily as male informants did. Another group that is largely missing from this study are Indigenous queer participants. Again, this is not because Indigenous women and men were not part of the queer worlds, but because the various oral history projects either did not ask people to self-identify as Indigenous, or did not locate sufficient numbers of Indigenous informants. Now that there is a renewed attention to the interactions between settler populations and Indigenous people in the prairies, the absence of Indigenous voices in the oral history collections needs scholarly attention. Such attention would further complicate the ways that these communities were stratified by gender, racial, class, and regional differences as much as they were unified by concepts of gay, lesbian, or queer identities.

In Winnipeg, starting in the 1930s, various urban spaces – the riverbanks, public toilets (tea rooms), hotel beverage rooms, and "the docks" – were inscribed as queer spaces by fairies, pansies, trade, and men in the know. Bert Sigurdson and his pals were flamboyant, creative, and not at all coy about these worlds, heading out in drag on the city's streetcars. Again, pre–Second World War this was partly facilitated by the naivety or willful ignorance of those around them. After the Second World War, gay male networks in Winnipeg would become more established, a number of house party circuits would be initiated, and with the loosening of laws governing public drinking, in particular the provision for "cocktail" lounges that enabled women to legally drink in public, more public spaces for lesbians became available. By the late 1960s, lesbians and gay men were starting to create dedicated gay bars, to think about creating organizations, and starting (however tentatively) to draw upon models of sociability and activism that were familiar in American cities, and in particular, those created in Minneapolis, Minnesota. They were also reading gay and lesbian periodicals and so increasingly tapped into a North American cultural world of gay and lesbian identities, social and organizational life.

In chapter 2, devoted to Saskatchewan, there were more sources to reconstruct lesbian worlds including the photos and suggestive history of Nan McKay's university world of female companionship. In addition, sources permitted better attention to the rural and small-town experience, illustrating that queer women and men could be highly resourceful in how they organized their lives. Prior to 1970, this took time and calibration and men and women used a variety of strategies. Some, like Nan McKay, would use the wonderful homosocial spaces of university to allow for queer lives. Others, such as Augustus Esch and a young Norman Dahl, successfully managed to find queer opportunities in rural areas but they were mindful of local norms, drew upon the naivety of the majority, and crafted individualistic solutions. As scholars for the American rural, southern, and small town have argued, queer people in Saskatchewan were highly creative in how they organized sexual experimentation and later queer sexualities. It was possible to live queer lives and reside in the countryside, either through a combination of travelling out of the community for sexual and social liaisons, finding discretionary strategies within the communities, and, in part, they were assisted by those who lived there. The importance of being "from there," as later oral interviews with Regina lesbians made very clear, could provide sufficient cover and protection provided people lived discreetly. The hapless Mounties of Carnduff had not managed that, but by the mid-twentieth century, small-town directories would be replete with bachelor farmers, "single" teachers and nurses, and same-sex small business owners who managed to carefully navigate local norms because they were "from there." I don't mean to suggest that this was an easy or liberatory situation, but such strategies for those who chose them did make particular sorts of middle-class queer lives possible.

One sees that model much in evidence in Saskatoon, where a whole coterie of middle-class professional lesbians – the campus lesbians, many of whom originally came from small towns to attend the University of Saskatchewan and later stayed there as employees – managed to hide in plain sight. They seldom talked about it outside their circle of friends, but they did live with long-term female companions, travelled, bought houses and cabins, and, in so doing, were couples. They did not welcome the attention of the activists who wanted to "out them," nor did they seek out the dances or organizational spaces. They did model a particular way to be lesbian in the prairies, though. And, ironically, unlike so many of the lesbians who did share their life histories with me, these women were unlikely to have married men, or had children, or come out later in life. Older informants like Dorothy might have been adamant that the on-campus lesbians were not part of the community but they were prairie lesbians. They did manage to coexist in the city of Saskatoon for years, which not only speaks to both their determination and discretion, but also to the accommodations and liberal-mindedness in Saskatoon, and on campus, that could be generated for euro-Canadian, middle-class women professionals.

By the late 1960s, in Saskatoon and in Winnipeg momentum was building for queer organizational developments. People like Gens Hellquist were in discussions with older queer mentors like Dan Nalbach about developments in Vancouver, Calgary, and in American cities, which led to their *Georgia Straight* ad intended to see what interest existed in Saskatoon for such a group. Calgary was the first to create a gay and lesbian membership club when they launched Club Carousel, and Edmonton followed shortly thereafter with Club 70. Winnipeg's community would launch Happenings Social Club, while queer students would emulate developments on the University of Minnesota campus, launching first the Campus Gay Club, later renamed Gays for Equality. Regina, alerted that Saskatoon had, by 1972, organized the Zodiac Fellowship Society, one part social club, one part activist organization, followed suit with their own Atropos Fellowship Society.

Throughout the 1970s and 1980s, as this book has enumerated in much detail, in all of the cities, even Regina, a wide range of organizations were created that branched out beyond social clubs with their drinks, dancing, and perhaps coffee house nights to include organizations and programs devoted to educational; activist; religious; counselling; sports; lesbian feminist issues; men's groups; and much cultural development in the form of newsletters, periodicals, radio programs, and, in Winnipeg, "Coming Out TV." With the exception of activist groups, which in all three cities remained limited to a dedicated core of gay men and lesbians, these various other groups and media could prove very popular. Some were relatively long-lived such as Saskatoon's gay community centre, which while moving around the city's downtown core nevertheless had a presence throughout the 1970s. GFE's media initiatives and their own prominence as an incubator and kick-starter for queer groups and organizations were important to Winnipeg. In both cases, the fact that key activists remained in Winnipeg and Saskatoon brought a sense of continuity that was missing in Edmonton, as activists tended to come and go throughout the decade. At the same time, Edmonton's gay organizational development was highly dependent on outsiders – those who came to work at the University of Alberta, or in the various governmental and civil service capacities in Alberta – who then volunteered their time to assist gay activist/organizational development and programming.

Separating the histories of 1970–85 prairie gay life into two thematic sections, one devoted to organizational development, the other to activism, resistance, violence, and backlash, was intended to serve two purposes. First this organization allows for an analytical overview of the major organizational developments, to offer specifics about the similarities and differences between cities and within the region. Second, any attempt to simplistically chart a narrative of "progress" is undercut by the reality that many of these organizations were short-lived. In the concluding part of the book, the activism and resistance in each city conclusively refutes a progressive, linear narrative. Activism came and went, and contained a variety of liberationist, progressive and later human rights–based strategies (and such approaches could and were argued by the same activists). And resistance to queer visibility, and certainly anything smacking of activism or "flaunting it," was persistent. In all cities, evidence of government or bureaucratic obstruction, of university silences and shunning, or local renegades taking matters into their hands – launching arson attacks, bashings, or even murder – could be found in the prairie cities. Edmonton and Calgary police were oppositional and often harassed the gay community, most notably in the bath raids in 1981. Saskatoon's police turned a blind eye to violence and proved unable to catch arsonists, yet they were willing to issue parade permits for gay activist parades. Winnipeg's police seemed ill-equipped, or unwilling, to police the hill or cruising areas, which led to numerous gay bashings. How to account for these multiple differences in experience and outcome? Queer people learned to be careful; even in Saskatoon, informants remembered going to the bar in groups, being prepared to make a quick entry or exit. In Edmonton, queer men characterized the experience of congregating in those early clubs, to dance and socialize, as akin to being "outlaws." Such situations fostered identity, built political networks, even as some claimed all they wanted was space to socialize. It would be the aftermath of Anita Bryant's tour, and the gay bath raids in Edmonton in 1981, that the folly of accommodation and tolerance would be exposed for what it was – a risky proposition. Much as middle-class women in western Canada learned that it was better to have the vote rather than influence, gay and lesbian activists, even those who hewed to older models of discretion and outward respectability, realized that such tactics would not protect one if a chinook of intolerance blew in. Having some basic human rights would. Or, at the very least, it would give gay men and lesbians avenues to pursue justice.

From 1970 to 1985, gay and lesbian activists in the prairies were well integrated into the Canadian movement, participating in conferences, periodicals, and organizations. At the same time, they demanded that their voices not merely support national, top-down strategies, but that the movement be inclusive enough to allow for different voices, notably lesbians and youth, and that it recognize the value of grass-roots work and multiple approaches to identity politics. Western activists did not believe that moving to a central metropolis was the only avenue to mature gay or lesbian identity, activist work, or life. They argued for the viability of small-town queer lives, recognized that this would look different than what was feasible in a big city, or queer ghetto, and tried to establish ways for prairie women and men to be proud queer people living, working, and loving in the prairies. Some, they knew, would move on in search of larger opportunities, but many, they realized, wanted to be both gay and western, lesbian and rural, and providing resources, spaces, organizations, and cultural groups acknowledged people's right to be gay and lesbian in their home region.

In 1985, it was AIDS that conclusively changed the activist terrain in the prairies. This epidemic, and the fear it caused, galvanized a wide-ranging number of queer people towards activism and support. It also removed the blinders from those mainstream residents who had persisted, or willfully ignored, the queer people in their midst. Deaths could not be ignored, lesbians and gay men threw themselves in AIDS advocacy and support groups, and vocally demanded that reluctant, conservative governments provide funding for research and educational campaigns. Getting little buy-in, they designed their own safe-sex campaigns, founded health organizations, and worked to assist those living with AIDS. This study concludes as that campaign began, in large part because it marked the end of one cycle of activism and organizational activity and the beginning of another. These histories of queer communities, politics, and resistance are not sequential and they are not linear, but as we collect more documents, oral and print, and as we write more inclusive histories, it is my hope that we not forget the queer people, communities, and organizations in the prairies who have made extensive contributions to this region. Delwyn Vriend's discrimination case, which went all the way to Canada's Supreme Court, was not entirely anomalous. In particular, it did not spring merely from one individual's quest for recognition and determination to fight discriminatory practices. Instead, it drew upon twenty years of activism in the prairies and a minimum of sixty years of identifiable queer subcultural life in the prairies.

In the end, reading the reflections of the *After Stonewall* collective, Liz Massiah, and Glen Murray it is evident the pride in the prairie queer accomplishments. A small band of volunteers, working against some insurmountable odds, put their shoulder into making queer lives possible and then, having established basic social and community structures, to working for changes. There were few funds, handfuls of people in each city, but what they lacked in funding and capacity they made up for in drive and determination. Prairie lesbians and gay men in the prairies knew, initially, that the odds were not in their favour, but they brought political, social, and cultural ideas of gay communities and activism to the region, tailoring the message for prairie residents. The irony in all of this is that they drew upon prairie norms of volunteerism, a rather pragmatic and at times unflappable approach to achieving what appear to be sizable goals, and a strong sense that, though small and isolated from larger queer centres, it was fully within their abilities to strive to achieve spaces, organization, and later activism geared to making life better for gays and lesbians in the prairies. In the words of Gays for Equality, to "love and let love." The communities were never as united as these recollections may suggest, but few communities of any sort, whether ethnic, gendered, religious, class-based, or political, ever are. The influence of Saskatchewan Gay Coalition's "grass-roots" campaigns and their support for queer people in small towns, mid-sized cities, and rural areas spoke volumes about the importance attached to place, sexuality, and identity. "Toward Gay Community," the slogan of the 1977 conference, with its image of a patchwork of prairie fields, which co-opted a familiar prairie agricultural image to symbolize regional gay and lesbian activism, sums up the difference of queer activism in the prairie west. These and other groups drew upon national and international developments in gay politics, culture, and activism, and then tailored and refined the messages to fit the local context.

Queer peoples' struggles to take lovers and carve out lives and social spaces are important because they offer insights into active resistance, accommodations, tolerance, and acceptance in the prairies. The stereotypes of the region as a bleak, persistently homophobic place scarred by violence and police persecutions has some basis in fact but queer women and men were not merely victims of a region noted for valorizing nuclear families, faith, and farming. Larger prairie cities provided refuge. This research challenges the preconceived narratives of queer and prairie histories, of the connections between the local, the national, and the international, and demonstrates how more nuanced, urban, and regional studies can enrich our histories of what liberation looked like beyond New York, San Francisco, and Toronto.

Notes

Introduction

1 Gens Hellquist, interview with author, 17 December 2002.

2 "Dorothy," interview with author, Saskatoon, 8 July 2003. Dorothy is a pseudonym chosen by my narrator for consistency with her other interviews.

3 Doug Wilson, "At the Grassroots," *After Stonewall: A Critical Journal of Lesbian and Gay Liberation in Prairie Canada* 9 (Fall 1979): 7.

4 "Dorothy" interview with author, Saskatoon, 8 July 2003.

5 Laura Doan, *Disturbing Practices: History, Sexuality and Women's Experiences of Modern War* (Chicago & London: University of Chicago Press, 2013), 61.

6 Matt Cook and Jennifer V. Evans, "Introduction" in *Queer Cities, Queer Cultures: Europe since 1945*, ed. Cook and Evans (London: Bloomsbury Academic, 2014), 3.

7 For a longer discussion of how queer history decentres the historiography of western Canada, including an acknowledgment that the contemporary west is an urban place, see: VJ Korinek "A Queer Eye View of the Prairies: Reorienting Western Canadian Histories," in *The West and Beyond: New Perspectives on an Imagined Region*, ed. Alvin Finkel, Sarah Carter, and Peter Fortna (Edmonton: Athabasca University Press, 2010), 278–96.

8 For a recent discussion of the difference between gay and lesbian social historical approaches and queer historicism, see Colin R. Johnson *Just Queer Folks: Gender and Sexuality in America* (Philadelphia, PA: Temple University Press, 2013), 17. "Queer" approaches have come to define the field, see: John Howard, *Men like That: A Southern Queer* History (Chicago: University of Chicago Press, 1999); Nan Alamilla Boyd, *Wide-Open Town: A History of Queer San Francisco to 1965* (Berkeley: University of California

Press, 2003) and Matt Holbrook, *Queer London: Perils and Pleasures in the Sexual Metropolis, 1918–1957* (Chicago: University of Chicago Press, 2005).

9 For an excellent overview of some of the major work on cities and sexuality, see: Matt Houlbrook, "Cities" in *Palgrave Advances in the Modern History of Sexuality*, ed. H.G. Cocks and Matt Houlbrook (London: Palgrave Macmillan, 2006). Starting with George Chauncey's groundbreaking *Gay New York: Gender, Urban Culture and the Making of the Gay Male World, 1890–1940* (New York: Basic Books, 1994) this approach has defined the field. Other notable entries in an ever-expanding literature are: Daniel Hurewitz, *Bohemian Los Angeles and the Making of Modern Politics* (Berkeley: University of California Press, 2007); Matt Houlbrook, *Queer London*; Matt Cook, *London and the Culture of Homosexuality 1885–1914* (Cambridge: Cambridge University Press, 2003); Nan Alamilla Boyd, *Wide Open Town: A History of Queer San Francisco to 1965* (Berkeley: University of California Press, 2003); Peter Boag, *Same-Sex Affairs: Constructing and Controlling Homosexuality in the Pacific Northwest* (Berkeley: University of California Press, 2003); Marc Stein, *City of Sisterly and Brotherly Loves: Lesbian and Gay Philadelphia, 1945–1972* (Chicago: University of Chicago Press, 2000); David Higgs, ed. *Queer Sites: Gay Urban Histories since 1600* (London: Routledge, 1999); Brett Beemyn, ed. *Creating a Place for Ourselves: Lesbian, Gay, and Bisexual Community Histories* (London: Routledge, 1997).

10 Chauncey, *Gay New York*; Nan Alamilla Boyd, *Wide Open* Town; Michel Foucault, *History of Sexuality, Vol. 2: The Use of Pleasure* (New York: Vintage Books, 1990); David Bell and Gill Valentine, eds. *Mapping Desire: Geographies of Sexualities* (London & NY: Routledge, 1995); Kath Weston, *Long, Slow Burn* (New York: Routledge, 1998); Jon Binnie and Gill Valentine, "Geographies of sexuality – A Review of Progress" *Progress in Human* Geography (London: Sage Publications, 1999), 23, 175; Mark Turner, *Backward Glances: Cruising the Queer Streets of New York and London* (London: Reaktion Books, 2003), Katherine McKittrick, *Demonic Grounds: Black Women and the Cartographies of Struggle* (Minneapolis: University of Minnesota Press, 2006).

11 Marc Stein, "Theoretical Politics, Local Communities: The Making of U.S. LGBT Historiography" *GLQ: A Journal of Lesbian and Gay Studies,* 11, no. 4 (2005): 608.

12 Matt Houlbrook, "Cities," 133.

13 Jennifer L. Pierce, "Introduction," in *Queer Twin Cities: Twin Cities GLBT Project* (Minneapolis: University of Minneapolis Press, 2010), xi–xii.

14 J. Jack Halberstam, *In a Queer Time and Place: Transgender Bodies, Subcultural Lives* (New York: New York University Press, 2005), 12. Also Kath Weston,

"'Get Thee to a Big City': Sexual Imagery and the Great Gay Migration," *GLQ: A Journal of Lesbian and Gay Studies*, 2, no. 3, (1995) 253–77.

15 Liz Millard, *Making a Scene: Lesbians and Community Across Canada, 1964–1984* (Vancouver: University of British Columbia Press, 2015), 233.

16 John Howard, *Men like That: A Southern Queer History* (Chicago: University of Chicago Press, 1999).

17 Howard, *Men like That*, xviii.

18 Colin R. Johnson, *Just Queer Folks*. For an earlier, Canadian oral history of rural couples, see Michael Riordan, *Out Our Way: Gay and Lesbian Life in the Country* (Toronto: Between the Lines Press, 1996).

19 Mary L. Gray, Colin R. Johnson, and Brian J. Gilley, eds, *Queering the Countryside: New Frontiers in Rural Queer Studies* (New York: New York University Press, 2016).

20 The earliest academic work on Canadian homosexuals was Maurice Leznoff's "The Homosexual in Urban Society" (master's thesis, McGill University, 1954) (which focuses on Montreal). Subsequently, there has been a sustained academic interest in histories of sexuality in Canada, see Gary Kinsman, *The Regulation of Desire: Homo and Hetero Sexualities*, 2nd ed. (Montreal: Black Rose Books, 1996); Karen Dubinsky, *Improper Advances: Rape and Heterosexual Conflict in Ontario, 1880–1929* (Chicago: University of Chicago Press, 1993); Becki L. Ross, *The House that Jill Built: A Lesbian Nation in Formation* (Toronto: University of Toronto Press, 1995); Carolyn Strange, *Toronto's Girl Problem: The Perils and Pleasures of the City, 1880–1930* (Toronto: University of Toronto Press, 1995); Ross Higgins, "Baths, Bushes, and Belonging: Public Sex and Gay Community in Pre-Stonewall Montreal" in *Public Sex/Gay Space*, ed. William L. Leaps (New York: Columbia University Press, 1999); Adele Perry, *On the Edge of Empire: Gender, Race and the Making of British Columbia, 1849–1871* (Toronto: University of Toronto Press, 2001); Elise Chenier, "Rethinking Class in Lesbian Bar Culture: Living 'The Gay Life' in Toronto, 1955–1965," *Left History* 9, no. 2 (Spring/Summer 2004): 85–117; David Churchill, "Mother Goose's Map: Tabloid Geographies and Gay Male Experience in 1950s Toronto" *Journal of Urban History* 30, no. 6 September (2004): 826–52; Gary Kinsman & Patrizia Gentile, *The Canadian War on Queers: National Security as Sexual Regulation* (Vancouver: University of British Columbia Press, 2010); Becki L. Ross, *Burlesque West: Showgirls, Sex, and Sin in Postwar Vancouver* (Toronto: University of Toronto Press, 2009); Elise Chenier, *Strangers in Our Midst: Sexual Deviancy in Postwar Ontario* (Toronto: University of Toronto Press 2008); Cameron Duder, *Awfully Devoted Women: Lesbian Lives in Canada, 1900–1950* (Vancouver: University of

British Columbia Press, 2010); and the extensive work of Steven Maynard on Toronto, including: "Through a Hole in the Lavatory Wall: Homosexual Subcultures, Police Surveillance, and the Dialectics of Discovery, Toronto, 1890–1930" in *Gender and History in Canada*, ed. Joy Parr and Mark Rosenfeld (Toronto: Copp Clark, 1996); Steven Maynard, "'Respect your Elders, Know Your Past': History and Queer Theorists" *Radical History Review* 75 (1999) 56–78.

21 There have been a few publications pertaining to histories of sexuality in western Canada, see: Terry L. Chapman, "'An Oscar Wilde Type': The Abominable Crime of Buggery in Western Canada 1890–1920," *Criminal Justice* History, 4 (1983): 97–118; Terry L. Chapman, "Male Homosexuality: Legal Restraints and Social Attitudes in Western Canada, 1890–1920" in *Law and Justice in a New Land: Essays in Western Canadian Legal History*, ed. Louise A. Knafla (Toronto: Carswell, 1986); Terry L. Chapman "Sex Crimes in the West, 1890–1920" *Alberta History* 35, no. 4 (October 1987): 6–21; Lyle Dick, "The 1942 Same-Sex Trials in Edmonton: On the State's Repression of Sexual Minorities, Archives, and Human Rights in Canada" *Archivaria* 68 (2009):183–217; Lyle Dick, "Same-Sex Intersections of the Prairie Settlement Era: The 1895 Case of Regina's 'Oscar Wilde'" *Histoire Sociale/Social* History 42 (May 2009): 107–45; Angus McLaren, "Sex Radicalism in the Canadian Pacific Northwest, 1890–1920,"*Journal of the History of Sexuality* 2, no. 4 (April 1992): 527–46, V.J. Korinek, "The Most Openly Gay Person for at Least a Thousand Miles': Doug Wilson and the Politicization of a Province, 1975–83," *Canadian Historical Review* 84, no. 4 (December 2003): 517–50.

22 Liz Millward, *Making a Scene.* See also Dale Barbour, *Winnipeg Beach: Leisure and Courtship in a Resort* Town (Winnipeg: University of Manitoba Press, 2011); Debra Shogan, "Queering Pervert City: A Queer Reading of the Swift Current Hockey Scandal," in *Queerly Canadian: An Introductory Reader in Sexuality Studies*, ed. Maureen Fitzgerald and Scott Rayter (Toronto: Canadian Scholars Press, 2012); Randal Rogers and Christine Ramsay, eds., *Overlooking Saskatchewan: Minding the Gap* (Regina: University of Regina Press, 2014), most notably see Krista Baliko and James McNinch's "Broken Borders, Broken Binaries: Two Spirit Youth in Saskatchewan in the Twenty-First Century"; Noelle Lucas, *Womanspace: Building a Lesbian Community in Edmonton Alberta* (master's thesis, University of Saskatchewan, 2002); Geoffrey Korfman, "The Wilde West: Homosexual Behaviours in the Court Records of SK, 1895–1930" (master's thesis, Trent University, 2007); Joe Wickenhauser, "Surprisingly Unexpected: Moose Jaw, Metronormativity and LGBTQ Activism" (master's thesis, York University, 2012).

23 While scholars have completed graduate theses on various queer topics set in Canada, these have not yet resulted in academic monographs. In Calgary, a community history is currently underway, and that promises to produce a valuable history of gay and lesbian spaces, places, and people in that city. See Calgary Gay History Project: http://calgaryqueerhistory.ca.

24 Edmonton's Queer History project was started in 2015 to celebrate thirty-five years of gay and lesbian organizing in the city, see: https://edmontonqueerhistoryproject.wordpress.com/.

25 Atlantic Canada is under-represented in histories of sexuality literature. For a good contemporary analysis of what it is like to be "queer" in Atlantic Canada, see Kelly Baker, "Out Back Home: An Exploration of LGBT Identities and Community in Rural Nova Scotia, Canada" in *Queering the Countryside: New Frontiers in Rural Queer Studies*, 25–48.

26 Archival resources for Calgary were limited, and I was only able to collect one interview in Calgary. For a time, it appeared that Calgary would not appear at all. However, the Edmonton sources, supplemented with the Glenbow Museum holdings, made possible episodic vignettes of Calgary. Those vignettes demonstrate how much more we need to know about Alberta queer history and the differences and similarities between the two major cities. Thankfully, Calgary's community history is well under way.

27 Cook and Evans, *Queer Cities/Queer Cultures*. Matt Cook and Alison Owram are lead researchers on a research grant entitled Queer Beyond London, intended to challenge the London-centric focus of LGBTTQ histories. They are currently at work on a monograph focused on the varied experiences in Brighton, Leeds, Manchester, and Plymouth. The Queer Localities Conference, held at Birkbeck College, University of London, 30 November–1 December 2017, brought researchers, collaborators, and community historians together for a workshop.

28 Lynn Hunt, *Writing History in the Global Era* (New York: WW Norton & Co, 2014), 6–9.

29 "Dorothy," interview with author, 8 July 2003.

30 Bill Waiser, "'All but Deserted Years Ago': Electricity and the Two Saskatchewans" in Overlooking Saskatchewan, ed. Rogers and Ramsay.

31 Bruce Garman, interview with author, Saskatoon, 25 July 2003.

32 The relaunch of the Western Canadian Studies Conferences in 2008 marks an important step forward in reinvigorating this field of scholarship. See, Sarah Carter, Alvin Finkel, and Peter Fortna, *The West and Beyond: New Perspectives on an Imagined Region* (Edmonton: Athabasca University Press, 2010).

33 See the articles listed in footnote 18.

34 See Sexual and Gender Diversity Library/Archival Resources on
   Campus, on the University Archives & Special Collections, University of
   Saskatchewan University Library page, https://library.usask.ca/archives/
   collections/sexualdiversity.php.

35 See V.J. Korinek, "We're the Girls of the Pansy Parade": Historicizing
   Winnipeg's Queer Subcultures, 1930s–1970s," *Histoire Sociale/Social History*
   45, no. 89 (May 2012): 125–7 for an expanded discussion of Winnipeg's
   oral interview projects. Provincial Archives of Manitoba (PAM), Manitoba
   Gay Lesbian Archives Committee, C1861–1903, 1990. Copies of thirty-three
   cassette tapes (twenty-five hours). C1869–70. In 2002, I was granted access
   to these tapes by both the archivists at PAM and by the Rainbow Resource
   Centre (RRC), 1–222 Osborne St, Winnipeg, Manitoba, which then held
   the originals. The original interviews are now part of the University of
   Manitoba Archives and Special Collections, Winnipeg Gay and Lesbian
   Archives Collection, (A.08–67, A.09–28).

36 For an extended commentary on the challenges of queer oral histories,
   see V.J. Korinek "Locating Lesbians, Finding 'Gay Women,' Writing
   Queer Histories: Reflections on Oral Histories, Identity, and Community
   Memory" in *Beyond Women's Words*, ed. K. Srigley, Stacey Zembrycki, and
   Franca Iacovetta (New York: Routledge, 2018).

37 E. Lapovsky Kennedy, "Telling Tales: Oral History and the Construction of
   Pre-Stonewall Lesbian History," *Radical History Review* 65 (1995): 59–79.

38 Historians have written evocatively about "crying in the archives"
   but those of us who do oral histories have our own challenges hearing
   harrowing material. Nothing prepares one adequately for such moments.
   See Ann Curthoys and Ann McGrath, *How to Write History That People
   Want to Read* (Sydney: UNSW Press, 2009) and Antoinette Burton, *Archive
   Stories: Facts, Fictions and the Writing of History* (Atlanta: Duke University
   Press, 2006).

39 The collective that organized the 1990 oral history project in Winnipeg
   selected twenty final participants from an initial response of two hundred
   individuals willing to discuss their histories of the gay and lesbian
   experiences in Winnipeg prior to 1970. The methodological notes on
   file with the interviews provides no insight into how that process was
   undertaken, just that the group sought to provide a "balanced" sampling
   of histories, and that women's participation rates were lower than they
   had hoped. Other historians have noted middle-class lesbian's desire for
   discretion, and have written persuasively about these choices and their
   impact upon the writing of lesbian history. See Cameron Duder, *Awfully
   Devoted Women*; Liz Kennedy, "'But We Would Never Talk About It':

The Structures of Lesbian Discretion in South Dakota, 1928–1933" in *Inventing Lesbian Cultures in America*, ed. Ellen Lewin (Boston, MA: Beacon Press, 1996); and Katie Gilmartin, "We Weren't Bar People': Middle-Class Lesbian Identities and Cultural Spaces," *Gay and Lesbian Quarterly* 3 (1996): 1–51.

40 LGBTTQ Archives, University of Manitoba Archives and Special Collections, MSS 383, EL 37, TC 160 A. 11–27, Sally Papso, "Introduction," in "Born between the Wars: Growing up Lesbian in Manitoba Before and After WW II: An Oral History," 1.

41 Papso, "Project Summary," "Born between the Wars," 2.

42 Marion, interview with author, Saskatoon, 26 August 2003.

43 Ibid.

44 Cook and Evans, "Introduction," *Queer Cities, Queer Cultures*, 6.

45 Scott Lauria Morgensen, *Spaces between Us: Queer Settler Colonialism and Indigenous Decolonization* (Minneapolis: University of Minnesota Press, 2011); Quo-Li Driskell, Chris Finley, Brian Joseph Giley, and Scott Lauria Morgensen, eds., *Queer Indigenous Studies: Critical Intervention in Theory, Politics and Literature* (Tucson: University of Arizona Press, 2011).

46 "Introduction." *What We Have Learned: Principles of Truth and Reconciliation* (Truth and Reconciliation Commission of Canada, 2015).

47 Morgensen, *Spaces between Us*, 78.

48 Scott Lauria Morgensen, "Unsettling Queer Politics: What Can Non-Natives Learn from Two Spirit Organizing?" in *Queer Indigenous Studies*, 135.

49 Ibid.,149.

50 Ma-Nee Chacaby, with Mary Louisa Plummer, *A Two-Spirit Journey: The Autobiography of a Lesbian Ojibwa-Cree Elder* (Winnipeg: University of Manitoba Press, 2016).

51 For an excellent discussion of such matters, and a model of how to map queer histories and terrain, see: Matt Houlbrook and Chris Waters, "*The Heart in Exile*: Detachment and Desire in 1950s London," *History Workshop Journal* 62 (2006):142–65 and Matt Houlbrook, *Queer London*.

52 Steven Maynard, "'Respect Your Elders, Know Your Past': History and the Queer Theorists" *Radical History Review* 75 (1999): 71.

53 Miriam Smith, *Lesbian and Gay Rights in Canada: Social Movements and Equality Seeking, 1971–1985* (Toronto: University of Toronto Press, 1999).

54 See Miriam Smith, *Lesbian and Gay Rights in Canada*; Tom Warner, *Never Going Back: A History of Queer Activism in Canada* (Toronto: University of Toronto Press, 2002); David Rayside, *Queer Inclusions, Continental Divisions: Public Recognition of Sexual Diversity in Canada and the U.S.* (Toronto: University of Toronto Press, 2008); Marc Stein, *Rethinking the Gay and*

Lesbian Movement (New York: Routledge, 2012); and Marc Stein, "Sex with Neighbours: Canada and Canadians in the U.S. Homophile Press" *Journal of Homosexuality*, 64, no. 7 (2017): 963–90, http://www.tandfonline.com/doi/full/10.1080/00918369.2017.1280999.
55 Other publications, move beyond this signpost to assess various campaigns for gay activism. See: V.J. Korinek, "'The Most Openly Gay Person for at Least a Thousand Miles'"; V.J. Korinek, "Activism=Public Education: The History of Public Discourses of Homosexuality in SK, 1971–1993" in *I Could Not Speak My Heart*, ed. J. McNinch and M. Cronin (Regina: Canadian Plains Research Center, 2004), 109–37.

1. "The torch of Golden Boy Burns Bright"

1 PAM, Manitoba Gay Lesbian Archives Committee, C1861–1903, 1990. Copies of thirty-three cassette tapes (twenty-five hours). C1869–70. Tapes 9 and 10. George M. Smith interviewed by David Theodore, 25 June 1990. Copies of these interviews and transcripts are available in the PAM. Originals are in the possession of the Manitoba Gay Lesbian Archive. In 2002, I was granted access to these tapes by the archivists at PAM and by the RRC, 1–222 Osborne St, Winnipeg, Manitoba, which held the originals. I am grateful to Donna Huen, then manager at RRC, for duplicating a copy of the transcript summaries for my use and providing me with access to the restricted interviews. According to the PAM finding aid, the "purpose of the project was to record the experiences of gay men and lesbian women in Manitoba to 1970, and to examine public attitudes about homosexuals and interactions with families and social institutions."
2 RRC, Manitoba Gay/Lesbian Oral History Project, Bert Sigurdson, interview with David Theodore, 29 June 1990. My thanks to Scott de Groot who reminded me of the raunchiness of the Sigurdson ditty and research assistant Erin Millions for tracking down the exact lyrics.
3 A queer theoretical approach resists the binarisms of gay/straight and instead seeks to understand a range of gendered and sexual behaviour. See Nan Alamilla Boyd, "Who is the Subject? Queer Theory Meets Oral History" *Journal of the History of Sexualities* 17, no. 2 (May 2008): 177–89; John Howard, *Men like That: A Southern Queer History* (Chicago: University of Chicago Press, 1999); Nan Alamilla Boyd, *Wide Open Town*, and David Halperin, *One Hundred Years of Homosexuality: And Other Essays on Greek Love* (New York: Routledge, 1989).
4 Although his work covers the pre–First World War era there are some parallels between Portland and Winnipeg. Peter Boag, *Same Sex Affairs*.

5 "The Golden Boy, a magnificently gilded 5.25M (17.2-foot) figure,
is probably Manitoba's best-known symbol. Embodying the spirit
of enterprise and eternal youth, he is poised atop the dome of the
building. He faces the north, with its mineral resources, fish, forest,
furs, hydroelectric power and seaport, where his province's future lies."
Source: Province of Manitoba Legislative BuildingTour: http://www.gov
.mb.ca/mit/legtour/golden.html.

6 George Chauncey and Nan Alamilla Boyd's research on New York City
and San Francisco's gay/lesbian/queer communities conclude that gay
and lesbian identities and social and geographical spaces were well
established in both cities *prior to* the Second World War. Chauncey argued
that "gay life in New York was less tolerated, less visible to outsiders and
more rigidly segregated in the second third of the century than in the first
and that the very severity of the postwar reaction has tended to blind us
to the relative tolerance of the pre-war years" (9). Such was not the case in
Winnipeg. My research on Winnipeg supports the research finding of John
D'Emilio and Allan Bérubé in which the Second World War was a stimulus
to homosocial opportunities and ultimately, homosexuality. See Chauncey,
Gay New York; Boyd, *Wide Open Town*; John D'Emilio *Sexual Politics, Sexual
Communities: The Making of a Homosexual Minority in the United States,
1940–1970* (Chicago: University of Chicago Press, 1983) and Allan Bérubé,
Coming Out under Fire: The History of Gay Men and Women in World War II
(New York: Free Press, 1990).

7 Gary Kinsman & Patrizia Gentile, *The Canadian War on Queers*, 200–9 maps
queer spaces in Ottawa during the post-war era.

8 Nan Alamilla Boyd, *Wide Open Town*.

9 John D'Emilio, *Sexual Politics, Sexual Communities*.

10 RRC, "Lesbians and Gays in Manitoba: The Development of a Minority.
Manitoba Gay/Lesbian Archives Committee Oral History Project 1990,
Project Summary."

11 Jerry Walsh, *Backward Glances: A Compilation of his Remembrances of a By-
Gone Era in the Gay Community of Winnipeg*, 27 pages, self-published, n.d.
This source contains much information about Winnipeg's community
prior to the establishment of exclusively gay clubs, from the 1940s to the
1970s, with shorter sections on the post-1972 era (specifically Happenings,
and other gay-owned or -operated spaces). Written for insiders, and in a
campy, humourous tone, it nevertheless offers much detailed information
about venues, locations, activities, and how the community defined itself.
Thanks to Mike Giffin for sending me a copy of this invaluable document.
Although it is undated, Mike Giffin believes the document dates from the

1990s. Jerry Walsh died in 2000 and regretfully I never had an opportunity to interview him. A "Gerry Walsh" was interviewed by the 1990 oral history project, and given the similar material in that interview they were likely the same individual.

12 David Churchill, the director of the University of Manitoba Institute for the Humanities, has worked to preserve the community histories in Winnipeg. The University of Manitoba Lesbian, Gay, Bisexual, Transgender, and Two-Spirited (LGBTT) Archival and Oral History Initiative has preserved the original 1990 and 1992 interviews, and added a contemporary oral history collection. The value of having these interviews in a secure, easily accessible location for scholars is tremendous.

13 Nan Alamilla Boyd, "Who is the Subject? Queer Theory Meets Oral History," 178. Nan Alamilla Boyd and Horacio N. Roque Ramirez, eds., *Bodies of Evidence: The Practice of Queer Oral History* (New York: Oxford University Press, 2012).

14 Boyd, "Queer Theory Meets Oral History," 189.

15 PAM, Finding Aid Manitoba Gay Lesbian Archives Committee, Gerry Berkowski, August 1991.

16 PAM, "Potential Oral History Project Questions: Manitoba Gay and Lesbian Archives, Oral History Project 1."

17 They were clearly indebted to the work of John D'Emilio, Allan Bérubé, and other foundational gay historians.

18 RRC, "Project Summary" Lesbians and Gays in Manitoba: The Development of a Minority, Oral History Project (Manitoba Gay/Lesbian Archives Committee, 1990).

19 Three women and one man. Two of these individuals indicated that their tapes were restricted, so there are only two usable interviews here, and both of those use pseudonyms.

20 RRC, "Project Summary," 2.

21 Contemporary studies illustrate an important link between the relatively high rate of youth suicide, homophobia, and GLBT orientation but sources pointing to a historic link with lesbianism are, to my knowledge, not available.

22 Cameron Duder, *Awfully Devoted Women*.

23 See "Born between the Wars: Women Who Grew Up Lesbian in Manitoba before and after WWII an Oral History," LGBTTQ Archives, Archives and Special Collections, Elizabeth Defoe Library, University of Manitoba.

24 The 1992 collection of oral interviews with Winnipeg lesbian and gay activists has a much better representation of women's voices. Similarly,

in the interviews I conducted in each prairie city, I prioritized collecting equal numbers of women's and men's histories. However, prioritizing collecting women's histories and actually managing to do so are not the same thing. While I did secure equal numbers of male and female narrators, it was much more challenging locating women to interview.

25 Among the many key books on Winnipeg see: Esyllt W. Jones & Gerald Friesen, eds., *Prairie Metropolis: New Essays on Winnipeg Social History* (Winnipeg: University of Manitoba Press, 2009); Alan Artibise, *Winnipeg: A Social History of Urban Growth 1874–1914* (Montreal and London: McGill-Queen's Press, 1975); Alan Artibise, *Winnipeg: An Illustrated History* (Toronto: James Lorimer & Co and The National Museum of Man, 1977); David Arnason & Mhari Mackintosh, eds., *The Imagined City: A Literary History of Winnipeg* (Winnipeg: Turnstone Press, 2005); David Jay Bercuson, *Confrontation at Winnipeg: Labour, Industrial Relations, and the General Strike*, rev. ed. (Montreal: McGill-Queen's, 1990); Christopher Dafoe, *Winnipeg: Heart of a Continent.* (Winnipeg: Great Plains Publishing, 1998); and Royden Loewen and Gerald Friesen, *Immigrants in Prairie Cities: Ethnic Diversity in Twentieth Century Canada* (Toronto: University of Toronto Press, 2009). Helpful are works on Manitoba or 'the West' more generally include: Ken Coates and Fred McGuiness, *Manitoba: The Province and the People* (Edmonton: Hurtig Publishers, 1987); Gerald Friesen, *River Road: Essays on Manitoba and Prairie History* (Winnipeg: University of Manitoba Press, 1996); Robert Collins, *Prairie People: A Celebration of My Homeland* (Toronto: McClelland and Stewart, 2003); W. Peter Ward, "Population Growth in Western Canada, 1901–71" in *The Developing West: Essays on Canadian History in Honour of Lewis H. Thomas*, ed. John E. Foster (Edmonton: University of Alberta Press, 1983).

26 Carl Abbott, *How Cities Won the West: Four Centuries of Urban Change in Western North America* (Albuquerque: University of New Mexico Press, 2008), 42.

27 Dominion Bureau of Statistics, *Seventh Census of Canada, 1931*, Volume II Population by Areas (Ottawa: Government of Canada, 1933), 9.

28 Artibise, *Winnipeg*; Rhonda Hinther, "The Oldest Profession in Winnipeg: The Culture of Prostitution in the Point Douglas Segregated District, 1909–1912" *Manitoba History* 41 (March 2001): 2–13; Mariana Valverde, *Age of Light, Soap and Water: Moral Reform in English Canada, 1885–1925* (Toronto: McClelland & Stewart, 1991).

29 RRC, "History of the Gay Lesbian Community," 1.

30 See Dale Barbour, *Winnipeg Beach: Leisure and Courtship in a Resort Town, 1900–1967* (Winnipeg: University of Manitoba Press, 2011) for an overview

of history of courtship, dating, and commercial amusements this resort community provided Winnipeggers.

31 Abbott, *How Cities Won the West*, 48.

32 Russ Gourluck, *The Mosaic Village: An Illustrated History of Winnipeg's North End* (Winnipeg: Great Plains Publications, 2010).

33 See Arnason and Mackintosh, eds., *The Imagined City: A Literary History of Winnipeg*.

34 Colin Johnson's *Just Queer Folks* features a queer couple from Minnesota who vacation in Winnipeg, so it was on the radar within queer Midwestern networks.

35 Artibise, *Winnipeg*, 109.

36 Census of Canada, 1931, Table 34, "Population of Cities and Towns 10,000 and over, classified according to racial origin," 499.

37 Ibid. Jewish citizens were the largest European "racial" origin in Winnipeg's 1931 Census statistics.

38 Census of Canada information, 1971, Ethnic Group by Census Metropolitan Areas.

39 Ibid., 176.

40 Hans Werner, *Imagined Homes: Soviet German Immigrants in Two Cities* (Winnipeg: University of Manitoba Press, 2007), 41.

41 Christopher Dafoe, *Winnipeg: Heart of a Continent*, 144–6.

42 1971 Census of Canada, Population, Volume I (Ottawa: Statistics Canada, August 1974), 8–4.

43 Werner, *Imagined Homes*, 51.

44 Abbott, *How Cities Won the West*, 177.

45 Ibid.

46 RRC, Manitoba Gay/Lesbian Oral History Project Bert Sigurdson, interview with David Theodore, 29 June 1990.

47 See George Chauncey, *Gay New York: Gender, Urban Culture, and the Making of the Gay Male World, 1890–1940* (New York: Basic Books, 1994), 65–97 and Matt Houlbrook, *Queer London*.

48 Chauncey, *Gay New York*, 54–5.

49 My thanks to Dr Ryan Eyford for his work tracking Bert Sigurdson through the Icelandic papers and commemorative books, Henderson Directories, and University of Manitoba yearbooks. And, surprisingly, Bert Sigurdson was still alive when that research project was concluded. An offer to interview him was received, and according to his niece he was mulling it over, but regretfully he was already in hospital and he died a few months later – in September 2012 at ninety years of age.

50 Bert Sigurdson Obituary, *Winnipeg Free Press*, 13 October 2012.

51 *Almanak Olafs S. Thorgeirssonar* (Winnipeg, 1950), 94.

52 Memorial postings for B. Sigurdson, "guest book," Neil Bardahl Funeral Centre, 2012. Website accessed 29 July 2014.

53 See Stewart Van Cleve, "Preface" in *Land of 10,000 Loves: A History of Queer Minnesota* (Minneapolis: University of Minnesota Press, 2012), xiii for a discussion of his own family's history of inclusion of his great aunt, Leslie Allen Van Cleve, and her partner, Evie Schaller, who were part of family photographs, celebrations et cetera, but whose relationship status was not discussed. Many oral informants mentioned similar treatment by close family members.

54 Mark Turner, *Backward Glances: Cruising the Queer Streets of New York and London*, 60.

55 RRC, Manitoba Gay/Lesbian Oral History Project, Bert Sigurdson interview with David Theodore, 29 June 1990.

56 Ibid.

57 University of Manitoba Archives and Special Collections (UMASC) "History of the G/L Community" Winnipeg Gay/Lesbian Resource Centre, 1–222 Osborne St. The "Events/Law" page lists a series of criminal cases, human rights events, landmark events (first pride events et cetera) and this one line, presumably referring to this incident: "Sidney Neil (arrested and tried in Calgary) 1956."

58 "Criminal Sexual Psychopath: Teacher Given Unique Sentence" *Calgary Herald*, 25 May 1956, 21 and 33.

59 Supreme Court of Canada, The Queen vs Sidney Keith Neil, 10, 11 June and 1 October 1957.

60 Methodological and theoretical observations about the value and challenges of utilizing oral history abound. A useful and accessible guide to the key issues is provided by Robert Perks and Alistair Thomson, eds., *The Oral History Reader* (London & New York: Routledge, 1998). See also Ann Cvetkovich, *An Archive of Feeling: Trauma, Sexuality and Lesbian Public Culture* (Durham & London: Duke University Press, 2003).

61 Steven Maynard, "'Horrible Temptations': Sex, Men, and Working-Class Male Youth in Urban Ontario, 1890–1935" *Canadian Historical Review* 78, no. 2 (June 1997): 235; Jeffrey Weeks "Inverts, Perverts, and Mary-Annes: Male Prostitution and the Regulation of Homosexuality in England in the Nineteenth and Early Twentieth Centuries" in *Hidden from History: Reclaiming the Gay and Lesbian Past*, ed. Martin Duberman, Martha Vicinus, and George Chauncey Jr (New York: Meridian, 1990); also G. Chauncey, *Gay New York*. For a similar argument about the uses working-class young women made of sexual favours and exchanges, see Christine Stansell, *City*

of Women: Sex and Class in New York, 1789–1860 (New York: Knopf, 1986)
and Kathy Peiss, *Cheap Amusements: Working Women and Leisure in Turn-of-
the-Century New York* (Philadelphia, PA: Temple University Press, 1986).

62 RRC, Manitoba Gay/Lesbian Oral History Project, George M. Smith
interview with David Theodore, 25 June 1990. Rainbow Resource Centre,
Winnipeg, Manitoba.

63 UMASC "History of the G/L Community," author unknown, n.d.
Winnipeg Gay/Lesbian Resource Centre, 1–222 Osborne St.

64 RRC, Manitoba Gay and Lesbian Oral History Project, "Gordon Clark"
(pseudonym, original name may not be used) interviewed by David
Theodore in Winnipeg, 4 June 1990.

65 RRC, Bruce Mitchell, born Winnipeg 1921, interviewed by David Theodore
in Winnipeg, 28 May 1990.

66 My own collection of oral interviews with gay men from Saskatoon,
Regina, and Moose Jaw also reported such activity, offering important
contextual information for the Winnipeg interviews. These were clearly
not isolated incidents.

67 RRC, Bruce Mitchell interviewed by David Theodore in Winnipeg, 28 May
1990.

68 Bruce Mitchell's recollections are similar to those reported in Paul
Jackson's work *One of the Boys*, which explores the range of experiences
queer servicemen experienced in the Canadian forces during the Second
World War. See P. Jackson, *One of the Boys: Homosexuality in the Military
during World War II* (Montreal and Kingston: McGill Queen's University
Press, 2004).

69 PAM, C1864 & C 1865, Manitoba Gay/Lesbian Archives Committee:
David B, pseudonym, born 1920, interviewed by David Theodore, 7 June
1990. No restrictions on the file.

70 Ibid.

71 By coincidence, the *Globe and Mail* recently published a gallop poll
indicating that Toronto was the least beloved Canadian city. Matt Demers,
"Toronto the Least Liked City in Canada, Especially by Westerners," *Globe
and Mail*, 9 November 2011. The poll conducted by Léger Marketing found
that 30 per cent of Albertans hate Toronto.

72 PAM C 1870, Manitoba Gay/Lesbian Archives Committee, George M.
Smith interviewed by David Theodore, 25 June 1990, Tape 2.

73 Ibid.

74 PAM C 1867, Manitoba Gay/Lesbian Archives Committee, David Swan
interviewed by David Theodore, 12 June 1990.

75 RRC, History of the Gay and Lesbian Community Appendix. This multipage document offers a list of social and political organizations (and their locations), special events, and a number of prominent gay and lesbian individuals in the city. The Bell entry (which corresponds to a very thin file in the biographical vertical file) restated the information provided in the oral interviews. A graduate student researcher was unable to locate any official archival materials from Dr Bell's tenure at the University of Manitoba that links his public, professional career to his private interests. Still, the multiple references to Bell in oral interviews (the 1990 and 1992 collections, along with my own interviews in Winnipeg) corroborate the story of Bell's private queer life.

76 PAM C 1867, Manitoba Gay/Lesbian Archives Committee, David Swan interviewed by David Theodore, 12 June 1990.

77 Author interview with "Frances Williamson" (pseudonym), Winnipeg, November 2002. Williamson mentioned Dean Bell in her interview, stating that Dr Bell "was always very careful but we knew he had lots of parties. The intern's residence was named for him. There were all kinds of rumours about Dr Bell but he had such a good record … He was one of the better people. Very sensitive. Very kind."

78 See Lyle Dick, "The 1942 Same-Sex Trials in Edmonton": Lyle Dick, "Same-Sex Intersections of the Prairie Settlement Era"; Scott F. de Groot, The Accused Have Not Indicated That They Intend to Fight Off This Disease: Moral Panic, the Imperiled Child, and the Regulation of Sexuality in Postwar Winnipeg, (master's cognate paper, Queen's University, 2008); "Terry Chapman, "'An Oscar Wilde type': 'The Abominable Crime of Buggery' in Western Canada, 1890–1920"; Terry Chapman, "Male Homosexuality: Legal Restraints and Social Attitudes in Western Canada, 1890–1920"; Terry Chapman, "Sex crimes in the West"; Chapman, Terry, "Sex Crimes in Western Canada, 1890–1920" (PhD dissertation, University of Alberta, 1984).

79 Scott de Groot, "The Accused Have Not Indicated That They Intend to Fight Off This Disease" (master's cognate paper, Queen's University, 2008), 27.

80 Lyle Dick, "The 1942 Same-Sex Trials in Edmonton: On the State's Repression of Sexual Minorities, Archives, and Human Rights in Canada" Archivaria 68 (2009): 183–217.

81 Mary Louise Adams, The Trouble with Normal: Postwar Youth and the Making of Heterosexuality (Toronto: University of Toronto Press, 1997); Gary Kinsman and Patrizia Gentile, The Canadian War on Queers; and Richard

Cavell, ed., *Love, Hate and Fear in Canada's Cold War* (Toronto: University of Toronto, 2004).

82 Walsh, *Backward Glances*, 17–18.

83 PAM C 1874, Manitoba Gay/Lesbian Archives Committee, Bert Sigurdson interviewed by David Theodore, 29 June 1990, Tape 1 Side B.

84 Elise Chenier has also noted the use of Chinese run restaurants in post-war Toronto. Elise Chenier, "Rethinking Class in Lesbian Bar Culture: Living 'The Gay Life' in Toronto, 1955–1965," *Left History* 9, no. 2 (2004): 85–118.

85 PAM C 1879, Manitoba Gay/Lesbian Archives Committee, "Peter" interviewed by David Theodore, 24 July 1990. Tape 1 Side A.

86 RRC Manitoba Gay/Lesbian Oral History Project, Peter interviewed by David Theodore, 24 July 1990.

87 PAM C 1869, Manitoba Gay/Lesbian Archives Committee, George Smith interviewed by David Theodore, 25 June 1990. Tape 1 Side B.

88 See Dale Barbour, "Drinking Together: The Role of Gender in Changing Manitoba's Liquor Laws in the 1950s" in *Prairie Metropolis: New Essays on Winnipeg Social History*, ed. Esyllt W. Jones and Gerald Friesen (Winnipeg: University of Manitoba Press, 2009), 187–99.

89 Jerry Walsh, *Backward Glances*, 2.

90 Ibid.

91 Ibid., 4–5.

92 Ibid., 8.

93 Russ Gourluck, *The Mosaic Village: An Illustrated History of Winnipeg's North End* (Winnipeg: Great Plains Publications, 2010), 168.

94 Jerry Walsh, *Backward Glances*, 9.

95 RRC, Manitoba Gay and Lesbian Oral History Project, Ted Patterson, interviewed by David Theodore in Winnipeg, 27 June 1990.

96 I am indebted to Matt Houlbrook's sections on the "pink shilling," where he astutely assesses how commercial opportunities, and consumer power, were critical facets of homosexual life in London for both middle-class and working-class men. Houlbrook, *Queer London*. Specifics regarding the Marlborough Hotel's Cocktail Bar, and its changing policy concerning gay patrons is taken from Jerry Walsh, *Back Ward Glances*, 2.

97 The 1992 community interviews as well as the author's research on the period between 1970–85 indicate more class and gender tensions, and particularly the creation of a number of women-only social and political organizations.

98 RRC, Manitoba Gay/Lesbian Oral History Project, Ted Patterson interviewed by David Theodore in Winnipeg, 27 June 1990.

99 RRC, Manitoba Gay/Lesbian Oral History Project, Peter interviewed by David Theodore, 24 July 1990.
100 Jerry Walsh, *Backward Glances*, p. 11–12.
101 Alan Miller, "Alan Miller's Winnipeg Years, 1969–1972," email to the author, 30 April 2007.
102 For an excellent analysis of the creation of heterosexual social spaces at Winnipeg Beach, see Dale Barbour, *If Heterosexuality Is the Norm, Why Do We Need to Go to Winnipeg Beach?: Making and Unmaking Safe Social Space: 1900–1965* (master's thesis, University of Manitoba, 2009) and Dale Barbour, *Winnipeg Beach: Leisure and Courtship in a Resort Town, 1900–1967* (Winnipeg: University of Manitoba Press, 2011).
103 Dale Barbour, *Winnipeg Beach: Leisure and Courtship in a Resort Town, 1900–1967*, 79–81.
104 American historians, most notably Elizabeth Lapovsky Kennedy and Madeline D. Davis, *Boots of Leather, Slippers of Gold: The History of a Lesbian* Community (New York: Rutledge, 1993), have offered considerable evidence of the importance of house parties within lesbian social networks in the city of Buffalo, New York. Cameron Duder offers similarly compelling evidence for middle-class Canadian lesbians, see *Awfully Devoted Women*. While the evidence presented here is partial and incomplete owing to the oral history project's failure to find sufficient female informants for the pre-1970 queer and lesbian history of Winnipeg nevertheless it seems logical that such venues were equally important in the city of Winnipeg.
105 Interestingly, Ruth Sells was interviewed twice, once in 1990 in the original set of oral interviews in Winnipeg, and then again in 2007, by Sally Papso, as part of the "Born between the Wars" collection of lesbian interviews.
106 Cameron Duder, *Awfully Devoted Women*.
107 Cameron Duder, in *Awfully Devoted Women*, focuses specifically on the strategies employed by middle-class women to be "discreet" and thus protect their lesbian relationships. For the United States, see Liz Kennedy, "'But We Would Never Talk about It': The Structures of Lesbian Discretion in South Dakota, 1928–1933" (Boston: Beacon Press, 1996), 15–39.
108 RRC, Manitoba Gay and Lesbian Oral History Project, Ruth B. Sells, interviewed by David Theodore in Winnipeg, 16 August 1990. For a discussion of the differences between respectable, middle-class homosexuals and working-class queers, see Houlbrook and Waters, "*The Heart in Exile*:

Detachment and Desire in 1950s London" *History Workshop Journal* 62, no. 1 (2006): 142–65, here 162. For a history of the Daughters of Bilitis, see Marcia Gallo, *Different Daughters: A History of the Daughters of Bilitis and the Rise of Lesbian Rights Movement* (New York: Carroll & Graf, 2006).

109 Dr A.M. Watts, Manitoba Gay/Lesbian Oral History Project II, interviewed in Winnipeg, 25 June 1992. Although not gay himself, Watts's influential work within the United Church contributed to gay and lesbian advocacy in the city and region during the 1980s. In explaining how he came to be an advocate for such issues in this quote he reflects on his youth and experiences at U of M.

110 RRC, Manitoba Gay/Lesbian Oral History Project, Jim H interviewed by David Theodore in Winnipeg, 12 July 1990.

111 Ross Higgins, "Baths, Bushes, and Belonging: Public Sex and Gay Community in Pre-Stonewall Montreal," in *Public Sex/Gay Space*, ed. William L. Leap (New York: Columbia University Press, 1999), 9.

112 Ibid.

113 PAM 1990–233 C 1883, Manitoba Gay and Lesbian Archives Oral History Project, Gerry 2/2.

114 RRC, Manitoba Gay and Lesbian Oral History Project, "Joe" and "Pat" (both names are pseudonyms, Joe is male, Pat female) interviewed by David Theodore in Winnipeg, 25 July 1990.

115 RRC, Manitoba Gay and Lesbian Oral History Project, Anonymous and Audrey interviewed by David Theodore in Winnipeg, 15 August 1990.

116 RRC, Manitoba Gay and Lesbian Oral History Project, "Kate" interviewed by David Theodore, 9 August 1990. This individual requested anonymity, so "Kate" is a pseudonym for the informant.

117 Elise Chenier, *Strangers in Our Midst: Sexual Deviancy in Post-war Ontario* (Toronto: University of Toronto Press, 2008).

118 Jane Smith interviewed by Sally Papso, 23 November 2006, interview transcript, 20.

119 Ibid.

120 PAM C 1868, Manitoba Gay/Lesbian Archives Committee: T. Frost interviewed by David Theodore, 19 June 1990.

121 Peter Carlyle-Gordge, "The Hill Is a Favourite Spot: Part I" *Winnipeg World*, Summer 1969, 36–41; and Peter Carlyle-Gordge, "The Hill Is a Favourite Spot: Part II" *Winnipeg World*, Winter 1969/Spring 1970, 36–41. Carlyle-Gordge is a Winnipeg based freelance journalist who has written for a wide-ranging number of local and national newspapers

and periodicals, including *Outwords*, a GLBT periodical produced in Winnipeg for members of the community and their allies. For more information about his career, see his website: http://www.gordge.com/.

122 Carlyle- Gordge, "The Hill Is a Favourite Spot: Part I," 37.

123 Ibid., 38.

124 Ibid., 37–8.

125 Ibid., 39.

126 Ibid., 40.

127 Carlyle-Gordge, "The Hill Is a Favourite Spot: Part II," 38.

128 In this respect, Winnipeg police officers were following similar policies and procedures as their counterparts in Toronto. Marcel Martel "'They Smell Bad, Have Diseases, and Are Lazy': RCMP Officers Reporting on Hippies in the Late Sixties" *CHR*, 90, no. 2 (June 2009): 215–45; and Stuart Henderson, *Making the Scene: Yorkville and Hip Toronto in the 1960s* (Toronto: University of Toronto Press, 2011).

129 Walsh, *Backward Glances*, 22.

130 PAM C 1892, Manitoba Gay/Lesbian Archives Committee, Murray W. interviewed by David Theodore, 22 August 1990, Tape 1 Side B.

131 Walsh, *Backward Glances*, 25.

132 Carlyle-Gordge, "The Hill Is a Favourite Spot: Part I," 38.

133 PAM C 1861, Manitoba Gay/Lesbian Archives Committee, Bruce Mitchell interviewed by David Theodore, 28 May 1990, Tape 1 Side A.

134 RRC, "Kate" Interviewed by David Theodore, 9 August 1990.

135 "History of the G/L Community," Winnipeg Gay/Lesbian Resource Centre, 1–222 Osborne St, author unknown, n.d., 2.

136 See Anne Hiebert and Margo Gunn interviews in the "Born between the Wars" Collection. Hiebert attempted suicide and was dishonourably discharged when the cause of her suicide attempt was revealed; Gunn left of her own volition. See the Maureen Irwin Edmonton interview later in this volume for a similar experience of lesbian affairs during the air force and then heterosexual marriage.

137 Evelyn Peters, *Native Households in Winnipeg: Strategies of Co-Residence and Financial Support* (Winnipeg, Manitoba: Institute of Urban Studies, University of Winnipeg, 1994); and Evelyn Peters, "'Our City Indians': Negotiating the Meaning of First Nations Urbanization in Canada, 1945–1975," *Journal of Historical Geography* 30 (1992): 75–92.

138 Peter Carlyle-Gordge, "The Hill Is a Favourite Spot: Part II," 40.

139 Ibid.

140 Peter Carlyle-Gordge, 'The Hill Is a Favourite Spot: Part I," 37.

2. A Kiss Is Never Just a Kiss

1 Peter Millard, *Or Words to That Effect*, unpublished manuscript. My thanks to Norman Zepp, the executor of Millard's estate, for providing me with a copy of this valuable autobiography. This work is now available at the University of Saskatchewan Archives and Special Collections.

2 See Mo Moulton's "*Bricks and Flowers*: Unconventionality and Queerness in Katherine Everett's Life Writing" in *British Queer History: New Approaches and Perspectives*, ed. Brian Lewis (Manchester: Manchester University Press, 2013); and Laura Doan, *Disturbing Practices: History, Sexuality, and Women's Experience of Modern War* (Chicago: University of Chicago Press, 2013).

3 Bill Waiser, *A World We Have Lost: Saskatchewan before 1905* (Calgary: Fifth House Press, 2016).

4 Bill Waiser, *Saskatchewan: A New History* (Calgary: Fifth House Press, 2005).

5 In addition to previously mentioned work by Bill Waiser, see: A.J. Ray, J.R. Miller, and Frank Tough, *Bounty & Benevolence: A History of Saskatchewan Treaties* (Montreal: McGill Queen's Press, 2000); J.R. Miller, *Compact, Contract, Covenant: Aboriginal Treaty Making in Canada* (Toronto: University of Toronto Press, 2009); Sarah Carter, *The Importance of Being Monogamous: Marriage and Nation Building in Western Canada* (Edmonton: University of Alberta Press, 2008), Gerald Friesen, *The Canadian Prairies: A History* (Toronto: University of Toronto Press, 1987).

6 Don Kerr and Stan Hanson, afterward by Alan F.J. Artibise, *Saskatoon: The First Half-Century* (Edmonton: NeWest Publishers, 1982).

7 Bill Waiser, *Saskatchewan: A New History*. Also Michael Hayden, *Seeking a Balance: The University of Saskatchewan, 1907–1982* (Vancouver: University of British Columbia Press, 1983).

8 Alan Anderson, "Population Trends" in *The Encyclopedia of Saskatchewan*, (Regina: Canadian Plains Research Centre, 2006), accessed 13 September 2016, esask.uregina.ca/entry/population_trends.html.

9 See studies from Waiser. A more popular perspective is offered in Saskatoon's Western Development Museum, which has as its focal point a recreation of an urban streetscape from "boomtown" Saskatoon in the 1920s.

10 Terry Chapman, "Male Homosexuality: Legal Restraints and Social Attitudes in Western Canada, 1890–1920," 267–292 contains a fuller analysis of criminal charges for buggery, sodomy, and gross indecency in the western provinces between 1890–1920.

11 "Homos on The Range Settled the West?" *The Body Politic*, March 1980, vol. 6, no. 1, page numbers unknown.

12 Geoffrey Korfman, "The Wilde West: Homosexual Behaviour in the Court Records of Saskatchewan, 1895–1930," (master's thesis, Trent University, 2007).

13 Lyle Dick, "Same-Sex Intersections of the Prairie Settlement Era."

14 Lyle Dick, "The Queer Frontier: Male Same-Sex Experiences in Western Canada's Settlement Era," *Journal of Canadian Studies* 48, no. 1 (Winter 2014): 15–52. Dick argues that "the frontier era afforded men some latitude within which to produce same-sex space, notwithstanding developing homophobic regimes and the risk of discovery, ostracism, and incarceration" (15).

15 See Peter Boag, *Same-Sex Affairs: Constructing and Controlling Homosexuality in the Pacific Northwest* (Berkeley: University of California Press, 2003); *Re-Dressing America's Frontier Past* (Berkeley: University of California Press, 2011); Adele Perry, *On the Edge of Empire: Gender, Race and the Making of British Columbia, 1849–1871* (Toronto: University of Toronto Press, 2001); Stewart Van Cleve, *Land of 10,000 Loves: A History of Queer Minnesota* (Minneapolis: University of Minnesota Press, 2012); Kevin P. Murphy, Jennifer L. Pierce, and Larry Knopp, eds., *Queer Twin Cities: Twin Cities GLBT Oral History Project* (Minneapolis: University of Minnesota Press, 2010).

16 Sarah Carter, *Imperial Plots: Women, Land and the Spadework of British Colonialism on the Canadian Prairies.* (Winnipeg: University of Manitoba Press, 2016), 222–37.

17 Provincial Archives of Saskatchewan (PAS) Neil Richards Collection A821 III.42 History 1918–1987, Letter from 21 Carnduff residents to The Commissioner, R.N.W.M.P, Regina, 12 January 1918.

18 PAS, NR A 821 III.42 History, "Record of the Investigation of Complaint Made by J.V. Millions and 18 others, that Reg. No. 4823 Corpl R. Bailey and Reg. No. 6397 F.W.J. Barker Behaved in an Ungentlemanly Manner, 21 January 1918, Carnduff, SK.

19 Ibid.; D.M. Lothian, Baker, Statement of Oath to Inspector Raven, January 1918.

20 PAS, NR A821 III. 42, Letter from Inspector Raven, Commanding Officer, Weyburn Sub-District to The Officer Commanding R.N.W.M.P, Regina District, Regina re. Complaint of J.V. Millions and 19 others at Carnduff, 28 January 1918.

21 PAS, NR A821 III.42, Memo to the Officer Commanding R.N.W.M.P, Regina District re Complaints against Police at Carnduff, from Assistant Commissioner, 2 February 1918.

22 For example, the work on E. Cora Hind often fails to engage with her gender presentation (beyond including a photo); see Katherine M.J.

McKenna, "E. Cora Hind's Feminist Thought: 'The Women's Quiet Hour' in the *Western Home Monthly*, 1905–1922," *Journal of the Canadian Historical Association* 22, no. 1 (2011): 69–98. Analysis of another interesting Saskatchewan farmer, British gentlewoman Georgina Binnie Clark, does mention that Clark was no fan of marriage, but given her more conventional gender presentation (while lecturing) she hasn't twigged sufficient interest in a queer reading. See Georgina Binnie Clark, *Wheat and Woman* with a new introduction by Sarah A. Carter (Toronto: University of Toronto Press, 2007) and S. Carter, *Imperial Plots*, 245–86.

23 McKenna, "E. Cora Hind's Feminist Thought," 93.

24 S. Carter, *Imperial Plots*, particularly chapter 4, which discusses women who bought their farmland.

25 Doan, *Disturbing Practices*, 61.

26 I am indebted to the generosity and encouragement of the late Professor Duff Spafford, who shared his research on Annie Maud (Nan) McKay with me. His work on McKay led to her inclusion in the 100 Alumnae of Influence cohort, and ultimately brought her exceptional, "queer" life to my attention.

27 Profile of Annie Maud (Nan) McKay, BA '15 (d. 1986); 100 Alumni of Influence, University of Saskatchewan, accessed 1 June 2012, http:// www.uofsalumni.ca/profile.cfm?type=6&name=&code=&startrow=57&id =163.

28 McKay had a lengthy career on campus, and was interviewed over the years about a series of matters – the First World War, the flu epidemic, the University Alumnae Association (of which she was a founding member), et cetera. As of yet, I have not seen evidence that she claimed a Metis or Indigenous heritage. My point here is not to critique the claims or to question them, merely to illustrate that many historical projects may be engaged in "claiming identities" for subjects that may not have, for a variety of reasons, claimed them for themselves.

29 Duff Spafford, "Nan McKay," unpublished essay, last accessed December 2017, https://library.usask.ca/indigenous/history_essays/nan_mckay. php. In our conversations about McKay, Professor Spafford willingly offered his perceptive comments about McKay's generation of students, life at the University of Saskatchewan, and the McKay family genealogy.

30 See D. Spafford, "Notes on Annie Maude (Nan) McKay and the McKay Family" University of Saskatchewan Archives, July 2011.

31 Spafford, "Annie Maud (Nan) McKay," Aboriginal Research Resources, University of Saskatchewan Library, 2012, accessed 12 September 2016, http://library.usask.ca/indigenous/history_essays/nan_mckay.php.

32 "Nan McKay Retires after 44 Years of Service in the University Library," *Saskatoon Star Phoenix*, 10 November 1959. My thanks to Vickie Lamb Drover for sharing this – and other documentation – about Nan McKay's life at the University of Saskatchewan.

33 There is a rich literature on such women, including Martha Vicinus' influential work *Independent Women: Work and Community for Single Women, 1850–1920* (Chicago: University of Chicago Press, 1985). Closer to home, the work of PearlAnn Reichwein and Karen Fox, eds., *Mountain Diaries: The Alpine Adventures of Margaret Fleming* (Calgary: Historical Society of Alberta, 2004) offers an intriguing history of women climbers.

34 Thanks to Neil Richards for flagging this photo and bringing it to my attention. To his knowledge, and my own, it is the only one of its kind yet located for the early years of the University of Saskatchewan. Martha Vicinus uses the term "lesbian like" to navigate around issues of both identity, and terminological specificity, in her work *Intimate Friends: Women Who Loved Women, 1778–1928* (Chicago: University of Chicago Press, 2004).

35 Duff Spafford, in conversation with the author, June 2012.

36 See the University of Saskatchewan Archives tribute to Spafford, who passed away in May 2014, accessed September 2014. https://library.usask .ca/archives/exhibitions-digital/exhibitions/a-tribute-to-dufferin-stewart -spafford.php.

37 Duff Spafford, "Annie Maude (Nan) McKay essay," last accessed December 2017, http://library.usask.ca/indigenous/history_essays/ nan_mckay.php.

38 The 1928 trial for Radclyffe Hall's *The Well of Loneliness* garnered widespread attention to the issues of "lesbianism." See Mo Moulton, "Bricks and Flowers," in *British Queer History*, ed. Lewis, 65.

39 Augustus Esch is a pseudonym. He contacted Saskatchewan Gay Coalition in 1978, and activist Doug Wilson wrote his biography in an article entitled "A Very Loving Man," *Pink Ink*, September 1983/19 in PAS, NR 821 III.42, History 1918–87.

40 Ibid.

41 Ibid.

42 Ibid.

43 Peter Boag's *Re-Dressing America's Frontier Past* provides an excellent analysis of the ways that gender inversion, cross-dressing, and what we would now call trans women and men were part of the fabric of the American West. In fact, Boag asserts that the American West's less hierarchical societies, frontier cities, wide-open spaces, and mobility attracted many individuals who were eager to re-invent themselves,

leaving behind their old names, gender identities, and families in the East. Western opportunities were not merely about immigration, farming, and the economy, they were also about gendered opportunities.

44 PAS, NR History file, "Scientists are Intrigued" *Regina Leader Post*, 2 March 1934, 19.

45 Ibid.

46 PAS, NR History file, "Our History – From the Saskatchewan Gay Coalition Newsletter," n.d.

47 Boag, *Re-Dressing America's Frontier Past*.

48 Bruce Garman, interview with author, 2003; T, interview with author, August 2003. This gay man requested the use of the initial T to identify him.

49 See the digital collection "All Frocked Up," University of Saskatchewan Special Collections, 2003, http://scaa.usask.ca/gallery/allfrockedup/.

50 I am indebted to Neil Richards for his work documenting these cultural moments of sexual play/theatre. The exhibit "All Frocked Up" contained many images of men dressed as women, including images of the popular cross-dressing First World War troupe the Dumbells on their tour through the West. Obviously, these activities were popular forms of entertainment for many, presumably straight, audiences and within the homosocial settings they no doubt filled a variety of goals – moments of release, "normality," and, potentially, same-sex sexual activity. Such entertainers were also popular in the United States; see Daniel Hurewitz, *Bohemian Los Angeles: And the Making of Modern Politics* (Berkeley: University of California Press, 2008).

51 Michael Taft, "Folk Drama on the Great Plains: The Mock Wedding in Canada and the United States," *North Dakota History* 56, no. 4 (Fall 1989):16–23.

52 Norman Dahl, interview with author in Gatineau, Quebec, 23 August 2006.

53 Following ethical best practices with oral interviews, while Norman Dahl has consented to have his name appear in this text, those who appear in his testimony may very well not provide their consent for such material. Hence "Brad S" is a pseudonym.

54 Norman Dahl, interview with author.

55 Ibid.

56 Randall Denley, "Leading the Way for Gay Couples: Gatineau Men Together 53 Years," *Ottawa Citizen*, 21 August 2003.

57 Gary Kinsman, "The Canadian Cold War on Queers: Sexual Regulation and Resistance" in *Love, Hate and Fear in Canada's Cold War*, ed. Richard

Cavell (Toronto: University of Toronto Press, 2004); and Patrizia Gentile and Gary Kinsman *Canada's War on Queers: National Security as Sexual Regulation* (Vancouver: University of British Columbia Press, 2009).

58 My thanks to Dr Justin Bengry for this observation about the tension between the "exceptional" queers who sought lives in cities and regions where it was possible to live in largely gay and lesbian worlds (Toronto, New York, San Francisco) and those more "ordinary" people who happened to be gay or lesbian. No value judgment is attached to these terms, merely an observation about the divergent nature of identity, its power to frame and determine the lives of some (perhaps the type A category), whereas for the type Bs this is but one identity or characteristic to be weighed against others.

59 Dorothy, interview with author, Saskatoon, 8 July 2003.

60 One of the well-known challenges with oral interviews concerns issues of dates and times. I have no doubt that Dorothy did read such information in the local paper, given what an impression it made upon her and that it both publicized sexual differences and provided the clear impression that one could easily be victimized if one was marked as different by mainstream society. According to Dorothy the female doctor in question moved to Calgary shortly afterwards. Despite our best efforts, my researchers could not find any mention in the papers of such an event. Nor had people at the University of Saskatchewan Archives heard of such an event.

61 Gallo, *Different Daughters*, confirms that Canadian women were members of DOB. One of the informants from Winnipeg reported attending DOB conventions in California as well as reading *The Ladder*.

62 Evelyn Rogers, interview with author, Regina, 29 July 2003.

63 Ibid. Rogers and her partner, Lilja Stefansson, gave a joint interview in 2003, both of them regaling me with stories, both tragic and humourous, about their lives together. That Evelyn's abusive marriage ended in 1975, the year the United Nations proclaimed as the Year of the Woman, was both a cherished tale that they enjoyed sharing, but also a bitterly ironic one about the challenges women continue to face.

64 Lilja Stefansson, interview with author, Regina, 29 July 2003.

65 Ibid.

66 Ibid.

67 They were aware that I had published a book on *Chatelaine* magazine and its feminist content but not my queer reading of the magazine's lesbian content. Hearing this, they said that they were those very women, who used an article from *Chatelaine* to initiate a conversation about

lesbian sexuality. See V.J. Korinek, "Don't Let Your Girlfriends Ruin Your Marriage": Lesbian imagery in *Chatelaine* magazine 1950–1969" in *Journal of Canadian Studies* 33, no. 3 (Fall 1998); *Roughing It in the Suburbs: Reading Chatelaine Magazine in the Fifties and Sixties* (Toronto: University of Toronto Press, 2001).

68 University of Saskatchewan Archives and Special Collections, Evelyn Rogers Fonds, Lilja Stefansson, "Our Family," personal essay, n.d.

69 University of Saskatchewan Archives and Special Collections, Evelyn Rogers Fonds, Lilja Stefansson, "My Coming Out Story," n.d.

70 Ibid.

71 Ibid.

72 Ibid.

73 Lilja Stefansson, obituary, *Regina Leader* Post, June 2013, http://www .legacy.com/obituaries/leaderpost/obituary.aspx?pid=165392152.

74 V.J. Korinek, "A Queer Eye View of the Prairies." For more detail on the queer content in *Chatelaine*, see V.J. Korinek, *Roughing It in the Suburbs* and Valerie Korinek, "'Don't Let Your Girlfriends Ruin Your Marriage': Lesbian Imagery in Chatelaine Magazine, 1950–1969," *Journal of Canadian Studies* 33, no. 3 (Fall 1998): 83–109.

75 Val Scrivener, interview with author, February 2003.

76 Gens Hellquist, interview with author.

77 Ibid.

78 Tom Waugh, *Hard to Imagine: Gay Male Eroticism in Photography and Film from Their Beginnings to Stonewall* (New York: Columbia University Press, 1996); Paul Deslandes, "The Cultural Politics of Gay Pornography in 1970s Britain," in *British Queer History*, ed. Lewis.

79 Gens Hellquist, interview with author.

80 David Rimmer, interview with author, July 2006.

81 "Nalbach Dies," *Perceptions*, 30 July 1997, 12.

82 Camp culture is a well-known "queer" form of cultural and social expression. While many have written of this phenomenon, David Halperin's recent book *How to Be Gay* (Cambridge, MA: Harvard University Press, 2014) offers a trenchant overview of this world and its legacy, particularly for queer men of a particular vintage.

83 "Nalbach Dies," *Perceptions*, 30 July 1997, 12.

84 Don McNamee, Saskatchewan Council for the Arts and Artists Exhibition, accessed 13 September 2016, http://scaa.usask.ca/gallery/art/artists -mcnamee.html.

85 Ibid.

86 McNamee obituary, *Perceptions*, 27 July 1994.

87 Garman, interview with author, 2003.

88 Ibid.

89 Peter Millard, *Words to That Effect*, 211.

90 Dorothy, interview with author. The "on-campus lesbians" group was the focus of much discussion in my Saskatoon interviews, as they were well known (indeed all interviewees could have named a large number of the women in question), but their decision to avoid socializing in gay or lesbian community events and to maintain their own private, exclusive friendship networks meant that while they were a part of the queer history of Saskatoon, many lesbians I interviewed claimed that they were not part of "the community."

91 Dorothy expressed both anger and sadness for members of this group. Anger because she herself had been left out and felt resentment toward a group that took a different approach, and perhaps had not paid some of the price that she paid for openness, which struck me as an honest reaction. However, she was mostly sad for them, because as a contemporary of some of the older members, she felt their excessive caution had been misplaced. Furthermore, she believed that they had paid a toll for their policy of silence. She could not fathom why they were not proud of who they were, or, in many cases, their decades-long relationships with other women within this network, which she felt should have been publicly acknowledged.

92 "Selena," interview with author, September 2003.

93 Ibid.

94 One of my informants was treated with a round of shock therapy after she experienced a "nervous breakdown" in the 1970s. See chapter 7 for discussion of her experiences.

95 Some residents of Saskatoon, or the University of Saskatchewan community, will recognize these women. However, in aggregating their demographic and professional data, it was intended to provide some sense of the group at large, which, despite concerns about their privacy, speaks to some fascinating issues around how queerness – in this case, lesbianism – was navigated in Saskatoon. I am so grateful that Selena chose to speak out, but given the ethics in place for my interviews, much of her interview remains off the official record.

96 I have chosen not to name this individual. As a second career he dedicated himself to the priesthood and social justice issues/focus. My narrator Bruce Garman felt that his work as priest was humanizing and a helpful sign for resident gays and lesbians.

97 T, interview with author, August 2003.

98 Colin R. Johnson, *Just Queer Folks*.
99 In May 2012 I had private conversations, and an extensive email
    exchange, about a case of two faculty members who left the university
    during the 1950s. Both accepted appointments elsewhere, and, in one
    case, this was a promotion. But suspicions about the motivation for
    those moves lingered with those familiar with the case. The archival
    trail lit up and then just as quickly went cold – no archival paper trail
    could be located because, experts claimed, such paperwork would
    not have been generated, or if it had, would have been purged at
    a later point. Many of the original participants were deceased, and
    one remaining source would not consent to an on-record interview.
    Ethically, this was the end of the research trail. But, given the passion
    with which this event was recalled, some sixty years later, it seems
    quite clear that something occurred and hence I felt confident to
    mention it here.
100 See V.J. Korinek, "The Most Openly Gay Man for at Least a Thousand
    Miles."
101 *U of S Greystone*, 1964, no page numbers provided.
102 Tom Warner, interview with author, March 2003. Also see Tom Warner's
    website for details about his career as a gay activist and author at *Tom
    Warner Books*, http://www.tomwarnerbooks.com.
103 There is an increasing fascination with lesbian and gay pulp fiction from
    the 1950s and 1960s. For an introduction, please see the resources at the
    University of Saskatchewan: http://library2.usask.ca/srsd/pulps/.
104 For an astute assessment of the destruction of such materials, see Estelle
    B. Freedman, "The Burning of Letters Continues": Elusive Identities and
    the Historical Construction of Sexuality," *Journal of Women's History* 9, no.
    4 (Winter 1998): 181–200.

3. *Wilde Times*

1 Canadian Lesbian and Gay Archives (CLGA), Winnipeg File, Jane Rule,
   "Go to Winnipeg for The People," *The Body Politic*, 1984.
2 Rainbow Resource Centre, Manitoba Gay and Lesbian Oral History II
   Interview Summary, Ted Millward interview, 23 June 1992.
3 Chris Vogel, interview with author, Winnipeg, 21 November 2002.
4 *Out and About* the newsletter of Project Lambda, Winnipeg, included
   a few ads for pen pals beginning in May 1979 through the early 1980s.
   Those men tended to be from smaller, more isolated communities in
   Manitoba and northwestern Ontario.

5 SAB, A 595 Neil Richards II.207, *Voices: A Survival Manual for Wimmin,*
1980–1981. The first issue appeared in 1980, or by their dating system,
Winter Solstice, 9980.

6 Debbie Simmons (pseudonym), interview with author, July 2006; Leonard
Lawrence, interview with author, August 2003.

7 There is a rich history of queer life in Minneapolis, see Murphy, Pierce,
and Knopp, eds., *Queer Twin Cities*; Stewart Van Cleve, *Land of 10,000
Loves*; and Ricardo J. Brown, *The Evening Crowd at Kirmser's: A Gay Life in
the 1940s* (Minneapolis: University of Minnesota Press, 2003).

8 Ad – "Super Spree Weekend in San Francisco" *Out and About*, no. 6 (July
1978), n.p.

9 Dr J.R.M. (Dick) Smith remains active in Winnipeg's medical and gay
community. He is the medical director of "Our Health" Centre, which
caters to gay, bisexual, and men who have sex with men within Winnipeg.
He founded the first gay men's health clinic in Winnipeg in 1983.

10 Dr J.R.M. (Dick) Smith, interview summary, 7.

11 Bill Lewis was part of a cohort of gay male student activists in Winnipeg
in the early 1970s. He later moved to Toronto where he became a tenured
professor at the University of Toronto, and an AIDS researcher and
activist. In 1987, at the age of thirty-seven he died of AIDS. See Ann
Silversides, *AIDS Activist: Michael Lynch and the Politics of Community*
(Toronto: Between the Lines Press, 2003), 121–4.

12 Don Fenwick, interview summary, 106.

13 Ibid.

14 Dr J.R.M. (Dick) Smith, interview summary, 8–11.

15 RRC, Manitoba Gay and Lesbian Oral History Project, Bill S interviewed
by David Theodore, Winnipeg, 22 July 1990.

16 RRC, Manitoba Gay and Lesbian Oral History Project, George Moore
interviewed by telephone by David Theodore, 19 August 1990.

17 PAS A595 II.142 Mutual Friendship Society: "Editorial: Club Almost Loses
Charter Through GFE Interference," *What's Happening?* 3, no. 6 (March
1974): 1.

18 Ibid.

19 RRC, George Moore interviewed by David Theodore.

20 U of M Archives and Special Collections, "Born between the Wars," Pearl
Wylie and Margaret Gunn interview with Sally Papso, 28 June 2007.

21 Ibid.

22 RRC, George Moore interviewed by David Theodore.

23 RRC, interview with Joe and Pat.

24 Lyle Dick, interview with author, November 2005.

25 RRC, Manitoba Gay and Lesbian Oral History Project, Jim T interviewed by David Theodore, Winnipeg, 4 July 1990.

26 PAS, A 595 Neil Richards II.142 Mutual Friendship Society 1972–5, 1980–91, "Editorial" *What's Happening?* 1, no. 2 (October 1971): 1.

27 PAS, Neil Richards Collection A 595I.2, Newspaper Clippings 1974; Susan White, "Struggling on: Winnipeg's Gay Liberation Movement: 2 Years after," *Manitoban*, 4 February 1974, 7.

28 PAS, A 595 II.142 Mutual Friendship Society, "Editorial: Club Almost Loses Charter Through GFE Interference," *What's Happening?* 3, no. 6 (March 1974): 1.

29 PAS, A 595 II.142 Mutual Friendship Society, Phil Graham, "II. A Note by Gays for Equality," *What's Happening?* 2, no. 8 (April 1973): 6.

30 Phil Graham, interview summary, 17.

31 Vogel, interview with author.

32 Vogel, interview with author.

33 PAS, A 595 II.142 Mutual Friendship Society: Phil Graham, "II. A Note by Gays for Equality," *What's Happening?* 2, no. 8 (April 1973): 6.

34 PAS, A 595 II.142 Mutual Friendship Society, "Editorial," *What's Happening?* 2, no. 7 (March 1973): 3.

35 Ibid.

36 PAS, A 595 II.142 Mutual Friendship Society, Bill Lewis, "II. A Note by Gays for Equality," *What's Happening?* 2, no. 8 (April 1973): 5.

37 Rich North, interview.

38 Sally Papso, in an editorial comment in the interview with "Jane Smith," noted the fears of this older generation, who experienced the Cold War purges and political chill, about liberationists and more open political battles. "Gays and lesbians at the time wanted to believe (naively) that if they just presented quietly and respectively, didn't demand things, kept silent, didn't 'flaunt' didn't make waves, worked hard, 'adjusted' and 'integrated' into society and so on, that sooner or later the heterosexual society would eventually come around and accept and tolerate them for the 'good' people that they are and that all would be well," in "Born between the Wars," Smith interview transcript, 23.

39 PAS, GFE Papers; Ted Millward, "Gays for Equality – A History / Appreciation," 4.

40 Millward article on GFE's tenth anniversary. See details in note 40.

41 Millward's *Making a Scene* covers the establishment of lesbian spaces across the country, including in the prairies. Given space limits there is not extensive coverage of any individual "scene" in Western Canada, but those interested in a national picture of lesbian organizing and cultural

development would be well served by reading her volume, Liz Millward, *Making a Scene: Lesbians and Community across Canada*.

42 CLGA Toronto, *Out and About*; Peter Crossley, "More than a Woman," *Out and About, no.* 8 (September 1978): 10.

43 Correspondence at the Canadian Women's Movement Archives indicates the foundation in September 1984 of The Lesbian Archives of Manitoba and North-West Ontario (LARC), located near Kenora. The intent of these archives, started by Erin Cole, Doreen Worden, and Isabel Andrews was to "preserve, honour and share the herstory of gay women and to make this herstory accessible to both rural and urban lesbians." Unfortunately, negotiations between the CWMA and LARC proved difficult, and thus LARC never provided more than a summation of their holdings, nor did they appear interested in allowing the larger archives to access their materials. LARC held the papers for a variety of early Winnipeg feminist and lesbian organizations, and because the paper trail goes cold with the correspondence in the CWMA files, it is uncertain what has happened to that material. This omission potentially accounts for the paucity of information about early Winnipeg women's liberation/lesbian organizations.

44 Canadian Women's Movement Archives (CWMA), *Long Time Coming*, HQ 75.6.C3 L66, "The National News," *Long Time Coming* 1, no. 6 (February 1974): 17.

45 CWMA, Box 129, Winnipeg Lesbian Society, Winnipeg, "undated flyer."

46 CWMA, Box 129, Winnipeg Women's Liberation Newsletter, *Winnipeg Women's Liberation Newsletter*, April/May 1976, 1.

47 CWMA, Box 135, The Women's Building, Winnipeg, Manitoba; "Canada's First Women's Building: Winnipeg," *Upstream* 3, no. 2 (January 1979): 2.

48 PAS NR A 821 III.54, Lesbianism (Canada) 1976–94, "Dyke Dynamics," *Harpies: Women's Building Newsletter: A Women's Monthly Periodical* 1, no. 1 (July): 15.

49 Ibid.

50 Graham Stinnett, Manitoba Gay and Lesbian Archives, 2012, "Manitoba Gay and Lesbian Archives – Lesbians."

51 Ibid.

52 CLGA, Toronto, Winnipeg Material, GFE Brochure, 1977, "Gay Friends of Brandon."

53 CLGA, Toronto, *Out and About* – Winnipeg $3218, "Gay Events," *Out and About, no.* 1 (February 1978): 1.

54 CLGA Toronto, *Out and About* – Winnipeg $3218, "Gay Friends of Brandon April Calendar," *Out and About, no.* 3 (April 1978): 9.

55 "Edward" is a pseudonym, interview with author, 2006.

56 CLGA, Toronto, Winnipeg Material, GFE Brochure, 1977, "Thompson Gay Group."

57 CLGA, Toronto, Gay Friends of Brandon – #1695, "Gay Friends of Brandon Newsletter, October 1978," 1.

58 CLGA Toronto, Winnipeg Material, "Coming Out" Gay Television Cablecast – Consolidated List of Programs Broadcast, 29 November 1984, 3.

59 CLGA Toronto Winnipeg Material, Letter from Bill Lewis, Manitoba Gay Conference to Winnipeg Lesbian Society, 6 April 1977.

60 CLGA Toronto Winnipeg Material, Manitoba Gay Directory 1977, "Council on Homosexuality and Religion: Origin and Precepts," 1.

61 CLGA Toronto Winnipeg Material, Manitoba Gay Directory 1977, "Dignity," 1.

62 CLGA Toronto Winnipeg Material, Manitoba Gay Directory 1977, "After Stonewall: A Gay Liberation Journal."

63 CLGA Toronto, Winnipeg Material, Manitoba Gay Directory 1977, "Gay Men's Discussion Group."

64 Interviews with Lyle Dick, Ted Millward, Frances Williamson, and others all mentioned the important role that the GFE counsellors played in their own awareness of diversity of sexual behaviours, and ultimately to their coming out as gay and lesbians.

65 Lambda Update – "Dollars and Sense: An Editorial" *Wilde Times* (June 1982): 6.

66 PAS, A 595 Neil Richards II. 142 Mutual Friendship Society 1972–75, 1980–1 (Winnipeg). Social Committee Report *What's Happening?* 2, no. 11 (Summer 1973): page unknown.

67 Social committee Report: "As far as this writer knows, we have the first gay bowling league in Canada … We bowl Tuesdays at 9pm at the Uptown Lanes on Academy Road," see *What's Happening?* 3, no. 3 (November 1973).

68 PAS, A 595 Neil Richards II. 142 Mutual Friendship Society 1972–75, 1980–1 (Winnipeg), Social Committee Report, *What's Happening?* 3, no. 3 (November 1973): 9.

69 Chris Vogel, interview with author.

70 Hilary Osborne-Hill, "Pink Notes from Blue Room," *What's Happening?* (August 1975): 6.

71 Don Fenwick, interview summary, 105–6.

72 PAS Neil Richards Collection A 595 II.100, Gays for Equality (Winnipeg), 1974–80, "Report on Activities for 1973–4 – Gays for Equality, Winnipeg."

73 CLGA: Manitoba Gay and Lesbian Archive, "Gays for Equality" brochure, n.d.

74 Manitoba Gay/Lesbian Oral History II: Interview Summary, Arthur E. (Ted) Millward, interviewed, Winnipeg, 23 June 1992, 1.

75 Rainbow Resource Centre: Clipping File 508: Chris Vogel, Barbara Huck, "Last Minority Making Strides," *Winnipeg Free Press*, 19 October 1982, 17.

76 PAS, Neil Richards A 595 II.100, Gays for Equality, 1974–80. "Report on Activities for 1973–4 – Gays for Equality, Winnipeg."

77 Further commentary on the activist agenda of GFE will be addressed in the final chapter.

78 In 1964, an American organization by the name of Council on Religion and the Homosexual was created in San Francisco. While it is logical that it might have been the model for Winnipeg's CHR, no evidence in the Winnipeg archival holdings confirms that supposition. See Marc Stein, *Rethinking the Gay and Lesbian Movement*, 67.

79 PAS, Neil Richards Collection A 595 II.46, Council on Homosexuality and Religion (Winnipeg), 1978–82. Ted Millward, "St. Stephens-Broadway Foundation: Preliminary Application for a Grant," 24 February 1982.

80 PAS, Neil Richards Collection A 595 II.46, Council on Homosexuality and Religion, Winnipeg, 1976–82; Harry Wiebe, "Witness Feature: Gay Mennonites A Brief Look at a Few of Our Experiences," *Gay Christian Witness* 3 (June 1982): 7–12.

81 Wiebe indicated that most of the men had been provided with pseudonyms to protect their privacy, including "Gerhard."

82 PAS, NRC A 595 II.46, Harry Wiebe, "Gay Mennonites," 11.

83 Frances Williamson, (pseudonym), interview with author, Winnipeg, 21 November 2002.

84 Doug Nicholson, interview summary, 2.

85 Rainbow Resource Centre, Manitoba Gay/Lesbian Oral History II, Chris Vogel, interview summary, 13 June 1992.

86 PAS, Neil Richards, File on University classes "Fall Session Calendar, 1979 for the University of Manitoba, Continuing Education Division."

87 PAS, NRC A 595 II.167, Project Lambda (Winnipeg) 1978–85, Project Lambda brochure, no date.

88 The Forty-Sixty Club was organized to combat the "loneliness and alienation some middle-aged gay men feel in a city as 'closeted' as Winnipeg." According to author Peter Crossley, some of the men in the club were married and unable to come out, others were openly gay but still preferred the less stressful setting than one might find at a club. "The 40-60 Club," *Out and About, no.* 5 (July 1978): 9.

89 PAS, NRC A 595 II.167, Project Lambda (Winnipeg) 1978–85, Crossley, "The 40-60 Club", 9.

90 PAS, NRC A 595 II.167, Project Lambda (Winnipeg) 1978–85. "Lesbians/ Gays of Fargo/Moorhead" announcement, *Out and About* (September 1980): 4.

91 Chris Vogel, interview with author.

92 Ms Purdy's closed its doors in 2001, having had a continuous run in the city from September 1979.

93 PAS, NRC A 595 II.167, Project Lambda (Winnipeg) 1978–85, "Regular Events at the Women's Building," *Out and About* (January 1980): 5.

94 CLGA Canadian Women's Music and Cultural Festival, Winnipeg, 1984; Maureen Medved, "Our Time is Now," *Herizons* 2, no. 7 (November 1984): 26–8.

95 CLGA Toronto, Winnipeg Gay Media Collective: "Coming Out" Gay Television Cablecast – Consolidated List of Programs Broadcast VPW (Winnipeg), Channel 13 west of Red River, Saturdays 6:00–6:30 p.m., 1–10.

96 For a detailed overview of the planning, programming, and personalities involved with Coming Out TV, see Saskatchewan Archives Board, Neil Richards Collection A 595 II.211, Winnipeg Gay Media Collective Collection, 1981–9.

97 CLGA Winnipeg Gay Media Collective, letter from Robert Dame to Friends, for Coming Out TV and the Gay Media Collective, Winnipeg, 1 March 1983.

98 CLGA Gay Media Collective, Winnipeg, letter from John Duggan, Gays of Ottawa, to Robert Dame, Winnipeg Gay Media Collective, 14 April 1983.

99 CLGA Toronto, Winnipeg Gay Media Collective, letter from Mrs. "J," Lynn Lake, Manitoba, to Take 30 Access, CBC, 11 March 1983.

100 CLGA Winnipeg Gay Media Collective, letter from Mr. "C," Vernon, BC, to CBC, 11 March 1983.

101 CLGA Winnipeg Gay Media Collective, letter from Mr S., London, Ontario, to CBC, 11 March 1983.

102 CLGA Winnipeg Gay Media Collective, unsigned letter, Kitchener, Ontario, to CBC, no date. Also, letter from Mrs C., Kitchener, Ontario, to CBC, n.d. Interestingly, out of the seventeen letters received, nine were from Ontario. Of those, the five negative ones all came from southwestern Ontario – Kitchener, London, Chatham, and Grand Bend versus the positive ones, which primarily came from the Toronto area.

103 CLGA Winnipeg Gay Media Collective, Mrs F, Garrick, Saskatchewan, to CBC, 14 March 1983.

104 CLGA Winnipeg Gay Media Collective, "Mrs B," Winnipeg, to CBC, 14 March 1983.

105 See Millward for the desire to shift to non-alcoholic spaces for lesbian community building.

106 PAS, Neil Richards Collection A 595 II.167, Project Lambda (Winnipeg) 1978–85; "Giovanni's Room – A Proposal Made to Project Lambda by Richard North," 26 August 1980.

107 PAS, A 595 II.167, Project Lambda (Winnipeg) 1978–85. "Giovanni's Room."

108 PAS, II.167 PL, "Giovanni's Room." Names of specific individuals appeared in the original text. However, by the terms of my agreement with the SAB, in return for unlimited access to all documents in the Neil Richards Collection, I agreed not to publish names of individuals listed in non-published documents (minutes of meetings, letters, et cetera) unless I could be confident that they were willing to have their names published. Thus, I have removed the names of these eleven men and women.

109 CLGA Toronto, Wilde Times – Winnipeg #4253. "Much Ado about Nothing or Beyond Beefcake," *Wilde Times: The Oscar Wilde Memorial Society* (October 1980): 5.

110 "Successful First Community Social!" *Wilde Times* (incorporating *What's Happening* and *Out and About*) January 1982: (8–9).

111 "Successful First Community Social!" *Wilde Times*, 8.

112 Doug Nicholson, interview summary. 3.

113 "What's Happening Board Notes," *Wilde Times* (March 1982): 6.

114 Lambda Update, "Dollars and Sense: An Editorial," *Wilde Times* (June 1982): 6.

115 Ibid.

116 Lambda Update, "Hands across the Street: An Editorial," *Out and About* (May 1983): 1.

117 "Happenings 12th Annual Meeting Heralds the Grand Opening Sum Quod Sum Building and Ends in a Smash Capacity Anniversary Social," *Out and About* (July 1983): 3.

118 Ibid.

119 See website for pictures of the last night at Happenings.

120 Stompin' Tom Connors beloved song, "Sudbury Saturday Night" alludes to the northern Canadian, small-town heterosexual pastimes of "the girls" at bingo, the boys getting "stinko" while not thinking about Inco – working in the mines. This working-class anthem was the antithesis of "Coming Out TV."

4. *Grassroots*

1 Marion Alexander, interview with author, Saskatoon, 2002.

2 Jeannine Locke, "Saskatoon: The Good Life City," *Maclean's* 82, no. 10 (October 1969): 24–35.

3 Richard Florida, *The Rise of the Creative Class: And How It's Transforming Work, Leisure, Community and Everyday Life* (New York: Basic Books, 2002).

4 For example, judged by attendance figures more residents of Saskatoon patronized the Mendel Art Gallery than Toronto inhabitants visited the AGO. Locke, "Saskatoon: The Good Life City," 26.

5 Alan F.J. Artibise, "Afterward: Saskatoon's History and the Usable Urban Past" in *Saskatoon: The First Half Century*, 313.

6 Ibid.

7 Locke, "Saskatoon: The Good Life City," 33.

8 David Rimmer, interview with author, 21 January 2003.

9 Bruce Garman, interview with author, 25 July 2003

10 Selena, interview with author, 8 September 2003.

11 Garman, interview with author.

12 Garman, interview with author.

13 Tom Warner, " Saskatoon," *The Body Politic*, February 1977, p. 11.

14 Gens Hellquist, interview with author.

15 "Nalbach Dies," *Perceptions*, 30 July 1997, 12.

16 In his autobiography, *Words to That Effect*, Peter Millard notes how much he disliked this system. This could also be part of what Warner, an activist then living in Toronto, also found objectionable with these parties.

17 Millard, *Words to That Effect*; Hellquist interview.

18 Leonard Lawrence, interview with author, 28 July 2003. Leonard Lawrence is a pseudonym.

19 Regina has a long history of protest, including, most famously, the 1935 Regina Riot. As the work of historian Roberta Lexier argues, the Regina Campus (later University of Regina) was the site of student activism in the 1960s and early 1970s. It is curious, then, that Regina's queer community was less vocal and less activist than Saskatoon's. See Roberta Lexier, "Dreaming of a Better World: Student Rebellion in 1960s Regina," *Past Imperfect* 10 (2004): 79–98.

20 A documentary film was produced of GLCR's move to their location on Broad Street in Regina in 1999. This film is an excellent resource as it also contains snippets of and interviews about their twenty-seven years in existence. See Glenn Wood, *Community Building*, (Viddy Well Films, Regina, 1999), DVD in the Neil Richards Collection of Sexual and Gender Diversity, University of Saskatchewan Archives and Special Collections.

21 Debbie Simmons (pseudonym), interview with author, Saskatoon, 12 July 2006.

22 Ibid.

23 Janet Harvey, interview with author, Regina, 28 July 2003.

24 Ibid.

25 Debbie Simmons, interview with author, 12 July 2006.

26 Correspondents to *Gay Saskatchewan/Grassroots* from North Dakota referenced trips to Regina. Again, it is worth reminding readers that prairie dwellers will drive long distances for long weekends, events, and even dinner, it is part of the regional culture and a means to mitigate the isolation of the place.

27 Leonard Lawrence, interview with author, July 2003.

28 Brian Gladwell, interview with author, 29 July 2003.

29 Paul Gessell, interview with author, 23 August 2006.

30 PAS, Neil Richards Collection: Darrel David Hockley, Esquire, "A History of the Gay Community of Regina," Regina, Saskatchewan, 1 October 1994, 6.

31 In 2015 the Copper Kettle celebrated their fiftieth anniversary. See http:// www.cbc.ca/news/canada/saskatchewan/copper-kettle-serves-up -50-years-1.3223241.

32 David Rimmer, interview with author, 21 January 2003.

33 Hellquist, interview with author.

34 Gens Hellquist, "Nalbach Dies," *Perceptions*, 30 July 1997, 12.

35 One of the joys of oral interviews is the wonderful moments when people just open up about their life experiences. Dorothy was a real character, and enjoyed our interview time immensely. Part of her sense of her self-identity, and her perception of her role in the Saskatoon community, derived from being the only and hence "original" lesbian to respond to this ad. It demonstrates how many people read alternative periodicals like the *Georgia Straight* carefully.

36 Neil Richards, *Celebrating a History of Diversity: Lesbian and Gay Life in Saskatchewan, 1971–2005. A Selected Annotated Chronology* (Saskatoon: The Avenue Community Centre for Gender and Sexual Diversity, 2005), 1.

37 Hellquist, interview with author.

38 PAS, NR A 821 IV.39 Newsletters, 1971–84, Doug Hellquist, "President's Report" *Gemini Club News*, 1, no. 1, 13 November 1971.

39 PAS, Doug Wilson Collection (DW) A 810 File #8 Original Correspondence, letter from Mavis Carleton to Doug Wilson, n.d. (but clearly from the early 1980s).

40 Paul Gessell, interview with author.

41 Ibid.

42 Hellquist, interview with author.

43 Gessell, interview with author.

44 Tom Warner, "Saskatoon: It Has One of the Biggest Gay Centres in the Country: A Report on the People Who Make It Work," *The Body Politic* 30 (February 1977): 11.

45 Millard, *Or Words to That Effect*, 214.
46 William Slights, "The Straight and Narrow" *Sheaf Special Supplement*, October 1975, p. 3.
47 Millard, *Words to That Effect*, 212.
48 Ibid.
49 Jean Hillabold and Cory Oxelrod interview with Global News reporter David Baxter in June 2016. See http://globalnews.ca/news/2770726/44 -years-of-the-gay-and-lesbian-community-of-regina-an-oral-history/.
50 Neil Richards, *Celebrating a History of Diversity*, 2.
51 PAS, Neil Richards Collection: Darrel David Hockley, Esquire "A History of the Gay Community of Regina," Regina, Saskatchewan, 1 October 1994, 3.
52 "Executive Directory: Gay Community of Regina Inc." (formerly known as the Atropos Friendship Society) Corporation No: 203098. My thanks to Neil Richards for providing me with a copy of this unpublished history. And, naturally, to the author of this document, a long-time member of the Odyssey Club for documenting the club's administrative history. Those individuals involved in running the Odyssey Club are named in the document but by agreement with the author their privacy has been maintained, and pseudonyms have been applied.
53 The building has long since been torn down to make way for a condo development. See http://globalnews.ca/news/2770726/44-years-of-the -gay-and-lesbian-community-of-regina-an-oral-history/.
54 Hockley, 10.
55 Brian Gladwell interview with author, Regina, 29 July 2003.
56 Heather Bishop, OC, OM, later moved to Winnipeg. She has been recognized for her role as an activist, folk musician, children's musician, and feminist. For more information about her various causes and career history, see *Heather Bishop* website, http://www.heatherbishop.com/.
57 Jean Hillabold, interview with Global News, 17 June 2016.
58 Rogers, interview with author 29 July 2003.
59 Hockley, 10.
60 PAS, A595II.154, "President's Message," *Odyssey News* (Regina) 5, no. 1 (February 1977): 3.
61 PAS, A595II.154 "Public Relations Committee Report," *Odyssey News* (Regina) 5, no. 1 (February 1977): 4.
62 Darrel David Hockley, "A History of the Gay Community of Regina," 11.
63 Ibid.
64 Ibid.
65 Saskatchewan Resources for Sexual Diversity, at the University of Saskatchewan Archives, has a copy of Glen Wood's 1999 film *Community Building*. My thanks to Neil Richards for sharing this DVD.

66 For full details about the Wilson case, see V.J. Korinek, "The Most Openly Gay Person for at Least a Thousand Miles," *Canadian Historical* Review 84, no. 4 (2003): 517–50. An abbreviated overview of this pivotal event is provided in chapter 7.

67 Neil Richards, interview with author, Saskatoon, December 2002.

68 Neil Richards, email to author, 14 November 2004.

69 In the mid-1970s, Doug Hellquist changed his name to Gens Hellquist. For consistency, and because this was his chosen name, I have used Gens Hellquist throughout this text; interview with author.

70 Millard recalled this as a formative experience for himself, see Millard's *Words to That Effect*.

71 Millard *Words to That Effect*, p 216.

72 Diana Rogers, "Gay, God, Man (and Woman) in Sexual Battle," *The Sheaf*, 29 January 1974, 3

73 Millard, *Words to That Effect*, p. 217

74 Peter Millard Papers, University of Saskatchewan Archives, P.T. Millard Fonds, MG 47.

75 Peter Millard Papers, University of Saskatchewan Archives, P.T. Millard Fonds, MG 47, *Words to That Effect*, p. 218.

76 Selena, interview with author, Saskatoon, 8 September 2003.

77 Debbie Simmons, interview with author, Saskatoon, July 12, 2006

78 Ibid.

79 Richards, *Celebrating a History of Diversity*, 5.

80 Ibid., 6.

81 Neil Richards, interview with author, 10 December 2002. This problem was exacerbated in the early 1980s by the funding issues, in particular the competition from commercial clubs (Numbers, later Diva's).

82 Hellquist, interview with author.

83 Ibid.

84 PAS, A595 II.2. Doug Wilson, "At the Grassroots" *After Stonewall* 9 (Fall 1979): 7.

85 Ibid., 8.

86 Ibid., 11.

87 The 2011 Canadian Census pegged Humboldt's population at 5,678 people, making them the fourteenth largest community in the province of Saskatchewan. See "Humboldt: Statistics & Demographics," accessed 27 September 2016, http://www.humboldt.ca/statistics-and-demographics. Humboldt was supported by the Saskatchewan Pride Network in this successful endeavour.

88 PAS, NR A595 II.2 After Stonewall, "Welcome to Saskatoon" *After Stonewall* 9 (Fall 1979): 2.

89 Ibid.

90 Hellquist, interview with author.

91 In June 1988 Artists for Human Rights presented "The Devine Comedy," which consisted of two nights of theatre intended to laugh Saskatchewan back to sanity. Neil Richards, *Celebrating a History of Diversity*, 27.

92 V.J. Korinek, "Activism=Education," 125.

93 Ibid.

94 "After 32 Years Diva's Kelly Faber Hangs up the Bar Towel," CBC Saskatoon, accessed July 2017, http://www.cbc.ca/news/canada/saskatoon/after-32-years-diva-s-kelly-faber-hangs-up-the-bartowel-1.2679768.

95 Hockley, 22.

96 Richards, *Celebrating a History of Diversity*, p 5

97 Hockley, 22.

98 Ibid., 23.

99 Ibid., 24.

100 Hockley, *A History of the Gay Community of Regina*, 26.

101 Jan Harvey, interview with author, Regina, 28 July 2003.

102 "The Challenges of Being Gay in a Homophobic Society," *Briarpatch*, June 1983, 21–3.

103 For an analysis of the importance lesbian feminists placed on creating spaces, see Liz Millward, *Making a Scene: Lesbians and Community across Canada, 1964–84*.

104 Ibid., 23.

105 PAS A595 Neil Richards II.125 Lesbian Newsletter Regina, 1984: February 1984, p. 1.

106 Jan Harvey, interview with author.

107 Ibid.

108 Brian Gladwell, interview with author.

109 PAS, NR A 821 VI.4, "Classified Ads" *Gay Saskatchewan* 2, no. 5 (May 1979).

110 PAS NR A 595 II.92, *Gay Saskatchewan* (formerly Saskatchewan Gay Coalition, 1980–1), "Regina," *Gay Saskatchewan*, November 1980, 3, no. 10, 3.

111 Neil Richards Collection for Sexual Diversity, University of Saskatchewan Archives and Special Collections, Glen Woods, *Community Building*.

112 PAS, Neil Richards fonds A821 VII-14-C, poster photo card.

113 PAS, Neil Richards fonds A821 VII.2., Metamorphosis, 1978.

114 Ibid.

115 SAB, Neil Richards A821 VI.4 Newsletters, 1978–82, "Metamorphosis Announcement," *Gay Saskatchewan: The Newsletter of the Saskatchewan Gay Coalition*, 1, no. 8 (September 1976): 2.

116 PAS, A821 Neil Richards fonds, V II.2 Metamorphosis, 1978, "Prairie Festival: Butterflies to Soar" *The Body Politic* 47 (October 1978): 13.

117 PAS, A821 Neil Richards fonds, V II.2 Metamorphosis, 1978, "Prairie Festival Soars to Success" *The Body Politic* 48 (November 1978): 9.

118 PAS, A821 VII.3, Metamorphosis, 1979.

119 PAS, NR A821 VII.4, Metamorphosis, 1980.

120 PAS, NR A821 VII.4, Metamorphosis, 1980, "Prairie Festival Blooms" *The Body Politic* 69 (December 1980/January 1981): 15.

121 Ibid.

122 PAS, NR A 821 VII.6 Metamorphosis, 1982, letter from Walter Davis to Metamorphosis volunteers, 19 October 1982.

123 Marion Alexander, interview with author, 26 August 2003.

124 PAS, A821 VII-14-C, heritage postcard image of 1980 poster and text.

125 Neil Richards, *Celebrating a History of Diversity*, 10.

126 Debbie Simmons, interview with author.

127 Ibid.

128 Ibid.

129 Ibid.

130 Raymond-Jean Frontain, "Peter Gregory McGehee (1955–1991)" in *The Encyclopedia of Arkansas History and Culture*, http://www.encyclopediaofarkansas.net/encyclopedia/entry-detail.aspx?entryID=3252; Raymond-Jean Frontain, "A Madhouse of Thanksgiving: Peter McGehee, AIDS, and Screwball Comedy" *Philological Review* 32 (Fall 2006): 79–109.

131 See the video *Sisters with a Difference: The Quinlan Sisters, 1981–1984* (Rudcat Productions, 2011), http://library2.usask.ca/srsd/media.php.

132 Listen to the clip at http://library2.usask.ca/srsd/media.php, accessed July 2017.

133 In addition to the documents in the P. McGehee Fonds at Saskatchewan Archives Board, his performing partner Fiji "Champagne" Robinson has created a website devoted to the work and life of Peter McGehee called The Resurrection of Peter McGehee, see http://library2.usask.ca/srsd/media.php.

134 VJ Korinek, "*Carousel Capers*: Queer and Feminist Activism in the Prairies, 1970–1985," *American Periodicals* (forthcoming).

135 Gens Hellquist, interview with author.

136 Tom Warner, interview with author.

137 Marcia Gallo, *Different Daughters*.

138 Dorothy, interview with author.

139 Richards, interview with author. Many community archives and libraries were established in the 1970s, and a number of influential queer

historians/academics began their careers as public historians – J. Ned
Katz, Alan Bérubé, Michael Lynch, Steven Maynard, Joan Nestle, et al.
The Canadian Lesbian and Archive, located in Toronto, where Richards
volunteered in summers, was also a key stimulus to the archiving of
Canadian papers and periodicals, starting with *The Body Politic*. See:
http://clga.ca/ accessed 17 December 2017.

140 Richards, *Celebrating a History of Diversity*.
141 Val Scrivener, interview with author.
142 PAS, NR A 821 VI.4, Saskatchewan Gay Coalition Newsletters, 1978–82;
"Classified Ads," *Gay Saskatchewan* 2, no. 8 (August 1979).
143 PAS, NR A821 VI.4, "Classified Ads," *Gay Saskatchewan* 2, no. 7 (July
1979).
144 PAS, NR A821 VI.4, "Classified Ads," *Gay Saskatchewan* 2, no. 5 (May
1979).
145 PAS, NR A 595.II.2, After Stonewall: Doug Wilson, "At the Grassroots,"
*After Stonewall: Critical Journal of Lesbian and Gay Liberation in Prairie
Canada* 9 (Fall 1979): 15.
146 Ibid.
147 Ibid.
148 PAS, NR A 595 II.2 After Stonewall, "Welcome to Saskatoon," *After
Stonewall: Critical Journal of Lesbian and Gay Liberation in Prairie Canada* 9
(Fall 1979): 2.
149 Ibid.
150 Walter Davis, "Gay Liberation in the Prairies: On to Saskatoon," *After
Stonewall: Critical Journal of Lesbian and Gay Liberation in Prairie Canada* 3
(1977): 28–9.
151 PAS, A821 NR I.126 "Editorial," *Perceptions* 40, 13April 1988, 3.
152 Ibid.
153 Ibid.
154 "Ritz Hotel Apollo Room Pass into City History" *Saskatoon Star Phoenix*,
24 April 1985, D11.
155 AIDS continues to cut a wide wake through the prairies, where
rates of HIV infections in Saskatchewan and Manitoba outpace all
other provinces (only the northern territories have worse rates of
infection). So, while we have a tendency to think of HIV as a chronic
disease, Saskatchewan and Manitoba rates of infections suggest
otherwise.
156 Erin Petrow, "Small Towns Not Small Minded" *Saskatoon Star Phoenix*, 17
September 2016, accessed 17 December 2017, http://thestarphoenix
.com/news/local-news/small-towns-not-small-minded.

5. "Outlaws"

1 City of Edmonton Archives, GATE records, verbatim transcript of taped phone interview between Gens Hellquist, Saskatoon, D.M. Winnipeg, and Walter Cavalieri, Edmonton, 3 July 1983.

2 Paul Gessell, interview with author.

3 Margaret Osler, interview with author, Calgary, March 2003.

4 Eliane Leslau Silverman, *The Last Best West: Women on the Alberta Frontier, 1880–1930* (Montreal: Eden Press, 1984), xiii and 90.

5 Margaret Osler, interview with author.

6 Margaret Osler, interview with author. Dr Osler put no restrictions on my interview with her other than that I was not to reveal her partner's name, which naturally I have respected.

7 Kevin Allen, the lead researcher and creator of *Calgary Gay History Project: Our Past Matters*, is at work on a community history of Gay/Queer Calgary. Please see: https://calgaryqueerhistory.ca/, accessed July 2017.

8 Glenbow Archives, Doug Young Fonds, M8397/10 Broach newsletter, Calgary 1985, n.d.

9 PAS, Neil Richards S-A 1067 145 correspondence, pamphlets, 1975–93: Letter from L.S., President of Club Carousel, Calgary, to Mr F, n.d. (likely 1974), 1.

10 Glenbow Archives, Doug Young Fonds, M8397/23 GIRC Gay Calgary Newspaper and Reach Newsletter, 1978–9, 1981, *Gay Calgary* 2, no. 4 (December 1978), 2.

11 Ibid.

12 City of Edmonton Archives: Maureen Irwin, "A Partial Chronology of the Edmonton Lesbian/Gay History," 1.

13 Ibid.

14 See Gloria Filax, *Queer Youth in the Province of the 'Severely Normal'* (Vancouver: University of British Columbia Press, 2006).

15 John Ibbitson, "In 1965, Everett Klippert Was Sentenced to a Life Behind Bars. His crime? Being Gay" *Globe and Mail*, 27 February 2016, Globe Focus, F1, F4–5.

16 Klippert refused attempts to get him to participate in gay activism, or to be visibly part of "gay pride" events. Kevin Allen, lead researcher of Calgary Gay History Project, with the help of Everett Klippert's family, has worked to document the Klippert's Calgary history. For an interesting photo essay of the family's life, and houses, in Calgary, please see: https://calgaryqueerhistory.ca/2016/06/02/the-homes-of-everett-klippert/, accessed July 2017.

17 Gloria Filax has produced a study of media and political impressions
    of queer youth in Alberta in the 1990s. For those interested in sociology,
    education, and social work, this is a valuable contemporary study: Gloria
    Filax, *Queer Youth in the Province of the Severely Normal*.
18 One would do well to contrast two contemporary municipal elections
    results from October 2010. Toronto voters elected Rob Ford as their mayor
    while Calgarians embraced the politics of Naheed Nenshi. Enough said,
    Alberta has changed, and so has Toronto.
19 "Notice This is a Private Newsletter," *Carousel Capers* 4, no. 6, June 1973.
20 Ibid.
21 Edmonton's gay organizational papers are available at the City of
    Edmonton Archives. My thanks to the archivists at the former armoury
    building for their assistance during this research, and in particular, to
    allow me and my research assistant, Erik Strikwerda, to access these as yet
    uncatalogued documents. Supplemented with the materials in the Doug
    Young Fonds at the Glenbow Archives, it has permitted the queer histories
    of Edmonton and Calgary to emerge here.
22 Edmonton Population Figures, provided by City of Edmonton Planning
    and Development Website, accessed 17 December 2017, https://www
    .edmonton.ca/city_government/facts_figures/population-history.aspx.
23 See Bill Waiser's *Saskatchewan: A New History* for an overview of the
    creation of the "twin" provinces, Alberta and Saskatchewan, in 1905. At
    the time they were admitted to Confederation, Saskatchewan was the third
    most populous province, and both economies were dominated by farming,
    with Alberta's leaning more towards ranching than the grain economy of
    Saskatchewan.
24 Edmonton Population Figures, provided by City of Edmonton Planning
    and Development Website.
25 GA Doug Young Fonds, Series II M8397/5 ALGRA newspaper *Gay
    Horizons*, 1979–80, see "Happy Birthday Swen!" *Gay Horizons* 14
    (December 1979): 6.
26 Dorothy, interview with author.
27 City of Edmonton Archives, MS 595 Box 1A GALA File List, Maureen
    Irwin, "A Partial Chronology of the Edmonton Lesbian/Gay History,"
    1996. Irwin based her chronology on newsletters from GATE and from
    Womonspace, as well as interviews and emails with older gays and
    lesbians in the community. She notes "in the spring and summer of 1996
    Michael Phair and I presented the information 3 times (to the Queer-Act-
    Queer Conference at the University of Alberta, to a pride event at Orlando
    Books and to the Prime Timers monthly meeting) and received input on

each occasion. Regretfully, Irwin died in 2000, and thus I was unable to interview her in person about her experiences.

28 City of Edmonton Archives, MS 595 Box 1A GALA File List. M. Irwin, A Partial Chronology, 1996, 1.

29 Marilyn Moysa. "Back When 'It' Was against the Law of the Land," *Edmonton Journal*, 2 March 1993, C7.

30 Ibid.

31 Selena ,interview with author; Garman, interview with author.

32 Irwin chronology, 2.

33 Marion Foster and Kent Murray, *A Not So Gay World: Homosexuality in Canada* (Toronto: McClelland & Stewart, 1972), 164.

34 Ibid.

35 Carolyn Anderson, "The Voices of Older Lesbian Women: An Oral History" (PhD diss., University of Calgary, 2001).

36 City of Edmonton Archives, GATE Files Box 1 Files 1–34, "Canadian National Canadian Pacific Telecommunications from W.H. Munro, Managing Editor, *Butch Magazine*, Sydney, Australia, to GATE P.O. Box 1352 Edmonton Alberta, 28 October 1972.

37 City of Edmonton Archives, GLA Edmonton Box 1 GATE, File #4, Correspondence 1985–1987, letter from K. King, GATE to Bill Munro, Managing Editor, Butch Magazine Monthly, Sydney Australia, 3 November 1972.

38 Ibid.

39 Ibid.

40 City of Edmonton Archives, Irwin, "Partial Chronology of the Edmonton Lesbian/Gay History," 1996, 2.

41 Ibid., 3.

42 *Butch Magazine* letter.

43 Irwin, 3.

44 Klondike Days is Edmonton's annual summer fair, which includes a parade, midway, concerts, et cetera. While the Calgary Stampede has parlayed their Stampede into a megarodeo, which is an international draw, Klondike Days (K-Days as they are now called) are focused in the Alberta capital region.

45 City of Edmonton Archives, GATE Files Box I Files 1–34, "Minutes of Prairie Regional Gay Activist Conference," Saskatoon, 18–20 May 1974, 2.

46 Irwin. 2.

47 City of Edmonton Archives, GATE Files Box I Files 1–34, "Minutes of Prairie Regional Gay Activist Conference, 2. The section on Lesbian Feminists of Edmonton did not provide any numbers for the group. When

such a group was described in the pages of *Club 70 News* four women's
names were attached to the nascent group.

48 City of Edmonton Archives, GATE Files Box I Files 1–34, "Minutes of
   Prairie Regional Gay Activist Conference, 4; Irwin Chronology, GATE
   closed, April 1978, 5.

49 Paul Gessell, interview with author.

50 Michael Phair interview with author, 11 September 2003.

51 Irwin Chronology, 1.

52 Anne Murray, the Grammy and Juno award-winning popular country
   singer from Springhill, Nova Scotia, had a consistently large number of
   lesbian fans of her music. "Snowbird," released in 1970, was one of her
   most popular cross over hits.

53 Copies of this newsletter are available in the GATE papers at the City of
   Edmonton Archives. As well, many of these materials are also available
   from the Canadian Lesbian and Gay Archives in Toronto, because of
   reciprocal exchanges between Canadian gay and lesbian organizations.

54 *Club '70 News* 3, no. 3 (April 1972).

55 "Editorial Comment," *Club '70 News* 3, no. 5 (June 1972): 1.

56 Paul Gessell, interview with author. Gessell recalled First Nations men in
   attendance, but also a couple of drag queens who were Indigenous. He
   could not recall seeing any First Nations women.

57 "Editorial," *Club '70 News* 3, no. 3 (April 1972): 1. Please note, by my
   access agreements with archives, I am obliged to protect the privacy of
   those named in these documents. Particularly in the early years of such
   newsletters, these were circulated only amongst members and to those in
   other local clubs – they were not "public" in the way that commercialized
   media publications are readily available today. However, if individuals
   were openly named/known (by appearing in conventional media reports
   or appearing as activists in public settings) then I am free to list their
   names.

58 "The President Speaks," *Club '70 News*, 14 June 1972, 1.

59 *Club '70 News*, June 1974.

60 "Roving Reporter," *Club '70 News*, 5 January 1974, 2.

61 "GATE Drop-ins," *Club '70 News*, 5 January 1974, no page.

62 *Club 70 News*, February 1974, 2.

63 BT (pseudonym), "Lesbian Lore," *Club '70 News* March 1974, no page.

64 Ibid.

65 City of Edmonton Archives, GALA Papers, Box 1, Ruth Gardner, "Former
   Resident Active in Gay Politics," *The Newsletter* 1, no. 1 (June 1981): 10–12.

66 Irwin Chronology, 2.

67 Ibid.

68 Neil Richards, interview with author, 2002.

69 Irwin Chronology, 2.

70 Edmonton newspaper articles re: Conrad, and his press conference with the Journal stating that women were to be barred from Boots and Saddles.

71 Source: University of Alberta Alumni Website Profile, "William Thorsell ('66 BA, '70 MA, '95 LLD Hon)."

72 Mitchel Raphel, "The Beauty of William Thorsell," *fab magazine*, no. 275.

73 Ibid.

74 Donald W. McLeod, Lesbian and Gay Liberation in Canada: A Select Annotated Chronology, 1964–1975 (Toronto: Homewood Books, 1996), 69.

75 Canadian Lesbian and Gay Archives, We Demand, 1971. See the new history site in Ottawa for further details of this groundbreaking event: http://www.villagelegacy.ca/items/show/8, accessed 17 December 2017.

76 City of Edmonton Archives, GATE Files Box 1, Files 1–34, "GATE Press Release," Vancouver, BC, 10 August 1971.

77 Canadian Lesbian and Gay Archives, Toronto, Edmonton Chronology.

78 City of Edmonton Archives, GALA Papers, Boxes 1–4, M.L.M., "Background on GATE," n.d.

79 City of Edmonton Archives, "Michael Roberts Press Release," *Club 70 News*, November 1972.

80 City of Edmonton Archives, GATE Records, Box 1, File 16, "Minutes from 1972."

81 City of Edmonton Archives, GATE Records, Box 1, File 16, "GATE Minutes 1973: Minutes of the Executive Meeting of GATE," Edmonton, 20 January 1973. From the minutes: "Michael [Roberts] gave a short resume of events to date – secretive and slanderous toward GATE Edmonton."

82 City of Edmonton Archives, GATE Records, letter from Michael Roberts, Regional Coordinator, GATE, Box 362 Pembina, University of Alberta Post Office, to "B," Gays for Equality, 14 March 1973.

83 Gary Kinsman and Patrizia Gentile, *The Canadian War on Queers: National Security as Sexual Regulation.*

84 My thanks to Dr Steve Hewitt for sharing the RCMP documents of their surveillance of the Moose Jaw Anita Bryant Rally in July 1977.

85 City of Edmonton Archives, GATE Records, letter from Michael Roberts to "B," 14 March 1973.

86 Ibid.

87 Tom Warner, *Never Going Back.*

88 Deborah Brock, "'Workers of the World Caress': An Interview with Gary Kinsman on Gay and Lesbian Organizing in the 1970s Toronto Left," *left history* 9, no. 2, 10, accessed 17 December 2017, http://www.yorku.ca/lefthist/online/brock_kinsman.html.

89 City of Edmonton Archives, GATE Records, Box 1, File 34, "GATE
    Administration Office: Letter from M.S. Power of Attorney for L.M.
    Roberts, dated 11 September 1973. "This will authorize the transfer of the
    telephone … to the GAY ALLIANCE TOWARD EQUALITY, the transfer
    to take effect, retroactively, on 1 September 1973."

90 City of Edmonton GALA Archives, Box 1-4, M.L. Mumert, "Background
    to GATE," no date.

91 City of Edmonton Archives, GALA Collection, Boxes 1–4, GATE
    Telephone Log, summary prepared by the Social Services Director, n.d. but
    presumably from 1979.

92 Ibid.

93 Summary of GATE lesbian drop in 16 February 1974, *Club 70 News*,
    March 1974.

94 Ibid.

95 City of Edmonton Archives, GATE Collection, "Former Resident Active
    in Gay Politics," n.d.

96 GATE Library, *Club '70 News*, August 1974.

97 City of Edmonton Archives, GATE Files, Jim Bentein, "Gays Quit the
    Shadows, Seek Place in the Sun," *Edmonton Journal*, 9 May 1975, 13.

98 City of Edmonton Archives, GATE Files, Jim Bentein, "'Get It Straight; We
    Don't Want to Change,'" *Edmonton Journal*, 9 May 1975, 13.

99 Glenbow Archives, Doug Young Fonds, "Homosexuals: A Minority
    without Rights," 1 March 1976. Presented by GATE Edmonton to the
    Alberta Human Rights Commission. More details about the various
    moments of discrimination and homophobic violence will be addressed
    in chapter 8.

100 City of Edmonton Archives, Letter from D.M., Winnipeg, to John,
    Edmonton, dated 1983.

101 "Background to GATE, by MLM."

102 Marc Stein, *Rethinking the Gay and Lesbian Movement*.

103 Sandra Martin, "Peter Lougheed, Mr. Alberta, Dies at 84," *Globe and Mail*,
    13 September 2012, https://www.theglobeandmail.com/news/politics/
    peter-lougheed-mr-alberta-dies-at-age-84/article4544369/.

104 City of Edmonton Archives, GALA Collection, Boxes 1–4, GATE
    application to the Alberta Law Foundation, Calgary, Alberta for financial
    assistance, 25 May 1982.

105 Glenbow Archives Doug Young Fonds, Series II M 8397/14, Dignity
    Calgary 1978: *Dignity Alberta*, September 1978, 1

106 Canadian Lesbian and Gay Archives, GARD Newsletter #1489. *GARD
    Newsletter*, 2 lists three contact organizations for lesbians and gays living

in Red Deer, Alberta: *Gay Calgary, Gay Saskatchewan,* and *Communigay,* the newsletter of GATE Edmonton.

107 City of Edmonton Archives, Letter from D.M., to John, 12 May 1983.

108 Ibid.

109 City of Edmonton Archives, W.C., Social Services Director, Gay Alliance Toward Equality, "GATE CONSIDERS MAJOR MOVE," August 1983.

110 City of Edmonton Archives, GATE records, verbatim transcript of taped phone interview between Gens Hellquist and Walter Cavalieri, 3 July 1983.

111 I am indebted to the work of my former graduate student, Noelle Lucas, whose excellent thesis on Womonspace's history forms the basis point for my abbreviated history. Please see Noelle M. Lucas, "Womonspace: Building a Lesbian Community in Edmonton, Alberta, 1970–1990" (master's thesis, University of Saskatchewan, 2002).

112 City of Edmonton Archives, GALA Collection Box 1, "Lesbians in Edmonton Organize: 'Womonspace,'" *Gay Gleaner,* June 1982, 3–4.

113 City of Edmonton Archives, GALA Collection Box 1, Linda Fontaine, "There's Room at Every Woman's Place" *Gay Gleaner,* June 1982, 4.

114 Internally, all members knew and acknowledged this was a lesbian organization. Outwardly, however, similar to Happenings in particular, they did not utilize the word lesbian, nor refer to themselves as a lesbian organization, and expected all members to agree to this position. When they did not, they were willing to force people out – particularly women who held positions in the group's executive. See Lucas, "Womonspace," (master's thesis, 2002).

115 Irwin Chronology, 7.

116 See Lucas, "Womonspace," (master's thesis, 2002) for an extended discussion of the class, educational, and political divisions between lesbians in Edmonton and, in particular, of how the feminists in the 1970s and 1980s were critical of the middle-class women who joined Womonspace to "socialize."

117 Lucas, "Womonspace," (master's thesis, 2002), 78–9.

118 Elizabeth Massiah, interview with author, 13 September 2003.

119 Ibid.

120 Elizabeth Massiah mentioned this individual stealing twelve thousand dollars from Womonspace, and this matter was also mentioned in many of N. Lucas's interviews for her master's thesis.

121 CLGA Files: GARD Newsletters #1489, "Resignation Announced," *Gay Association of Red Deer, Supplement to the June Newsletter,* 5 June 1979, 2.

122 Ibid.

123 CLGA Files: GARD Newsletter #1489, *GARD Newsletter*, February 1979, 1.

124 CLGA Files: GARD Newsletter #1489, "GARD Holds First Meeting,"
    GARD Newsletter, March 1979, 1.

125 CLGA Files: GARD Newsletter #1489, "Calgary Gays Attend Meeting,"
    GARD Newsletter, April 1979, 1.

126 CLGA Files: GARD Newsletter #1489, "Bar Going Gay," *GARD
    Newsletter*, June 1979, 2.

127 Ibid,

128 Glenbow Archives, Doug Young Fonds, "Doug Young," *The Body Politic*,
    September 1980, 2.

129 Gloria E. Miller, *Lesbian and Gay Life in Alberta*, Research Project Summary,
    prepared for the Red Deer and District Museum, June 1999, 3.

130 Miller, 27.

131 Ibid., 6–7.

132 It was a curious situation, to be welcomed to Red Deer, provided space
    to view the transcripts, and access to all the confidential information they
    collected, but not then to be able to utilize them in published work. In
    the end, I have had to utilize the fragments of interviews provided in the
    research project summary and press commentary about the project.

133 Miller, 15.

134 Ibid., 20.

135 Ibid., 24.

136 Ibid., 24.

137 Ibid., 25.

138 City of Edmonton Archives, GLA Edmonton Box 1, GATE File 3: GATE
    Correspondence, 1977–83, W. Cavalieri, Social Services Director, GATE to
    GB, GAYFEST coordinator, Vancouver, BC, 28 July 1983.

139 Mariam Ibrahim, "Former City Councillor Michael Phair Named
    Chairman of the University of Alberta Board of Governors," *Edmonton
    Journal*, 25 February 2016, http://edmontonjournal.com/news/politics/
    former-city-councillor-michael-phair-named-new-chairman-of-university
    -of-alberta-board-of-governors.

6. "Love and Let Love"

 1 PAS NR A 595 II.2, *After Stonewall: A Critical Journal of Lesbian and Gay
    Liberation in Prairie Canada, 1977–80*. "So Much to Do," *After Stonewall* 1
    (Spring 1977): 1.

 2 Chris Vogel, interview with author.

3 Canadian Lesbian and Gay Archives Toronto (CLGA) "Out and About" – Winnipeg – #3218, Darryl Kippen, "After Stonewall," *Out and About*, 2.

4 Ibid.

5 Graham Stinnett, Manitoba Gay and Lesbian Archives, "Homophobic Violence," University of Manitoba Library and Special Collections: Manitoba Gay and Lesbian Archives History, http://umanitoba.ca/ libraries/units/archives/digital/gay_lesbian.

6 Vogel, interview with author.

7 University of Manitoba Archives and Special Collections, Manitoba Gay and Lesbian Archives, Gays for Equality: "Love and Let Love," http:// hdl.handle.net/10719/2721, no date.

8 Ibid.

9 PAS A595 II.100, "Manitoba Homosexuals: A Minority Without Rights," 10.

10 PAS, Neil Richards Collection A 595I.2 Newspaper Clippings 1974, Susan White, "Struggling on: Winnipeg's Gay Liberation Movement: 2 Years After," *Manitoban*, 4 February 1974, 7.

11 Ibid.

12 PAS, Neil Richards Collection A 595I.2 Newspaper Clippings 1974, "Prairie Lib a Long, Slow Process," *The Advocate*, 13 March 1974.

13 PAS, A 595 Neil Richards II. 142 Mutual Friendship Society 1972–5, 1980–1 (Winnipeg), "Am I an Uncle Tom," *What's Happening?* 3, no. 6 (March 1974): 8–9.

14 Ibid.

15 PAS, A 595 Neil Richards II. 142 Mutual Friendship Society 1972–5, 1980–1 (Winnipeg), Hilary Osborne-Hill, "Pink Notes from the Blue Book," *What's Happening?* 3, no. 6 (March 1974): 12.

16 Vogel, interview with author.

17 Between June 2003 (Ontario) and July 2005 all the Canadian provinces and territories legalized gay and lesbian marriages. Manitoba was the fifth province to do so in September 2004. See Elise Chenier, "Liberating Marriage: Gay Liberation and Same-Sex Marriage in Early 1970s Canada," in *We Still Demand: Redefining Resistance in Sex and Gender Struggles*, ed. P. Gentile, G. Kinsman, and L. P. Rankin (Vancouver: UBC Press, 2017).

18 Gay and Lesbian marriage became legal in Manitoba on 16 September 2004.

19 "Gays Wed in Canada," The Advocate 137, 8 May 1974.

20 CBC Digital Archives, Gay and Lesbian Emergence: Out in Canada, 1974. Barbara Frum interviewed Vogal and North on 21 February 1974 for the CBC program *As it Happens*. http://www.cbc.ca/archives/entry/ gay-winnipeg-couple-marries

21 Ibid.

22 Interviews with gay and lesbian activists in Winnipeg, 1992.

23 Vogel, interview with author.

24 Interestingly, both couples are still together. See CBC coverage of Vogel and North's "marriage" and the new book about Jack Baker and Mike McConnell's fifty years of marriage. See Erik Eckholm, "The Same Sex Couple Who Got a Marriage Licence in 1971," *New York Times*, 16 May 2015; Michael McConnell with Jack Baker, *The Marriage Heard 'Round the World: America's First Gay Marriage* (Minneapolis: University of Minnesota Press, 2016).

25 Eckholm, "The Same Sex Couple Who Got a Marriage Licence in 1971," 16 May 2015.

26 Hilary Osborne-Hill, "Pink Notes from the Blue Book," *What's Happening* 3, no. 6 (March 1974): 12.

27 CLGA Winnipeg, "Legal Defence Fund Seeks Rights Trial," *The Body Politic* 110 (January 1988): 14–15.

28 CBC Manitoba interviewed them in February 2015. See: http://www .cbc.ca/news/canada/manitoba/chris-vogel-richard-north-fight-for -manitoba-to-recognize-41-year-same-sex-marriage-1.2961152. They are also profiled in the Canadian Museum of Human Rights History in Winnipeg, see "As Long as Love Shall Last," https://humanrights.ca/ blog/long-love-shall-last.

29 "Canadian Printer Continues His Private War," *The Advocate* 145, 28 August 1974, 18.

30 CBC Winnipeg and CBC National covered this event. See "Thousands Take Part in the 1st Pride Parade in Steinbach Manitoba," 9 July 2016, http://www.cbc.ca/news/canada/manitoba/steinbach-first-pride -1.3671878.

31 "Steinbach-Area Politicians Will Be No-Shows at City's 1st Pride Parade," CBC Manitoba, 20 June 2016, http://www.cbc.ca/news/canada/manitoba/ steinbach-first-pride-1.3671878.

32 Miriam Toews's novels mine a vein of dark, complicated humour about life in Steinbach, Manitoba where the novelist was raised. This scene could very well have appeared in *A Complicated Kindness* (2004) where it is not difficult to imagine sixteen-year-old heroine Nomi Nickel, a resident of "East Village," sardonically viewing and commenting upon this event.

33 "Canadian Printer Continues His Private War," *The Advocate*, 18.

34 PAS, A 595 II.100 Gays for Equality, "Report on Activities for 1973–4 – Gays for Equality, Winnipeg," 2.

35 Ted Millward, "Gays for Equality – A History/Appreciation," 5.

36 Ibid.

37 Miriam Smith, *Lesbian and Gay Rights in Canada*, 31.

38 Graham Stinnett, Manitoba Gay and Lesbian Archives, "Local Gay
Liberation Movement," 2012 University of Manitoba Libraries, http://
umanitoba.ca/libraries/units/archives/digital/gay_lesbian/local
_liberation.html.

39 Ibid.

40 Heather Bishop, interview summary, 1992 Oral History Project,
Winnipeg, 133.

41 Winnipeg Lesbian Society, *After Stonewall: Manitoba's Critical Journal of Gay
Liberation* 3 (1980): 4.

42 Heather Bishop, interview summary, 134.

43 Robert Wilson, interview summary, 1992 Oral Interviews, Winnipeg, 101.

44 In my interviews with gay activists in Saskatoon and Winnipeg, and
in particular, with Vogel and Hellquist, both were quite clear about the
"costs" of being an activist – in terms of employment, health, and lives.
Vogel was quite direct, in our interview, that he had not had much fun in
his twenties and thirties, so consumed was he by civil service work and
gay activism. He had, ironically, largely missed the sexual adventures of
the gay liberation that he was fighting so hard to preserve.

45 Graham Stinnett, Manitoba Gay and Lesbian Archives, "Lesbians," 2012.

46 D. Wood/jhesekah interview summary, 1992 Manitoba Oral Interview
Project, 74–5.

47 Ibid., 76. Wood was a student at the University of Winnipeg, and
participated in the Women's Resource Centre.

48 Sally Papso, interview summary; also K. Louise Fulton interview
summary, Manitoba Oral Interviews, 1992 Collection.

49 PAS, A 595 Neil Richards II.207, *Voices: A Survival Manual for Wimmin*, Yvette
Parr, "The Closet's Getting Stuffy," *Voices*, no. 3 (Spring/Summer 9981): 1–2.

50 PAS, A 595 Neil Richards II.207, *Voices: A Survival Manual for Wimmin*, no. 6
(9981), Isabel Andrews, "A Plea to Gay Women in Kenora and Elsewhere,"
Voices, no. 6 (Winter Solstice 9981): 7.

51 PAS, A 595 Neil Richards II.207, *Voices: A Survival Manual for Wimmin*,
1980–1, Doreen and Isabel, "A Response to the Combahee River Collective
Statement on Lesbian Separatism," *Voices*, no. 6 (9981): 19.

52 PAS, A 595 Neil Richards II.207, *Voices: A Survival Manual for Wimmin*,
1980–1, Doreen Worden, "Nobody Cheered for Me," in "Three Views
of International Women's Day, Winnipeg 1981," *Voices*, no. 3 (Spring/
Summer 9981): 1.

53 PAS, A595 Neil Richards II.207, *Voices: A Survival Manual for Wimmin*,
1980–1, Yvette Parr, "The Closet's Getting Stuffy," in "Three Views of

International Women's Day, Winnipeg 1981," *Voices*, no. 3 (Spring/ Summer 9981): 1 and 22.

54 Ibid., 22.

55 PAS, NR A595 II.207, *Voices: A Survival Manual for Wimmin, 1980–1981*, no. 3 (Spring/Summer 9981): 1.

56 Lee Lanning, *Maize: A Lesbian Country Journal* 3 (1984 Winter): 84–5.

57 Ibid.

58 Women's Movement Archives (WMA), University of Ottawa, The Lesbian Archives, Press Release, Spring 1984.

59 WMA, University of Ottawa, Ottawa, Box 53, LARC.

60 Ibid and letter from Andrews to Women's Movement Archives, Toronto, 19 February 1985.

61 PAS, NR A 821 I.84, Gays of Thunder Bay, letter from Isabel Andrews and Doreen Worden, R.R. 2, Kenora, Ontario to Readers, *Thunder Gay*, April– May 1983, 3.

62 Margaret Doreen Worden, Kenora, Ontario, obituary, 25 September 2011. Originally published in the *Kenora Daily Miner and News*, 29 September 2011, accessed 25 April 2014, http://yourlifemoments.ca/sitepages/ obituary.asp?oid=538607.

63 Marilyn Fortier online condolence/memory for Worden obituary; see also Nancy Janovicek, *No Place to Go: Local Histories of the Battered Women's Shelters* (Vancouver: University of British Columbia Press, 2007).

64 *Sensible Shoes News* started publishing in 1995.

65 Please see V.J. Korinek, "*Carousel Capers*: Queer and Feminist Activism in the Prairies, 1970–1985," *American Periodicals* (forthcoming Fall 2018).

66 Anita Bryant's campaigns in Dade County, Florida were national news in the United States. She and her then husband, Bob Green, were instrumental in getting an anti-gay ordinance passed; emboldened by this success, they took their Christian tour/anti-gay activism on the road, including an international tour in Canada, see Marc Stein, *Rethinking the Gay and Lesbian Movement*.

67 See Tom Warner, *Never Going Back*, 136–7 for more details on Bryant's tour of Canadian cities and the implosion of her crusade in 1979.

68 Walter Davis, "A Spirit of Unity," *After Stonewall: A Critical Journal of Gay Liberation* 6 (Summer 1978): 7.

69 RRC, Manitoba Gay/Lesbian Oral History II, interview summary, R. Glenn Fewster, Winnipeg, 6 November 1992.

70 Graham Stinnett, Manitoba Gay and Lesbian Archives, "Lesbians," 2012.

71 Ibid.

72 Lyle Dick, interview with author.

73 "Calgarians Against Anita," newspaper unknown 2, no. 3 (September 1978): unknown page, accessed July 2017, https://calgaryqueerhistory. ca/2013/04/25/orange-juice-vs-gay-rights/.

74 Ibid.

75 Isabel Andrews, "Responses from Wages Due," *After Stonewall* 7 (Fall 1978): 13.

76 Ken DeLisle, Winnipeg, letter to the editor, *Winnipeg Free Press*, reprinted in *Out and About* 4 (July 1978): 10–11.

77 Bill Fields, "Images in Pink and Blue," *After Stonewall* 7 (Fall 1978): 11.

78 Bill Fields, "Queer Bashing in Winnipeg: A Survivor Talks to A.S." *After Stonewall* 7 (1978): 8.

79 Ibid.

80 Ibid., 9.

81 Stinnett, Manitoba Gay and Lesbian Archives, "Homophobic Violence," 2012.

82 Bill Fields, "Queer Bashing in Winnipeg: A Survivor Talks to A.S." *After Stonewall*, 9.

83 Ibid.

84 Frances Williamson, interview with author.

85 Jane Rule and Helen Sonthoff were very popular hosts at Galliano, and the recent publication of the letters between Jane Rule and *The Body Politic* activist Rick Bébout provides a window into their world there. See Marilyn R. Schuster, ed., *A Queer Love Story: The Letters of Jane Rule and Rick Bébout* (Vancouver: University of British Columbia Press, 2017).

86 Frances Williamson, interview with author.

87 Ibid.

88 See Colin R. Johnson, *Just Queer Folks*, 108–28 for an intriguing discussion of community standards, "benevolent toleration," and small-town life.

89 Stinnett, Manitoba Gay and Lesbian Archives, "Lesbians," 2012.

90 The book in question was *Flaunting It!*, see Jackson and Stan Persky, eds., *Flaunting It!: A Decade of Gay Journalism from the* Body Politic (Vancouver: Star Books, 1982).

91 PAS, A595 I.78 July 1983, "Book on Homosexuality Upsets School Principal," *Moose Jaw Times Herald*, 1.

92 PAS, A595 I. 91 Newspaper Clippings File, March–April 1985, "Feminist Magazine Banned," *Saskatoon Star Phoenix*, A6.

93 See Jane Rule, *Detained at Customs: Jane Rule Testifies at the Little Sister's Trial* (Vancouver: Lazara Press, 1995); Janine Fuller and Stuart Blackley, *Restricted Entry: Censorship on Trial* (Vancouver: Press Gang Publishers, 1995); and Janine Fuller and Pat Califia, *Forbidden Passages: Writings Banned in Canada* (Pittsburgh, PA: Cleis Press, 1995).

94 See Catherine A. MacKinnon and Andrea Dworkin, eds., *In Harm's Way: The Pornography Civil Rights Hearings* (Cambridge, MA: Harvard University Press, 1999).

95 Manitoba Gay and Lesbian Archives, Graham Stinnett overview of North and Vogel activism.

96 Graham Stinnett, Manitoba Gay and Lesbian Archives, "Gay Rights," 2012.

97 PAS, A 595 I. 128 Prior to August 1989, "It's the Gay Pressure," *Winnipeg Sun* 9 February 1986, 4.

98 Darryl Kippen interview, Manitoba Gay/Lesbian Interviews, 1992.

99 Joyce Rankin interview, Manitoba Gay/Lesbian Interviews, 1992.

100 Cogill interview, Manitoba Gay/Lesbian Interviews, 1992.

101 Papso interview, Manitoba Gay/Lesbian Interviews, 1992.

102 In my interview with Frances Williamson she specifically mentioned the importance of the Manitoba Conference Study called "Homosexuality and the Church," which focused on openly homosexual members and ministers within the United Church of Canada (UCC). Dr A.M. Watts chaired the group. While the outcome of these various studies was ultimately supportive of homosexual members, and would pave the way for the ordination of openly gay and lesbian clergy in the UCC, this was not achieved without significant internal turmoil and debate, both in the prairies and elsewhere. Interestingly, though, it was in southwestern Ontario that the key dissenting group, the Community for Concern, was formed. Interviews conducted in Winnipeg in 1992 indicate that many people participated in religious gay and lesbian support/activist groups (Dignity, Affirm, Chutzpah – a Jewish group), and that their religious and political work often converged.

103 DeLisle interview, interview summary, Manitoba Gay/Lesbian Interviews 1992, 47.

104 V.J. Korinek, "Activism=Education."

105 Lyle Dick, interview with author.

106 Interview with Donn Yuen, Manitoba Gay/Lesbian Interviews, 1992, 14.

107 PAS, A 595 I.106 July 1987, "Manitoba Passes Gay Rights Law," *Globe and Mail*, 18 July 1987, A5.

108 PAS, A595 I.106 July 1987, "Schreyer Criticizes Gay Bill," *Regina Leader Post*, 15 July 1987, A12.

109 Kippen interview, Manitoba Gay/Lesbian Interviews, 1992.

110 PAS, A 595 I. 107 Aug 1987, "Homosexual Clause Infuriating Natives," *Moose Jaw Times Herald*, 8 August 1987.

111 Bev Baptiste, Manitoba Gay/Lesbian Interviews 1992, 132.

112 Stinnett, Manitoba Gay and Lesbian Archives, "Community Centres,"
      2012.
113 Ibid.
114 See Rainbow Resource Centre, accessed 17 December 2017, http://www
      .rainbowresourcecentre.org/about/history.

7. "Towards a Gay Community"

 1 See image from 1977 Conference: Towards Gay Community button
     (figure 7.1, page 301).
 2 Warner article, *TBP*, February 1977, 11.
 3 Paul Gessell, interview with author.
 4 Lilja Stefansson, interview with author.
 5 See: V.J. Korinek, "The Most Openly Gay Person for at Least a Thousand
     Miles" and "Activism= Public Education."
 6 PAS, A821 NR IV.39 Newsletters, 1971–84, Doug Hellquist, "President's
     Report," *Gemini News* 1, no. 3 (February 1972): 1.
 7 Ibid., 23.
 8 PAS, NR, "Western Canadian Clubs Conference," *ZFS News* 1 (December
     1972): 1–2.
 9 Donald W. McLeod, *Lesbian and Gay Liberation in Canada: A Selected
     Chronology, 1964–1975* (Toronto: ECW Press/Homewood Books, 1996),
     169.
10 Richards, *Celebrating a History of Diversity*, 2.
11 Ibid., 3.
12 Ibid.
13 As many will know, Roy Romanow would later become premier of
     Saskatchewan. It was during his time as premier that sexual orientation
     was added to the provincial human rights legislation. He is currently the
     chancellor of the University of Saskatchewan.
14 PAS, NR Clipping Collection, *Saskatoon Star Phoenix*, 25 August 1978, 3.
15 PAS, A 595 Richards I. Newspaper Clippings 1, 1966–73, "Saskatoon
     Won't Be Gay" *Saskatoon Star Phoenix*, 14 August 1973, 4.
16 Currently gay pride events in most Canadian cities are held in June. The
     June date commemorates the anniversary of the Stonewall Riots in New
     York City in June 1969. It is important to note that this was not always the
     case, and initially some Canadian cities chose to mark the date the federal
     government decriminalized consenting homosexual acts between adults.
17 PAS, A 595 Richards I. Newspaper Clippings 1, 1966–73, "Saskatoon
     Won't Be Gay," 4.

18   Ibid.
19   Phil Tank, "Mayor Denies He Avoids Pride Festival Events" *Saskatoon Star Phoenix*, 7 June 2016.
20   PAS, A 821 Neil Richards IV.41 Political and Human Rights – General 1972–7, "New Release – For Immediate publication Saskatoon Gay Action-Zodiac Friendship Society SK Human Rights Complaint re. Western Producer," contact G. Hellquist, P. Millard, B. Garman.
21   PAS, A 595 Richards I. Newspaper Clippings 2, 1974, "Ex Husband Steals Kids from Lesbian," *The Advocate*, 11 September 1974.
22   PAS, A821 Neil Richards, III.96 Saskatchewan, 1974–93, "Sexual Orientation Raised in Saskatchewan Legislature," *The Body Politic*, May/June 1974.
23   PAS, A595 Richards I. Newspaper Clippings, January–October 1975, Vern Greenshields, "*Star Phoenix* Picketed: Gay Community Protests Ad Decision" *Saskatoon Star Phoenix*, 11 June 1975.
24   Ibid.
25   Ibid.
26   PAS, A 595 Richards I. Newspaper Clippings January–October 1975, "Phoenix Burns Gay Centre Survey," *Saskatonian*, 13 June 1975.
27   Ibid.
28   R. Nordahl, interview with author, 2003.
29   "Out of the Closet, Into the Archives," *Perceptions* 25 (1986): 20 and 22.
30   Neil Richards, interview with author.
31   PAS, A821 N.R. IV.29 General Meeting Minutes, Peter Millard, "Gay Community Centre of Saskatoon – President's Report 1975."
32   For a more detailed appraisal of this case see: V.J. Korinek "The Most Openly Gay Person for At Least Thousand Miles."
33   After the publication of my CHR article, Wilson's story and history attracted new attention. He was the only openly gay or lesbian person included in a special centennial 100 top Saskatchewan people, and subsequently the filmmaker produced a docudrama about his life and times, see "Stubblejumper," directed by David Geiss (Regina: Da Vid Films, 2008).
34   *The Sheaf* Volume 66, numbers 18, 19, September 1975.
35   The University of Saskatchewan archives is, perhaps not surprisingly, silent about previous cases of gay professors or students. Over the years, I have had a series of discussions with archivists, archival staff, and local campus historians/researchers (notably, the late Duff Spafford, with whom I had many conversations) about evidence of campus homosexuality prior to the early 1970s. In the absence

of archival material (other than the tantalizing images from a few yearbooks, and Nan McKay's wonderful photo album) what I have heard are fragmentary stories. Stories of a handful of faculty members invited to take up positions elsewhere (but no records of the reasons for those moves). Stories of faculty members invited to think about retirement (but no records). And speculation about why the archival holdings are so unbalanced between male faculty, staff, and administrators and early female academic, administrative, and staff members. Estelle Freedman's article "The Burning of Letters Continues: Elusive Identities and the Historical Construction of Sexuality," *Journal of Women's History* 9, no. 4 (Winter 1998): 181–200 potentially explains the gap in archival holdings. It is merely conjecture but it appears that there has been some active archival purging prior to records being deposited and, additionally, a number of situations where concern about what records might reveal, or suggest, meant that whole record collections were not deposited.

36 Neil Richards, interview with author.

37 PAS, A821 III.64 Millard 74–93, "An Interview with Peter Millard," *Vox* 12 (March 1993): 3.

38 Ibid., 4.

39 See the University of Saskatchewan Archives, "Events in the History of the University of Saskatchewan," http://scaa.usask.ca/gallery/uofs_events/articles/1995.php.

40 PAS, A821 Richards IV. 40 Tom Warner, "Saskatoon: It Has One of the Biggest Gay Centres in the Country: A Report on the People Who Make It Work" *The Body Politic* 30 (February 1977): 11.

41 Ibid.

42 Ibid.

43 PAS, NR A595 II.76, Gay Community Centre of Saskatoon, 1974–8, *Newsletter* (Fall 1976): 6.

44 Richards's *Celebrating a History of Diversity*, 8.

45 Warner, interview with author.

46 Richards, interview with author.

47 Scrivener, interview with author.

48 Ibid.

49 Tom Warner, *Never Going Back*.

50 Warner, interview with author.

51 Richards, *Celebrating a History of Diversity*.

52 PAS, A821 Richards IV. 40 Paul Trollope "High Spirits and Hard Work," *The Body Politic* 36 (September 1977): 6–7.

53 PAS, A595 II. 175 Pat M, "National Gay Rights Conference," *Saskatoon Women's Liberation Newsletter*, 1977.

54 PAS, A821 Neil Richards IV. 19 Correspondence 1971–82, 6 of 8, Parade Permit signed by James G. Kettle, Chief of Police.

55 PAS, A821 Richards IV. 40 Paul Trollope, "High Spirits and Hard Work," *The Body Politic* (September 1977): 6–7.

56 Trollope, *TBP*, September 1977.

57 Bill Fields, "Reflections on NGRC," *After Stonewall* 4 (1978): 4.

58 Deborah Brock, "'Workers of the World Caress': An Interview with Gary Kinsman on Gay and Lesbian Organizing in the 1970s Toronto Left," *left history* 9, no. 2, online feature, 10.

59 Ibid.

60 PAS, NR A595 II.2 Weisia, "NGRC/Halifax: Crossroads," *Prairie Woman*, September 1978. *Prairie Woman* was described as the "excellent newspaper of the Saskatoon Women's Liberation." Subscription cost $4 per year.

61 Weisia, "NGRC/Halifax: Crossroads," *Prairie Woman*, September 1978.

62 PAS, NR A821 IV.19 (7), Correspondence, letter from Douglas Wilson to *Body Politic*, 20 August 1978.

63 Richards, *Celebrating a History of Diversity*.

64 PAS, A595 II. 175, Kay Bierweiler, "Gay Rights Coalition Founded," *Saskatoon Women's Liberation Newsletter*, 1978.

65 PAS, NR A821 VI.2a Saskatchewan Gay Coalition Correspondence, 1977–82, "Letter from Douglas Wilson to the Annual Meeting of Lesbian and Gay Saskatchewan, 1 September 1982.

66 PAS, NR A 595 II. 76, "Saskatchewan Gay Coalition Formed," *Gay Community of Saskatoon Newsletter*, 1978.

67 Dick Smith, "My First Gay March," in "Prairies Coming Out Strong," special issue, *After Stonewall* (1979): 17–19.

68 Smith, "My First Gay March," 19.

69 PAS, NR A 821 VI.2a Saskatchewan Gay Coalition Correspondence, 1977–82, letter from Doug Wilson to Yorkton contacts, 10 May 1981.

70 Doug Wilson, "Regional Report," *The Body Politic* (December 1979/January 1980): 14.

71 Ibid.

72 PAS, NR A821 Saskatchewan Gay Coalition, VI.2.b Correspondence, 1979–82, Restricted, letter from General Delivery, Tisdale, SK, to D. Wilson, 1 March 1979.

73 Doug Wilson, "At the Grassroots: The Outreach Program of the Saskatchewan Gay Coalition," *After Stonewall* (1979): 7.

74 Ibid., 11.

75 See Warner's book about Saskatoon, *Never Going Back*. For evidence of the split, and those GCCS members who were not in agreement with opting opt of CLGRC, see SAB A821 IV.19(7), letter from Board of Directors of the Gay Community Centre of Saskatoon to *The Body Politic*, 8 June 1979. From the letter: "In response to the letters from Messers Carriere, Hellquist, Garman and Demchinsky, the Board of Directors of the Gay Community Centre of Saskatoon freely acknowledges that the decision to leave the CLGRC may not reflect the opinion of *every* member of our community. Our position is a principled one, based upon a majority consensus … which involved a seven month dialogue within this community, with other prairie groups and with other groups and individuals across the country sharing our concerns."

76 Gens Hellquist, "Indications of Pride," *Perceptions*, 30 July 1997, 8.

77 Neil Richards, interview with author.

78 David Rimmer, interview with author, 21 January 2003.

79 Lynn Hunt, *Writing History in the Global Era* (New York: W.W. Norton and Company, 2014), 69.

80 Peter Millard, "The Fundamentalist Crusade," *Briarpatch*, October 1989, 10.

81 Ibid.

82 Lyle Dick, interview with author, November 2005.

83 Joe Wickenhauser, "Surprisingly Unexpected: Moose Jaw, Metronormativity and LGBTQ Activism" (master's thesis, York University, 2012), 44; SAB video of 1978 Moose Jaw Rally, "Video – Gay Liberation, 1978," NR, Saskatchewan Gay Coalition, A821.V1.6 SAB, Saskatoon.

84 Barb Clay, interview with author, 29 August 2003.

85 PAS, A821 III.96, Peter Millard, "The Fundamentalist Crusade," *Briarpatch*, October 1989, 11.

86 Ibid.

87 My thanks to Steve Hewitt for sharing these secret, RCMP surveillance documents with me. SS-306 Saskatchewan Security Service (by mail), re: Protests and Demonstrations Saskatchewan, 29 June 1978, 1–2.

88 Ibid., 2.

89 PAS, A821 III.96, Peter Millard, "The Fundamentalist Crusade," *Briarpatch*, October 1989, 10–13.

90 Ibid.

91 See Joseph Wickenhauser, "Surprisingly Unexpected."

92 Wickenhauser, "Surprisingly Unexpected," 42–6.

93 "Welcome to Saskatoon," *After Stonewall* 9 (Fall 1979): 2.

94 See V.J. Korinek, "The Prairies Coming Out Strong," NOTCHE(s) blog, 11 May 2017, http://notchesblog.com/2017/05/11/ after-stonewall-and-gay-and-lesbian-liberation-in-western-canada/.

95　"Gay Community Centre," *After Stonewall* 9 (Fall 1979): 3.

96　PAS, A 821 Richards IV.40 Ross Irwin, "Teacher Fired in Saskatchewan: Trustee Resignations Demanded," *The Body Politic* (1979).

97　PAS, A 821 Richards IV.40, "Teacher Wins Appeal, Forced to Resign," *Gay Calgary* 13, October 1979, 1.

98　PAS, A 821 Richards IV.40, Ross Irwin, "Board Orders Teacher Reinstated after Dismissal for 'Immorality,'" *The Body Politic* 57 (October 1979): 13.

99　Ibid.

100　PAS, A 821 Richards IV.40 Ross Irwin, "Teacher Fired in Saskatchewan: Trustee Resignations Demanded," *The Body Politic* (1979).

101　PAS, A-595 II.92, Gay Saskatchewan (formerly Saskatchewan Gay Coalition, 1980–1), editor's note, *Grassroots: Voice of Gay Saskatchewan*, Spring 1981, 2.

102　Mcleod, *Gay and Lesbian Liberation in Canada*, 110.

103　Erin Shoemaker, interview with author, 28 July 2003.

104　Ibid.

105　PAS, A 595 II.76 Gay Community Centre SK, 1974–8, *GayWest*, DH "Our Story (Part 3), 1976, 6.

106　Erin Shoemaker, interview with author, 28 July 2003.

107　Canadian Women's Movement Archives, Saskatoon Women's Liberation Newsletter, X10–89 CWMA Periodicals, *Saskatoon Women's Liberation Newsletter* Feb 1974.

108　Canadian Women's Movement Archives, Ottawa, *Saskatoon Women's Liberation Newsletter*, X10–89 CWMA Periodicals, *Saskatoon Women's Liberation Newsletter*, February 1974, 13.

109　PAS, A 595 II.77, *GCCS Newsletter*, 1981, Diane "A Proposal."

110　Ibid.

111　Shoemaker interview with author, 28 July 2003.

112　Marion Alexander, interview with author, 26 August 2003.

113　Barb Clay, interview with author, Saskatoon, 29 August 2003.

114　Ibid.

115　Ibid.

116　T, interview with author, 25 August 2003.

117　Ibid.

118　Ibid.

119　PAS, A595 Neil Richards I Newspaper Clippings, February–May 1975–6, "Gays Seek Protection," *Saskatoon Star Phoenix*, Tuesday April.

120　PAS, A 821 Richards IV.40, "Fire Destroys Library, Cops Suspect Arson," *The Body Politic* 57 (October 1979): 13.

121 PAS, A 821 Richards IV.40, Paul Trollope, "RCMP Raid Home, Seize Porn Collection," *The Body Politic* 61 (March 1980): 6.

122 Gary Kinsman and Patrizia Gentile have documented many episodes of such RCMP behaviour in Ottawa, in their book *The War on Queers*.

123 T, interview with author, 25 August 2003.

124 David Rimmer, interview with author, 21 January 2003.

125 PAS, A 821 VI.4 Newsletters, 1978–82: Gay Saskatchewan, "Native Gay Group Forming," *Gay Saskatchewan* 1, no. 10 (December 1978).

126 *Gay Saskatchewan* 3, no. 1 (March 1980): 2.

127 David Rimmer did name three Cree men who were leaders, dancers, and proud Indigenous gay men. Because he was the only narrator who did, and because I was not able to interview those men or their families, ethically I could not release their names in this book. I have mentioned the reserves and communities from which they came, hopeful that future work will recover their stories.

128 Ma-Nee Chacaby, with Mary Louisa Plummer, *A Two Spirit Journey: The Autobiography of a Lesbian Ojibwa-Cree Elder* (Winnipeg: University of Manitoba Press, 2016).

129 Leonard Lawrence (pseudonym), interview with author, 28 July 2003.

130 PAS, A 821 IV.19(4), Neil Richards to Huntley Schaller, Saskatchewan Association on Human Rights, 28 November 1975.

131 Ibid.

132 Marion Alexander, interview with author, 26 August 2003. Marion was proud of her life, and she generously shared with me a very candid narrative of her experiences. I am grateful for her bravery in telling this story – it has personalized and enriched the history of lesbians in the prairies.

133 Marion A, interview with author.

134 Ibid.

135 *Perceptions* 27, 1986, 9.

136 Gens Hellquist, "Editorial," *Perceptions*, 27 July 1994, 3.

137 Ibid.

138 PAS, A821 Neil Richards IV. 40 Bill Kobewka, "Community Centre: Not Just a Building," *The Body Politic* 85 (July/August 1982): 13.

139 PAS, NR A595 II.77, Gay Community Centre of Saskatoon, 1979–81, "Outgoing Board Report Presented by Walter Davis at the Annual General Meeting January 25, 1981."

140 Ibid.

141 Ibid.

142 PAS, A821 Neil Richards, IV.19 Correspondence, 1971–82, 8 of 8. Letter from Brenda Vallelle and Douglas Wilson, to members, 23 March 1982.
143 Kobekwa, *The Body Politic* 85 (July/August 1982): 13.
144 PAS, A595 II.79 Gay Community Centre 1979–81, *Gayline*, December 1981.
145 Importantly, Hellquist was not done with gay and lesbian community organizations when GLSS folded. In 1991 he returned with Gay and Lesbian Health Services, located at 241 2nd Avenue South in Saskatoon. That group, in 2005, was renamed the Avenue Community Centre for Sexual Diversity, and in 2015 the name changed again to OUTSaskatoon. While their mandate – and locations – have changed during those years, it is important to stress that such services continue to be part of the contemporary Saskatoon queer experience, a point that speaks both to the continued necessity for such wide-ranging agencies, but also of the commitment to the queer community. See OUTSaskatoon website for more details of their current programming, and history: *OUTSaskatoon*, http://www.outsaskatoon.ca/, accessed July 2017.
146 Brigadoon was a popular Broadway musical with score written by Lerner and Lowe. The play was released as a feature film in 1954, staring Gene Kelly. The setting, "Brigadoon," was a fictional Scottish village that appeared for one day every hundred years – it was, then – a magically idyllic place.

8. Found-Ins at the Pisces Spa

1 "Notice This is a Private Newsletter," *Carousel Capers* 4, no. 6, Calgary, Alberta, June 1973.
2 Elizabeth Massiah, interview with author, 13 September 2003.
3 "Reluctant Gay Rights Hero Seeks Serenity Abroad," *Edmonton Journal*, 30 March 2008.
4 Vriend's parents were organic farmers and vegans. See ibid.
5 V.J. Korinek, "'Beef Stinks/Eat Beef Dyke': Coming Out as a Lesbian in Alberta," in *Edible Histories/Cultural Politics: Towards a Canadian Food History*, ed. Franca Iacovetta, V.J. Korinek, and Marlene Epp (University of Toronto Press, 2012).
6 See Bruce MacDougall, *Queer Judgments: Homosexuality, Expression and the Courts in Canada* (Toronto: University of Toronto Press, 2000) and Tom Warner, *Never Going Back: A History of Queer Activism in Canada* (Toronto: University of Toronto Press, 2002) for more details on this case.
7 City of Edmonton Archives, "Michael Roberts Press Release," *Club 70 News*, November 1972.

8 It is noteworthy that the second piece of legislation the Lougheed government introduced was the IRPA.

9 Ken Norman, "Saskatchewan Bill of Rights," *Saskatchewan Encyclopedia*, http://esask.uregina.ca/entry/saskatchewan_bill_of_rights.html.

10 V.J. Korinek, "A Queer Eye View of the Prairies," in *The West and Beyond* provides more details about the human rights campaigns.

11 Miriam Smith, *Lesbian and Gay Rights in Canada*, 115.

12 Glenbow Archives, Doug Young Fonds, M8397 File #16, Gate 1976–81, "Homosexuals a Minority Without Rights," a brief presented by the Gay Alliance towards Equality (Edmonton) to the Alberta Human Rights Commission, 1 March 1976.

13 "Homosexuals a Minority without Rights," 3

14 Ibid., 5.

15 Ibid., 6–7.

16 See Smith for a discussion of GATE Vancouver's censorship case against the *Vancouver Sun*, 53–5.

17 "Homosexuals a Minority without Rights," 14.

18 Ibid.

19 Ibid., 15.

20 Ibid., 26; Carole Fogel, director, Saskatchewan Human Rights Commission to R.E. Radke, Gay Alliance for Equality, Edmonton, 15 January 1976.

21 Glenbow Archives, Doug Young Fonds, Alberta Lesbian and Gay Rights Association, presentation to the Alberta Human Rights Commission, 2 August 1979, 1.

22 Ibid., 2.

23 Ibid., 6.

24 Ibid., 8.

25 Glenbow Archives, Doug Young Fonds, Series II M 8397/23 GIRC Gay Calgary Newspaper and Reach Newsletter, 1978–9, 1981, "Red Deer Ad Refused," *Gay Calgary* 10 (March 1979): 1.

26 Ibid.

27 Glenbow Archives, Doug Young Fonds, "Human Rights: The Gay Minority in Alberta," presented to Alberta Minister of Labour, GIRC, 28 January 1980.

28 Letter from Doug Young to Minister of Labour, 28 January 1980, 2.

29 Robert Harris, "Victoria Park," *Gay Horizons*, June 1980, 6.

30 Glenbow Archives, Doug Young Fonds, "Human Rights: The Gay Minority in Alberta," presented to Alberta Minister of Labour, GIRC, 28 January 1980, 2.

31 PAS, A821 VI.4, Newsletter of Saskatchewan Gay Coalition, William Thorsell, "The Anita Syndrome," *Gay Saskatchewan* 1, no. 5 (June 1978): 2–3. Reprinted from the *Edmonton Journal*, 28 April 1978.

32 Ibid., 2
33 Ibid., 3.
34 Ibid., 3
35 Glenbow Archives, Doug Young Fonds, "The Hat Comes Out," *Gay Calgary*, October 1979, 1.
36 Ibid.
37 Ibid.
38 Glenbow Archives, Doug Young Fonds Series II. M 8397/5 ALGRA newspaper, *Gay Horizons*, 1979–80, C. Rochon, "Medicine Hat," *Gay Horizons* 14 (December 1979): 11.
39 Ibid.
40 Glenbow Archives, Doug Young Fonds, *Gay Horizons*, "Lethbridge Dance" June 1980, 11.
41 Ibid.
42 Glenbow Archives, Doug Young Fonds, *Gay Horizons*, "GALA Meeting," June 1980, 11.
43 Ibid.
44 Glenbow Archives, Doug Young Fonds, J. Cooper "Doug Young Papers," 2 indicates that GIRC was mismanaged in the early 1980s. Financially they were in difficult circumstances and the organization failed. For whatever reason, Cooper notes that "the files of GIRC were destroyed."
45 Glenbow Archives, Doug Young Fonds, J. Cooper "Doug Young Papers," 1
46 Glenbow Archives, Doug Young Fonds, "Doug Young," *The Body Politic*, September 1980, 2.
47 Ibid., 2.
48 Patrizia Gentile and Gary Kinsman, *The Canadian War on Queers*, see in particular the chapter devoted to Ottawa life.
49 Doug Young, *The Body Politic*, September 1980, 2
50 Ibid.
51 Glenbow Archives, John Cooper Fonds: M8371 f.159, notes from Interviews with Doug Young: Young Obituary, 9 June 1994.
52 Glenbow Archives, John Cooper Fonds: M8371 f.159, notes from Interviews with Doug Young: Brian Brennon, "Gay Warrior Led by Example, Courage" *Calgary Herald*, 14 June 1994, B2.
53 Ibid.
54 Glenbow Archives, Doug Young Fonds, "Doug Young Papers," 5.
55 Doug Young was ahead of his time. Such arguments are now beginning to gain traction academically, see Johnson, *Just Queer Folks* and Gray, Johnson, and Gilley, eds, *Queering the Countryside*.

56 Glenbow Archives, Doug Young Fonds, Series II: M8397/16 GATE
(Edmonton), 1976–81, letter from GS (Secretary) GATE Edmonton to
GIRC, 13 May 1980.

57 Glenbow Archives, Doug Young Fonds, Series V M8397/56, News
clippings, 1983–4, Don Truckey, "Gays, Police Try to Talk Down Barriers,"
Calgary Herald, 26 May 1984, B3.

58 Glenbow Archives, Doug Young Fonds, Series II: M 8397/35, Right to
Privacy Committee, Calgary, 1981–3, Sheila Pratt, "Sawyer Gets Control of
Parade Permits," *The Calgary Herald*, 15 September 1981, page unknown.

59 See Gay Calgary History Project for an expanded discussion of Klein and
political controversies concerning his initial support and then the backlash
from "the majority," as represented by the *Calgary Sun* newspaper. Kevin
Allen, "Mayor Ralph Klein's Gay Rights Tempest," 14 July 2016, https://
calgaryqueerhistory.ca/?s=klein.

60 Glenbow Archives, Doug Young Fonds Series II, M8397/5 ALGRA
newspaper, *Gay Horizons*, 1979–80 (incomplete), Robert Harris, "Press,"
Gay Horizons, 16 (June/July 1980): 2.

61 Glenbow Archives, Doug Young Fonds Series II, M8397/5 ALGRA
newspaper, *Gay Horizons*, 1979–80 (incomplete), "GIRC Cancels March," 3.

62 *Gay Horizons*, June 1980, 2; letter from David Garmaise, Coordinating
Office, Canadian Lesbian and Gay Rights Coalition to Bob Harris, "Gay
Information and Resources Calgary" 2 April 1980.

63 Robert Harris, "Alger," *Gay Horizons*, June 1980, 3.

64 Robet Harris, "Victoria Park," *Gay Horizons*, June 1980, 6.

65 George Edin, letter to the editor, *Gay Horizons*, June 1980, 10.

66 Bill Holmes a Court, letter to the editor, *Gay Horizons*, June 1980, 10.

67 See Calgary Gay History Project, "Infighting in 1980," 11, August 2016,
https://calgaryqueerhistory.ca/2016/08/11/split-on-parades-in-1980/.

68 Peter P. Pratt, interview with author, 11 September 2003.

69 Michael Phair, interview with author, 11 September 2003.

70 Ibid.

71 PAS, Neil Richards Collection A 595 I.56, Newspaper Clippings June 1981,
Rae Hull, "Gay Gave Police Tip on Spa," *Edmonton Journal*, June 1981, B1.

72 An educator, employed with the Department of Education, Phair would
go on to be the founder of the AIDS Network of Edmonton, and later an
elected city councillor from 1992 to 2007. He was the first openly gay city
councillor in Edmonton.

73 City of Edmonton, GALA fonds MS 595, Box 21 Clipping Files, Clippings
Bawdy House – Bath Raids, handwritten notes, n.d., from the Privacy
Defence Committee Meeting on 9 September1981, held at Flashback's.

74 CLGA, Toronto: Gay and Lesbian Awareness (GALA) Edmonton, Chris Bearchell, "Edmonton: Taking Chances, Facing Changes," *The Body Politic*, October 1984, 13.

75 PAS, Neil Richards Papers, A595 I.46 August 1980, "Gay Prostitutes Warn of Bloodbath," *Edmonton Journal*, 11 August 1980, B1.

76 Ibid.

77 Phair, interview with author.

78 Ibid.

79 City of Edmonton Archives, GATE records, "Gay Alert," June 1981.

80 Ibid.

81 City of Edmonton Archives, GATE records, "Press Release: Edmonton Gays Establish Privacy Defence Committee," 19 June 1981. On the thirtieth anniversary of the bathhouse raids in Toronto, in February 2011, there were many websites, articles, and retrospectives produced, see *Xtra* newspaper, et cetera.

82 PAS, Neil Richards Collection, A595 I.56 Newspaper Clippings June 1981, "Spa Raid Sparks Rally for Liberties," *Edmonton Journal*, 2 June 1981, 1.

83 PAS, A595 II.92, "Attack on Edmonton Gays," *Grassroots*, Fall 1981, 3

84 Glenbow Archives, Doug Young Fonds, Series IV M8397/52 Pisces Health Spa, Edmonton, 1981, "Feature: The Pisces Health Spa Raid," *Gay Moods*? n.d.

85 Phair, interview with author.

86 City of Edmonton Archives, GALA Fonds MS 595, Box 21 Clipping Files, Clippings – Bawdy House – Bathhouse Raids, handwritten notes, n.d., but presumably from the Privacy Defence Committee Meeting on 9 September 1981, held at Flashback's.

87 City of Edmonton Archives, GATE records, 630 AM CHED radio, transcript of the Eddie Keen Commentary, aired 8 June1981, at 12:00 and 5:00 p.m.

88 City of Edmonton Archives, GATE records, letter from N.C. Civil Rights Director, GATE, to Manager, The Courtyard Club, Edmonton, 9 July 1983.

89 Ibid.

90 City of Edmonton Archives, GATE records, 630 AM CHED radio, transcript of the Eddie Keen Commentary, aired 8 June 1981, at 12:00 and 5:00 p.m.

91 City of Edmonton Archives, GALA Fonds MS 595, Box 21 Clipping Files – Bawdy House – Bath Raids, Cathie Bartlett, "Pisces a Refuge for Closet Gay, Trial Judge Told," *Edmonton Journal*, 28 August 1981, page unknown.

92 City of Edmonton Archives, GALA Fonds MS 595, Box 21, Clipping Files – Bawdy House – Bath Raids, Robin Barstow, "Raid Drove Gays Back into the Closet," *Edmonton Sun*, 30 May 1982, Sunday City section, B1.

93 City of Edmonton Archives, GALA Fonds MS 595, Box 21, Michael Phair, "Pisces Revisited: The Conclusion," *Fine Print*, April 1983, 8.

94 City of Edmonton Archives, GALA Fonds MS 595, Box 21, Gilbert Bouchard, "Effects of '81 Spa Raid Still Concern Local Gays," *Edmonton Journal*, G12.

95 Ibid.

96 City of Edmonton Archives, GALA Fonds, Box 1, "After the Raid," *The Newsletter* 1, no. 1 (June 1981): 12–13.

97 City of Edmonton Archives, GALA Fonds MS 595, Box 21, Clipping File, "Crown Calls Pisces Place for 'Depraved.'" *Edmonton Journal*, 31 July 31 1981, B6.

98 City of Edmonton Archives, GALA Fonds MS 595, Box 21, Michael Phair, "Pisces Revisited: The Conclusion," 8.

99 City of Edmonton Archives, GALA Fonds MS 595, Box 21, Gilbert Bouchard, " Effects of '81 Spa Raid Still Concern Local Gays," G12.

100 Feature – Pisces Raid in Edmonton.

101 City of Edmonton Archives, GALA Collection Box 1, Lena, "The Pink Triangle Strikes Again," *The Newsletter* 1, no. 2 (August 1981): 1.

102 City of Edmonton Archives, GALA Collection Box 1, "Edmonton Gays Celebrate Gay Pride Week," *Gay Gleaner*, June 1982, 1.

103 Ibid.

104 Phair, interview with author.

105 Peter P. Pratt, interview with author.

106 PAS, A595 II.81 *The Gay Gleaner* (Edmonton), 1981–2, Stephen, "Television," *Gay Gleaner*, December 1981, 8; Edmonton's Queer History Project, https://edmontonqueerhistoryproject.wordpress.com/, is working on securing permission to link to this documentary.

107 PAS, A595 II.81 *The Gay Gleaner* (Edmonton), 1981–2, Walter, "Television," *Gay Gleaner*, December 1981, 6.

108 Ibid., 8.

109 PAS, A595 II.81 *The Gay Gleaner* (Edmonton), 1981–2, Bonnie, "Television" *Gay Gleaner*, December 1981, 7.

110 Walter, "Television," 7.

111 PAS, A595 II.81 *The Gay Gleaner* (Edmonton), 1981–2, Lena letter to the editor, "Fewer Hustlers, More Lesbians, Please," *Gay Gleaner*, January 1982, 3.

112 PAS, NR A 595 II.81, "Editorial," *The Gay Gleaner*, January 1982, 2.

113 Ibid.

114 Ibid.

115 Elizabeth Massiah, interview with author, p. 9 of interview transcript.

116 One prominent lesbian activist, who many had recommended would be an essential narrator for historicizing women's experiences in

Edmonton, declined an interview. With regret she informed me that she had given and given to the city's queer politics for years, and now she was dedicated to her career, her own health, personal life, and experiences. While one understands and respects such individual decisions, in the end it produces some gaps within the record that simply cannot be papered over.

117 Glenbow Archives, Doug Young Fonds, Bob Harris, "Alberta Gays Move Forward," *Gay Calgary*, May 1979, n.p.

118 Elizabeth Massiah, interview with author.

119 Eliza Barlow, "Maureen Irwin Fought for Society's Underdogs: Opinionated and Outspoken: LIFE AND TIMES," *Edmonton Journal*, 6 August 2002, B3.

120 City of Edmonton Archives, GALA fonds, MS #595 Box 12 Conferences, Maureen Irwin, "Panel Address – Flaunting It," 1 December 1990.

121 Marina Jimenez, "Gays 'Deserve Equality' Now, Conference Told," *Edmonton Journal*, 3 December 1990, B4.

122 "Lesbian Given Award," *Perceptions*, 28 July 1993, 13.

123 Ibid.

124 City of Edmonton, "Naming Committee," Michael Phair Park, 2014, 10, March 2015, see https://www.edmonton.ca/city_government/documents/MichaelPhair_Bio_Map.pdf.

125 Mariam Ibrahim, "Former City Councillor Michael Phair Named Chairman of University of Alberta Board of Governors," *Edmonton Journal*, 25 February 2016.

126 Some will think Calgary is the obvious choice. Because the history presented here only includes fragments of Calgary's history, I am choosing Edmonton, since this portrait is more fully formed than the impressions I have collected of Calgary. Given Calgary's community history project, we may ultimately find that Calgary had more varied experiences than we currently realize.

Conclusion

1 The Collective, "Editorial," *After Stonewall* #2 mid 77, p. 2. PAS, 595 II.2

2 Liz Massiah, interview with author.

3 Glenn Murray interview, *Outlooks*, April 1999, 6, as quoted in Dawn Johnston, "Sites of Resistance, Sites of Strength: The Construction and Experience of Queer Space in Calgary" (master's thesis, University of Calgary, 1999).

Bibliography

Primary Sources

Archival Collections:

Canadian Lesbian and Gay Archives, Toronto
Canadian Women's Movement Archives, Ottawa

City of Edmonton Archives, Edmonton:

Gay and Lesbian Archives of Edmonton Fonds

Glenbow Archives, Calgary:

Cooper Family Fonds
Doug Young Fonds

Saskatchewan Archives Board, Saskatoon:

Doug Wilson Collection
Neil Richards Collection

University of Manitoba Libraries and Special Collections, Winnipeg:

Manitoba Gay and Lesbian Archives
Sally Papso Fonds

University of Saskatchewan Archives and Special Collections, Saskatoon:

Neil Richards Collection of Gender and Sexual Diversity
Evelyn Rogers Fonds

Oral History Collections:

1990   Winnipeg Gay and Lesbian Histories, Pre-Liberation, 1930s–70
       University of Manitoba Collection
1992   Winnipeg Gay and Lesbian Political Histories, 1970–92
       University of Manitoba Collection
2011   Born Between the Wars, Winnipeg Lesbians interviewed by Sally Papso
       University of Manitoba Collection

Narrators Interviewed by Author:

Alexander, Marion. Saskatoon, 26 August 2003.
Clay, Barb. Saskatoon, 29 August 2003.
Dahl, Norman. Gatineau, QC, 23 August 2006.
Dick, Lyle. Ottawa, 11 November 2005.
*Dorothy, Saskatoon 8 July 2003.
Dousse, Bernard. Edmonton, 12 September 2003.
*Edward. Ottawa, August 2006.
Garman, Bruce. Saskatoon, 25 July 2003.
Gessell, Paul. Chelsea, Quebec, 23 August 2006.
Gladwell, Brian. Regina, 29 July 2003.
Harvey, Janet. Regina, 28 July 2003.
Hellquist, Gens. Saskatoon, 17 December 2002
*Kingsway, Jenny. Regina, 19 July 2006.
*Lawrence, Leonard. Regina, 28 July 2003.
Massiah, Elizabeth. Edmonton, 13 September 2003.
Miller, Alan. Email correspondence with author, 2007–10.
Nordahl, Richard. Toronto, 27 January 2003.
Osler, Margaret. Calgary, 20 March 2003.
Phair, Michael. Edmonton, 11 September 2003.
Pratt, Peter P. Edmonton, 11 September 2003.
Richards, Neil. Saskatoon, 10 December 2002.
Rimmer, David. Ottawa, 21 January 2003.
Rivera, Mirtha. Regina, 19 July 2006.
Rogers, Evelyn J. Regina, 29 July 2003.

Scrivener, Val. Saskatoon, 18 Feb 2003.
*Selena. Saskatoon, 8 Sept 2003.
Shoemaker, Erin. Regina, 28 July 2003.
*Simmons, Debbie. Saskatoon, 12 July 2006.
Stefansson, Lilja. Regina, 29 July 2003.
*T, Saskatoon, 25 August 2003.
Vogel, Chris. Winnipeg, 21 Nov 2002.
Warner, Tom. Toronto, 8 March 2003.
*Williamson, Frances. Winnipeg, 21 Nov 2002.

* Indicates an alias, at the request of the narrator. Individuals who requested a particular name/initial appear as requested; otherwise I have selected a first name and surname.

Print/Publications:

Foster, Marion, and Kent Murray. *A Not So Gay World: Homosexuality in Canada*. Toronto: McClelland and Stewart, 1972.

Gordge, Peter Carlyle. "The Hill Is a Favourite Spot." Part 1 and 2. *Winnipeg World*, 1969.

Walsh, Jerry. "Backward Glances: A Compilation of His Remembrances of a By-Gone Era in the Gay Community of Winnipeg." Undated, but likely mid-1990s.

Secondary Sources

Abbott, Carl. *How Cities Won the West: Four Centuries of Urban Change in Western North America*. Albuquerque: University of New Mexico Press, 2008.

Adams, Mary Louise. *The Trouble with Normal: Postwar Youth and the Making of Heterosexuality*. Toronto: University of Toronto Press, 1997.

Anderson, Carolyn. "The Voices of Older Lesbian Women: An Oral History." PhD diss., University of Calgary, 2001.

Arnup, Katherine. "'Mothers Just like Others': Lesbians, Divorce, and Child Custody in Canada." *Canadian Journal of Women and the Law* 3 (June 1989): 18–32.

Artibise, Alan J. *Winnipeg: A Social History of Urban Growth 1874–1914*. Montreal: McGill Queen's University Press, 1975.

Artibise, Alan. *Winnipeg: An Illustrated History*. Toronto: James Lorimer, 1977.

Barbour, Dale. *Winnipeg Beach: Leisure and Courtship in a Resort Town, 1900–1967*. Winnipeg: University of Manitoba Press, 2011.

Beemyn, Brett, ed. *Creating a Place for Ourselves: Lesbian, Gay and Bisexual Community Histories*. London: Routledge, 1997.

Bell, David, and Gill Valentine, eds. *Mapping Desire: Geographies of Sexualities.* London: Routledge, 1995.

Bérubé, Allan. *Coming Out under Fire: The History of Gay Men and Women in World War II*. New York: Free Press, 1990.

Binnie, Jon, and Gill Valentine. "Geographies of Sexuality – A Review of Progress." *Progress in Human Geography* 23, no. 2 (1999): 175–87.

Boag, Peter. *Same Sex Affairs: Constructing and Controlling Homosexuality in the Pacific Northwest*. Berkeley: University of California Press, 2003.

– *Re-Dressing America's Frontier Past*. Berkeley: University of California Press, 2011.

Boyd, Nan Alamilla. *Wide Open Town: A History of Queer San Francisco to 1965*. Berkeley: University of California Press, 2005.

– "Who Is the Subject? Queer Theory Meets Oral History" *Journal of the History of Sexuality* 17, no. 2 (May 2008): 177–89.

Boyd, Nan Alamilla, and Horacio N. Roque Ramîrez, eds. *Bodies of Evidence: The Practice of Queer Oral History*. New York: Oxford University Press, 2012.

Burke, Kathryne, Angela Davis, and Kathryn Gleadle. "Introduction: Space, Place and Gendered Identities: Feminist History and The Spatial Turn." *Women's History Review* 21, no. 4 (September 2012): 523–32.

Burton, Antoinette. *Archive Stories: Facts, Fictions and the Writing of History*. Atlanta: Duke University Press, 2006.

Brock, Deborah. "'Workers of the World Caress': An Interview with Gary Kinsman on Gay and Lesbian Organizing in the 1970s Toronto Left." *left history* 9, no. 2 (2005): online feature.

Brown, Ricardo J. *The Evening Crowd at Kirmser's: A Gay Life in the 1940s*. Minnesota: University of Minneapolis Press, 2003.

Burring, Daneel. *Lesbian and Gay Memphis: Building Communities behind the Magnolia Curtain*. New York: Garland Publishing, 1997.

Cavanaugh, Catherine, and Jeremy Mouat, eds. *Making Western Canada: Essays on European Colonization and Settlement*. Toronto: Garamond Press, 1996.

Cavell, Richard, ed. *Love, Hate and Fear in Canada's Cold War*. Toronto: University of Toronto Press, 2004.

Chacaby, Ma-Nee, with Mary Louisa Plummer. *A Two-Spirit Journey: The Autobiography of a Lesbian Ojibwa-Cree Elder*. Winnipeg: University of Manitoba Press, 2016.

Chapman, Terry. "'An Oscar Wilde Type': The Abominable Crime of Buggery in Western Canada, 1890–1920." *Criminal Justice History* 4 (1983): 97–118.

– "Male Homosexuality: Legal Restraints and Social Attitudes in Western Canada, 1890–1920." In *Law and Justice in a New Land: Essays in Western Canadian Legal History*, edited by Louise A. Knafla, 267–92. Toronto: Carswell, 1986.

– "Sex Crimes in the West, 1890–1920." *Alberta History* 35, no. 4 (October 1987): 6–21.

Chauncey, George. *Gay New York: Gender, Urban Culture and the Making of the Gay Male World, 1890–1940*. New York: Basic Books, 1994.

Chenier, Elise. "Rethinking Class in Lesbian Bar Culture: Living 'the Gay Life' in Toronto, 1955–1965." *left history* 9, no. 2 (Spring/Summer 2004).

Churchill, David S. "Mother Goose's Map: Tabloid Geographies and Gay Male Experience in 1950s Toronto." *Journal of Urban History* 30, no. 6 (September 2004): 826–52.

Churchill, David. "Personal Ad Politics: Race, Sexuality, and Power at *The Body Politic*." *left history* 8, no. 2 (Spring 2003).

Cocks, Harry, and Matt Houlbrook. *Palgrave Advances in the Modern History of Sexuality*. Basingstoke, England: Palgrave Mcmillan, 2006.

Collins, Robert. *Prairie People: A Celebration of My Homeland*. Toronto: McClelland and Stewart, 2003.

Cook, Matt and Jennifer Evans, eds. *Queer Cities, Queer Cultures: Europe since 1945*. London: Bloomsbury, 2014.

Cooper, Danielle. "Beyond Liberation: Conceptualization of History at the Canadian Lesbian and Gay Archives." *left history* 19, no. 1 (Spring/Summer 2015).

Curthoys, Ann, and Ann McGrath. *How to Write History That People Want to Read*. Sydney: UNSW Press, 2009.

Cvetkovich, Ann. *An Archive of Feelings: Trauma, Sexuality, and Lesbian Public Cultures*. Durham, NC and London: Duke University Press, 2003.

Dafoe, Christopher. *Winnipeg: Heart of the Continent*. Winnipeg: Great Plaines Publications, 1998.

De Groot, Scott. "The Accused Have Not Indicated That They Intend to Fight Off This Disease." MA cognate, Queen's University, 2008.

D'Emilio, John. *Sexual Politics, Sexual Communities: The Making of a Homosexual Minority in the United States, 1940–1970*. Chicago: University of Chicago Press, 1983.

Dick, Lyle. "Same Sex Intersections of the Prairie Settlement Era: The Case of Regina's 'Oscar Wilde,'" *Histoire Sociale/Social History* 42, no. 83 (2009) 107–45.

– "The 1942 Same Sex Trials in Edmonton: On the State's Repression of Sexual Minorities, Archives, and Human Rights in Canada." *Archivaria* 68 (2009): 183–217.

Doan, Laura. *Disturbing Practices: History, Sexuality and Women's Experience of Modern War*. Chicago: University of Chicago Press, 2013.

Dubinsky, Karen. *Improper Advances: Rape and Heterosexual Conflict in Ontario, 1880–1920*. Chicago: University of Chicago Press, 1993.

Duder, Cameron. *Awfully Devoted Women: Lesbian Lives in Canada, 1990–85* (Vancouver: UBC Press, 2010)

Filax, Gloria. *Queer Youth in the Province of the 'Severely Normal.'* Vancouver: UBC Press, 2006.

Friesen, Gerald. *River Road: Essays on Manitoba and Prairie History*. Winnipeg: University of Manitoba Press, 1996.

Gale, Patrick. *A Place Called Winter*. London: Tinder Press, 2015.

Gallo, Marcia. *Different Daughters: The History of the Daughters of Bilitis and the Rise of the Lesbian Rights Movement*. New York: Carol and Graff Publishers, 2006.

Gilmartin, Katie. "We Weren't Bar People': Middle-Class Lesbian Identities and Cultural Spaces." *Gay and Lesbian Quarterly* 3 (1996): 1–51.

Goldie, Terry, ed. *In a Queer Country: Gay and Lesbian Studies in the Canadian Context*. Vancouver: Arsenal Pulp Press, 2001.

Gourluck, Russ. *The Mosaic Village: An Illustrated History of Winnipeg's North End*. Winnipeg: Great Plains Publications, 2010.

Gray, Mary L., Colin R. Johnson, and Brian J. Gilley. *Queering the Countryside: New Frontiers in Rural Queer Studies*. New York: New York University Press, 2016.

Halberstam, J. Jack. *In a Queer Time and Place: Transgender Bodies, Subcultural Lives*. New York: NYU Press, 2005.

Halperin, David. *How to Be Gay*. Boston, MA: Harvard University Press, 2014.

Henderson, Stuart. *Making the Scene: Yorkville and Hip Toronto in the 1960s*. Toronto: University of Toronto Press, 2011.

Higgins, Ross. "Baths, Bushes and Belonging: Public Sex and Gay Community in Pre-Stonewall Montreal." in *Public Sex/Gay Space*, edited by William L. Leap, 187–202. New York: Columbia University Press, 1999.

Higgs, David. *Queer Sites: Gay Urban Histories since 1600*. London: Routledge, 1999.

Hinther, Rhonda. "The Oldest Profession in Winnipeg: The Culture of Prostitution in the Point Douglas Segregated Districts, 1909–1912." *Manitoba History* 41 (March 2001).

Houlbrook, Matt. "Toward a Historical Geography of Sexuality." *Journal of Urban History* 27, no. 4 (May 2001): 497–504.

– "*Queer London: Perils and Pleasures in the Sexual Metropolis, 1918–1957*. Chicago: University of Chicago Press, 2005.

Houlbrook, Matt, and Chris Waters. "The Heart in Exile: Detachment and Desire in 1950s London." *History Workshop Journal* 62 (2006): 142–65.

Howard, John. *Men like That: A Southern Queer History*. Chicago: University of Chicago Press, 1999.

Hubbard, Philip. *Sex and the City: Geographies of Prostitution in the Urban West*. Aldershot: Ashgate, 1999.

Hunt, Lynn. *Writing History in the Global Era*. New York: WW Norton and Co, 2014.

Hurewitz, Daniel. *Bohemian Los Angeles: And the Making of Modern Politics*. Berkeley: University of California Press, 2008.

Hurtado, Albert L. *Intimate Frontiers: Sex, Gender and Culture in Old California*. Albuquerque: University of New Mexico Press, 1999.

Jackson, Ed, and Stan Persky, eds. *Flaunting It! A Decade of Gay Journalism from the* Body Politic. Vancouver: Star Books, 1982.

Jackson, Paul. *One of the Boys: Homosexuality in the Military during World War II*. Montreal: McGill University Press, 2004.

Johnson, Colin R. *Just Queer Folks: Gender and Sexuality on Rural America*. Philadelphia: Temple University Press, 2013.

Johnston, Dawn Elizabeth. "Sites of Resistance, Sites of Strength: The Construction and Experience of Queer Space in Calgary." MA thesis, University of Calgary, 1999.

Jones, Esyllt W., and Gerald Friesen. *Prairie Metropolis: New Essays on Winnipeg Social History*. Winnipeg: University of Manitoba Press, 2009.

Katz, Jonathon. *Love Stories: Sex between Men before Homosexuality*. Chicago: University of Chicago Press, 2001.

Kennedy, Elizabeth Lapovsky, and Madeleine D. Davis. *Boots of Leather, Slippers of Gold: The History of a Lesbian Community*. New York: Routledge, 1993.

Kennedy, Elizabeth Lapovsky. "But We Would Never Talk about It: The Structures of Lesbian Discretion in South Dakota, 1928–1933." In *Inventing Lesbian Cultures in America*, edited by Ellen Lewin, 15–39. Boston: Beacon Press, 1996.

– "Telling Tales: Oral History and The Construction of Pre-Stonewall Lesbian History." In *The Oral History Reader*, edited by Robert Perks and Alistair Thomson, 344–56. London: Routledge, 1998.

Kerr, Don, and Stan Hanson. *Saskatoon: The First Half-Century*. Edmonton: NeWest Publishers, 1982.

Kinsman, Gary. *The Regulation of Desire: Homo and Hetero Sexualities*. Montreal: Black Rose Books, 1996.

Kinsman, Gary, and Patrizia Gentile. *The Canadian War on Queers: National Security as Sexual Regulation*. Vancouver: UBC Press, 2010.

Korfman, Geoffrey. "The Wilde West: Homosexual Behaviour in the Court
Records of Saskatchewan, 1895–1930." MA thesis, Trent University, 2007.

Kramer, Jerry Lee. "Bachelor Farmers and Spinsters: Gay and Lesbian
Identities and Communities in Rural North Dakota." In *Mapping Desire*,
edited by David Bell and Gill Valentine, 182–94. London: Routledge, 1995.

Lewis, Brian, ed. *British Queer History: New Approaches and Perspectives*.
Manchester: Manchester University Press, 2013.

Leznoff, Maurice. "The Homosexual in Urban Society." MA thesis, McGill
University, 1954.

Limerick, Patricia Nelson, Clyde A. Milner II, and Charles E. Rankin, eds. *New
Trails: Toward a New Western History*. Lawrence: University Press of Kansas, 1991.

Lucas, Noelle. "Womanspace: Building a Lesbian Community in Edmonton
Alberta." MA thesis, University of Saskatchewan, 2002.

Martel, Marcel. "'They Smell Bad, Have Diseases, and Are Lazy': RCMP
Officers Reporting on Hippies in the Late Sixties." *Canadian Historical Review*
90, no. 2 (June 2009): 215–45.

Maynard, Steven. "Through a Hole in the Lavatory Wall: Homosexual
Subcultures, Police Surveillance, and the Dialectics of Discovery, Toronto
1890–1930." In *Gender and History in Canada*, edited by Parr and Rosenfeld.
Toronto: Copp Clark, 1996.

– "'Horrible Temptations': Sex, Men, and Working-Class Male Youth in Urban
Ontario, 1890–1935." *Canadian Historical Review* 78, no. 2 (June 1997).

– "'Respect Your Elders, Know Your Past': History and Queer Theorists."
Radical History Review 75 (1999): 56–78.

– "'Hell Witches in Toronto': Notes on Lesbian Visibility in Early 20th Century
Canada." *left history* Volume 9, no. 2 (Spring/Summer 2004): 191–205.

– "Without Working? Capitalism, Urban Culture and Gay History." *Journal of
Urban History*, 30, no. 3 (March 2004): 378–98.

McDonald, Robert A.J. *Making Vancouver: Class, Status and Social Boundaries,
1863–1913*. Vancouver: UBC Press, 2000.

McLeod, Donald W. *Lesbian and Gay Liberation in Canada: A Selected Chronology,
1964–1975*. Toronto: ECW Press/Homewood Books, 1996.

McKittrick, Katherine. *Demonic Grounds: Black Women and the Cartographies of
Struggle*. Minneapolis: University of Minnesota Press, 2006.

Millward, Liz. *Making a Scene: Lesbians and Community across Canada, 1964–1984*.
Vancouver: UBC Press, 2015.

– "Making a Scene: Struggles over Lesbian Place Making in Anglophone
Canada, 1964–1984." *Women's History Review* 21, no. 4 (2012): 553–69.

Morgensen, Scott Lauria. *Spaces between Us: Queer Settler Colonialism and
Indigenous Decolonization*. Minneapolis: University of Minnesota Press, 2011.

Oakley, Janice. "Postcards from The Edge: Decoding Winnipeg's 'One Gay City' Campaign." *Ethnologies* 2, no. 2 (1999): 177–92.

Owram, Alison. "Sexuality in Heterotopia: Time, Space and Love between Women in the Historic House." *Women's History Review* 21, no. 4 (September 2012): 533–51.

Peiss, Kathy. *Cheap Amusements: Working Women and Leisure in Turn-of-the-Century New York*. Philadelphia: Temple University Press, 1986.

Perks, Robert, and Alistair Thomson, eds. *The Oral History Reader*. London: Routledge, 1998.

Perry, Adele. *On the Edge of Empire: Gender, Race and the Making of British Columbia, 1849–1871*. Toronto: University of Toronto Press, 2001.

Richards, Neil. *Celebrating a History of Diversity: Lesbian and Gay Life in Saskatchewan, 1971–2005. A Selected Annotated Chronology*. Saskatoon: The Avenue Community Centre for Gender and Sexual Diversity, 2005.

Riordan, Michael. *Out Our Way: Gay and Lesbian Life in the Country*. Toronto: Between the Lines, 1996.

Ross, Becki L. *The House that Jill Built: A Lesbian Nation in Formation*. Toronto: University of Toronto Press, 1995.

– *Burlesque West: Showgirls, Sex and Sin in Postwar Vancouver*. Toronto: University of Toronto Press, 2009.

Rogers, Randal, and Christine Ramsay, eds. *Overlooking Saskatchewan: Minding the Gap*. University of Regina Press, 2014.

Rupp, Leila J. *A Desired Past: A Short History of Same-Sex Love in America*. Chicago: University of Chicago Press, 1999.

Schuster, Marilyn, ed. *A Queer Love Story: The Letters of Jane Rule and Rick Bébout*. Vancouver: University of British Columbia Press, 2017.

Sheftel, Anna, and Stacey Zembrzycki. "Only Human: A Reflection on the Ethnical and Methodological Challenge of Working with 'Difficult' Stories." *The Oral History Review* 37, no. 2 (2010): 191–214.

Silversides, Ann. *AIDS Activist: Michael Lynch and the Politics of Community*. Toronto: Between the Lines Press, 2003.

Simon, Bryant. "New York Avenue: The Life and Death of Gay Spaces in Atlantic City, New Jersey, 1920–1990." *Journal of Urban History* 28, no. 3 (March 2002): 300–27.

Smith, Miriam. *Lesbian and Gay Rights in Canada: Social Movements and Equality Seeking, 1971–1995*. Toronto: University of Toronto Press, 1999.

Spence, Alex. *Perceptions: The First Fifteen Years, 1983–1997: An Index to the Canadian Gay and Lesbian Newsmagazine*. Saskatoon: Perceptions Publications, 2003.

Stansell, Christine. *City of Women: Sex and Class in New York, 1789–1860*. New York: Knopf, 1986.

Stein, Marc. *City of Sisterly and Brotherly Loves: Lesbian and Gay Philadelphia,
    1945–1972*. Philadelphia: Temple University Press, 2004.
– *Rethinking the Gay and Lesbian Movement*. New York: Routledge, 2012.
Strange, Carolyn. *Toronto's Girl Problem: The Perils and Pleasures of the City,
    1880–1930*. Toronto: University of Toronto Press, 1995.
Stryker, Susan. *Transgender History*. Berkeley, CA: Seal Press, 2008.
Truth and Reconciliation Commission of Canada. *What We Have Learned:
    Principles of Truth and Reconciliation*. Ottawa: Truth and Reconciliation
    Commission of Canada, 2015.
Turner, Mark. *Backward Glances: Cruising the Queer Streets of New York and
    London*. London: Reaktion Books, 2003.
Twin Cities GLBT Oral History Project. *Queer Twin Cities*. Minneapolis:
    University of Minneapolis Press, 2010.
Van Cleave, Stuart. *Land of 10,000 Loves: A History of Queer Minnesota*.
    Minneapolis: University of Minnesota Press, 2012.
Waiser, Bill. *Saskatchewan A New History*. Calgary: Fifth House Press, 2005.
– "All but Deserted Years Ago: Electricity and the Two Saskatchewans." In
    Overlooking Saskatchewan: Minding the Gap, edited by Rogers and Ramsay.
    Regina: University of Regina Press, 2014.
Walsh, John C., and Steven High. "Rethinking the Concept of Community."
    Histoire Sociale/Social History 64, no. 32 (November 1999): 255–73.
Ward, W. Peter. "Population Growth in Western Canada, 1901–71." In *The
    Developing West: Essays in Canadian History in Honour of Lewis H. Thomas*,
    edited by John E. Foster. Edmonton: University of Alberta Press, 1983.
Warner, Tom. *Never Going Back: A History of Queer Activism in Canada*. Toronto:
    University of Toronto Press, 2002.
Weeks, Jeffery. "Inverts, Perverts, and Mary-Annes: Male Prostitution and
    the Regulation of Homosexuality in England in the Nineteenth and Early
    Twentieth Centuries." in *Hidden from History: Reclaiming the Gay and Lesbian
    Past*, edited by M. Duberman, M. Vicinus and G. Chauncey Jr. New York:
    Meridian, 1990.
Werner, Hans. *Imagined Homes: Soviet German Immigrants in Two Cities*.
    Winnipeg: University of Manitoba Press, 2007.
Weston, Kath. *Long, Slow Burn*. New York: Routledge, 1998.
Weston, Kath. "'Get thee to a big city': Sexual Imagery and The Great Gay
    Migration." *GLQ: A Journal of Lesbian and Gay Studies* 2, no. 3 (1995): 253–77.
Wickenhauser, Joseph. "Surprisingly Unexpected: Moose Jaw,
    Metronormativity and LGBTQ Activism." MA thesis, York University, 2012.

STUDIES IN GENDER AND HISTORY

General Editors: Franca Iacovetta and Karen Dubinsky